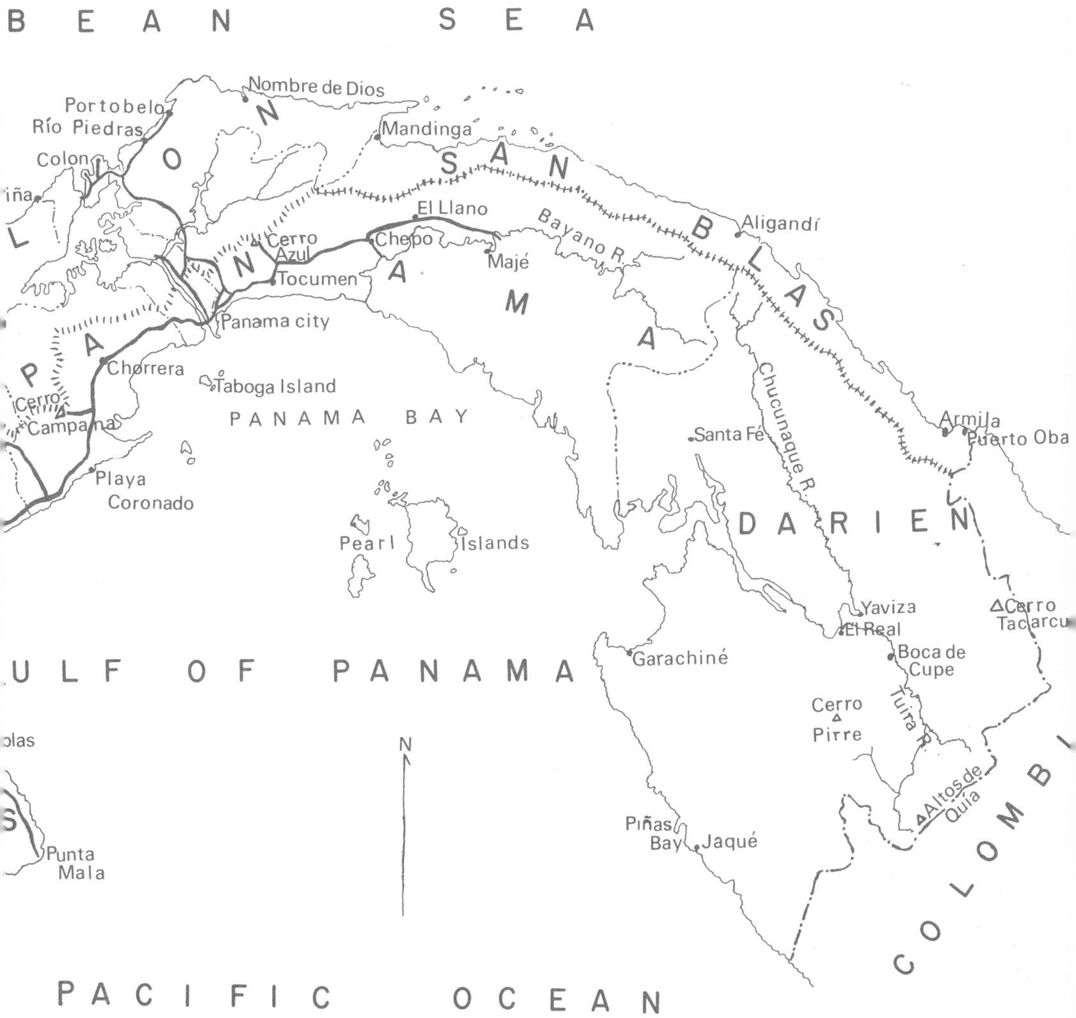
BEAN SEA
Nombre de Dios
Portobelo
Río Piedras
Colon
iña
Mandinga
SAN BLAS
El Llano
Bayano R.
Aligandí
Cerro Azul
Chepo
Majé
Tocumen
PANAMA
Panama city
Chorrera
Taboga Island
Cerro Campana
PANAMA BAY
Playa Coronado
Santa Fé
Chucunaque R.
Armila
Puerto Oba
Pearl Islands
DARIEN
Yaviza
El Real
Cerro Tacarcu
Garachiné
Boca de Cupe
ULF OF PANAMA
Cerro Pirre
Tuira R.
olas
N
Altos de Quía
Piñas Bay
Jaqué
Punta Mala
COLOMBI
PACIFIC OCEAN

A GUIDE TO THE BIRDS OF PANAMA

A GUIDE TO THE

Birds of Panama

BY ROBERT S. RIDGELY

ILLUSTRATED BY

JOHN A. GWYNNE, JR.

Sponsored by the
International Council for Bird Preservation
(Pan American and United States sections)
with the support of the
Marcia Brady Tucker Foundation

PRINCETON UNIVERSITY PRESS

*Published by Princeton University Press,
Princeton, New Jersey*

*In the United Kingdom: Princeton University Press,
Guildford, Surrey*

Library of Congress Cataloging in
Publication Data will be found on the last
printed page of this book

This book has been composed in Times Roman

3rd printing, with corrections and additions, 1981

Printed in the United States of America
by Princeton University Press,
Princeton, New Jersey

DEDICATED TO THE MEMORY OF

DR. ROBERT H. MACARTHUR

Professor in the Department of Biology at Princeton University, who showed us a new way of looking at the natural world, and whose enthusiastic support and counsel during the early stages of this project were invaluable.

CONTENTS

FOREWORD

The long isthmus of Panamá offers a varied and attractive avifauna to the birdwatcher, amateur and professional. In its western and central areas there are representatives of tropical kinds found through Central America, and in the east in San Blas and Darién, those of affiliation with South America. Among the residents at the proper season there appear many migrants from the north, present in this warmer climate as a winter home, or in passage to and from more distant regions farther to the south. The avifauna in total, as compiled by the author, includes over 880 species that have been recorded by naturalists through a period of more than one hundred years. Valuable additions to the text are the 32 color plates and numerous line drawings in which the artist, John Gwynne, Jr., carefully portrays details of color and form from museum specimens, photographs, and his personal field experience.

The common birds of the lowlands in Panamá are widely distributed, and many are easily found. On first encounter some immediately suggest kinds familiar in more northern haunts. (If the period is that of winter, examine them carefully to make certain they are not northern migrants). Others in appearance and mannerism may be at once strange and unusual. Species of the highlands are seen most readily in a journey west to Boquete and Cerro Punta in the mountains of Chiriquí. Those of Darién may require longer time and special arrangements.

Local interest in birds has increased in recent years, and there is now an active chapter of the Florida Audubon Society. Travelers remaining in Panamá for a period may find its scheduled meetings and bird walks helpful.

The present volume, based on broad field experience of the author throughout the isthmus, is certain to be a guide of value to the bird student, be he tyro or expert in the field.

Alexander Wetmore
Smithsonian Institution

INTRODUCTION

The Republic of Panama comprises an area of 29,208 square miles (somewhat smaller than South Carolina), which includes a strip about 10 miles wide bordering the Panama Canal leased "in perpetuity" to the United States, and has long been a region of special interest to persons interested in birds. Located at the southern end of Middle America, Panama is a land bridge where the faunas of North and South America meet and intermingle. Largely due to this geographical position, Panama's avifauna is exceptionally large: at this writing, some 883 species have been reported from the Republic, considerably more species than are recorded from all of North America north of Mexico. People have been studying Panama's birdlife for over a century, and today it is one of the best known (in an ornithological sense) countries in the neotropics. Nonetheless, as will be noted repeatedly on the following pages, there is still a great deal to be learned and some areas remain little explored. The conscientious observer is in a position to add materially to our knowledge.

The first man to make large bird collections in what is now the Canal Zone was James McLeannan, who in the mid-nineteenth century was stationmaster at Lion Hill on the Panama Railroad (now submerged under Gatun Lake). He collected many birds around Lion Hill (Harpy Eagles were then not uncommon) and sent them to leading American and British ornithologists; from these specimens a number of new species were described, chiefly by George Lawrence and Osbert Salvin. Other collectors worked in different parts of Panama, most notably Enrique Arcé in "Veragua," which then encompassed much of present-day western Panama (including Bocas del Toro and Chiriquí). Available data were included in the *Aves* volumes of *Biologia Centrali-Americana* by O. Salvin and F. DuC. Godman (1879–1904). But it was the influx and interest of North Americans, partly stimulated by Canal construction, that prompted the intense zoological exploration of Panama and the beginning of popular study.

A number of bird collections were made in little-known regions of the country during the first third of the century, notably by W. W. Brown, T. Barbour, E. A. Goldman, L. Griscom, R. R. Benson, H. Wedel, H. E. Anthony and W. B. Richardson, F. H. Kennard, J. Aldrich, and others. These collections established the distributional outlines of Panama's avifauna and were used in publications by either the collectors or such leading ornithologists as O. Bangs, F. M. Chapman, J. L. Peters, and C. Hellmayr. Robert Ridgway's great, though uncompleted, multivolume work, *The Birds of North and Middle America* (1901–1919), provided the descriptive and taxonomic foundation for subsequent Middle

American studies. In 1918 W. Stone produced the first checklist of Canal Zone birds, based partly on a collection made by L. L. Jewel. In 1935 L. Griscom published the first complete checklist of the birds then known from the Republic. Work on seabirds in the Gulf of Panama was done by R. C. Murphy, and collections over many years by T. B. Mönniche on the Volcán de Chiriquí massif were later reported upon by E. R. Blake (1958). Detailed ecological and behavioral studies, as well as public interest, were promoted by the establishment in 1923 of a biological research station on Barro Colorado Island, Canal Zone, under the supervision of James Zetek. This former hilltop, isolated by rising waters when the Chagres River was dammed to form Gatun Lake, has been a mecca for naturalists, many of whom have repeatedly returned to Panama, or have sent their students. Its fame was spread by F. M. Chapman's delightful books, *My Tropical Air Castle* (1929) and *Life in an Air Castle* (1938). Some personnel associated with the operation or defense of the Canal developed an interest in the varied avifauna of the area, and this was markedly assisted by the preparation of a popular book, *Field Book of Birds of the Panama Canal Zone* in 1928 (long since out of print) by B. B. Sturgis, wife of a former Canal Zone commanding general.

Succeeding decades have seen an increase in the number of visiting naturalists and residents interested in the local birdlife. Of these, the two who have made by far the most significant contributions are Dr. Alexander Wetmore and Dr. Eugene Eisenmann. Since the 1940's, Wetmore, one of the world's leading ornithologists, has collected birds virtually throughout Panama, and it is largely through his efforts and those of his collaborators in the Gorgas Memorial Laboratory that something is known about the birds found in certain of the less accessible parts of the country. Dr. Wetmore's research is culminating in the publication of a lengthy multi-volume treatise on the birds of the country, three volumes of which have been published, with the fourth in preparation. Eisenmann has also been conducting personal field work in Panama since the 1940's (in addition to having been born in the country), gathering distributional, ecological, and behavioral data, publishing on Panama birds, and encouraging and assisting students of its ornithology. Barro Colorado Island was placed under the jurisdiction of the Smithsonian Institution, and subsequently (particularly in the last fifteen years under its recent director, Dr. Martin Moynihan) the Smithsonian has greatly expanded its local organization until it is now a major center for research into many aspects of tropical biology. During the early 1960's, Florida State University established a branch in the Canal Zone, and under its auspices the Center for Tropical Studies was created in 1963, directed until recently by Dr. Horace Loftin. This organization has sponsored many research visits by graduate students and others, and offers a course in ornithology. Popular nonprofessional clubs and societies have existed sporadically through the period, and recently the Panama Audubon Society (chartered in 1968 as an affiliate of the Florida Audubon Society) has done a great deal to foster the study and appreciation of Panama's birdlife. In 1973 a chapter of the Amigos de la Naturaleza was also organized in Panama city.

I arrived in Panama as an Army lieutenant in the fall of 1967, and, as a birder from early boyhood in the United States, was elated at the prospect of several years in the neotropics. But being accustomed to North America's superbly written and illustrated bird guides, I was not fully prepared for the difficulties in field recognition that I would encounter in Panama. Toucans and the other large showy species were no problem, but what of the many more difficult groups such as the hummingbirds, woodcreepers, antbirds, and above all the wealth of confusing flycatchers? The then-available references—the Sturgis book mentioned above and de Schauensee's *Birds of Colombia*—were both useful up to a point, but neither was easy to use in the field. I now remember those first few months as being greatly exciting but also rather frustrating. A growing friendship with Dr. Eisenmann proved invaluable at this point. I soon was given permission to copy his unpublished "Diagnostic List of Panama Birds" with its 100 pages of brief field diagnoses of Panama birds, this in return for making available to him any of my personal field observations. I found this manuscript to be immensely valuable over the next few years, and with time I gained in field proficiency. But its use was highly restricted by the author, who at the time was still considering expanding and publishing it. I and many others felt that what was needed was a generally available, more comprehensive and detailed book, and above all one which would include color illustrations.

Soon after my return to Princeton University in the fall of 1969, I made the decision to write the book I would have liked to have had myself. Eisenmann agreed to let me use his "Diagnostic List" as the basis for the projected work, having by then realized that with his other commitments he would never find the time to do the work himself, on the understanding that all royalties would accrue to some nonprofit ornithological or conservation organization. Since then he has given freely of his vast storehouse of knowledge, providing information on distribution, morphology, behavior, and taxonomy, and has labored untold hours over the pages of manuscript I sent him to examine. By a stroke of good fortune, a fellow undergraduate at Princeton, John Gwynne, Jr., had an interest in birds and a remarkable artistic talent, and he agreed to do the illustrations. Gwynne had never done such work, but his proficiency increased rapidly, and I feel certain the results are a valuable contribution to neotropical ornithology.

It has taken five years to complete the work, far more time, and effort, than either Gwynne or myself had anticipated. All along we have been students with many other concerns, and never have we been able to devote any extended, full-time effort to our project. Throughout that period, assistance, direct and indirect, has been rendered by a great many individuals and organizations, in this case far too many for all to be mentioned here, but the following are among the most important.

A trip to Panama during the summer of 1970 for Gwynne and myself was financed in part by a grant from the National Science Foundation undergraduate summer study program at Princeton, and in part from funds made available by Dr. Robert MacArthur of the Princeton Biology Department. While in Panama, Captain and Mrs. Gaylord Lyon USN furnished us with accommodations, while Mr. and Mrs. Roy Sharp loaned us one of their cars; both these couples, as well as many other persons, extended many kindnesses to us during that delightful sojourn. On that and my subsequent visits, the staff of STRI have gone out of their way to be helpful, as have Drs. Edwin Tyson and Horace Loftin of the Florida State branch, and several members of the Panama Audubon Society, especially Dr. Jaime Pujals. Dr. Pedro Galindo, of the Gorgas Memorial Laboratory, kindly afforded Eisenmann, Gwynne, and myself the hospitality of the Gorgas camp above the Bayano River near Majé in late January 1973, and he also provided invaluable assistance in setting up my trip to Santa Fé, Veraguas, in early January 1974. Dr. Jorge Campabadal, director of the Organization for Tropical Studies in Costa Rica, was helpful in providing transportation and lodging during my visit to that country during the winter of 1972–1973. An abundance of information has been gleaned from Eisenmann's copious unpublished data, compiled by him over the years from his personal observations, study of specimens and the literature, and notes given him by numerous observers. A comprehensive listing of these contributors would be too lengthy (they are credited in the text when the observation is unusual), but I owe all of them a great debt of gratitude, in particular (other than those mentioned elsewhere in this introduction): James E. Ambrose, Major F. O. Chapelle, Eugene S. Morton, Richard Ryan, Dennis R. Sheets, and Edwin O. Willis. Dr. Wetmore's volumes have of course been invaluable, and he has graciously taken the time to answer many specific queries as well. Peter Alden, David O. Hill, James R. Karr, Neal G. Smith, F. Gary Stiles, and Guy Tudor have all been very patient in replying to my persistent queries. Many persons thus contributed information and advice, but responsibility for all the statements made in this book rests, of course, with the author.

Several persons (among them Alden, John Dunning, Karr, Michel Kleinbaum, Hill, and Smith) have kindly lent photographs of certain species needed by Gwynne for more accurate portrayals. Guy Tudor, one of the finest living bird artists, has also given Gwynne much technical advice for which Gwynne is grateful. We are indebted to the American Museum of Natural History (in particular to Dr. Dean Amadon and Charles O'Brien), the Museum of Comparative Zoology (and Dr. Raymond A. Paynter, Jr.), and the Smithsonian Institution (and Dr. George E. Watson) for access to and loan of specimens in their collections. Both of us are immensely grateful to Eugene Eisenmann, without whose aid and encouragement the book would never have gotten off the ground. Drs. S. Dillon Ripley and Thomas Lovejoy have given valuable advice, and Warren King has also been helpful. The Pan American and United States Sections of the International Council for Bird Preservation provided a needed boost by agreeing to sponsor the book, while the generosity of Mrs. Carll Tucker and the Marcia Brady Tucker Foundation helped make its actual publication possible; Mrs. Tucker's deep interest is greatly appreciated. Both Gwynne's and my parents gave support and encouragement when needed. Finally to my wife Julie, who not only prepared the maps, but also had to endure many late nights and the grouchy husband that all too often resulted, I owe a special thanks for bearing with me through a few difficult times.

Robert S. Ridgely
August 1974

A GUIDE TO THE BIRDS OF PANAMA

CLIMATE

Panama lies between 7° and 10° north of the Equator, hence its climate is essentially warm tropical; only the highlands of the west and east have cooler conditions. This is not to say that the climate of the country is uniform; it varies significantly between regions, and in most areas also fluctuates seasonally.

In a tropical climate one finds that the variation between the average daily maximum and minimum temperatures is greater than the variation in the average monthly figures. Table I demonstrates this for Balboa and Cristobal, representative localities on the Pacific and Caribbean coasts of the Canal Zone, respectively. Variation in the monthly averages at Balboa is only 3°F, and at Cristobal is even less. Variation between daily highs and lows is greater on the Pacific slope than on the Caribbean, primarily because of its lower humidity and less persistent cloud cover. In general, temperatures in the Panama lowlands are hot during daylight hours and pleasant during the hours of darkness; one should plan one's activities accordingly.

A major factor of most tropical lowland climates is the seasonal variability in precipitation; i.e., there is a definite alternation between dry and rainy seasons. Table II shows that this is clearly the pattern in Panama. For the five localities given (placed in order from Balboa on the Pacific coast to Cristobal and Portobelo on the Caribbean), considerable differences in the average annual totals can be seen (ranging from 68.9 in. in Balboa to 158.6 in. at Portobelo). For each locality, however, there is a distinctly drier period (January–April) and a rainier period (May–December). The same annual pattern holds for most of the Panama lowlands, with heaviest precipitation occurring in Caribbean western and eastern (not central) Panama; in Bocas del Toro the rainfall tends to be more uniformly distributed. As the table indicates, the

TABLE I

TEMPERATURE DATA FOR CANAL ZONE (DEG. F.)

	Jan.	Feb.	Mar.	Apr.	May	June	July	Aug.	Sept.	Oct.	Nov.	Dec.
BALBOA												
Avg.	80.0	80.5	81.6	82.2	80.9	80.2	80.4	80.3	79.8	79.2	79.2	79.9
Avg. Max.	88.3	89.4	90.7	90.5	87.5	86.2	86.9	86.7	85.9	85.2	85.4	87.0
Avg. Min.	71.7	71.7	72.6	73.9	74.4	74.1	74.0	73.8	73.7	73.3	72.9	72.6
CRISTOBAL												
Avg.	80.3	80.3	80.8	81.4	81.1	80.8	80.5	81.9	80.7	80.3	79.5	80.1
Avg. Max.	83.9	83.8	84.4	85.2	85.6	85.5	84.9	84.9	85.8	85.6	84.0	84.1
Avg. Min.	76.6	76.7	77.3	77.6	76.7	76.0	76.2	75.9	75.5	75.0	75.0	76.1

SOURCE: Panama Canal Company, Meteorological and Hydrographic Branch

TABLE II
PRECIPITATION DATA FOR CANAL ZONE AND VICINITY (INCHES)

	Jan.	Feb.	Mar.	Apr.	May	June	July	Aug.	Sept.	Oct.	Nov.	Dec.	Ann.
BALBOA													
Avg.	1.1	0.6	0.6	3.0	7.8	7.8	7.3	7.7	7.5	10.2	9.9	5.4	68.9
Max.	5.2	4.9	5.0	7.8	15.2	16.3	15.8	15.6	17.3	20.8	20.5	15.0	93.1
Min.	0	0	0	Tr.	2.2	2.4	3.4	1.3	2.5	3.4	3.2	0.2	48.9
SUMMIT													
Avg.	0.9	0.4	0.4	3.1	10.1	9.2	10.1	10.0	9.9	12.2	12.6	5.8	84.8
Max.	5.3	2.9	3.0	8.9	22.8	16.4	20.4	18.7	14.8	18.8	31.4	24.4	111.2
Min.	0	0	0	0	3.3	3.6	2.9	5.2	4.5	4.3	6.0	0.5	67.6
BARRO COLORADO ISLAND													
Avg.	2.2	1.3	1.2	3.4	11.0	10.9	11.7	12.5	10.3	14.0	17.9	10.6	107.3
Max.	9.0	7.3	5.5	18.3	19.0	19.4	28.6	21.9	20.0	22.2	41.6	28.2	143.4
Min.	0.2	Tr.	Tr.	Tr.	3.1	3.8	5.4	5.9	5.7	6.1	7.2	1.2	76.6
CRISTOBAL													
Avg.	3.3	1.6	1.5	4.0	12.4	13.2	15.6	15.3	12.5	15.7	22.5	12.2	129.7
Max.	12.2	12.4	9.0	21.4	20.4	21.2	27.7	26.6	23.0	42.2	43.1	34.4	183.4
Min.	0.3	Tr.	Tr.	0.1	1.6	5.9	4.4	5.8	3.1	5.8	6.6	0.9	86.5
PORTOBELO													
Avg.	5.1	3.0	2.6	6.4	17.5	16.9	18.3	19.3	13.2	15.6	24.5	16.1	158.6
Max	20.9	11.6	9.7	30.2	30.6	25.9	29.0	33.5	23.0	42.2	53.3	58.2	237.3
Min.	0.7	0.4	0.6	0.5	5.0	6.5	7.4	8.7	6.5	4.8	7.7	2.2	118.0

SOURCE: Panama Canal Company, Meteorological and Hydrographic Branch

dry season on the Caribbean slope is much less pronounced than on the Pacific, though here, too, notably less precipitation falls than during the rainy season. A pattern somewhat similar to that of the Caribbean slope also prevails on the Pacific slope in most of Darién and in western Chiriquí and on the western side of the Azuero Peninsula. The remainder of the Pacific slope has a more pronounced dry season, most severe in southern Coclé, Herrera, and adjacent Veraguas. Here many trees then lose their leaves (this happens to relatively few species in Caribbean slope forests), the grass turns brown, and many areas are burned over. Not surprisingly, this seasonal fluctuation in rainfall has a pronounced effect on birdlife. Many species time their breeding cycles so that they will be feeding young at about the time when the rains begin, when food is most abundant, this peaking April–June. Furthermore, a growing body of evidence indicates that a number of species engage in local movements correlated with seasonal change; e.g. they migrate to more humid areas during the dry season and then back again (see section on Migration and Local Movements). One other interesting point can be made about rainfall in Panama and in some other tropical areas. Rainfall in much of the temperate zone characteristically occurs during storms that often last for a day or more. In the Panama lowlands, by contrast, rain may come down unbelievably hard, but usually it lasts no more than an hour or two, frequently less. The classic rainy season pattern is for clouds to build during the day, and for a heavy shower to fall in the late afternoon or evening, followed by nighttime clearing. This "schedule" is by no means invariable—especially during October–November, the peak of the rainy season, when it often rains in the morning—but is of regular enough occurrence to take into consideration when planning a day's trip.

The main cause of this annual cycle of dry and rainy seasons is the trade winds. In Panama the northeast trades blow most strongly during the dry season, when they drop their moisture chiefly on the Caribbean slope of the highlands. The winds build up during the day so that on some afternoons there may be a gusty breeze blowing, especially over the open Pacific savannas where they further dessicate an area already made dry by a lack of rain and a hot sun unobstructed by clouds. The constant trades at this season also sometimes cause an upwelling in the Gulf of Panama: warm surface waters are pushed away from the land by the wind, and cooler, more nutrient-rich, underlying water is forced up to take the warm water's place, thereby creating a rich feeding ground for great flocks of birds. During the rainy season, the trades subside and are more variable, though on most afternoons a breeze will spring up; strong gusty winds may occur around squalls and showers. It should finally be pointed out that Panama lies well south of the normal hurricane track, though very occasionally a weak tropical depression may skirt the Caribbean coast.

Most of the preceding description is especially applicable to the lowlands, but some of the same patterns hold in the highlands as well. Temperatures in the highlands are, expectedly, lower, and at high elevations can become rather cold. One notices a significant and pleasant drop in temperature at elevations over 2000 feet, as on Cerro Campana and Cerro Azul. In Chiriquí at elevations over 4000 feet, nights can be cold, and frosts are not unknown, especially at higher elevations, while days are usually in the 60s or low 70s F (lower in inclement weather). Seasonal fluctuations in rainfall are not as marked as in most of the lowlands. The Caribbean slopes tend to be more humid than those on the Pacific, in part a result of frequent low-hanging mist and clouds. Series of several rainy, unpleasant days are not infrequent in the highlands, especially on the Caribbean slope. A typical pattern is for the sky to be crystal clear at daybreak, for clouds to form rapidly during the morning, and for the clouds to lower and precipitation to occur off and on through the afternoon, often in the form of a drenching mist or drizzle (locally called *bajareque*). Some days, though, are delightful and sunny, especially invigorating after the heat of the lowlands. At elevations above 7000 feet, temperatures become progressively colder, clouds and precipitation are likely at any time of the year, and freezes are of at least occasional occurrence, especially during the dry season. Snow has been reported falling briefly on the summit of the Volcán de Chiriquí (*fide* Eisenmann).

MIGRATION AND LOCAL MOVEMENTS

Out of Panama's total avifauna (here considered) of 883 species, and excluding its 23 hypothetical species, 127 species occur only as long-distance migrants, i.e., they are not known or likely to breed in the country. This total (Table III) includes only those species that prob-

TABLE III
REGULAR MIGRANTS
(not known to breed in Panama)

Great Blue Heron	Common Dowitcher
Glossy Ibis	Long-billed Dowitcher
American Wigeon	Common Snipe
Northern Pintail	Wilson's Phalarope
Blue-winged Teal	Ring-billed Gull
Northern Shoveler	Herring Gull
Ring-necked Duck	Laughing Gull
Lesser Scaup	Franklin's Gull
Mississippi Kite	Black Tern
Sharp-shinned Hawk	Gull-billed Tern
Swainson's Hawk	Common Tern
Broad-winged Hawk	Least Tern
Northern Harrier	Royal Tern
Osprey	Sandwich Tern
Peregrine Falcon	Black Skimmer
Merlin	Black-billed Cuckoo
American Kestrel	Yellow-billed Cuckoo
Sora	Chuck-will's-widow
American Coot	Chimney Swift
Black-bellied Plover	Belted Kingfisher
American Golden Plover	Yellow-bellied Sapsucker
Semipalmated Plover	Scissor-tailed Flycatcher
Killdeer	Eastern Kingbird
Solitary Sandpiper	Gray Kingbird
Greater Yellowlegs	Sulphur-bellied Flycatcher
Lesser Yellowlegs	Great Crested Flycatcher
Spotted Sandpiper	Olive-sided Flycatcher
Willet	Eastern Wood-Pewee
Ruddy Turnstone	Western Wood-Pewee
Surfbird	Yellow-bellied Flycatcher
Red Knot	Acadian Flycatcher
Least Sandpiper	Willow Flycatcher
Baird's Sandpiper	Alder Flycatcher
White-rumped Sandpiper	Bank Swallow
Pectoral Sandpiper	Barn Swallow
Semipalmated Sandpiper	Cliff Swallow
Western Sandpiper	Purple Martin
Sanderling	Brown-chested Martin
Stilt Sandpiper	Gray Catbird
Buff-breasted Sandpiper	Wood Thrush
Upland Sandpiper	Swainson's Thrush
Whimbrel	Gray-cheeked Thrush
Marbled Godwit	Veery

TABLE III—Continued

Cedar Waxwing	Northern Waterthrush
Yellow-throated Vireo	Kentucky Warbler
Red-eyed Vireo	Mourning Warbler
Philadelphia Vireo	MacGillivray's Warbler
Black-and-white Warbler	Common Yellowthroat
Prothonotary Warbler	Yellow-breasted Chat
Worm-eating Warbler	Hooded Warbler
Golden-winged Warbler	Wilson's Warbler
Blue-winged Warbler	Canada Warbler
Tennessee Warbler	American Redstart
Yellow Warbler	Orchard Oriole
Magnolia Warbler	Northern (Baltimore) Oriole
Yellow-rumped (Myrtle) Warbler	Bobolink
Black-throated Green Warbler	Summer Tanager
Cerulean Warbler	Scarlet Tanager
Blackburnian Warbler	Rose-breasted Grosbeak
Chestnut-sided Warbler	Blue Grosbeak
Bay-breasted Warbler	Indigo Bunting
Palm Warbler	Painted Bunting
Ovenbird	Dickcissel
Louisiana Waterthrush	

ably occur regularly, though some may occur only in small numbers. Another 33 species (Table IV) have been recorded on but a few occasions, some of them being purely casual or accidental (e.g., Snowy Plover, Vermilion Flycatcher), while others may have only been overlooked (e.g., Elegant Tern, Black-whiskered Vireo). Another 13 species are basically pelagic (Table V) and occur only as nonbreeding visitants; most are rarely seen from shore, and several are known from very few

TABLE IV
VERY RARE OR CASUAL VISITANTS
(not breeding in Panama)

American Bittern	Whip-poor-will
Jabiru	White-chinned Swift
Buff-necked Ibis	Ashy-tailed Swift
Fulvous Tree-Duck	Ruby-throated Hummingbird
Cinnamon Teal	Vermilion Flycatcher
Bay-winged Hawk	Least Flycatcher
Snowy Plover	Tree Swallow
Wandering Tattler	Southern Martin
Dunlin	White-eyed Vireo
Ruff	Black-whiskered Vireo
Long-billed Curlew	Cape May Warbler
Band-tailed Gull	Yellow-throated Warbler
Bonaparte's Gull	Blackpoll Warbler
Large-billed Tern	Connecticut Warbler
Elegant Tern	Western Tanager
Caspian Tern	Lincoln's Sparrow
Burrowing Owl	

TABLE V
PELAGIC VISITANTS

Least Storm-Petrel	Red-footed Booby
Wedge-tailed Shearwater	Northern Phalarope
Sooty Shearwater	Great Skua
Wilson's Storm-Petrel	Pomarine Jaeger
Wedge-rumped Storm-Petrel	Parasitic Jaeger
Black Storm-Petrel	Sabine's Gull
Masked Booby	

(or even one) records. More collecting in Panama waters will undoubtedly add to this pelagic list.

Practically all of the long-distance migrants are temperate or arctic North American breeders; only one landbird breeding in South America is known to migrate regularly to Panama (Brown-chested Martin), though a few others (e.g., Southern Martin, Ashy-tailed Swift, and the Patagonian race of the Blue-and-white Swallow) may be more regular than the few records would indicate. Migration from South America and from farther north in Middle America may be more extensive but in numerous cases involves populations of species or even subspecies that also breed in Panama, and separating migrants from local breeders is difficult or impossible without having marked birds (examples include Fork-tailed Flycatcher of Middle America, Streaked Flycatcher, Gray-breasted Martin). Only 5 species that breed in Panama are definitely thought to migrate out of the country during their nonbreeding season, all 5 being generally absent during the peak of the rainy season and returning in January or later (Swallow-tailed and Plumbeous Kites, Common Nighthawk, Piratic Flycatcher, Yellow-green Vireo).

At some times of the year, especially during the northern autumn and spring migration periods, migrant passerines constitute a conspicuous element in the Panamanian avifauna. As yet relatively little attention has been paid to them in other than a casual way, though their impact at least locally must be great. Some northern breeding species (e.g., Yellow Warbler, Orchard Oriole) arrive in Panama so early and leave so late that they spend considerably more of their year on their winter quarters than on their breeding grounds. In general, most northern migrants shun the forest interior in favor of borders, lighter woodland, and man-disturbed areas such as clearings and gardens. In more wooded areas migrant passerines frequently join mixed flocks of resident species, while in more open areas they are apt to occur in groups of their own species or with other migrants. Northern migrants are most numerous during their periods of transience in the fall and spring, often occurring in marked waves; they are strikingly less numerous during the northern winter months (December–February). However, some migrants remain common, notably in the foothills and highlands, all through the winter, though the reasons for this marked contrast with the lowlands are uncertain. Several other migrant groups besides the passerines occur in significant numbers in Panama. Migrant ducks, though limited in species, are in the aggregate more numerous than all the resident waterfowl put together. Certain species of diurnal raptors (Turkey Vulture, Broad-winged and Swainson's Hawks) provide an almost unbelievable spectacle during their migrations (for photos see N. G. Smith, *American Birds 27*: 3–5, 1973). Many of the shorebirds also gather in impressive flocks, and the variety of species is often notable.

Some Panamanian breeding species may engage in local movements, in most cases of an unknown magnitude. Information on this phenomenon is scant, for it requires long-term observations, population studies, and banding of individuals at specific areas. One problem is that the entire population of a species may not take part in the local movement; i.e., the presence of a few individuals may "mask" the absence of others. What we see for some species is a seasonal fluctuation in abundance, probably caused by seasonal variations in the food supply, or by dispersal of immatures, or both. The Ruddy-breasted and Yellow-bellied Seedeaters are good examples, both seemingly "disappearing" from their breeding areas from the end of the rainy season through most of the dry season. Other species also fluctuate markedly on a local basis, e.g., in the Canal Zone, Blue Ground-Dove and Lesser Elaenia. Various species of hummingbirds almost unquestionably engage in similar local movements (e.g., White-necked Jacobin), probably in order to find sufficient flowering trees and other plants. Again it must be emphasized that these comments are of a preliminary nature, and are included merely to indicate how much has yet to be learned about this interesting and until recently unrecognized phenomenon.

Altitudinal movements are also undertaken by some Panamanian breeding species, in all known cases involving birds that breed in the highlands or foothills and descend to the lowlands in their nonbreeding seasons. Again these movements are little documented in Panama except in the case of two large cotingas, the Three-wattled Bellbird and Bare-necked Umbrellabird, both of which breed in the western highlands and subsequently descend to the lowlands, especially during the peak of the rainy season. Movements of this type are most likely to be noted in lowland areas adjacent to some mountains, which largely eliminates central Panama, where most of the sustained bird observation work to date has taken place. Also, because most of the species involved are forest birds, areas that are still largely covered with forest are required, thus eliminating much of Pacific western Panama. Other species besides the bellbird and umbrellabird that may in part move down-slope after the breeding season include several parrots (Sulphur-winged and Barred

Parakeets and Red-fronted Parrotlet), several hummingbirds (Violet-headed Hummingbird, Snowcap), White-ruffed Manakin, Olive-striped Flycatcher, Pale-vented and White-throated Robins, Silver-throated Tanager, and probably a number of others (in part as to Costa Rica, *fide* G. Stiles, oral comm.). Much further field work will be required before the extent of these movements is known. Bocas del Toro, Caribbean slope Veraguas, and Darién would seem the most promising areas for such studies.

CONSERVATION

There is perhaps no better area in Latin America than Panama where one can easily see within a rather short distance a variety of relatively unspoiled and accessible tropical habitats, each with corresponding abundant bird, mammal, and plant life. For the traveler this situation is made even better by the excellent accommodations available at a number of strategically placed localities (see Appendix II). But as in the rest of Latin America—and throughout the tropics—there are serious and increasing conservation problems in Panama that merit discussion here.

Of pre-eminent concern is the unnecessary and often wanton destruction of the forest that at one time covered the greater part, if not all, of Panama. The extent of forest cover has varied over the millennia, influenced in part by climatic fluctuations (dry periods favoring the spread of savannas, rainy periods the spread of forest) and in part by human population. Though it comes as a surprise to most people, some evidence indicates that at the time of the Spaniard's arrival around 1500 A.D., the Indian population was so large that less of Panama was forested than was the case until very recently (see Bennett, 1968). It is likely, thus, that Balboa passed through planted fields and not through solid forest in crossing the isthmus to "discover" the Pacific. Much of the forest, in eastern Panama especially (where the Indian population was apparently very large), appears to be essentially a regrowth from that period, when for a variety of reasons the Indian population was substantially reduced. But given the technology of Indian society at that time, and the shifting slash-burn type of agriculture then employed (far less damaging to the soil or to potential regrowth than present methods), forest clearing was surely not as total as it usually is today. Unquestionably forest pockets would have remained from which rapid reforestation could take place. The Pacific slope of much of the more humid parts of western Panama was, until the early decades of the present century, covered with extensive forest. Today almost all has been removed from the lowlands except along some watercourses and on some steep hillsides, and the only area where much forest remains is the still roadless western side of the Azuero Peninsula. The usual pattern, often repeated in Panama and elsewhere in Latin America, is for a road to be cut through a formerly "virgin" area. The land near the road is soon cleared, usually by squatters, and within a few years virtually no forest remains except on the far-off slopes or sometimes along water courses. A striking example of this destruction can be seen along the Trans-Isthmian Highway between Panama city and Colon: cut through largely uninhabited, forested country during World War II by the U.S. Army as an alternate means of crossing the isthmus, the road was opened to the public after the war, and now one sees no forest anywhere (not even on the far slopes), except where the road passes through a short stretch of the Canal Zone.

Panama's population continues to grow rapidly, and the people must go somewhere. What better place than into newly opened country? There is still a considerable amount of virtually untouched forested land away from the roads, though this area is obviously being chipped away. But surely controls can be applied to this process of colonization of newly accessible areas. Especially on the steep slopes, where permanent agriculture is almost impossible, rapid erosion certain, and the danger of flooding great, forests should be retained. Failure to preserve such forests has already resulted in a lack of water in some areas during the dry season. Much of the soil in the lowlands is poorly suited for conventional agriculture anyway—a large proportion of the available nutrients are tied up in the naturally occurring vegetation, and are lost when that vegetation is removed. In most areas the soil is so thin that it will produce crops for only a season or two and then must be abandoned. Because of this, the highest economic use for many areas would probably be retention in forest, perhaps with periodic selective cutting of marketable trees, or with growing of certain crops, such as cocoa and coffee, in which most forest canopy trees are retained.

Most of the Canal Zone presents a striking contrast to the picture so far presented. As part of its Canal defense policy, the U.S. government has for years carefully restricted the number of private individuals allowed to farm or settle within Zone limits; there are minor exceptions, but essentially all land is owned and controlled by the government. Because of this exclusionary policy, much of the Zone remained in or reverted to woodland or forest, and now is a virtual island of forest in the midst of generally cleared countryside. The contrast is especially impressive on the road that winds through Madden Forest in the Canal Zone and then suddenly emerges into Panama province. As a result, the Canal Zone now has probably the most extensive, readily accessible lowland forests in Middle America. A great variety of birds, and even many of the larger mammals, can be easily seen, the latter especially on Barro Colorado Island, where protection from hunters is provided. Hunting is allowed generally, and, as the Zone is adjacent to heavily populated areas, some of the larger fauna have been locally extirpated. A newly enacted (1973) hunting law, totally protecting all bird species other than the Blue-winged Teal, Gray-headed Chachalaca, Common Snipe, and doves and pigeons, may, if enforced, greatly aid some species. At present, native waterfowl, the larger eagles, curassows, macaws, as well as such mammals as the jaguar, tapir, and manatee are either gone from the Canal Zone or are very scarce and local. Virtually everything else remains, however, and the Zone continues to be a naturalist's paradise.

Political considerations may soon drastically alter this situation, however. The Republic of Panama understandably resents the large American presence and its obvious affluence. A major change in the status of the Zone has been anticipated for years and is bound to come sooner or later. This surely will mean an end to the Canal Zone as it is presently known, and (unless the Panamanian government takes protective measures) will probably also mean an end to most of its forest. Certain areas, among them Madden Forest and Barro Colorado Island, will, it is hoped, continue to be preserved in their natural state. It is not out of place to make a plea here for preservation of a few additional areas, most notably Fort Sherman and San Lorenzo, the Achiote Road area, and particularly the Pipeline Road area near Gamboa. Even a brief perusal of the main body of this book will reveal how often Pipeline Road is mentioned. For variety of birdlife, it is without question the outstanding, easily accessible forest area in Panama. As such it would make a wonderful wildlife reserve, and if properly protected could become a fine tourist attraction for Panama. For the present, it remains in the hands of the U.S. military, and the forests are intact (though hunting is allowed); its future, like the future of the rest of the Canal Zone, is decidedly uncertain.

Latin America lags considerably behind the rest of the world in setting aside suitable areas as national parks and biological reserves, though some countries are making commendable strides in the right direction, despite severe budgetary restrictions (a fine example is Panama's neighbor, Costa Rica). Panama, unfortunately, trails even most of its sister republics. To date only one national park has been established (in 1968), a small but interesting tract of cloud forest on Cerro Campana, about thirty miles west of Panama city. Regrettably, even this area is inadequately protected and has been invaded by squatters. It is much to be hoped that Panama establish a system of parks, both for its own people and as part of an effort to attract more tourists from abroad. Probably top priority should go to the area in western Chiriquí around Volcán Barú (the Volcán de Chiriquí of much zoological literature), a long extinct volcano that reaches above timberline and is Panama's highest mountain at 11,410 feet. Actual establishment of this long discussed park would protect what remains of a fine highland forest (rapidly being destroyed by squatters), and the faunas that are dependent upon it, including the Resplendent Quetzal (perhaps the most beautiful bird in the New World, and still probably easier to see here than anywhere else) and numerous other species endemic to the highlands of western Panama and adjacent Costa Rica. Adequate samples of other forest habitats should also be set aside before they are totally destroyed; the situation in the lowlands of western Chiriquí is the most critical in this respect. Reservation is relatively easy today because much of the land involved is still owned by the government. Areas should be set aside as forest reserves along the Pan-American Highway as it is extended east through the so-called "Darién Gap," and also along the several trans-isthmian highways now under construction or projected. Government plans for the reservation of sizable areas surrounding the body of water that will be impounded behind the dam on the Bayano River above El Llano are commendable. Protection of the as yet remote Darién highlands, which also contain endemic birds and other animals, and of the many seabird colonies in the Gulf of Panama, is also needed.

A number of bird species have decreased drastically in Panama, especially in recent decades; several have already been mentioned. The Resplendent Quetzal depends upon the highland forests of western Panama, which are rapidly being cleared for new agricultural land. Although it is illegal, males are still shot as trophies, both sexes still find their way into the pot, and young still are removed from nests to be caged, where most promptly die. This bird's potential as a tourist attraction is being realized only slowly. Despite hunting laws regulating the season and bag limits for most gamebirds, a number of species have been overshot, and the laws remain virtually unenforced. The relatively unsuspicious Great Curassow is probably the most endangered, and has been extirpated over wide areas, though it apparently remains fairly numerous in remote inaccessible forests. The somewhat warier and more arboreal Crested Guan seems better able to withstand hunting pressure, and remains in reduced numbers wherever the forest cover it depends on is retained. The Black Guan, endemic to the highland forests of the western highlands and Costa Rica, has become decidedly scarce in western Chiriquí, and probably has declined to at least an equal degree in other parts of its Panama range, though there are no recent data. Tinamous and wood-quail are also hunted assiduously, but their overall decline is probably more due to forest destruction than to direct hunting pressure. Wood-quail are considerably less furtive, however, and consequently are more vulnerable; the Marbled Wood-Quail has for example declined considerably even in the forested Canal Zone. Populations of the resident species of waterfowl have been decimated in many areas by unrestricted year-round shooting. The once abundant Band-tailed Pigeon of the western highlands has also decreased dramatically due to heavy hunting, though it is still reasonably common at least locally. Many diurnal birds of prey remain fairly numerous in Panama, though again all species dependent on forest have seen their potential ranges shrink drastically. However the larger species, in particular the huge Harpy Eagle, have become very rare in recent years, and the Harpy appears to have decreased even in remote areas despite its official protection.

The group whose status gives greatest cause for alarm is the macaws. Though at one time widespread in Panama, today they are restricted entirely to remote forested areas. One species, the Scarlet Macaw, once ranged over the Pacific slope east to the Canal Zone, but is now found regularly only on Coiba Island off the coast of Veraguas, and if that island's status as a penal institute should be altered and the area opened to settlement, the macaws would undoubtedly be swiftly eliminated. The other Panamanian members of the genus are not yet in such a precarious situation, but all species have been greatly reduced in overall numbers. Macaws are sometimes shot for food, but the primary cause of their rapid decrease (other than the usual forest destruction) has been the taking of young from nests to be kept as pets or sold into the cagebird traffic. If there are to be any macaws at all in Panama a few decades hence, measures prohibiting their exportation from the country will have to be implemented.

The picture is not entirely bleak, though. In recent years a number of persons residing in Panama have become aware of the conservation problem, and are organizing ever more effectively to do something about it. The Comisión Nacional de Protección de la Fauna Silvestre (National Commission for Wildlife Protection) was formed in 1967 under the Ministry of Agriculture and was instrumental in obtaining presidential decrees protecting various animals, including the Quetzal and the Harpy Eagle. In 1967 Panama organized a national section of the International Council for Bird Preservation (ICBP). The Panama Audubon Society has striven to interest more people in the country's birdlife and the need for its protection. An increasing number of persons visit Panama each year for the express purpose of seeing its birds and other wildlife. But any such progress will inevitably be short-lived if the present rapid rate of population increase (over 3 percent annually) continues for any length of time. In the long run, curbing this increase will not only be of great benefit to Panama's marvelously rich avifauna, it will also be much in the interest of the Panamanian people, for only then will real social and economic progress for all the people become possible.

PLAN OF THE BOOK

Persons who have had field experience observing birds, especially in the neotropics, will find this book much easier to use than those who are just starting out in this fascinating study. A certain amount of knowledge has had to be assumed. However, I have tried to make the book both understandable to the beginner and useful to the experienced amateur and professional. Thus, some information is included that only the beginner will need (such as how to tell an ibis from a heron), and also data that only those with experience will know how to use (such as how to distinguish the two dowitcher species).

In this section I will discuss the major headings found under each family and species account, and define the more important terms used.

Family Accounts

The sequence of families followed is essentially that of Wetmore (1960), with a few minor deviations. The family accounts themselves follow a relatively standardized format in order to facilitate comparison. First, the general distribution of the family is given, and its approximate size is indicated. Generalizations about the family that may be helpful to the field student are made, with emphasis on distinctive family characteristics. Data on food preferences, general behavior, and style of nest are included here for the Panamanian members of the family as a whole, rather than in the individual species accounts. Finally, where appropriate, special identification problems in the family are outlined, and its current status in Panama is discussed. The number of species recorded for the family in Panama is given in parentheses in the heading.

Species Accounts

Some discussion of classification and nomenclature is essential at this juncture. The species is the basic unit in biology. Most zoologists now accept the view that an animal species consists of a group of populations whose members interbreed freely, or would do so if their ranges met. Different species are usually also morphologically distinct, i.e., they "look different," though this is not a prerequisite, and some geographical populations of the same species look very different and yet interbreed freely where their ranges meet. Many species contain several such subspecies or geographic races, which inhabit different portions of the range of the species. Subspecies generally differ only slightly in appearance. Only those subspecies occurring in Panama that differ markedly from each other are mentioned in the main text. This all seems simple in theory, but in practice it often proves difficult. The problem that most concerns the nonsystematist arises when zoologists differ as to whether or not a particular population or populations, usually isolated and of distinctive appearance, represents a valid species or is merely a subspecies or group of subspecies. In the neotropics, where knowledge of bird distribution and behavior is still inadequate, this kind of disagreement occurs frequently. Differences in the names used then cause a great deal of confusion among some amateurs, who cannot understand why names vary from book to book.

This book attempts to steer a middle-of-the-road course in scientific nomenclature, for I make no pretense of being a taxonomist. I have accepted the recommendations of Eisenmann, who strongly urged that no taxonomic innovations be adopted in a book of this sort, even though he might personally favor them. In general, the policy has been to retain most reasonably distinct forms as valid species where such treatment has been customary in the literature. In most disputed cases at the species level, I follow the recommendations of Wetmore to the extent published in parts I–III of his Panama work; also followed are all recommendations of the American Ornithologists' Union Checklist Committee (including the supplement published in the April 1973 *Auk*). Some recent authors (for example, Meyer de Schauensee and R. A. Paynter, Jr.) tend to merge species (and genera) somewhat more, i.e., they often combine in one species related representative forms unless there is evidence of overlap without interbreeding. In this book, when a serious taxonomic question at the species (or sometimes higher) level involves Panama populations, it is always mentioned in the hope that work in Panama might help to resolve it.

Most nonprofessionals are not usually concerned with the scientific name except insofar as they generally wish to list only what are regarded as full species. Of greater concern to them is the common or English name that each species has been given. In temperate North America and Europe these names have been generally standardized and accepted, though a few changes will always have to be made in order to conform with new taxonomic findings. But in the neotropics, where ornithology is hardly more advanced than it was in the United States at the turn of the century, a single species may have been given several different English names by various authors. This obviously creates difficulties for those who are not accustomed to using the Latin names—one often cannot be sure what bird the other person is talking about. A giant step toward the standardization of these names for neotropical birds was taken with the publication of Eisenmann's *The Species of Middle American Birds* (1955) and de Schauensee's *The Species of Birds of South America* (1966), the latter prepared with considerable assistance from Eisenmann. These names have been followed, more or less, by most recent authors, and have been recommended by the Checklist Committee of the American Ornithologists' Union, though a few recent authors have employed rather different names. The problem of common names is a thorny one: everyone has their personal preferences, and one usually wants to retain names that are familiar to him. But the primary issue is one of utility and standardization. Therefore the names used in this book are those of Eisenmann and de Schauensee with but very few exceptions. Widely used alternate names, including those of Wetmore, are also indicated.

After much consideration, I decided not to include Spanish names, as there seems as yet to be little agreement on the subject. A few widely used popular names have been mentioned.

The sequence of species within each family is essentially that of Eisenmann (1955), with a few deviations.

Each species account is divided into up to six headings, as follows; one or more may be omitted where there is insufficient information.

DESCRIPTION

First the species' average total length in inches (from tip of bill to end of tail) is given; other lengths are also mentioned when appropriate (hummingbird bills, elongated tail feathers, etc.). The first sentence is designed as a "warning sentence," and is included when the species is not widespread in its Panama range. For example, "found only in western highlands" means that in Panama it ranges only in the highlands of Chiriquí, Veraguas, and sometimes Bocas del Toro. Thus any observation away from this area would be highly unusual and should be carefully checked. Another phrase, "known only from . . . ," is similar, but implies that while the species has been recorded only from the area given, the species is little known and may be more widespread. The next sentence gives distinguishing features of shape and soft-part colors, when these are particularly helpful in species recognition.

Adult males are described first, followed by females, immatures, juvenals, and aberrant plumages where appropriate (often all that is indicated is how they differ from the adult male). For each, a diagnosis of the entire plumage is given. Species that also occur in North America have been fully treated (though very few are illustrated) as it was thought desirable to have in one reference data needed for field recognition of *any* species occurring in Panama. The description is kept simple, with minor details not considered important to identification omitted. The most distinctive characters of the species are italicized. In a few cases where a less well-known species closely resembles another better known bird, reference is made to the latter and only distinguishing points are given. Many North American migrants (but, interestingly, very few resident species: one is the male Red-legged Honeycreeper) have a breeding and a nonbreeding ("winter") plumage. In Panama these migrants are most often seen in nonbreeding plumage, hence that is usually treated first.

SIMILAR SPECIES

Comparison is made here between the species under discussion and others known from Panama with which it might be confused. For a few difficult groups, wing and tail measurements (in millimeters) are included as an aid to mist-netters. When the species is not likely to be confused, this paragraph is omitted.

STATUS AND DISTRIBUTION

In this sometimes lengthy paragraph, the known range of the species in Panama, its relative abundance, its period of occurrence when not a resident, and its known habitat preferences are given. For some species, specific, accessible localities where they may be more easily found than elsewhere are included. If information on some (or all) of these points is scanty, this is clearly indicated in the hope that further work will fill in some of these gaps in our knowledge. For many of the less common species, specific, almost always otherwise unpublished, records are mentioned. In the case of sight reports of such rarities, the name of the observer(s) is given. Collector's names are included only when the record was not mentioned by Wetmore or when some special situation is involved. Emphasis has been placed on documenting reports not included in Wetmore's volumes, or which occurred subsequent to preparation of his volumes, when such reports have significantly altered the status or range of that species in Panama.

Accents have been included only on proper names thought not to be well known to English readers. Thus Panama, Galapagos, Peru, Yucatan, Colon have not been accented (though they are in Spanish, e.g. Panamá, Colón, Yucatán), while other, less familiar names have had their accent retained, in part as a pronunciation guide (e.g. Chiriquí, Darién, Coclé, Calovévora, etc.).

Abundance Terms

The abundance terms used here are necessarily subjective and thus require considerable explanation. Many species in Panama, especially those of forest and undergrowth, are very difficult to see; one hears them many times for each time seen. In estimating relative abundance of these species, I have relied heavily on their often very distinctive vocalizations, and this fact must be borne in mind. For example, I have listed the Streak-chested Antpitta as "fairly common" though I personally have not seen it (other than in mist-nets) more than a half-dozen times. Nonetheless it is known to be fairly common in suitable habitat because its distinctive far-carrying call is so often heard. The numerical abundance of certain furtive, undergrowth species is much better indicated by mist-net captures than by sight observations (the leaftossers are prime examples), and consideration has also been given to this factor.

Two further qualifications must be made. First, my field experience is strongly biased toward the Canal Zone and adjacent areas, where I have spent most of my time in Panama. The abundance terms used tend to be slanted to an indeterminable extent by my experiences in that area. Oral or published opinions of others (especially Wetmore and Eisenmann) have been somewhat helpful in this respect, but it must be pointed out that little concentrated observation has been done in Panama away from the Canal Zone and vicinity (except very locally in the western Chiriquí highlands and the lowlands of western Bocas del Toro). In some cases the problem has been overcome by separating ranges into several parts, while in others no abundance term has been used at all. One should also remember that, in general, as one approaches the geographical limit of the range of a species, the species becomes less numerous (for example, the Black-tailed Trogon and Sirystes are both rather scarce at the northwestern limit of their range in the Canal Zone area, but become more numerous as one moves into eastern Panama). Second, abundance terms must be approached in a relative sense: hawks should be compared with hawks, and flycatchers with flycatchers, but not hawks with flycatchers. The Double-toothed Kite and Forest Elaenia are both listed as fairly common, but there are not nearly as many kites per acre as there are elaenias. There is thus a double standard, one for large birds, another for smaller ones. In general, moreover, birds of open situations, being more easily seen, will appear more numerous than those of forest or woodland, though again they may not be any more numerous per acre. Here, too, there is a double standard, one for more or less open country, one for wooded areas.

The abundance terms used here are explained below. A "trip" is considered to be a day's field work. The terms must be viewed in a relative, not absolute, sense. It should be emphasized that the terms refer to the frequency with which the experienced observer, especially one familiar with their vocalizations, notes them; clearly the beginner will not be as successful.

Abundant. Recorded on all field trips in proper habitat and season, often in large numbers. These are usually birds of open areas or water habitats. Examples: Tropical Kingbird, Western Sandpiper.

Very common. Almost invariably recorded on trips in proper habitat and season, but not observed in as large numbers as the preceding category. Examples: Slaty Antshrike, Lesser Greenlet.

Common. Recorded on most (at least 75%) trips in proper habitat and season, but usually not in large numbers. Examples: Boat-billed Flycatcher, Slaty-tailed Trogon.

Fairly common. Recorded on about half of trips in proper habitat and season. Examples: Blue-chested Hummingbird, White-winged Tanager. From this category on, numbers recorded on any trip are usually small.

Uncommon. Recorded on less than half (between 25 and 50%) of trips in proper habitat and season. Examples: Ocellated Antbird, Gray-headed Kite.

Rare. Recorded on fewer (usually considerably fewer) than 25% of trips in proper habitat and season. Examples: Wilson's Phalarope, Dull-mantled Antbird.

Very rare. Records extremely few anywhere in Panama, and always in small numbers, but presumed to be a resident within the country, or within the expected range of a migrant or wanderer. Examples: Least Flycatcher, Lanceolated Monklet.

The following terms relate to distributional status or regularity, rather than primarily to numbers.

Casual. Records very few in Panama; a migrant or wandering species that ranges regularly not too far from Panama, but that cannot be expected to occur in the country except at intervals (usually long). Examples: Buff-necked Ibis, Yellow-throated Warbler.

Accidental. Usually only one record for Panama, and hardly to be expected again though possible; a species whose normal range is a considerable distance from Panama. Examples: Burrowing Owl, Vermilion Flycatcher.

Hypothetical. A species for which there is no incontrovertible proof of occurrence in Panama. Species have been admitted to full status on the Panama list if: a) a specimen has been collected and preserved, or b) a recognizable photograph has been taken, or c) there are at least three independent sight reports by at least three competent observers of a species that can be identified in the field. Failure to meet one of these criteria relegates a species to the hypothetical list for Panama. A few additional species have been placed on the hypothetical list because there is doubt as to whether it reached Panama unassisted or whether the specimen attributed to Panama was actually collected in the country. By these criteria, 23 species are on Panama's hypothetical list. In the text the English names for each of these species is placed in brackets.

Local. A relatively subjective term indicating that a species seems not to be found in all areas that, on the basis of present knowledge, appear suitable. Numerous forest species seem to be local, though this may at least in part be due to the furtive habits of many and a lack of sufficient field work (some may have very narrow ecological tolerances). Examples: Wing-banded Antbird, Short-billed Marsh-Wren.

Irregular. A migrant or wandering species whose numbers fluctuate considerably from year to year, i.e. in some years it may be locally numerous while in others it is rare or even absent. Examples: Cedar Waxwing, Yellow-rumped (Myrtle) Warbler.

Scarce. Used occasionally as a general term to refer to an uncommon or rare species, especially in the case of migrants.

Altitude Terms

To indicate elevation, four terms have been used. There is considerable overlap between adjacent zones, and a good deal of variation occurs depending on local climatic conditions. On the more humid Caribbean slope the upper zones tend to extend somewhat lower. For still controversial reasons, many birds of higher elevations tend to occur somewhat lower where the mountain ranges are low than where the mountains are high; thus many basically montane species occur notably lower in Veraguas and Darién than they do in Chiriquí. The unit of measurement used throughout is feet, not meters.

Lowlands. Areas ranging from sea level up to about 2000 feet.

Foothills (Sometimes hill country). Areas ranging between about 1500 and 4000 feet.

Highlands. Areas above about 3000 feet; used in a general sense.

Mountains. Areas above about 6000 feet (found chiefly in Chiriquí). Timberline in Chiriquí occurs at about 10,000 feet.

Habitat Terms

The habitat terms used also require some discussion. As will be seen, many species occur in more than one, and the habitats themselves often merge almost imperceptibly. The following are the terms most frequently employed.

Forest, humid forest, and deciduous forest. In mature tropical forest the trees are tall (averaging about 100 feet in height with occasional taller emergent trees), and in fairly level areas they form a more or less solid canopy that so reduces the amount of sunlight reaching the ground that there is little undergrowth. *Forest* is used in a general sense for tall mature canopied woodland, and has been subdivided into two major types. *Humid forest* is luxuriant and occurs where the climate is sufficiently wet that most trees retain their leaves throughout the year. *Deciduous forest* occurs where the climate is drier; here the dry season is marked, at which time a larger number of trees lose their leaves. *Humid forest* includes Holdridge's "rain forest," "wet forest," and "moist forest"; *deciduous forest* is equivalent to Holdridge's "dry forest." Humid forest is found (where not removed by man) in the Caribbean lowlands, in much of the foothill zone on both slopes, and in parts of eastern Panama province and Darién. Deciduous forest occurred on most of the Pacific slope lowlands, but much of it has been destroyed except on the western side of the Azuero Peninsula, in eastern Panama province, and in western and southern Darién. The term *cloud forest* has not been used in the descriptions; the forests found in the highlands of Panama are simply called *forest,* though in the sense that many other authors use the term, it is cloud forest. It should be mentioned that unless one is willing to mount a full-fledged "expedition," one is not going to see much "virgin" forest in Panama, for virtually all of the reasonably accessible forest has been cut over at one time or another. But much forest is fully mature, and mature and virgin forest are actually scarcely distinguishable from each other in their structure (though in tree species composition they may differ).

In a structural sense, forest can be divided into five components, each with its own characteristic set of birds: ground (Great Tinamou); undergrowth, within about 10 feet of the ground (Spotted Antbird); lower tree levels, between about 5 and 20 feet of the ground (Olivaceous Flatbill); middle tree levels, roughly 15 to 50 feet above the ground (Rufous Piha); and upper levels, everything higher, including the top of the canopy (Green Shrike-Vireo, Blue Cotinga). These divisions are, of course, generalizations, but are useful in describing where a bird is most apt to be found, and are frequently employed throughout the text. Tropical forests are noted for their remarkable diversity of tree species, and also for their profuse growth of epiphytes, lianas, and many species of orchids. In tropical forests is also found the highest diversity of bird species, and many of the most interesting to the average observer.

Second-growth woodland. A relatively mature regrowth stage found over large areas, which in time will develop into true forest. Woodland eventually covers an area that was cleared in the fairly recent past but has subsequently been allowed to grow back to trees. The trees in woodland are not as tall as in forest, averaging not more than 50 or 75 feet in height. In its more mature stages, the canopy is more or less closed, but a greater amount of light gets through than in forest and hence there is more undergrowth, which at borders may be very dense.

Dry woodland. Here the trees are even smaller and spaced farther apart than in second-growth woodland, and the undergrowth is often very dense. Many species of trees lose their leaves during the dry season. Dry woodland occurs near the Pacific coast of the Canal Zone and on many of the Pearl Islands; again much of it has been highly disturbed. If left alone for sufficiently long periods of time, even this woodland will develop into tall deciduous forest, as it has on Coiba Island.

Gallery woodland or forest. A special type of woodland or forest (depending on the size of the trees), referring to the growth of trees along streams or other watercourses in otherwise mostly open country. In Panama, gallery forest or woodland is usually a remnant of a more extensive forest that has been largely destroyed. Good examples can be seen in the Tocumen/Chepo area of eastern Panama province, and in the Chiriquí lowlands.

Forest or woodland borders. Describes the edge of either forest or woodland with a more open area such as a road, clearing, stream or river, or even where a tree has fallen, taking down many of its neighbors. The vegetation is usually dense, in humid areas often with *Heliconia* and other big-leaved monocots, and it more closely resembles the popular conception of a "jungle" than does the interior of forest or woodland. Borders are interesting habitats for the bird observer, for the variety is often great, visibility is usually better than inside forest or woodland, and many upper-level or canopy species often come lower, while many undergrowth species may venture briefly into the open.

Shrubby areas and clearings. The regrowth stage preceding woodland. Here an area that had been recently cleared is being allowed to grow up with shrubs, small trees, and dense thickety growth with interspersed areas of tall grass. Many stages of this habitat occur, of course, and with time trees slowly become dominant. Shrubby clearings have a surprisingly rich avifauna, though many species are difficult to observe clearly because of the dense growth. Bird activity during the first few hours of the day is high, but afterwards seems to taper off even more markedly than in forest.

Scrubby areas. A distinctive habitat of the Pacific lowlands. It is a relatively permanent growth (probably in whole or in part maintained by fire) of low and often scraggly bushes and small trees with grass interspersed, usually found in areas with a relatively dry climate and poor or much eroded soil. In its relative permanence, it is unlike the shrubby growth found in clearings in more humid areas or areas with better soil, which if undisturbed can revert to woodland and forest. Characteristic areas occur in southern Coclé and adjacent western Panama province.

Savannas and grassland. Also found most extensively on the Pacific slope, although there are increasingly large grassy clearings on the Caribbean as well. The two terms are used here more or less interchangeably to describe the open grassy plains that dominate much of the Pacific lowlands except in eastern Panama. Such habitat in Panama is apparently not natural, though some of it is ancient, being artificially maintained through seasonal burning. Trees are found along fencelines (the "live fences"), along watercourses (gallery woodland), and a few are planted around habitations or are retained to shade cattle.

Residential areas and gardens. The man-maintained areas around habitations, with planted trees and shrubs and lawns. A surprisingly rich bird habitat, especially if it is near an undeveloped area. The best such areas are found in the Canal Zone, notably at Ancon Heights and Summit Gardens.

Swamps. Low areas where water stands most of the year with considerable tree growth. Natural fresh water swamps are rare in Panama except in Bocas del Toro and Darién.

Marshes. Low areas where water stands most of the year, supporting emergent vegetation, but where trees do not grow. Likewise not extensive in Panama, found primarily in the Pacific lowlands.

Mangroves. A distinctive association found locally in the intertidal zone on both slopes, consisting of a few species of trees, flooded to varying depths at high tide, characterized by their stilt-like roots. Rather extensive in Panama, but usually difficult of access. In Chiriquí and along some other coasts, the mangroves are tall and form an impressive forest.

Ocean. The Gulf of Panama comprises that section of the Pacific lying north of a line connecting the Azuero Peninsula with Darién; Panama Bay is that portion of the Gulf lying north of the Pearl Islands. The largest numbers of seabirds usually occur around driftlines, often found south of the Pearl Islands and off Darién and the Azuero.

HABITS

This paragraph includes various supplementary facts about the species, most of which should aid in identification (such as whether or not it ocurs in groups or mixed foraging flocks). Special attention is given to transcriptions of the vocalizations of the species, recognition of which is so important to bird identification in the tropics. In most cases where a transcription is given with no credit, that credit belongs to Eisenmann.

RANGE

A summary indication of the entire range of the species is included here. This information is derived basically from published sources, with de Schauensee's *The Species of Birds of South America* (1966) being especially useful.

NOTE

When there is a current dispute as to the taxonomic status of the species, this is briefly noted. Also included under this heading are other more or less similar species that have not yet been recorded from Panama, but that seem rather likely to occur, and for which one should be alert. In general, these are species known to migrate or wander extensively, or are species whose known ranges closely approach Panama either in Costa Rica or northwestern Colombia. For each, a brief diagnosis of its appearance and range is given.

PENGUINS: Spheniscidae (1)

The penguins are a well-known group of flightless seabirds of colder waters of the Southern Hemisphere. They hardly merit inclusion here as Panama's only recorded species is certainly at most an accidental visitor, and probably would never have occurred but for the aid of man.

[GALAPAGOS PENGUIN]
(*Spheniscus mendiculus*)

Description: 19–20. One record from coast of Chiriquí. *Face black bordered above, behind, and below by white stripe;* otherwise slaty above (becoming more brownish as feathers wear); white below with *two slaty bands across chest.* Immature has blackish areas paler, with pattern more obscure but already present.

Status and distribution: Only record is an immature captured alive in the surf at Puerto Armuelles, Chiriquí, by a local fisherman in February 1955. The bird was kept alive for a month, then died, and was ultimately prepared as a specimen, now at the Smithsonian. It seems likely that the bird was captured by some visiting vessel in the Galapagos, then released (or escaped) off Chiriquí.

Range: Galapagos Islands; possibly wanders to Panama.

Note: Humboldt Penguin (*S. humboldti*) of coastal Peru and northern Chile is similar though larger (26–28″), with one slaty band across chest. Either species could conceivably wander north in Niño Current (warm water) years.

TINAMOUS: Tinamidae (4)

The tinamous are an exclusively neotropical group of terrestrial birds much sought after as game; Panama's four species range in size from that of a quail to a grouse. They are compact in build, with thin slightly decurved bills, small heads, slender necks, and very short tails. All are cryptically colored in shades of brown and gray, often barred or spotted with darker. Panama's representatives are shy and infrequently seen inhabitants of forest, woodland, or brushy areas (others in South America are found in open country). None flies often or particularly well. Many have beautiful, tremulous, whistled calls; all are heard much more often than seen. Their food is primarily vegetable matter. Tinamous are known for their lovely unicolored eggs with a glazed, almost enamel-like surface. So far as known, incubation is exclusively by the male; females may lay eggs at several sites for different males to incubate, and two or more females may lay at one site for a single male.

GREAT TINAMOU
(*Tinamus major*) Pl.1

Description: 16–18. *Large. Mostly olive brown,* barred with dusky especially on upperparts and flanks. Birds from western Caribbean slope (*fuscipennis*) have crown sooty olive brown; on Pacific slope and in eastern Panama crown chestnut brown; *distinctly crested* from eastern Colon and eastern Panama provinces eastward (*saturatus*).

Similar species: Much larger than Little or (in extreme eastern Darién) Chocó Tinamous. Highland Tinamou of Chiriquí highlands is browner above with blackish cap, rufescent below.

Status and distribution: Fairly common in forest in lowlands and foothills on both slopes, ranging up in smaller numbers into lower highlands (to about 5000 feet) in Chiriquí and Darién; absent from dry open Pacific lowlands from eastern side of Azuero Peninsula to western Panama province. A highly esteemed table bird, it becomes less numerous and more wary near settled areas. Still reasonably common in forested areas on Caribbean slope of Canal Zone, particularly on Pipeline Road and in the Achiote/Escobal area.

Habits: Usually shy and not often observed, normally walking away quietly or hiding, but occasionally flushes with a great rush like a grouse. Roosts at night on a branch or liana. Heard far more often than it is seen; the call consists basically of two beautiful, long, tremulous whistles, the first slightly lower pitched and sometimes repeated two or three times, the second note sliding down; it calls chiefly at dawn and dusk, occasionally during the day or at night. The eggs, placed between the buttresses of a large forest tree, are a beautiful glossy turquoise blue or blue-green.

Range: Southern Mexico to northern Bolivia and Amazonian Brazil.

HIGHLAND TINAMOU
(*Nothocercus bonapartei*) Pl.1

Description: 15–16. Known only from Chiriquí highlands. *Crown and sides of head blackish;* otherwise dark brown above, finely vermiculated with black, more rufous on nape; wings and rump spotted with buff; *almost uniform rufous below,* brightest on throat, buffier on belly, narrowly and sparsely barred with black except on throat, more heavily barred black on sides and flanks.

Similar species: Slightly smaller than Great Tinamou and richer brown and rufous generally (not so olive), especially on underparts; Great Tinamou in Chiriquí has chestnut brown (not black) crown.

Status and distribution: Rare (at least very infrequently recorded in recent years) in forest in highlands of western Chiriquí, mostly above 5000 feet.

Habits: Little known but apparently the highland counterpart of the Great Tinamou. The call is reported to consist of two notes and to be wholly different from the tremulous whistling of other Panama tinamous (Wetmore). In Venezuela the call is a loud, deep, harsh, even nasal *caw-oh* or *kooyoó* repeated over and over (Eisenmann).

Range: Costa Rica and western Panama; Colombia to northern Venezuela and northern Peru.

LITTLE TINAMOU
(*Crypturellus soui*) Pl.1

Description: 9–9½. *The smallest Panama tinamou. Nearly uniform brown with no barring,* more rufous on rump and tail, whitish on throat and more gray on chest. Some birds are more grayish brown. Females are brighter brown, especially below.

Similar species: Easily identified by its small size, lack of barring, and usually its non-forest habitat. In extreme eastern Darién see Chocó Tinamou.

Status and distribution: Common in forest borders, second-growth woodland, overgrown clearings, and scrubby areas in lowlands and foothills on both slopes, ranging up in reduced numbers to lower highlands (to about 5000 feet) in western Chiriquí; found also on Pearl Islands (Rey) where possibly introduced by Amerindians.

Habits: Extremely furtive, and though frequently heard rarely seen. Almost exclusively terrestrial, keeping to dense thickets, and rarely flying. There are two main calls, one a series of clear tremulous whistles, each higher in pitch than the preceding, increasing in volume and rapidity and usually ending abruptly; the other somewhat resembling that of the Great Tinamou, sliding up about a half tone, then down about a full tone; neither call is nearly as resonant as the Great Tinamou's.

Range: Southern Mexico to northern Bolivia and southern Brazil.

CHOCO TINAMOU
(*Crypturellus kerriae*)

Description: 12. Known only from eastern Darién. *Legs reddish. Crown blackish, sides of head slaty gray;* otherwise dark warm brown above indistinctly barred with dusky; upper throat white, lower throat gray, remaining underparts dull cinnamon brown. Female has breast and flanks slaty gray and is somewhat darker above.

Similar species: The only Panamanian tinamou with reddish legs. Little Tinamou is smaller and almost uniform brown, with no black or gray on head.

Status and distribution: Recently discovered "in heavy forest" in lower foothills (1000–2500 feet) of extreme eastern Darién on steep slopes of Cerro Quía on trail from Río Mono; two specimens have been taken, one on March 13, 1970, the other on February 21, 1971 (Wetmore and P. Galindo, 1972).

Habits: Very little known, even in its Colombian range. Its voice is reported to be a "low, tremulous, single-noted whistle, repeated constantly at two or three second intervals" (Wetmore and P. Galindo).

Range: Eastern Panama and extreme northwestern Colombia.

Note: Eisenmann believes *kerriae* is closely allied to, or possibly even conspecific with, *C. boucardi* (Slaty-breasted Tinamou) of southern Mexico to Costa Rica.

GREBES: Podicipedidae (2)

Panama's two members of this widespread family are found exclusively on fresh water lakes, ponds, and marshes. They have lobed toes and are expert divers, feeding on aquatic invertebrates and to a lesser extent fish. Their nests are floating structures attached to aquatic vegetation.

Least Grebe

LEAST GREBE
(*Podiceps dominicus*)

Description: 9. *Slender black pointed bill.* Cap and throat black, sides of head and neck sooty, with *prominent pale orange to yellow eye;* otherwise brownish gray above; paler below, whitish on center of breast and belly, more cinnamon on chest. In flight shows white wing patch. Juvenal has whitish throat, striped face and neck.

Similar species: Smaller and slenderer than Pied-billed Grebe with narrower black bill (not stout and whitish) and darker head. The pale eye often stands out at a distance.

Status and distribution: Fairly common on shallow ponds and lakes, especially those with marshy borders, in lowlands on both slopes; ranges up to lower highlands of western Chiriquí on Volcán Lakes; found also on Coiba Island. Widespread in Canal Zone in suitable habitat.

Habits: Almost invariably seen swimming, usually singly or in pairs, in favorable areas in scattered groups. Obtains most of its food by diving underwater. Often seen on same lakes as Pied-billed Grebe, but will occupy small ponds too shallow for that species. Has a high pitched nasal *"yank."*

Range: Southern Texas and Mexico to central Argentina; West Indies.

PIED-BILLED GREBE
(*Podilymbus podiceps*)

Description: 12–14. *Thick short white bill,* with black ring in breeding plumage. *Mostly grayish brown,* somewhat paler below, with black throat patch in breeding plumage and white under tail-coverts. Shows no white on wing in flight. Juvenal has dusky and white stripes on sides of head and neck.

Similar species: Least Grebe is smaller and darker on head and neck, with narrow pointed black bill.

Status and distribution: Fairly common locally on ponds and lakes in lowlands on both slopes in western and central Panama; some individuals are northern migrants, but the species is known to breed in western Bocas del Toro, western Chiriquí (Volcán Lakes in lower highlands), Herrera, Canal Zone, and eastern Panama province (La Jagua). Not recorded from Darién or San Blas but seems likely to occur. Widespread in Canal Zone in suitable habitat.

Habits: Much like Least Grebe but more reluctant to fly and favors somewhat deeper and more open water. Like other grebes often submerges slowly, leaving only the head and neck above water. The usual call, often heard in the breeding season, is a loud *cuk-cuk, cuk-cuk, cuk-cuk, cow-cow-cow.*

Range: Canada to southern South America; West Indies

ALBATROSSES: Diomedeidae (3)

Albatrosses are very large seabirds found primarily in southern oceans, with three species in the North Pacific and one other nesting on the Galapagos Islands. All are characterized by their exceptionally long and very narrow wings and stout, strongly hooked bills; several species are among the largest flying birds in the world. They feed on squid and other marine animals. Albatrosses are best known for their marvelous powers of flight, gliding without a flap over the water for extended periods of time. They are entirely pelagic except when nesting on small islands; apparently no member of the group is regular in Panamanian waters.

[WANDERING ALBATROSS]
(*Diomedea exulans*)

Description: 40–50. One record. *Very large* with long narrow wings (spread of 9–10 feet, sometimes more). Heavy pinkish bill. Old adult is *all white* with black wing tips and tipping to secondaries; adult female has brown rear crown and some brown vermiculations on back. Juvenal brown with *white facial area* and *white under wing surface* (as in adults); they become progressively whiter with age, requiring more than 10 years to attain full adult plumage.

Similar species: So much larger than most other albatrosses that confusion is most unlikely; one of the largest flying birds. In all plumages, *entire* under wing surface is white except for dark tip to primaries and line along rear edge.

Status and distribution: One yearling was captured alive in Panama Bay in August 1937 and brought to Balboa, where it was photographed and released. No subsequent records. This bird possibly was captured in southern waters, kept on a ship coming north to transit the Canal, and then released (or escaped) in Panama Bay.

Range: Breeds on subantarctic islands; in America, wanders north to Chile and southern Brazil; one recent record from southern California, where possibly also a released bird.

[GALAPAGOS (WAVED) ALBATROSS]
(*Diomedea irrorata*)

Description: 35. Two sight reports. *Heavy yellow bill. Head and neck yellowish white; otherwise sooty with narrow wavy white barring above and narrow white freckling below;* under wing-coverts grayish white with dusky markings.

Similar species: Gray-headed Albatross has partly or mainly black bill and adults have white underparts (whitish in immatures). Wandering Albatross is much larger.

Status and distribution: Apparently an occasional wanderer to Pacific offshore waters; no specimens. Two reports: one seen west of Piñas Bay, Darién on February 26, 1941 (R. C. Murphy, who also collected one just south of the Panama-Colombia border near the Octavio Rocks on March 8, 1941); three seen during gale SW of Pearl Islands (Galera) on September 27, 1964 (N. G. Smith). The albatross most likely to be seen in Panamanian waters.

Range: Breeds in Galapagos Islands; ranges at sea off Peru, Ecuador, Colombia, and casually Panama.

[GRAY-HEADED ALBATROSS]
(*Diomedea chrysostoma*)

Description: 32–36. One somewhat dubious published report from Pacific coast. *Bill black* with orange-yellow stripe down culmen and another on underside of lower mandible. *Head and neck light bluish gray* (though becoming whiter with age and wear), back and tail gray, wings blackish; rump and *underparts white; under wing-surface mostly white* with broad black leading edge and narrower black trailing edge.

Similar species: See Galapagos Albatross. Probably not safely identified in the field in Panamanian waters as confusion is likely with other "mollymawk" albatrosses (some of which are actually more likely to occur than this far southern species).

Status and distribution: One old record of a bird supposedly collected on the "Coast of Panama" (variously later attributed to "Bay of Panama" or "off coast of Chiriquí") in 1855 or 1856. Wetmore doubts whether the bird was taken in Panamanian waters at all, and could not find the specimen in the British Museum.

Range: Breeds on subantarctic islands; ranges north off coasts of Chile and Argentina with sight reports off Peru; hypothetically reported from Panama, California, and Oregon.

SHEARWATERS AND PETRELS: Procellariidae (5)

The shearwaters and petrels are pelagic birds found throughout the oceans of the world, coming ashore only to nest on islands, usually in burrows. A number of species are highly migratory. Only one species breeds in Panama, with the others occurring only as migrants off the Pacific coast. Typical shearwaters have a characteristic stiff gliding flight low over the water on set wings, interspersed with short flaps, similar to but less accomplished than the flight of albatrosses. Some of the smaller shearwaters have a weaker, more fluttery flight, while the gadfly-petrels have a distinctive dashing flight, often well above the surface. All feed on various marine organisms and also on refuse. Field identification in Panama presents considerable difficulty, in part because of variability in color and pattern, in part because the status of so many species is still inadequately known. Additional pelagic field work, especially off the Azuero Peninsula and also off Darién, is needed and will surely result in the addition of several species not as yet recorded from Panama.

[PARKINSON'S BLACK PETREL]
(*Procellaria parkinsoni*)

Description: 17–18. Several sightings off Pacific coast. *Bill mostly pale,* varying from greenish yellow to bluish horn with dark tip and line on culmen; *legs black. Entirely brownish black.* Immature somewhat browner, with whitish edging on mantle; bill ivory whitish.

Similar species: Larger than any recorded all-dark *Puffinus* shearwater; Flesh-footed Shearwater (possible off Pacific Panama, see under Sooty Shearwater) is similar but has pale flesh legs. See also Sooty (smaller, with dark bill and usually pale under wing-linings) and dark phase Wedge-tailed Shearwaters (also smaller, with pale legs, wedge-shaped tail).

Status and distribution: One bird almost surely this species was seen 35 miles SE of Punta Mala, Azuero Peninsula on April 27, 1965 (G. Watson). Another probably this was seen west of Punta Mala on March 31, 1935 (J. Chapin), and "a large, all-black shearwater" seen in the Gulf of Panama on November 9–10, 1958 (C. R. Robins) suggests this species (*fide* Eisenmann). Perhaps a regular visitant off Pacific coast; a specimen would be desirable.

Habits: Attracted to boats, where it feeds on scraps thrown overboard (J. Jehl).

Range: Breeds on islands off New Zealand, ranging east in tropical Pacific to near Galapagos Islands and off Central America (J. Jehl, *Auk 91:* 687–689, 1974) and Ecuador and Peru.

WEDGE-TAILED SHEARWATER
(*Puffinus pacificus*)

Description: 16–17. Recorded off Pacific coast. Tail rather long and wedge-shaped, but this is usually not a useful field character (when sitting on water, tail extends beyond wing-tips). Bill varies from *pinkish to slaty gray; feet flesh.* Two phases. In dark phase, dark brown above; grayish brown below, *including entire under-wing.* In light phase, dark brown above, cheeks brownish gray; *mostly white below, including under wing-linings,* with brownish gray sides and under tail-coverts.

Similar species: Dark phase distinguished from Sooty Shearwater by its dark under wing-linings (whitish in Sooty) and sometimes pale bill (always dark in Sooty). Light phase birds resemble several other possible though unrecorded species (see below).

Status and distribution: Only one specimen record, that of two birds (one in each phase) taken off southern Darién on March 5, 1941 (R. C. Murphy). Murphy also saw large flocks of 60 to 80 birds of both phases off Piñas Bay on February 26, 1941. Shearwaters believed to be light phase Wedge-tails were seen off Pearl Islands on April 21, 1930 (J. Chapin), and off Taboga Island on July 13, 1952 (Eisenmann and J. Bull).

Range: Breeds on various islands in Pacific and Indian Oceans, ranging east as far as off coasts of Mexico to Ecuador.

Note: Pink-footed Shearwater (*P. creatopus,* sometimes treated as a race of the all-dark but otherwise similar *P. carneipes,* Flesh-footed Shearwater) ranges to eastern Pacific off both North and South America and is possible off Panama. It differs from Wedge-tail in its larger size (19–20″), short rounded tail, mostly yellowish to flesh bill (never all dark), somewhat paler more brownish gray upperparts, and in having under wing-linings and often underparts mottled with grayish. Flesh-footed Shearwater, also possible, differs from dark phase Wedge-tail in its larger size, short rounded tail, and yellowish to flesh bill (never all dark).

SOOTY SHEARWATER
(*Puffinus griseus*)

Description: 16–18. Apparently the only numerous medium-sized shearwater in Panama waters. *Bill slender, slaty; feet blackish.* Wings long and narrow, back-swept; tail short and rounded. *Sooty brown,* somewhat paler and more grayish below, with *whitish* (occasionally pale gray) *under wing-linings* (showing well as the bird banks). A rare light phase has throat whitish and breast mottled gray and grayish white.

Similar species: Dark phase Wedge-tailed Shearwater has dark under wing-linings, somewhat longer tail, and sometimes pale bill. See also Flesh-footed and Short-tailed Shearwaters (below).

Status and distribution: Apparently a fairly common transient along Pacific coast, recorded mostly June–September with a few at other times. Occasionally seen from shore. Though not recorded from Caribbean, perhaps occurs.

Habits: Usually seen well offshore, scaling low over the water on stiff wings, flapping only occasionally, banking to change direction. On calm days frequently seen swimming.

Range: Breeds on islands off extreme southern South America, Falkland Islands, and New Zealand, dispersing northward as far as arctic regions of Pacific and Atlantic Oceans.

Note: Flesh-footed Shearwater (*P. carneipes*), possible off the Pacific coast, is similar to Sooty but is larger (19–20″) with yellow to flesh (never dark) bill and feet, and dark (not whitish) under wing-linings. Short-tailed (Slender-billed) Shearwater (*P. tenuirostris*), erroneously recorded from Panama though possible, closely resembles Sooty but is smaller (14–15″) and has shorter bill and dark grayish under wing-linings.

AUDUBON'S (DUSKY-BACKED) SHEARWATER

(*Puffinus lherminieri*)

Description: 11–12. *Panama's smallest shearwater.* Bill black; legs mostly flesh. *Blackish brown above, sharply demarcated on sides of head from white underparts,* including under wing-linings (which are sometimes gray); under tail-coverts dusky.

Similar species: So much smaller than other recorded Panama shearwaters that confusion with them is unlikely. On Pacific see the possible Manx Shearwater (below).

Status and distribution: Breeds on Tiger Cays off western Bocas del Toro, and recorded occasionally off entire Caribbean coast; the Galapagos breeding race is fairly common in Gulf of Panama (not known to breed) from south of Pearl Islands to off Darién, but rare in Panama Bay.

Habits: Has a distinctive sloppy flight, not long sustained, with 5–10 shallow flaps interspersed with a short glide; may approach and circle boats. Frequently feeds over schools of small fish, often with flocks of terns, the terns hovering and plunging headfirst or plucking from the surface, the shearwaters swimming and making short thrusts into the water.

Range: Breeds in Bermuda, West Indies, and on islands off Caribbean coast of Panama and Venezuela and off Tobago; also on Galapagos Islands and many islands in tropical Pacific and Indian Oceans; recorded off both coasts of Panama and Costa Rica.

Note: Two forms of the Manx Shearwater, *P. puffinus auricularis* and *P. p. opisthomelas* (both perhaps distinct species) possibly occur south to Panama waters; both breed off Pacific Mexico. Field identification within this group of small "black-and-white" shearwaters is so difficult that collection of specimens would be required to confirm their presence. Both forms are larger than the Audubon's, with *auricularis* being more blackish (less brown) above, *opisthomelas* more mottled on sides of head and breast (lacking Audubon's sharp contrast).

[DARK-RUMPED PETREL]

(*Pterodroma phaeopygia*)

Description: 16–17. Three sightings from off Pacific coast. Bill blackish; legs and most of feet flesh, tipped black. Tail wedge-shaped and rather long. *Cap and wings blackish* with brown back; *forehead, sides of head, sides of upper tail-coverts, and entire underparts white;* upper wing-coverts sometimes edged with whitish; underside of wings mostly white with blackish leading and trailing edges and tip. Said to look white-headed at a distance.

Similar species: White forehead and cheeks distinguish it from other recorded Panama shearwaters; see especially light phase Wedge-tail. See also other *Pterodroma* petrels (below).

Status and distribution: Three sightings believed to be this species: one seen off Azuero Peninsula on March 31, 1935 (J. Chapin); several seen south of Pearl Islands (Rey) on September 9, 1937 (R. C. Murphy); and 11 seen SW of Pearl Islands (Galera) on September 27, 1964 (N. G. Smith). Specimen confirmation needed in this difficult genus.

Habits: As a group the *Pterodroma* (or gadfly) petrels have short but very stout deep bills, long wings, and a very fast dashing flight with broad sweeping arcs, rapid wingbeats, and lengthy glides; they bank more frequently than shearwaters, sometimes swinging as much as 100 feet above the water.

Range: Breeds on Galapagos Islands and Hawaii (considered endangered on both); specimens of Galapagos race (nominate *phaeopygia*) have been taken off Mexico, Costa Rica, Ecuador, and Peru, with sightings from off Panama.

Note: The *Pterodroma* petrels are a large group of seabirds found mostly in the southern hemisphere; many species closely resemble each other and are difficult to identify at sea. Several other members of the genus are possible off the Pacific coast (e.g. White-necked Petrel (*P. externa*), Blue-footed (Cook's) Petrel (*P. cookii*), and Sooty-capped (Mas Afuera) Petrel (*P. masafuerae*), perhaps others); see other references for descriptions, etc. Collection of specimens would be necessary. Black-capped Petrel (*P. hasitata*) is possible off Caribbean coast (breeds Hispaniola); it is somewhat smaller (14–15″) than Dark-rumped Petrel, with white forehead, black cap, sooty brown upperparts with white rump, and white underparts; in dark phase entirely sooty brown with white rump.

STORM-PETRELS: Hydrobatidae (5)

Storm-petrels are small seabirds found on oceans throughout the world. Several species are highly migratory, most notably the Wilson's which is also reputed to be one of the most numerous birds in the world (though rare in Panama). Most have an erratic and fluttering flight, somewhat swallow-like, frequently pausing to "dance" on the surface with their feet touching the water; others have longer wings and a more swooping flight. The feed primarily on zooplankton, and some species often follow ships. No member of the family is known to breed in Panama; elsewhere they nest in burrows or crevices on islands. As in the previous family, field identification is critical and often requires the collection of specimens.

WILSON'S STORM-PETREL
(*Oceanites oceanicus*)

Description: 7–7½. Very rare; only one recent specimen but would be easily overlooked among Wedge-rumps. Bill black; *legs long* (feet extending well beyond tail), black *with yellow on webs of feet* (sometimes visible as bird "walks" on surface of water). Sooty black with paler wing-coverts and *white band across rump* to lower flanks; *tail square*. Some individuals have feathers of lower belly and under tail-coverts edged with white.

Similar species: Very similar to Wedge-rump but when close comparison is possible can be distinguished by its larger size, square (not slightly forked) tail, rectangular (not triangular) rump band, and the yellow feet webbing. Even more closely resembles the hypothetical White-vented Storm-Petrel.

Status and distribution: One record, a bird collected in Pearl Islands (near San José) on August 29, 1969 (H. Loftin, Smithsonian Pacific seabird project), identified as the subspecies *chilensis* by Eisenmann. Might also occasionally occur off Caribbean coast.

Habits: Has a more fluttery flight than the *Oceanodroma* storm-petrels; the long legs are often dangled loosely.

Range: Breeds in Antarctica and on subantarctic islands off southern tip of South America; migrates regularly to North Atlantic, Pacific (where it is very rare or casual north of the Equator), and Indian Oceans.

Note: White-faced Storm-Petrel (*Pelagodroma marina*) is possible off Pacific coast; it breeds off Australia and New Zealand and on eastern Atlantic islands, and is known to range north in Pacific to the Galapagos and south of Cocos Island. It is somewhat larger (8″) than Wilson's, which it does not at all resemble, being gray above with blackish spot in front of and below eye and with white forehead, stripe above eye, and underparts (in pattern somewhat suggesting a nonbreeding phalarope).

[WHITE-VENTED STORM-PETREL]
(*Oceanites gracilis*)

Description: 5¾–6¼. One report from Gulf of Panama. Closely resembles Wilson's Storm-Petrel (and likewise has yellow on webs of feet) but smaller and with white well up to middle of belly and sometimes middle of breast (Wilson's sometimes shows white edging but only on lower belly and sides of under tail-coverts).

Similar species: See Wilson's Storm-Petrel; the two species would be difficult to distinguish in the field.

Status and distribution: Attributed to Panama on the basis of a report by R. C. Murphy, who told Eisenmann that in early September 1937 he saw this species "in the Gulf of Panama and southward" and definitely observed two at Humboldt Bay, just south of the Darién border, on September 11. This was before the very similar Wilson's Storm-Petrel was known to occur at least casually in the Pacific north of the Equator. Collection will probably prove that both species occur.

Range: Breeds on Galapagos Islands and perhaps elsewhere; ranges off coast of western South America from Colombia to Chile.

Note: Wetmore calls it Graceful Storm-Petrel.

WEDGE-RUMPED (GALAPAGOS) STORM-PETREL

(*Oceanodroma tethys*)

Description: 6–7. Generally the most numerous storm-petrel off Pacific coast. Fairly small. Mostly sooty black, paler below and on wing-coverts; *triangular white rump-patch* and very slightly forked tail (normally not noticeable in the field).

WEDGE-RUMPED STORM-PETREL

Similar species: The larger Black and smaller Least Storm-Petrels both lack white rump-patches; closely resembles the very rare Wilson's (which see), and the possible Band-rumped and white-rumped Leach's Storm-Petrels (below).

Status and distribution: Often fairly common to common off Pacific coast, sometimes coming well up into Panama Bay, and occasionally visible even from shore. Apparently most numerous May–November, and either rare or absent January–February.

Habits: Usually flies low over the ocean surface, generally maintaining a steady course, alternating flapping and gliding, pausing occasionally to drop over some morsel in the water. On calm days flocks often rest on the water. Less wary than other Panama storm-petrels.

Range: Breeds on Galapagos Islands and islands off coast of Peru; disperses north to off Pacific coast of Mexico (casually California), Panama, Colombia, and Ecuador, and south to central Chile.

Note: Both Band-rumped (Harcourt's or Madeiran) Storm-Petrel (*O. castro*) and white-rumped races of Leach's Storm-Petrel (*O. leucorhoa*) may occur off Pacific coast. Band-rumped breeds in eastern Atlantic, on the Galapagos (possibly also on Cocos Island), Hawaii, and Japan, while the Leach's breeds on small islands of the North Atlantic and Pacific Oceans. Both are somewhat larger (Band-rumped 8½–9"; Leach's 7½–8") than Wedge-rumped, have white like a band across rump, and have more deeply forked tails (especially in Leach's). It is extremely difficult to separate the two in the field, though Band-rump's white rump has some black speckling, while Leach's white rump is narrower and usually shows a dusky stripe down center. Either might be picked out by their more bounding, swooping (less fluttery) flight (especially marked in Leach's). Specimen confirmation would be necessary. Leach's might also occur off Caribbean coast.

BLACK STORM-PETREL

(*Oceanodroma melania*)

Description: 9. Regular off Pacific coast. Bill and rather long legs black. A *large* storm-petrel, *all brownish black* with somewhat paler brown wing-coverts; tail deeply forked.

Similar species: Large size and lack of white rump sets it apart from all other recorded Panama storm-petrels (Least is *much* smaller), but see dark-rumped Leach's and Sooty Storm-Petrels (below).

Status and distribution: Uncommon but apparently regular in small numbers through the year in Gulf of Panama and off Darién, only rarely coming inshore into Panama Bay.

Habits: Unlike the smaller Panama storm-petrels, usually solitary, only occasionally gathering in small loose groups. Has longer wings, slower wingbeats, and more bounding flight but with steady flaps (suggesting a nighthawk); usually flies well above surface of water.

Range: Breeds on islands off Baja California, ranging at sea north to central California and south to central Peru.

Note: By some authors placed in a separate genus *Loomelania* because of its long legs. At least one of the dark-rumped races of Leach's Storm-Petrel (*O. leucorhoa*) probably occurs off Pacific coast. The race *chapmani* (breeding off southern Baja California, wintering south to Galapagos area) is known near Panama from 4 specimens taken by W. Beebe on March 30, 1925, then en route from Balboa to the Galapagos; Eisenmann plotted his position on that date as some 100–150 miles from the Azuero Peninsula. It resembles Black but is distinctly smaller (7–7½″) and has shorter wings and less deeply forked tail. Sooty Storm-Petrel (*O. markhami*) is a somewhat less likely possibility; it very closely resembles Black (the two are probably not safely distinguished in the field) but is slightly larger (9–10″), has much shorter legs, and is more sooty brown (not as black); it ranges chiefly in the Humboldt Current off Peru and Chile (breeding grounds unknown), with records from the Galapagos and Cocos and Clipperton Islands.

LEAST STORM-PETREL
(*Halocyptena microsoma*)

Description: 5–6. Regular off Pacific coast. Bill and legs black. *The smallest storm-petrel.* Sooty black, paler on wing-coverts, with characteristic *long wedge-shaped tail.*

Similar species: Wedge-rumped and Wilson's Storm-Petrels are both larger and have white rumps. Other all blackish storm-petrels are much larger (7″ or more) with forked tails.

Status and distribution: Uncommon to fairly common in the Gulf of Panama and off Darién, occasionally ranging north into Panama Bay, and very rarely seen even from mainland. Apparently less numerous July-October.

Habits: Often found with Wedge-rumped Storm-Petrel. Has a fluttery, somewhat erratic flight, usually very close to the surface of the water.

Range: Breeds on islands off Baja California; ranges at sea to southern California and south to Ecuador.

TROPICBIRDS: Phaethontidae (1)

The tropicbirds are a small group of beautiful seabirds found in warmer waters throughout the world. Adults are characterized by their extremely long central tail feathers, which when fully developed may exceed the length of the body. They nest on small islands, usually in crevices or shady places, at other seasons dispersing at sea where they are generally encountered individually. Their food is fish and squid, obtained by diving from considerable heights.

RED-BILLED TROPICBIRD
(*Phaethon aethereus*)

Description: 18–22, excluding *extremely long central tail feathers (1–2 feet in length). Heavy red bill. Mostly white* with black stripe through eye, *fine black barring on back and rump,* and black primaries. Immature lacks the long tail feathers, has yellow bill and coarser barring on back.

Status and distribution: Breeds in small numbers on Swan Cay off western Bocas del Toro; not reported elsewhere on Caribbean coast though possible; rare visitant to Gulf of Panama (including single individuals collected by H. Loftin on Smithsonian Pacific seabird project on September 20 and October 12, 1968), usually seen singly and well offshore; not known to breed in Pacific Panama waters, but does nest on nearby Malpelo Island off Colombia.

Habits: Strong, dove-like flight. When swimming, the tail is cocked up out of the water.

Range: Breeds on small islands in warmer parts of eastern Pacific Ocean (off Baja California, Malpelo Island, Galapagos Islands), Caribbean Sea, Red Sea, and Indian Ocean; ranges widely in tropical oceans.

Note: White-tailed Tropicbird (*P. lepturus*) might wander to Caribbean coast as it breeds in the Antilles and has been taken off Caribbean coast of Colombia. It resembles Red-billed but is smaller; adult White-tail differs in having unbarred back and black on scapulars, secondaries, and wing-coverts; immature White-tail differs from immature Red-bill in size and black mark on scapulars and wings.

PELICANS: Pelecanidae (1)

Pelicans are very large, heavy seabirds with characteristic, long bills and throat pouches. They are widely distributed in tropical and to some extent temperate areas. Most species are found on lakes, marshes, and coastal lagoons, but Panama's sole representative is a coastal bird. Pelicans feed primarily on fish, obtained either by plunging into the water or by submerging the bill and head while swimming. They nest in colonies, often large, in some species on the ground, but in the Brown Pelican in bushes and trees. Several species have declined drastically in the past few decades, among them the Brown Pelican in the United States, this decrease apparently a result of pesticide contamination. So far the Panamanian population appears stable and very large (especially in Panama Bay), but it should be monitored carefully.

BROWN PELICAN
(*Pelecanus occidentalis*)

Description: 46–54. Unmistakable. *Very large.* Heavily built with *long bill* and *pouch on lower mandible.* Mostly gray above, the feathers outlined darker; *dark brown below; crown and stripe down sides of neck white.* Nonbreeding adults have head and neck whitish. Immature is brownish above and on head and neck, whitish below.

Status and distribution: Abundant along Pacific coast, especially in Panama Bay and around Pearl Islands and other islands off Pacific coast; less numerous but still fairly common along Caribbean coast. Breeds on many islands off Pacific coast and on some of Pearl Islands, in largest numbers on the south side of Taboga Island; no known breeding colonies along Caribbean coast or from western Panama. Frequently seen crossing the isthmus over Canal (occasionally elsewhere).

Habits: The head is drawn back so that the bill rests on the neck, both perched and in flight. Flies with a characteristic few flaps and a sail. Lines of pelicans are often seen scaling low over the water; at other times they soar high on thermals. When feeding they fly roughly 30 to 50 feet above water, then plunge down headfirst, extending neck just before entering water. Upon resurfacing, Laughing Gulls often attempt to snatch away their quarry. In shallow water pelicans also feed without diving by submerging and opening the bill.

Range: Coasts of southeastern and western United States to the Guianas and extreme northeastern Brazil and southern Chile; West Indies.

BOOBIES AND GANNETS: Sulidae (4)

Boobies and gannets are large seabirds with long pointed wings and narrow, wedge-shaped tails. Boobies are found in tropical oceans throughout the world, gannets in temperate oceans except the North Pacific. They have a strong flight, often gliding on set wings like a shearwater or albatross, but are less pelagic, being found primarily near islands rather than far out to sea. All feed on fish captured in a spectacular plunge from considerable heights. They are colonial breeders, most boobies nesting on the ground on small islands, with two species nesting in trees. The common name "booby" is derived from the birds' unsuspicious behavior on their breeding grounds, which enabled early sailors to kill them easily for food.

MASKED (BLUE-FACED) BOOBY
(*Sula dactylatra*)

Description: 32–36. Bill orange-yellow to dull yellow with horn tip in male, pinkish with horn to dull yellow tip in female; legs grayish, greenish, or yellow. Bare facial skin black. Adult *white* with black flight feathers (tip and broad rear border) and *black tail* (except middle pair of feathers). Immature mostly grayish brown with white lower underparts and whitish patches on lower hindneck and rump; legs lavender blue.

Similar species: Adult can be confused with white phase adult Red-footed Booby but is notably larger with black (not white) tail, and lacks Red-foot's red legs. Immature resembles Blue-footed Booby but is more grayish brown (not cinnamon brown). Brown Booby also somewhat resembles immature Masked but is considerably smaller and much more clearly patterned, lacks whitish areas on hindneck and rump.

Status and distribution: Occasionally observed off Caribbean coast, rarely seen from Colon harbor; regular and sometimes quite numerous in Gulf of Panama south of Pearl Islands and off Darién, rarely noted around Pearl Islands, and very rare in Panama Bay. Though regular in occurrence at least off Pacific coast, apparently does not breed in Panama waters.

Habits: Distinctly pelagic. Often in small groups, frequently seen perched on floating debris in drift lines.

Range: Breeds on islands in warmer parts of Atlantic, Pacific, and Indian Oceans; known breeding sites closest to Panama are Malpelo Island off Pacific coast of Colombia and Los Monjes off Caribbean coast of Colombia (breeds also on Galapagos).

BLUE-FOOTED BOOBY
(*Sula nebouxii*)

Description: 32–36. Occurs off Pacific coast. Bill dull greenish or grayish blue; *legs bright blue* (somewhat duller in immatures). *Head and neck pale cinnamon brown streaked with whitish, white patch on lower hindneck; back, wings* (including underside), *and tail brown,* back and rump somewhat mottled with white; underparts white. Immature similar but with some brownish on throat. In flight adult's head looks whitish.

Similar species: Immature Masked Booby resembles immature Blue-footed but is more grayish brown above (without cinnamon tones), and has darker head, neck, and throat. Brown Booby is smaller and uniform brown above and on throat and chest. See also Peruvian Booby (below).

Status and distribution: Breeds on a number of small islands off Pacific coast in Panama Bay and on some of the smaller Pearl Islands; disperses to some extent but generally seems rather sedentary around its favored islands. Apparently breeds on San José Rock off Flamenco Island at Pacific entrance to Canal.

Habits: Seems somewhat crepuscular, feeding mostly in early morning and late afternoon, perching inactively most of the day. Sometimes soars high over the water or over its roosting and nesting islands.

Range: Breeds on islands off Baja California, and from Panama to central Peru; recorded off Costa Rica.

Note: Peruvian Booby (*S. variegata*), inhabiting the Humboldt Current from Peru to central Chile, might occur as a casual wanderer on Pacific coast (has been recorded north to Bahía de Malaga in southwestern Colombia). It resembles Blue-foot but is smaller (28–30") with entire head, neck, and underparts white; back, wings, and rump dark brown, feathers broadly edged with white; tail largely white; bill bluish to pinkish, legs bluish gray; immature with white areas tinged buffy.

BROWN BOOBY
(*Sula leucogaster*)

Description: 26–30. Bill and legs greenish to yellow. Adult *dark brown with sharply contrasting white breast and belly;* under wing-coverts also white. Immature mostly dark grayish brown but already with an indication of adult's pattern below (throat and chest distinctly darker than breast and belly). Adult males of Pacific race (*etesiaca*) have white forehead, darkening on forecrown.

Similar species: Immature Red-footed Booby somewhat resembles immature of this species but lacks the contrast below. See also the larger Blue-footed Booby.

Status and distribution: The most numerous booby on both coasts. Known to breed on islands off Bocas del Toro and eastern Colon province, and on various small islands off Pacific coast and some of the smaller Pearl Islands. Quite frequently seen from shore on both coasts.

Habits: Looks tapered at all ends, with long pointed bill, narrow pointed wings, and long wedge-shaped tail. Sails on rather stiff outstretched wings, usually rather low over the water, much like a large shearwater. Often attempts to fly off with bait being trolled behind fishing boats; occasionally one becomes hooked and must be hauled in to be released.

Range: Breeds on islands in warmer parts of Atlantic, Pacific, and Indian Oceans.

RED-FOOTED BOOBY
(*Sula sula*)

Description: 26–30. Definitely recorded only off Caribbean coast. Bill mostly bluish (in some areas partly yellow) with pinkish base; *legs bright red.* White phase adult, entirely white with black flight feathers; *tail usually white,* sometimes light grayish brown (never black). Gray phase adult, *gray above* with golden tinge on hindneck and *usually with white rump and tail;* pale brownish gray below. Brown phase adult has brown replacing gray. Immature mostly grayish brown, *usually contrastingly darker on belly;* legs yellowish.

Similar species: Adults of all phases can be known by their red legs and feet; many also have white tail (black in adult Masked Booby, dark in other, immature boobies). Immature resembles immature Brown Booby but is more grayish brown (not chocolate brown) and whereas Brown Booby is paler on belly, this species usually has belly darker brown than remainder of underparts. Immature Masked Booby is similar but larger with whitish patches on lower hindneck and rump.

Status and distribution: Regular at sea a few miles off Caribbean coast, but rarely seen from shore; not satisfactorily reported from Pacific though may possibly occur (the several sight reports from the Gulf of Panama probably refer to the Masked Booby).

Habits: More pelagic than most boobies. Feeds chiefly on flying fish. The only Western Hemisphere booby to roost and nest in trees.

Range: Breeds on islands in warmer parts of Atlantic, Pacific, and Indian Oceans; closest known breeding sites to Panama are islands off Belize and Honduras and off Venezuela in Caribbean Sea, and on Revilla Gigedo Islands off Mexico and Cocos and Galapagos Islands in the Pacific.

CORMORANTS: Phalacrocoracidae (2)

The cormorants are a widespread group of aquatic birds, the various species being found both on fresh water rivers, lakes, and marshes, and on seacoasts. They feed primarily on small fish, captured after diving from the surface of the water. Cormorants are colonial breeders, nesting on cliffs, the ground, or in trees (which are slowly killed by their profuse droppings). Several species, notably the Guanay, are extremely important producers of guano.

NEOTROPIC (OLIVACEOUS) CORMORANT
(*Phalacrocorax olivaceus*)

Description: 25–27. Long slender blackish bill, hooked at tip; legs black. Adult *entirely black;* in breeding season bare facial skin dull yellow to orange, bordered behind by narrow line of white feathers. Immature more grayish brown above, paler below, almost white on breast. Juvenal almost entirely white below, including sides of head.

Similar species: With its long slender neck, rather long wedge-shaped tail, and blackish plumage easily recognized. See Anhinga and the casual Guanay Cormorant.

Status and distribution: Common and generally widespread along both coasts and (chiefly immatures) on larger bodies of fresh water (occasionally even small rivers) on both slopes; most abundant on Pacific coast and on Pearl Islands where at times in huge flocks of tens of thousands; ranges occasionally (immatures) up into lower Chiriquí highlands. Only known breeding colonies are on two of the Pearl Islands (Pacheca and Saboga) but may nest on mainland as well.

Habits: May occur in staggering numbers in Panama Bay soon after the onset of the dry season when upwelling in inshore waters (caused by constant NE trade winds) attracts schools of small fish. Swims low in water, sometimes with no more than head and neck visible, bill tilting upwards. Has a strong steady flight (though some difficulty in becoming airborne) with outstretched head and neck slightly angled upward. Perches upright, often with wings outstretched to dry its nonwaterproof plumage.

Range: Very wide-ranging, breeding from extreme southern United States to extreme southern Chile (Cape Horn) and high on Andean lakes; also Bahamas and Cuba.

[GUANAY (PERUVIAN) CORMORANT]
(*Phalacrocorax bougainvillii*)

Description: 27–28. One sighting from off Darién. Adult *glossy black above* with bare red facial skin and *elliptical area of white on throat separated from white underparts by black collar across foreneck and sides of throat.* Immature dusky rather than black. Juvenal dusky brown above including sides of head and foreneck; mostly white below finely mottled with brown.

Similar species: See Neotropic Cormorant.

Status and distribution: Only one report, a flock of about 100 seen flying north off Enseñada de Guayabo Chiquito on coast of southern Darién near Colombian border on May 21, 1941 (R. C. Murphy). The same observer collected several not far to the south off Colombia in March and April of the same year. Not correlated with any unusual Niño current (*fide* Murphy).

Range: Breeds on islands off coast of Peru and northern Chile; disperses chiefly in Humboldt Current, north to Ecuador, occasionally to Colombia and casually to eastern Panama, south to southern Chile.

DARTERS: Anhingidae (1)

The darters are a small group of fresh water aquatic birds found in subtropical and tropical areas of the world. They resemble cormorants, differing in their long pointed (unhooked) bill, small head, very long and slender neck, and long tail. Like cormorants they feed mostly on fish, but rather than grasp their prey, darters spear it underwater and then, upon resurfacing, flip it up into the air and catch it as it falls. They nest in small colonies in swamps and along wooded rivers, sometimes with various herons and ibis.

ANHINGA
(*Anhinga anhinga*)

Description: 32–36. Long pointed bill, small head, very long slender ("*snaky*") neck, and *long fan-shaped tail.* Male *glossy black with large silvery area on wing;* tail tipped with brown. Female similar but with *head, neck, and chest pale brown.*

Similar species: Somewhat cormorant-like, but longer and more slender, with pointed (not hooked) bill, silvery wing-patch, and fan-shaped (not wedge-shaped) tail.

Status and distribution: Uncommon to fairly common around fresh water marshes, ponds, lakes, and wooded rivers in lowlands on both slopes (not yet reported from Chiriquí or San Blas). In Canal Zone most easily seen in the Pedro Miguel/Miraflores area. Two partially developed young were observed being fed by two adults at Tocumen, eastern Panama province, on January 7, 1974 (Ridgely, C. Leahy); as yet no nest has been reported from Panama.

Habits: Usually seen perched on branches of bushes and trees bordering water, often with wings outstretched to dry like a cormorant. Flies with alternating flaps and long glides, but unlike cormorants also often soars high overhead with tail spread wide. Swims low in water, frequently with only snake-like head and neck visible, diving for food while swimming.

Range: Southeastern United States to Bolivia, northern Argentina, and Uruguay; Cuba and Grenada.

FRIGATEBIRDS: Fregatidae (1)

The frigatebirds are a small group of spectacular seabirds found in tropical oceans. They are typically seen soaring high overhead with no apparent movement of their very long pointed wings. Some of their food is obtained by harrying other seabirds (boobies, gulls, terns, etc.), but a good proportion is found independently, the birds swooping rapidly over the surface and capturing small fish or animal refuse, without plunging into the water and remaining dry in the process. Frigatebirds breed in colonies on islands, the nest usually being placed in bushes and trees. Generally they are not found far from land.

MAGNIFICENT FRIGATEBIRD
(*Fregata magnificens*)

Description: 38–42. Very large with *very long narrow pointed wings* (spread up to 7½ feet), bent back at the "shoulder," and *long deeply forked tail* (often folded so as to appear pointed). Adult male *entirely black* with red throat pouch, which is inflated like a balloon in breeding season (often not apparent at other times). Adult female also mostly black (including throat), but lacks throat pouch and has *sides of neck and entire breast white,* and brown band on upper wing-coverts. Juvenal resembles female but in addition has *entire head white.*

Status and distribution: Very common along Pacific coast, offshore islands, and on Pearl Islands; less numerous but still common along Caribbean coast. Breeds on many small islands off Pacific coast, including Pearl Islands and off Veraguas; not recorded as a breeder on Caribbean though possible in Bocas del Toro (ballooning males have been seen). Regularly seen crossing the isthmus along the Canal, less often elsewhere.

Habits: Generally seen soaring high overhead on motionless wings, sometimes in very large congregations, particularly over its nesting and roosting islands.

Range: Breeds on small islands in tropical Atlantic and eastern Pacific Oceans.

Note: Very similar Great Frigatebird (*F. minor*) is possible on Pacific coast though so far unrecorded (would likely be overlooked); it breeds on the Revilla Gigedos, Cocos, and Galapagos Islands, and elsewhere in the Pacific, Indian, and eastern Atlantic Oceans. Adult male has brown band on upper wing-coverts and (sometimes) red legs; adult female has gray or whitish throat (black in Magnificent) and red (not blue) orbital skin; immature has head and often breast washed with rusty, and a broad blackish chest band. The two species are about the same size, despite their apparently contradictory common and Latin names.

HERONS: Ardeidae (18)

Herons are long necked and long legged wading birds with pointed straight bills found throughout the world. They vary considerably in size, among Panamanian species from the large Great Blue and White-necked Herons and the heavy tiger-herons to the diminutive Least Bittern. Virtually all the Panamanian species favor the vicinity of water, fresh or salt, though the Cattle Egret regularly forages in dry pastures. They fly with neck retracted and legs extended. Most feed primarily on fish and small vertebrates, obtained on shores and in shallow water. Many species are gregarious and highly colonial during the breeding season, nesting in trees in inaccessible swamps; a few, including the tiger-herons, bitterns, and the Green and Striated Herons, nest solitarily or in small groups, the bitterns on or near the ground in dense vegetation. At present only roosts are known from mainland Panama (though several species have been found nesting on islands in Panama Bay and the Pearl Islands), but breeding colonies almost certainly exist in coastal swamps of eastern Panama province, Herrera and southern Coclé, and perhaps elsewhere.

GREAT BLUE HERON
(*Ardea herodias*)

Description 40–50. A *very large,* long-necked, *mostly gray* heron. Bill dull yellow to dusky; legs dark. Adult has black crown with *white central stripe,* in breeding dress also with two long black occipital plumes; neck grayish streaked in front with black and white; back and wings bluish gray; lower underparts streaked black and white with *rufous thighs.* Immature is similar but dingier, crown dusky without white.

Similar species: Large size and mostly gray appearance sets it apart from all Panama herons except White-necked, which is much whiter generally and has a solid black crown.

Status and distribution: Uncommon winter visitant (mostly September–April) on larger bodies of fresh water in lowlands on both slopes, ranging occasionally to Volcán Lakes in lower highlands of western Chiriquí; a few birds, apparently immatures, are present throughout the year with nesting unproved though possible (not known to breed on continental Middle America south of Mexico); recorded also from Coiba Island, Taboga Island, and the Pearl Islands.

Habits: Usually solitary and rather wary.

Range: Breeds from North America to southern Mexico and in West Indies and islands off Venezuela and on Galapagos Islands; northern birds winter south to northern Colombia and Venezuela (where also may breed).

WHITE-NECKED (COCOI) HERON
(*Ardea cocoi*) Pl.1

Description 40–45. Superficially like more widespread Great Blue Heron but *much whiter generally. Entire crown black* (no white central stripe) with breeding occipital plumes tipped white; *neck and most of wings white; thighs white* (not rufous). Immature dingier but still essentially white below with white thighs, a little black on breast.

Similar species: See Great Blue Heron.

Status and distribution: Rare in fresh water marshes and along rivers in lowlands of eastern Panama province (Tocumen to Bayano River) and eastern Darién (lower Tuira River valley, where more numerous). Though nesting unrecorded as yet, almost certainly breeds in Darién and probably farther west.

Habits: Similar to Great Blue Heron, which it replaces in South America.

Range: Central Panama to southern Chile and southern Argentina.

GREAT (COMMON) EGRET
(*Casmerodius albus*)

Description 36–40. A large, slender, long-necked heron with *yellow bill* and *black legs. Entirely white;* long aigrettes spring from back during breeding season.

Similar species: Snowy Egret and immature Little Blue Heron are also all white, but both are much smaller and have black or partly dark bills.

Status and distribution: Common and widespread on both fresh and salt water in lowlands on both slopes, ranging rarely to Volcán Lakes in lower highlands of western Chiriquí; found also on all offshore islands; local population augmented by northern migrants during northern winter, but numerous the entire year, occasionally in large flocks of several hundred or more individuals. So far nesting colonies have only been reported from various islands in Panama Bay and Gulf of Panama (including Changamé, Taboga, and Pearl Islands), but surely breeds locally on mainland as well.

Habits: Remains motionless for long periods of time when feeding, often with straight neck so that it stands well above other herons and egrets.

Range: Virtually cosmopolitan in warmer areas; in America from United States (wandering north to Canada) to extreme southern Chile and in West Indies.

SNOWY EGRET
(*Egretta thula*)

Description: 23–27. *Bill black;* black legs with *bright yellow feet* ("golden slippers"). *Entirely white;* filmy recurved aigrettes spring from crown, back, and chest during breeding season. Immature often shows greenish yellow stripe down back of leg.

Similar species: Great Egret is larger and has longer neck and all yellow bill. Immature Little Blue Heron has bicolored bill and greenish legs.

Status and distribution: Fairly common along both coasts; less numerous in fresh water marshes and along shores of lakes and rivers (though a number are often found at Gatun Dam spillway), ranging occasionally to Volcán Lakes in lower highlands of western Chiriquí; recorded also on Coiba Island and the Pearl Islands; more numerous during northern winter when some northern migrants are present. To date found breeding only on islands in Panama Bay but almost certainly colonies exist on the mainland as well, particularly near Pacific coast.

Habits: An active and graceful feeder.

Range: United States (wandering north to Canada) to central Chile and northern Argentina; West Indies.

LITTLE BLUE HERON
(*Florida caerulea*)

Description: 22–26. *Bill bluish with blackish tip; legs greenish.* Adult *bluish slate* with dull maroon head and neck (lacking in subadults). Juvenal white except for dusky tips to flight feathers. Immature white splotched irregularly with slaty, giving a pied appearance.

Similar species: Snowy Egret rather resembles juvenal but has all black bill (not bicolored) and black legs with yellow feet (though immature Snowy's legs show greenish stripe down back, which can cause confusion). See also Great Egret and Tricolored Heron.

Status and distribution: Common and widespread on fresh and salt water in lowlands on both slopes, ranging in small numbers to Volcán Lakes in lower highlands of western Chiriquí; found also on Coiba Island and all larger islands in Panama Bay and Gulf of Panama; more numerous during northern winter when local population augmented by northern migrants. No confirmed breeding record for Panama, but surely does so. The most numerous member of its family in the Canal Zone.

Habits: Immatures and juvenals predominate. A fairly active feeder but less graceful in its movements than Snowy Egret.

Range: Eastern United States and Mexico to central Peru, southeastern Brazil, and Uruguay; West Indies.

TRICOLORED (LOUISIANA) HERON

(*Hydranassa tricolor*)

Description: 22–26. *Very slender,* with long neck. *Mostly bluish slate* with some dull chestnut on head and white occipital plumes; maroon stripe down front of neck; rump and *belly contrastingly white.* Immature similar in pattern but brown above, lacking occipital plumes.

Similar species: Adult Little Blue Heron is stockier, entirely dark (bluish slate and maroon) without white belly.

Status and distribution: Fairly common on fresh and salt water in lowlands on both slopes, most numerous on or near Pacific coast, ranging rarely to Volcán Lakes in lower highlands of western Chiriquí; found also on larger Pearl Islands; more numerous during northern winter when northern migrants are present. No definite breeding record though almost certainly nests in Panama.

Habits: Usually rather solitary. An active, graceful feeder.

Range: Eastern United States and Mexico to Peru and central Brazil; Greater Antilles.

GREEN HERON

(*Butorides virescens*) Pl.1

Description: 16–18. *Small and chunky.* Legs bright orange in breeding adult; yellow otherwise. Crown (with shaggy crest, sometimes raised) black; *sides of head, neck, and chest rich chestnut,* with narrow white stripe bordered with black down front of neck; upperparts otherwise greenish black; lower underparts gray. A melanistic phase occurs on Caribbean slope (especially in Bocas del Toro) with blackish neck and lacking white central stripe on underparts (also lacking in some Pearl Islands birds). Immature is duller, with chest and breast whitish streaked brown.

Similar species: Adult Striated Heron has neck gray or dull grayish brown (never rich chestnut). Immatures of the two species are not always separable but Green tends to be browner on sides of neck (Striated more grayish).

Status and distribution: Fairly common and widespread on fresh and salt water, but particularly on wooded shores of lakes and rivers, in lowlands on both slopes, breeding east at least to Canal Zone, with resident population augmented during northern winter by northern migrants; ranges up to Volcán Lakes in lower highlands of western Chiriquí; found also on Pearl Islands where mostly in mangroves.

Habits: Usually solitary. Normally hunts by standing on perch just out of water (not wading); quite arboreal. Frequently gives a loud complaining *kyow,* especially as it flies off after having been disturbed.

Range: North America to central Panama and West Indies; northern birds winter to northern Colombia and Venezuela, casually to Surinam.

Note: Closely related (probably conspecific) to Striated Heron.

STRIATED HERON

(*Butorides striatus*) Pl.1

Description: 16–18. Resembles Green Heron. Adult differs in having head, neck, and chest *gray or dull grayish brown* (not chestnut). Immature is difficult to distinguish from immature Green but tends to be more grayish on sides of head and neck. In eastern Panama adult Striateds tend to be grayer-necked than most found in Canal Zone.

Similar species: See Green Heron.

Status and distribution: Fairly common in situations similar to Green Heron in eastern Panama province and Darién; somewhat less numerous in Canal Zone and recorded west on Caribbean slope to western Colon province, on Pacific slope to eastern side of Azuero Peninsula. Situation somewhat confused due to probable hybridization with Green Heron in central Panama. Good gray-necked birds can easily be observed in the Tocumen/La Jagua area.

Habits: Similar to Green Heron. Though the two species are generally regarded as distinct, interbreeding seems likely in central Panama as most birds are of brown-necked form; however, definite instances of mixed pairs have not been recorded, perhaps because of lack of study.

Range: Central Panama to northern Argentina and Uruguay (casual central Chile); also warmer parts of Africa, Asia, Australia, and islands in western Pacific Ocean.

CHESTNUT-BELLIED (AGAMI) HERON
(*Agamia agami*) Pl.1

Description: 28–32. Slender with very long neck and *very long slender bill;* legs short. *Mostly dark glossy green above* with black face and long bluish gray crest; *neck and most of underparts rich chestnut,* with throat and stripe down front of neck white, and patch of bluish gray on chest; bluish gray plumes also spring from back in breeding plumage. Immature dark brown above with blackish crown; throat white, remaining underparts buff.

Status and distribution: Rare; recorded along forested streams in lowlands on entire Caribbean slope (not reported from San Blas, but surely occurs); on Pacific slope known from Canal Zone (Miraflores Lake, one specimen) east through Darién (where perhaps more numerous); one record from Pearl Islands (Rey). In Canal Zone recently reported seen only from Pipeline Road and Barro Colorado Island.

Habits: A solitary, shy, and very infrequently encountered heron of shady forest streams and wet depressions; rarely in the open. When disturbed will sometimes fly up to a perch fairly high in the trees.

Range: Southeastern Mexico to northern Bolivia and central Brazil.

CATTLE EGRET
(*Bubulcus ibis*)

Description: 18–20. A small *white* heron with characteristic *heavy jowl,* giving a heavy-headed appearance. Breeding adult has varying amounts of buff on crown, back, and breast, lost at other seasons. *Bill yellow,* becoming red (except at tip) for short period at onset of breeding season; legs dull yellow to greenish, also becoming red at beginning of breeding season. Immatures lack the buff.

Similar species: Snowy Egret and immature Little Blue Heron are larger and slenderer, never have yellow or red bills.

Status and distribution: Common in open country, especially near water and invariably near where cattle or other livestock are present, in lowlands on both slopes, ranging into lower highlands around Volcán in western Chiriquí; reported from Taboga Island in 1964 (G. Harrington). More numerous and widespread on Pacific slope. Only report of nesting is a small colony of about 6 pairs at La Jagua in eastern Panama province on July 18, 1968 (Ridgely, N. G. Smith, J. Karr); certainly breeds elsewhere as large numbers are seen in breeding plumage. First recorded in 1954, it has spread rapidly in Panama, as it has elsewhere in suitable areas of the New World.

Habits: Notably gregarious, flocks usually feeding among cattle or other grazing animals, sometimes even perching on their backs.

Range: Eastern and southern North America to Bolivia and northern Brazil and in West Indies, still spreading; also warmer parts of Old World (its original habitat).

CAPPED HERON
(*Pilherodius pileatus*) Pl.1

Description: 22–24. *Bill and facial skin blue,* becoming more intense in breeding plumage; legs gray. White with *black crown* (not forecrown) and long white occipital plumes. In breeding plumage underparts become strongly tinged with buff. Immature has crown streaked with gray.

Similar species: A striking heron, not to be confused. Rather chunky, in flight often suggesting a white Black-crowned Night-Heron.

Status and distribution: Rare to uncommon in fresh water marshes, swamps, and along rivers in lowlands on Pacific slope in eastern Panama province (Tocumen eastward) and Darién; one nineteenth-century specimen from Caribbean side of Canal Zone, and apparently still occurs in small numbers along Chagres River above Gamboa, with one collected at Juan Mina on October 30, 1962 (G. Van Horn, *fide* Wetmore), and another seen in same general area on January 15, 1972 (V. Miller). Probably regular, but in very small numbers, in the Tocumen/La Jagua area.

Habits: Usually seen singly, but otherwise not differing greatly in habits from most other herons. May be at least partially crepuscular.

Range: Central Panama to northern Bolivia, northern Paraguay, and southeastern Brazil.

BLACK-CROWNED NIGHT-HERON
(*Nycticorax nycticorax*)

Description: 24–26. Rather stocky with short neck and rather short bill and legs. *Crown and back glossy black* with long white occipital plumes (even longer during breeding season); *wings and tail gray;* sides of neck pale gray, *underparts white.* Immature brown above streaked and spotted with white; white below streaked with brown.

Similar species: Boat-billed Heron somewhat resembles adult in pattern but has gray back and is not white below; the bills, of course, are very different. Immature closely resembles immature Yellow-crowned Night-Heron but is browner (not as slaty) with comparatively longer and more slender bill and shorter legs (in flight only feet project beyond tail). See also American Bittern.

Status and distribution: Uncommon on salt and fresh water in coastal lowlands on both slopes, more numerous on Pacific side; somewhat more plentiful during northern winter months when northern migrants are present; found also on Taboga Island and the Pearl Islands. So far found breeding only on a few small islands in Panama Bay but almost surely nests on mainland as well.

Habits: Nocturnal, only rarely seen abroad by day, usually roosting in leafy trees. Often heard is an abrupt *quok,* given most frequently in the evening as it flies to its feeding area, also when disturbed.

Range: Virtually cosmopolitan except in holarctic regions and in Australia; in New World from southern Canada to Tierra del Fuego and in West Indies.

YELLOW-CROWNED NIGHT-HERON
(*Nyctanassa violacea*)

Description: 24–26. Similar in shape to Black-crowned Night-Heron but with stouter bill and longer legs. *Mostly gray; head black with white crown and white patch behind eye* and long white occipital plumes (even longer in breeding season). The yellow is restricted to a very small spot on the forecrown. Immature resembles immature Black-crowned Night-Heron but is slatier (not so brown) with finer streaking above; in flight feet and part of legs project beyond tail in Yellow-crown (only feet in Black-crown).

Similar species: See Black-crowned Night-Heron.

Status and distribution: Common along Pacific coast, less numerous along Caribbean coast and inland in fresh water marshes and along rivers in lowlands on both slopes; resident population augmented during northern winter by northern migrants; common also on Coiba Island, Taboga Island, the Pearl Islands, and other smaller islands off Pacific coast. To date found breeding only on Changamé Island off Pacific entrance to the Canal but certainly nests elsewhere as well. Can generally be seen, even during mid-day, on mud flats and rocks exposed at low tide on Pacific coast around the Canal entrance and Panama City.

Habits: Not as nocturnal as Black-crowned Night-Heron. The call is similar but somewhat higher pitched, *quak.*

Range: Eastern United States and Mexico to northern Peru and eastern Brazil (primarily in coastal areas) and in West Indies and Galapagos Islands.

RUFESCENT TIGER-HERON
(*Tigrisoma lineatum*) Pl.1

Description: 24–27. Heavy-bodied, with stout bill. *Head and neck rich rufous,* neck barred with black; stripe of white from throat down front of neck; upperparts otherwise brownish finely barred with black; underparts otherwise rufous, streaked with white on chest, banded black and white on flanks. Juvenal mostly cinnamon-buff coarsely barred with black; *throat and lower belly white.* Immature intermediate in pattern.

Similar species: Adults of other two tiger-herons look gray (not rufous) on sides of head and neck. Juvenals present more of a problem. Bare-throated, while somewhat similar, in all plumages has a prominent featherless yellow throat. Juvenal Fasciated is so similar that the two cannot be distinguished with any certainty in the field (in the hand, note its somewhat shorter and heavier bill, shorter legs, and presence of powder downs on back). See also American Bittern.

Status and distribution: Apparently rare (certainly not often seen) in swampy forest and along forested streams in lowlands on entire Caribbean slope; on Pacific slope known from eastern Panama province (one adult seen near Chepo on July 9, 1952; Eisenmann and J. Bull) and Darién. Scarce in Canal Zone, with recent reports including one taken at Juan Mina, several sightings from Barro Colorado Island, and an adult seen at Achiote Road on July 5, 1970 (Ridgely and R. Sharp).

Habits: Rather solitary and generally not conspicuous, as in Panama it forages mostly inside forest. The bird seen at Achiote Road was disturbed as it was attacking a Gray-chested Dove caught in a mist-net set in swampy woodland; the heron flew up heavily and perched high in a nearby tree, the pigeon had several deep puncture wounds in its breast and wings.

Range: Honduras (one doubtful record from southern Mexico) to northern Argentina and Uruguay.

Note: Members of the genus *Tigrisoma* are sometimes called tiger-bitterns. Wetmore calls this species Banded Tiger-Bittern.

FASCIATED TIGER-HERON
(*Tigrisoma fasciatum*) Pl.1

Description 23–25. Bill shorter and stouter, with more arched keel, than in other tiger-herons. Adult suggests Bare-throated in pattern with black crown, mainly blackish barred neck and upperparts, and unbarred slaty flanks, but differs in *feathered white throat,* darker (more slaty) face, *predominantly black neck and upperparts* (with pale buff bars narrower and more widely spaced), and less rufous lower belly. Juvenal most like juvenal Rufescent and not usually separable in the field, though less sharply banded on flanks and under wing-coverts and, in relation to age and sex, bill shorter. Subadult and immature are similar to adult but head barred black and buff, some white bars on flanks, and lower belly grayer. Fasciated, like Bare-throated, but unlike Rufescent, has concealed interscapular (mid-back) powder downs.

Similar species: Bare-throated Tiger-Heron in all plumages has wholly bare throat; adult has paler gray face and less black neck with broader buff bars than this species. Adult Rufescent Tiger-Heron has rufous head and neck; immature is more rufescent than this species and has a longer bill; juvenal is not surely separable in the field as juvenal Rufescents have rather short bills.

Status and distribution: Rare to locally uncommon chiefly along rapid forested streams and rivers in lowlands and foothills on Caribbean slope (recorded Bocas del Toro, Coclé, eastern Colon province, and San Blas); on Pacific slope known from eastern Panama province (one adult seen near Aguas Claras on Bayano River on July 21, 1973; D. Hill) and Darién. Not known from Canal Zone, though one has been collected as close as just above Madden Lake.

Habits: Little known but probably similar to Rufescent Tiger-Heron, with which it was long confused. Favors forested hill country, not swampy lowlands.

Range: Costa Rica south locally to northwestern Argentina and southeastern Brazil.

Note: The Panama form (*salmoni,* Costa Rica to Bolivia) is sometimes treated as a distinct species, Salmon's Tiger-Heron.

BARE-THROATED TIGER-HERON
(*Tigrisoma mexicanum*) Pl.1

Description: 28–32. *Wholly bare throat in all plumages.* Crown black; *face light gray;* sides of neck and upperparts barred blackish and buff; *bare throat greenish yellow to orange;* broad stripe of white bordered with black down front of neck; dull rufous brown below. Juvenal buff barred coarsely with black. Immature and subadult similar but more finely banded.

Similar species: Other tiger-herons (adults and juvenals) have feathered white throats. Adult Fasciated is somewhat similar in pattern but has stouter and shorter bill (more like a night-heron's) and wider black bars on neck and upperparts, making it appear much darker.

Status and distribution: Uncommon to locally fairly common in Pacific coastal lowlands from Chiriquí to eastern Panama province, both on coast and in nearby fresh water swamps and marshes; found also on Coiba Island and the Pearl Islands (where quite numerous on rocky and sandy shorelines); only one record from Caribbean slope, that a bird taken at Permé, San Blas, on July 25, 1929. No definite recent reports from Canal Zone, but still fairly common in the Tocumen/La Jagua area.

Habits: Usually solitary and at times surprisingly unsuspicious. Like other tiger-herons, often rests with neck hunched and bill angled skyward.

Range: Mexico to northwestern Colombia.

Note: Formerly placed in the genus *Heterocnus.*

LEAST BITTERN
(*Ixobrychus exilis*)

Description: 11–13. *Easily the smallest Panama heron.* Crown and back black; *wings rufous and buff* (especially prominent in flight); sides of head and neck rufous; underparts buffy white. Female has brownish crown and back. Immature is somewhat streaked below.

Similar species: Might be confused with several of the rails, especially in brief flight after having been flushed from the marsh, though no rail shows the conspicuous buffy patch on the wing-coverts. Green and Striated Herons are notably larger and have dark wings.

Status and distribution: Uncommon and very local in fresh water marshes, so far recorded mostly from Chagres River valley in Canal Zone, but surely more widespread. Known from several old records from Lion Hill, and recently from marshy areas on southwestern shore of Barro Colorado Island in Gatun Lake and on Chagres River above Gamboa near Juan Mina. Only report away from this area is a sighting of two birds flushed at Tocumen, eastern Panama province on July 11, 1973 (D. Hill). Resident population (the primarily South American *erythomelas*) is augmented by northern migrants (*exilis*) during winter.

Habits: Very secretive, usually remaining in dense marsh vegetation. Often escapes detection by "freezing" with bill pointed upward. When flushed, flies weakly for a short distance before dropping back into the marsh.

Range: North America to Bolivia, Paraguay, northeastern Argentina, and southeastern Brazil.

AMERICAN BITTERN
(*Botaurus lentiginosus*)

Description: 25–30. Only one old record. Brown above mottled with buff and with *broad black stripe down sides of neck; flight feathers slaty,* contrasting with brown wing-coverts; whitish buff below streaked with brown.

Similar species: Immatures of both night-herons are superficially similar but lack the black neck stripe and the slaty flight feathers. See also Pinnated Bittern (below).

Status and distribution: Known only from a specimen taken by McLeannan in 1862, presumably on what is now Caribbean side of Canal Zone. To be watched for in marshes during northern winter months.

Range: Breeds in North America; winters rarely south through Middle America, casually to Panama, also in West Indies.

Note: Pinnated Bittern (*B. pinnatus*), recorded locally in marshes from southeastern Mexico to Costa Rica and in South America, is unreported from Panama but may occur. It resembles American Bittern but lacks black neck stripe and is barred as well as streaked on sides of neck and upperparts (thus somewhat resembling juvenal tiger-herons but more finely barred above and streaked, not barred, below).

BOAT-BILLED HERONS: Cochleariidae (1)

Boat-billed Herons are little-known, neotropical wading birds, closely allied to the true herons, considered by some authors as best treated within the Ardeidae, most closely related to the night-herons. Their most remarkable feature is the broad shovel-like bill. The function of this curious bill is as yet uncertain, for all available information indicates a diet not appreciably different from the true herons, though the bill would seem more fitted to sifting in mud or aquatic vegetation. Boat-bills are usually found in small groups roosting in trees near water, from which they fly out at dusk to feed.

BOAT-BILLED HERON
(*Cochlearius cochlearius*)

Description: 18–20. *Very broad and flat bill.* Crown (except white forehead), long and wide crest, and upper back black; wings and lower back gray; *gray below,* becoming rusty on belly, with *large area on sides and flanks black.* Birds from extreme southern Darién at Jaqué (the South American form *cochlearius*) have *sides of head and chest white* and paler gray on wings and lower back. Immature is strongly washed with cinnamon above, buff below, and lacks crest.

Similar species: In pattern somewhat like adult Black-crowned Night-Heron.

Status and distribution: Uncommon and rather local (but strictly nocturnal and hence probably somewhat overlooked) in colonies in wooded swamps, river borders, and mangroves in lowlands on entire Caribbean slope; on Pacific slope known only from western Chiriquí, eastern side of Azuero Peninsula, and from Canal Zone (perhaps only formerly) east through Darién.

Habits: Nocturnal, feeding solitarily, roosting by day in groups in trees with thick foliage, usually not with other herons. Seems to decrease or even disappear as human population increases, though on the Bayano River (at least) they are apparently

BOAT-BILLED HERON

not shot for food. When disturbed while feeding at night sometimes utters a low quacking call.

Range: Mexico to Bolivia, northern Argentina, and southeastern Brazil.

Note: Birds from Middle America (*C. zeledoni* group), ranging as far south as the Tuira River valley in Darién, are sometimes considered a distinct species.

STORKS: Ciconiidae (2)

The storks are a widespread group of large, long legged wading birds. Resembling herons in many respects, they differ obviously in flying with neck extended. Only three species are found in the New World, of which but two are known in Panama. All storks feed on fish, small animals, and to some extent insects, generally in shallow water or wet grassy areas. The Wood Stork often feeds in a cooperative manner, a group more or less lining up and muddying the water in front of them with their feet, grabbing the fleeing prey with their bill. Some storks (notably the Wood Stork) are highly colonial, often nesting in association with herons and ibises; other species (among them the Jabiru) are solitary nesters.

WOOD STORK (WOOD IBIS)
(*Mycteria americana*)

Description: 35–42. Very large, with heavy somewhat decurved bill. Mostly white with *bare blackish head and upper neck* and *black flight feathers* and tail. Immature similar but with head and neck more or less feathered, brownish.

Similar species: Egrets and white herons lack black on wings and dark bare skin on head and neck. White Ibis is much smaller, has red bill and facial area, black restricted to wing-tips. Soaring birds somewhat resemble King Vulture in pattern.

Status and distribution: Locally fairly common but erratic (occasionally in large flocks, especially in Herrera and adjacent Coclé and in the Tocumen/La Jagua area) in marshes and swamps in lowlands on Pacific slope; less numerous on Caribbean slope (chiefly recorded in Bocas del Toro). No nesting colonies have been reported, but surely breeds in coastal swamps along Pacific coast, possibly on western Caribbean. Rather infrequent in the Canal Zone and then often only flying overhead.

Habits: Gregarious. Though rather awkward on the ground or perched in a tree, they are exceptionally graceful in the air, particularly when circling high overhead on outstretched wings.

Range: Southern United States (where decreasing) to northern Argentina and Uruguay.

JABIRU
(*Jabiru mycteria*)

Description: 48–55. *Huge size* makes this very rare species unmistakable. Bill very heavy, slightly upturned. *Entirely white* with bare head and neck blackish becoming red on lower neck. Immature is more brownish gray.

Similar species: Wood Stork is much smaller with black flight feathers and tail.

Status and distribution: Only one definite record, a bird taken at Cricamola, Bocas del Toro, on August 11, 1927. Wetmore mentions that Baldomiro Meno, a native hunter, said that he had seen this species once at La Jagua, eastern Panama province (date not given). Favors extensive marshy areas.

Habits: Usually solitary or in pairs, unlike Wood Stork. Like that species, the Jabiru often soars to great heights.

Range: Occurs from southern Mexico (accidental in southern Texas, with one recent record) south locally to northern Argentina and Uruguay; definitely recorded breeding in Middle America only in Belize and Costa Rica.

IBISES AND SPOONBILLS: Threskiornithidae (6)

Ibises and spoonbills are large, long legged wading birds, widespread in distribution but particularly numerous in tropical areas. Ibises are known by their long decurved bills, spoonbills by their broad flat bills widened at the tip. They fly with neck outstretched, and a number of species alternate a series of flaps with short glides on somewhat downcurved wings. Their food consists mostly of fish and crustaceans, usually obtained by probing in mud, or (in the case of spoonbills) by sideways movements in mud and shallow water. Many species are gregarious, forming large roosts and nesting colonies in inaccessible swamps; others (among them the Green and Buff-necked Ibises) are more solitary and are found in at most small groups.

BUFF-NECKED IBIS
(*Theristicus caudatus*)

Description: 28–32. Casual. *Large.* Bill decurved. *Head, neck, and chest buffy white,* more orange-rufous on crown and chest, whiter on throat; upperparts otherwise dark gray, wings black with *conspicuous white wing-coverts;* lower underparts black.

Status and distribution: One definite record, a bird killed near Pacora, eastern Panama province on September 18, 1950; another was reported seen in the same general area in September 1958 (Baldomiro Meno, *fide* Wetmore). Favors savannas and open fields, especially near marshes.

Range: Colombia (casual in Panama) to Tierra del Fuego.

Note: Wetmore calls it White-throated Ibis.

GREEN IBIS
(*Mesembrinibis cayennensis*)

Description: 20–22. Decurved greenish bill; *short greenish legs. Dark bronzy green, brightest on neck and chest,* with bushy crest (usually not prominent); belly dull black.

Similar species: At a distance or in poor light, Glossy Ibis is superficially similar, but it has a more slender build, lacks crest, and adults are purplish chestnut when seen in good light (not as black as this species). See also Bare-faced Ibis (below).

Status and distribution: Fairly common to common but local in swampy forest and along forested rivers in lowlands of western Bocas del Toro (Almirante Bay), eastern Panama province (Bayano River; one record from near Pacora on September 15, 1958), and Darién (Chucunaque/Tuira River valleys); a single sighting from eastern Colon province (Río Guanche; N. G. Smith), and two reports from San Blas (Mandinga, Puerto Obaldía). In Canal Zone known from several nineteenth-century specimens but not recorded since.

Habits: Usually found singly or in pairs. Often rather secretive and hard to see, but sometimes feeds in the open on gravel bars on banks of rivers, probing deeply in

Green Ibis

mud and water between rocks. In some areas best known from their mellow rolling calls, heard at sunrise and dusk, *kro, kro,* or *koro, koro.*

Range: Costa Rica to Paraguay, northeastern Argentina, and southeastern Brazil.

Note: Wetmore calls it Cayenne Ibis. Bare-faced Ibis (*Phimosus infuscatus*) of South America is possible in eastern Panama; it ranges as close as the Río Sinú in northern Colombia. It resembles Green Ibis but is smaller and more slender (18–20″); adult is blackish, slightly glossed green above, more sooty below; facial skin including bare forehead and upper throat red, bill reddish.

WHITE IBIS
(*Eudocimus albus*)

Description: 23–25. *Decurved bill and bare facial skin red;* legs pink. Adult *white with black wing-tips.* Immature has pinkish bill with dark tip, pinkish legs; is grayish brown somewhat streaked with white, with *contrasting white rump and belly.*

Similar species: Egrets and white herons lack black in wings; Wood Stork is larger and has all of flight feathers black. Glossy and Green Ibises are *all* dark, lacking white rump and belly of immature. See also Limpkin.

Status and distribution: Fairly common in mangroves and on coastal mudflats (only occasionally in fresh water marshes; inland chiefly on tidal rivers) in lowlands on Pacific slope from eastern Chiriquí (sighting of two at Las Lajas on July 16, 1964; Eisenmann and N. G. Smith) east through Darién; apparently not known from Caribbean slope; fairly common also on Coiba Island and the Pearl Islands. To date found breeding only on Isla Changamé in Panama Bay but may nest on mainland as well. A number can almost always be seen on mudflats exposed at low tide at the Pacific entrance to the Canal.

Habits: Rather gregarious. Often become quite soiled by the mud in which they habitually forage. A flock of adults in flight presents an especially attractive sight.

Range: Southeastern United States and Mexico to northwestern Peru and Venezuela; Greater Antilles.

[SCARLET IBIS]
(*Eudocimus ruber*)

Description: 22–24. One report. Unmistakable. Decurved bill, bare facial skin, and legs red (sometimes blackish in breeding plumage). *Entirely scarlet* with black wing-tips. Immature closely resembles immature White Ibis.

Status and distribution: Only report is an adult seen on the Farfan mudflats at the Pacific entrance to the Canal "off and on" from January 25, 1967 to February 17, 1967, and again on March 14, 1967 (N. G. Smith). The origin of the bird must remain suspect; the species is often kept in captivity.

Range: Colombia, Venezuela, the Guianas, and eastern Brazil; casual or accidental in southeastern United States (perhaps all escapes) and West Indies.

GLOSSY IBIS
(*Plegadis falcinellus*)

Description: 22–24. Rare. *Long decurved bill.* Bare facial skin and lores slaty. *Mostly bronzy chestnut,* with purplish reflections in good light, greener on wings and lower back. Breeding birds have border of facial skin bluish white. Winter adults have whitish streaks on head and neck. Immature like winter adult but duller and grayer.

Similar species: Appears blackish in poor light. Green Ibis is stockier with shorter legs, slight bushy crest, and is greener on neck and chest. Immature White Ibis has white rump and belly. See also White-faced Ibis (below).

Status and distribution: A rare but possibly regular migrant in small numbers to fresh water marshes and ponds and wet grassy areas in lowlands locally on Pacific slope (Herrera, eastern Panama province); on Caribbean slope only in Canal Zone and adjacent eastern Colon province (Puerto Pilón). Though only one specimen has been taken (near La Jagua on March 18, 1949), there have been a number of recent sight reports, perhaps reflecting the species' recent increase in the United States and West Indies. Though apparently most frequent during fall and winter months, there are also sightings from northern breeding season (May 23 and July 16, 1968; Ridgely). Many of the birds sighted could be identified only as *Plegadis,* chiefly immatures, but all that could be identified to species seemed to be Glossies.

Range: Coastal eastern and southern United States and Greater Antilles; migrating or wandering birds have been recorded with increasing frequency in Middle America and northern South America, though status in these areas uncertain due to confusion with White-faced Ibis, which had erroneously been thought to be resident in Colombia and Venezuela. Recently found breeding in Venezuela (*fide* P. Schwartz); breeding in Middle America possible but unrecorded. Also found locally in warmer parts of southern Europe, Africa, Asia, and Australia.

Note: White-faced Ibis (*P. chihi*) of western North America and southern South America might possibly occur as a wanderer. It closely resembles the Glossy (some regard the two as conspecific), but adults have bare red facial skin and lores, and in breeding season this area is narrowly edged with white *feathers*. Immatures of the two are not separable in the field.

ROSEATE SPOONBILL
(*Ajaia ajaja*)

Description: 28–32. Long flat bill, broadening at tip into the *unmistakable "spoonbill."* Adult has featherless head and white neck; *otherwise mostly pink, wing-coverts red;* tail buffy-orange. Immature has head largely feathered, is more whitish, becoming pinker with age.

Similar species: Even the whitish immatures can be instantly recognized by the spoonlike bill.

Status and distribution: Uncommon and local in mangroves and fresh water swamps and marshes in coastal lowlands on Pacific slope from Chiriquí to Darién; only a rare wanderer to Caribbean slope, with one bird shot on Changuinola River, Bocas del Toro, prior to 1962 (de la Guardia, *fide* Eisenmann); one seen at Almirante, Bocas del Toro, on March 27, 1965 (N. G. Smith); one taken at Gatun, Canal Zone, in November 1911; and one seen at France Field, Canal Zone, on January 26, 1973 (J. Pujals). Now very scarce in Canal Zone (though reported to breed until about 1930 in mangroves near Cocoli), but can still be seen in small numbers in the Tocumen/La Jagua area; most numerous near coast of Gulf of San Miguel (salinas south of Aguadulce, Santa María marshes, mudflats off Chitré).

Habits: Usually seen in small flocks. Forages by swinging bill from side to side in shallow water and mud.

Range: Coasts of southeastern United States and Mexico south locally to northern Argentina and Uruguay (casual in central Chile); Greater Antilles.

DUCKS, GEESE, AND SWANS: Anatidae (14)

Well known and worldwide in distribution, the waterfowl need no introduction. Most of the ducks found in Panama feed primarily on vegetable matter, a few on crustaceans and other small aquatic animals. Nests of the Panamanian breeding species are generally located in hollows in trees, the exception being the Masked Duck, which conceals its nest in dense vegetation on the ground near water. Due to a scarcity of good habitat and the intense hunting pressure on much of what exists, ducks do not form a conspicuous part of Panama's avifauna.

WHITE-FACED TREE-DUCK (WHISTLING-DUCK)
(*Dendrocygna viduata*)

Description: 16–18. Now very rare. Bill black. *Forepart of head white* (sometimes stained by mud), remainder of head and neck black (sometimes with patch of white on foreneck); back brown; rump, tail, and most of wings black; chest rufous-chestnut, center of lower underparts black, sides and flanks brown barred with black. In flight shows *no white on wings.* Juvenal has no black or white on head; head mainly gray with rusty face, below light gray barred with darker.

Similar species: Other tree-ducks lack white on head.

Status and distribution: Uncertain. Recorded only from Canal Zone and eastern Panama province, chiefly at La Jagua where it was formerly quite numerous but now appears to have disappeared with no recent reports. One was shot on Gatun Lake in June 1924; two were taken (one in 1928, the other in 1931) on marshes near Pacora, eastern Panama province (in or near the area presently known as La Jagua). Reported to have invaded La Jagua in numbers in the 1930's and to have nested there, but had essentially disappeared by the early 1940's (many were shot).

Habits: Similar to Black-bellied Tree-Duck and usually consorts with them; less arboreal.

Range: Northwestern Costa Rica; irregular

in central Panama; Colombia to northern Argentina and Uruguay; also warmer parts of Africa.

FULVOUS TREE-DUCK (WHISTLING-DUCK)
(Dendrocygna bicolor)

Description: 18–21. Only one record. Bill slaty gray. *Mostly cinnamon brown,* paler and buffier below, with patch of whitish streaks on sides of neck and *prominent creamy white stripes down sides and flanks.* In flight, wings appear very dark and it shows *conspicuous white ring on upper tail-coverts.*

Similar species: See other tree-ducks. Female *Anas* ducks are differently shaped (shorter neck, shorter legs), show some pattern on wings, and are generally mottled with dusky; female Pintail is most similar but shows white on wing in flight and lacks creamy white flank stripe.

Status and distribution: A casual wanderer. Only record is a bird shot at La Jagua, eastern Panama province on June 14, 1936. To be watched for among groups of Black-bellied Tree-Ducks.

Range: Southern United States south locally to Honduras; casual in Costa Rica (recent sightings—G. Stiles) and central Panama; Colombia to central Argentina (casually to Chile); also in eastern Africa and southern Asia.

BLACK-BELLIED TREE-DUCK (WHISTLING-DUCK)
(Dendrocygna autumnalis)

Description: 20–22. *Bill and legs reddish.* Mostly reddish brown with sides of head and upper neck gray and wash of gray on lower chest; *breast and belly black; wings show broad white band across coverts* (visible at rest and very prominent in flight). Immature is duller and more grayish brown but already shows adult's pattern; bill and legs dusky.

Similar species: See other tree-ducks. On the ground, tree-ducks give a gangly impression, with long neck and legs; in the air the wings beat relatively slowly, the neck is drooped, and the long legs extend well beyond the tail.

Status and distribution: Local and now generally uncommon (formerly much more widespread and numerous) in fresh water marshes and ponds (occasionally salt water) in lowlands on entire Pacific slope; rare (perhaps only a wanderer) on Caribbean slope where known only from eastern San Blas and two nineteenth-century specimens probably taken in Chagres basin of Canal Zone. Now largely extirpated in Canal Zone (though occasional wandering birds have been seen recently on Pacific side) but still present in small numbers in the Tocumen/La Jagua area; more numerous in western Panama, particularly in southern Coclé near Aguadulce, Santa María marshes of Herrera, and coastal Veraguas. Constant hunting has greatly reduced their numbers; formerly they occurred in flocks of hundreds (C. A. Rogers, oral comm.).

BLACK-BELLIED TREE-DUCK

Habits: Unlike the other two Panama tree-ducks, this species perches readily in trees, especially on dead branches. Usually in small groups. Has loud high semi-whistled calls, varying in speed and quality, given mostly in flight; these result in its local name of "wíchity" or "güíchiti." Often kept in captivity around farmyards and pools.

Range: Southern Texas and Mexico to northern Argentina and southeastern Brazil.

COMB DUCK
(Sarkidiornis melanotos)

Description: ♂28–30; ♀22–24. Large. Adult male has *black fleshy comb* on upper mandible. Crown and hindneck mostly black, feathers recurved forming slight crest; *rest of head and neck and most of underparts white,* the head flecked with black; remaining upperparts (including entire wing) black glossed with green and purple. Female much smaller.

Similar species: Muscovy is all dark with prominent white wing-coverts. Some domesticated Muscovies have white on underparts (and elsewhere) but always show white on wings.

Status and distribution: Fairly common on the Chucunaque River in lowlands of eastern Darién; very rarely wanders to marshes at La Jagua, eastern Panama province where one out of a band of five was shot on March 30, 1949 (others seen until May).

Habits: Similar to Muscovy, like that species often perching in trees.

Range: Eastern (rarely central) Panama south locally to northern Argentina and Uruguay; also in Africa and southern Asia.

Note: American birds are by some authors considered distinct, *S. sylvicola* (South American Comb-Duck).

MUSCOVY DUCK
(*Cairina moschata*)

Description: ♂ 32–35; ♀ 24–26. *Large.* Adult male has fleshy red caruncles over eye and at base of bill. *Glossy black* with slight bushy crest; *upper wing-coverts and entire undersurface of wing white* (very conspicuous in flight). Female similar but much smaller, with no red on bill or face and no noticeable crest. Immature has much less white on wing.

Similar species: Comb Duck has mostly white head, neck, and underparts, and has wholly black wings. Immature in flight showing little white on wings might be confused with Neotropic Cormorant.

Status and distribution: Uncommon and local in fresh water swamps and marshes in lowlands of eastern Panama province (Tocumen eastward) and Darién; one sighting from Coiba Island (Wetmore), but otherwise, curiously, not recorded from western Panama; known formerly from Chagres River valley in Canal Zone, but now apparently extirpated except for occasional wandering birds; unrecorded elsewhere on Caribbean slope. Surprisingly local in Panama; now much reduced in numbers where it does occur by incessant hunting. A few still survive in the Tocumen/La Jagua area.

Habits: Muscovies are frequently domesticated and kept at liberty by country people, so it is sometimes questionable whether or not a bird is truly feral. Wild birds are usually very wary, often a good distinction from captive ones. The species favors wooded swamps and rivers, and perches readily in trees.

Range: Mexico south locally to northern Argentina and Uruguay.

MUSCOVY DUCK

AMERICAN WIGEON
(*Anas americana*)

Description: 18–22. Bluish gray bill. Male has *white crown and green patch behind eye;* throat and neck buff with small black dots; otherwise brown above; chest and sides pinkish brown, center of underparts white; white patch in front of black rump and under tail-coverts. Female *mostly ruddy brown with contrasting grayish head and neck.* In flight, both sexes show *prominent white wing-coverts* and a green speculum.

Similar species: Pale bluish wing-coverts of Shoveler and Blue-winged Teal can look white in some lights. Male's white crown is usually very conspicuous.

Status and distribution: Locally fairly common but somewhat irregular winter visitant (October–April) to ponds, lakes, and fresh water marshes in lowlands of western and central Panama; recorded from Bocas del Toro, Chiriquí (sight report of two east of David on November 9, 1968; Ridgely and J. Karr), Canal Zone (most numerous and regular in the Miraflores Lake/Pedro Miguel area), and eastern Panama province (La Jagua); one band recovery from southern Los Santos in December 1957.

Habits: Swims with more upright carriage than other *Anas* ducks. Males frequently give an easily recognized whistled *whee whee whew* (R. T. Peterson).

Range: Breeds in western North America; winters south to northern Colombia and Venezuela, and in West Indies.

Note: By some separated in the genus *Mareca.*

NORTHERN PINTAIL
(*Anas acuta*)

Description: 26–30. *Long slender neck* and *pointed tail* (much longer in male). Bill gray. Male has *brown head and white stripe extending up foreneck ending in point;* upperparts and sides mostly pale gray; underparts mostly white with black under tail-coverts. Female is mottled light brownish all over. In flight, both sexes show *white stripe on rear edge only* of green speculum.

Similar species: Females can be known by their streamlined appearance and pointed tail (longer than in other similar female ducks). See Fulvous Tree-Duck.

Status and distribution: A very local and irregular, but sometimes common, winter visitant (mostly December–February), reported mostly from Bocas del Toro and eastern Panama province (La Jagua, where large flocks have occasionally appeared), also from Los Santos and Coclé (band recoveries). Very few reports from Canal Zone though it was listed by McLeannan in the nineteenth century (no specimens); a female was seen on Chagres River above Juan Mina on December 18, 1962 (Eisenmann).

Range: Breeds in North America, Europe, and Asia; American birds winter south to northern South America and in West Indies.

[MALLARD]
(*Anas platyrhynchos*)

Description: 22–26. Old reports. Bill yellow in male, *orange and dusky in female.* Male has *glossy green head, narrow white collar around neck, rufous chest,* and mostly pale gray body with black rump and under tail-coverts and white tail. Female mottled brownish with *whitish tail.* In flight, both sexes show violet-blue speculum *bordered in front and behind by a white stripe.*

Similar species: Female can be told from female Pintail by orange on bill, whitish tail, and stripe in front of wing speculum (Pintail has stripe only to rear).

Status and distribution: Only definite report is of "one seen" on one of the lakes near Miraflores in the Canal Zone on November 26, 1911 (L. Jewel); also listed as occurring by McLeannan in nineteenth century (no specimens).

Range: Breeds in North America, Europe, and Asia; in America winters south to Mexico, rarely to Honduras, reported seen in Nicaragua, Costa Rica, and Panama.

CINNAMON TEAL
(*Anas cyanoptera*)

Description: 15–17. Rare. Bill gray. Male *mostly bright cinnamon red* with black mottling on back and blackish rump and tail. Female almost identical to female Blue-winged Teal and cannot be distinguished in the field. In flight, both sexes show prominent pale blue wing-coverts and green speculum (as in Blue-winged Teal).

Similar species: See Blue-winged Teal. Only males in breeding plumage (assumed during northern winter) are safely identified (they otherwise resemble females).

Status and distribution: A rare winter visitant, perhaps overlooked. Known from one old Canal Zone record, a recent sight report of a male at Gamboa in Canal Zone on January 5, 1967 (N. G. Smith), and from three band recoveries, two from La Jagua (January 20, 1955; January 7, 1956) and one from near Chame, western Panama province (November 8, 1957). Males should be watched for among flocks of Blue-winged Teal, especially after January when they have molted into nuptial plumage.

Range: Breeds in western North America south to central Mexico, Colombia, and from southern Peru and southeastern Brazil to the Straits of Magellan; northern birds winter south rarely to northern South America.

BLUE-WINGED TEAL
(*Anas discors*)

Description: 15–16. Bill gray. Male has head and upper neck dark gray (blacker on crown) with *prominent white crescent on forepart of face;* otherwise mostly blackish above, brownish below spotted with blackish; black rump, tail, and under tail-coverts. Female mottled light brownish. In flight, both sexes show *prominent pale blue wing-coverts* (may look white at a distance) and green speculum.

Similar species: Noticeably smaller than most of the ducks with which it consorts;

see Cinnamon Teal. Northern Shoveler has similar pale blue wing-coverts but is larger with spoon-shaped bill.

Status and distribution: Though a migrant, easily the most numerous and widespread duck in Panama. Locally common on fresh water marshes, ponds, and lakes in lowlands on both slopes, ranging up to Volcán Lakes in lower highlands of western Chiriquí; reported also from Coiba Island. Recorded mostly September–April, a few lingering into May and even into June: e.g., a male at Pedro Miguel in Canal Zone on June 20, 1970 (Ridgely and J. Gwynne), perhaps a crippled bird.

Habits: Found wherever there is suitable marshy or shallow water habitat and an absence of excessive disturbance. Like most other *Anas* ducks feed by tipping up, submerging the front half of the body. Also like other *Anas* ducks, springs directly into flight, without preliminary pattering along the surface of most of the others. Usually silent, like most other migrant ducks in Panama.

Range: Breeds in North America; winters from southern United States to central Argentina and Uruguay.

NORTHERN SHOVELER
(*Anas clypeata*)

Description: 17–20. *Oversize spoon-shaped bill* distinguishes both sexes. Male has *head and neck dark green,* back black, chest white, *most of lower underparts dark chestnut* with white area on flanks. Female is mottled brownish. In flight, both sexes show pale blue wing-coverts and green speculum.

Similar species: Told from all other Panama ducks by the large spatulate bill. Female resembles female Blue-winged Teal but is larger with the oversize bill.

Status and distribution: Rare to uncommon winter visitant (October–March) to fresh water marshes and shallow ponds in lowlands on both slopes; rather local and reported only from Chiriquí (David), Bocas del Toro (Changuinola), Canal Zone, and eastern Panama province (La Jagua). In Canal Zone, known from only two sight reports, the more recent being a female at Pedro Miguel on December 17, 1967 (Ridgely).

Habits: Usually holds bill angled downward, almost touching the water. Feeds by sifting through mud and shallow water as it slowly paddles forward.

Range: Breeds in North America, Europe, and Asia; in America winters south to northern Colombia, rarely to northern Venezuela (sightings—P. Alden).

Note: By some separated in the genus *Spatula.*

RING-NECKED DUCK
(*Aythya collaris*)

Description: 16–18. *Bill bluish gray with white ring* and black tip. Male has head and neck black (glossed purple) with inconspicuous narrow chestnut collar around neck; chest and *back black;* sides light gray with *prominent vertical white mark in front of wing;* center of lower underparts white. Female mostly brown, darkest on crown and back, with *whitish face and white eye-ring;* belly white. In flight, both sexes show broad gray stripe on flight feathers.

Similar species: Both sexes resemble Lesser Scaup but have ring on bill (absent in scaup). Male known by its black (not gray) back and white vertical mark in front of wing (lacking in scaup); female by its lack of female scaup's distinct white patch at base of bill (though face is vaguely whitish).

Status and distribution: First reported in February 1951, now known to be an occasional winter visitant (December–February) in very small numbers to ponds, lakes, and fresh water marshes. No Panama specimens; reported from Chiriquí (sighting of a female on Volcán Lakes on February 23, 1971; R. V. Clem, J. H. Dick, and G. Stout), Canal Zone (a number of sight reports, principally from Miraflores Lakes and Pedro Miguel), and eastern Panama province (reportedly shot occasionally at La Jagua).

Habits: A diving duck, preferring open and relatively deep fresh water. Favors company of Lesser Scaup.

Range: Breeds in North America (increasing in recent decades, especially to east); winters from United States to Panama (once Venezuela) and in West Indies.

LESSER SCAUP
(*Aythya affinis*)

Description: 16–18. Bill bluish. Male has black head (glossed with purple in some lights), neck, and chest; *otherwise mostly grayish* (paler below). Female is brown, darker above, with *well-defined white patch at base of bill.* In flight, both sexes show prominent white stripe on flight feathers.

Similar species: See much less numerous Ring-necked Duck.

Status and distribution: Locally fairly common winter visitant (November–March) to less disturbed portions of larger bodies of water in lowlands on both slopes, ranging up to Volcán Lakes in lower highlands of western Chiriquí; recorded also on Coiba Island; apparently not recorded from Darién or San Blas. Most numerous in Canal Zone on Madden and Gatun Lakes, Chagres River above Gamboa.

Habits: Usually seen in flocks on open water, diving frequently.

Range: Breeds in western North America; winters south to Colombia and Venezuela (once Ecuador) and in West Indies.

MASKED DUCK
(male left, female right)

MASKED DUCK
(*Oxyura dominica*)

Description: 13–14. *Bill blue* (brighter in male); long stiff tail usually submerged (sometimes cocked into air). Male has *black face; otherwise mostly chestnut,* paler and buffier below, speckled with black. Female is mostly dark brown above with sides of head more grayish buff and *crossed by two dusky stripes;* buffy brownish below mottled with black. Immature male resembles female but blacker on crown. In flight, both sexes show *prominent white patch on secondaries.*

Status and distribution: Fairly common but very local in fresh water marshes and on shallow ponds in lowlands on Pacific slope; on Caribbean slope known only from Chagres River above Gamboa and eastern San Blas (Puerto Obaldía); recently found on Volcán Lakes in lower highlands of western Chiriquí, where possibly only a winter resident (8 seen on February 23, 1971, by R. V. Clem, J. H. Dick, and G. Stout; at least 19 seen February 16–18, 1973, by Eisenmann and J. Pujals). Irregular in Canal Zone; about 30 were on Miraflores Lake in early August 1972 (Ridgely), and some were seen subsequently (J. Pujals), but none seemed to be present in late January 1973 (Ridgely), perhaps having been shot out. Numerous on some ponds in the Santa María marshes of Herrera.

Habits: Often rather shy and difficult to see, usually remaining in areas of water with thick emergent vegetation. Swims low in the water. Adult males are considerably outnumbered by female-plumaged birds.

Range: Southern Texas and Mexico to northern Argentina and Uruguay; West Indies (rarely Florida).

AMERICAN VULTURES: Cathartidae (4)

The American Vultures are a well known group of carrion eaters found only in the New World, in greatest numbers in warmer regions. Two species, the Turkey and the Black, are familiar birds in Panama, as elsewhere in the warmer parts of America. Black Vultures in particular are especially numerous around towns and cities; they and the Turkey Vulture roost in large numbers in places such as Ancon Hill. The Panamanian vultures apparently nest in shaded crevices, such as hollow trees or logs on or very near the ground and cavities in rocks. Vultures locate their food primarily through keen eyesight, though recent evidence indicates that, at least in the Turkey Vulture, the sense of smell also plays a role.

KING VULTURE
(*Sarcoramphus papa*) page 56

Description: 30–34. Very large. Adult *mostly creamy white* with black rump, tail, and flight feathers; at short range *multicolored featherless head and neck* can be seen. Immature blackish brown, becoming progressively whiter on underparts with age.

King Vulture (adult)

Flight profile of long broad flat wings, short tail, and almost headless look is characteristic at great distances.

Similar species: Adults are unmistakable. Immature might be confused with Turkey Vulture but generally shows at least some white and soars with flat (not uptilted) wings.

Status and distribution: Uncommon to fairly common, but thinly spread, in lowlands and foothills on both slopes, mostly in relatively unsettled wooded areas; found also on Coiba Island. Though most numerous in forested areas, also occasionally seen flying over cleared areas and savannas. To be seen regularly (almost daily) in small numbers (usually no more than one or two) on Caribbean side of Canal Zone, particularly on Pipeline Road and at Barro Colorado Island.

Habits: Almost invariably seen soaring effortlessly high overhead, only occasionally perched. Usually seen singly, occasionally in pairs, very rarely more; generally keeps apart from other soaring vultures.

Range: Southern Mexico to Bolivia, northern Argentina, and Uruguay.

BLACK VULTURE

(*Coragyps atratus*)

Description: 24–27. *Black,* including featherless head and neck, with *white patch at base of primaries* (prominent in flight).

Similar species: Compared to Turkey Vulture has relatively broad and short wings and tail; Turkey Vulture has red (not solid black) head in adults and lacks the white wing patch.

Status and distribution: Very common to abundant in more or less inhabited and open country and in smaller numbers at forested borders (rare in areas of unbroken forest, occasionally flying over) virtually throughout; particularly numerous around towns and cities; found also on Coiba Island, Taboga Island, the Pearl Islands, and other smaller islands in Panama Bay.

Habits: A familiar carrion feeder in settled areas and around sea bird colonies. In some places (e.g., Panama city) it becomes very unsuspicious and serves a useful function as a supplementary garbage collector. Very large numbers are also to be seen on updrafts around Ancon Hill or going to roosts about Panama city. Ordinary flight consists of several flaps and a sail, unlike Turkey Vulture, which mainly soars; soars on flat wings (not in dihedral). There appears to be some migratory movement through Panama; soaring flocks flying eastward are regularly seen in November, and recently movement toward the west has been recorded in March and April (Eisenmann).

Range: Central United States to central Chile and southern Argentina.

TURKEY VULTURE

(*Cathartes aura*)

Description: 28–32. Black, with *featherless head and neck reddish* (blackish in young birds). The breeding race (*ruficollis*) has several narrow dull yellow bands across back of neck (may look like a pale patch at a distance). *Soars with wings held slightly above the horizontal;* from below contrast between black under wing-coverts and *silvery gray flight feathers* is apparent.

Similar species: Black Vulture has shorter and broader wings and tail, white patch on primaries, and alternates flapping with sailing (soaring much less). Lesser Yellow-headed Vulture is similarly shaped but has mostly yellow head (not just on rear part of neck), usually has whitish patch at base of primaries, and is smaller. Immature King Vulture shows some white below except when very young. Zone-tailed Hawk is smaller with larger feathered head, has white tail bands.

Status and distribution: Common resident

throughout, abundant on migration, in greater numbers during northern winter months; probably somewhat more numerous in open country than in forested areas; found also on the Coiba, Taboga, and Pearl Islands. In October and November and again from late February to early April large (sometimes tremendous) flocks of migrants breeding in north pass overhead, providing the observer who is in the right place at the right time with a breathtaking spectacle; these flocks often number in the many thousands. The greatest flights have been observed in coastal Bocas del Toro and on Pacific slope of Canal Zone and eastern Panama province, in early March and in October.

Habits: More widespread than Black Vulture, but less numerous around towns and cities. Less gregarious (except on migration) than Black Vulture. A masterful flier, soaring for long periods without a flap, tilting from side to side to take advantage of every favorable air current.

Range: Breeds from southern Canada to Tierra del Fuego; Greater Antilles. Many northern birds winter in Middle America and northwestern South America.

LESSER YELLOW-HEADED VULTURE
(*Cathartes burrovianus*)

Description: 23–25. Resembles more familiar Turkey Vulture but slighter and *smaller;* at close range bare head can be seen to be *mostly yellow or orange-yellow* with red forecrown and nape and blue-gray midcrown (skin colors somewhat variable). In flight shows whitish patch on upper surface of wing at base of primaries, as well as two-toned underwing pattern as in Turkey Vulture. Immature has dusky head with whitish nape.

Similar species: See Turkey Vulture.

Status and distribution: Fairly common locally over savanna grasslands and open marshes in lowlands on Pacific slope from Chiriquí and eastern side of Azuero Peninsula to eastern Panama province. Scarce in Canal Zone and vicinity, though occasional single birds or small groups have been seen in Panama city and in grassy open areas of Zone. Fairly numerous in Tocumen/La Jagua area though most common in Coclé and eastern Azuero Peninsula. Seems seasonally more numerous, so perhaps in part migratory; evidently breeds in Panama, however, as juvenals have been observed.

Habits: Usually seen sailing low over a grassy area or marsh, or perched on a low branch or fence post; only rarely soars high (when sometimes hard to distinguish from Turkey Vulture).

Range: Eastern Mexico; spottily in Central America; Colombia to northern Argentina and Uruguay.

HAWKS, EAGLES, AND KITES: Accipitridae (37)

This is a varied group of diurnal birds of prey, worldwide in distribution and well represented in Panama. All are characterized by a strongly hooked bill and gripping feet; most species have rather rounded wings (the exceptions being chiefly several species of kites). The female is larger, sometimes considerably larger, than the male, and a few species show sexual dimorphism in coloration as well. Their food is live prey, ranging in the various species from sizable mammals and birds to insects. Though many Panama species, especially the medium-sized members of the group, are generalists (i.e. they feed relatively opportunistically), a number of others have more specialized feeding habits; several feed mainly on insects captured on the wing, a few feed on snails, several mainly on birds, a number chiefly on snakes and other reptiles, and one on fish. Though they are more conspicuous and easily observed on the open savannas and in gallery woodland, there is a greater diversity of species in humid forest and woodland. Many neotropical birds of prey are very difficult to identify in the field, for one often does not get a close or long look at them, and in numerous species there are several plumage phases or age stages to contend with. Most resident species are still poorly known and would amply repay detailed and sustained study. The larger species, in particular the huge Harpy Eagle, have been greatly reduced in numbers around settled areas, and though the Harpy is now officially protected, it as well as other species are still usually shot when the opportunity arises.

WHITE-TAILED KITE
(*Elanus leucurus*)

Description: 15–16. Wings fairly long, pointed; tail long, square-tipped. *Mostly white* with pearly gray back and wings and a *black shoulder patch*. Juvenal similar but tinged with brown above, on breast, and on tail.

Similar species: Should be easily recognized. Plumbeous Kite has similar shape but is uniform leaden gray with black tail crossed by white bands; see also Mississippi Kite. Male Northern Harrier is also mostly pale gray and white, but is considerably larger with prominent white rump, lacks black shoulders, and has different proportions.

Status and distribution: A recent arrival in Panama. First observed in early 1967; now fairly common to common in open grassy areas and savannas on Pacific slope from western Chiriquí to eastern Panama province, ranging in smaller numbers up into lower highlands of western Chiriquí around Volcán and Boquete; recorded also from cleared areas on Caribbean slope in Bocas del Toro and in increasing numbers in Canal Zone and vicinity; also spreading locally into foothills in central Panama (Cerro Santa Rita, Cerro Azul). First recorded breeding in 1970. Easily observed along Pan-American Highway both east and west of Panama city, especially in early morning; most numerous in eastern Panama province. This species' dramatic range expansion and population increase through Middle America in the last decade is fully documented by Eisenmann (*American Birds 25:* 529–536, 1971).

Habits: Generally very conspicuous. Has a graceful flight with deep wingbeats; often hovers, the body then angled at about 45° (not horizontal as in kestrel). At least partially crepuscular, hunting mostly in the early morning and late afternoon, perching most of the day, often in an exposed situation.

Range: Southwestern United States to central Panama; northern Colombia to the Guianas; coastal Brazil through Paraguay, northern Argentina, and Chile.

WHITE-TAILED KITE

SWALLOW-TAILED KITE
(*Elanoides forficatus*)

Description: 21–24. Unmistakable. *Head, neck, and underparts white;* back, wings, and tail black, glossed with green on upper back and shoulders (gloss becoming duller blue in worn plumage); *tail very long and deeply forked.*

Status and distribution: Fairly common in forest and forest borders in lowlands and foothills on both slopes, more numerous on Caribbean; ranges up in Chiriquí highlands to over 6000 feet. Breeds in Panama, and also occurs as a transient in fairly large numbers (flocks of up to several hundred birds, regularly in association with Plumbeous Kite) late January–February and late July–early September; appears to be absent mid-September–early January. Breeding birds of southern United States (nominate *forficatus*) unrecorded but possibly occur as transients en route to their wintering grounds in South America east of the Andes (though perhaps only moving via the West Indies or Caribbean); they cannot be separated in the field from Middle American breeders (*yetapa*).

Habits: A beautiful bird, the most graceful of all birds of prey. Pre-eminently a bird of the sky, only infrequently seen perched, then mostly in cloudy dull weather. Quite gregarious, even when breeding gathering in groups of a dozen or so individuals.

Range: Breeds from southern United States to Bolivia, northern Argentina, and southeastern Brazil; North and Middle American birds withdraw to South America during northern winter; transients recorded in Cuba and Jamaica.

GRAY-HEADED KITE
(*Leptodon cayanensis*) Pl.2

Description: 18–22. Cere, bare facial area, and legs gray. Adult has *pale gray head contrasting with black upperparts and white underparts;* tail black with two nar-

All adults. Top row, left to right, Double-toothed Kite, Hook-billed Kite (female), Gray-headed Kite, Plumbeous Kite; second row, Broad-winged Hawk, Gray Hawk, Swallow-tailed Kite; third row, Short-tailed Hawk (light phase), White-tailed Hawk, White Hawk; bottom row, Savanna Hawk, Black-collared Hawk, Swainson's Hawk (typical phase), Red-tailed Hawk row white bands (a third rarely visible) and white tipping. In flight from below, wings rather broad and rounded, black with white barring on flight feathers, black wings contrasting strongly with white body. Immatures have two very different and variable plumage phases and have facial skin, cere, and legs yellow to orange-yellow. In pale phase, *most of head, neck, and underparts white* with brown on midcrown and small black streak over and behind eye; back and wings dark brown; tail black with grayish bands; under wing-linings white (not black as in adult). In dark phase, very variable, upperparts (including sides of head and neck) dusky brown (sometimes with rusty collar on hindneck); underparts buffy whitish variably streaked with dusky, usually heavily so, sometimes so coarsely that chest is almost blackish. In an intermediate phase, only a few fine, dusky shaft streaks on throat and breast, these sometimes coalescing into a central throat stripe. Subadult resembles adult but still has yellow legs and white under wing-lingings.

Similar species: Adults are distinctive and should not be confused when seen clearly. Pale phase immature, however, resembles Black-and-white Hawk-Eagle in pattern but is slenderer and somewhat smaller, browner above (not black), and lacks eagle's short crest and its black in front of eye. Pale phase immature might also be taken for a Collared Forest-Falcon but has most of head white (falcon has black crown and crescent down sides of head) and lacks falcon's long graduated tail. Immature Hook-billed Kite in normal phase is smaller, has entire crown dark and some barring below. Dark phase immatures may also present problems. Heavily streaked individuals resemble immature Black-Hawk but have two or three grayish or brownish tail bands (not numerous narrow buffy bands). Immature Gray Hawk is also rather similar but is smaller and more spotted below.

Status and distribution: Uncommon in forest, second-growth woodland, and borders in more humid lowlands and foothills on both slopes; not reported from dry Pacific lowlands from eastern side of Azuero Peninsula to extreme western Panama province. Thinly spread throughout Canal Zone in more wooded areas, but more numerous on Caribbean side.

Habits: Usually rather unobtrusive, often remaining perched hidden from view for long periods of time. Usually perches rather high, sometimes in the open in the early morning. Soars regularly, though usually not very high. The most frequently heard call is a loud *kek kek kek kek* (Wetmore), uttered when perched in the canopy and in flight.

Range: Eastern Mexico to Bolivia, northern Argentina, and southern Brazil.

Note: Wetmore calls it Cayenne Kite.

HOOK-BILLED KITE — Pl.2
(*Chondrohierax uncinatus*) — *page 59*

Description: 16–18. *Heavy strongly hooked bill,* with *cere and bare skin in front of eye usually greenish* but varying to yellow or blue; legs yellow or orange. Adult male in normal phase is *slaty gray, usually lightly barred with white or buffy below;* upper tail-coverts whitish; tail dark gray with two broad white bands; wings from below slaty barred white. Some birds are plain gray below and on wing linings, with one tail band. Adult female in normal phase is dark brown to slaty gray above with *tawny collar on hindneck; coarsely barred brown and white or buffy below;* tail dark gray with two indistinct grayish bars; underwing gray barred white. Black phase (occurs in both sexes but relatively uncommon) is *brownish black all over, tail with one broad white band,* underwing also black but unbarred. Immature dark brown above edged with rufous and with *white or buff collar on hindneck;* creamy white below, narrowly barred with dusky on breast and flanks; tail with three or four grayish bands; underwing prominently barred. Immature of black phase is sooty black with white tail bands. In flight, note distinctive oval wings (long and fairly broad, but narrowing at base), longish tail.

Similar species: Gray males may be confused with adult Gray Hawk but are much darker, more coarsely barred below, and have long hook on bill. Black phase rather resembles Plumbeous Hawk but lacks white under wing-linings and bright orange cere and legs. Black-Hawk adults are larger with relatively broad and short wings and tail, less hooked bill, and show white patch at base of primaries in flight. See also Slender-billed Kite. Rufous females are easily known by their rufous collar and boldly barred underparts. Immatures may be confused with light phase adult of longer and lankier Collared Forest-Falcon or with light immature Bicolored Hawk, both of which lack barring below. See also intermediate phase Gray-headed Kite.

Status and distribution: Uncommon in forest and second-growth woodland (especially in humid or swampy areas) in lowlands on both slopes, but not recorded on Caribbean slope outside Canal Zone and vicinity except for one Bocas del Toro sighting (N. G. Smith); also unrecorded from Azuero Peninsula, Coclé, and Darién. Most frequently reported from Chagres River valley of Canal Zone.

Habits: Usually unsuspicious, allowing a close approach. Feeds primarily on tree snails. Soars occasionally, usually not very high.

Range: Northern Mexico (casually southern Texas) to Bolivia, northern Argentina, and southern Brazil; Cuba and Grenada.

DOUBLE-TOOTHED KITE Pl.2
(*Harpagus bidentatus*) page 59

Description: 13–15. Cere and base of lower mandible greenish; legs greenish yellow. Slaty above, more brownish on back; *throat white with dusky central stripe; remaining underparts mostly rufous* barred with grayish or whitish (amount of barring variable; females are much more uniform rufous with little barring); tail black with three narrow whitish bars. In flight from below, under wing-coverts white or pale buff, usually contrasting with dark body; flight feathers barred grayish and white; white under tail-coverts "puffy"-looking. Immature has yellow cere and legs and brown upperparts; *throat as in adult,* remaining underparts streaked (usually broadly) with dusky, usually with some barring on sides.

Similar species: Shaped like an Accipiter, with short rather rounded wings and fairly long tail. The characteristic dusky throat stripe is easy to see; the "double-tooth," two notches on the upper mandible, is not. Some immature Gray-headed Kites show dusky central throat stripe but are much larger.

Status and distribution: Fairly common in forest, second-growth woodland, and borders in more humid lowlands on both slopes; apparently absent from dry Pacific lowlands from eastern side of Azuero Peninsula to southern Coclé; ranges in reduced numbers up into foothills; found also on Coiba Island. Quite numerous on Caribbean side of Canal Zone, notably so on Pipeline Road.

Habits: Usually seen perched quietly at medium heights, often at edge of forest or woodland. Rather unsuspicious. Soars regularly, though usually fairly low. Chases lizards and large insects in trees; sometimes accompanies troupes of White-faced Monkeys (*Cebus*), catching prey the monkeys disturb as they move through the forest.

Range: Southern Mexico to Bolivia and southern Brazil.

PLUMBEOUS KITE
(*Ictinia plumbea*) page 59

Description: 14. Bill black, cere dark gray; *legs orange. Mostly leaden gray;* wings and tail black, *tail with two white bands, wings with rufous patch in primaries* (conspicuous in flight). Juvenal slaty above edged with buffy whitish; whitish below, heavily streaked with grayish; tail with three white bands; wings usually with some rufous in primaries. Wings long and narrow, usually pointed, but when soaring primaries often spread; rather long tail.

Similar species: See Mississippi Kite. When seen perched can resemble other mostly gray hawks, but note long wings, which extend beyond tip of tail.

Status and distribution: Uncommon to locally fairly common in forest, forest borders, and second-growth woodland in lowlands on both slopes (less numerous in drier areas), ranging up in smaller numbers into lower foothills. More numerous during migration, even passing over open areas. Migrating flocks of up to several hundred birds pass through in early February–mid-March and early August–late September, with stragglers into early October; the species appears to be absent mid-October–January. Recorded also on Pearl Islands, perhaps only as a migrant.

Habits: Often associates with the Swallow-tailed Kite, especially on migration. Usually seen in flight overhead, sometimes high. Regularly occurs in small groups, even when not migrating.

Range: Breeds from eastern Mexico to Bolivia, northern Argentina, and southern Brazil; Middle American birds withdraw to South America during northern winter, but exact distribution unknown.

MISSISSIPPI KITE
(*Ictinia mississippiensis*)

Description: 14. Resembles the much more numerous Plumbeous Kite. *Legs dusky* in all plumages. Leaden gray above, *paler gray on head* and below; tail black with *no white bands;* wings with *no rufous in pri-*

maries, but with *pale gray patch on secondaries.* Juvenal more brownish than juvenal Plumbeous Kite, heavily streaked rusty brown below, with three whitish tail bands. Immature resembles adult but retains tail bands.

Similar species: Caution is urged in distinguishing this species from the Plumbeous Kite. *Ictinia* kites are usually seen in flight overhead, when the two major field marks of adult Mississippis (lack of white tail bands, lack of rufous in wing) can often not be unquestionably determined. Perched adults can be known by their paler head (contrasting with back), pale wing patch, solid black tail, and dusky (not orange) legs. Immature is usually not distinguishable in the field, and juvenal is difficult, though it is browner than juvenal Plumbeous Kite.

Status and distribution: No specimen has been taken in Panama, but there are a number of recent sight reports of migrating flocks and individuals from Bocas del Toro, both slopes of Canal Zone, and Darién (mid-March–mid-April; October), in both periods migrating *later* than the Plumbeous Kite (Wetmore, Eisenmann, Ridgely). As it is known to winter in southern South America, and as it has been taken in Costa Rica and Colombia (specimen in Field Museum of Natural History at Chicago, originally identified as *plumbea; fide* Eisenmann), it surely occurs, but specimen confirmation desirable. When migrating, most often seen alone or in small groups, sometimes among other transient birds of prey.

Range: Breeds in central and southern United States (recently increasing in numbers and regaining its former range); recorded in winter in Paraguay and northwestern Argentina, but winter range and migration routes not well known; probably migrates through Middle America but few specimen records.

SNAIL (EVERGLADE) KITE
(*Rostrhamus sociabilis*)

Description: 16–17½. Apparently rare. *Bill black, slender, very sharply hooked. Facial area and legs red* (orange in immature). Adult male slaty black with *upper and under tail-coverts, basal half of tail, and tip of tail white.* Adult female brownish black above; buffy below streaked and mottled with brown; *tail as in male.* Immature like female but brown above and more prominently streaked below.

Similar species: Brightly colored facial skin and legs, strongly hooked bill, and white basal half of tail distinguish any plumage of this species. Slender-billed Kite of Darién lacks white in tail. Hook-billed Kite also has sharply hooked bill but in any plumage lacks reddish facial area. See also female and immature Northern Harrier.

Status and distribution: Only one specimen, an immature taken at Permé, San Blas, on March 22, 1929. Several recent sightings: an adult male and an immature at Guataca, eastern Chiriquí on September 27, 1965 (Eisenmann and N. G. Smith); an immature at Tocumen, eastern Panama province in March 1971 (P. Alden and R. Forster); and several pairs apparently breeding (one nest seen) in a marsh along Pan-American Highway near Remedios, Chiriquí, on June 19, 1973 (D. Hill). Whether a regular breeder in Panama remains to be determined; there is relatively little suitable habitat for it in the country.

Habits: A bird of open fresh water marshes where it feeds on *Pomacea* snails, hunting by quartering low over the marsh. The tail is constantly in motion as the bird flies, at an angle different from that of the wings.

Range: Southern Florida; eastern Mexico south locally to Bolivia, northern Argentina, and Uruguay; Cuba.

SLENDER-BILLED KITE
(*Helicolestes hamatus*)

Description: 15–16½. Known only from eastern Darién. *Bill black, slender, very sharply hooked; facial area and legs orange-red;* iris pale. *Slaty all over* with wing-tips and tail black. Immature similar but with some whitish barring on underparts and rufous edging on wings; tail with two to four white bands.

Similar species: All plumages of Snail Kite have prominent white base of tail; Slender-billed Kite is chunkier than Snail, with relatively short broad wings and short tail; Slender-bill is found in wooded swampy areas, Snail in open marshes. Black phase of Hook-billed Kite has one broad white tail band and lacks orange-red facial area and legs. See also Plumbeous Hawk.

Status and distribution: Known only from two specimens taken at Río Paya in the Tuira River valley of eastern Darién.

Habits: Frequents swampy forest or woodland, usually seen perched on low branches overlooking shaded pools. Generally found inside forest, but sometimes soars above it.

Feeds on *Pomacea* snails, like Everglade Kite apparently exclusively.

Range: Eastern Panama locally to Surinam, Amazonian Brazil, and eastern Peru.

Note: The genus is often merged in *Rostrhamus.*

BICOLORED HAWK
(*Accipiter bicolor*) Pl.2

Description: ♂14; ♀17. Wings short and rounded; tail fairly long, rounded at tip. Dark slaty gray above (more blackish on head and wings); *uniform pale gray below with contrasting chestnut thighs;* tail blackish with three narrow whitish bands and whitish tip. Immature variable, dusky brown above, blacker on crown, sometimes with narrow indistinct whitish or buffy collar on hindneck; *underparts varying from buffy white to ochraceous.* Subadult is brown above and pale gray below.

Similar species: Contrasting chestnut thighs of the two-toned gray adults are characteristic. Much larger than Tiny Hawk. Immature is rather similar to adult Collared Forest-Falcon but latter is larger with longer legs, has longer more graduated tail, and a black crescentic cheek stripe.

Status and distribution: Rare; in recent decades recorded very infrequently. In past, recorded locally from forest in lowlands and foothills on both slopes, but not from eastern side of Azuero Peninsula, Coclé, Colon province, or San Blas; most records are from western Panama. Only recent records are two on Coiba Island in January 1956 (Wetmore) and an adult male collected at Majé, eastern Panama province on January 10, 1973 (P. Galindo, specimen in Gorgas collection). Only one twentieth-century report from Canal Zone, a sighting in Madden Forest in 1942 (T. Imhof).

Habits: Little known in Panama; evidently even less numerous in this country than elsewhere in its vast range. Reported to be a bold and rapacious bird, feeding chiefly on birds, keeping to dense lower growth of forest and woodland borders (Brown and Amadon).

Range: Eastern Mexico to Tierra del Fuego.

TINY HAWK
(*Accipiter superciliosus*) Pl.2

Description: ♂8; ♀11. *Very small.* Slaty gray above, blackish on crown; *white below narrowly barred throughout with brownish gray;* tail blackish with three or four grayish brown bands. Immature has two phases. In dark phase, dusky above, buff below narrowly barred with buffy brown. In rufous phase, bright rufous brown above except for blackish crown; buff below narrowly barred with brown, washed with rufous on sides and flanks.

Similar species: Should be known in any plumage by its small size; the smallest Panamanian hawk. Double-toothed Kite is larger and lacks the even, narrow barring below. See also Sharp-shinned Hawk and Barred Forest-Falcon.

Status and distribution: Rare in forest borders and second-growth woodland in more humid lowlands on both slopes. Recorded mostly from Caribbean slope; on Pacific slope known only from old specimens from Chiriquí and Veraguas, a sighting of an adult near Chepo, eastern Panama province, on July 9, 1952 (Eisenmann and J. Bull), and one recent specimen from eastern Darién. In Canal Zone known from two nineteenth-century specimens and recent sight reports from Pipeline Road (J. Karr), near Summit Gardens (Ridgely, J. Gwynne, V. Miller), and Achiote Road (Ridgely).

Habits: Usually remains hidden in dense lower growth but occasionally perches fairly high on an exposed branch at forest edge; much more likely to be seen under the latter condition.

Range: Nicaragua to eastern Peru, Paraguay, northeastern Argentina, and southern Brazil.

SHARP-SHINNED HAWK
(*Accipiter striatus*)

Description: ♂10; ♀14. Recorded only in west. Short rounded wings and rather long tail as in other Accipiters. *Dark bluish gray above,* darkest on crown; *white below barred with rufous brown;* tail black with 3 gray bands and white tip. Immature is dusky brown above, whitish below heavily streaked with dusky and brown.

Similar species: Adults most resemble dark phase immature Tiny Hawk, but latter is dusky (not bluish gray) above. Double-toothed Kite is rather similar but has distinctive black throat stripe in both adult and immature. See also Cooper's Hawk (below).

Status and distribution: Uncommon winter resident in western Chiriquí highlands (late October–late March); single sightings from lowlands of Herrera and Los Santos (Wetmore), and Bocas del Toro (N. G. Smith).

Habits: Favors woodland borders and clearings; usually inconspicuous, perching in concealment of foliage, but also circles and flies in the open, especially on migration. A bird eater.

Range: Breeds in North America and Mexico, also in Greater Antilles; northern birds winter to western Panama.

Note: Resident forms of northern Middle America (*A. chionogaster*) and South America (*A. erythronemius*) are sometimes considered conspecific. Cooper's Hawk (*A. cooperii*) of North America has been recorded in winter to Costa Rica and once in Colombia, and is possible in Panama. It resembles Sharp-shin but is larger (♂14; ♀18), with tip of tail rounded (not square).

WHITE-TAILED HAWK

(*Buteo albicaudatus*) *page 59*

Description: 21–25. A large Buteo with broad wings and ample tail. *Slaty gray above* with blackish sides of head and *prominent rufous area on shoulders;* white below with indistinct brownish bars on flanks; *rump* and *tail white, tail with broad black band near tip.* In flight from below, under wing-coverts white, flight feathers grayish. A rare dark phase is gray above and below, without rufous shoulders, but with white tail as in normal phase. Immature brownish black with variable amounts of white below, especially on lower belly; rump whitish barred with brown; tail brownish or grayish with numerous narrow blackish bars, gradually becoming whiter with age.

Similar species: Pattern of adult from below is rather like that of the forest inhabiting White Hawk (very different from above). Immatures are difficult, though in most birds the rump and tail are sufficiently pale, at least toward base (in contrast to remaining plumage), to make recognition possible. Sometimes helpful is a hint of rusty wing-edging. White-tailed is only Panama Buteo that regularly hovers. See especially dark phase Red-tailed, Swainson's, and Short-tailed Hawks.

Status and distribution: Uncommon and rather local on grassy savannas and open hillsides on Pacific slope from western Chiriquí (a number of sightings on Llanos del Volcán above Volcán, up to about 6000 feet) to western Panama province, including eastern side of Azuero Peninsula; only two records from Caribbean slope (Cricamola, Bocas del Toro; Calovévora, Veraguas). Unrecorded from Canal Zone; a sighting of an immature on lower slopes of Cerro Azul on December 4, 1954 (F. O. Chapelle) is sole report from east of Canal Zone; one sighting also from Taboga Island (Wetmore). Most easily seen in Coclé and on the open eroded hillsides of Cerro Campana.

Habits: A handsome hawk of open, rather dry or scantily vegetated country, regularly seen in pairs circling high overhead. Often perches on or near the ground.

Range: Southern Texas and Mexico to Colombia, Venezuela, the Guianas, and northeastern Brazil; also in southern South America.

RED-TAILED HAWK

(*Buteo jamaicensis*) *page 59*

Description: 19–24. Large and chunky, with broad wings and rounded tail. In adults, the *rufous tail,* brighter from above, is distinctive. Plumage in northern populations highly variable. Dark brown above; whitish below with varying amounts of black streaking, especially on belly (in some birds almost forming a band). Adult of western Panama breeding race (*costaricensis*) has *rufous thighs and usually flanks and lower belly.* Some individuals of northern races entirely blackish except for the red tail, or even are solid rufous brown below. Immature of Panama race more streaked below than adult, with tail dull cinnamon (grayish in young northern birds) with many narrow dusky bars.

Similar species: The rufous-tailed adults are easily identified; much smaller and slighter Roadside Hawk also has reddish tail in most of Panama but shows reddish on wings in flight. Immatures very difficult, resembling several other large immature Buteos, usually not safely identified away from western mountains. Swainson's Hawk (the most similar) has somewhat more slender proportions, longer and narrower wings, and longer less fan-shaped tail.

Status and distribution: Fairly common resident in forest and adjacent cleared areas in highlands of Chiriquí (above 5000 feet) and Veraguas. Has also been recorded (probably northern migrants) in lowlands of Bocas del Toro (once, Changuinola), Veraguas, Pacific slope of Canal Zone, and eastern Panama province (twice on Cerro Azul—J. Karr, P. Alden; once near El Llano—Eisenmann and J. Strauch). Whether these recent lowland sightings represent North American migrants or wanderers from the western mountains is uncertain, but all such reports are from northern winter months. One bird identified as of the western North American race (*calurus*) has been taken in Veraguas, and an adult which lacked the rufous thighs and lower underparts of the resident race was seen west of Santiago, Veraguas, on February 20, 1960 (Eisenmann).

Habits: In the Chiriquí highlands, an individual or pair can often be seen soaring over forested ridges or clearings, sometimes high. Elsewhere seen only rarely, in open or semi-open areas, usually soaring high overhead (often with other Buteos) or resting on a high exposed perch.

Range: Breeds from North America to western Panama and in West Indies; northern birds winter, at least occasionally, to Panama.

ZONE-TAILED HAWK

(*Buteo albonotatus*) *page 67*

Description: 18–23. Wings and tail fairly long. Entirely black, with *3 or 4 white tail bands* (grayer from above; sometimes only 2 show). In flight from below, *wings noticeably two-toned,* with black under wing-coverts and grayish flight feathers. Immature similar but browner and lightly spotted below with white; tail grayish brown above with narrow black bars, inner webs whitish or pale gray so that from below tail looks whitish.

Similar species: In flight, looks superficially much like a Turkey Vulture, and like that species usually flies with *wings held slightly above horizontal* (and with similar two-toned effect below); Zone-tail is smaller, has white tail bands, and larger feathered black head. Dark phase Short-tailed Hawk has more typical Buteo proportions (relatively broader wings and tail) and lacks conspicuous tail bands. Perched Common and Great Black-Hawks look rather like a Zone-tail but are chunkier with shorter tail with only 1 or 2 white bands. See also immature White-tailed Hawk and Crane Hawk.

Status and distribution: Uncertain. Uncommon, with reports scattered, mostly from lowlands; specimens few. Reported from western Chiriquí (David airport; E. O. Willis), western Bocas del Toro (N. G. Smith), Cerro Campana, both slopes of Canal Zone, eastern Panama province, San Blas, and Pearl Islands. Most often reported from central Panama, especially Pacific slope Canal Zone. Most reports are from September to March, and apparently migrating birds have recently been seen from Ancon Hill in October (N. G. Smith); however, there are also reports during northern summer months (Pearl Islands, Cerro Campana, near Chepo, San Blas) that suggest possibility of a local breeding population, though as yet there is no definite indication of nesting in Panama.

Habits: Usually seen flying fairly low over open or broken country. Appears to mimic the Turkey Vulture, thus presumably luring its prey into a very false sense of security. Zone-tails are often almost passed by as Turkey Vultures.

Range: Southwestern United States south very locally to Venezuela and the Guianas, western Peru, Bolivia, and Paraguay.

SWAINSON'S HAWK

(*Buteo swainsoni*) *page 59*

Description: 19–22. A rather large Buteo with fairly broad wings. Pale phase adult dark brown above; whitish below usually with *broad brown band across chest,* contrasting with white throat; tail brownish gray with numerous blackish bands. In flight from below, under wing-coverts buffy whitish contrasting with dark flight feathers. In dark phase, more or less sooty brown all over, including wings from below. Intermediates between these two phases often occur. Immature is brown above, buffy below streaked to varying degrees with dusky.

Similar species: Typical pale phase adults are relatively easily recognized and usually predominate. Other phases can be very confusing: note lack of prominent tail banding, and that rump and basal half of tail (as seen from above) can look whitish. Dark individuals closely resemble immature White-tailed Hawk, but that species usually shows some white below. Dark phase Short-tailed Hawk is smaller with white on forehead and pale flight feathers contrasting with dark under wing-coverts. See also dark phase Red-tailed Hawk. Swainson's *often carries wings angled in slight dihedral,* suggesting the narrower-winged Zone-tailed Hawk (which somewhat resembles dark phase of this species but has white tail bands and two-toned underwing).

Status and distribution: Common to abundant transient through Panama, occurring in sometimes enormous flocks, passage being mostly March–early April (sometimes late February) and October–early November (sometimes late September). Most birds winter in southern South America, but a few stragglers, usually immatures, sometimes linger in open country on Pacific slope. Usual migration route appears to be primarily along Pacific slope, in central Panama near the coast, in west and east along central mountain range; heavy flights also occur along Caribbean slope, at least in fall passage, in Bocas del Toro and San Blas (Eisenmann); in Chiriquí highlands, heavy flights have been noted only during spring migration.

Habits: Generally remains separate from the migrant flocks of Broad-winged Hawks, though there are often a few Swainson's among the Broad-wings and vice versa. It is thought that they may not feed at all while migrating.

Range: Breeds in western North America; winters mostly in southern South America, migrating through Middle America; small numbers (probably mostly immatures) winter locally in southern United States, Middle America, and northern South America.

SHORT-TAILED HAWK

(*Buteo brachyurus*) *pages 59, 67*

Description: 17–18. A typically proportioned Buteo. Light phase adult dusky brown above, blackish or slaty on head, *this coming well down over sides of head;* small patch on forehead and entire underparts white; *tail dark brownish to grayish with dusky barring.* In flight from below, wing white except for dark tipping to flight feathers. Dark phase adult entirely sooty black except for whitish sides to forehead and some spotting below; tail as in light phase; wings from below with *whitish flight feathers* contrasting with dark under wing-linings. Immatures resemble adults of respective phases but have more bars on tail; light phase has head streaked whitish, dark phase has more white spotting below.

Similar species: Often confused. In light phase (which predominates in Panama) note contrasting dark upper and white lower surfaces, blackish sides of head, and lack of definite tail bands. Semiplumbeous Hawk is somewhat similar but has orange cere and legs, a distinct white tail band, and is grayer above; it rarely if ever soars or leaves forest. From below, light phase also suggests White-tailed Hawk without the white tail. Dark phase is somewhat like several other species: dark phase Swainson's has uniform dark wing from below; Zone-tailed and Common and Great Black-Hawks all show at least one distinct white band on tail.

Status and distribution: Uncommon to fairly common in mostly open or partially wooded country in lowlands and foothills on both slopes, apparently more numerous on Pacific side. Though most published records are from northern fall and winter months, there are many sight reports from throughout the year. One breeding record, a pair at a nest on Escobal Road in Canal Zone on February 16, 1960 (Eisenmann and G. Carleton). Widespread but not especially numerous at any one locality.

Habits: A rather active hawk, often soaring to great heights, diving down on its prey. Not often seen perched.

Range: Florida; Mexico to Bolivia, northern Argentina, and southern Brazil.

GRAY HAWK

(*Buteo nitidus*) Pl.3, *page 59*

Description: 15–18. *Mostly pale gray above,* indistinctly barred with darker gray; *white below narrowly barred with gray;* tail blackish with two white bands (upper one narrow and usually hard to see) and narrow white tip. In flight from below, wings whitish with gray barring on wing-coverts. Immature mostly dusky brown above edged with rusty; head and hindneck buffy streaked with dusky and with broad buff superciliary; *buffy below with heavy tear-shaped elongated spots of dark brown,* dusky moustache stripe, and often a central throat stripe; tail blackish with 3 or 4 grayish bars.

Similar species: Attractive pearly gray adults are easily recognized: highland inhabiting Black-chested Hawk is much larger and distinctly darker; Roadside Hawk has solid grayish throat and chest, rufous on primaries. Immatures are more difficult: immature intermediate phase Gray-headed Kite is larger and more streaked (not so spotted) below; immature Common Black-Hawk has numerous narrow buff and black bands on tail; immature Broad-winged Hawk is not as dark brown above generally, head lacks Gray Hawk's buffy, and is much less heavily marked below.

Status and distribution: Uncommon to locally fairly common in forest borders, lighter woodland (often along watercourses), and clearings in lowlands on both slopes, though not reported from Bocas del

All adults. Top row, left to right, ORANGE-BREASTED FALCON, SHORT-TAILED HAWK (dark phase), CRANE HAWK, BLACK-CHESTED HAWK; second row, ZONE-TAILED HAWK, COMMON BLACK-HAWK, GREAT BLACK-HAWK, GREAT BLACK-HAWK (eastern race); third row, BLACK HAWK-EAGLE; bottom row, HARPY EAGLE, CRESTED EAGLE, ORNATE HAWK-EAGLE

Toro; more widespread on Pacific slope; in western Chiriquí reported up to about 4000 feet; only report from Darién is an adult at Santa Fé in April 1967 (Eisenmann).

Habits: Favors vicinity of water. Soars fairly often, usually not at great heights. Sometimes allows a close approach when perched, but unlike Roadside Hawk does not seem sluggish, remaining alert and watchful.

Range: Extreme southwestern United States to Bolivia, northern Argentina, and southern Brazil.

Note: Sometimes placed in the genus *Asturina.* Birds from southwestern Costa Rica south, *nitidus* group, are sometimes considered specifically distinct.

BROAD-WINGED HAWK

(*Buteo platypterus*) *page 59*

Description: 15–18. A chunky small Buteo. Dark grayish brown above; whitish below *broadly barred or mottled with dull grayish rufous;* tail blackish with *two broad white bands* (a third may show near base of tail) and narrow white tip. In flight from below, underside of wings mostly whitish. Immature brown above, whitish below sparsely streaked with dark brown; tail more narrowly banded with dusky and whitish.

Similar species: Double-toothed Kite is smaller and more slender, with dusky throat stripe. Immature resembles immature Gray Hawk but is less heavily streaked below. Roadside Hawk is much grayer generally with prominent rufous in wings.

Status and distribution: Abundant transient in huge migrant flocks, passage occurring mostly in October (some late September and early November) and March–early April, following same routes as Swainson's Hawk; also a common winter resident in forest borders, second-growth woodland, and clearings in lowlands and foothills on both slopes, ranging up to about 6500 feet. During winter months perhaps the most numerous hawk in Panama woodlands (certainly the most often seen), although essentially solitary at this season.

Habits: Regularly occurs in aggregations of thousands of individuals while on migration; the passage of this species and the Swainson's Hawk and Turkey Vulture is Panama's most spectacular avian sight: occasionally the sky seems literally "blackened." At the proper season, migrating flocks can be seen settling to roost from mid-afternoon onward, and rising up in the early morning, in woodland on Pacific slope of Canal Zone. Though it soars frequently, when perched it is usually rather sluggish, allowing a close approach. Calls fairly often, a loud shrill whistled *p-teeeeeeee.*

Range: Breeds in North America and West Indies; winters in southern Florida and from southern Mexico to Peru and northern Brazil.

ROADSIDE HAWK

(*Buteo magnirostris*) Pl.2

Description: 14–16. *Slaty grayish above* (browner on back) *and on throat and chest;* breast and belly barred gray and dull rufous; tail banded inconspicuously with rufous and dusky, *often appearing essentially reddish;* in flight shows *prominent rufous patch in primaries,* visible from above and below. Birds from Bocas del Toro (*argutus*) and extreme eastern Panama (*insidiatrix*) have pale tail bands mainly gray (not reddish). Immature resembles adult but is browner on breast with some dusky streaking, tail with more blackish bands. Juvenal has more brown streaking below, less barring.

Similar species: Grayish general appearance and conspicuous rufous wing patch identify this small open country Buteo. See Gray Hawk.

Status and distribution: Common in fairly open and scrubby areas and in light gallery woodland in lowlands on Pacific slope from Chiriquí to central Darién; on Caribbean slope found in smaller numbers in clearings and woodland borders in western Bocas del Toro and from northern Coclé east through San Blas; in Chiriquí highlands found regularly up to around 5000 feet; common also on Coiba Island and the Pearl Islands. Rather scarce and local in Canal Zone (due perhaps to considerable woodland regrowth), but common and easily seen in drier areas to east and west along Pan-American Highway.

Habits: Usually seen perched fairly low, often on telephone poles or even wires. A sluggish hawk, often very unsuspicious, and a weak flier with very shallow rapid wingbeats interspersed with short periods of gliding. Soars only rarely. Its distinctive call is a squealing buzzy *kzweeeeooo* or *zhweeeeyoo.* Eats mainly reptiles and insects.

Range: Central Mexico to central Argentina and Uruguay.
Note: Wetmore calls it Large-billed Hawk.

BAY-WINGED (HARRIS') HAWK
(*Parabuteo unicinctus*)

Description: 19–22. Apparently rare. Rather long and narrow wings and tail. Mostly blackish brown with *bright chestnut shoulders* and thighs; tail black with *white rump and basal area* and tip. In flight from below shows chestnut under wing-coverts and black flight feathers. Immature is similar but with upperparts somewhat edged with rufous; underparts variable, ranging from chocolate brown streaked with buff to buffy streaked with dusky; *shows chestnut shoulders* (though not as prominent as in adult) and *whitish base of tail from above* (from below tail more grayish barred with dusky).
Status and distribution: Uncertain. Known only from three old specimens (Santa Fé, Veraguas; Pacora, eastern Panama province; Almirante, Bocas del Toro) and recent sight reports of small numbers apparently on migration seen from Ancon Hill in Canal Zone in October 1970 and 1971 (N. G. Smith). All dated records are from northern winter or migration months; probably a rare (perhaps only irregular) winter visitant or transient from farther north.
Habits: Favors savanna country and open areas with scattered trees, often near water and marshes. Forages chiefly by sailing low over the ground, somewhat suggesting a dark harrier; sometimes soars. Frequently perches low, even on the ground. Sometimes eats carrion.
Range: Southwestern United States south locally to central Chile and central Argentina.

WHITE HAWK
(*Leucopternis albicollis*)

Description: 22–24. Buteo-like in shape, with broad rather rounded wings and fairly short tail. *Entirely white* with black markings on primaries and secondaries and a broad black subterminal band on tail.
Status and distribution: Fairly common in forest and forest borders in more humid lowlands and foothills on both slopes to about 4000 feet, rarely higher; apparently absent from drier woodland on eastern side of Azuero Peninsula. Its conspicuousness probably makes it seem more numerous than other forest hawks.

WHITE HAWK

Habits: Soars freely, sometimes quite high, presenting a beautiful contrast against blue of sky or dark green of forest canopy. When soaring, often utters a semi-whistled hissing or buzzy *sheeeer,* somewhat like call of Red-tailed Hawk. Often perches on fairly low branches at forest borders and usually rather unsuspicious.
Range: Southern Mexico to Bolivia, central Brazil, and the Guianas.

BLACK-CHESTED (BARRED) HAWK
(*Leucopternis princeps*) Pl.3, *page 67*

Description: 23–25. Known only from highlands of west and east. Broad wings and short tail (in shape, rather like a White Hawk). Base of bill, cere, and legs yellow. *Blackish slate above and on throat and chest; breast and belly white narrowly barred with black;* tail black with one white band. In flight from below, wings whitish barred with gray and dusky.
Similar species: Large size and sharp contrast between black chest and pale lower underparts distinguish this handsome species. The barring below is not prominent at a distance. See the smaller, paler Gray Hawk of lowlands.
Status and distribution: Apparently rare; known primarily from humid forest and forest borders in highlands of Bocas del Toro and Chiriquí (3000–5000 feet); recorded also from highlands of Veraguas (seen once above Santa Fé in February 1974; S. West), southern Los Santos (Cerro Hoya) and eastern Darién (Cerro Pirre). In western Panama known primarily from Caribbean slope.
Habits: Little known in Panama, apparently more numerous in Costa Rica. Soars regularly, sometimes rather high. The usual

call is a screaming *kee-aaarr,* often given in flight.
Range: Costa Rica to northern Ecuador.

SEMIPLUMBEOUS HAWK
(*Leucopternis semiplumbea*) Pl.2

Description: 15–16. Wings short, broad, and rounded. *Cere, base of bill, and legs bright orange to reddish orange. Slaty gray above; white below,* sometimes with a few fine dusky streaks on chest (immatures especially); tail blackish with *one broad white band* (a second narrower one sometimes visible near base). Underside of wings mostly white.

Similar species: Light phase Short-tailed Hawk is superficially similar but lacks orange cere and legs, has indistinctly banded tail, very different habits. Slaty-backed Forest-Falcon is quite similar and is a forest bird like Semiplumbeous, but has 3 narrow tail bands (not a single broad one) and does not have orange soft-parts.

Status and distribution: Uncommon to fairly common in forest and more humid second-growth woodland in lowlands on entire Caribbean slope; on Pacific slope rare west of eastern Panama province (Bayano River valley), with one old specimen from Veraguas and one recent sighting from Canal Zone (Fort Clayton—Ridgely). Widespread in forested areas on Caribbean side of Canal Zone.

Habits: A bird of the interior of forest and shady woodland, rarely leaving their borders. Usually very unsuspicious, generally seen perched on an open branch beneath the canopy (sometimes quite low), in the early morning sometimes on a high exposed perch. Seems never to soar, or even to circle above the canopy.

Range: Honduras to northwestern Ecuador.

PLUMBEOUS HAWK
(*Leucopternis plumbea*) Pl.2

Description: 16–17. In shape like more numerous Semiplumbeous Hawk. *Cere, lores, and legs orange. Mostly dark slaty gray;* tail black with *one prominent white band* (in some, especially immatures, another shows). In flight shows *white under wing-coverts.* Immature has under wing-coverts and thighs somewhat barred, belly somewhat flecked with white.

Similar species: Superficially resembles several other dark forest hawks but note orange soft parts and the white tail band. Black phase Hook-billed Kite has strongly hooked bill, greenish cere and lores, and black underside of wing (no white). Plumbeous Kite has dark gray cere, long wings projecting beyond tail at rest, no white on underside of wing. In Darién see also Slender-billed Kite.

Status and distribution: Apparently rare; recorded locally in humid forest in lowlands on Caribbean slope from Veraguas to San Blas; on Pacific slope known only from single sightings from Cerro Azul and Santa Fé, Darién (both Eisenmann). Only recently (1968) found in Canal Zone; now known to be a rare resident along Pipeline and Achiote Roads (Ridgely, J. Karr, *et al.*)

Habits: Similar to Semiplumbeous Hawk. An unsuspicious bird of the forest interior, usually seen at low and middle levels, but in the early morning occasionally perching high on an open branch. Apparently never soars.

Range: Western Panama to extreme northwestern Peru.

BLACK-COLLARED HAWK
(*Busarellus nigricollis*) Pl.3, *page 59*

Description: 18–22. Wings broad and long; tail very short and broad. *Mostly bright cinnamon-rufous,* with *head and hindneck buffy whitish* and *a black patch on upper chest;* tail barred black and chestnut with broad black subterminal band. In flight from below, under wing-coverts chestnut, flight feathers mostly black. Immature similar but duller, buffier below, streaked throughout with dusky.

Similar species: A handsome, distinctive hawk; likely to be confused only with Savanna Hawk, which has white tail bands, mostly rufous undersurface of wing, and lacks whitish head and black collar. When perched, Black-collared Hawk seems to have a small head.

Status and distribution: Uncommon and local in fresh water marshes and along sluggish rivers in lowlands on Pacific slope from Veraguas to Darién; only record from Caribbean slope is one collected at Lion Hill in Canal Zone in 1900 (not reported from Canal Zone since). Most often noted in eastern Panama province (Tocumen/La Jagua area) and Darién.

Habits: Usually seen perched on trees or bushes near water, but also soars majestically on broad flat wings. Feeds mostly on fish, which it captures near the surface of the water. Spends much time drying its nonwaterproof plumage.

Range: Western and southern Mexico to Bolivia, northern Argentina, and southern Brazil.

SAVANNA HAWK
(*Heterospizias meridionalis*) Pl.3, *page 59*

Description: 23–25. Long broad wings and fairly short tail. Rather long legs. *Mostly rufous,* more gray on upper back, paler (more cinnamon) below and narrowly barred with dusky; *tail black with broad white band* and white tip; wings mostly rufous, with flight feathers tipped black. Immature blackish brown above with buff forehead and superciliary, mottled with rufous on wings; buffy below with blackish spotting. Older immatures have head and underparts more rufous.

Similar species: A large hawk with distinctive, mostly rufous coloration. Black-collared Hawk has somewhat similar proportions and rufous color but has whitish head, black collar, and lacks white in tail.

Status and distribution: Uncommon to locally common in open grassy savannas in lowlands on Pacific slope from Chiriquí to eastern Panama province; few records from western Chiriquí and not known from Darién (though may appear with clearing of forest). Only a few reports from Caribbean slope: a sighting of an immature near Changuinola, Bocas del Toro (Eisenmann); a specimen from Permé, San Blas; and several recent (1973 on) reports from Canal Zone and vicinity (D. Engleman, J. Pujals, *et al.*), where it may be in the process of colonizing the increasingly large clearings of Colon province. Very local on Pacific side of Canal Zone, restricted to the few existing large open grassy areas, but easily seen in the Tocumen/Chepo area.

Habits: Rather sluggish, usually seen perched on the ground or on a low branch or fencepost. Walks on ground. Soars regularly, sometimes high. Follows grass fires.

Range: Western Panama (one Costa Rica sighting) to central Argentina and Uruguay.

COMMON (LESSER) BLACK-HAWK
(*Buteogallus anthracinus*) Pl.3, *page 67*

Description: 20–23. Very broad, rounded, relatively short wings; tail rather short. *Cere, lores, and legs bright yellow to orange-yellow.* Mostly black; *tail with one broad white band* and white tip. Wings from below usually show small whitish patch at base of primaries. Juvenal blackish brown above with buff superciliary; *tawny-buffy below with blackish elongated drop-like spots;* tail mostly buffy with *5 to 8 narrow wavy black bands,* subterminal band widest; sometimes shows rufous or whitish patch on underside of primaries. Older birds are darker with fewer tail bands. In Darién some immatures have been taken in a peculiar pale phase: mostly dull grayish buff (chamois color), finely streaked with dusky on crown and underparts; flight feathers and tail pale brownish gray, latter with 5 or 6 irregular dull whitish bands.

Similar species: Often difficult to distinguish from Great Black-Hawk. Note this species' smaller size, considerable yellow area in front of and above eye (Great Black's lores slaty in most of Panama), and lack of white upper tail-coverts (feathers sometimes narrowly tipped with white). Immature even harder, but note Great Black's more numerous (10–14) black tail bands, and its larger size. Unless seen well the two species often cannot be distinguished in the field with certainty. Zone-tailed Hawk is also similar (especially when perched), but has much longer and narrower two-toned wings in flight. See also Crane Hawk and dark phase Short-tailed Hawk. At a distance somewhat resembles Black Vulture. Immature Gray Hawk is also easily confused with immature Common Black but it is smaller and lacks the numerous tail bands.

Status and distribution: Fairly common to common along both coasts, along larger streams and rivers on both slopes, in mangroves, and in fresh water swamps and marshes; common also in Coiba Island and the Pearl Islands. Especially numerous in the lower Tuira River valley of Darién.

Habits: Soars often, frequently uttering its typical call, a series of high-pitched ("spinking") whistled notes, quite different from the Great Black-Hawk's harsh scream. Usually rather unsuspicious, sometimes perching rather low in trees, especially when hunting for its primary food, crabs.

Range: Southwestern United States to northwestern Peru and Guyana; Cuba (possibly a distinct species) and St. Vincent.

Note: Some authors consider birds of the Pacific coast from southern Mexico to northwestern Peru a distinct species, *B. subtilis* (Mangrove Black-Hawk).

GREAT BLACK-HAWK
(*Buteogallus urubitinga*) Pl.3, *page 67*

Description: 24–28. Very like Common Black-Hawk, but larger. Cere and legs yellow; *lores slaty* in northern race (*ridgwayi*) of most of Panama (yellow in Common Black), but lores yellow (as in Common Black) in southern race (nominate *urubitinga*) of extreme eastern Panama. Adult mostly black with white upper tail-coverts (usually hard to see clearly, feathers sometimes only white-tipped); tail with *two white bands* (upper one narrow and often concealed) and white tip; *usually shows narrow white barring on thighs.* Southern race has *basal half of tail entirely white.* Juvenal closely resembles juvenal Common Black except for its larger size and more numerous (10–14) narrow black tail bands.

Similar species: Distinguishing between the two black-hawks is difficult unless they are seen well. White thigh barring of Great Black adult is diagnostic when present. Note also Great Black's larger size, longer legs, less yellow on facial area in northern race (though *both* species have a yellow cere), and white upper tail-coverts and second tail band (when visible). Southern race with its broad white basal half of tail is relatively easy. See also Solitary Eagle.

Status and distribution: Uncommon to locally fairly common in forest borders and second-growth woodland, most often near water, in lowlands on both slopes; ranges locally up into foothills, in western Chiriquí into highlands (to about 6200 feet). The mainly South American race *urubitinga* is found in eastern San Blas, with one recent specimen from eastern Darién (see discussion below). Rather scarce in Canal Zone.

Habits: Similar to Common Black-Hawk but less restricted to immediate vicinity of water. Soars freely, often giving its rather long screaming whistle, *wheeeeeeeer.*

Range: Northern Mexico to Bolivia, northern Argentina, and Uruguay.

Note: A specimen from near El Real, Darién, taken in November 1966 (P. L. Slattery) is an adult of the mainly South American race *urubitinga* (*fide* Eisenmann). Wetmore attributes other specimens from the Tuira River vally to the Middle American race *ridgwayi.* The possible overlap or integradation of these forms requires investigation. "Ridgway's Black-Hawk" has been considered a distinct species by some authors.

SOLITARY EAGLE

(*Harpyhalietus solitarius*)

Description: 28–32. Very rare. In shape much like Great Black-Hawk with broad wings and short tail. Cere, lores, and legs yellow. *Dark slaty gray* with slight bushy crest on nape; *tail black with one broad white band* and white tip. In flight from below, underside of wing uniformly dark slaty gray, somewhat paler toward base of primaries but with no white spot. Immature blackish brown above edged and mottled with buff and with buff superciliary; buffy whitish below, heavily streaked with black, almost solid on chest; *tail buffy grayish speckled with dusky.* In flight from below, under wing-coverts buffy mottled with blackish, flight feathers blackish.

Similar species: Adult resembles adult Great Black-Hawk but is larger and less black overall (more slaty) with proportionately shorter tail and broader wings, tail with single white band (no white upper tail-coverts), wings without small white spot at base of primaries (usually present in Great Black). Immature Great Black differs in its smaller size, buff tail with many narrow black bands.

Status and distribution: Uncertain, evidently very rare. Known only from two nineteenth-century specimens taken in Veraguas foothills (Calobre); a bird seen in hills north of Chepo, eastern Panama province, on April 14, 1949 (Wetmore); and a recent report of two birds seen in hills north of El Llano, eastern Panama province, on September 9, 1972 (N. G. Smith). Little known.

Range: Northern Mexico south very locally to northern Venezuela and central Peru.

Note: Wetmore separates it in the genus *Urubitornis.*

CRESTED EAGLE

(*Morphnus guianensis*) *pages 67, 73*

Description: 31–35. *A large eagle* with broad rounded wings and *very long tail.* Adult and immature have *prominent pointed crest.* Adult has two distinct phases, formerly regarded as separate species. In normal phase *head, neck, and chest brownish gray,* feathers of crest blackish; otherwise brownish black above, white or buffy white below, sometimes lightly banded with brown on underparts; tail black with three grayish bands. In flight from below, under wing-coverts whitish, *flight feathers conspicuously banded black and gray.* In banded phase *head, neck, and chest dark gray; lower underparts boldly barred black and white;* otherwise as in normal phase; wings from below *entirely banded black and white.* Intermediates between the two phases occur. A rare phase with almost wholly blackish underparts is also known. Immature has head, neck, and entire underparts white; back and wings blackish with whitish mottling; wings and tail as in adult. Several years are required to attain adult plumage, and several intermediate plumages occur.

Similar species: Despite the many plumage variations, adults are recognizable by their large size and long tail, in flight by the boldly banded wings. Immature is easily confused with immature of even larger Harpy Eagle, but has slimmer proportions and single-pointed crest (two-parted in Harpy). Immature Ornate Hawk-Eagle is much smaller, browner above.

Status and distribution: Rare, with scattered records in extensive humid forest in lowlands and foothills on Caribbean slope; on Pacific slope recorded from eastern Panama province and Darién, with sightings from Boquete, Chiriquí and Coiba Island (both Wetmore). In Canal Zone reported in recent years from near Achiote Road (subadult photographed at close range on January 8, 1975—W. Cornwell) and Barro Colorado Island; has also been collected and seen in the Cerro Azul/Jefe area.

Habits: Not well known despite its wide range. Soars regularly, often very high. Perches conspicuously in tall forest trees.

Range: Honduras to Bolivia, northeastern Argentina, and southern Brazil.

HARPY EAGLE

(*Harpia harpyja*) *pages 67, 73*

Description: 38–42. A huge, massively built eagle, the most powerful bird of prey in the world, with tarsi two inches thick. Very broad rounded wings; fairly long tail. *Head and neck gray* with *prominent two-pointed blackish crest;* back and wings black, somewhat edged with gray; chest black, lower underparts white; tail black with three broad, pale gray bands (whiter from below). In flight from below, wings white with black axillars and flight feathers barred with black. Juvenal has head, neck, and underparts white with *dark bushy two-parted crest;* back and wings pale gray marbled with blackish; tail gray with narrow dusky bands; underside of wings as in adult except for white axillars.

Similar species: Young birds require several years to attain adult plumage and then may be confused with young Crested Eagle despite their markedly greater size; Crested has proportionately longer tail, single-

Left, Crested Eagle (adult); right, Harpy Eagle (adult)

pointed crest, and is darker above and marbled with whitish.

Status and distribution: Rare and local in extensively forested and little settled areas on Caribbean slope; on Pacific slope recorded from western Panama province (sighting from La Campana; Wetmore) east through Darién. Formerly more numerous and found regularly in the Canal Zone area, this spectacular eagle has decreased greatly in recent decades, with few recent verified reports except from Darién. Remarkably, there is one recent sighting from the Canal Zone, that an adult seen perched along the outer part of Pipeline Road on March 2, 1974 (Ira Joel Abramson). Unfortunately the Harpy presents too tempting a target for most hunters to resist, despite its legally protected status.

Habits: Evidently very inconspicuous despite its size, generally remaining in or below the forest canopy, though known to soar at least occasionally.

Range: Southeastern Mexico to Bolivia, northern Argentina, and southern Brazil.

BLACK-AND-WHITE HAWK-EAGLE
(*Spizastur melanoleucus*)

Description: 22–24. Rather Buteo-like proportions. Cere and base of bill orange; legs feathered to toes. *Head, neck, and entire underparts white* with *short bushy black-tipped crest* and *black patch in front of eyes;* back and wings black; tail blackish with three grayish bands. In flight from below, *underside of wings essentially white,* with a little black barring on flight feathers. Immature 'has back and wings mixed with brownish gray.

BLACK-AND-WHITE HAWK-EAGLE

Similar species: A handsome, rather small, black and white eagle. Pale phase immature Gray-headed Kite is similar in pattern but is less robust, browner above, has bare tarsi, and lacks this species' black "mask" and short crest. Immature Ornate Hawk-Eagle is brown (not black) above, lacks black mask, and has longer crest and black barring on flanks and thighs.

Status and distribution: Rare and local in forest borders and clearings on both slopes; recorded only from Bocas del Toro, Chiriquí highlands, Veraguas, Canal Zone, eastern Colon province (sighting from Cerro Santa Rita; N. G. Smith), and eastern Panama province. Apparently scarce throughout its range. One was recently (1968–1970) seen around Summit Gardens, and a pair nested (unsuccessfully) on the Platanares–Jesús María road east of Chepo, eastern Panama province, in late 1972 (J. Strauch, Jr.).

Habits: Generally conspicuous where it does occur, though it does not seem to call as much as the *Spizaetus* hawk-eagles. Soars regularly.

Range: Southern Mexico south locally to northeastern Argentina and southern Brazil.

ORNATE HAWK-EAGLE
(*Spizaetus ornatus*) Pl.3, *page 67*

Description: 23–25. Wings broad, rather short and rounded; tail rather long. Legs feathered to toes. *Crown and long pointed crest black; sides of head, hindneck, and sides of chest tawny;* back and wings black; throat and center of chest white, bordered with black malar stripe; *lower underparts white heavily barred with black;* tail black with three grayish bands; underside of wings barred black and white. Immature has head, neck, and underparts white with *long crest* usually white with black tip, *flanks and thighs barred with black;* dark brown above; wings and tail as in adult.

Similar species: Immature can be confused with Black-and-white Hawk-Eagle, which has black area around eye, lacks long crest and black barring on flanks. Immature Black Hawk-Eagle is much darker below. Crested Eagle is much larger.

Status and distribution: Uncommon in forest and forest borders on both slopes, but not known from Azuero Peninsula nor from dry areas on Pacific slope; in Chiriquí and Darién ranges up into lower highlands. In Canal Zone apparently found only on Caribbean slope; everywhere outnumbered by the Black Hawk-Eagle.

Habits: Does not soar as much nor as high as the Black-Hawk Eagle. The call is distinctive and often given in flight, *whee-er, whip, whip, whip, whip,* with slurred note first; in pattern the reverse of the Black Hawk-Eagle's call, which has slurred note last. The crest is laid out flat at rest, stands straight up "like a Prussian helmet" when the bird is disturbed or annoyed (Slud).

Range: Eastern Mexico to Bolivia, northern Argentina, and southern Brazil.

Note: Wetmore calls it Barred Hawk Eagle.

BLACK HAWK-EAGLE

(*Spizaetus tyrannus*) *page 67*

Description: 25–28. Wings broad and rounded, *narrower* at base; tail rather long. Legs feathered to toes. *Mostly black* with short bushy crest, some white about head and white barring on thighs; tail black with three whitish bands. In flight from below, *flight feathers prominently barred black and white.* Immature is mostly dark chocolate brown with white to buff mottling, especially on head, and white barring on back; throat white, most of lower underparts barred with white.

Similar species: A large but rather slender eagle with a very distinctive flight appearance: wings and long tail prominently banded, wing-tips often held forward of head, with rear of wing often seemingly "cut-out" near body. No other mostly dark hawk or eagle has such conspicuous banding or underside of wings (sometimes difficult to see against the light).

Status and distribution: Fairly common locally in forest, second-growth woodland, and borders in lowlands and foothills on entire Caribbean slope and in more humid forested areas on Pacific slope; apparently absent from Azuero Peninsula; in western Chiriquí ranges at least occasionally up into highlands (Finca Lerida above Boquete). On Pacific slope published records are few, but there are many recent sight reports from Coclé (El Valle), Cerro Campana, Canal Zone (nesting; N. G. Smith), eastern Panama Province (Cerro Azul, Bayano River, etc.) and Darién (near El Real, April 1967; Eisenmann *et al.*). Frequently noted in Canal Zone area, where, for a bird its size, it is numerous and widespread in or near wooded areas on both slopes.

Habits: Very conspicuous, frequently seen soaring high overhead, even in the heat of the day; rarely seen perched. Calls regularly when soaring, an unmistakable loud, mellow *wheet, wheet, wheeteeeeeeea,* with long slurred note last; sometimes the last note is given alone.

Range: Eastern Mexico to northern Bolivia, northeastern Argentina, and southern Brazil.

NORTHERN HARRIER (MARSH HAWK)

(*Circus cyaneus*)

Description: 18–22. Wings long and narrow, *in flight usually held slightly above horizontal in dihedral;* tail long. Characteristic *white rump patch* in both sexes. Adult male, *mostly pale gray,* white on breast and belly. In flight from below, wings whitish with primaries tipped black. Female mostly dark brown above and on face and chest, paler brown below streaked with darker; tail grayish brown barred with blackish; underside of wings strongly barred with grayish brown. Immature like female but more uniform rufous below with less streaking.

Similar species: Note the conspicuous white rump. Female and immature Snail Kite are somewhat similar but have broader wings and heavier body, sharply hooked bill, brightly colored facial area and legs, and white on base of tail. At a distance male might be confused with White-tailed Kite.

Status and distribution: Uncommon to rare transient and winter resident in open grassy areas and marshes throughout, most numerous in Pacific lowlands (mid-October–late April); most spring migrants pass through in March. On migration a small number can sometimes be seen among the huge flocks of Broad-winged and Swainson's Hawks as they pass overhead.

Habits: Usually seen quartering low back and forth over the ground with uptilted wings. Not often seen perched.

Range: Breeds in northern and central Eurasia and in North America; American birds winter south to Panama, rarely to Colombia and Venezuela.

CRANE HAWK

(*Geranospiza caerulescens*) Pl.3, *page 67*

Description: 17–20. *Lanky slender appearance* with *long orange to reddish orange* *legs; cere and lores gray.* Wings rather long and rounded, tail long; in shape suggests Zone-tailed Hawk. *Slaty blackish in west, becoming paler and grayer eastward;* more or less barred with white on lower belly, thighs, and under tail-coverts; tail with two broad white bands (upper one sometimes hidden) and white tip. In flight from below, wings black narrowly banded with white on under wing-coverts and with *prominent white band across primaries* (this also visible from above). Immature is browner, with whitish eye-stripe and sides of head, more prominent buff barring on lower belly and thighs, white bars on upper tail-coverts.

Similar species: When perched, suggests a Black-Hawk in color but has a slender, small-headed appearance, gray (not yellow) cere, and strikingly long orange legs. In flight, most resembles Zone-tailed Hawk (though not flying with dihedral) but note white band on primaries and lack of Zone-tail's two-toned wings.

Status and distribution: Rare to locally uncommon in humid forest, second-growth woodland, borders, and swamps and marshes in lowlands on both slopes. Almost always found near water. Decidedly scarce in Canal Zone, recently reported mostly from Achiote Road; more numerous in gallery woodland and swamps and marshes in the Tocumen/La Jagua area.

Habits: When feeding in forest hops about rather awkwardly from branch to branch, sometimes even hanging upside down, searching for frogs, lizards, snakes, and large insects in epiphytes and crevices. Also goes to the ground, then seeming very long-legged. At times quarters over open marshy areas much like a harrier; occasionally soars, then appearing rather Buteo-like.

Range: Mexico to Bolivia, northern Argentina, and Uruguay.

Note: Formerly split into 2 or 3 species, now generally regarded as one; Panama birds were included in *G. nigra* (Blackish Crane-Hawk) of Middle America to western Ecuador. Wetmore uses the generic name *Ischnoceles,* considered barred by the International Code of Nomenclature.

OSPREYS: Pandionidae (1)

The Osprey is a virtually cosmopolitan species, nesting on every continent except South America, where it does occur as a nonbreeder. It feeds almost exclusively on fish, and its feet have been modified with a rough spiny surface to assist in grasping such prey. In some parts of North America it has in recent years decreased drastically, a decline apparently due to pesticide residues concentrated in its fishy prey.

OSPREY
(*Pandion haliaetus*)

Description: 21–24. Mostly *dark brown above, white below; crown and nape white,* broad stripe through eye black. Immature is similar but more streaked and edged with white and buffy above, washed with buffy below. In flight, wings appear long and rather narrow, with terminal half bent back ("kinked"); underside of wings mostly whitish with *black "wrist" mark* (carpal joint).

Similar species: Contrasting dark upperparts and white underparts and attachment to larger bodies of water are characteristic.

Status and distribution: Fairly common during northern winter months around larger bodies of water in lowlands on both slopes; smaller numbers present throughout the year, especially on or near coast ("summering" birds being immatures); on migration, occurs elsewhere, sometimes accompanying other migrating hawks; noted regularly on Volcán Lakes in western Chiriquí highlands; occurs also on Coiba Island, Taboga Island, and the Pearl Islands. Does not breed in Panama.

Habits: Regularly rests on a high exposed perch from which it flies out to fish; it plunges into the water feet first, often from considerable heights and with a great splash, and seems successful a good proportion of the time. Often hovers heavily while hunting. Flies with deep deliberate wingstrokes interspersed with gliding on set wings.

Range: Virtually cosmopolitan, breeding on every continent except South America; during northern winter, North American birds occur south to southern South America (with some individuals "summering" even there); in New World not known to breed south of Guatemala and Belize.

FALCONS AND CARACARAS: Falconidae (13)

This family includes a large and widespread group of diurnal birds of prey, separated in most species from the Accipitridae by their notched upper mandible and various anatomical characters. The true falcons (genus *Falco*), a world-wide group, are known by their pointed and rather narrow wings; some of the smaller falcons often hover, while many of the larger ones kill their avian prey by a spectacular stoop from above. Most of the caracaras (entirely American in distribution) eat largely carrion, but one Panamanian species (the Red-throated) specializes in wasp and bee larvae. The forest-falcons (also exclusively American) are inconspicuous accipiter-like birds of dense forest lower growth; they have short rounded wings, long tails (in some strikingly graduated), and an owl-like facial ruff (sometimes not very apparent), and feed mostly on birds. Nesting sites selected by the members of the family are varied, ranging from cliff ledges to old nests of other birds, holes in trees, and stick nests in trees. Interestingly, no record of the nest of any of the forest-falcons is known, a tribute to their secretive habits.

LAUGHING FALCON
(*Herpetotheres cachinnans*)

Description: 18–22. Appears large-headed. Wings rather short and rounded; tail long and rounded. *Head, neck, and underparts buffy white to buff* with *prominent broad black mask through eyes and around hindneck;* crown with a few black shaft streaks; upperparts dark brown; tail black with numerous buffy white bands. In flight shows caracara-like buffy patches on primaries.

Similar species: Yellow-headed Caracara is smaller and lacks the broad mask (only a thin black line through eye).

Status and distribution: Uncommon and local in woodland and forest borders, gallery woodland, and clearings in lowlands on Pacific slope; on Caribbean slope apparently recorded only from Bocas del Toro; unreported from drier Pacific lowlands from eastern side of Azuero Peninsula to western Panama province; ranges up into foothills to about 4000 feet in western Chiriquí. Only recent Canal Zone reports are from southwestern sector (Empire Range area; S. West *et al.*), where rare; still found in small numbers in the Tocumen/Chepo area; most numerous in Chiriquí and southern Veraguas.

Habits: Rather inactive, remaining perched for long periods of time. Notably unsuspicious, which may account for its diminished abundance in more settled areas. Flies with rapid and stiff wing-beats (recalling those of an Amazon parrot) alternating with short glides; does not soar. Best known from its far-carrying calls, most often a loud *gua-co, gua-co . . .*, first note higher, with variations (sequence sometimes reversed); this is repeated many times, initially rather slowly, then increasing in tempo. It calls most often in the early morning and late afternoon. Other less frequently heard vocalizations do somewhat suggest maniacal laughter, *hah, hah, hah-hah-hah-hahhahhah-hah.* Some vocalizations are reminiscent of calls of Collared Forest-Falcon.

Range: Mexico to Bolivia, northern Argentina, and southern Brazil.

LAUGHING FALCON

COLLARED FOREST-FALCON
(*Micrastur semitorquatus*) Pl.2

Description: 20–24. Slender with short broad wings; *long graduated tail.* Bill blackish; bare facial skin and cere dull greenish; legs yellow. Three phases in adults. In light phase, blackish above, *black of crown extending down over face in crescent;* white below, extending up over sides of head and neck and forming *collar on hindneck;* tail black with narrow white bands and white tip. Buffy phase similar but with *white replaced by buff to tawny.* Rare dark phase is all sooty black except for white tail banding and small amount of white barring on flanks. Immature variable, with greenish bill; upperparts dark brown edged with tawny, and *whitish to tawny collar;* underparts varying from whitish to deep buff, brightest on chest, and coarsely barred with blackish or dark brown; tail as in adult. Dark phase immature brownish black with white barring on lower underparts.

Similar species: All phases except dark show contrasting collar. Immature Bicolored Hawk resembles this species' white and buffy phases but is smaller and has shorter ungraduated tail, shorter legs, and lacks white or buff face and dark facial crescent. Barred Forest-Falcon is much smaller and lacks prominent collar, is evenly barred below in adults.

Status and distribution: Uncommon to fairly common in forest, second-growth woodland, and borders in more humid lowlands on both slopes, ranging up to 5300 feet in Chiriquí; apparently absent from dry Pacific lowlands of southern Coclé and western Panama province. In Canal Zone more numerous on Caribbean side.

Habits: Usually remains in dense undergrowth and lower trees, thus difficult to observe. A bold rapacious hunter. Reported to run on the ground with half-open wings (H.-J. Peters). The call is a slowly repeated, resonant *ow . . . ow . . . ow . . .,* somewhat suggestive of Laughing Falcon but without the acceleration; it is sometimes given from a high perch near the canopy.

Range: Mexico to Bolivia, northern Argentina, and southern Brazil.

SLATY-BACKED FOREST-FALCON

(*Micrastur mirandollei*) Pl.2

Description: 16–18. Shape similar to Collared Forest-Falcon, but tail not as proportionately long and graduated. Base of bill, cere, and legs yellow. *Dark slaty gray above and on sides of neck* (*with no collar on hindneck*); below varying from whitish to pale buff with very fine dark shaft streaks; tail blackish with three narrow whitish bands. Immature has mainly yellow bill, is browner above, whitish below with broad dusky scalloping.

Similar species: Caution is urged in identifying this rare and confusing species. Immature Barred Forest-Falcons that lack black barring below somewhat resemble adults of this species with light buff underparts, but are much smaller, with more graduated tail, are browner or dusky above, and have pale face and yellow orbital area. This species also resembles immature Bicolored Hawk but has facial ruff, shorter legs, slaty (not rusty) upperparts, and never has a collar (present in most Bicoloreds). Semiplumbeous Hawk has similar color pattern but is chunkier with one prominent white tail band (not three narrow inconspicuous ones).

Status and distribution: Apparently rare in humid forest and second-growth woodland in lowlands on Caribbean slope (though not recorded from Bocas del Toro or Veraguas, it probably occurs); on Pacific slope known from eastern Panama province and Darién. In and near Canal Zone has recently been reported from various areas near Caribbean coast (Río Piedras, Ft. San Lorenzo, Achiote Road) and from middle Chagres River valley (Pipeline Road, Gamboa, Juan Mina), in most cases only one report per locality.

Habits: Inconspicuous, usually seen rather low, inside humid forest or at heavily overgrown borders. Reported to do some of its hunting on the forest floor (Wetmore). The usual call is a rather subdued, somewhat nasal *aah,* repeated 5 to 8 times, not as loud as Collared Forest-Falcon.

Range: Costa Rica to eastern Peru, Amazonian Brazil, and the Guianas.

BARRED FOREST-FALCON

(*Micrastur ruficollis*) Pl.2

Description: 13–15. Short rounded wings; tail very long and graduated. Cere, *orbital area,* lores, and legs orange-yellow. Blackish slate above (browner in female); throat pale gray, *remaining underparts white finely and evenly barred with black;* tail black with three narrow white bands and narrow white tip. Immature variable, dark brown above with narrow buff collar (sometimes broken or hidden); varying shades of buff below, usually with irregular dusky barring (much coarser than in adult); in a few individuals, underparts uniform deep buff with no barring; tail as in adult.

Similar species: Adult's even barring below is characteristic, but see Tiny Hawk (smaller, with different shape, habits).

Collared Forest-Falcon is much larger. Immature Bicolored Hawk lacks barring below, has shorter legs and shorter less graduated tail. See also Slaty-backed Forest-Falcon.

Status and distribution: Apparently uncommon (probably overlooked because of furtive habits) in humid forest in lowlands and foothills on entire Caribbean slope; on Pacific slope found in humid forested areas (mostly in foothills) from Chiriquí to Darién, ranging up in western Chiriquí in lower highlands to 5400 feet. More numerous on Caribbean side of Canal Zone.

Habits: A bird of dense forest undergrowth, shy and not often seen. Reported following army ants on Barro Colorado Island (E. O. Willis); also reported to hunt to some extent on forest floor. Like Collared Forest-Falcon appears to be at least partially crepuscular. The usual call is a sharp staccato *our,* like the bark of a small dog (Slud), repeated at intervals. This often reveals the bird's presence, but it is extremely difficult to track down, the calling bird being very wary and usually slipping away at one's approach; the call is also ventriloquial. When excited the note is repeated more rapidly becoming *kĕo-kĕo-kĕo. . . .* Most vocal in the early morning and late afternoon.

Range: Southern Mexico to Bolivia, northern Argentina, and southern Brazil.

RED-THROATED CARACARA
(*Daptrius americanus*) Pl.3

Description: 20–21. Very distinctive in appearance, looking almost like a curassow. *Mostly glossy black* with *white belly;* bill yellow; *bare skin of face and throat, and legs, red.*

Status and distribution: Uncommon to locally fairly common in humid forest and borders in lowlands on entire Caribbean slope; on Pacific slope found in lowlands of Chiriquí and Veraguas to western side of Azuero Peninsula, and in Darién (where it ranges rarely up to about 4500 feet). Formerly rather numerous in forest on Caribbean side of Canal Zone (including Barro Colorado Island), but for unknown reasons has greatly decreased of late; recorded in recent years only from Achiote/Escobal area.

Habits: Generally travels above the forest in small groups, regularly low inside forest, otherwise usually rather high. Often unsuspicious, sometimes even seeming curious, approaching the observer closely. Feeds mostly on wasp and bee larvae, which it obtains by tearing open their nests. A very noisy bird, with loud raucous calls, *ca-ca-ca-cáo,* and variations; hence known locally as "ca-cao."

Range: Southeastern Mexico to Peru and southern Brazil.

YELLOW-HEADED CARACARA
(*Milvago chimachima*) Pl.3

Description: 16–17. Wings rather long, somewhat pointed; tail fairly long, rounded at tip. *Head, neck, and underparts pale buffy* with *narrow dark brown streak behind eye;* back and wings blackish brown; tail with numerous blackish and buff bands; in flight wings dark with *prominent pale buffy patch on base of primaries.* Immature streaked with brown and buff on head and neck and with brown back; mostly brown below streaked with buff or whitish; tail brownish barred with white; wings as in adult, with primaries barred with cinnamon.

Similar species: Immatures, though less distinctive, can still be recognized by caracara shape, wing patch, and habits. See Crested Caracara and Laughing Falcon.

Status and distribution: Fairly common to common in open grasslands with scattered trees and scrubby areas in lowlands on Pacific slope from western Chiriquí to eastern Panama province (not yet recorded from Darién but will likely spread there), in Chiriquí ranging up occasionally to slightly over 3000 feet; only reports from Caribbean slope are two sightings at Gamboa, Canal Zone, in 1973 and 1974 (Ridgely *et al.*) but likely will spread and become more numerous with increased clearing of forest; found also on Pearl Islands. In Canal Zone occurs in but small numbers (around Corozal, Balboa, etc.), but numerous and easily seen along Pan-American Highway from about Playa Coronado westward, less numerous in eastern Panama province.

Habits: Rather unsuspicious; often in small groups. Much of its food is carrion of all sorts: a good proportion is obtained by patrolling the highways for road-killed animals. Sometimes also seen picking ticks from backs of cattle. The usual call is a harsh *krrr-krrr-krrr;* also heard is a peculiar (part whistle, part hissing) *ksyeh, ksyeh.*

Range: Southwestern Costa Rica to Bolivia, northern Argentina, and Uruguay.

CRESTED CARACARA
(*Polyborus plancus*) Pl.3

Description: 20–24. Rather long legs. Somewhat crested. *Bare skin of face and base of bill red. Crown black; sides of head, neck, and throat whitish;* otherwise blackish above; breast whitish barred with dusky, becoming solid dusky on belly; *rump and most of tail white* narrowly barred with dusky and with broad black subterminal band; in flight shows *conspicuous white patches on primaries.* Immature recognizably similar though buffier and browner overall and more streaked below.

Similar species: Yellow-headed Caracara is much smaller and less robust, lacks white rump and wing patch (buffy instead) and has head and underparts mostly buffy.

Status and distribution: Fairly common to common in open grasslands with scattered trees and in scrubby areas in lowlands on Pacific slope from western Chiriquí to eastern Panama province; single records (probably stragglers) from Taboga Island and the Pearl Islands (Pacheca). Rather scarce in Canal Zone, with only occasional individuals appearing in open areas, particularly at Albrook AFB; more numerous and easily seen in the Tocumen/Chepo area and from Coclé westward. Recently (1973 on), odd individuals have been turning up in open areas on Caribbean side of Canal Zone and vicinity (France Field, just east of Puerto Pilón, outer Escobal Road; J. Pujals *et al.*); in time may become established and regular in this area.

Habits: Like Yellow-headed Caracara, most common in cattle country. A rather powerful bird of prey whose food is not limited to carrion. Usually forages in pairs or small groups, often seen walking on the ground. Flies strongly but does not seem to soar.

Range: Southwestern United States to Tierra del Fuego; southern Florida and Cuba.

Note: Generic name *Caracara* is sometimes used. Northern birds (ranging south to Peru and northern Brazil) are sometimes separated under the species name *P. cheriway.*

PEREGRINE FALCON
(*Falco peregrinus*)

Description: 15–20. *Long pointed wings;* rather pointed tail. *Slaty gray above,* blacker on head, with *broad black moustache stripe running down sides of throat;* whitish below, washed with buff and irregularly barred with dusky on breast and belly; tail barred gray and blackish. Immature similar but is dark brown above, buffy whitish below streaked with brown.

Similar species: Large size and long pointed wings mark this species as the largest of Panama's falcons. See the very rare Orange-breasted Falcon.

Status and distribution: Uncommon transient and winter resident (October–early May), with records scattered throughout, but chiefly coastally or near water. Very few inland records, those probably transients, except around Gatun Lake and the Canal; seen several times at Aligandí, San Blas (P. Alden). Only two reports from Chiriquí: one bird collected above Boquete on April 23, 1905, and one seen at Volcán Lakes on February 16, 1973 (Eisenmann and J. Pujals); recorded also from Pearl Islands and Coiba Island. Most often reported along shore of Panama Bay, where it feeds on the abundant shore and water birds. Several individuals have often passed the winter around the Pacific entrance to the Canal.

Habits: Nearly always found singly, in the air or on an exposed perch. Stoops on its prey with terrific speed and force. North American birds have greatly decreased in the last several decades, apparently as a result of breeding abnormalities caused by various persistent pesticides and industrial products.

Range: Virtually cosmopolitan, though not breeding in tropical America.

ORANGE-BREASTED FALCON
(*Falco deiroleucus*) *page 67*

Description: 13–16. Very rare. A large version of the much more numerous Bat Falcon. Black above and on sides of head, feathers margined with slate; throat white, *chest and breast rufous, upper belly black barred with buff,* lower belly rufous; tail black with very narrow whitish bands.

Similar species: Bat Falcon is smaller (though a large female Bat Falcon approaches the size of a small male Orange-breast), has blackish chest, breast, and upper belly, with rufous only on throat (sometimes) and lower belly. Resembles a small Peregrine in flight.

Status and distribution: Known definitely only from two nineteenth-century specimens from Chiriquí. Two recent sight observations were believed to refer to this species, though both birds were seen only in flight: near Penonomé, Coclé, on March 29, 1957 (Wetmore) and near Cerro Jefe, eastern

Panama province on June 25, 1970 (Ridgely). Griscom's account (*Bull. AMNH, 64,* 1932, p. 164) of nesting in church towers and belfries in towns in western Panama (Santiago and Las Palmas, Veraguas, and Aguadulce, Coclé; in letter to Eisenmann) probably refers to the Bat Falcon.

Habits: This little known falcon is often considered the neotropical equivalent of the Peregrine. It seems to be scarce and local throughout its range.

Range: Southeastern Mexico south very locally to northern Argentina and southern Brazil.

BAT FALCON

(*Falco rufigularis*) Pl.2

Description: 9–12. Very long, narrow, pointed wings. Dark bluish slate above and on sides of head; *throat, upper chest, and sides of neck white,* sometimes tinged with tawny; *lower chest, breast, and upper belly black,* narrowly barred with white; lower belly rufous.

Similar species: A small falcon that appears dark in the field; readily recognized by the contrastingly colored underparts. See the very rare Orange-breasted Falcon.

Status and distribution: Uncommon to locally fairly common in forest and woodland borders and nearby clearings in lowlands on both slopes, occasionally ranging up into the lower highlands; found also on Coiba Island, Taboga Island, and the Pearl Islands (San José). Rather scarce (unaccountably so) in Canal Zone.

Habits: Usually seen perched on an exposed branch, often in pairs, rather unsuspicious. Seems to feed mostly in early morning and late afternoon; catches its food (larger insects, bats, small birds) in very swift and graceful flight, often even eating its prey while on the wing. Nests in tree holes.

Range: Mexico to Bolivia, northern Argentina, and southern Brazil.

APLOMADO FALCON

(*Falco femoralis*)

Description: 14–17. Local in Pacific western Panama. Mostly bluish gray above with *narrow pale buffy line extending back over eye and meeting on hindneck;* narrow black moustache stripe on sides of throat; throat, sides of neck, and chest white or pale buffy merging into *buffy breast and tawny belly, band across upper belly and sides black* narrowly barred with white; tail black with narrow white bars. Immature similar but duller, browner above and with chest and breast streaked blackish.

Status and distribution: Uncommon on open plains and grassy savannas in lowlands on Pacific slope in Herrera and southern Coclé; one old specimen labeled as from "Veraguas" may actually have been taken farther east; one sight report of a bird believed this species on Barro Colorado Island on February 19, 1954 (Wetmore), and another sighting near Pedasí, Los Santos (also Wetmore).

Habits: Usually perches low and in the open, typically on fence posts, sometimes on telephone poles. Has a rapid flight, usually close to the ground; often hovers.

Range: Extreme southwestern United States (where now very rare) south very locally to Tierra del Fuego.

MERLIN (PIGEON HAWK)

(*Falco columbarius*)

Description: 10–13. Male *dark bluish gray above,* tinged with rusty on sides of head and nape; buff to whitish below, *streaked with blackish brown;* tail black with three gray bands and white tip. Female and immature are similar but browner above.

Similar species: Note falcon shape and habits, fairly small size, and streaked underparts. American Kestrel has bright rufous back and tail; Peregrine is much larger with prominent dark moustache.

Status and distribution: Uncommon transient and rare winter resident (late September–mid-April), spottily reported throughout, mostly from coastal lowlands including Pearl Islands. Favors semi-open country.

Habits: Usually seen in swift flight fairly low over the ground or on an exposed perch.

Range: Breeds in northern Eurasia and northern North America; American birds winter from southern United States to Venezuela and northern Peru and in West Indies.

AMERICAN KESTREL (SPARROW HAWK)

(*Falco sparverius*)

Description: 9–12. Male *mostly rufous above* with most of crown and *wings bluish gray;* sides of head white with narrow black moustache stripe and a vertical stripe through eye; buff below, spotted with black on breast and sides; *tail rufous* with broad black subterminal band and white tip. Female has head pattern as in male, *en-*

tirely rufous above (including wings), barred with black; buffy below, lightly streaked with brown; *tail rufous* with many narrow black bands.

Similar species: Striking facial pattern and mostly rufous tail and upperparts will identify both sexes.

Status and distribution: Fairly common transient and local winter resident (early October–early April) in lowlands on Pacific slope from Chiriquí to eastern Panama province; in smaller numbers in suitable habitat on Caribbean slope, mainly during migration; ranges well up into Chiriquí highlands; recorded also on Pearl Islands (San José) and Coiba Island.

Habits: Usually seen perched conspicuously on telephone poles or wires or on an exposed branch, favors open or semi-open country. Often jerks tail up and down upon alighting. Regularly seen hovering while hunting, especially just before it plunges down after its predominately insect prey.

Range: Breeds from northern North America south locally to Nicaragua and through much of South America; northern birds winter south at least to northern South America.

CURASSOWS, GUANS, AND CHACHALACAS: Cracidae (4)

This group of superficially pheasant or turkey-like birds is found only in the warmer parts of the New World. Most species are primarily arboreal; curassows, however, do much of their foraging on the ground. Although most species range in forest, chachalacas favor overgrown clearings and woodland borders. They feed chiefly on vegetable matter, particularly fruit. The nest is a simple structure of twigs or sticks and leaves, usually situated rather low in trees. All are much desired gamebirds, and populations of the larger species (especially the unsuspicious curassows) are quickly reduced by even light hunting pressure.

GREAT CURASSOW
(*Crax rubra*)

Description: 34–38. Restricted to more remote forest. *Very large.* Male *black* with rounded crest of recurved feathers and *globular yellow knob on base of upper mandible;* belly and under tail-coverts white. Female lacks yellow knob on bill,

Left, two Crested Guans; center top, Black Guan; center bottom, two Great Curassows (female left, male right); right top, two Gray-headed Chachalacas

is variable in color, mostly rufous brown or blackish washed with rufous, *head, neck, and rounded crest black barred with white;* tail barred buff and brown; belly barred buff and black. Subadult male lacks yellow knob on bill.

Similar species: This magnificent bird should not be confused. Crested Guan is more lightly built, with bare red throat, white streaking below.

Status and distribution: Formerly widespread in heavy lowland forest on both slopes, this species is one of the first birds to disappear when a region is settled or becomes accessible to hunters. Now found locally in humid forest on Caribbean slope; on Pacific slope in forest locally in southern Veraguas and on western side of Azuero Peninsula (formerly occurring in Chiriquí, ranging rarely to over 5000 feet), and in eastern Panama province and Darién. Now rare in Canal Zone, but small numbers apparently persist, with sightings from near Rodman Ammunition Dump in 1967 but not since (N. G. Smith), and recent sightings on Pipeline Road, including a female seen with young in March 1974 (N. Gale, S. West, *et al.*).

Habits: Frequently found in pairs. Mostly terrestrial, though rising into trees when disturbed, also roosting and nesting in trees. Males have a long low boom or humming noise (rather tuba-like), *oom-m-m-m,* very ventriloquial (Wetmore), and also often give a high pitched whistled *wheep, wheep, wheeeew,* or any of these notes alone (Eisenmann). Rather unsuspicious and highly esteemed as a table bird.

Range: Eastern Mexico to western Colombia.

Note: Wetmore calls it Central American Curassow.

CRESTED GUAN
(*Penelope purpurascens*)

Description: 34–36. Very large but rather slender with long neck and tail. Mostly dark olive brown with short, bushy crest and *prominent bare red throat; chest and breast lightly streaked with white;* lower back and tail more chestnut.

Similar species: As long as a curassow, but much more slender with proportionately longer neck and tail. See Baudó Guan (below).

Status and distribution: Still found locally in forest in lowlands and foothills on both slopes, ranging (perhaps only formerly) well up into western Chiriquí highlands (to about 7000 feet). Recorded from entire Caribbean slope; on Pacific slope known only from Chiriquí (very possibly extirpated), southern Veraguas and western side of Azuero Peninsula, Canal Zone (formerly), and eastern Panama province and Darién. In Canal Zone, still found locally on Caribbean side; most likely to be seen on Barro Colorado Island (small groups sometimes visible from clearing in early morning) and in Ft. Sherman/San Lorenzo area.

Habits: Arboreal and more wary than the curassow, the guan seems better able to withstand hunting pressure. Usually found in small groups in the treetops. Has a loud metallic honking or yelping, *quenk, quenk, quenk,* or *keelp, keelp, keelp.*

Range: Mexico to northern Venezuela and western Ecuador.

Note: Baudó Guan (*Penelope ortoni*) of western Colombia and Ecuador may occur in eastern Darién as it has been recorded close to the Panama border (Río Jurado). It is much smaller (26″) than the Crested Guan, and feathers of underparts are less conspicuously edged with whitish.

BLACK GUAN
(*Chamaepetes unicolor*)

Description: 21–23. Found only in western highlands. Iris red; *bare blue skin in front of eye and on sides of face;* legs light reddish. *Wholly black.* Immature has breast and belly somewhat more brownish. Unmistakable in its range.

Status and distribution: Rare to uncommon in forest and forest borders in highlands of Chiriquí, Bocas del Toro (where recorded as low as 1500 feet), and Veraguas (Calovévora and Santa Fé); recorded mostly 4000–7500 feet. Best known from western Chiriquí, though its numbers there have been reduced by excessive hunting; can still be seen occasionally on Finca Lerida above Boquete.

Habits: Favors heavily wooded humid ravines and slopes. Mostly arboreal though sometimes goes to ground. Usually in pairs, quite wary where under hunting pressure.

Range: Costa Rica and western Panama.

GRAY-HEADED CHACHALACA
(*Ortalis cinereiceps*)

Description: 19–21. Slender with small head (somewhat crested), long neck, long tail. *Mostly grayish brown* with small patch of red skin on throat; *head and neck distinctly gray;* somewhat paler below, becoming whitish on lower belly; *bright chestnut* *primaries conspicuous in flight;* tail tipped buff.

Similar species: Crested Guan is much larger, has white streaking below, lacks chestnut on wings.

Status and distribution: Fairly common to common in second-growth woodland and borders, clearings, and shrubby areas in lowlands and foothills on both slopes, though has not been reported from Darién; found also on larger Pearl Islands. Quite numerous and widespread in wooded areas on both slopes of Canal Zone.

Habits: Usually seen in groups of up to about a dozen individuals; primarily arboreal. Not particularly shy where they are not under intense hunting pressure. Has a variety of vocalizations: groups often greet the dawn with a harsh repeated *chack* or *chacalaca;* also has a soft *hoit, hoit,* or *hweet, hweet* and a *kt-kt-kt,* both given especially when the birds are disturbed.

Range: Honduras to extreme northwestern Colombia.

Note: By some authors considered conspecific with *O. garrula* (Chestnut-winged Chachalaca) of northern Colombia.

PHEASANTS, PARTRIDGES, AND QUAIL: Phasianidae (7)

This family is most highly developed in the Old World, especially in southern Asia, with only a few genera native to America. It is not very well represented in Panama: one species in Pacific western savannas is obviously related to the Northern Bobwhite group, and there are six species of infrequently seen wood-quail in humid forests. All Panama species are terrestrial, ranging in small groups (coveys), and are best known from their far-carrying calls. They eat a variety of food, largely seeds and berries, supplemented with insects and other invertebrates. The simple nest is placed on the ground.

CRESTED BOBWHITE
(*Colinus cristatus*)

Description: 8–9. *Crown, prominent pointed crest, and face buff to white;* hindneck and sides of neck black spotted with white; otherwise brown above spotted and vermiculated with black; buff to chestnut below, with *prominent white spots on breast and flanks,* barred with black on belly. Female similar but duller, crown black and crest brown, throat streaked with black.

Status and distribution: Fairly common in savannas and open scrubby areas in lowlands on Pacific slope from western Chiriquí to western Panama province (Playa Coronado to base of Cerro Campana), ranging to above 4000 feet around Boquete in western Chiriquí; commonest in Herrera, less numerous east of Coclé. Two nineteenth-century specimens labeled "Panama Railroad" may be attributable to the then more open conditions of that area; the only subsequent report from Canal Zone is a sighting of a small covey near Contractor's Hill in southwestern sector on August 10, 1969 (H. A. Hespenheide). Apparently absent from savannas of eastern Panama province though they would seem to be suitable.

Habits: Similar in most respects to the Northern Bobwhite (*C. virginianus*). Usually found in small coveys on ground; rather shy, generally keeping in or close to cover. Males have an unmistakable, whistled call similar to the northern bird's, though it is faster and huskier, usually triple-noted *quoit bob-white?,* sometimes double-noted, *oh, wheet.*

Range: Pacific western and central Panama; northwestern Colombia to the Guianas and northwestern Brazil. Can be expected to extend its range to southwestern Costa Rica.

CRESTED BOBWHITE

MARBLED WOOD-QUAIL
(*Odontophorus gujanensis*) Pl.1

Description: 9–11. *Bare skin around eye orange to red.* Short, bushy crest varying from brown to blackish; *otherwise mostly dark brown,* finely barred and vermiculated with black and buff; neck often gray and scapulars streaked with whitish.

Similar species: More uniformly colored than other Panama wood-quail. Rufous-fronted Wood-Quail is mostly chestnut below and has purplish or black orbital area (not red or orange) and rufous forecrown. Tinamous are differently shaped, with smaller heads, longer and more slender necks, tail-less appearance.

Status and distribution: Rare to locally fairly common in humid forest in lowlands and foothills (to about 3000 feet) on Caribbean slope from Coclé east through San Blas; on Pacific slope known from eastern Panama province (Tocumen eastward) and Darién; formerly found in lowlands of western Chiriquí but no recent reports and probably extirpated due to felling of most lowland forest. Formerly numerous on Caribbean slope of Canal Zone area, it has greatly decreased in recent years; still found in small numbers on Pipeline and Achiote Roads.

Habits: Usually found in small groups on the forest floor. Rather shy in most areas, keeping to dense cover and usually preferring to escape by crouching and hiding or by running (not flying). Best known from its very fast rollicking ringing musical call, *córcorovado, córcorovado, córcorovado . . .* (also interpreted as "perro-mulato"), repeated many times for up to several minutes, given most often at dawn or dusk. The call is antiphonal, the male giving the *córcoro,* the female the *vado.*

Range: Costa Rica to Bolivia and Amazonian Brazil.

RUFOUS-FRONTED WOOD-QUAIL
(*Odontophorus erythrops*) Pl.1

Description: 9–10. *Bare orbital area purplish blue in male, black in female. Crown and short crest refous,* feathers of crest tipped with blackish brown; otherwise dark olive brown above mottled with black and buffy; *sides of head, throat, and foreneck blackish; remaining underparts chestnut.* Female similar but without black on sides of head, throat, and foreneck.

Similar species: Marbled Wood-Quail is more uniform dark brown (not chestnut below), lacks rufous crest, and has red or orange (not dark) orbital area.

Status and distribution: Rare and local in humid forest in lowlands and especially in foothills (1500–3000 feet) on Caribbean slope where recorded from Bocas del Toro, Veraguas, eastern Colon province (Cerro Bruja), and San Blas: on Pacific slope recorded from Veraguas foothills (Santa Fé), Panama province (Cerro Azul/Jefe area, Cerro Campana), and eastern Darién (Cerro Pirre, where recorded to over 5000 feet). Apparently decreases rapidly near inhabited areas, with only one recent report from Cerro Campana (1 on January 4, 1975; S. West), and one from Cerro Jefe (3 on January 11, 1974; Ridgely).

Habits: Little known in Panama. The Cerro Jefe birds were rather unsuspicious, and uttered soft peeping notes before scurrying up the rather open slope of a forested ravine. In Costa Rica reported to forage on the forest floor in small bands; the call, heard mostly in the early morning but also in the late afternoon, is a repeated *kláwcoo kláwcoo . . . ,* sometimes reversed to *kook-láwk* (Slud).

Range: Honduras to western Ecuador.

Note: Wetmore calls it Rufous-breasted Wood Quail (which name is also in current use for a South American species, *O. speciosus*).

BLACK-BREASTED (WHITE-THROATED) WOOD-QUAIL
(*Odontophorus leucolaemus*) Pl.1

Description: 9–9½. Known only from western highlands. Dark brown above (more blackish on crown and short crest) finely vermiculated with black; *throat usually white; sides of head and neck and most of underparts black* with dull white barring on belly. Considerable individual variation: some birds blacker above with throat speckled with black or even wholly black, others brighter brown above and below (especially on breast).

Similar species: The only Panama wood-quail with largely black head and underparts.

Status and distribution: Rare and local in humid forest in foothills and lower highlands (3500–5200 feet) of Bocas del Toro, Chiriquí, Veraguas, and Coclé (one old specimen); most records are from Caribbean slope.

Habits: Little known in Panama. Said to favor steep wooded slopes. The call in Costa Rica is reported to be a rushing gabble which breaks out suddenly from several individuals, two sets of paired syllables, the first accented, repeated over and over (Slud).

Range: Costa Rica and western Panama.

TACARCUNA WOOD-QUAIL
(*Odontophorus dialeucos*) Pl.1

Description: 9–10. Found only in highlands of eastern Darién. *Crown and crest black* spotted very lightly with white, *superciliary white,* neck brown becoming buff on hindneck; otherwise dull brown above, vermiculated with black; *throat and upper chest white, lower throat crossed by a blackish band;* remaining underparts dull buffy brown mottled with black.

Similar species: The only wood-quail recorded in its restricted range.

Status and distribution: Reported fairly common in forest in highlands of eastern Darién (Cerro Tacarcuna, Cerro Malí), above 3500 feet. Discovered only in 1963.

Habits: Little known. A terrestrial forest species, found in pairs or small groups. One was seen perched 25 feet up in a small tree (Wetmore).

Range: Eastern Panama. Probably also found on same mountain range in adjacent northwestern Colombia.

SPOTTED WOOD-QUAIL
(*Odontophorus guttatus*) Pl.1

Description: 9½–10½. Found only in western Chiriquí highlands. Mostly dark olive brown with blackish crown and rufous crest, wings speckled with white spots; *throat and foreneck blackish streaked with white;* remaining underparts grayish brown *with small elongated black-bordered white spots.* Some birds are brighter brown above and below.

Similar species: The only Panama wood-quail that is spotted below (though the spots are sometimes hard to see in the dim light of the forest). Black-breasted Wood-Quail has white throat (usually) and mostly black sides of head and underparts (no rufous on head).

Status and distribution: Fairly common in forest and forest borders in highlands of western Chiriquí, mostly 4000–7000 feet.

Habits: Like other wood-quail shy and not often seen, ranging the forest floor in small coveys. The call somewhat resembles the Marbled Wood-Quail's, a loud rapidly repeated series of whistled phrases, often antiphonal, *whípa, wipeé-o . . .,* · heard mostly in the early morning.

Range: Southern Mexico to Pacific western Panama.

TAWNY-FACED QUAIL
(*Rhynchortyx cinctus*) Pl.1

Description: 7–8. Male has *sides of head bright tawny* with narrow dark brown stripe through eye; otherwise brown above, mottled with gray and buff on back, wings barred and spotted with black and buff; *throat and breast gray,* lower underparts cinnamon-buff to whitish, flanks lightly barred with black. Female mostly brown with *narrow, pale buffyish superciliary;* throat whitish, chest brown, *lower underparts whitish barred with black.*

Similar species: *Odontophorus* wood-quail are considerably larger. Male easily recognized by its bright tawny face, female by its overall brown appearance and barred lower underparts.

Status and distribution: Rare and local in humid forest in lowlands and foothills on Caribbean slope from at least Canal Zone eastward; on Pacific slope known from Cerro Campana (one sight report, *fide* Wetmore) and eastern Panama province east through Darién, where ranges up to at least 4400 feet. Not recorded from any definite locality in western Panama, though the original nineteenth-century specimens came from "Veragua," a term that then encompassed most of the western area. Only recently (1968) found in Canal Zone, now known to occur in small numbers on Pipeline Road (once mist-netted and photographed, seen repeatedly; J. Karr *et al.*).

Habits: Usually found in pairs; terrestrial, rather shy, and not often seen. Flies rarely, prefering to run or hide when discovered. A peeping note has been heard (J. Karr).

Range: Honduras to northwestern Ecuador.

Note: Wetmore calls it Banded Wood-Quail.

LIMPKINS: Aramidae (1)

The Limpkin is a large, brown, superficially ibis-like wading bird of riverbanks and tree-bordered marshes. It is rather scarce and not well known in Panama, though it enjoys a wide range in the warmer parts of the New World. It feeds largely on *Pomacea* snails. The nest is placed on the ground or low in a bush or tree, always near water.

LIMPKIN
(*Aramus guarauna*)

Description: 26–28. Long dark legs, slender neck, and *long slightly drooping bill* impart a somewhat ibis-like appearance. Brown with *white streaks on head and neck.* Bocas del Toro birds (*dolosus*) are also streaked with white on wings and body.

Similar species: Ibises have more slender and much more decurved bills with bare facial areas. Immature and winter adult Glossy Ibis also have white streaks on head and neck but are smaller with bare facial area, and are darker and glossier on back and underparts.

Status and distribution: Rare to uncommon and local in fresh water swamps and tree-bordered marshes and along rivers in lowlands of western Bocas del Toro (east to Cricamola), Herrera (sight report of one south of Santa María on May 23, 1968; Ridgely), Canal Zone (along Chagres River above Gamboa; along banks of Canal near Miraflores Locks, and at Howard AFB; N. G. Smith), and Darién.

Habits: Infrequently seen in Panama, and very local, apparently due to lack of much suitable habitat. Often perches in bushes and low trees. Rather noisy, with a variety of loud wailing calls, *car-rr-rao, car-rr-rao* (Wetmore). Their flight is jerky and awkward and usually not long sustained, with outstretched neck and dangling legs.

Range: Florida; southern Mexico locally to Bolivia, northern Argentina, and Uruguay; Greater Antilles.

RAILS, GALLINULES, AND COOTS: Rallidae (12)

This is a cosmopolitan group of small to medium-sized, mostly marsh and swamp inhabiting, birds. Many species are secretive (some are crepuscular and even nocturnal) and difficult to study, and a number of the species recorded from Panama are still very poorly known. Wood-rails are relatively large, brightly patterned, almost chicken-like birds of wet forests, swamps, and mangroves. Typical rails have fairly long bills; the crakes have short bills and are smaller; both groups favor marshes and wet meadows. Gallinules and coots are more birds of open water, swimming regularly and the coot (with lobed toes) diving expertly. All members of the family eat a variety of plant and animal matter. The nest is generally on or near the ground in dense vegetation, though in the wood-rails it is placed in a bush or low branch of a tree.

[SPOTTED RAIL]
(*Pardirallus maculatus*) Pl.1

Description: 10. One sight report. Rather long slightly decurved bill, mostly greenish with red at base of lower mandible; legs red. Mostly black above, *spotted and streaked with white;* wings brown streaked with white; throat white dotted with black, *chest black spotted with white, breast and belly barred black and white.* Juvenal has black replaced by brown, and underparts almost uniform sooty to dark grayish olive with indistinct bars.

Status and distribution: Only report is a sighting of a bird believed this species at Mandinga, San Blas, on January 22, 1957 (Wetmore). To be watched for especially in marshes on Caribbean slope.

Habits: In Costa Rica, the call has been reported to consist of four whistled notes, the first longer, the other three given in rapid succession (D. A. Jenni). The bird seen by Wetmore was flushed from tall grass bordering an abandoned airfield.

Range: Eastern Mexico; Belize; Costa Rica; Colombia locally to Bolivia, northern Argentina, and Uruguay; Cuba and perhaps formerly Jamaica (J. Bond).

Note: By some authors included in the genus *Rallus.*

GRAY-NECKED WOOD-RAIL
(*Aramides cajanea*) Pl.1

Description: 14–16. Bare skin around eye and iris red; *rather long bill, basally yellow, terminally green; legs red. Head and rather long neck mostly gray,* browner on crown and paler on throat; back olive brown; breast and sides cinnamon-rufous; *belly, rump, and tail black* (tail usually cocked up). Juvenal duller with dusky bill and legs.

Similar species: The largest rail in Panama, relatively brightly colored and patterned.

Very local Rufous-necked Wood-Rail is smaller and has rufous head and neck.

Status and distribution: Fairly common and widespread along forested streams and rivers, in swampy wooded areas, and in mangrove swamps in lowlands on both slopes; ranges locally up into forested foothills (to about 4000 feet) in Chiriquí, Los Santos, and Darién; found also on Coiba and Cébaco Islands and the Pearl Islands. In Canal Zone more numerous on Caribbean slope.

Habits: Usually keeps to thick cover and not regularly seen; sometimes, however, feeds partially in the open though never far from concealment. Often feeds at night, but also roosts well above ground. Coastally feeds largely on crabs. Best known from its loud cackling calls, often given in a duet, a rather deliberate repeated *cok, cok,* and a hoarse cackling *co haak* or *co wéy hee* over and over. Calls most often in early morning, late afternoon, and at night. Known in Panama as "cocaleca" or "coclé" because of its calls.

Range: Central Mexico to Bolivia, northern Argentina, and Uruguay.

RUFOUS-NECKED WOOD-RAIL

(*Aramides axillaris*) Pl.1

Description: 10–11½. Very local. Bill mostly greenish, red basally; legs red. Resembles Gray-necked Wood-Rail but smaller with *head, neck, breast, and sides rufous brown to chestnut;* triangular gray area on upper back; *rump, lower belly, and under tail-coverts black;* primaries rufous. Juvenal similar but without rufous except on primaries; head, neck, and underparts grayish brown.

Similar species: See Gray-necked Wood-Rail. Uniform Crake is rather similar but smaller with shorter bill and legs, is uniform rufous brown, lacking black on lower underparts.

Status and distribution: Known only from mangrove swamps around Almirante, Bocas del Toro, and on Río Pocrí at Puerto Aguadulce, southern Coclé. Possibly occurs elsewhere in mangrove swamps but overlooked.

Habits: Little known. Probably like Gray-necked Wood-Rail. In South America found in dense forest undergrowth as well as in mangroves.

Range: Mexico and Yucatan south very locally to western Ecuador and the Guianas.

UNIFORM CRAKE

(*Amaurolimnas concolor*) Pl.1

Description: 8–8½. Rare. *Bill short,* thick, yellowish green; legs red. *Mostly dull rufous brown,* more olive brown on rear crown, hindneck, and back; *brighter rufous brown below,* paler on throat.

Similar species: Should be recognized by uniform brown color and the short bill. See Rufous-necked Wood-Rail.

Status and distribution: Apparently rare or local, at least infrequently reported. Known from western Chiriquí (Boqueron), western Bocas del Toro (where not infrequently mist-netted around Almirante), Veraguas (Chitra), Caribbean slope Canal Zone (1 seen at Achiote Road on January 4, 1975; Ridgely), San Blas, Darién, and the Pearl Islands (San José).

Habits: Apparently not primarily a marsh or swamp inhabitant, preferring damp thickets and second-growth woodland near water or marshy areas. Extremely furtive and difficult to see, skulking in dense vegetation.

Range: Southern Mexico south locally to Bolivia, Amazonian and southeastern Brazil, and Guyana; Jamaica (perhaps extinct).

SORA

(*Porzana carolina*)

Description: 8–9. A plump little rail with *stout, short, yellow bill* and greenish legs. *Black face patch and throat* (smaller in female); brownish above streaked with black and white; *sides of head and most of underparts gray,* barred with black and white on sides and flanks, lower belly white. Immature lacks black facial area and is buffier below.

Similar species: Larger than the breeding crakes of Panama. Can be known in any plumage by the yellow bill, barred sides, and lack of rufous brown in plumage.

Status and distribution: Uncommon and local winter resident (late September–early April), apparently somewhat irregular in numbers, in fresh water marshes and damp grassy and sedgy areas in lowlands; on Caribbean slope recorded from Bocas del Toro (fairly common), Veraguas, Canal Zone, and San Blas; on Pacific slope recorded from Chiriquí highlands (several heard at Volcán Lakes on February 7, 1973; C. Leahy and A. Morgan) and eastern Panama province; recorded also on Coiba Island.

Habits: Generally keeps to cover and not

easily seen, though sometimes skulks partially in the open. More easily flushed than most rails. Utters a sharp *keek* when disturbed; also gives a distinctive descending whinny.

Range: Breeds in North America; winters from southern United States to central Peru and Guyana.

YELLOW-BREASTED CRAKE (RAIL)
(*Porzana flaviventer*) Pl.1

Description: 5½. Local in marshes. *Very small.* Short, dusky bill; *legs yellow.* Crown and stripe through eye black, superciliary white; otherwise buffy brown above streaked with whitish and black; throat and belly white, *sides of neck and breast buffy;* sides, flanks, and belly barred boldly with black.

Similar species: A tiny mostly buffy crake, the smallest rail in Panama, and easily recognized.

Status and distribution: Very local, in fresh water marshes and grassy water borders. Fairly common in marshes along Chagres River between Gamboa and Juan Mina. Elsewhere known only from one collected and another seen at Playa Jobo south of Las Lajas in eastern Chiriquí on January 8, 1955; and from two sight reports: two near Changuinola, western Bocas del Toro on June 30, 1956 (Eisenmann), and one at Tocumen, eastern Panama province, on July 2, 1970 (Ridgely and J. Gwynne). Probably occurs elsewhere in suitable habitat.

Habits: On Chagres River, small numbers perch and forage in the open in the early morning, but retire to cover for most of the day (Wetmore). When flushed, the dangling yellow legs are prominent. In West Indies reported to give a high-pitched *peep* (J. Bond).

Range: Southern Mexico south locally to northern Argentina and central Brazil; Greater Antilles.

Note: Ocellated Crake (*Micropygia schomburgkii*) of tropical South America has been recently collected in southwestern Costa Rica and should be watched for in Panama. It is slightly larger (5½–6″) and mostly rufescent brown with prominent black-edged white spots on nape, back, and breast; legs red.

GRAY-BREASTED CRAKE (RAIL)
(*Laterallus exilis*) Pl.1

Description: 6. Apparently very rare. Short greenish and gray bill; legs greenish yellow or brown. *Crown, sides of head and neck, and breast gray; nape and upper back bright chestnut;* otherwise olive brown to brown above, wing-coverts sometimes narrowly barred with white; throat white; sides and belly barred black and white.

Similar species: White-throated Crake has head and breast rufous brown (not gray). See also Colombian Crake, and the Black Rail (below).

Status and distribution: Only two definite locality records: one taken on Coiba Island on January 28, 1956; and another collected at Puerto Obaldía, San Blas, on March 14, 1963. A third was purchased alive at the Panama city market early in 1961 by Mrs. Ricardo Marciaq and lived at the Summit Gardens Zoo at least into 1964; it probably had been captured somewhere in Panama.

Habits: Very difficult to observe, keeping to dense cover in marshes and wet grassy areas. The call appears to be unrecorded, though the Tocumen bird mentioned below was tape-recorded and was similar to the usual call of the Black Rail in New Jersey, except for an extra initial syllable, *dídidee-dunk* (G. Reynard).

Range: Belize south locally to eastern Peru and Amazonian Brazil.

Note: The Black Rail, or Crake (*L. jamaicensis*), was reported flushed and a domed nest with 3 eggs collected in a damp grassy field northest of Tocumen along the road to Chepo on July 6, 1963 (S. T. Harty *et al.*). The report likely pertains to the Gray-breasted Crake, though the Black Rail is not inconceivable (it has not, however, been definitely recorded in Middle America south of Belize). It resembles Gray-breasted Crake but is darker overall with black (not greenish) bill and white dots on mid-back.

WHITE-THROATED CRAKE (RAIL)
(*Laterallus albigularis*) Pl.1

Description: 6. Short blackish bill; legs brown. *Mostly warm brown,* brighter chestnut on hindneck; throat white; *sides of throat, breast, and upper belly bright rufous* (center of breast and belly sometimes white); belly barred black and white. Bocas del Toro and western Caribbean Veraguas birds (*cinereiceps*) have crown and sides of head gray, in contrast to chestnut of nape. Juvenal is dark dull brown above, feathers tipped with lighter on head; cheeks, sides of neck, and breast gray, throat white; belly dark brown with very narrow whitish bars.

Similar species Uniform Crake is larger, with

red legs, lacks black and white barring on belly. Gray-breasted Crake has head and breast gray (no rufous below).

Status and distribution: Common and widespread, though infrequently seen, in marshes and damp grassy places in more humid lowlands on both slopes, in Chiriquí ranging up to about 4000 feet, in Coclé up to El Valle (2000 feet); not recorded from Azuero Peninsula or lowlands of Pacific Coclé and western Panama province; found also on Coiba Island. In Canal Zone much more numerous on Caribbean slope.

Habits: The most numerous rail in Panama. The call is very distinctive, and will be heard many times for each time the bird is seen, a long rattling churring, *chirrrrrrrrr*. Birds often call within a few meters of the observer and yet remain invisible.

Range: Honduras to western Ecuador.

Note: By some authors considered conspecific with *L. melanophaius* (Rufous-sided Crake) of South America east of the Andes.

COLOMBIAN CRAKE
(*Neocrex columbianus*) Pl.1

Description: 7½–8. Very rare. Bill dull yellowish with some orange at base; *legs red. Mostly slaty gray,* more brownish olive on back, wings, and tail; throat white, lower belly and under tail-coverts buffy whitish.

Similar species: The only largely gray Panama crake without barring below; see Sora.

Status and distribution: Only one record, a bird collected by G. Van Horn in a small marshy area on Achiote Road (just beyond Canal Zone border in western Colon province) on November 8, 1965 (described as the race *ripleyi* by Wetmore, 1967). The same race has been taken just east of San Blas border at Acandí, Colombia, so should be watched for in San Blas.

Range: Central Panama to northern and western Colombia and western Ecuador.

Note: By some authors considered a race of *N. erythrops* (Paint-billed Crake) of South America east of the Andes.

COMMON GALLINULE
(*Gallinula chloropus*)

Description: 13–14. A chunky somewhat duck-like (swimming) or chicken-like (perched) bird with *stout red bill* (with yellow tip) *and frontal shield;* legs greenish. Mostly slaty gray, browner on back and wings, with *white stripe on sides and flanks* and white on under tail-coverts. Immature is paler, more olive or brownish gray, with whitish sides of head and throat, gray underparts with white streaks on flanks and belly; bill brown.

Similar species: Purple Gallinule is deep violet-blue (not slaty gray) on head and underparts and lacks white flank stripe; immature Purple is brown above (not olive or grayish) and whitish on breast and belly (not grayish). American Coot has white bill and lacks the flank stripe.

Status and distribution: Rather local on fresh water lakes, ponds, and marshes in lowlands on both slopes (numbers may increase as a result of migration from the north). Recorded from western Bocas del Toro (breeding), western Chiriquí (one seen on Volcán Lakes on March 6, 1954; Wetmore), Herrera (one seen on Río Santa María east of Divisa on September 22, 1958; Eisenmann), Canal Zone (breeding commonly on both slopes), eastern Colon province (one seen at Río Piedras on March 3, 1968; Eisenmann and Ridgely), and eastern Panama province (one seen at La Jagua on March 4, 1968; Eisenmann, Ridgely, N. G. Smith). Fairly common on the Chagres River and parts of Gatun Lake and in the Miraflores Lake/Pedro Miguel area.

Habits: Usually seen swimming (unlike Purple Gallinule), with head nodding back and forth. Flies relatively little. Has a variety of clucks and cackles.

Range: Nearly cosmopolitan except for Australia; in America from extreme southern Canada to northern Chile and northern Argentina.

PURPLE GALLINULE
(*Porphyrula martinica*)

Description: 13–14. *Brilliantly colored.* Bill rather stout, red, tipped yellow; *frontal shield pale blue;* legs yellow. *Head, neck, and entire underparts deep purple to violet-blue;* back and wings bronzy green; under tail-coverts white. Immature *brown above,* bluer on wings; mostly whitish below; bill dusky.

Similar species: Beautiful adults are unmistakable; immature might be confused with immature Common Gallinule but is not as grayish. Immature jacanas, though also basically brown above and whitish below, are very differently shaped, have extremely long toes, and show much yellow on wings in flight.

Status and distribution: Fairly common in fresh water marshes and along edges of small ponds, larger lakes, and slow-flowing rivers (the requirement being abundant marshy vegetation) in lowlands on both slopes, including entire Pacific slope (recorded Chiriquí, Santa María marshes of Herrera, and Canal Zone east); recently (1971 on) found also at Volcán Lakes in lower highlands of western Chiriquí, apparently breeding (juvenals seen January 1974; Ridgely, C. Leahy). Much more widespread than Common Gallinule though not as numerous as that species in most of Canal Zone.

Habits: Less apt to be seen swimming than Common Gallinule; more often seen walking on floating vegetation, along shores, even perching and climbing about in bushes and emergent vegetation.

Range: Southeastern United States and Mexico to northern Argentina (recorded once in Uruguay and northern Chile); West Indies.

AMERICAN COOT
(*Fulica americana*)

Description: 13–14. *Stout, white bill* with dark ring near tip; inconspicuous reddish brown frontal shield. *Entirely slaty gray* (blacker on head and neck) except for white under tail-coverts and white tips to secondaries (visible in flight). Immature is paler, more olive gray, with whitish on throat; bill whitish.

Similar species: Rather duck-like but note bill shape, small head and short neck pumped back and forth when swimming. Adult gallinules have red bills; immature Common Gallinule is browner than immature Coot and has dark bill and at least a suggestion of a white flank stripe.

Status and distribution: Locally common winter resident (October–late April) on lakes, ponds, and larger sluggish rivers in lowlands on both slopes in western and central Panama; most numerous in Bocas del Toro; recorded east to eastern Panama province (La Jagua); ranges regularly to Volcán Lakes in lower highlands of western Chiriquí. In Canal Zone some usually winter in the Miraflores Lake/Pedro Miguel area and on Chagres River above Gamboa, smaller numbers on Gatun Lake. Not known to breed in Panama.

Habits: Usually seen swimming in open water, frequently in flocks. Dives for its food. Has various cackling notes.

Range: Breeds from North America to Nicaragua and from Colombia to central Chile and northwestern Argentina; northern birds winter at least to Panama and in West Indies.

FINFOOTS: Heliornithidae (1)

The finfoots are a small family of tropical aquatic birds, one species being found in the Americas, one in Africa, and one in southern Asia. They are shy and usually not easily observed, and are not very well known. They feed on a variety of aquatic animal life. The nest is a platform of twigs placed in a bush or low tree overhanging the water.

SUNGREBE (AMERICAN FINFOOT)
(*Heliornis fulica*) Pl.1

Description: 11–12. Slender reddish bill; black-and-yellow banded webbed feet. Small head and slender neck. *Crown and hindneck black with white superciliary, a black stripe on cheeks and down sides of neck, and another white stripe down neck;* otherwise olive brown above; white below; rather wide tail black narrowly tipped white. Female has buffy cheeks.

Similar species: More slender than a grebe or duck; black and white striped head and neck is characteristic. Sunbittern is mostly brown with white striping only on face, does not swim or dive.

Status and distribution: Uncommon and local in lowlands on fresh water ponds, lakes, and quiet streams and rivers with abundant bordering vegetation; recorded only from western Bocas del Toro, Chagres River valley, eastern Panama province (La Jagua), and Darién (Tuira River). Best known from Gatun Lake and the Chagres; can be found regularly in esteros on Gigante Bay on southwestern shore of Barro Colorado Island and on middle Chagres above Gamboa.

Habits: Essentially aquatic; usually seen swimming, but not far from protective shoreline vegetation. Perches on branches hanging low over the water. Dives freely. Sometimes swims, like a grebe, with body submerged and only head and neck above

water. When disturbed, flies and patters rapidly along the surface of the water. Reported to give a peculiar "bark" of one, two, or three notes (L. Jewel); in Mexico the call has been described as a *eeoó, eeoó, eeoó-eeyéh, eeyéh* (M. Alvarez del Toro).
Range: Southern Mexico to northern Bolivia, northeastern Argentina and southern Brazil.

SUNBITTERNS: Eurypygidae (1)

The Sunbittern is an interesting and beautifully marked bird found along forested streams in the New World tropics. Superficially resembling a heron (but with different proportions and shorter legs), it also looks something like a large sandpiper. It is terrestrial, sedately walking and wading along streams and rivers, feeding on aquatic animal life. The nest, however, is placed on a branch of a tree some ten to twenty feet above the ground.

SUNBITTERN
(*Eurypyga helias*) Pl.1

Description: 17–18. *Bill long and straight,* upper mandible black tipped orange-yellow, lower mandible orange; *short orange legs.* Head notably small, neck long and slender; *long fan-shaped tail.* Head black with narrow white stripe over eye and another across cheeks; *neck and upperparts dull chestnut vermiculated and barred with black,* wing-coverts spotted with white; tail broadly banded chestnut and black and with black vermiculations; throat white, most of remaining underparts buff narrowly barred with black, becoming whitish on belly; *wings with bright orange-rufous patches,* conspicuous in flight and in display.

Similar species: Not likely to be confused. Sungrebe (a swimming, diving bird) has black and white striped neck and white underparts.

Status and distribution: Rare to locally uncommon along forested streams in lowlands and foothills (to about 3000 feet) on both slopes (recent records mostly from Caribbean slope and Darién); unreported from dry Pacific lowlands from eastern side of Azuero Peninsula (but recorded from Cerro Hoya in Los Santos) to western Panama province. Rare in Canal Zone where recorded in recent years only from Pipeline Road (Ridgely, J. Karr, N. Gale *et al.*).

Habits: Usually seen walking deliberately on the ground along or near a stream; sometimes alights on low tree branches, especially when disturbed. Very unsuspicious and tames easily. Has a beautiful display with lowered neck, spread wings, and raised and fanned tail, thus exposing the subtle plumage details and the "sunbursts" on the wings. Utters a low hissing sound like a tire going flat when disturbed (Ridgely, J. Karr); also has an alarm call *ka, ka, ka . . . ,* repeated 6 or 8 times; and a sweet and high but very penetrating double note (heard often in captivity).

Range: Southern Mexico to northern Bolivia and central Brazil.

JACANAS: Jacanidae (2)

Jacanas are found in marshes in tropical and subtropical regions throughout the world. They are conspicuous noisy birds, best known for their extremely elongated toes, which enable them to walk with ease upon lily pads and other floating vegetation. Most species have a sharp spur on the carpal joint of the wing, the exact function of which is uncertain. They feed on a variety of animal and vegetative life. The nest is usually located on floating vegetation. The American species, at least, appear to be polyandrous, the female having two or more mates, each of which incubates a separate clutch of eggs.

NORTHERN (MIDDLE AMERICAN) JACANA
(*Jacana spinosa*) Pl.1

Description: 9. Found only in western Panama. Bill yellow with *three-lobed yellow frontal shield;* long grayish legs and *extremely long toes.* Head, neck, and chest black; *otherwise rich chestnut; pale greenish yellow flight feathers very conspicuous in flight.* Immature very different with buffy white stripe above eye and dusky stripe behind eye; otherwise grayish brown above; sides of head and entire underparts whitish; yellow flight feathers as in adult; bill brownish with *rudimentary frontal shield yellowish green.*

Similar species: Adult Wattled Jacana (in Panama) is usually mostly black, with two-lobed frontal shield and short wattles on sides of bill dull purplish red. Immatures of the two are very similar but Wattled is blacker on crown and has rudimentary pinkish or blue frontal shield and wattles.

Status and distribution: Common in fresh water marshes and on slow flowing rivers and streams with abundant floating vegetation in lowlands of western Bocas del Toro and lowlands of Chiriquí and extreme western Pacific Veraguas, ranging up to Volcán Lakes in lower highlands of western Chiriquí. Readily seen in marshes and ponds along Pan-American Highway in Chiriquí. Eastern limit of range on Caribbean slope unknown.

Habits: Similar to Wattled Jacana.

Range: Southern Texas and Mexico to western Panama; West Indies.

Note: Some authors prefer to recognize only one species of jacana in America, *J. spinosa* (American Jacana). The two forms occur together in extreme western Veraguas and possibly in eastern Chiriquí, with some hybridizing (Eisenmann).

WATTLED JACANA
(*Jacana jacana*) Pl.1

Description: 9. Resembles the preceding species. Bill yellow with *two-lobed frontal shield and short wattles on sides of bill dull red to purplish red* (sometimes lavender); long grayish legs and *extremely long toes. Mostly black* (a few birds with maroon-chestnut on wing-coverts, sometimes also on back and even rump, then resembling Northern Jacana); *pale greenish yellow flight feathers very conspicuous in flight.* Immature very different, sooty brown above, *more blackish on crown* with buffy whitish stripe over eye and black stripe behind eye; sides of head and entire underparts whitish; yellow flight feathers as in adult; bill brownish with *rudimentary pinkish or lilac frontal shield and wattles.*

Similar species: Easily recognized as a jacana; in western Panama see Northern Jacana.

Status and distribution: Common in fresh water marshes and along shores of lakes, ponds, and rivers with abundant emergent vegetation in lowlands on Caribbean slope from at least northern Coclé east through San Blas; on Pacific slope from western Veraguas (possibly eastern Chiriquí) east through Darién; once recorded from Coiba Island. Recorded with Northern Jacana on ponds near Remedios, eastern Chiriquí by Griscom in 1920's, but only Northern Jacanas seen there recently. Common and conspicuous in suitable habitat throughout Canal Zone, particularly on Chagres River and Gatun Lake.

Habits: Usually seen walking on floating vegetation, using their extremely long toes to advantage. Sometimes also feeds in adjacent grassy areas. Rather noisy, with various chatters and clacking calls.

Range: Western Panama to Bolivia, northern Argentina, and Uruguay (casually central Chile).

Note: Sometimes treated as conspecific with *J. spinosa* (Northern Jacana).

OYSTERCATCHERS: Haematopodidae (1)

Various species of oystercatchers (the exact number is still disputed) inhabit coastlines virtually throughout the world. They are characterized by their stout, laterally compressed bills, used to pry open oysters and other shellfish. The nest is a slight hollow in the ground or beach, sometimes lined with grasses or bits of seaweed.

AMERICAN OYSTERCATCHER
(*Haematopus palliatus*)

Description: 17–19. A *large* shorebird, with *stout, bright red bill,* fairly short pink legs, and rather prominent yellow iris. *Head, neck, and chest black;* remaining upperparts dark brown; *lower underparts white.* In flight shows *very prominent white wing-stripe.*

Status and distribution: Fairly common resident on rocky coasts of Pearl Islands; rare and very local on Pacific coast (perhaps formerly more numerous), breeding in Los Santos, reported from "Veragua," Pacific entrance to Canal (once), Panama Viejo (in 1920's, not since), extreme eastern Panama province (Río Majé), and Coiba and Taboga Islands. One bird seen repeatedly and photographed at Coco Solo, C.Z. September 27–October 5, 1973 (J. Pujals *et al.*) is of uncertain origin (could have been a northern migrant).

Habits: Usually in pairs; wary. Extremely noisy, the birds often calling in the middle of the night, a shrill piercing *kleeep!*, repeated over and over. Favors areas where oyster beds are exposed at low tide.

Range: Locally on coasts of United States, Middle America, and South America; also in West Indies and Galapagos Islands.

Note: By some authors considered conspecific with *H. ostralegus* (Common Oystercatcher) of the Old World.

PLOVERS: Charadriidae (8)

The plovers are a generally distributed group of shorebirds, many favoring coastlines and fresh water borders but with other species inhabiting fields, open plains, and marshes. Most species differ from typical sandpipers in their shorter and heavier bills and chunkier proportions. Many species are highly migratory and most are gregarious. They eat a wide variety of animal matter. Most of the species recorded from Panama breed only in North America (mostly in arctic regions), occurring in Panama as transients and winter residents; some individuals of these northern breeding species also pass the summer months in Panama, without breeding (most are apparently first year birds). Two species do breed locally (Collared and Thick-billed), the nest being a slight depression in the ground or beach, usually with no lining.

SOUTHERN LAPWING
(*Vanellus chilensis*)

Description: 13–14. Known only from savannas of east. *Long pointed crest.* Mostly brownish gray above; *forehead, throat patch, and breast black;* belly white. In flight shows *broad rounded wings* with prominent white band, black tail with white terminal band and rump.

Status and distribution: Uncertain. Rare and irregular in savannas and fresh water marshes in eastern Panama province around La Jagua and Chepo; one record from Puerto Obaldía, San Blas, and one from El Real, Darién. Perhaps only a wanderer from South America, though breeding is possible ("pairs" have been seen).

Habits: This boldly patterned species is quite conspicuous, favoring open short grassy areas. Flies with slow floppy wing-beats. The usual call is a loud *kehhoo, kehhoo.*

Range: Central Panama to Tierra del Fuego.

Note: Sometimes placed in the genus *Belanopterus.*

SOUTHERN LAPWING

BLACK-BELLIED (GRAY) PLOVER
(*Pluvialis squatarola*)

Description: 10–12. Fairly large and chunky; short, stout bill. Nonbreeding plumage: *light grayish above* (sometimes more brownish), *white below,* somewhat mottled with dusky on breast. Breeding plumage: upperparts mottled black and white (looking pale gray at a distance); white forehead extending as stripe around sides of head to sides of breast; *black below and on face,* under tail-coverts white. In flight shows *white rump and largely white tail,* white wing-stripe, and *black axillars* under the wing.

Similar species: See the much less common American Golden Plover, and also nonbreeding Knot.

Status and distribution: Common transient and winter resident on both slopes; uncommon in summer.

Habits: Occurs on beaches, flats, and grassy areas, though most numerous on large expanses of mudflats such as at Panama Viejo. Usually scattered, not in compact flocks, and wary, not allowing a close approach. Its distinctive call, a plaintive slurred whistle, *whee-er-eee,* is often heard.

Range: Breeds in high arctic; winters in southern United States, Middle and South America, southern Europe and Africa, southern Asia, Australia, and islands in South Pacific.

Note: Sometimes separated in the genus *Squatarola.*

AMERICAN (LESSER) GOLDEN PLOVER
(*Pluvialis dominica*)

Description: 9–11. Stocky; short, stout bill. Nonbreeding plumage: *brown above,* speckled with yellow and with dusky cap; brownish white below, more or less mottled with brownish. Breeding plumage: *brown above spangled with golden yellow;* narrow white stripe extending from forehead around cheeks to sides of breast; *black below and on face.* In flight note *absence of pattern above* (dark rump, no wing-stripe) and pale grayish axillars.

Similar species: Black-bellied Plover in any plumage is larger, grayer above, and in flight shows conspicuous white rump and black axillars. At rest the two can look similar (there is overlap in size and coloration) so the best policy is to flush the bird when possible.

Status and distribution: Much less numerous than Black-bellied Plover; recorded primarily as rare to uncommon transient on both slopes, a few individuals straggling in winter and summer. All reports are from Canal Zone and adjacent areas.

Habits: Prefers grassy fields to mudflats. Usually less shy than Black-bellied Plover, with which it often occurs.

Range: Breeds in arctic North America and northern Siberia; winters mostly in southern South America.

SEMIPALMATED PLOVER
(*Charadrius semipalmatus*)

Description: 6½–7½. Small and chunky. *Short yellow bill* with black tip; *yellowish legs.* Brown above; forehead, *collar around hindneck,* and underparts white; breast crossed by narrow black band. Immature duller, with black bill and brownish breast band.

Similar species: See Collared Plover. Thick-billed Plover has stouter all black bill and pinkish (not yellowish) legs.

Status and distribution: Very common transient and common winter resident; fairly common in summer.

Habits: Largely coastal (especially Pacific), on beaches and mudflats, gathering in huge flocks at Panama Viejo in September and April. The distinctive call is a musical two-noted *toor-lee.*

Range: Breeds in northern North America; winters from southern United States south coastally through most of South America.

Note: By some authors considered conspecific with *C. hiaticula* (Ringed Plover) of Old World.

SNOWY PLOVER
(*Charadrius alexandrinus*)

Description: 6. Accidental. *Slender black bill* and *slaty gray legs. Very pale sandy gray above,* with black forecrown and ear-coverts; forehead, sides of head, and underparts white; sides of breast black (forming an incomplete collar). Immature lacks the black and shows a mere trace of the collar.

Similar species: Much paler above than any of the other small plovers; most like Collared Plover but with dark gray (not pale) legs. See also the equally pale nonbreeding Sanderling.

Status and distribution: Only one record, a bird collected at Cocoplum, Bocas del Toro on October 30, 1927, by R. R. Benson (specimen AMNH).

Habits: In its normal range found primarily on sand flats, beaches, alkaline ponds, etc.

Range: Breeds locally in southern and western United States, Mexico, the West Indies, and coastal Peru and Chile; also in Europe, North Africa, and Asia; North American birds winter to Honduras, accidentally to Costa Rica (sighting—*fide* G. Stiles) and Panama.

COLLARED PLOVER
(*Charadrius collaris*)

Description: 5½–6. A small plover, reminiscent of the Semipalmated. *Bill slender and all black;* legs yellowish to pinkish. Grayish brown above with fairly large patch of white on forehead; *crown and nape tinged cinnamon, sometimes forming a cinnamon-rufous band around hindneck;* white below, breast crossed by black band. Immature duller with less cinnamon on head.

Similar species: Resembles the more numerous migrant Semipalmated Plover. Collared is a smaller, more dapper bird; it has a

COLLARED PLOVER

narrower, longer, all black bill, lacks the white collar of the Semipalmated, and has a larger white patch on forehead and rufous on head. Thick-billed Plover is larger with white superciliary and heavy bill. See also very rare Snowy Plover.

Status and distribution: Fairly common locally after breeding season on sandy and gravelly beaches and on short grass areas in central Panama from July (rarely June) to early March. At other seasons, disperses, apparently to breeding areas on sand and gravel banks in streams and rivers, but actual breeding evidence lacking from Panama. During nonbreeding season readily found on the grass at Coco Solo and Gatun Dam, and at Fort Amador.

Habits: Always less numerous than the migrant plovers. Curiously little is known about their breeding, though birds collected and others seen on rivers in Bocas del Toro were thought to be nesting.

Range: Western and southern Mexico to Chile and central Argentina.

KILLDEER
(*Charadrius vociferus*)

Description: 9–11. Fairly long black tail. Bill black; legs flesh. Brown above with *buffy-orange rump;* forehead, eyestripe, collar on hindneck, and underparts white; *breast crossed by two black bands.*

Similar species: Larger than the other "ringed" plovers, and easily recognized by its *two* breast bands.

Status and distribution: Uncommon to fairly common transient and winter resident throughout, mostly late October–late March, occasionally to mid-April.

Habits: Favors savannas, short grass areas, golf courses and the like, often far from water. Generally found as scattered individuals or small groups, not in large flocks. The call is a loud insistent *kil-deé* or *kil-deéah,* often repeated.

Range: Breeds in North America and West Indies, also in coastal Peru; northern birds winter south to Ecuador and Venezuela.

THICK-BILLED (WILSON'S) PLOVER
(*Charadrius wilsonia*)

Description: 7–8. *Rather long heavy black bill; legs dull pinkish.* Brown above, sometimes tinged with cinnamon on back of head and ear-coverts; forehead, broad eyestripe, narrow collar on hindneck, and underparts white; *breast crossed by single broad black band.* Female has brownish breast band.

Similar species: Immature Semipalmated Plover also has all black bill but it is shorter and slimmer than Thick-bill's and it has yellowish (not dull flesh) legs. See also Collared Plover.

Status and distribution: Fairly common locally as transient and winter resident coastally; breeds locally in small numbers along Pacific coast. Particularly numerous (flocks of well over a hundred) in Canal Zone at Farfan Beach and Fort Amador; breeds at the latter locality (and probably the former as well) and is also known to breed at Playa Coronado and on Aguadulce salt flats in Coclé. Resident birds are greatly augmented by northern migrants. Less numerous on Caribbean coast, and not yet known to breed there.

Habits: Prefers sandy or pebbly beaches, not mudflats. The call is an emphatic whistled *whit* or *wheep* (R. T. Peterson).

Range: Coastal southeastern United States, Middle America, northern South America to Guyana, western South America to Peru, and in West Indies; winters to Brazil.

SNIPES, SANDPIPERS, AND ALLIES: Scolopacidae (27)

The vast majority of the members of this family breeds in the Northern Hemisphere, mostly at high latitudes, and none nests in Panama. Most species are highly migratory, however, and thus a good variety occurs in Panama as non-breeders. As with the plovers, first-year immatures of a number of species summer over. Most individuals seen in Panama are in confusing nonbreeding plumage (though some older birds on spring passage have attained full breeding dress), and thus are sometimes difficult to identify. It must be kept in mind that many species are rather particular in their habitat requirements, and thus may occur only locally. Almost all species are found exclusively in the lowlands, largely on or near either coast. A number have been recorded primarily (or only) from central Panama, this due in part to the greater number of observers in the Canal Zone and vicinity than elsewhere, in part to the accessibility of coastal areas, and in part to the abundance of short grass fields in the Canal Zone, a favored habitat of many shorebirds during fall migration.

SOLITARY SANDPIPER
(*Tringa solitaria*)

Description: 8–8½. Long slender black bill; *dark greenish legs. Dark olive brown above* with fine whitish streaks and small spots and a *white eye-ring;* white below, lightly streaked with dusky on chest. In flight shows *dark rump, white sides of tail with blackish bars, and no wing-stripe.*

Similar species: Spotted Sandpiper teeters more (nods less), flies with stiff wing-beats showing white stripe lacking in Solitary. Lesser Yellowlegs has yellow (not dark) legs, white rump in flight.

Status and distribution: Fairly common transient and less numerous winter resident (late August–early April, rarely in late July and to mid-April) throughout, ranging up to Volcán Lakes in lower highlands of western Chiriquí.

Habits: As the name implies, usually found alone, at most in small scattered groups. Occurs mostly around fresh water, margins of ponds, sluggish streams. Flies with deep wing-strokes, almost swallow-like; when flushed often calls *peet* or *peet-weet,* similar to but sharper than Spotted Sandpiper's call.

Range: Breeds in Alaska and Canada; winters from southern Mexico to Peru and central Argentina.

LESSER YELLOWLEGS
(*Tringa flavipes*)

Description: 10–11. Slender straight bill; *legs yellow.* Grayish brown above, spotted and barred with white; white below, streaked with dusky on sides of neck and chest. In flight, shows dark wings and whitish rump and tail.

Similar species: Very like Greater Yellowlegs; see comparison under that species. Solitary Sandpiper is darker above with white eye-ring, dark rump, and dark greenish legs. Nonbreeding Stilt Sandpiper resembles a yellowlegs in flight but is smaller than even a Lesser, with prominent white eyestripe and greenish legs. Nonbreeding Wilson's Phalarope is also similar, but it too is smaller and is strikingly white below, with greenish legs and thin needle-like bill.

Status and distribution: Fairly common transient (locally common in fall) and uncommon winter resident; a few may summer but mostly late August to late April.

Habits: Prefers fresh water and wet grassy areas. Not as shy as Greater Yellowlegs. Often feeds very actively.

Range: Breeds in Alaska and Canada; winters from southern United States to Straits of Magellan.

GREATER YELLOWLEGS
(*Tringa melanoleuca*)

Description: 12–14. Identical to Lesser Yellowlegs in plumage. Somewhat larger (useful chiefly when the two species are together); bill somewhat heavier and slightly upcurved (latter not always apparent).

Similar species: The very similar Lesser Yellowlegs has a slender straight bill, is somewhat smaller (though largest Lessers are virtually the size of the smallest Greaters), and has a different call (often the best point): Greater's is a loud ringing three- or four-noted whistle *tew-tew-tew;* Lesser's is a softer whistle, characteristically one or two-noted *yew* or *wheep-wheep* (R. T. Peterson).

Status and distribution: Common transient (especially in fall) and uncommon winter resident; a few summer but mostly early August to early May.

Habits: Favors coastal mudflats and in largest numbers at Panama Viejo, but quite widespread, occurring even at Volcán Lakes in lower highlands of western Chiriquí.

Range: Breeds in Alaska and Canada; winters from southern United States to Straits of Magellan.

SPOTTED SANDPIPER
(*Actitis macularia*)

Description: 7–8. Bill flesh, tipped black; legs flesh. Nonbreeding plumage: olive brown above with white eyestripe; white below, with *brownish smudge on sides of chest.*

Breeding plumage: similar, but somewhat barred with blackish above, *distinctly spotted with black below* (female usually with more spots). In any plumage easily recognized by *almost constant teetering*. In flight shows whitish wing-stripe, *stiff wing-beats*.

Similar species: Solitary Sandpiper is darker above, bobs its head more than it teeters its rear end, and has dark wing and dark rump with white on sides of tail.

Status and distribution: Very common transient and winter resident (mostly early August–mid-May, rarely in late July and to late May) throughout, occurring wherever there is water. Apparently does not over-summer.

Habits: Found scattered individually, not in flocks. Usually stands with body tilted forward, head low, bobbing tail up and down. When flushed, flies low over the water with short stiff wing-strokes below the horizontal, often calling a shrill *peet-weet*.

Range: Breeds in North America; winters from southern United States to southern South America.

WANDERING TATTLER
(*Heteroscelus incanus*)

Description: 10–10½. Casual. Bill black; *rather short yellow legs*. Nonbreeding plumage: dark gray above with whitish eyestripe; white below tinged grayish on neck and breast. Breeding plumage: similar but with white *underparts barred with black*. In flight shows *dark wings, rump, and tail*.

Similar species: Sometimes bobs like a Spotted Sandpiper, but latter is much smaller, browner above (not so gray), and shows white wing-stripe in flight.

Status and distribution: Only two reports: one bird collected on Valladolid Rock in Panama Bay between Chame and Otoque Islands (not far from Taboga) on March 3, 1969, by H. Loftin and R. Crossin (Smithsonian Pacific seabird project); and another almost certainly this species in nonbreeding plumage seen at Fort Kobbe, Canal Zone, on April 22, 1973 (S. West).

Habits: Favors rocky shorelines and pebbly beaches. Usually tame and rather noisy. Associates with other rock-inhabiting shorebirds such as turnstones and Surfbirds.

Range: Breeds locally in mountains of Alaska and northwestern Canada; winters mostly on islands in South Pacific, but also locally on rocky Pacific coasts and islands from California to Peru, and on the Galapagos Islands.

WILLET
(*Catoptrophorus semipalmatus*)

Description: 14–16. Fairly heavy long blackish bill; *bluish gray legs*. Nonbreeding plumage: *pale gray above*, whitish below. Breeding plumage: more grayish brown above, barred with dusky; white below spotted and barred with dusky. In any plumage shows unmistakable *very bold white wing-stripe* in flight.

Similar species: Rather nondescript at rest but cannot be confused in flight. Greater Yellowlegs always has yellow (not gray) legs, lacks nonbreeding Willet's contrast between gray upperparts and white underparts.

Status and distribution: Very common transient and winter resident on both coasts though more numerous on Pacific; common also in summer.

Habits: This species and the Whimbrel are easily the two commonest large shorebirds in Panama. Both often roost in mangroves at high tide, up to fifteen or twenty feet above the ground or water. Usually occurs in compact flocks but scatters out to feed. The calls are loud and shrill, a repeated *kip-kip-kip*, also *klee-wee-wee*.

Range: Breeds in North America and in West Indies; winters from southern United States south coastally to northeastern Brazil and Peru, occasionally to northern Chile and southeastern Brazil.

RUDDY TURNSTONE
(*Arenaria interpres*)

Description: 8–9. Bill black, very slightly upturned; *short orange legs*. Nonbreeding plumage: head, upperparts, and chest brownish; remaining underparts white. Breeding plumage: much brighter, with *rusty red back and wings*, white head, *chest and stripes on sides of head black*, lower underparts white. In flight in any plumage shows *striking wing and tail pattern* of black, brown, and white.

Similar species: Its pied pattern, though difficult to describe, renders it unmistakable, particularly in breeding dress. See Surfbird.

Status and distribution: Common transient and winter resident along both coasts, more numerous on Pacific; rather uncommon but regular in summer.

Habits: Though characteristically a bird of

pebbly beaches and rocky shores, in Panama it also occurs regularly in other habitats such as the mudflats at Panama Viejo and even on grassy fields near the coast such as those at Coco Solo. Generally not found any distance inland.

Range: Breeds in Arctic; winters from southern United States south coastally to southern South America and in West Indies, in Old World to southern Africa, Asia, Australia, and New Zealand, also on islands in South Pacific.

Note: The species is by some placed in the Charadriidae.

SURFBIRD
(*Aphriza virgata*)

Description: 9–10. Bill rather short, yellowish tipped black; legs yellowish or greenish. Nonbreeding plumage: *almost entirely dark brownish gray* with whitish superciliary, throat, and belly (latter streaked or spotted with dusky). Breeding plumage: blackish above streaked with gray and brownish; *white below scallopped with blackish.* In flight in any plumage shows white wing-stripe, *white rump and tail with black triangle at tip.*

Similar species: Ruddy Turnstone (with which this species often occurs) in nonbreeding plumage is brown above and on chest, and has bright orange legs. See also very rare Wandering Tattler.

Status and distribution: Fairly common but localized on rocks along Panama Bay at or near Panama City, particularly at Panama Viejo and San Francisco de la Caleta; present throughout the year but in greatest numbers on migration; recorded also at Playa Coronado, western Panama province, and Piñas Bay, Darién. To be watched for elsewhere on Pacific coast. Oddly, it has not yet been reported from the Canal Zone proper.

Habits: Usually feeds on rocks, but sometimes spreads out onto adjacent mudflats.

Range: Breeds in Alaskan mountains; winters on Pacific coast from western North America south very locally to Tierra del Fuego.

Note: The species is by some placed in the Charadriidae.

RED KNOT
(*Calidris canutus*)

Description: 10–11. Rather short black bill; greenish legs. *Chunky shape,* somewhat reminiscent of a plover. Nonbreeding plumage: *gray above,* lightly barred with dusky, with whitish rump and tail; white below, sometimes spotted with dusky on breast. Breeding plumage: grayish brown above, streaked and barred with black and buffy; *cinnamon-rufous below,* fading to white on lower belly. In flight shows pale wing-stripe, whitish rump.

Similar species: In breeding plumage likely to be confused only with the dowitchers, which have longer bills and white rump extending narrowly up back. Nonbreeding Knots are more nondescript and are often confusing, but note stocky shape, overall gray appearance, short bill, and in flight less contrasty whitish rump.

Status and distrbiution: Rather rare transient, in spring apparently mostly on mudflats and beaches (e.g. Panama Viejo), in fall also on damp grassy fields near coast (e.g. Coco Solo); recorded mostly September–October and March–May, but small numbers may winter at least occasionally (e.g. 6 on Panama city waterfront near Paitilla Point on January 8, 1974; Ridgely and C. Leahy), and 5 were on the salinas at Aguadulce, Coclé on June 26, 1971 (Eisenmann and J. Pujals). Reported mostly from Canal Zone and vicinity.

Habits: One of the less numerous shorebirds in Panama. Often associates with Black-bellied Plover, both on flats and fields.

Range: Breeds in high arctic; winters in small numbers and locally on coasts of southern United States and Middle America, but mostly on coasts of southern South America; in Old World winters to Africa, southern Asia, Australia, and New Zealand.

LEAST SANDPIPER
(*Calidris minutilla*)

Description: 5¾–6¼. *Bill short and slender; legs yellowish or greenish. Dark brown above* margined with rufous; whitish below streaked with brownish on chest and breast. Somewhat grayer in nonbreeding plumage but still looks rather brown. In flight shows faint white wing-stripe, dark center to white rump.

Similar species: Generally looks browner than Western or Semipalmated Sandpipers but check diagnostic leg color (not blackish) and slighter bill. Pectoral Sandpiper has similar coloration but is much larger.

Status and distribution: Very common transient (mostly September–October and March–April) and common winter resident along both coasts and locally in lowlands;

recorded early August to mid-May; no evidence of any over-summering birds.

Habits: Widespread but usually much outnumbered by Western Sandpipers on shores and mudflats; the commonest small "peep" on grassy and marshy fields and vegetated borders. The call is a high *kree-eep.*

Range: Breeds in northern North America; winters from southern United States to northern Chile and central Brazil and in West Indies.

Note: Sometimes placed in the genus *Erolia.*

BAIRD'S SANDPIPER
(*Calidris bairdii*)

Description: 7. Bill rather short; *legs dark. Rather buffy brown above, the feathers edged with paler usually giving a scaly appearance* (especially in immatures); *breast buffy* (especially in fall) with a few fine dusky streaks, underparts otherwise white. At rest wing-tips extend slightly beyond tip of tail (in other "peep" wing-tips barely reach tip of tail). In flight shows faint wing-stripe, dark center to white rump.

Similar species: Must always be identified with care, but fortunately it can often be observed closely in Panama. In size and shape most like White-rumped Sandpiper but that species can always be known by its white rump (no dark center); in nonbreeding plumage White-rump is mostly gray, not the brown and buffy of the Baird's (breeding White-rumps are rustier, however). Sanderling in full breeding plumage (very infrequently seen in Panama) is orange-buffy about head and chest and hence looks somewhat like a Baird's, but can always be known by its heavier bill and bold white wing-stripe; it favors sandy beaches and not grassy fields. Pectoral Sandpiper often occurs with Baird's, but is a little larger and longer-necked, striped (not scaly) above, with yellow (not dark) legs. See also the smaller "peeps."

Status and distribution: Uncommon and very local on damp grassy fields during fall migration (September–October); rare on spring migration (several sightings in April and early May 1966; N. G. Smith). Reported only from Canal Zone except for one sighting from a wet meadow at Panama Viejo. Most numerous on grassy expanses of Coco Solo and Gatun Dam, in smaller numbers at Albrook AFB.

Habits: Usually seen at rain pools on grassy areas, not on open mudflats or beaches. Found singly or in small groups, often associating with Pectoral and Buff-breasted Sandpipers.

Range: Breeds in northeastern Siberia and arctic North America; winters mostly in southern South America, also in Andes from Ecuador south.

Note: Sometimes placed in the genus *Erolia.*

WHITE-RUMPED SANDPIPER
(*Calidris fuscicollis*)

Description: 7. In any plumage the key mark is the *all-white rump* (no dark center), visible only in flight. Legs dark. Nonbreeding plumage: *mostly gray above;* white below with blurry grayish streaks on breast. Breeding plumage: rusty brown above; white below with dusky streaking on breast. In flight shows faint wing-stripe.

Similar species: Can be distinguished from any of the "peep" by its entirely white rump. Larger than Least, Semipalmated, or Western Sandpipers, though this is most helpful when they are together. In rusty breeding plumage looks rather like similarly sized Baird's but is not as buffy above, never looks scaly, and of course shows the white rump.

Status and distribution: Rather rare transient (early September–mid-October; late April–mid-May) on both coasts (recorded Bocas del Toro, Canal Zone, and eastern Panama province); occasional reports of summering individuals.

Habits: Reaches Panama in but very small numbers; probably most numerous on coastal mudflats, but also seen on wet grassy areas. Has a distinctive two-noted mouse-like squeak, *jeet-jeet,* often given in flight.

Range: Breeds in high arctic; winters in southern South America, mostly east of the Andes.

Note: Sometimes placed in the genus *Erolia.*

PECTORAL SANDPIPER
(*Calidris melanotos*)

Description: 8–9½, male considerably larger than female. Bill slender; *legs greenish yellow.* Rather long neck. Brown above streaked with black; *neck and breast buffy and streaked brownish, ending abruptly against white belly.* Wing-stripe in flight faint or lacking; center of rump black.

Similar species: Sharp contrast between streaked breast and pure white belly is characteristic. Small females especially can be confused with Baird's Sandpiper, but latter is always smaller and buffier, usually scaly on back, and has black legs. Least Sandpiper is almost exactly like a Pectoral in plumage, but is hardly half the size. See also Upland Sandpiper.

Status and distribution: Locally common fall transient on grassy fields (late August–mid-November) but uncommon as spring transient (early March–late May, a few occasionally lingering into June). Very small numbers occur also on coastal mudflats (especially if bordered by vegetation), particularly at Panama Viejo in fall.

Habits: Often in very large numbers at the top shorebird fields on Caribbean slope of Canal Zone, especially Coco Solo and Gatun Dam, with flocks of hundreds. The usual call is a creaky *krrik* or *prrit,* often doubled.

Range: Breeds in northeastern Siberia and arctic North America; winters mostly in southern South America.

Note: Sometimes placed in the genus *Erolia.*

SEMIPALMATED SANDPIPER
(*Calidris pusilla*)

Description: 6–6½. *Rather short, fairly stout bill; blackish legs.* Brownish gray above; white below, tinged brownish and somewhat streaked on neck and chest. In nonbreeding plumage somewhat grayer. In flight shows light wing-stripe, dark center of rump.

Similar species: Very difficult to separate from the much more numerous Western Sandpiper. The Western's bill is longer (usually longer than head) and often has distinct droop at tip; nonbreeding grayish Westerns sometimes show contrasting rusty scapulars. Either the bill droop or the presence of rusty scapular feathers can confirm an individual bird as a Western; unfortunately, however, there is no way to confirm a Semipalmated, as they look almost exactly like a short-billed (male) winter (grayish) Western that lacks the rusty scapulars. Thus the Semipalmated is probably not safely identified in the field in Panama except perhaps in breeding plumage, at which time it is slightly less rusty than Western and lacks rufous shoulders. In the hand, unsexed birds with exposed culmen under 20 mm can be called Semipalmateds; exposed culmen of 20–22 mm may be either species (if female, probably Semipalmated); 23 mm or more, probably Westerns. See also Least Sandpiper.

Status and distribution: Uncertain due to difficulty mentioned above. Regular, probably fairly common transient and winter resident on both coasts, a few also summering.

Habits: Found among the huge flocks of Western Sandpipers, chiefly on coastal mudflats. Usual call is a short *cherk* (R. T. Peterson).

Range: Breeds in arctic North America, migrating chiefly east of the Rockies; winters coastally from Florida south through Middle America and West Indies to southern South America.

Note: Sometimes placed in the genus *Ereunetes.*

WESTERN SANDPIPER
(*Calidris mauri*)

Description: 6¼–6¾. *Rather long bill* (shorter in males), *stout especially at base, often with distinct droop at tip;* legs blackish. Rusty brown above; white below, streaked with brownish on neck and chest. In nonbreeding plumage, grayer above but *often retaining some rusty on scapulars.*

Similar species: Semipalmated Sandpiper has a shorter bill that lacks drooping tip; it never shows rusty scapulars. Westerns tend to wade in deeper water. For full discussion of the great difficulties in distinguishing between the two species see under the Semipalmated. Least Sandpiper is smaller and browner with greenish or yellowish (not blackish) legs.

Status and distribution: Abundant transient and winter resident on both coasts, more numerous on Pacific; large numbers also over-summer, also mainly on Pacific.

Habits: Often present in tremendous numbers on the flats at Panama Viejo, with flocks in the many tens of thousands, particularly on spring passage (peaking late April–early May). The usual call is a thin *jeep.*

Range: Breeds in northeastern Siberia and western Alaska; winters coastally from southern United States south through Middle America and West Indies to the Guianas and Peru.

Note: Sometimes placed in the genus *Ereunetes.*

SANDERLING
(*Calidris alba*)

Description: 7½–8½. Rather stout black bill and black legs. Nonbreeding plumage: *pale gray above with black shoulders; white below.* Breeding plumage: rusty brown above, *almost orange-buffy on head and breast,* belly white. In flight in any plumage shows *bold white ling-stripe* the length of the wing.

Similar species: In nonbreeding plumage, the palest of the sandpipers; in breeding plumage, brighter than most. The conspicuous wing-stripe helps to distinguish it from any of the "peeps."

Status and distribution: Fairly common transient and uncommon winter resident on Pacific coast, much less numerous on Caribbean coast; no reports of over-summering as yet.

Habits: Prefers sandy and pebbly beaches, often with flocks of Semipalmated Plovers and Western Sandpipers. A very active feeder, chasing the waves back and forth.

Range: Breeds in high arctic; winters coastally from United States to Tierra del Fuego, and in southern Europe, Africa, southern Asia, Australia, and islands in South Pacific.

Note: Sometimes separated in the genus *Crocethia.*

DUNLIN

(*Calidris alpina*)

Description: 7½–8½. Casual. *Bill rather long, stout at base, slightly decurved toward tip;* legs dark. Nonbreeding plumage: *nondescript,* gray above, whitish below with gray smudge on breast. Breeding plumage: *bright rusty above;* white below, lightly streaked with gray, with *prominent black patch on belly.* In flight shows white wing-stripe and dark center of rump.

Similar species: The drooping bill is the best mark. Nonbreeding Red Knot is larger, paler gray, with straight bill and greenish legs. Western Sandpiper also has drooping bill but is considerably smaller; nonbreeding White-rumped Sandpiper is also gray but has straight bill and shows prominent all-white rump in flight. See also nonbreeding Stilt Sandpiper and Curlew Sandpiper (below).

Status and distribution: Very rare, with three sightings of birds believed this species from Pacific coast (all Wetmore), one at Panama Viejo on December 3 and another on December 28, 1955, and five at the mouth of the Río Chico, eastern Panama province on March 5, 1956. One recent record from the Caribbean coast at Coco Solo, Canal Zone: three birds seen and one photographed January 19–24, 1974 (D. Engleman, R. Johnson, and J. Pujals). Specimen confirmation desirable.

Range: Breeds in northern North America and Eurasia; winters mostly in southern North America, Europe, North Africa, and southern Asia, occasionally further south (in Middle America casually to western Nicaragua and Panama).

Note: Sometimes placed in the genus *Erolia.* The Curlew Sandpiper (*C. ferruginea*) is not inconceivable in Panama as it has been recorded in the Lesser Antilles and Argentina and is reported regularly in small numbers on the eastern coast of the United States; it is normally Old World in distribution, breeding in arctic Eurasia, wintering in tropical areas. In non-breeding plumage (most unlikely in its unmistakable rufous-red breeding plumage) closely resembles non-breeding Dunlin, then best known by its all-white rump (like White-rumped Sandpiper), readily seen in flight; other points are the more slender evenly decurved bill, whiter underparts, and more upright stance with longer neck (less dumpy-looking than Dunlin) and longer legs. The only certain mark is the rump.

STILT SANDPIPER

(*Micropalama himantopus*)

Description: 8–9. Long slender straight bill, sometimes with slight droop at tip; *long greenish legs.* Nonbreeding plumage: *gray above with narrow white eyeline;* mostly white below. Breeding plumage: brownish gray above with *rusty crown and cheek patch; underparts white uniformly barred with dusky.* In flight shows dark wings and whitish rump and tail.

Similar species: Confusing in nonbreeding plumage. Compared to nonbreeding dowitchers of either species, it is longer-legged and shorter-billed, and is whiter below; in flight white of rump does not extend up lower back as it does in the dowitchers. In proportions more like a Lesser Yellowlegs, but with greenish (not yellow) legs and a white eyestripe.

Status and distribution: Rare transient (mostly August and March, one May 11 report), recorded mostly from shallow fresh water areas near either coast, particularly at the Gatun Dam spillway; a few may occasionally winter, as 4 were seen at Fort Amador on January 9, 1974 (C. Leahy and Ridgely). All reports so far are from the Canal Zone or nearby areas.

Habits: Generally found singly or in small groups, associating with dowitchers and yellowlegs. Feeds like a dowitcher, wading out into water up to its belly and submerging its head.

Range: Breeds in arctic North America;

winters mostly in southern South America, rarely in southern United States and Middle America.

BUFF-BREASTED SANDPIPER
(*Tryngites subruficollis*)

Description: 7½–8½. Bill short; *legs yellowish.* Rather slender-necked and small-headed. *Mostly buffy,* brownish above with buffy feather edgings, *uniform buffy below; whitish eye-ring.* In flight, note absence of pattern above, white under wing-linings.
Similar species: Somewhat like a small Upland Sandpiper but much more buffy. Baird's Sandpiper is buffy on breast only and has black legs. See also Pectoral Sandpiper.
Status and distribution: Locally fairly common fall transient (late August–late October) on grassy fields on both slopes of Canal Zone and vicinity; rare on spring passage, with one March 29 report and reported from Paitilla Airport in Panama city in March–April (N. G. Smith). Not reported from elsewhere in Panama though probably occurs where there is proper short grass habitat. Most numerous at Coco Solo and on grassy slopes of Gatun Dam.
Habits: Very tame. Has a distinctive wide-eyed, innocent-looking appearance. Usually occurs in flocks of its own species, sometimes in fairly large numbers (25–75 individuals). When flushed, usually twists and turns like a snipe, circling several times, often as not returning to the spot from which it was put up.
Range: Breeds in western arctic North America; winters in southern South America; rather a scarce and local transient inbetween.

RUFF (♀, REEVE)
(*Philomachus pugnax*)

Description: ♂ 11–12; ♀ 9. Two sight reports. *Bill short, usually yellowish or orangey at base; legs yellowish or reddish.* Female and nonbreeding male: mostly brown, feathers of upperparts edged with buff giving scaly appearance; dull buffy below, somewhat barred with dusky especially on sides. In flight note *diagnostic pair of oval white patches on sides of rump.* Males in breeding plumage (most unlikely in Panama) have enormous erectile ruffs and ear tufts, variously colored black, white, chestnut, or combinations of the three.
Similar species: Rather variable in size and plumage, so must be identified carefully. Looks like a brownish yellowlegs with a short bill, or a Pectoral Sandpiper without the sharp contrast below; see also Upland Sandpiper. Flush the bird to be certain.
Status and distribution: One sighting of a male in nonbreeding plumage on the wet grassy fields at Coco Solo, Canal Zone on September 29, 1968 (Ridgely), observed 3 days later by H. Loftin; another male was seen and adequately photographed at Howard AFB, Canal Zone on November 19–20, 1974 (S. West).
Habits: In the New World usually associates with yellowlegs or dowitchers.
Range: Breeds in northern Eurasia; winters in southern Europe, Africa, and southern Asia; a regular though rare transient in eastern North America and on Barbados, one record from Colombia, sightings from Panama and Trinidad.

UPLAND SANDPIPER (PLOVER)
(*Bartramia longicauda*)

Description: 11–12. Rather short bill; legs yellowish. Distinctive proportions: *small head, long slender neck, and rather long tail.* Brown above streaked with buff; white below heavily streaked and marked with brown and dusky on chest and breast. Essentially unpatterned in flight; often flies with stiff wingbeats like a Spotted Sandpiper.
Similar species: Though it has no single diagnostic mark, this species can be recognized by its characteristic shape and overall brown appearance.
Status and distribution: Uncommon to fairly common fall and rather rare spring transient (mid-August–late December; mid-March–late May) on grassy fields and pastures in lowlands on both slopes.
Habits: Found singly or in small groups, usually apart from other shorebirds. Has habit of briefly holding wings up upon alighting.
Range: Breeds in North America; winters in southern South America.

WHIMBREL
(*Numenius phaeopus*)

Description: 16½–18. *Bill long* (3–4″) *and decurved; legs grayish.* Mostly grayish brown with *blackish and white stripes on crown.*
Status and distribution: Common transient and winter resident; fairly common in summer; most numerous on beaches and mudflats on both coasts (especially on Pacific), but also on damp grassy fields in lowlands not far from shore.

Habits: Scatters out over flats and beaches to feed, but gathers in large flocks of up to several hundred birds to roost at high tide, at times perching well up in mangroves. Usually wary. When flushed often gives a rapidly repeated series of musical whistles; also has a sharp *kee-kee-kee-kee-kee-kee.*

Range: Breeds in arctic North America and Eurasia; winters from southern United States south coastally through most of South America, and in Europe, Africa, and Australasia.

LONG-BILLED CURLEW
(*Numenius americanus*)

Description: 22–26. Very rare. *Very long* (5–8″), *decurved bill;* legs grayish. Larger and buffier than Whimbrel, without that species' bold head striping. In flight overhead, note this species' *bright cinnamon under wing-linings.* To be identified with care as bill length varies considerably, but longer extremes can be picked out at once.

Status and distribution: Probably a casual winter visitant. One was collected (out of two seen) on September 24–30, 1966, on Fort Sherman airstrip in Canal Zone (H. Loftin, G. V. N. Powell, C. L. Wallis, and S. G. Martin); another was seen at the same place on December 4, 1967 (Ridgely). To be watched for on grassy fields.

Range: Breeds in western North America; winters from southern United States south rarely to Guatemala and Honduras, casually to Panama.

MARBLED GODWIT
(*Limosa fedoa*)

Description: 17–19. *Long (4–5″) somewhat upturned bill,* pinkish on basal half, blackish on terminal half; legs grayish. *Brown above* mottled with buff and whitish; *buffy below,* more whitish on throat, indistinctly barred with brown. In flight from below shows cinnamon under wing-linings.

Similar species: A large, buffy brown shorebird with a distinctly upcurved bill. Likely to be confused only with the Whimbrel, which has a decurved bill and is not as buffy (this apparent even at a distance when bill shape cannot be made out). See also Hudsonian Godwit (below).

Status and distribution: A regular transient and summer and winter visitant to the vast mudflats at Panama Viejo; single reports from Fort Clayton and Fort Amador in Canal Zone; one recently observed and photographed at Coco Solo on Caribbean coast of Zone in October 1971 (J. Pujals). Apparently occurs in largest numbers on spring passage when up to 150 have been observed at Panama Viejo (F. O. Chapelle); usually no more than a dozen are present there, with smallest numbers apparently during northern winter months. No specimens have been taken in Panama.

Range: Breeds in western North America; winters from southern United States to Panama, rarely on west coast of South America.

Note: Hudsonian Godwit (*L. haemastica*) is unrecorded but may eventually be noted; it breeds in arctic North America, and winters in southern South America. It is smaller (17–19″) than the Marbled, with similar slightly upturned bill; in breeding plumage, reddish chestnut below; in nonbreeding plumage, gray above, whitish below; at all seasons shows a bold white wing-stripe, white rump, and black and white tail.

COMMON (SHORT-BILLED) DOWITCHER
(*Limnodromus griseus*)

Description: 10–11. *Long straight bill* (2–2½″); legs greenish. Nonbreeding plumage: grayish above, whitish below. Breeding plumage: brown above edged with blackish and buffy and with white eyestripe; mostly rusty below, spotted with black, barred on flanks. In flight, note *white trailing edge to secondaries, white rump and tail* (latter barred with blackish) *extending up lower back in a "V."*

Similar species: Most of the foregoing applies equally well to either species of dowitcher; the two are very difficult to differentiate in the field: see full discussion under the Long-billed. Dowitchers in the broad sense are easily recognized by their long straight snipe-like bills and the white rump extending up the back. See Stilt Sandpiper.

Status and distribution: Fairly common transient and winter resident on both coasts (more numerous on Pacific); small numbers summer. This is much the more common of the two dowitchers in Panama.

Habits: Prefers mudflats, gathering in rather large flocks where conditions are favorable. Feeds by wading belly-deep into shallow water and rapidly jabbing bill into mud with perpendicular motions, entirely submerging head. The usual call is a metallic *tu-tu-tu,* given in flight or when flushed.

Range: Breeds in northern Canada; winters

from southern United States south coastally to Peru and central Brazil.

LONG-BILLED DOWITCHER
(*Limnodromus scolopaceus*)

Description: 10½–11½. Long straight bill (2–3″); legs greenish. Very similar to Common Dowitcher and usually not safely distinguished in the field. Bill measurements overlap, though long extremes of this species (females) can usually be picked out. In breeding plumage, this species is darker above and richer rusty below; tail has black bars broader than white; *foreneck and breast with dusky bars instead of spots.* In nonbreeding plumage, the two resemble each other very closely though this species is darker; they can be distinguished only by bill length (when apparent), voice (often the best clue), and habitat (helpful but not diagnostic; see below). In the hand, birds with exposed culmen of 68 mm or more are Long-bills; those with less than 56 mm are Commons; the Long-billed has relatively shorter wings so that the difference between wing length and exposed culmen is 77 mm or less (in Common difference is 77 mm or more because of relatively longer wing).

Status and distribution: Probably a rare winter resident though definite records are few; collected in Bocas del Toro in October, November, and January; only sight reports from the Canal Zone.

Habits: Normally not found on coastal mudflats, preferring fresh water situations, pond margins, flooded or wet grassy fields, etc. However, the Common Dowitcher is not *restricted* to mudflats, and also often occurs inland. Some arriving dowitchers in August and September are still in breeding plumage and should be carefully checked for this species. The usual call is a thin *keek,* sometimes trebled, quite different from the Common's almost yellowlegs-like *tu-tu-tu.*

Range: Breeds in northeastern Siberia and western arctic North America; winters from southern United States to Guatemala, rarely to Panama and probably only casually to South America (where all published records require confirmation in the light of modern criteria).

COMMON SNIPE
(*Gallinago gallinago*)

Description: 10½–11½. *Long straight bill* (2½–2¾); short legs. Dark brown above, streaked with buff and with *buff and black striped head;* chest and breast mottled buff and brown, belly white. When flushed, flies off in a zigzag, displaying brown rump and short orange tail, holding bill pointed downward.

Similar species: Rather like a dowitcher in general proportions, but with different habits and with striped head and brown rump. No other shorebird has proportionately such a long bill.

Status and distribution: Locally fairly common transient and winter resident (October–April) in boggy areas and fresh water marshes and wet spots in lowlands on both slopes, ranging up to Volcán Lakes in lower highlands of western Chiriquí.

Habits: Cryptically colored and a close sitter, this species is usually not noticed until it flushes and dashes off with a grating *scaip.*

Range: North and South America, Europe, and Asia; withdraws southward in winter, North American birds to northern South America.

Note: North American birds, *G. delicata* (Wilson's Snipe), are often considered specifically distinct from Old World birds; so too are the South American breeding forms. All are sometimes placed in the genus *Capella.*

STILTS AND AVOCETS: Recurvirostridae (1)

The stilts and avocets are a small group of large, elegant shorebirds, found locally throughout the world. They are characterized by very long slender bills (upturned in the avocets), long legs (exceptionally so in the stilts), and bold, basically black and white plumage patterns. They are gregarious and nest in colonies; as yet the stilt has not actually been found breeding in Panama, but it may well do so locally on the Pacific coast.

BLACK-NECKED STILT
(*Himantopus mexicanus*)

Description: 14–15½. A striking black and white shorebird with a long (2¼–2¾″), thin, black bill and *extremely long red-to-pink legs. Black above,* including wings; *white below* and on rump.

Status and distribution: Uncommon, local, and apparently somewhat erratic on coastal mudflats and fresh water ponds and marshes near both coasts (more numerous on Pacific); probably at least in part migratory from the north as most records are from late August to March; no definite evidence of breeding, though this is likely locally on the Pacific coast (e.g. Río Chico in eastern Panama province and at the Aguadulce salinas in Coclé).

Habits: Feeds actively in shallow water; rather noisy, with several short sharp notes, often given in a series, especially when bird is alarmed. The long legs trail far beyond the tail in flight.

Range: Breeds locally from southern United States south through Middle America and most of South America, also in West Indies; northern birds withdraw southward during northern winter.

Note: By some authors considered conspecific with *H. himantopus* (Black-winged Stilt) of Old World and called Common Stilt.

PHALAROPES: Phalaropodidae (2)

The phalaropes are a small group of sandpiper-like birds which are adapted through lobed toes to an aquatic environment. In all three species, the usual sexual roles are reversed: females are larger and more colorful and leave incubation and the rearing process to the more subdued male. In breeding plumage the phalaropes are among the most brightly colored of the shorebirds; most individuals seen in Panama are in the duller winter dress. Flocks of sandpipers seen swimming out at sea are virtually certain to be phalaropes, and those swimming in a pond are likely to be so.

WILSON'S PHALAROPE
(*Steganopus tricolor*)

Description: 8½–9½. *Very slender, black bill;* legs greenish or yellowish. Nonbreeding plumage: plain gray above, *strikingly white below,* with *grayish smudge through eye.* Breeding plumage: gray above with *broad rufous stripes on back and another up sides of neck blending into black patch behind eye;* whitish below; female much brighter than male. In flight, in any plumage, note *dark unpatterned wings.*

Similar species: Breeding plumage birds are easily recognized. More difficult at other seasons, as it resembles Lesser Yellowlegs or Stilt Sandpiper, but can always be known by its thin almost needle-like bill and very white underparts. Northern Phalarope has whitish back stripes, dark legs, and a prominent white wing-stripe.

Status and distribution: A rare and apparently irregular fall transient (late August–late September), thus far reported only from Canal Zone and vicinity, mostly on Caribbean side. No specimens have been taken in Panama.

Habits: Favors fresh water margins. Extremely active and nervous and can often be picked out on that character alone; does little swimming.

Range: Breeds in western North America; winters from Peru to Chile and Argentina; a rather rare and local transient in Middle America.

NORTHERN (RED-NECKED) PHALAROPE
(*Lobipes lobatus*)

Description: 6½–7½. *Slender, black bill;* dark legs. Nonbreeding plumage: dark gray above, *striped with whitish on back;* face and underparts white with *dark gray patch through and behind eye.* Breeding plumage: largely dark gray with *white throat* and *rusty patch on sides of neck and upper chest;* breast and belly whitish; female brighter than male. In flight shows a *bold, white wing-stripe.*

Similar species: Breeding plumage is distinctive; at other seasons marked as a phalarope by the dark patch through the eye. Nonbreeding Wilson's Phalarope is similar but has unpatterned gray back, yellowish legs, and no wing-stripe; the two are not normally found together, the Wilson's not being pelagic. See also Red Phalarope (below).

Status and distribution: An irregular but at times very numerous transient and winter resident off Pacific coast (mid-August–early May); in recent years has been recorded in rather large flocks in the Gulf of Panama; sometimes seen from land (especially at Fort Amador), but more numerous further offshore; no reports from Caribbean coast, though possible.

Habits: Very active, flying rapidly over the ocean, then dropping lightly to the surface where it spins around like a top and daintily plucks food from the surface.

Range: Breeds in arctic North America and Eurasia; winters at sea in Atlantic, Pacific, and Indian Oceans.

Note: When not in breeding dress, this species is most likely to be confused with the Red (Gray) Phalarope (*Phalaropus fulicarius*), a species that has not yet been recorded from Panama but that seems likely to occur at least occasionally (it has been reported at sea well to the west of the Gulf of Panama). In breeding plumage, Red would be easily known by its rufous underparts and white face, but in nonbreeding plumage the two are quite similar. Red is somewhat larger (7½–9″) with shorter, stouter bill that is yellow basally, paler plain gray back (no stripes), and yellowish legs.

SKUAS AND JAEGERS: Stercorariidae (4)

Skuas and jaegers are piratic seabirds, breeding in polar regions, spending the remainder of the year well out to sea, only infrequently coming near shore. They are somewhat gull-like but have strong hooked bills (with a horny cere unlike gulls and terns), long and pointed (in the jaegers) wings showing a flash of white in the primaries, and in adults lengthened central tail feathers. They are aggressive birds with powerful rapid flight, easily capable of overtaking gulls and terns and other seabirds, forcing them to disgorge their food; they also eat dead fish and other carrion. Identification within the group usually presents a problem. The skua and adults of the three jaeger species are relatively easy when seen clearly (assuming the central tail feathers have not been broken off). However, several years are required for young birds to attain adult plumage, and immatures of the three jaegers are very similar and frequently cannot be identified to species in the field. Immatures of the Parasitic and Long-tailed are the most similar; using the criteria of H. Walter (*J.F.O.* 103: 166–179, 1962), many older records especially of Long-tails, based on relative length of supra-nasal saddle, wing length, and number of primaries showing white shaft, are erroneous because of overlap in these characters. Length measurements given do *not* include the lengthened tail feathers.

GREAT SKUA
(*Catharacta skua*)

Description: 22–24. Recorded off Pacific coast; no specimens, and exact form uncertain. A stocky seabird with *broad wings* and *wedge-shaped tail.* Variable in color, the most southern birds being the palest. Dark to light brown above, darker birds streaked and edged with buff, lighter birds with head and neck "chamois"-colored; dark brown to cinnamon-rufous to light brown below; wings with *prominent white patch at base of primaries.*

Similar species: A larger and heavier bird than any of the jaegers, with broader wings and more ample tail without projecting central feathers; more Buteo-like, the jaegers being more falcon-like. Most resembles a dark immature Pomarine Jaeger, which see.

Status and distribution: Uncertain, apparently an uncommon and irregular visitant off Pacific coast in Gulf of Panama and off Azuero Peninsula, rare inshore; reported February, March, September, and early November. No specimens have been taken in Panama waters, and collection is desirable in order to determine which of the various southern forms is involved. Antarctic-breeding *maccormicki* (often given full species status, South Polar Skua) is the most likely, as it engages in an extensive trans-equatorial migration into the North Pacific. Over 20 skuas were counted in a movement of over a thousand jaegers "pouring past" Punta Mala on March 30, 1970 (N. G. Smith).

Habits: A powerful seabird with deceptively swift flight, easily overtaking other pelagic birds, forcing them to disgorge their food. Also scavenges for refuse around ships and in harbors.

Range: Breeds locally on islands in North Atlantic, coast of southern South America, subantarctic islands, and Antarctica; North Atlantic and Antarctic forms wander widely toward and even beyond the equator.

POMARINE JAEGER
(*Stercorarius pomarinus*)

Description: 18–20. A hawk-like, piratical seabird with narrow pointed wings and wedge-shaped tail; *distinctly larger than Laughing Gull.* Plumages vary. Adults have *fairly long (up to 4″) twisted central tail feathers, rounded at tip* ("spoon-shaped"), extending beyond rest of tail. In light phase, dark grayish brown above with black cap and white collar on hindneck; whitish below with varying amounts of brown barring, usually with a brown band across chest; *prominent white flash in wings* at base of primaries. In dark phase, uniform sooty brown with white flash in wings. Immature brownish with white wing flash, without projecting central tail feathers.

Similar species: Closely resembles Parasitic Jaeger but larger and heavier with more white on wing. Adult can usually be known by the round-tipped central tail feathers, but these are often broken off; the twist is normally not apparent in the field. Immature is very difficult and, unless there is size comparison, often impossible to identify with certainty (even then it is often very difficult). Great Skua is larger and heavier than the Pomarine, with notably broader wings and heavier bill.

Status and distribution: An uncommon to locally fairly common transient and winter visitant to offshore waters in both Pacific and Caribbean, rare during northern summer months; sometimes coming within sight of land, regularly at Colon harbor. Only one specimen from Panama: a bird taken at Puerto Obaldía, San Blas, on April 15, 1935; also one immature photographed on beach at Fort Amador, Canal Zone, on March 25, 1968 (Ridgely). Numerous recent sightings from Colon harbor and Coco Solo (where also photographed; J. Pujals), with up to 20 or more being seen at once; immatures predominate, though adults have also been seen.

Range: Breeds in arctic; winters southward, mostly at sea, in New World south to Peru and Guyana.

PARASITIC JAEGER
(*Stercorarius parasiticus*)

Description: 16–18. Very similar to Pomarine Jaeger but smaller and less stocky; *about same size as Laughing Gull* (not distinctly larger). Tarsus black in adults; gray in immatures. Light phase is more frequent in adults than it is in Pomarine Jaeger. Adults have *fairly long (up to 3½") straight, pointed central tail feathers* extending beyond rest of tail. In light phase, grayish brown above, darker on crown, with whitish collar on hindneck; white below with grayish brown band across chest, usually with no barring; *prominent white flash in wings* at base of primaries (3–4 white shafts, occasionally only 2). In dark phase, dark sooty brown all over, darkest on crown, also with white flash in wings. Immature is brownish (usually with rusty tones) with white wing flash and very slightly projecting central tail feathers (usually not visible in the field); first-year birds show pale bars above.

Similar species: See Pomarine Jaeger; as with that species, adult's projecting central tail feathers are frequently broken off, compounding an already difficult identification problem. Even greater difficulties arise in conjunction with young Long-tailed Jaeger, which is smaller and more slender than the Parasitic, and has less white in the wing (usually), but which is usually not separable in the field.

Status and distribution: Generally an uncommon but regular transient and winter visitant to offshore waters on both coasts, usually not coming within sight of land though it is apparently fairly regular in small numbers at Colon harbor (where outnumbered by the Pomarine); also several winter sightings from Gatun Lake (E. O. Willis, R. MacArthur, Ridgely). Immatures seem to predominate. Three specimens have been taken in Panama: one at Puerto Obaldía, San Blas, on November 27, 1934; one in Gulf of Panama south of Pearl Islands (Rey) on November 2, 1968 (H. Loftin and Ridgely, Smithsonian Pacific seabird project); and another in Gulf of Panama south of Pearl Islands on March 3, 1969 (H. Loftin and R. Crossin, also Smithsonian Pacific project). N. G. Smith reports seeing between 900 and 1300 passing west along south shore of Azuero Peninsula off Punta Mala on March 30, 1970. One immature, probably this species, was closely observed as it flew in and landed on a small pond along the Pan-American Highway west of Penonomé, Coclé on January 6, 1974 (Ridgely and G. Stiles).

Range: Breeds in northern North America, Europe, and Asia; winters southward, primarily at sea, in New World south to Tierra del Fuego.

[LONG-TAILED JAEGER]
(*Stercorarius longicaudus*)

Description: 14–16. Only one old sighting. *Central feathers very long and pointed* (4½–10"), but they are often broken off. *Smaller and slimmer than Parasitic Jaeger.* Brownish gray above with black cap and white collar on hind-neck; white below; *small white flash in wings* at base of primaries (usually less extensive than in Parasitic, showing on only 2 shafts, rarely 3). Dark phase is not known in America. Young immature is brownish with pale barring on mantle; older immature has *grayish back* with pale barring; both lack the long central tail feathers, but show small white flash in wing.

Similar species: The adult with long tail is unmistakable; it is usually whiter below than Parasitic, with no chest band, and has cleaner-cut black cap contrasting with white collar and underparts. Immatures pose the problem. Contrary to some sources, leg color is no help, being grayish in immatures of both species (in adult leg color does differ: black in Parasitic, grayish in Long-tailed). Older immature Long-tail can be distinguished at close range from immature Parasitic by its grayish (not brownish) back crossed by paler barring. First and second year immature Long-tails are more difficult and are only dubiously identified in the field. A small jaeger with white showing on only one primary is a Long-tailed, but many individuals show white on 2 or 3 primaries and these can be either Long-tailed or Parasitic (H. Walter, *J.f.O. 103:* 166–179, 1962). In the hand measurements of bill, wings, and tarsus are useful but all these characters overlap according to Walter; hence many older specimen identifications are probably erroneous.

Status and distribution: One old sight report of a bird seen with other jaegers in Colon harbor on February 9, 1927 (Griscom and Crosby). Even this report is doubtful, for Griscom seemingly relied on the number of primaries showing white but failed to state how many actually did; he was unaware of the overlap in this character. Nonetheless this species will probably prove to be a rare migrant off both coasts.

Range: Breeds in arctic North America and Eurasia; winters southward at sea, in New World to central Chile and northern Argentina.

GULLS AND TERNS: Laridae (22)

Gulls and terns are familiar and cosmopolitan birds, most prominent along coasts but also found inland on larger lakes, rivers, and marshes, with a few species well offshore except during the breeding season. Though birds of the family are conspicuous on Panama coasts, no gull breeds in Panama, and there is no irrefutable proof that any of the terns do so. The two subfamilies Larinae and Sterninae are readily differentiated. Gulls generally are larger, with heavier somewhat hooked bills, rather broad wings, and usually square tails. Most terns are smaller and slimmer, with slender straight bills, rather narrow pointed wings, and usually (except noddies) forked tails. Gulls are often seen swimming; terns rarely do. Most terns dive into the water after small fish; most gulls eat animal matter on shores or floating on the water. In the following descriptions, the term *mantle* is frequently used to describe the back and upper surface of the wings. Identification is not always easy in this family, and caution is urged.

[GRAY GULL]
(*Larus modestus*)

Description: 17–18. Two sightings. Bill and legs black. Slightly larger than Laughing Gull. *Uniform plain gray* with *front of head white* (brownish gray in nonbreeding plumage); flight feathers blackish, secondaries with white tips forming *broad white band along rear edge of wing;* tail gray with black subterminal band and white tip. Immature more brownish below, without white head. Juvenal uniform dull brown, with buff edging on blackish wings and tail.

Similar species: Adult resembles no other Panama gull. Immature is not safely identified in the field, though some stages are grayer below than other Panama gulls. Some immature Laughing Gulls can look largely gray.

Status and distribution: Reported seen south of Pacific entrance to the Canal on November 28, 1945 (R. C. Murphy); three seen south of Isla Otoque in Panama Bay on February 6, 1956 (Wetmore).

Range: Breeds in northern Chile and probably western Peru; ranges north regularly to Ecuador (in largest numbers May–November), occasionally to Colombia, probably casually to Panama.

BAND-TAILED GULL
(*Larus belcheri*)

Description: 20–22. Rare. A large, heavy-looking gull. *Bill heavy, yellow with outer* *third red and black spot on upper mandible;* legs yellow. Breeding plumage: head and underparts white; mantle brownish black; tail white with *broad black subterminal band.* Nonbreeding plumage (and subadult): similar, but with duller bill and dusky hood extending over neck and pale gray area between hood and mantle. Immature resembles nonbreeding adult but has *yellow bill with black tip.*

Similar species: Easily recognized by its heavy appearance, brightly colored bill, and banded tail; mantle darker than any other gull known from Panama.

Status and distribution: Three recent reports from Pacific coast of Canal Zone and Panama city: a nonbreeding adult or subadult at Panama Viejo on December 20, 1962 (Eisenmann); one at Fort Amador on May 10 and August 24, 1964 (W. Belton and H. Loftin, photographed); one at Albrook AFB on December 2, 1967 (H. Loftin). No specimens from Panama.

Range: Breeds on Pacific coast from northern Peru to central Chile and on Atlantic coast of central Argentina, wandering north rarely to Panama and south to Tierra del Fuego.

RING-BILLED GULL
(*Larus delawarensis*)

Description: 18–20. Rare. Somewhat larger than Laughing Gull. Adult has *yellow bill with black ring near tip; legs yellowish green.* Mostly white with pearly gray mantle (much paler than dark gray of Laughing) and blackish wing-tips with white spots near tip; in winter, head and neck lightly streaked with brownish dusky. Subadult like adult but lacks white spots on wing-tips, and sometimes has dusky tip to bill. Immature grayish brown above, whitish below, with *narrow black band near tip of white tail;* bill flesh with dusky tip.

Similar species: Winter and immature Laughing Gulls are darker generally with dark smudging on neck and breast and blackish bill and legs. Herring Gull is larger; first-year immatures are much darker (including underparts), while second-year immatures (which often seem to have a ring on bill) have much broader black band on tail (tail appearing essentially dark, with whitish rump).

Status and distribution: Rare but perhaps regular winter visitant on or near both coasts in central Panama. First recorded from a banded first year bird captured alive (molting) on Pacific coast of Coclé on July 11, 1954 (it could not fly because it was "sin plumas," i.e. without flight feathers). Recently there have been a number of sightings from Panama city waterfront and Gatun Dam spillway (where also photographed; Ridgely); recorded November–June.

Habits: Usually associates with the omnipresent Laughing Gull.

Range: Breeds in southern Canada and northern United States; winters from northern United States to Mexico and in West Indies, rarely to Panama.

HERRING GULL
(*Larus argentatus*)

Description: 22–25. Rare. *Considerably larger than Laughing Gull* and easily picked out on that basis alone. Adult has yellow bill with red spot near tip of lower mandible; *legs flesh.* Mostly white with pearly gray mantle and blackish wing-tips with white spots near tip; in winter head and neck lightly streaked with brownish dusky. First-year immature *predominantly grayish brown,* marked with buff; wings and tail dusky; bill dark. Second-year immature whiter, especially below and on rump, bill dull yellow, often with black ring near tip. Only immatures have been reported from Panama, most of these in their first winter.

Similar species: Considerably larger and heavier than the otherwise rather similar Ring-billed Gull. See also Band-tailed Gull.

Status and distribution: Rare but possibly regular winter visitant on both coasts. First recorded from three recoveries (two in Bocas del Toro) of birds banded in the United States. More recently there have been a number of sightings from both coasts of Canal Zone and vicinity (Panama Viejo, Balboa, Colon, Coco Solo) and Gatun Lake; recorded December–late April.

Range: Breeds in North America and Eurasia; in New World winters south to Mexico, rarely to Panama, West Indies, and other Caribbean islands.

LAUGHING GULL
(*Larus atricilla*)

Description: 15–17. By far the commonest gull in Panama. Bill and legs blackish, dusky red in breeding plumage. Nonbreeding plumage: head and underparts white, mottled with brownish gray around eyes and on ear-coverts and back of head; *mantle dark gray blending into black wing-tips,* with white trailing edge to wing. In breeding plumage hood black. Subadult like nonbreeding adult but with black tail band. Immature dark grayish brown to grayish with *contrasting white rump* and rear edge to wing, whitish belly.

Similar species: Can be known by its small size and dark general appearance. Adult Franklin's Gull has smaller bill and considerable white near wing-tips; in nonbreeding plumage has well defined gray "half-hood" on rearcrown; immatures of the two are not safely distinguished.

Status and distribution: Very common, often locally abundant, transient and winter visitant on both coasts (especially Pacific) and larger bodies of fresh water; smaller numbers, but still locally common, in summer months, especially around Panama city (all birds then being immatures or nonbreeding adults). Does not breed in Panama.

Habits: Easily outnumbers all other gulls in Panama put together, sometimes gathering in very large flocks. Regularly feeds on insects over land. Habitually lands on the heads of pelicans that have just surfaced after diving; they then attempt to rob the pelican of its catch as it attempts to swallow.

Range: Breeds locally along Atlantic and Gulf coasts of North America, in Bahamas and on many Caribbean islands including those off Venezuela, and in southeastern California and northwestern Mexico; winters from southern United States to Peru and northern Brazil.

[GRAY-HOODED GULL]

(*Larus cirrocephalus*)

Description: 16½–17½. One sight report. Bill dark red; legs red (both yellowish in first year immatures). Breeding plumage: *hood pale gray;* mantle gray, *primaries largely black with large white patches basally;* underside of wings largely dusky; rump, tail, and underparts white. Nonbreeding plumage: similar but head white with *pale gray half-hood on rear crown, dusky crescent-shaped mask in front* and spot behind eye. First-year immature has brownish gray head paling to whitish on forecrown and hindneck; mantle light brown, outer primaries dusky; tail with blackish subterminal band; white below, tinged brown on sides.

Similar species: Differs from both Laughing and Franklin's Gulls in its larger area of white on wings, paler hood (breeding season), and dusky area in front of eyes (nonbreeding season).

Status and distribution: One sight report of a bird in nonbreeding plumage at a sewer outlet into Panama Bay in Panama city on September 25, 1955 (M. Moynihan). To be watched for on Pacific coast.

Range: Breeds on coast of western Peru and from Bolivia and southern Brazil to northern Argentina, also in central and southern Africa; ranges commonly north to off Ecuador and northern Brazil.

FRANKLIN'S GULL

(*Larus pipixcan*)

Description: 13½–15. Resembles Laughing Gull but somewhat smaller, especially bill. Bill and legs reddish, brighter in breeding plumage. Nonbreeding plumage: head and underparts mostly white with *dusky area on mid and rear crown down over sides of head to below and behind eyes* (forming a "half-hood," absent in Laughing Gull); mantle gray (slightly paler than Laughing Gull) with *broad, irregular band of white on outer primaries crossed by a black subterminal band* and white trailing edge to wing. In breeding plumage, hood black. Subadult resembles nonbreeding adult but has dusky tail band and less white on wing. First-winter immature is brownish gray above with white rump, head mottled with dusky and white, largely white below.

Similar species: Adult can be distinguished from Laughing Gull by wing pattern; subadult and winter adult by distinct half-hood (Laughing Gull has some head mottling). Immature is almost indistinguishable in the field from some stages of immature Laughing Gull.

Status and distribution: Uncommon to fairly common transient (April–May; November–December) and less numerous winter visitant to both coasts, most numerous along shore of Panama Bay (especially about Panama city); immatures and subadults remain throughout the summer, often showing almost complete black hoods. Also occurs well offshore, and often noted inland on Gatun Lake and other Canal waters, especially on migration.

Habits: Has a more buoyant, graceful flight than Laughing Gull.

Range: Breeds in western North America; winters along Pacific coast from Guatemala to northern Chile, on Caribbean coast in Panama.

BONAPARTE'S GULL
(*Larus philadelphia*)

Description: 12–14. Two recent records. Bill slender, black; legs red in breeding adult; dull flesh to pinkish gray in winter adult and immature. *A small, tern-like gull.* Nonbreeding plumage: head and underparts white, with *conspicuous black spot behind eye;* mantle gray with *broad white wedge on front part of outer wing.* Breeding plumage: similar but head black. Immature resembles nonbreeding adult but has dusky diagonal band across wing-coverts, more black on edges of wing, and *narrow black band on tip of tail.*

Similar species: Sabine's is only other Panama gull as small: it has conspicuous black wedge on front part of wing (where this species is white) and has slightly forked tail. See also Black-headed Gull (below).

Status and distribution: One immature photographed at Coco Solo, Canal Zone on December 26–29, 1972 (J. Pujals); and another immature seen at Gatun Dam spillway on January 13, 1974 (C. Leahy and Ridgely).

Range: Breeds in Alaska and western Canada; winters mostly coastally in United States, Mexico, and in smaller numbers in West Indies, with two recent reports from Panama.

Note: Black-headed Gull (*L. ridibundus*) of Eurasia is possible in Panma, for it occurs rarely but regularly in eastern North America and casually in West Indies; it resembles Bonaparte's but is slightly larger (14–15″) and has heavier red to dull yellowish orange bill in any plumage.

SABINE'S GULL
(*Xema sabini*)

Description: 13–14. The only gull definitely recorded from Panama with a *forked tail.* Bill blackish *with yellow tip;* legs black. Nonbreeding plumage: head and underparts white, back of head smudged with gray; striking pattern on mantle, with *broad black wedge on front part of outer wing, white triangular area behind it, and pale gray wing-coverts and back.* Breeding plumage: similar but hood slaty gray with black ring around neck. Immature is like nonbreeding adult but with black along inner edge of forked tail and grayish brown back and wing-coverts.

Similar species: The striking pattern of this species is unlike that of any other Panama gull except the hypothetical (and much larger) Swallow-tailed Gull. Bonaparte's Gull has a white wedge on front part of wing.

Status and distribution: Uncommon to occasionally fairly common transient and occasional winter visitant (October–May) in offshore waters of Gulf of Panama, very rarely seen from shore; a few birds possibly remain though summer. Several specimens taken by H. Loftin and associates in 1968–1969 on the Smithsonian Pacific seabird project; also a number of sight reports, most of them recent.

Habits: Has a buoyant, rather tern-like flight. Found singly or in small groups, often in association with terns and other pelagic birds.

Range: Breeds in arctic; winters southward at sea, in New World to Peru (no records from tropical Atlantic coast, and only one from West Indies).

[SWALLOW-TAILED GULL]
(*Creagrus furcatus*)

Description: 21–23. One sight report. A *very large* gull (almost size of Herring Gull) with a *deeply forked tail.* Bill black, tipped greenish or bluish in breeding plumage; legs pinkish, more brownish in nonbreeding season. In pattern, reminiscent of the much smaller Sabine's Gull. Breeding plumage: hood slaty with white spot at base of bill; mantle mostly gray, *primaries blackish with white triangle on wings and narrow white stripe on either side of back* (scapulars); white below. Nonbreeding plumage: similar but head white with *broad black ring around eyes.*

Similar species: Large size, striking wing pattern, and forked tail should make recognition easy. Sabine's Gull is much smaller with slender black bill with yellow tip and no black around eyes at any stage.

Status and distribution: One report of a bird believed this species seen ten miles north of Piñas Bay, Darién on July 18, 1957 (C. R. Robins).

Range: Breeds on Galapagos Islands and on Malpelo Island off Colombia; ranges to coasts of Ecuador and Peru, perhaps casually to Panama.

BLACK TERN
(*Chlidonias niger*)

Description: 9–10. A *small* tern with an *only slightly notched tail.* Bill black. Nonbreeding adult and immature: forecrown, neck, and underparts white, with *dusky patches around eye, on ear-coverts, and rearcrown; mantle and tail gray.* Breeding plumage adult (seen only briefly in Panama): *entire head, neck, and underparts black;* mantle and tail gray; under wing-coverts pale gray, under tail-coverts white.

Similar species: Small size (among Panama terns only Least is as small), gray upperparts, and pied facial pattern are distinctive.

Status and distribution: Common, at times locally abundant, transient and winter resident on all areas of open water, most numerous along Pacific coast (especially during migration) and offshore in Gulf of Panama (especially during northern winter months, when sometimes gathering in flocks of tens of thousands); present throughout the year, but numbers fluctuate markedly, often seeming to "disappear" locally for short periods.

Habits: Has a graceful flight, sometimes swooping, sometimes fluttery; does not dive, rather pauses to hover briefly while it daintily picks up some morsel from the water's surface. Sometimes catches insects over land.

Range: Breeds in North America, Europe, and southwestern Asia; in New World winters from Panama to Surinam and Peru, accidentally to central Chile.

LARGE-BILLED TERN
(*Phaetusa simplex*)

Description: 15. Casual. A *large* tern with a *stout yellow bill;* legs greenish. Forehead and underparts white, crown black; *back and rather short almost square* (slightly forked) *tail dark slaty gray;* contrasting wing pattern in flight, with dusky primaries and *prominent triangular white area on secondaries and wing-coverts.* Immature similar but mantle mottled with brownish, dusky wing-band, less black on crown.

Similar species: No other Panama tern shows the striking wing pattern; no gull has a heavy yellow pointed bill. Somewhat suggests immature Black Skimmer, but that species has a red and black bill and lacks the large, white area on wing.

Status and distribution: Recorded only very recently: 2 immatures seen repeatedly and well photographed at Coco Solo, Canal Zone, from June 15 to July 7, 1973 (J. Pujals *et al.*), with one seen intermittently through December 1973 at various localities along Caribbean coast of Canal Zone; another (?) was well seen at a fresh water pond near El Rincón, Herrera, on March 27, 1974 (J. Pujals, Eisenmann, A. Skutch).

Range: Larger rivers and coastlines of South America east of the Andes (west of them only in Ecuador; ranges as close as the Magdalena River valley in northern Colombia); recorded from central Panama and once each from Cuba, Bermuda, and United States (Illinois).

GULL-BILLED TERN
(*Gelochelidon nilotica*)

Description: 13–14. *Heavy, black, almost gull-like bill;* legs dark. Nonbreeding plumage: *mostly white* with *dusky patch on ear-coverts;* mantle silvery gray; *tail only slightly forked.* Breeding plumage: similar but lacks dusky ear patch, has black crown and nape.

Similar species: Very pale, at a distance sometimes looking almost all white. Nonbreeding Common Tern has black patch on rearcrown and nape (not just on ear-coverts), more slender bill, darker mantle. Sandwich Tern (which also looks very white) has a slender bill that usually shows yellow tip (often hard to see), more deeply forked tail, and in nonbreeding plumage has black rearcrown.

Status and distribution: Uncommon to fairly common transient and winter visitant on Pacific coast, somewhat erratic and variable in numbers; on Caribbean coast much less numerous and apparently known only as a scarce transient; occasionally found on fresh water (Miraflores Lake and Gatun Dam spillway); a number of reports of nonbreeding birds on Pacific coast during northern breeding season (Panama city, Canal Zone, Aguadulce).

Habits: Unlike most terns, rarely dives into deep water, sometimes catching insects in the air or by walking on the ground. Its call is a rasping *za-za-za;* also *kay-weck, kay-weck* (R. T. Peterson).

Range: Breeds locally on coast of southern United States and western Mexico, Bahamas and Virgin Islands, and on Atlantic coast from the Guianas to central Argentina; also locally in many warmer areas of the Old World; in New World northern birds winter south to the Guianas and Peru.

COMMON TERN
(*Sterna hirundo*)

Description: 13–15. Bill blackish, often with some reddish or (immatures) yellowish near base (coral red with black tip in breeding season); *legs reddish to dull orange.* Nonbreeding plumage: mostly white with *black patch on rearcrown and nape;* mantle gray with *blackish bend of wing and primaries;* tail deeply forked. Breeding plumage similar but with black cap and nape and paler wings without dark shoulders.

Similar species: Sandwich Tern is whiter generally (especially so in flight), and has slender black bill usually with a yellow tip; it has black legs (not reddish or orange—a useful character on perched birds). Gull-billed Tern has heavy black bill and dark legs, lacks black on rear of head (only on ear-coverts). See also Roseate and Arctic Terns (below).

Status and distribution: Common transient and fairly common winter resident on both coasts, more numerous on Pacific, with non-breeders present through the summer; regularly occurs also on Gatun Lake and other Canal waters; most numerous October–November and April.

Habits: Calls consist of a drawling *kee-arr,* a *kik-kik-kik,* and *kirri-kirri* (R. T. Peterson), but usually rather quiet in Panama.

Range: Breeds in North America and on islands in southern Caribbean, also in Europe and southern Asia; in New World winters coastally from Mexico to central Peru and southern Argentina.

Note: Two other very similar species are possible though unrecorded. Roseate Tern (*S. dougallii*) should be watched for, especially on Caribbean coast; it breeds locally on Atlantic coast of North America, in West Indies, off coast of Belize and Honduras, and on southern Caribbean islands (also in Old World), wintering south to Colombia, Venezuela, and Brazil. A nestling banded on Great Gull Island off Long Island, New York, on August 8, 1969, was recovered on Isla Gorgona off Pacific coast of Colombia on October 27, 1969 (H. Hays), and its likeliest route would have taken it across Panama. In nonbreeding plumage resembles nonbreeding Common Tern, but is paler with much longer outer tail feathers (when sitting tail extends far beyond wing-tips) with outer web on outermost pair white (not blackish), has less prominent blackish margin on bend of wing, and has wholly black bill (mostly black with red base in breeding plumage). Arctic Tern (*S. paradisaea*) regularly migrates off coasts of Ecuador and Peru to its wintering grounds off Antarctica, and doubtless also migrates well off Pacific coast of Panama; it breeds in northern North America and Eurasia. Field identification in non-breeding plumage is usually unreliable, though on sitting birds Arctic's shorter tarsus (13.5 mm vs. Common's 16) can sometimes be discerned; in breeding plumage, bill wholly blood red with no black tip.

BRIDLED TERN

(*Sterna anaethetus*)

Description: 14–15. Known only from off Pacific coast. Bill black. Forehead, superciliary, and underparts white; cap black, *hindneck white (forming a distinct collar); mantle dark brownish gray;* tail deeply forked, outer feathers white, others brownish gray.

Similar species: A pelagic tern, dark gray above with characteristic collar on hindneck. Sooty Tern is blacker above with no collar.

Status and distribution: Reported in numbers (possibly breeding?) on February 6, 1956, on Los Frailes del Sur, a pair of rocky islets off Punta Mala (Wetmore); flocks seen off Punta Mala in February 1961 (E. O. Willis) and on March 30, 1970 (N. G. Smith). Otherwise reported to occur in small flocks in drift lines in Gulf of Panama from south of Pearl Islands to Darién (rarely in Panama Bay), mostly September–November, occasionally in other months. So far not reported from Caribbean.

Habits: Primarily pelagic when not breeding.

Range: Breeds locally on islands in tropical oceans, ranging quite widely at sea when not breeding. Recently found breeding off Pacific coast of northwestern Costa Rica (G. Stiles).

SOOTY TERN

(*Sterna fuscata*)

Description: 15–16. Recorded rarely off both coasts. Bill black. Forehead, superciliary, and underparts white; *otherwise black above;* tail deeply forked, mostly black, outer feathers white. Immature mostly dark brown, feathers of upperparts white-tipped, somewhat whiter on lower belly.

Similar species: Bridled Tern is dark gray above (not black), with white collar around hindneck. Immature Sooty might be confused with Brown Noddy (especially immatures, lacking white forecrown), but has deeply forked (not wedge-shaped) tail.

Status and distribution: Apparently breeds on Los Frailes del Sur off Punta Mala (flying birds seen on March 18, 1962;

Wetmore). Otherwise reported only occasionally from off Pacific coast (4 seen near Islas Secas off Chiriquí on April 1, 1970, by N. G. Smith; one specimen from Santiago, Veraguas) and once (only) in Gulf of Panama (about 40 seen SW of Galera Island on September 27, 1964; N. G. Smith). Caribbean records are apparently all of storm-driven birds: one picked up near Cristobal on January 3, 1956 (J. Ambrose); one banded bird recovered at Galeta Island in September 1963; one banded bird picked up on Trans-Isthmian Highway near Gatuncillo on November 19, 1970; 4 picked up in clearing on Barro Colorado Island about November 30, 1970 (*fide* E. S. Morton); and one banded bird picked up on Colon waterfront on October 10, 1972 (all banded birds had been tagged at Dry Tortugas, Florida).

Habits: Like Bridled Tern, primarily pelagic when not breeding. In at least some areas its breeding is not annual but at 9-month intervals.

Range: Breeds locally on islands in tropical oceans, ranging widely at sea when not nesting.

LEAST TERN
(*Sterna albifrons*)

Description: 8–9. *Panama's smallest tern. Bill yellow usually tipped with black* (breeding season), blackish at other times; legs yellow to orange (sometimes dusky in immature). Breeding adult has white forehead, stripe over eye, and underparts; cap and stripe from bill to eye black; mantle pale gray with outer primaries mostly black; tail deeply forked, white. Immature and non-breeding adult similar but with black cap reduced to blackish patch on nape, immature with dusky on scapulars.

Similar species: Black Tern is somewhat larger with uniform gray back, wings, and tail. See also Yellow-billed and Peruvian Terns (below).

Status and distribution: Uncommon fall transient on both coasts (mid-August–late December) and in Gulf of Panama; one report from Gatun Lake (one seen on August 11 and 17, 1961; E. O. Willis); only one spring report (two seen at Piña, western Colon province on April 7, 1968; Ridgely); 6 to 10 birds believed this species were seen at the Aguadulce salinas in southern Coclé on June 26, 1971 (Eisenmann and J. Pujals). Only one specimen from Panama, a bird taken in Gulf of Panama on November 4, 1968 (H. Loftin and Ridgely, Smithsonian Pacific seabird project).

Habits: Often found offshore, usually with flocks of Black Terns. When together the Least can be picked out at great distances by its habit of flying well above the flock of milling Blacks. Often hovers before it dives headfirst after prey.

Range: Breeds in North America and locally on Pacific coast of Mexico, Caribbean coast of Honduras, and on southern Caribbean islands; also in Europe, Africa, Asia, and Australasia; New World birds winter south to Atlantic coast of northern Brazil (rarely to Argentina), and recorded on Pacific coast of Panama.

Note: Two similar South American species are possible though unrecorded; possibly some of the many sightings of Leasts in Panama refer to one or the other of these. Yellow-billed Tern (*S. superciliaris*) occurs on rivers and Caribbean and Atlantic coasts of South America east of the Andes; it resembles Least but is somewhat larger (9–10″), with stouter and longer bill entirely yellow, olive legs (not yellow or orange), and more black on outer primaries. Peruvian Tern (*S. lorata*), breeding on coast of Peru, migrating north at least to Ecuador and south to Chile, also resembles Least but has longer more slender and largely black bill (even in breeding season, when only base of lower mandible yellow), darker mantle but with little black on wings, and pale gray (not white) underparts. Exposed culmen of Yellow-billed 30–34 mm, of Peruvian 29–34 mm, of Least 24–31 mm.

ROYAL TERN
(*Thalasseus maximus*)

Description: 19–21: A large tern, larger than Laughing Gull. *Bill heavy, reddish orange to orange.* Mostly white with rearcrown black (often with some white streaks), the feathers forming a bushy crest often standing out from back of head; mantle pale gray; tail moderately forked, white. For a short period at onset of breeding season entire cap solid black (rarely seen in Panama).

Similar species: The stout, orange bill is distinctive among the terns regularly occurring in Panama. See the very rare Caspian and Elegant Terns (easily confused with latter in particular).

Status and distribution: Fairly common to common along both coasts (more numerous on Pacific); nonbreeders present throughout the year but species probably most numerous during northern winter. Also occurs well offshore in Gulf of Panama and inland on larger bodies of water, especially Gatun Lake.

Range: Breeds on coasts of southern United States, Mexico, West Indies, islands in southern Caribbean, and coast of western Africa; in New World winters south to Peru and southern Argentina.

Note: Sometimes placed in the genus *Sterna.*

ELEGANT TERN
(*Thalasseus elegans*)

Description: 16–17. Rare. Closely resembles Royal Tern but smaller; the two can be distinguished only under favorable circumstances. *Bill longer and much more slender* (in shape very like Sandwich Tern's), *yellow to orange-yellow* (more reddish orange at onset of breeding season). The crest is slightly longer, and the solid black crown of breeding plumage is retained longer; underparts of breeding adults have a rosy flush; rear part of cap solid black even in nonbreeding plumage (no white streaking visible as in Royal).

Similar species: See Royal Tern.

Status and distribution: A rare transient and visitant to Pacific coast and offshore waters, probably overlooked until recently. Still no Panama specimen but there are a number of reports: 2 believed seen in Gulf of Panama south of Pearl Islands (Rey) on September 8, 1937 (R. C. Murphy); 1 photographed in flight at Fort Amador, Canal Zone, on January 23, 1969 (Ridgely); a group of 55 seen at the Aguadulce salinas, Coclé, on June 26, 1971 (Eisenmann and J. Pujals); 1 seen among a group of Sandwich Terns at Panama city on February 7, 1973 (Eisenmann); and 12 seen on rocks with 2 Royals on coast south of Aguadulce on January 6, 1974 (G. Stiles and Ridgely).

Habits: Migration appears to be mainly pelagic, but to be watched for among flocks of terns on the Pacific coast.

Range: Breeds on coast of extreme southern California, Baja California, and islands in Gulf of California; winters on coast from Ecuador to central Chile (nonbreeders remaining throughout the year); wanders north along coast of California and recorded rarely (but increasingly regularly) on Pacific coast of Central America.

Note: Sometimes placed in the genus *Sterna.*

SANDWICH TERN
(*Thalasseus sandvicensis*)

Description: 15–16. *Bill long and slender, black, with yellow tip* (at distance pale tip hard to see, occasionally even lacking). Nonbreeding plumage: mostly white with pale gray mantle and deeply forked tail; forecrown white, rearcrown and nape black, somewhat crested. In breeding plumage, crown all black.

Similar species: Most apt to be confused with Gull-billed Tern; Gull-bill has much heavier all-black bill, only slightly forked tail, and in non-breeding plumage lacks black on rearcrown (only on ear-coverts). The smaller Common Tern in nonbreeding plumage has a blackish bill (sometimes showing reddish at base) and reddish (not black) legs; its mantle is darker gray, with blackish on front edge of wing.

Status and distribution: Fairly common transient and winter resident on both coasts (somewhat more numerous on Pacific) and in Gulf of Panama; nonbreeders are found throughout the year on Pacific coast; occasionally reported from fresh water on Gatun Lake and along the Canal.

Range: Breeds on coasts of southeastern United States and on Bahamas and islands off Yucatan, also in Europe, North Africa, and southwestern Asia; in New World winters south to Ecuador and northern Argentina.

Note: Sometimes placed in the genus *Sterna.*

CASPIAN TERN
(*Hydroprogne caspia*)

Description: 21–23. Rare. *Very heavy red bill.* Nonbreeding plumage: *crown black streaked with white;* otherwise mostly white with light gray mantle, the primaries darker (visible especially from below); tail only slightly forked. In breeding plumage, crown all black.

Similar species: Resembles much more numerous Royal Tern; Royal has slimmer more orange bill, white forehead in nonbreeding plumage (black only on rearcrown), more deeply forked tail, and lacks Caspian's blackish underside of primaries.

Status and distribution: Rare, but apparently becoming more numerous in recent years, with a number of sightings and recoveries of banded birds, mostly on Caribbean coast: one banded bird recovered at Aligandí, San Blas, on November 12, 1955; banded birds recovered on Caribbean coast of Canal Zone on November 19, 1964, and

November 27, 1967; one seen on Chagres River near Gamboa on February 19, 1968 (C. Leck); one banded bird picked up on coast of Bocas del Toro in January 1969; one banded bird recovered on Pacific coast of Coclé (near mouth of Río Grande) in March 1971; one seen on Caribbean coast of Canal Zone in November 1972 (M. Perrone, J. Pujals *et al.*).

Range: Breeds locally in North America, Europe, Africa, and Asia; in New World winters south in Caribbean to Belize and northern Colombia, rarely to Panama.

BROWN NODDY
(Anous stolidus)

Description: 15. Recorded off both coasts. Bill black. *Entirely dark brown* except for *white forecrown,* becoming grayer on rear-crown; *tail wedge-shaped.* Immature darker and lacks white forecrown (restricted to superciliary and narrowly on forehead).

Similar species: Adults are a "negative" of other terns and should not be confused. Immature Sooty Tern is also essentially all brown, but has deeply forked (not wedge-shaped) tail.

Status and distribution: Probably breeds on Los Frailes del Sur off Punta Mala (photographed on May 6, 1949, *fide* Wetmore; seen in February 1961 by E. O. Willis). At times fairly common in drift lines in Gulf of Panama south of Pearl Islands to Darién (breeds on Octavio Rocks off Colombia, just south of Panama border); rare in inshore waters. Several records of Atlantic race (nominate *stolidus*) from Caribbean coast, including specimens from Bocas del Toro and San Blas, and four recent sightings (once photographed; D. Sheets) of up to 6 individuals at once on Caribbean coast of Canal Zone.

Habits: Primarily pelagic when not breeding. Often seen among flocks of Black Terns where its larger size and heavier less graceful flight make it stand out. The noddy, like the Black Tern, does not dive, rather picking up its food from the surface.

Range: Breeds locally on islands in tropical oceans, dispersing at sea when not nesting.

SKIMMERS: Rynchopidae (1)

The skimmers are a small group of tern-like birds, three species being found locally in warmer parts of the world (one in America). They differ most strongly from terns in their unusual bill in which the mandibles are laterally compressed to thin blades, with the lower mandible considerably longer than the upper. Skimmers are often seen flying low over the water with bill open and the lengthened lower mandible "ploughing" the water, in this way picking up small fish and other small aquatic life. Most skimming occurs late in the afternoon or evening; the remainder of the day is spent resting on a sandbar or beach, often consorting with terns, especially the larger species.

BLACK SKIMMER
(Rynchops niger)

Description: 16–18. *Bill compressed, bright red tipped with black, the lower mandible considerably longer than the upper. Black above* except for white forehead and rear edge to wing; white below. Tail of North American race (nominate *niger*) mostly white, of northern South America race (*cinerascens*) mostly dark gray (this a good field mark in flight); tail of southern South America race (*intercedens*) is white as in North American race (and would not be distinguishable in the field). Immature like adult but browner and somewhat streaked above.

Status and distribution: A rare and apparently irregular visitant to both coasts, always in small numbers; reported from Bocas del Toro, Veraguas, Colon and Panama provinces, and both coasts of Canal Zone. Migrants from both North and South America probably occur; the only specimen taken (at Cocoplum, Bocas del Toro on October 28, 1927) is of the northern South America race. Two birds of the northern South America race were present at Coco Colo, Canal Zone, in late June and July 1973 (well photographed by J. Pujals). Recorded mostly June–October.

Habits: Usually seen with gulls or terns.

Range: Breeds on coasts of eastern United States and both coasts of Mexico, and on coasts and along larger rivers in much of South America; scattered records from Central America and West Indies.

PIGEONS AND DOVES: Columbidae (23)

The pigeons and doves are a widespread group of birds, well represented in Panama. They are heavy-bodied with small heads, rather short necks, and short legs. Most Panamanian species are plainly though attractively attired in various soft shades of brown and gray, often with some irridescence on head or breast (in some of the quail-doves also on back). Most species are found individually or in pairs; however, some of the pigeons (especially the Band-tailed) and the *Columbina* ground-doves regularly flock. They all feed chiefly on various sorts of vegetable matter. The nest is a flimsy structure of twigs usually placed in a bush or tree; young are fed by regurgitating "crop-milk." Several species are considered good gamebirds, and one, the Band-tailed, has been greatly reduced in numbers.

WHITE-CROWNED PIGEON
(*Columba leucocephala*)

Description: 13–14. Known only from Bocas del Toro. Bill with red base and whitish tip. *Mostly dark slaty gray* with *prominent white crown* (pale grayish in female). Not likely to be confused; looks black at a distance.

Status and distribution: Fairly common locally along coast of western Bocas del Toro and on offshore islands (Swan Cay, Escudo de Veraguas). Possibly only a post-breeding wanderer from the West Indies; no definite proof of breeding in Panama.

Habits: Frequents tall mangroves and adjacent forest growth. The call is a deep throaty *crooo-cru-cru-crooo* (J. Bond).

Range: Southern Florida; islands off Yucatan, Belize, Honduras, Nicaragua, and Caribbean western Panama.

PALE-VENTED PIGEON
(*Columba cayennensis*) Pl.4

Description: 12–13. Bill black. *Mostly deep ruddy brown,* head more grayish and with crown and nape glossed with green and bronze; breast and upper belly reddish brown, *fading to whitish on lower belly and under tail-coverts;* lower back and rump gray.

Similar species: A large dark arboreal pigeon, quite easily confused with Short-billed Pigeon but note larger size, noticeably paler lower belly (not uniformly rufous brown), and different habitats (Pale-vent in lighter woodland and borders, Short-bill in humid forest). Scaled Pigeon is about same size and often occurs with Pale-vent but is conspicuously scaled below and has red bill.

Status and distribution: Fairly common to common in lighter woodland and borders, clearings, mangroves, and residential areas with large trees in lowlands on both slopes, ranging in smaller numbers up into foothills to about 3500 feet; common also on Coiba Island, Taboga Island, Pearl Islands, and other islands off Pacific coast.

Habits: Usually rather shy, perching high in tall trees, often in small groups. The usual call is a mournful hooting, *coó-oo, cuk-tu-cóoo, cuk-tu-cóooo,* etc., sometimes with the *coó-oo* omitted or with only one *cuk-tu-cóoo.*

Range: Southeastern Mexico to Bolivia, northern Argentina, and Uruguay.

BAND-TAILED PIGEON
(*Columba fasciata*) Pl.4

Description: 13–14. Found only in western highlands. Bill yellow. Dark brown above with conspicuous *white band across hindneck;* vinaceous below; *basal half of tail dark grayish, outer half pale grayish* (the contrast prominent, especially in flight).

Similar species: Only other large arboreal pigeon found in western highlands is the smaller and more uniformly ruddy brown Ruddy Pigeon.

Status and distribution: Fairly common to common in forest, forest borders, and clearings with large trees in highlands of western Chiriquí (4000–10,000 feet); recorded also from eastern Chiriquí and Veraguas highlands.

Habits: Breeds in mountain forests, descending in flocks in May, June, and July. Still locally common but numbers have greatly decreased in recent years due to a combination of intense hunting pressure and extensive habitat destruction. Formerly, flocks were reported to be enormous, up to a thousand birds; today, however, a flock of fifty is large. Most often seen flying high above the valleys and mountain slopes. Usually perches high, but sometimes comes lower to feed in fruiting trees. The hooting call of Chiriquí birds has been paraphrased as *look for paw-paw* (R. Ward).

Range: Western North America to western

Panama; Venezuela and Colombia to northwestern Argentina.

Note: Birds from Costa Rica, western Panama, and South America are by some treated as a distinct species, *C. albilinea* (White-naped Pigeon).

SCALED PIGEON
(*Columba speciosa*) Pl.4

Description: 11–13. *Bill bright red.* Mostly chestnut with *neck, upper back, throat, and chest with white spots and black markings, giving an unmistakable scaly effect;* lower underparts whitish, somewhat scallopped with dusky; tail dark brownish black. Female somewhat duller.

Similar species: In poor light or in flight, scaly effect may not be evident, but red bill can usually be seen.

Status and distribution: Common in forest borders, second-growth woodland, and shrubby clearings in lowlands and foothills on both slopes to about 4000 feet; sometimes comes out into more open country to feed.

Habits: Single birds or pairs often perch conspicuously on high dead branches; sometimes occurs in small groups when feeding. The usual call is a single deep *coo.*

Range: Southern Mexico to Bolivia, northern Argentina, and southern Brazil.

RUDDY PIGEON
(*Columbia subvinacea*)

Description: 11–12. Known only from western highlands and extreme eastern Panama. Closely resembles more widespread Short-billed Pigeon. Bill black, short. *Entirely ruddy brown,* glossed with purplish on hindneck.

Similar species: Short-billed Pigeon is very similar but is duller on back and wings; the two can only be distinguished at very close range or by voice; they overlap only in a limited area.

Status and distribution: Uncommon to fairly common in forest and forest borders in highlands of Chiriquí and Veraguas above 3500 feet; a smaller race is found in lowlands of eastern Darién (Tuira/Chucunaque River valley) and eastern San Blas (Puerto Obaldía).

Habits: Primarily a forest bird, usually seen in pairs or small groups perching high in trees. The call in Chiriquí resembles Short-billed Pigeon's but is faster and somewhat higher, with different rhythm, *cook, wocoocoo,* also has growling *krrrow.* Darién birds are reported to give a soft plaintive *whoo-oo-a hoo hoo* (Wetmore).

Range: Costa Rica and western Panama; eastern Panama to Bolivia and central Brazil.

Note: Wetmore suggests that the eastern Panama form *berlepschi* (ranging to western Ecuador) may prove to be specifically distinct.

SHORT-BILLED PIGEON
(*Columba nigrirostris*) Pl.4

Description: 10–11. Bill black, very short. *Mostly warm brown,* duller and *more olive brown on back, wings, and tail.*

Similar species: Pale-vented Pigeon is larger and has whitish lower belly. Closely resembles Ruddy Pigeon: Short-bill is a lowland forest bird, while, in west, Ruddy is a highland forest bird. In western foothills and in Darién and San Blas, they may occur together and then are very difficult to distinguish, though the Ruddy is a more uniform ruddy brown bird; their calls differ slightly.

Status and distribution: Common in humid forest and borders on entire Caribbean slope; on Pacific slope known from lowlands and foothills (to about 4500 feet) in Chiriquí and western Veraguas and from eastern Panama province (Cerro Azul/Jefe area, Bayano River) and Darién. Widespread and numerous in forest on Caribbean side of Canal Zone.

Habits: Usually seen in pairs at middle and upper tree levels, sometimes coming lower and out into small clearings to feed. Relatively lethargic, and often quite unsuspicious. Unlike Pale-vented and Scaled Pigeons, rarely perches conspicuously in the open. Heard far more often than it is seen, the far-carrying musical call of this species is one of the characteristic sounds of the Panamanian forest, typically a mellow mournful *ho, cu-cu-coóo* (Eisenmann) or *oh-whit-mo-gó* (Wetmore); also has a growling *grrrrr.*

Range: Southern Mexico to northwestern Colombia.

Note: The specimen from which *C. chiriquensis* was described is, according to Wetmore, a slightly aberrant example of this species.

MOURNING DOVE
(*Zenaida macroura*)

Description: 11–12. A slender dove with a *long, pointed white-bordered tail.* Mostly light brown, paler on throat and belly, with small black spot on ear-coverts and black spotting on wings.

Similar species: White-winged Dove has shorter, more rounded tail, and large white patch on wing, prominent in flight.

Status and distribution: Locally fairly common in savannas and scrubby areas in lowlands on Pacific slope from Chiriquí to western Panama province, ranging up occasionally to about 4800 feet in Chiriquí highlands. Resident population is augmented during northern winter by migrants from temperate North America (November–early April), at which time it has also been reported once each from Bocas del Toro and Canal Zone (latter a sight report of one at Balboa on February 18, 1941; R. C. Murphy).

Habits: Usually found in small groups and rather wary. Feeds mostly on ground.

Range: Breeds from North America south locally to central Panama; Bahamas and Greater Antilles; northern birds winter south to Panama, accidentally to Colombia.

Note: Inca Dove (*Scardafella inca*) of southwestern United States to Costa Rica has been extending its range southward on Pacific slope of Costa Rica and may spread into western Panama. It is a rather small (8″), essentially terrestrial dove of open country, grayish with scaled upperparts and long white-bordered tail.

[EARED DOVE]

(*Zenaida auriculata*)

Description: 9–10. One recent record. Superficially resembles Mourning Dove but *notably smaller and without pointed tail* (tip rounded). Crown gray with small black spot behind eye and a larger one below ear-coverts; olive brown above with black spots on wing-coverts; forehead, sides of head, and underparts vinaceous; *in flight, outer tail feathers show conspicuous cinnamon-rufous in northern races.* Female lacks gray crown. Some South American races (less likely in Panama) have white (not cinnamon) in tail.

Similar species: Mourning Dove is larger with pointed, white-bordered tail.

Status and distribution: Only record is an immature (still with scaling on back and wing-coverts, and very tame) seen and photographed at Coco Solo, Canal Zone on February 3, 1973 (Ridgely, Eisenmann, J. Gwynne and C. Leahy). While there is no question as to the bird's specific identity, its provenance is uncertain; it perhaps escaped from captivity. In its normal range found in open, often semi-arid, country.

Range: Most of South America; southern Lesser Antilles; one recent record from Panama.

WHITE-WINGED DOVE

(*Zenaida asiatica*)

Description: 11. Known only from mangroves and adjacent scrubby areas in Herrera and Coclé. Mostly brown with crown and hindneck glossed with purplish and small black spot on ear-coverts; *large white patch on wing-coverts* (visible both at rest and in flight); lower underparts grayish; tail gray, not pointed, tipped white.

Similar species: Easily known by the conspicuous white patch on the wing. Somewhat resembles the more widespread Mourning Dove.

Status and distribution: Uncommon and local in or near mangrove swamps of Herrera and southwestern Coclé (chiefly around Gulf of Parita); feeds in adjacent fields and scrubby areas. No definite proof of breeding, though probable. It perhaps retreats to mangrove swamps during dry season, at other times dispersing and probably breeding in dry scrubby areas as elsewhere in its range (Eisenmann).

Habits: Rather shy and difficult to find in Panama. Occasionally gathers in flocks: 30 in scrub on coast near Monagre, Herrera on June 4, 1967 (H. Loftin). The usual call is a series of soft cooing notes, for example *who hoó hoó-ah* (Wetmore).

Range: Southwestern United States south locally to northern Costa Rica; west-central Panama; western Ecuador to northern Chile; Bahamas and Greater Antilles. Northern birds winter at least occasionally to Costa Rica.

PLAIN-BREASTED GROUND-DOVE

(*Columbina minuta*) Pl.4

Description: 5–6. Small. Head and nape bluish gray; upperparts otherwise grayish brown; *light grayish below;* wing-coverts with a few spots of steel blue, *primaries chestnut* (very prominent in flight); outer tail feathers narrowly tipped white. Female is duller.

Similar species: Male of more widespread Ruddy Ground-Dove is mostly ruddy brown, with only head gray. Females of the two species approach each other and are sometimes very difficult to distinguish, but female Ruddy is always ruddier on back than female Plain-breast. Plain-breast is far more local and less numerous, favoring dry short grass areas; Ruddy is widespread in both dry and humid areas.

Status and distribution: Locally common in dry or open areas with extensive grassland in lowlands on Pacific slope from Chiriquí to eastern Panama province; on Caribbean slope recorded locally and infrequently only from Canal Zone. Rather scarce in Canal Zone, even on Pacific slope, but numerous in some areas of savannas to east and west.

Habits: Usually in pairs though occasionally gathers in small groups. Generally less confiding than Ruddy Ground-Dove. Calls *whoop, whoop, whoop*... from 5 to 30 times without a pause.

Range: Southeastern Mexico locally to Peru, northern Paraguay, and southern Brazil.

RUDDY GROUND-DOVE

(*Columbina talpacoti*) Pl.4

Description: 6–7. Male *mostly ruddy brown* with *gray head;* wings with a few black spots; primaries and secondaries flash rufous in flight. Female duller brown and paler below, but *back still distinctly brown.*

Similar species: Male's ruddy coloration with contrasting gray head in distinctive; female more easily confused, especially with the grayer Plain-breasted Ground-Dove, but usually can be known by the company they keep. Female Blue Ground-Dove is larger.

Status and distribution: Abundant in clearings, shrubby areas, and around habitations in lowlands on both slopes, ranging up in smaller numbers into foothills and rarely to lower highlands (to about 5300 feet, in Chiriquí); found also on Coiba Island and the Pearl Islands.

Habits: One of the most numerous birds in open and settled parts of Panama. Small flocks gather on grassy lawns and fields where they crouch close to the ground while feeding; at one's approach they walk away with bobbing heads, flying off with a whirr when one gets too close. The male's call is a soft *hoo-whoop, hoo-whoop* . . ., repeated 3 to 10 times at a slower pace than Plain-breasted Ground-Dove's call; it is usually given from a low perch.

Range: Mexico (casually southern Texas) to Bolivia, northern Argentina, and Uruguay (sight reports); accidental in Chile.

BLUE GROUND-DOVE

(*Claravis pretiosa*) Pl.4

Description: 8. Male unmistakable, *bluish gray,* paler below and on head; wings spotted with black; outer tail feathers black. Female brown above with rufous rump; *wings spotted with chestnut;* dull brownish below with white throat and lower belly; *tail rufous and black.*

Similar species: Female somewhat resembles female Ruddy Ground-Dove but is larger with dark chestnut spots on wing, rufous rump, and bicolored tail. This species is almost always seen in pairs, which simplifies identification.

Status and distribution: Fairly common in forest borders, second growth woodland, and shrubby clearings in lowlands and foothills on both slopes, ranging in small numbers to about 5300 feet in lower highlands.

Habits: Because it usually perches in thick undergrowth or in trees, less often seen than the *Columbina* ground-doves. Pairs sometimes come out onto woodland trails and roads, especially in early morning. The male's call, an abrupt *boop* or *woop,* usually given singly but sometimes in a series, is very difficult to track down to its source; it is usually given from a perch at middle tree heights.

Range: Eastern Mexico to Bolivia, northern Argentina, and southern Brazil.

MAROON-CHESTED GROUND-DOVE

(*Claravis mondetoura*) Pl.4

Description: 8–9. Local in western highlands. Male slaty gray above with white forehead and two violet-black wing-bars; throat white, *sides of neck and chest purplish chestnut,* remaining underparts grayish; tail grayish with *outer feathers white.* Female olive brown above with *two violet-black wing-bars;* buffy below, browner on chest and flanks; tail grayish with black subterminal band and *outer feathers tipped white.*

Similar species: Handsome males are easily recognized; female somewhat resembles female Blue Ground-Dove but has bars (not just spots) on wings and shows white on tail.

Status and distribution: Rare in forest and forest borders in highlands of western Chiriquí (3000-8000 feet, chiefly above 5000 feet); recently discovered in forest on

Cerro Campana (2500 feet), where also rare (Blue Ground-Dove is more numerous). Not recorded from eastern Panama though seems possible.

Habits: Favors forest with heavy undergrowth and especially bamboo; shy and difficult to observe. The call resembles Blue Ground-Dove's, a deep and resonant *hwoop* (Eisenmann), or with a rising inflection *coo-ah* (Wetmore).

Range: Southern Mexico south locally to northwestern Venezuela and Bolivia.

WHITE-TIPPED (WHITE-FRONTED) DOVE

(*Leptotila verreauxi*) Pl.4

Description: 11. Grayish brown above, paler on forehead and with *light grayish blue orbital and loral skin; pale pinkish brown below,* becoming white on lower belly; tail blackish, *broadly tipped white.*

Similar species: Gray-headed Dove of western Panama has contrasting bluish gray head, less white on tail. See also Gray-chested Dove.

Status and distribution: Very common in lighter second-growth woodland and borders, shrubby clearings, and (where not overly persecuted) around habitations in lowlands and foothills on Caribbean slope in western Bocas del Toro and from western Colon province to western San Blas; on entire Pacific slope, though scarce in Darién, following clearings up into lower highlands to about 6000 feet in western Chiriquí; found also on Taboga Island, Pearl Islands, and other islands off Pacific coast (but not on Coiba). Very numerous and widespread in Canal Zone, often coming out onto residential lawns.

Habits: Mostly terrestrial, pottering about with head nodding back and forth; usually quite wary, flying off with a white flash in the tail before one gets too close. The call is a soft *hoó-oo* or *hoo-oo, hoo-oo,* sometimes a *tip-too-whoó.* Often called "rabiblanco."

Range: Southern Texas and Mexico to central Argentina and Uruguay.

GRAY-HEADED DOVE

(*Leptotila plumbeiceps*) Pl.4

Description: 10–11. Found locally in west. *Crown and hindneck bluish gray* with gray orbital skin and red loral skin; otherwise olive brown above (more chestnut brown in birds from Pacific slope); *pinkish white below,* more vinaceous on chest, becoming white on belly; tail dusky with outer feathers tipped white.

Similar species: Gray on head contrasting with brown back and pale underparts should distinguish this local species.

Status and distribution: Uncommon in forest and second-growth woodland in lowlands of western Bocas del Toro; also uncommon on western side of Azuero Peninsula in southern Veraguas and western Herrera, and on Cébaco Island; common on Coiba Island.

Habits: Similar to other *Leptotila* doves. Feeds on forest floor, when disturbed flying up to a low branch. Wetmore describes the call of the Bocas del Toro birds as a low note *cwuh-h-h-a* with a reedy quality suggestive of the Broad-billed Motmot, while Pacific slope birds gave a very slow *hoo-hoo,* with quality of White-tipped Dove.

Range: Eastern Mexico to western Panama; western Colombia.

Note: Wetmore treats birds from Pacific western Panama as a distinct species, *L. battyi* (Brown-backed Dove), mostly on the basis of their different vocalizations.

GRAY-CHESTED DOVE

(*Leptotila cassinii*) Pl.4

Description: 10–11. Olive brown above with *gray crown* and *red loral and orbital skin; foreneck, chest, and breast gray,* darkest on breast, pale grayish on throat, belly whitish; tail grayish with outer feathers *narrowly* tipped white. Birds from western Chiriquí (*rufinucha,* formerly sometimes treated as distinct, Rufous-naped Dove, ranging also in southwestern Costa Rica) have nape rufous brown.

Similar species: More numerous White-tipped Dove has more conspicuous white tail-tipping, pinkish brown (not gray) underparts, and bluish eye-ring and loral skin. See also Gray-headed Dove.

Status and distribution: Uncommon to locally fairly common in forest, second-growth woodland, and borders in lowlands on Caribbean slope in western Bocas del Toro and from northern Coclé east through San Blas; on Pacific slope in lowlands and foothills (to about 4200 feet) of western Chiriquí, Veraguas foothills, and from Canal Zone east through Darién. Widespread in forested parts of Canal Zone, more numerous on Caribbean side, especially in Fort Sherman/San Lorenzo area and on Achiote Road.

Habits: Everywhere less familiar than the common White-tipped Dove. A terrestrial forest dove that either walks away at one's approach, or flies up to a low branch where it nods nervously. The call is a deep low-pitched, long drawn *cooooooh* (E. O. Willis).

Range: Southern Mexico to northern Colombia.

Note: Wetmore calls it Cassin's Dove.

OLIVE-BACKED QUAIL-DOVE
(*Geotrygon veraguensis*) Pl.4

Description: 9–10. Mostly dark olive brown above glossed with dull green; *forehead white; crown and nape gray* glossed with dull purplish; *broad white facial stripe* bordered below by indistinct dark grayish stripe; brownish gray below, whitish on throat, with cinnamon flanks. Female darker, with buff forehead.

Similar species: A very dark quail-dove; the white forehead and broad facial stripe stand out in the deep forest shade. See Purplish-backed Quail-Dove.

Status and distribution: Rare to locally uncommon in undergrowth of humid forest and adjacent second-growth woodland in lowlands on Caribbean slope; on Pacific slope known from eastern Panama province (pair seen near Aguas Claras on Bayano River on July 21, 1973; D. Hill) and eastern Darién. Only recently (1968) found in Canal Zone, with nest and a number of observations from Pipeline Road (J. Karr *et al.*) and Achiote Road (Ridgely).

Habits: Usually seen walking about on the forest floor, generally quite unsuspicious, sometimes flushing and perching on low branches. Found singly or in pairs.

Range: Costa Rica to northwestern Ecuador.

RUFOUS-BREASTED QUAIL-DOVE
(*Geotrygon chiriquensis*) Pl.4

Description: 11–12. Known only from western highlands. *Crown and nape dark gray;* otherwise chestnut brown above; whitish facial stripe bordered below by prominent black moustache stripe, sides of neck giving effect of fine radial lines; throat buffy white, *becoming cinnamon-rufous on chest; remaining underparts cinnamon-buff.* Immature is brown above, darker on crown, with dusky bars on scapulars; like adult below but breast with black barring.

Similar species: Buff-fronted Quail-Dove has buff forehead and dark green crown and nape (not dark gray), more purple back, and mostly gray underparts (not rufous and cinnamon).

Status and distribution: Uncommon in undergrowth of forest and coffee plantations in highlands of Chiriquí and Veraguas, recorded 4000-10,000 feet, but mainly below 6500 feet. The most numerous quail-dove in the Bambito/Nueva Suiza area at 5200–5400 feet.

Habits: Found singly or in pairs on ground; rather shy. When flushed usually flies to a low branch. The call is a mournful one-syllabled *hoooo* (Slud).

Range: Costa Rica and western Panama.

Note: Considered by some authors to be a race of the *G. linearis* (Lined Quail-Dove) group of South America, or of *G. albifacies* (White-faced Quail-Dove, sometimes also included in *G. linearis*) of Mexico to Nicaragua. Wetmore calls it Chiriquí Quail-Dove.

RUSSET-CROWNED QUAIL-DOVE
(*Geotrygon goldmani*)

Description: 10–11. Found only in eastern Panama. Resembles Purplish-backed Quail-Dove. *Crown and hindneck russet brown;* sides of neck giving effect of fine radial lines; center of back purplish, otherwise dull brown above; *broad facial stripe cinnamon-buff,* bordered below by narrow black moustache stripe; throat white, foreneck and breast gray, lower underparts buffy white with sides and flanks brownish.

Similar species: Purplish-backed Quail-Dove has gray crown and hindneck (not brown) and white (not cinnamon) facial stripe.

Status and distribution: Known only from undergrowth in humid forest in foothills of eastern Panama province (Cerro Jefe—sighting of a single bird on July 27, 1973 by D. Hill; Serranía de Majé—one specimen) and in foothills and lower highlands of Darién (2800–5000 feet).

Habits: The call is reported to be a soft cooing, similar to the sound made by blowing across the top of a bottle (Wetmore).

Range: Eastern Panama and extreme northwestern Colombia.

Note: Wetmore calls it Goldman's Quail-Dove. Probably a member of the *G. linearis* complex (Eisenmann).

PURPLISH-BACKED QUAIL-DOVE
(*Geotrygon lawrencii*) Pl.4

Description: 10–11. Forehead grayish white, *crown and hindneck gray;* otherwise mostly olive brown above, with *contrasting triangular purplish area on upper back; facial stripe and throat white,* separated by *con-*

spicuous black moustache; foreneck and breast gray, belly buffy white; tail dusky.

Similar species: See Buff-fronted and Russet-crowned Quail-Doves.

Status and distribution: Uncommon and apparently local in undergrowth of humid forest in foothills on Caribbean slope in Bocas del Toro and eastern Colon province (Cerro Bruja); on Pacific slope recorded from Veraguas, Panama province (Cerro Campana, Cerro Azul/Jefe area), and Darién; recorded mostly 2000-3500 feet, occasionally to 1500 and 4400 feet.

Habits: Mostly terrestrial and difficult to observe in the dense undergrowth it favors. The call is a loud nasal or croaking *coo-ah,* somewhat frog-like in quality (Wetmore), given from a perch several meters above the ground.

Range: Southern Mexico; Costa Rica to eastern Panama.

Note: Wetmore calls it Lawrence's Quail-Dove.

BUFF-FRONTED QUAIL-DOVE
(*Geotrygon costaricensis*) Pl.4

Description: 10–11. Found only in western highlands. *Forehead buff, crown and nape dark green;* otherwise chestnut above, *strongly glossed with purple on back;* facial stripe white bordered below by a conspicuous black moustache; throat white, becoming *gray on foreneck and breast,* lower belly pale buff; tail grayish. Immature has whitish forehead, grayish crown; otherwise dull chestnut above barred with dusky; mainly cinnamon below with dark barring.

Similar species: A beautifully colored quail-dove, partially sympatric with the Rufous-breasted, which is rufous and cinnamon below (not mostly gray) and lacks buff forehead and purple on back. Purplish-backed Quail-Dove is mostly olive brown above (not rich chestnut), lacks buff forehead, and has gray (not green) crown.

Status and distribution: Uncommon to locally fairly common in undergrowth of forest in highlands of western Chiriquí (4000–10,000 feet); recorded also from adjacent Bocas del Toro (specimen from Camp Cylindro, 5200 feet; Mönniche) and Veraguas (two specimens from Chitra, 4000–4300 feet; Benson). Can be regularly seen in forest on Finca Lerida above Boquete.

Habits: As in other quail-doves; mostly terrestrial, usually encountered singly.

Range: Costa Rica and western Panama.

Note: Wetmore calls it Costa Rican Quail-Dove.

VIOLACEOUS QUAIL-DOVE
(*Geotrygon violacea*) Pl.4

Description: 9–10. Crown gray; otherwise *purplish chestnut brown above, strongly glossed with violet on back;* sides of head and throat gray; foreneck dull lilac, becoming vinaceous on chest and *whitish on rest of underparts. No moustache stripe.* Female duller, with olive brown wings.

Similar species: The only Panama quail-dove without a moustache stripe. Gray-chested Dove is dull olive brown above without the violaceous back and has white-tipped outer feathers.

Status and distribution: Rare and very local (except apparently in Darién) in undergrowth of humid forest in lowlands and foothills; records few, a nineteenth-century specimen from Chagres basin in present Canal Zone, specimens from eastern Colon province (Portobelo) and eastern Panama province (slopes of Cerro Azul) and a number of specimens from Darién (to 5000 feet). Not reported from western Panama, though should occur. In Canal Zone recorded recently only from sightings on Barro Colorado Island (E. O. Willis) and one reported mist-netted on Pipeline Road on February 25, 1963 (T. C. Crebs).

Habits: Somewhat more arboreal than other Panama quail-doves. When flushed from ground flies without whirr of wings to branch of a tree and utters a short hollow *cooo,* repeated at intervals, higher than call of Ruddy Quail-Dove or Gray-chested Dove (E. O. Willis). Slud reports a sort of double-stopped *oo-oo,* the first syllable higher.

Range: Nicaragua south locally to Bolivia and northern Argentina.

RUDDY QUAIL-DOVE
(*Geotrygon montana*) Pl.4

Description: 9–10. *Bill, orbital skin, and legs purplish red.* Male *rufous-chestnut above,* glossed with purple on back; *pinkish cinnamon facial stripe* bordered below by chestnut moustache; throat cinnamon, becoming buff on remaining underparts. Female much duller, mostly olive brown above with *cinnamon forehead and facial stripe;* cinnamon to buffy below, sometimes mottled with dusky on breast; tail grayish olive. Immature like female but with dusky bars and rufous spots on back and wings.

Similar species: Rufous-breasted Quail-Dove of western highlands has gray crown.

Status and distribution: Fairly common in undergrowth of forest and second-growth woodland in lowlands and foothills (to about 4000 feet in Chiriquí) on both slopes, less numerous or lacking in dry Pacific lowlands from eastern side of Azuero Peninsula to western Panama province; found also on Coiba Island and reported from Pearl Islands (San José). The most numerous and widespread quail-dove in Panama. Widespread in wooded areas of Canal Zone, but more numerous on Caribbean side.

Habits: A largely terrestrial forest dove; like other quail-doves shy and not often seen, favoring dense tangled undergrowth. Often caught in mist-nets. The call is a low soft resonant *cooo* (Ridgely) or humming moan *mmmmm* (Eisenmann), similar to but shorter than call of Gray-chested Dove (E. O. Willis).

Range: Southern Mexico to Bolivia, northeastern Argentina, and southern Brazil.

PARROTS: Psittacidae (21)

Parrots are widespread chiefly in tropical and south temperate areas of the world, but reach their greatest development in the neotropics and Australia. They are noisy and gregarious birds, familiar and widely distributed in Panama, though most numerous in forested lowlands. Most Panamanian species are basically green, the major exception being the macaws, some of which are clad in red or blue and yellow. Macaws are also characterized by their huge bills and bare facial skin; they, like the *Aratinga* parakeets, have long pointed tails. Panama's representatives vary in size from the large macaws with a length of over three feet to the tiny sparrow-sized Spectacled Parrotlet. They all feed mostly on fruit and nuts, and nest in hollows in trees or in termitaries. Many species are still quite numerous and easily seen, especially in the early morning when they fly to their feeding areas, generally in groups numbering in multiples of two, the pairs remaining together throughout the year. Macaws, however, have been greatly reduced throughout Panama, and now occur only in remote mostly unsettled areas, especially in the forested eastern third of the country. Not only have the macaws been affected by the reduction in their habitat, but in some areas they are shot for food and the young are taken from nest holes to be sold as pets or to dealers. Without increased protection, several species will probably become extinct in Panama in the near future: a sad loss, as there are few grander sights than a pair or flock of these great birds flying by with their long tails streaming behind.

BLUE-AND-YELLOW MACAW
(*Ara ararauna*)

Description: 32–34. Known only from eastern Panama. Unmistakable. Very long pointed tail. *Rich blue above;* small area on throat black; ear-coverts, sides of neck, and *entire underparts orange-yellow*. Bare skin on sides of head white with narrow lines of blackish feathers.

Status and distribution: Uncommon to locally still fairly common in extensively forested and essentially unsettled areas in lowlands on Pacific slope in eastern Panama province (upper Bayano River valley, above Majé) and Darién. Decreasing in numbers, rapidly so near inhabited areas.

Habits: As with other large macaws, most often seen in pairs or small flocks during flight overhead in the early morning and late afternoon, en route between their roosts and feeding areas. Their extremely loud, raucous calls are very often given in flight, and frequently are the first indication that a pair or two of these truly spectacular birds are coming your way. Macaws are generally silent when feeding, however, and at such times can be difficult to see.

Range: Eastern Panama to Bolivia, Paraguay, and southeastern Brazil.

GREAT GREEN MACAW
(*Ara ambigua*)

Description: 32–34. Very long pointed tail. *Mostly green,* with red forehead, pale blue lower back and rump, and some red feathers in tail; *from below wings and tail yellow*. Bare skin on face whitish with narrow lines of black feathers.

Similar species: Chestnut-fronted Macaw is also mostly green, but has underside of wings reddish and is hardly half the size.

Status and distribution: Local, but now the most numerous large macaw in Panama; found in relatively remote forested areas in lowlands and foothills on both slopes. Reported in recent years from Bocas del Toro,

GREAT GREEN MACAW

western Los Santos, eastern Panama province (Bayano River valley; also seen in November 1973 on the Platanares-Jesús María road east of Chepo by N. Gale), and Darién. Formerly occurred in Canal Zone but unknown in this century except for one possible sighting in 1911 and another reported to have been killed around 1950.

Habits: Similar to other large macaws, usually seen in pairs flying over in early morning and late afternoon, with raucous far-carrying calls. Relatively tame in undisturbed areas.

Range: Nicaragua (perhaps Honduras) to western Ecuador.

Note: Wetmore calls it Green Macaw.

SCARLET MACAW
(*Ara macao*)

Description: 35–38. Now found regularly only on Coiba Island and southwestern Azuero Peninsula. Very long pointed tail. *Mostly scarlet* with *yellow wing-coverts* (prominent at rest and in flight) and blue flight feathers and rump. Bare skin on sides of head white.

Similar species: Red-and-green Macaw (with which it is not now known to occur in Panama) is darker red and has green (not yellow) wing-coverts. Otherwise unmistakable at virtually any distance if light is adequate.

Status and distribution: Fairly common on Coiba Island, where protected by the lack of shooting (the whole island is a penal institute). Apparently still ranges in small numbers in western Los Santos, and possibly a few survive in western Chiriquí (or birds wander in from southwestern Costa Rica). Formerly more widespread on Pacific slope, and known to have occurred on Caribbean slope of Canal Zone, but curiously there are no records from eastern Panama.

Habits: Similar to other large macaws. In most areas this species favors light and gallery woodland and savannas, not humid forest. In Panama (and elsewhere in Latin America) all the large macaws are known as "guacamayos."

Range: Southern Mexico to northern Bolivia and Amazonian Brazil.

RED-AND-GREEN MACAW
(*Ara chloroptera*)

Description: 35–38. Now found only in eastern Panama. *Very large* with long pointed tail. *Mostly red* with *green wing-coverts* (prominent at rest and in flight); flight feathers, most of outer tail feathers, and rump blue. Bare skin on sides of head white with lines of small red feathers. Bill proportionately larger than in other Panamanian macaws.

Similar species: The similar Scarlet Macaw is more scarlet in color and has yellow (not green) wing-coverts. The two are not known to occur together in Panama.

Status and distribution: Found locally in heavily forested and little settled areas in lowlands and foothills of eastern Panama province (Bayano River valley above Majé), Darién, and eastern San Blas; formerly (in nineteenth-century) occurred west to Caribbean slope of Canal Zone. Decreasing in numbers.

Habits: Similar to other large macaws.

Range: Eastern Panama to northern Argentina, Paraguay, and southern Brazil.

Note: Wetmore calls it Red-blue-and-green Macaw.

CHESTNUT-FRONTED MACAW

(*Ara severa*) Pl.5

Description: 18–20. Long pointed tail. *Mostly green* with *dull chestnut forehead* and bluish green crown; *underside of wings and tail dull reddish.* Bare skin on sides of head creamy white with lines of very small, blackish feathers.

Similar species: The smallest Panamanian macaw; the Great Green is almost twice as large. Told from the larger parrots, even at a great distance, by the long pointed tail.

Status and distribution: Fairly common in generally forested areas in lowlands of eastern Panama province (Bayano River above Majé) and Darién; formerly occurred west to Caribbean slope of Canal Zone and may occasionally still do so. This is the macaw most likely to be seen in the Canal Zone area; there are several recent sightings from the Canal Zone, including one from the Pacific slope (one flying overhead with Blue-headed Parrots on K–6 Road in southwestern sector on June 14, 1971; Ridgely, Eisenmann and T. Lovejoy), which are either wandering birds from further east or escaped cage birds (though the species, with its relatively dull plumage and small size, is not common in captivity).

Habits: Seems to favor partially wooded areas, often swampy, with many dead trees. Like other macaws most likely to be seen flying overhead in early morning or late afternoon; has faster wingbeats than the large macaws. Its calls are shriller than those of other Panamanian macaws.

Range: Central Panama to northern Bolivia and Amazonian Brazil.

CRIMSON-FRONTED PARAKEET

(*Aratinga finschi*) Pl.5

Description: 11–12. Found only in western Panama. Green with *red forecrown and front edge of wing;* in flight from below under wing-coverts red and primaries yellow.

Similar species: The largest Panama parakeet and the only one with red forecrown and on the wing. Red-fronted Parrotlet is much smaller and has square tail. See also Sulphur-winged Parakeet.

Status and distribution: Locally common in lowlands of western Bocas del Toro, western Chiriquí, and Pacific western Veraguas; on Pacific side wanders up to lower highlands to over 5000 feet. Apparently increasing in recent years.

Habits: Primarily a bird of open woodland and borders; roosts in large numbers in palms at Almirante, Bocas del Toro, and in patches of tall bamboo above Concepción, Chiriquí. Rather noisy, with loud screeching calls, *keerr, keerr,* given particularly in flight and at roosting areas.

Range: Nicaragua to western Panama.

Note: Wetmore calls it Finsch's Parakeet. Considered by some authors to be a race of *A. leucophthalmus* (White-eyed Parakeet) of South America. Aviculturists call members of the genus *Aratinga* "Conures."

OLIVE-THROATED (AZTEC) PARAKEET

(*Aratinga astec*)

Description: 9–10. Known only from western Bocas del Toro. Green above, *buffy-olive below,* somewhat greener on chest with dusky streaks; in flight, shows blue band on upper part of wing.

Similar species: Rather like Brown-throated Parakeet (a Pacific slope bird) but more olive (not brown) below, without bluish on head, and without adult Brown-throat's patch of orange feathers below eye.

Status and distribution: Rare in lowlands of western Bocas del Toro. Four specimens were taken between April and October 1927, and one was taken at Almirante on April 6, 1963 (S. Olson); no other reports. Possibly only a wanderer from further north.

Habits: Keeps rather low in trees in clearings and at forest borders. Has a high-pitched screeching.

Range: Eastern Mexico to Caribbean western Panama.

BROWN-THROATED PARAKEET

(*Aratinga pertinax*) Pl.5

Description: 9–10. Green above, the crown usually more bluish green, with *prominent patch of orange feathers below eye; sides of head, throat, and chest buffy brownish,* fading to yellowish green on lower underparts; underside of wings mostly slaty. Immature lacks the orange beneath eye.

Similar species: Widely sympatric with the smaller and shorter-tailed Orange-chinned Parakeet. Olive-throated Parakeet of Bocas del Toro lacks the orange below the eye, and is not as brown on throat and chest. Crimson-fronted Parakeet is larger with red on crown and red and yellow on wing.

Status and distribution: Locally common in savannas and open scrubby areas on Pacific slope from western Chiriquí to western Panama province; an irregular wanderer in small numbers further east to Pacific side of Canal Zone and Panama city area, occurring mostly in dry season (December–April), rarely wandering even to Caribbean side of Canal Zone (some of these reports may represent escaped cage birds). Commonly seen along the Pan-American Highway from about Playa Coronado westward.

Habits: Usually seen in small flocks flying by rapidly, chattering loudly as they go. Often rather unsuspicious.

Range: Western and central Panama; Colombia to northern Brazil and the Guianas.

Note: The Panama form (*ocularis*) has sometimes been treated as a distinct species, Veragua Parakeet.

SULPHUR-WINGED PARAKEET

(*Pyrrhura hoffmanni*) Pl.5

Description: 9–10. Found only in western highlands. Slender and long-tailed. Mostly green, somewhat brownish on head with *dull red ear-coverts; yellow wing-coverts, inner primaries, and outer secondaries* conspicuous in flight but more or less hidden at rest; yellow area on underside of flight feathers; tail tinged brownish red.

Similar species: Crimson-fronted Parakeet (with which it occasionally occurs) is larger with red forecrown and none on cheeks, lacks yellow on upperside of wings.

Status and distribution: Common (though somewhat erratic) in highlands of western Chiriquí above 4000 feet; found also in foothills and highlands of Bocas del Toro, occasionally wandering even down to the lowlands, and recently reported from Veraguas (small flock above Santa Fé in February 1974; S. West).

Habits: Most often noted in small flocks as they wing by rapidly with high-pitched chatters and screeches, *kreey-kreey-kreey* or *keeyik-keeyik-keeyik*. Usually rather wary, but sometimes a feeding group can be approached closely.

Range: Costa Rica and western Panama.

Note: Wetmore calls it Hoffmann's Parakeet. Aviculturists call members of the genus *Pyrrhura* "Conures."

BARRED PARAKEET

(*Bolborhynchus lineola*) Pl.5

Description: 6–6¾. Known only from western Panama highlands. Tail short, wedge-shaped. Green *more or less barred all over with black;* black bend of wing.

Similar species: In shape, rather like the much more abundant Orange-chinned Parakeet of lowlands; in flight or in poor light the black barring of this species is hard to see. Very rare Red-fronted Parrotlet has a square tail, lacks the barring, and has much red on wing.

Status and distribution: Rather rare and very erratic in highlands of western Chiriquí above 4500 feet; also recorded from adjacent highlands of Bocas del Toro down to about 2000 feet, and recently from above Santa Fé, Veraguas (flock of 6 seen on April 8, 1975; N. G. Smith).

Habits: Usually in flocks, sometimes large. Very difficult to see perched when it "vanishes" into the green foliage of the upper parts of large trees. Has a soft musical chattering.

Range: Southern Mexico to western Panama; Andes of western Venezuela, Colombia, and Peru.

Note: Wetmore calls it Banded Parakeet.

SPECTACLED PARROTLET

(*Forpus conspicillatus*) Pl.32

Description: 5. Known only from eastern Panama. A *tiny* parrot, sparrow-sized, with very short, wedge-shaped tail. Male green with *bright blue ocular region* (often not very conspicuous) and *dark blue wing-coverts and rump.* Female lacks the blue, but both sexes have bluish green under wing-coverts.

Similar species: The smallest Panamanian parrot. Orange-chinned Parakeet is larger, with longer tail, lacks the blue, and has brown shoulders.

Status and distribution: Uncommon and rather local in lighter woodland, borders, and clearings in lowlands of eastern Panama province (Bayano River around Majé: first noted on August 3–4, 1972, by Ridgely and J. Pujals, then already fairly numerous with flocks of up to 25 seen; 2 collected on February 9, 1973 by P. Galindo, specimens in Gorgas Lab coll.) and eastern Darién (reported mostly from lower Tuira River valley; also a flock of 8 seen at Piñas Bay on June 20, 1969 by Ridgely). May be spreading westward and increasing in numbers with clearing of more forest.

Habits: Usually seen flying by in small groups with buzzing or chattering calls. Upon alighting in a tree they become exceedingly difficult to see.

Range: Eastern Panama through northern Colombia to western Venezuela.

ORANGE-CHINNED (BROWN-SHOULDERED) PARAKEET
(*Brotogeris jugularis*) Pl.5

Description: 6½–7¼. *Fairly short, wedge-shaped tail.* Mostly green with small spot of orange on chin (usually difficult to see in the field) and *brown shoulders;* under wing-coverts yellow.

Similar species: *Aratinga* parakeets are considerably larger, with long pointed tails. *Touit* parrotlets have square tails and lack the brown shoulders. See also Spectacled Parrotlet (much smaller) and Barred Parakeet (barred with black).

Status and distribution: Abundant and widespread in lowlands on both slopes except in Bocas del Toro and Caribbean slope Veraguas; most numerous in cleared areas with trees and in second-growth woodland, but also found in canopy and borders of humid forest; ranges in reduced numbers up into foothills; found also on Coiba and Taboga Islands, but not known from Pearl Islands.

Habits: The most familiar of Panama's parrots and a popular cage bird, known locally as "perico" (as are the other parakeets). Abundant throughout the Canal Zone where it roosts in large numbers in stands of banyans or palms. Often occurs in large flocks. Very noisy, flocks give an almost incessant chattering.

Range: Southern Mexico to northern Colombia and northern Venezuela.

RED-FRONTED PARROTLET
(*Touit costaricensis*) Pl.5

Description: 6–6½. Apparently very rare; found only in western Panama. *Tail short and square.* Green with *red forecrown,* lores and narrow streak below eye also red; *wing-coverts and outer edge of wing red* (very prominent in flight from above), primaries and outer secondaries black (visible in flight); tail light greenish yellow tipped with black; under wing-coverts yellow (conspicuous in flight from below). Female has less red on wing-coverts.

Similar species: Blue-fronted Parrotlet of eastern Panama is similar but has blue forecrown. Orange-chinned Parakeet has wedge-shaped tail, lacks the red, and has brown shoulders. See also Barred Parakeet.

Status and distribution: Uncertain; only two Panama records. One collected above Boquete, Chiriquí (4000 feet) on February 17, 1905; another taken at Cocoplum, Bocas del Toro (at sea level) on November 5, 1927.

Habits: In Costa Rica, where it seems more numerous, this species favors very humid forested foothill areas, perhaps descending seasonally to lowlands. Usually noted in the early morning as it flies overhead in pairs or small groups to the day's feeding area (Ridgely).

Range: Costa Rica and western Panama.

Note: Considered by some authors to be a race of the following species, in which case the enlarged complex should be called Red-winged Parrotlet.

BLUE-FRONTED PARROTLET
(*Touit dilectissima*)

Description: 6–6½. Known only from eastern Panama. Closely resembles Red-fronted Parrotlet of western Panama (sometimes regarded as conspecific). Male differs in having inconspicuous *blue forecrown* (no red), and more blue and less red below eye. Female resembles male but has less red on wing-coverts.

Similar species: See Red-fronted Parrotlet. Spectacled Parrotlet is smaller with no red, has blue rump and wing-coverts.

Status and distribution: Recorded from forest in foothills and lower highlands of eastern Darién (Cerro Pirre and near Cana); two recent sightings from Cerro Jefe, eastern Panama province: one flying from its nest in an arboreal termitary on January 11, 1974 (Ridgely and C. Leahy), and a family group of 2 adults and 3 juvenals photographed on July 24, 1975 (Ridgely).

Range: Eastern Panama to northwestern Venezuela and northwestern Ecuador.

BROWN-HOODED PARROT
(*Pionopsitta haematotis*) Pl.5

Description: 8–9. Rather chunky, with short tail. Pale bill; bare orbital skin bluish white. *Head brownish slate or brownish olive* with *small red patch on ear-coverts;* otherwise mostly green above and below, male sometimes with a broken collar of red on foreneck; upper and under wing-coverts dark blue, *axillars red* (conspicuous in flight from below). Female somewhat duller.

Similar species: A small parrot, likely to be confused only with the Blue-headed, though lacking the blue. See also the *Touit* parrotlets.

Status and distribution: Locally fairly common in forest and forest borders in lowlands and foothills on entire Caribbean slope; on Pacific slope known from lowlands and foothills in Chiriquí and Veraguas, and from Panama province (Chorrera, Tocumen, Cerro Azul eastward) east through Darién. In Canal Zone quite numerous on Pipeline Road; also easily seen on Cerro Azul.

Habits: Usually seen in small groups. Has a distinctive rapid flight, tossing from side to side, lifting wings above the horizontal. The calls are quite high-pitched, a *check-check* or *cheek-cheek,* and a thin *tseek.*

Range: Southern Mexico to western Ecuador.

Note: Wetmore calls it Red-eared Parrot.

SAFFRON-HEADED PARROT
(*Pionopsitta pyrilia*) Pl.32

Description: 8–9. Known only from eastern Darién. *Head, neck, and shoulders orange-yellow;* otherwise green above; chest olive, breast and belly green; bend of wing, axillars, and under wing-coverts red.

Similar species: No other Panama parrot has entire head yellow. Panama race of Yellow-headed Amazon has only forecrown yellow and is much larger.

Status and distribution: Uncertain. Apparently rare, known only from two specimens taken in lower Tuira River valley of eastern Darién (near Boca de Cupe and Tapalisa) in 1915.

Range: Eastern Panama through northern Colombia to western Venezuela.

BLUE-HEADED PARROT
(*Pionus menstruus*) Pl.5

Description: 9½–10. Base of bill reddish. *Head, neck, and chest blue,* with blackish ear-coverts; otherwise mostly green, with red under tail-coverts and base of underside of tail.

Similar species: No other Panama parrot has an all-blue head (though this can be difficult to see in poor light). White-crowned Parrot of extreme western Panama is somewhat similar but has a white crown.

Status and distribution: Common in forest, second-growth woodland, and adjacent clearings with some trees left standing in lowlands on both slopes, in western Chiriquí ranging up to around 4000 feet near Volcán; found also on Coiba Island and the larger Pearl Islands. Widespread in forested areas in the Canal Zone, though in larger numbers on the Caribbean side.

Habits: In most areas the most numerous of the larger parrots. In flight, easily told from the Amazon parrots (which are larger) by its deeper wing-stroke. Flight calls are relatively high-pitched and characteristically doubled, *keeweenk, keeweenk, keeweenk . . .* ; when perched, gives other calls, typically a *krrreeeck.* Often kept in captivity, and known locally as "casanga."

Range: Costa Rica to northern Bolivia and central Brazil.

WHITE-CROWNED PARROT
(*Pionus senilis*)

Description: 9½-10. Found only in western Panama. *Forecrown white* (conspicuous in the field); remainder of head, neck, and chest greenish blue; otherwise mostly green above, wing-coverts edged and spotted with buff; throat white; breast and belly dark green, somewhat edged with blue; under tail-coverts and base of tail red. Female usually duller than male.

Status and distribution: Uncommon in second-growth woodland and clearings with large trees in lowlands, foothills, and lower highlands (to about 5000 feet) of western Chiriquí and in lowlands of western Bocas del Toro. Small numbers can regularly be seen in the remnant patches of forest around Volcán.

Habits: Similar to Blue-headed Parrot. Like that species, very noisy, with the usual flight call a raucous *krreeck, krreeck, krreeck. . . .* (Ridgely). Has a very deep wingstroke, even deeper than Blue-head's.

Range: Eastern Mexico to western Panama.

RED-LORED (RED-FRONTED) AMAZON (PARROT)
(*Amazona autumnalis*) Pl.5

Description: 12–13. Red forehead and lores; otherwise mostly green, *more yellowish green on face* and throat, with crown and nape feathers edged lavender; red patch on secondaries (visible in flight) and some red at base of tail.

Similar species: The red area on the fore-

WHITE-CROWNED PARROT

head is small and not easy to see, which makes this species easy to confuse with the other Amazons, especially in flight; often the yellowish cheeks (a character not shared by other Panama Amazons) are more prominent at a distance. When together can be told from Mealy Amazon by its smaller size.

Status and distribution: Common and widespread in forest and more humid woodland in lowlands and foothills on both slopes, though absent from drier areas on eastern side of Azuero Peninsula, southern Coclé, and western Panama province; found also on Coiba Island, the larger Pearl Islands, and Escudo de Veraguas. More numerous in less settled areas, and still present in large numbers at least locally (e.g., at least 600–800 came in to roost near Majé, eastern Panama province, on August 2–4, 1972; Ridgely and J. Pujals). In Canal Zone rather scarce on Pacific side, but common and widespread in forested areas on Caribbean.

Habits: Relatively catholic in its choice of habitat. As with other larger parrots, almost invariably seen in multiples of two. Like other Amazons, flies with shallow stiff wing-strokes, very striking in the field and making the genus easy to recognize even if the various species often are not. The Red-lore's flight calls are very loud and harsh, the most strident of Panama's three Amazons, a repeated *keekorák, keekorák, keekorák* . . . (Ridgely), or *chikák, chikák, oorák, oorák, ooerk* (F. Chapman).

Range: Eastern Mexico to western Ecuador and northwestern Brazil.

YELLOW-HEADED AMAZON (PARROT)

(*Amazona ochrocephala*) Pl.5

Description: 12–13. *Forehead and midcrown yellow;* otherwise mostly green; red patch on secondaries (visible in flight), and some red at base of tail.

Similar species: Unless seen clearly can easily be confused with other Amazons, especially the Red-lored. Yellow-headed generally favors more open country than the other two Amazons, and in flight the somewhat shorter tail and different voice can be helpful.

Status and distribution: Locally fairly common in gallery woodland and savannas in lowlands on Pacific slope from Chiriquí to western Darién; on Caribbean slope known only from a few sightings from Bocas del Toro (Wetmore), Barro Colorado Island (Eisenmann), above Madden Lake (Wetmore), and eastern San Blas, where, oddly, it is the most numerous parrot (Wetmore); found also on Coiba Island and the larger Pearl Islands. Primarily, however, a Pacific slope bird, though much reduced in central Panama. Apart from the Barro Colorado observations not reported recently from Canal Zone. In early morning, readily observed between Penonomé and Divisa on the Pan-American Highway.

Habits: Usually outnumbered by the Red-lored Amazon. Its calls are not as raucous as those of the other Panama Amazons, being deeper and more variable, *chuck, week-weeah,* and *chíckwah, chíckwah,* also a musical *wheeawhit.* Highly prized as a cagebird, and considered the best talker among the Panama parrots; for this reason, it has been much reduced about more populated areas. This and the other Amazons are known collectively as "loros."

Range: Mexico to eastern Peru and Amazonian Brazil.

Note: Some authors consider Mexican birds, *A. oratrix* (Yellow-headed Amazon), and Central American birds, *A. auropalliata* (Yellow-naped Amazon), as species distinct from Panamanian and South American birds, *A. ochrocephala* (Yellow-crowned Amazon).

MEALY AMAZON (PARROT)

(*Amazona farinosa*) Pl.5

Description: 14–16. *Mostly green,* feathers of crown and nape edged with bluish often giving a powdery look; *white* (featherless) *eye-ring;* red patch on secondaries (visible in flight).

Similar species: Notably larger than the other two Amazons, though this usually cannot be discerned without direct comparison. Note lack of either red or yellow on head.

Status and distribution: Fairly common in humid forested lowlands and foothills on both slopes, but largely absent from more open Pacific slope lowlands from western Veraguas to western Panama province; ranges up in smaller numbers to lower highlands (to about 5000 feet) of Chiriquí; numerous also on Coiba Island. In Canal Zone widespread in Caribbean side forests, though less numerous than Red-lored.

Habits: More strictly a forest bird than the

Red-lored, but also found locally in gallery woodland in savanna areas. Generally similar in habits to other Amazons. Its very loud flight calls rather resemble the Red-lore's, but can usually be recognized by the phrase *chop-chop* or *cookyüp-kyüp*.

Range: Southern Mexico to northern Bolivia and southern Brazil.

CUCKOOS: Cuculidae (11)

The cuckoos are a widespread group of generally rather inconspicuous birds, occurring in a wide range of habitats in Panama. Most Panamanian species are slender, long-tailed birds, rather solitary and of furtive habit. Various Old World species are well known for their parasitic habits; however, most New World cuckoos are not parasitic, the exceptions being the Striped Cuckoo *Tapera* and the two species of *Dromococcyx*. Anis are conspicuous black birds that occur in groups and lay their eggs in large communal nests and then share in the duties of incubation and nestling care. All other American (non-parasitic) species construct flimsy twig nests in bushes and trees. All are largely insectivorous.

BLACK-BILLED CUCKOO
(*Coccyzus erythropthalmus*)

Description: 12. Slender, smooth profile with rather long tail. *Bill all black. Bare orbital skin red in adult,* yellow in immature. Olive brown above; white below, somewhat buffier on throat; tail feathers narrowly tipped white. Immature buffier below with some rufous on primaries.

Similar species: Yellow-billed Cuckoo has yellow lower mandible (except in immatures), a prominent rufous flash in wing, and has tail feathers more broadly tipped white; adult's orbital skin is gray.

Status and distribution: A rare to uncommon fall transient, recorded mostly in October (once September 27); much less numerous in spring (only two records, April 20 and 28); reports scattered, but mostly in coastal lowlands.

Habits: Like the other Panama *Coccyzus* cuckoos, rather furtive, rarely leaving dense cover. Can occur almost anywhere on migration, but prefers open woodland and edges, clearings with scattered bushes and trees.

Range: Breeds in eastern North America; winters in northwestern South America.

YELLOW-BILLED CUCKOO
(*Coccyzus americanus*)

Description: 12. Resembles Black-billed Cuckoo. *Lower mandible yellow;* upper mandible dusky. *Bare orbital skin gray in adult,* yellow in immature. Grayish brown above; white below; wings with *primaries edged rufous* (especially visible in flight); tail feathers broadly edged white (most visible from below). Immature is similar but has less white on tail, occasionally has all blackish bill.

Similar species: See Black-billed Cuckoo. Immature Yellow-bill resembles Black-bill but almost always shows at least some yellow on lower mandible and has more white on tail (though somewhat less than as adults). Mangrove Cuckoo has prominent black mask through eyes and is buffy below.

Status and distribution: Uncommon to occasionally fairly common transient, more numerous in fall (mid-September–early December, mostly October, once August 14; early–late April, once May 11); recorded mostly in lowlands. A few evidently winter locally, with 1 seen at Tocumen, eastern Panama province on January 29, 1973, and several seen at Tocumen and on Pacific side of Canal Zone in late December 1973 (Ridgely *et al.*).

Habits: Like Black-billed Cuckoo: quiet, secretive, not often seen. Does not seem to call in Panama.

Range: Breeds in North America, Mexico, and West Indies; winters mostly in South America, a few in Costa Rica (perhaps) and Panama.

MANGROVE CUCKOO
(*Coccyzus minor*) Pl.6

Description: 12. Lower mandible yellow; upper mandible dusky. Bare orbital skin yellow. Grayish brown above with *broad black mask through eyes and over ear-coverts; buffy below,* varying in intensity; tail feathers broadly tipped white.

Similar species: Black and Yellow-billed

Cuckoos both lack black mask and have white (not buffy) underparts.

Status and distribution: Uncertain. Local and rare in lighter woodland and borders and in clearings with thickets and trees in lowlands on Pacific slope from Chiriquí to Canal Zone and Panama city; one recent sight report from near Summit Gardens on June 19, 1970 (Ridgely); another sight report is from Pearl Islands (Contadora) on February 5, 1970 (Ridgely, R. MacArthur and H. Hespenheide). No proof of breeding in Panama, though Wetmore took a female in breeding condition on May 22 in Veraguas; perhaps only a migrant from further north.

Habits: Similar to other *Coccyzus* cuckoos. Does not appear to be particularly attracted to mangroves in Panama, though most records are from rather near the Pacific coast.

Range: Primarily in West Indies; also Florida, spottily in Middle America (breeding status uncertain), islands in southern Caribbean, the Guianas, and northern Brazil, perhaps in Colombia and Venezuela.

SQUIRREL CUCKOO

(*Piaya cayana*) Pl.6

Description: 17–19. Larger than other true cuckoos, with *very long tail* that often seems to be loosely connected to the rest of its body. Somewhat decurved bill and *bare orbital skin yellowish green. Chestnut above;* throat and chest pinkish cinnamon, *breast and belly gray,* becoming black on under tail-coverts; underside of tail black with feathers broadly tipped white.

Similar species: This widespread species is easily recognized by its large size, spectacular long tail, and chestnut upperparts. See Little Cuckoo.

Status and distribution: Common in forest borders, second-growth woodland, shrubby clearings with trees, and even groves of trees in rather open country in lowlands on both slopes, ranging in smaller numbers up into foothills, and in western Chiriquí recorded in highlands to over 6000 feet.

Habits: Usually rather quiet and furtive, but sometimes runs rapidly along a branch (like a squirrel). Forages at all levels in bushes and trees. Has a number of distinctive and arresting calls, among them a dry *chick, kwah* and a loud *trrt-trrt-trrt-trrt;* also a loud *kikerah* or *geep-kareer,* rather reminiscent of a Great Kiskadee; and others.

Range: Mexico to Bolivia, northern Argentina, and Uruguay.

LITTLE CUCKOO

(*Piaya minuta*) Pl.6

Description: 10–11. Resembles Squirrel Cuckoo but *much smaller* with proportionately shorter tail. Bill greenish yellow; *bare orbital skin red.* Rufous brown above; throat and chest tawny, blending into brownish gray breast, grayish belly, and black under tail-coverts; underside of tail black with feathers tipped white.

Similar species: Squirrel Cuckoo is much larger with longer tail, greenish (not red) orbital skin, and shows more contrast between pinkish cinnamon chest and gray breast.

Status and distribution: Uncommon and rather local in thickets and shrubby areas usually near water in lowlands on Pacific slope from eastern Panama province east through Darién; on Caribbean slope rare, known only from Canal Zone area (Chagres River, Achiote Road, Río Piedras). In central Panama most regularly found in the Tocumen/La Jagua area.

Habits: Quiet and secretive, usually remaining in dense undergrowth. Most often seen singly. Probably often overlooked.

Range: Central Panama to northern Bolivia and central Brazil.

Note: Wetmore calls it Dwarf Squirrel Cuckoo.

GREATER ANI

(*Crotophaga major*) *page 134*

Description: 18–19. *Bill arched only on basal two-thirds of upper mandible* (giving characteristic "broken nose" effect), and laterally compressed. *Eye conspicuously whitish. Glossy blue-black all over,* glossed somewhat greener on wings and purplish on tail.

Similar species: The other two anis are considerably smaller and duller black (without the gloss), and have dark eyes.

Status and distribution: Fairly common in thickets and trees along larger rivers and lakes, and in fresh water swamps and marshes, in lowlands on Caribbean slope from western Colon province east, and on Pacific slope from Canal Zone (where uncommon) east. Quite numerous on shores of Chagres River and Gatun Lake, also in the Tocumen/La Jagua area.

Habits: Looks sleek and well-groomed, unlike the other two anis. Usually found in groups of 4 to 12 individuals. The most characteristic call is a bubbling *prrrr* or *brrrr;* also has an almost mammal-like growl *grrwa*.

Range: Central Panama to Bolivia, northern Argentina, and southern Brazil.

SMOOTH-BILLED ANI
(*Crotophaga ani*)

Description: 13–14. Bill arched and laterally compressed, with high narrow ridge. Eye dark. Dull black all over.

Similar species: Distinguishing between this species and the Groove-billed Ani is often not easy; see discussion under that species. The Greater Ani is much larger and glossier than either, and has a prominent pale eye.

Status and distribution: Common in open areas, clearings, and residential areas in lowlands on both slopes, ranging in smaller numbers up into the foothills, in western Chiriquí occasionally to about 5000 feet; not found in Bocas del Toro or Caribbean slope Veraguas; common also on Coiba Island, and the Pearl Islands. Regularly found in small clearings made in otherwise forested areas. Much the more numerous of the two small anis in the Canal Zone, less common in drier Pacific lowlands from eastern Veraguas to western Panama province (where probably outnumbered by the Groove-bill).

Habits: Almost always found in small groups, perching in bushes and low trees and on fences and wires. Their flight is laboured and awkward, with frequent periods of gliding, the long tail often looking "loose-jointed." Can look incredibly shaggy and disheveled. The most characteristic call is a whining querulous *oooo-eeeek?,* often given in flight; also has a variety of other whining and clucking vocalizations.

Range: Florida; West Indies and islands in western Caribbean; southwestern Costa Rica to western Ecuador and northern Argentina.

Upper left, two GREATER ANIS. Heads: upper, GREATER ANI; middle, SMOOTH-BILLED ANI; lower, GROOVE-BILLED ANI

GROOVE-BILLED ANI
(*Crotophaga sulcirostris*)

Description: 11–12. Bill arched and laterally compressed, with upper mandible grooved. Eye dark. Entirely dull black, but somewhat glossier than Smooth-billed Ani.

Similar species: Closely resembles the Smooth-billed Ani; the presence or absence of bill grooving is usually difficult to discern in the field, and the Smooth-bill under some lighting conditions gives an illusion of grooving. A better mark is the Groove-bill's unbroken arc on culmen; the Smooth-bill usually has a thin irregular hump at the base of the culmen, breaking the smooth arc. The Groove-bill is a little smaller and often looks sleeker. The two are generally best differentiated by their rather different calls.

Status and distribution: Common on open savannas and in dry scrubby areas in lowlands on Pacific slope from Chiriquí to eastern Panama province (not recorded from Darién, but may spread there with clearing of forest); on Caribbean slope abundant in clearings and open areas in lowlands of western Bocas del Toro (to which it presumably spread following clearing for bananas), and found locally in small numbers in middle Chagres River valley of Canal Zone. Rather scarce in Canal Zone proper, but numerous in drier and more open areas just to the east and west. On the Pacific slope this species occurs in some areas with the Smooth-bill, but the two seem never to actually associate with each other.

Habits: Similar to Smooth-billed Ani. Like that species, often forages around cattle, feeding on insects disturbed by the animals. Has a variety of guttural clucking calls (some rather similar to certain vocalizations of the Smooth-bill), and a distinctive sharp dry *kwik* or *hwilk,* usually given in a series and often accelerated into an almost flicker-like *"wicka-wicka-wicka."*

Range: Extreme southwestern United States to Peru, northwestern Argentina, and Guyana; not found in Amazon basin or Brazil.

STRIPED CUCKOO

(*Tapera naevia*) Pl.6

Description: 11–12. *Short bushy crest;* tail fairly long and graduated. *Brown above* streaked with buff and blackish, with whitish superciliary; *whitish below,* buffier on throat and chest.

Similar species: See Pheasant Cuckoo.

Status and distribution: Fairly common in open areas and clearings with scattered bushes and thickets in lowlands on Pacific slope from Chiriquí to eastern Panama province, ranging in smaller numbers up into the foothills, in western Chiriquí to about 5000 feet; on Caribbean slope found in cleared areas from northern Coclé east to San Blas. Widespread in suitable habitat in the Canal Zone.

Habits: Usually rather secretive, remaining hidden in dense underbrush. Best known from its calls, the most frequent being a pure melancholy two-noted whistle, the second note a half-tone higher than the first, *püü-peeee,* highly ventriloquial and far-carrying; also has a 5 or 6-noted call of similar quality, falling off at the end. A calling bird often perches in the open on top of a bush or fencepost, elevating its crest with each vocalization. A parasitic species, apparently mostly on species building domed nests, in Panama especially the Pale-breasted Spinetail, Black-striped Sparrow, *Thryothorus* wrens, and *Myiozetetes* flycatchers (N. G. Smith).

Range: Southern Mexico to Bolivia and central Argentina.

PHEASANT CUCKOO

(*Dromococcyx phasianellus*) Pl.6

Description: 15–16. *Rather small head* with short pointed crest, giving unusual profile. *Tail long and fan-shaped; feathers of upper tail-coverts greatly elongated* and almost twice as long as the tail itself. Dark brown above, the feathers with whitish edging; mostly white below with *band of dusky streaking across chest;* tail brown with whitish tipping.

Similar species: Striped Cuckoo is smaller and paler brown above, lacks streaking below, and has more normal tail.

Status and distribution: Uncommon and local in dense undergrowth and thickets in second-growth woodland and forest borders in lowlands on Pacific slope (recorded from Chiriquí, Los Santos, Canal Zone, and eastern Panama province); on Caribbean slope recorded only from Canal Zone to western San Blas. Probably more widespread but little known due to its very secretive habits.

Habits: Rarely seen but often heard in proper habitat. The call resembles the short call of the Striped Cuckoo, but with an added third note that is either trilled or broken into two or three short notes, *püü, peee, pr'r'r'r;* also has a long call of 4–6 whistles much like than of Striped Cuckoo but usually ending in a tremulo and not falling in pitch. Parasitic, mainly on species building cup nests, but also on those constructing closed nests (N. G. Smith).

Range: Southern Mexico to northern Bolivia, Paraguay, northeastern Argentina, and southern Brazil.

RUFOUS-VENTED GROUND-CUCKOO

(*Neomorphus geoffroyi*) Pl.6

Description: 19–20. *A large, prominently crested, long-tailed terrestrial cuckoo,* somewhat resembling a roadrunner (*Geococcyx sp.*). Heavy pale greenish bill; bare blue skin behind eye. *Mostly bronzy olive brown above* with blue-black crest; buffy brown below, with *narrow band of black spots across chest,* becoming rufous on lower belly and under tail-coverts; tail dark bronzy olive.

Status and distribution: Rare and apparently local in humid forest in lowlands and foothills; on Caribbean slope recorded from Bocas del Toro (specimen from Almirante in Gorgas collection) east to San Blas, on Pacific slope recorded in foothills from eastern Chiriquí eastward, in Darién also in lowlands. Very rare in Canal Zone, with two early 20th century specimens but only one recent report (1 at an antswarm near Achiote Road on December 25, 1974; W. Cornwell); has also been seen in recent years on both Cerro Campana and Cerro Azul.

Habits: Primarily terrestrial, but also perches on branches in undergrowth. Most likely to be found at an army ant swarm. Snaps its bill loudly, somewhat like the wing-snapping of the Golden-collared Manakin (Slud). Nest unrecorded, but believed not to be parasitic, as adults have been seen with young in Brazil (H. Sick).

Range: Nicaragua to northern Bolivia and central Brazil.

BARN OWLS: Tytonidae (1)

The barn owls are a small but cosmopolitan group, closely allied to the typical owls but differing outwardly in the strongly marked heart-shaped facial disk and the long slender legs. Like the typical owls, barn owls are mainly nocturnal. They favor the vicinity of human habitations, where they often nest. Agriculturally valuable birds, they feed almost exclusively on various rodents.

BARN OWL
(*Tyto alba*)

Description: 14–16. *Heart-shaped facial area buffy or white* and encircled by narrow line of black; otherwise mixed grayish and golden buff above, lightly dotted with white and black; *buff or white below,* lightly dotted with blackish.

Similar species: Has an unusual narrow profile when perched, with large head and slender body. Characteristic pale ghostly appearance at night. See Great Potoo (which also looks very pale at night).

Status and distribution: Uncommon to locally fairly common in semi-open country in lowlands on Pacific slope, ranging occasionally into highlands; on Caribbean slope recorded only from western Bocas del Toro and Canal Zone; found also on Pearl Islands (San José). Usually seen around human habitations where it obtains diurnal shelter and nesting sites in towers and other structures.

Habits: Primarily nocturnal but sometimes active in the early morning and late afternoon, when it can be observed perched on fence posts and flying about low over the ground. Its calls are varied, with a loud rasping shriek being most characteristic.

Range: Virtually cosmopolitan in temperate and tropical regions.

OWLS: Strigidae (14)

Owls are universally known birds, the nocturnal counterparts to the hawks and eagles. Because many species are so strictly nocturnal (and hence only rarely seen), and because they have a variety of far-carrying vocalizations, owls are the subject of many superstitious beliefs. As a group they are characterized by their forward-facing eyes, strong hooked bill, powerful sharp talons, and fluffy plumage; many species have ear-like tufts ("horns"). Their flight is noiseless. They feed on a variety of small mammals and birds, some of the smaller species mostly on large insects; prey is located primarily through their keen sense of hearing. Food is swallowed whole, the undigestible parts later being cast up as pellets. The nest is placed in a variety of situations: in tree hollows (most Panamanian species), on an old stick nest of another bird, or on the ground.

VERMICULATED SCREECH-OWL
(*Otus guatemalae*) Pl.6

Description: 8. A small owl with *ear-tufts* resembling the more numerous Tropical Screech-Owl. Iris yellow. Dark grayish brown above vermiculated with dusky, wing-coverts spotted with white; pale brown to whitish below, *densely and coarsely vermiculated with wavy dusky brown barring,* with only a few vertical streaks. Rufous phase has grayish brown replaced by chestnut-rufous and underparts vermiculated white and rufous, the rufous predominating on throat and chest.

Similar species: Tropical Screech-Owl has a whitish face with dark rim (no distinct facial rim in this species), well-marked white superciliary (lacking in Vermiculated), and is conspicuously streaked below (not with predominately *horizontal* vermiculations); the calls differ characteristically. Juvenal Tropical and Vermiculated Screech-Owls are both barred with dusky brown above and below, but Tropical already shows black facial rim. In highlands, see also Bare-shanked Screech-Owl.

Status and distribution: Apparently local and uncommon in forest and second-growth woodland in lowlands and foothills on both slopes; recorded on Pacific slope from Chiriquí, Veraguas, Canal Zone, eastern Panama province, and Darién; on Caribbean slope from Bocas del Toro and Canal Zone.

Habits: Relatively little known in Panama. The call is a prolonged whinnying whistle, on one pitch and without emphasis, suggestive of the Common Screech-Owl (*O. asio*) of eastern temperate North America.

Range: Mexico to Venezuela and Ecuador; Bolivia.

Note: Birds from Costa Rica southward (*O. vermiculatus*) have been considered specifically distinct from northern *O. guatemalae*.

TROPICAL SCREECH-OWL

(*Otus choliba*) Pl.6

Description: 8½–9½. A small grayish brown owl with *ear tufts*. Iris yellow. *Facial area including superciliary dirty whitish, bordered by black rim;* otherwise grayish to cinnamon brown above, somewhat streaked and vermiculated with dusky; cinnamon mottling and banding on wings; whitish or pale grayish below (bases of feathers golden buff) with *prominent herring-bone pattern of dusky streaks and angled bars.* Rare rufous phase is rufous brown above and on face; buffy or cinnamon below, marked as in normal phase.

Similar species: Vermiculated Screech-Owl is smaller and darker, lacks the superciliary and facial rim and the prominent vertical streaking below, and is a forest or humid woodland bird. In highlands see also Bare-shanked Screech-Owl.

Status and distribution: Fairly common in light second-growth woodland and woodland borders, clearings and open areas with scattered trees, and residential areas in lowlands on Pacific slope from Chiriquí to Canal Zone and Panama city; on Caribbean slope recorded only from Canal Zone and eastern San Blas (Armila); found also on Pearl Islands (Rey, Pedro Gonzalez). Has been heard at night in Boquete in lower highlands of western Chiriquí. Not recorded from eastern Panama province or Darién though probably occurs in cleared areas.

Habits: The commonest owl on the Pacific slope, but strictly nocturnal and hence infrequently recorded except by call at night. The call is a distinctive dry purring trill, *prrrrrrr* or *hoorrrrrr,* usually, but not always, terminating in an abrupt querulous *ook?* or *ook?ook?*—most often heard in the evening soon after dark, also at night and in early morning before dawn.

Range: Costa Rica to Bolivia, northern Argentina, and southern Brazil.

Note: Wetmore calls it Choliba Screech Owl.

BARE-SHANKED SCREECH-OWL

(*Otus clarkii*) Pl.6

Description: 9–10. Known only from highlands of west and east. A rather large *spotted* screech-owl with *ear-tufts.* Iris yellow. *Facial area cinnamon-tawny;* otherwise *dark reddish brown above* with black mottling, streaks, and vermiculations; white spots on scapulars and wing-coverts; light brown below with *black streaks and bars and white spotting or short bars,* becoming paler on lower belly. Most of tarsus bare (but not a field character).

Similar species: Has a big-headed appearance. Note prominent squarish white bars or spots below. The only screech-owl in the mountain forests.

Status and distribution: Apparently rare (perhaps overlooked) in forest in highlands of western Chiriquí, Veraguas (one old specimen from Calobre), and eastern Darién; recorded 4000–7000 feet.

Habits: Nocturnal. Little known in Panama. The call is a rather high musical hooting in two parts, *coo, coo-coo-coo* (Wetmore).

Range: Costa Rica to eastern Panama.

CRESTED OWL

(*Lophostrix cristata*) Pl.6

Description: 16. A large owl with *very long whitish or buffy ear-tufts.* Iris variable, yellow or brown. Sooty brown above mottled with rufous; *prominent white or buffy eyestripe,* which extends onto ear-tufts in an unbroken line; wings conspicuously spotted with white; underparts buffy to tawny with narrow dusky barring giving mottled appearance.

Similar species: No other Panama owl has such prominent ear-tufts. Striped Owl is prominently streaked below, inhabits more or less open areas (not forest). See also the rare Great Horned Owl.

Status and distribution: Apparently rare and local in forest and second-growth woodland in more humid lowlands on both slopes. No specimens from central Panama east of Coclé or west of Darién and San Blas, but there are sightings from Barro Colorado

Island, and a few recent sight reports from Pipeline Road (including family group of 3 seen on July 17, 1972, by Gard Otis).

Habits: Strictly nocturnal and little known in Panama apart from the specimens taken. Pipeline Road birds have been seen in thickets bordering small streams, within 10 to 30 feet of the ground. In Venezuela, the call was a distinctive, low-pitched, rather frog-like *k'k'k'k-krrrrrr,* sometimes suggesting a turkey gobble; at a distance sounded like *tkrrrrrr* (Eisenmann).

Range: Southern Mexico to Bolivia and Amazonian Brazil.

GREAT HORNED OWL
(*Bubo virginianus*)

Description: 19–21. Very rare. *Panama's largest owl,* with *prominent ear-tufts.* Iris yellow. Sooty brown above mottled with tawny and grayish and streaked with black; facial area buffy bordered by black facial rim; *lower throat and foreneck white;* remaining underparts tawny to whitish, *barred with blackish.*

Similar species: Crested Owl has conspicuous pale superciliary and ear-tufts and lacks the white throat patch; it is much smaller and slenderer than this species. Striped Owl is also smaller and is streaked (not barred) below.

Status and distribution: Uncertain. Known only from one nineteenth-century specimen taken at Chitra, Veraguas; and from one sight report of a bird perched at the edge of a swamp on Isla Ranchería, off Coiba Island, on February 4, 1956 (Wetmore). Possibly resident in forest or woodland on Pacific slope of west, perhaps only a "winter" vagrant from farther north.

Range: Northern North America to Tierra del Fuego; rare and very local in tropical Middle and South America.

SPECTACLED OWL
(*Pulsatrix perspicillata*) Pl.6

Description: 17–19. No ear-tufts. Iris yellow. Dark brown above with *broad white eyebrow and area about bill* (the "spectacles"); throat white, *face and chest blackish brown, lower underparts buffy white to buff.* Juvenal has buff head with broad blackish brown mask.

Status and distribution: Uncommon to fairly common in forest and second-growth woodland in more humid lowlands and foothills (to about 4000 feet) on both slopes, but not often seen.

SPECTACLED OWL (juvenal)

Habits: Usually rests by day in thick foliage, but occasionally active on dark cloudy early mornings and late afternoons. The commonest call is a rapid series of about six low short dry rattling hoots (lacking in resonance), almost like an imitation of a machine gun. Also utters a much slower series of three or four low-pitched dry hoots, suggesting the beating of wings. Juvenals have a rather hoarse call, *kweeew.*

Range: Southern Mexico to Bolivia, northern Argentina, and southern Brazil.

LEAST PYGMY-OWL
(*Glaucidium minutissimum*)

Description: 5½. Apparently rare; recorded mostly from eastern Panama. *Head grayish with small whitish dots;* broken band of white on hindneck terminating on either side in a *small black eye-like spot;* otherwise brown above, unspotted except sometimes for a few small buff or whitish spots on scapulars and wings; white below *broadly streaked with rufous brown on chest, sides, and lower belly;* tail black with narrow whitish bars. Immature has head without whitish spots.

Similar species: Not known to occur in habitats of either of the other Panama pygmy-owls. Andean Pygmy-Owl is somewhat larger and barred or spotted (not streaked) below; head of adult Ferruginous Pygmy is streaked (not spotted) with whitish or buff.

Status and distribution: Probably overlooked and not uncommon at least locally; recorded definitely only from forest and forest borders in lowlands on Caribbean slope

Left to right, UNSPOTTED SAW-WHET OWL, ANDEAN PYGMY-OWL, FERRUGINOUS PYGMY-OWL; LEAST PYGMY-OWL

in eastern Panama province (Río Boqueron above Madden Lake) and eastern San Blas (Permé, Puerto Obaldía); on Pacific slope in eastern Panama province (Bayano River at Majé—1 seen and at least 1 other heard on January 28, 1973, by Ridgely and J. Gwynne; and 1 collected on March 23, 1973 by P. Galindo, specimen in Gorgas coll.) and eastern Darién (Chucunaque River). One old specimen labeled only as from "Veragua" was probably taken somewhere in the Caribbean lowlands of western Panama.

Habits: Like other pygmy-owls, abroad both by day and by night. The call is a series of 3 to 5 *poop's,* sometimes more (up to 8 or 9) when the bird is excited; often a calling bird can be decoyed in by imitating the call.

Range: Mexico and locally in Central America; northwestern Colombia; Guyana; spottily in northern and central Brazil; southeastern Peru; Paraguay.

ANDEAN (MOUNTAIN) PYGMY-OWL
(*Glaucidium jardinii*)

Description: 6. Known only from western highlands. Brown above, *crown with small whitish to buff spots,* back spotted and wings barred with white and buff; short white eyebrow and *small black eye-like spot on either side of back of head;* mostly white below with band of brown across chest (sometimes broken in middle); sides and flanks bright brown, *barred or spotted with buff or whitish* and sometimes with black; tail blackish with narrow white bands. In rufous phase, mostly rufous below with little or no barring and no streaking. Immature has gray crown without spots or with spots restricted to forecrown.

Similar species: Both other Panama pygmy-owls have broadly streaked underparts.

Status and distribution: Rare in forest and forest borders in highlands of western Chiriquí and Veraguas, mostly above 5000 feet. Not well known in Panama but can be seen occasionally in the Cerro Punta area.

Habits: Similar to the better known Ferruginous Pygmy-Owl, and likewise partly diurnal.

Range: Costa Rica and western Panama; Andes of northwestern Venezuela and Colombia to Bolivia.

Note: Possibly conspecific with *G. brasilianum.*

FERRUGINOUS PYGMY-OWL
(*Glaucidium brasilianum*)

Description: 6½. Brown or rufous above, *crown narrowly streaked with buff or whitish,* wings with white or buff spots; short white eyebrow and *black eye-like spot on either side of back of head;* white below, broadly streaked with rufous or brown, especially on flanks; tail blackish with narrow whitish bands. Immature lacks crown streaks.

Similar species: The only frequently encountered pygmy-owl in Panama. In its range, the small size and chunky shape, black "eyes" on back of head, and fairly long tail (often cocked at a perky angle) are distinctive. Both other pygmy-owls in Panama have crown spotted, not streaked, but this is not always easy to see.

Status and distribution: Uncommon to locally fairly common in scrubby and light woodland and in open areas with scattered thickets and trees in lowlands on Pacific slope (chiefly in drier regions) from Veraguas and eastern side of Azuero Peninsula to western Panama province; one recent sight report from southwestern Canal Zone (Rodman Ammunition Dump) and another from Panama city (both N. G. Smith).

Habits: Often active during the day, perching out in the open on fence posts or even telephone wires. Small birds come regularly to mob it. The usual call is a low whistle, repeated a number of times, heard mostly at night, sometimes during the day.

Range: Extreme southwestern United States to northern Chile and central Argentina.

BURROWING OWL

(*Speotyto cunicularia*)

Description: 9–10. Accidental. *Long legs;* quite short tail. Iris yellow. Brown above spotted with whitish, forehead and superciliary white; whitish below with blackish band across chest, and barred irregularly with brown on breast and sides. *Terrestrial.*

Status and distribution: Only one record, a bird taken at Divalá, Chiriquí on Dec. 13, 1900.

Habits: Active by day as well as by night, perching on the ground or on low vantage points, bobbing up and down on its long legs when nervous.

Range: Breeds locally in western North America and Mexico, wintering (perhaps breeding) to Honduras, accidentally to Costa Rica and western Panama; also breeds in Florida, West Indies, and locally in open parts of South America.

Note: Short-eared Owl (*Asio flammeus*) has been recorded in northern winter casually as far south as Costa Rica; it breeds in temperate North America, South America, and the Old World, favoring open marshy and grassy country. It is fairly large (15–16") and mostly tawny brown, lightly streaked below, with short ear-tufts; buffy wing-patches and black patch at carpal joint show in low flopping flight.

MOTTLED OWL

(*Ciccaba virgata*) Pl.6

Description: 13–14. A medium-sized owl *without ear-tufts.* Iris brown. *Brown above* mottled with grayish buff and dusky and with whitish superciliary; wings and tail dusky mottled and barred with paler gray; *buffy below mottled and streaked with dusky.* In dark phase, darker above and more cinnamon below with irregular dusky barring. Juvenal plain cinnamon-buff except wings and tail as in adult.

Similar species: Black-and-white Owl is distinctly barred below with black and white. Striped Owl has prominent ear-tufts and is found in open country, not in forest and woodland.

Status and distribution: Fairly common in forest and second-growth woodland on both slopes, ranging well up into the highlands. Infrequently seen due to its strictly nocturnal habits.

Habits: In Panama gives a rather long-drawn cat-like screech *keeooweéýo* or *cowooáoo* and a gruff growl *grrr.* In Venezuela also heard uttering a low deep *whoó-oo,* slightly modulated downward, usually repeated three times (Eisenmann).

Range: Northern Mexico to Bolivia, northern Argentina, and southern Brazil.

BLACK-AND-WHITE OWL

(*Ciccaba nigrolineata*) Pl.6

Description: 14–15. A medium-sized owl *without ear-tufts.* Iris light brown. *Face and upperparts sooty black* with an indistinct white superciliary; throat black, remaining *underparts white banded narrowly with black.*

Similar species: Mottled Owl is essentially brown and is not barred below.

Status and distribution: Uncommon and local in forest and forest borders; recorded only from Bocas del Toro, Chiriquí, Veraguas, Caribbean slope of Canal Zone, and eastern Panama province but probably found elsewhere in suitable habitat; recorded up into lower highlands in western Chiriquí. Strictly nocturnal and hence not often seen. Recorded often from edge of clearing at Barro Colorado Island.

Habits: Has two very different calls. One is a long-drawn, nasal, whining, rather cat-like *oo-weh* with an *upward* inflection (L. Ingles); it resembles the louder call of the Mottled Owl. The other is a very deliberate, deep, resonant *whoof, whoof, whoof.*

Range: Southern Mexico to northwestern Venezuela and northwestern Peru.

STRIPED OWL
(*Rhinoptynx clamator*) Pl.6

Description: 13–15. A medium-sized owl with *conspicuous, blackish ear-tufts.* Iris light brown to orange-yellow. Tawny-buff above coarsely streaked and vermiculated with blackish; facial area whitish bordered by black rim; whitish to buffy below, *heavily streaked with brownish black.*

Similar species: The only medium-sized owl with ear-tufts that is streaked below. Very rare Great Horned Owl is much larger and is barred below. See also Stygian Owl (below).

Status and distribution: Uncommon to fairly common locally in open grassy areas and shrubby clearings in lowlands on Pacific slope from Chiriquí to eastern Panama province, ranging occasionally up to about 3500 feet; on Caribbean slope recorded only in Canal Zone.

Habits: Rests by day in low trees or thickets, but nests on the ground. Can sometimes be seen flying low over the ground at dusk. Has a loud, penetrating, semi-whistled *wheeeyoo;* also a stacatto series of barking hoots *ow, ow, ow, ow* (P. Schwartz).

Range: Southeastern Mexico south locally to Bolivia, northern Argentina, and Uruguay.

Note: Stygian Owl (*Asio stygius*) is possible in highlands; very local, it is known from wooded highlands of Mexico to Nicaragua and in South America, also Greater Antilles. It resembles Long-eared Owl (*A. otus*) of temperate North America and Eurasia, but is mainly blackish above with dusky (not rufous) facial area; buffy below, strongly streaked and barred with blackish.

UNSPOTTED SAW-WHET OWL
(*Aegolius ridgwayi*) *page 139*

Description: 7. Apparently rare; known only from western Chiriquí mountains. Dark brown above, including face, with *forehead and narrow line above eye white; buff below* with indistinct cinnamon band across breast.

Similar species: A small and plain owl, with no streaking, barring, or spotting (except on inner secondaries). See Andean Pygmy-Owl. In appearance strikingly like juvenal plumage of Northern Saw-whet Owl (*A. acadicus*).

Status and distribution: Known only from one bird taken in a mist-net set in forest on west flank of Volcán de Chiriquí, at about 7000 feet, on February 17, 1965.

Habits: Little known. Apparently rare throughout its range, though possibly only overlooked. In Costa Rica, the call is reported to be a series of rhythmic whistles of equal pitch, similar to but seemingly somewhat lower in pitch than the call of the Northern Saw-whet (Foster and Johnson).

Range: Southern Mexico to western Panama.

Note: Wetmore calls it Central American Saw-whet Owl.

OILBIRDS: Steatornithidae (1)

To date, the presence of oilbirds in Panama rests solely on the two records mentioned below, but it is probable that a colony exists in some yet undiscovered cave or grotto in eastern Panama. In South America, oilbirds are found locally, usually in limestone caves, and in some areas are still persecuted, the very fat young being taken as a source of oil. In appearance they are something between a large nightjar and a hawk, with strong hooked bills and sharp claws. When disturbed in their caves, they emit loud screams; in these caves they also utter clicking sounds used as echo-locators, but probably they find their food (various fruits, mostly palm) primarily through their sense of smell (D. Snow). Oilbirds are the only nocturnal fruit-eating birds.

OILBIRD (GUACHARO)
(*Steatornis caripensis*)

Description: 18. Only two records. Eyes reflect bright red. *Heavy, hooked bill. Rufous brown above,* spotted with rusty on head, *spotted with white on wing-coverts,* wings lightly barred with blackish; *pale rusty brown below,* spotted with white; tail long and graduated, brown barred narrowly with blackish.

Similar species: Somewhat nightjar-like, but much larger with hawk-like bill and rather large, white, black-encircled spots.

Status and distribution: Uncertain, only two records: one taken in a mist-net set for bats over the Río Tacarcuna in eastern Darién (1750 feet) on March 19, 1959, and one seen and photographed as it rested on a branch in humid forest along Pipeline Road in Canal Zone on May 11, 1974 (N. Gale, J. Pujals). Probably a colony exists in some as yet undiscovered cave in eastern Panama.

Range: Eastern Panama locally to Guyana and northern Bolivia.

POTOOS: Nyctibiidae (2)

The potoos are a small family of exclusively neotropical, rather little known birds. They resemble the nightjars in many respects, especially in their large eyes, cavernous mouths, and nocturnal habits, but differ in their greater size and more or less upright (not horizontal) posture. They are rarely seen by day, for they then rest motionless, often high in a tree, looking like an extension of a dead snag or stump. If the bird is unaware of one's presence, its head is hunched into its body and its bill is in a natural, forward position. Usually, however, the potoo will see the observer before it is noticed, and it then slowly assumes the typical stretched-out position with the bill pointing skyward. More easily seen at night (especially when the moon is full), when the birds may be calling and may be seen perching on a prominent look-out. They feed on insects caught on the wing, usually returning to their original perch after a sally. The nest is non-existent: a single egg is laid in the small depression or crevice created by a broken-off branch.

GREAT POTOO
(*Nyctibius grandis*)

Description: 19–20. *Looks very pale, virtually white, in the field.* Eyes large, dark brown, but reflecting orange at night. Pale brownish above, spotted and margined with buffy and whitish; whitish below, finely barred with dusky, spotted with dusky on breast.

Similar species: Common Potoo bulks only half as large and is much darker overall. Barn Owl also looks very pale at night, but has different shape (large head).

Status and distribution: Apparently rare; recorded in humid forest, second-growth woodland, and borders in lowlands on Caribbean slope, on Pacific slope in eastern Panama province (several heard and seen in forest just beyond Bayano River Bridge on January 1–2, 1975; Ridgely) and Darién. In Canal Zone has been reported recently from Barro Colorado Island (where it can sometimes be seen by paddling around the island at night) and Pipeline Road.

Habits: Apparently similar in most respects to the better known Common Potoo. Nocturnal, resting by day high in a forest tree, at night coming out more into the open, often to forest borders and adjacent clearings. In Venezuela the call was noted as a growling *ahrrr* (Eisenmann); in Surinam reported as a strange *oorrroo* or *oorrr* (F. Haverschmidt).

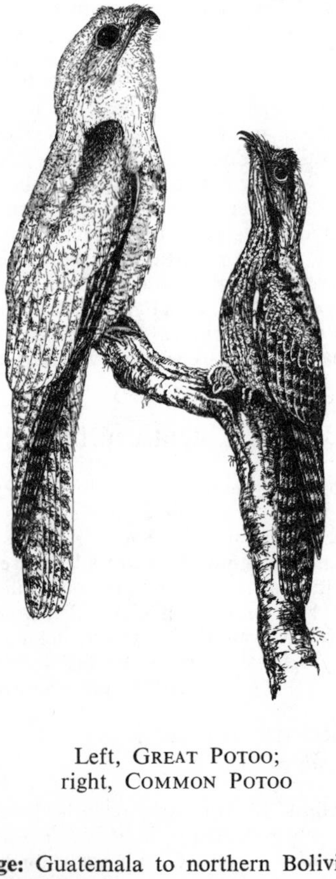

Left, GREAT POTOO; right, COMMON POTOO

Range: Guatemala to northern Bolivia and southern Brazil.

COMMON POTOO
(*Nyctibius griseus*)

Description: 15–16. Eyes very large, yellow, *reflecting intense glowing orange at night.* Bill notably small, but opening wide, exposing huge flesh-colored mouth. *Grayish brown to brown,* intricately patterned above and below with tawny, black, and white; a broken band of scattered black spots across chest in some birds. Upstanding feathers above eyes sometimes resemble horns.

Similar species: Most likely to be mistaken for an owl but of different proportions, with smaller head and long tail. Great Potoo is larger and appears much whiter.

Status and distribution: Uncommon to fairly common but seemingly local in forest borders, second-growth woodland, and clearings in lowlands on both slopes, ranging up to about 4000 feet in western highlands; absent from drier and more open parts of western Pacific slope, but fairly common in Canal Zone.

Habits: Active only by night, especially in hours just after dusk and just before dawn. Very difficult to see during the day, then resting motionless but often fully in the open, usually at moderate heights on bare branch of a tree, relying on its cryptic coloration and lack of movement for protection. The beautiful haunting call is one of the most memorable of Panama bird sounds, and is heard particularly on moonlit nights. It is a deep, melancholy, wonderfully modulated series of 4 to 8 wailing notes, falling in pitch, loudest at first and falling off at the end. Many Panamanians attribute this to a sloth! This vocalization seems to be known only north to eastern Nicaragua (T. Howell).

Range: Mexico to Bolivia, northern Argentina, and Uruguay; Jamaica and Hispaniola.

Note: Wetmore calls it Lesser Potoo. At least two species are probably involved.

NIGHTJARS: Caprimulgidae (9)

Except for the crepuscular nighthawks, members of this family are strictly nocturnal; by day they are almost never seen except when flushed accidentally. The family is virtually worldwide in occurrence. Most are best known from their calls, in most species readily recognized, given primarily by males during the breeding season. Nightjars as a group are characterized by their short bills, large mouths, which open wide, and loose fluffy plumage; most species resemble each other closely and are difficult to separate on visual characters alone. By day, nighthawks and nightjars rest either on the ground or lengthwise on a branch, their cryptic coloration making them almost invisible. They eat insects, captured on the wing. Eggs are laid directly on the ground, there being no attempt at a nest.

SHORT-TAILED (SEMICOLLARED) NIGHTHAWK
(*Lurocalis semitorquatus*) *page 145*

Description: 9–9½. *Very short, square tail;* rather long, somewhat pointed wings. *Blackish above,* speckled with rufous; throat white, remaining underparts dark brown barred with black; tail dark brown; wings dark *without white band.* At rest, wings extend well beyond tail.

Similar species: Looks very dark in the field, with no white in wings or tail; characteristic silhouette of short tail and long wings is almost reminiscent of a huge swift. *Chordeiles* nighthawks have longer slightly forked tails, more pointed wings with a conspicuous pale band, and usually frequent open country (not forest and adjacent areas).

Status and distribution: Uncommon and local; found in humid forest in lowlands and foothills on both slopes, more widespread on Caribbean side; on Pacific slope known only from Veraguas (Cébaco Island), western Los Santos (Río Guánico, Cerro Hoya), and Darién. Can be seen fairly regularly at dusk along Pipeline Road in Canal Zone.

Habits: Crepuscular; usually seen around dusk or dawn as it feeds in and above the forest canopy, sometimes coming out over adjacent clearings. Flight is erratic and shifting, rather bat-like. Sometimes feeds lower over rivers and streams, where occasionally in the company of *Chordeiles* nighthawks. Apparently roosts by day in forest trees. Generally silent, but in Venezuela heard to give a stacatto semi-whistled *wheep, wheep, wheep, wheep,* varied to to *wookeéup* or *coo-coó-queet* (Eisenmann).

Range: Nicaragua to northern Argentina and southern Brazil.

LESSER NIGHTHAWK
(*Chordeiles acutipennis*)

Description: 8–9. Long, slender, pointed wings; fairly long, somewhat notched tail. Dark grayish brown to buffy brown above, marbled and spotted with buff, whitish, and black; throat white, remaining underparts buff barred with dusky; *band of white across primaries nearer to tip than to bend of wing;* tail barred whitish and dusky, with white band near tip. Female has throat and wing-band pale buffy (but looks white at any distance) and lacks white tail-band. At rest wings reach end of tail.

Similar species: Smaller than Common Nighthawk, with wing-band nearer tip of wing. Female Lesser is only nighthawk with buff wing-band (white in both sexes of Common), but this rarely of any use in the field. Pauraque and other nightjars have broader rounder wings that at rest do not reach end of tail.

Status and distribution: Locally fairly common in lowlands on Pacific slope, breeding in drier more open areas, especially in eroded and scrubby savanna country of Coclé and western Panama province; local breeders augmented by northern migrants late July–April, and during this season also occurs on Caribbean slope (particularly on migration) and up into lower highlands.

Habits: Both *Chordeiles* nighthawks have a rapid bounding flight with deep wing-strokes, swerving and changing speeds abruptly. Active in the late afternoon and evening and before dawn, feeding over open areas, usually flying low (not high as in Common Nighthawk). On migration flies higher and in broad daylight, frequently in loose flocks. Generally spends day roosting lengthwise on a tree branch, especially in mangroves and swampy areas. Much less vocal than Common Nighthawk, never booming nor giving that species' nasal *peent;* during breeding season gives a frog-like trilling on the ground, and a bleeting or whinnying call in flight.

Range Southwestern United States to northern Bolivia, Paraguay, and southern Brazil; northern breeders winter from Mexico to Colombia.

COMMON NIGHTHAWK
(*Chordeiles minor*)

Description: 9–10. Very similar to Lesser Nighthawk. Larger and usually somewhat darker and more coarsely marked, particularly below; as in Lesser only male has white throat and only adult male has white tail band; white wing-band in this species is *about midway between tip and bend of wing* (in Lesser it is nearer the tip) and is white in both sexes.

Similar species: See Lesser Nighthawk. When perched, often very difficult to separate, but Lesser females and some males have basal half of primaries barred or spotted with buff (all blackish, except for white band, in Common). Migrating nighthawks flying overhead are not safely identified as to species; at other times possible but often difficult.

Status and distribution: Fairly common but local breeder in open areas in lowlands and foothills on Pacific slope from Chiriquí (probably) to eastern Panama province (actual breeding records only from Panama province). Various northern races migrate through both slopes but no records known from northern winter months (November 4–March 24); even the local breeding race apparently migrates to South America during nonbreeding season.

Habits: Tends to fly high, whereas the Lesser skims low over the ground, but both species fly high overhead when migrating, and this species sometimes forages low. During much of the year (less outside of breeding season) utters an unmistakable nasal *peent* or *beezhnt;* males in courtship display give a loud booming sound when diving toward the ground.

Range: Breeds from North America to Panama; winters in South America.

PAURAQUE
(*Nyctidromus albicollis*)

Description: 9½–11. Rounded wings; *rather long, rounded tail.* Brownish above, mottled and spotted with dusky and buff; chin dusky, throat buff, remaining underparts buffy, finely barred with dusky; wings with *broad white band across primaries; sides of tail mostly white* (very prominent in flight). Female has narrower white wing-band and white in tail reduced to tipping. At rest wings extend only half the length of the tail.

Similar specis: Superficially like a *Chordeiles* nighthawk but with rounded and shorter wings and unforked tail. White-tailed Nightjar is considerably smaller with buff or tawny collar on hindneck and almost square tail. Rufous Nightjar and Chuck-will's-widow are both much ruddier and lack white wing-band.

Status and distribution: Common in clearings, shrubby areas, roadsides, and second-growth woodland in lowlands and foothills on both slopes, less numerous and more local on Caribbean side; found also on larger Pearl Islands.

Habits: Strictly nocturnal, this species' true abundance is best indicated during breeding season (February–May) when at night in proper habitat its calls may resound from all around. The typical call is a hoarse whistle, *whe-wheéee-oo;* this is sometimes slurred into a *por-weéeeeer* or preceded by a series of *bup*'s; occasionally the *bup*'s are given alone in a series. At night often seen resting on little-traveled dirt or gravel roads where its bright orange-red eye reflects the light of a car's headlights; at such times it can be approached closely. Only rarely encountered by day, when it flushes up from the ground and flies off like a large moth.

Range: Southern Texas and Mexico to Bolivia, northern Argentina, and southern Brazil.

CHUCK-WILL'S-WIDOW
(*Caprimulgus carolinensis*)

Description: 11–12. *Rufous brown above,* vermiculated and spotted with buff and black; paler brown below, barred with dusky, lower throat buffy white; terminal half of three outer tail feathers white in male, buff in female; no wing-band.

Similar species: Best told by combination of large size (the largest nightjar in Panama) and dark brown overall appearance. Rufous Nightjar is very similar in plumage but notably smaller; in the hand, note lateral filaments on rictal bristles (lacking in Rufous Nightjar). Pauraque has white wing-band.

Status and distribution: Rare (at least infrequently noted) winter resident (October–March) in forest, second-growth woodland, and borders; recorded almost throughout. Records are few, but it appears to be somewhat more numerous in western Panama, particularly in Chiriquí.

Habits: Strictly nocturnal. By day rests on the ground, at night sometimes comes out into clearings. Also feeds in forest canopy (Wetmore). Not known to call in Panama.

Range: Breeds in southeastern United States; winters through Middle America to Colombia (once Venezuela) and in Florida and Greater Antilles.

RUFOUS NIGHTJAR
(*Caprimulgus rufus*)

Description: 10. Very similar to the Chuck-will's-widow but *smaller* and ruddier brown, with less white in tail of male. In the hand, note this species' smooth rictal bristles (like other nightjars), without lateral filaments of the Chuck-will's-widow.

Similar species: See Chuck-will's-widow. Pauraque, with which this species often occurs, has a white wing-band, more white in tail, and is much less rufous generally.

Status and distribution: Locally fairly common in second-growth woodland and borders in lowlands and foothills on Pacific slope in Canal Zone and eastern Panama province; elsewhere on Pacific slope apparently less numerous, though recorded from Chiriquí to Darién; on Caribbean slope known only from middle Chagres River

Left to right, WHITE-TAILED NIGHTJAR (male), SHORT-TAILED NIGHTHAWK, RUFOUS NIGHTJAR (male)

valley in Canal Zone and single Bocas del Toro and San Blas records; found also on Coiba Island. During breeding season (late January–early May) can easily be heard in the Curundu/Fort Clayton area of Canal Zone and on lower slopes of Cerro Azul.

Habits: Strictly nocturnal. During breeding season calls frequently, a fast resonant *chuck, wick-wick-weéoo,* the first syllable inaudible except at close range, the whole call reminiscent of that of the Chuck-will's-widow but considerably faster and higher pitched. Does not sit on roads as often as Pauraque.

Range: Southeastern Costa Rica (once) to northern Argentina and southeastern Brazil.

WHIP-POOR-WILL
(*Caprimulgus vociferus*)

Description: 9–10. Recorded only from Chiriquí highlands. *Grayish brown above,* vermiculated and spotted with tawny and black; upper throat blackish, *lower throat buffy white,* remaining underparts brownish mottled with dusky; outer tail feathers broadly tipped white in male, more narrowly tipped buff in female.

Similar species: Dusky Nightjar male is blacker, without whitish lower throat. Rufous Nightjar is ruddier generally, as is the larger Chuck-will's-widow.

Status and distribution: Two records from western Chiriquí highlands: one collected on slopes of Volcán Barú above Cerro Punta (6500 feet) on March 8, 1955; and one flushed from woodland at Volcán Lakes on January 15, 1974 (Ridgely).

Habits: Like other nightjars, strictly nocturnal; as with Chuck-will's-widow silent on its wintering grounds and hence usually overlooked.

Range: Breeds in eastern North America and from southwestern United States to Honduras; winters from extreme southern United States to Costa Rica (rare), casually to western Panama.

DUSKY NIGHTJAR
(*Caprimulgus saturatus*)

Description: 9. Known only from Chiriquí highlands. Male *blackish* spotted throughout with cinnamon-rufous; belly buff barred with blackish. Female has larger cinnamon-buff spots so that general effect is of a *very dark rufous* bird. Outer tail feathers broadly tipped white in male, more narrowly tipped buffy in female.

Similar species: Whip-poor-will is grayer overall (not blackish or dark rufous) with distinct narrow whitish band across lower throat. Rufous Nightjar is more uniform and paler rufous brown, not spotted.

Status and distribution: Uncommon in forest and forest borders in highlands of western Chiriquí around Volcán Barú, mostly above 5000 feet.

Habits: Little known in Panama. Often rests on branches a few feet off the ground in bamboo thickets in humid mountain forest. The call is a distinctive *tk, cheer-for-will,* rather similar to call of western race of Whip-poor-will (L. I. Davis).

Range: Costa Rica and western Panama.

WHITE-TAILED NIGHTJAR
(*Caprimulgus cayennensis*) *page 145*

Description: 8–8½. Pale grayish above mottled with buffy brown, finely streaked with black, and vermiculated with dark brown; *buff collar across hindneck;* throat and superciliary white; underparts otherwise buffy barred with dusky; *broad white band across primaries* (like band of Lesser Nighthawk); *tail slightly forked, mostly white* (especially from below), middle feathers mottled gray and dusky, others with black tip. Female is darker and browner, with *tawny collar on hindneck, buff wing-band,* and no white on tail, which is brown and buff.

Similar species: Nighthawks have longer pointed wings that at rest extend to tip of tail; in this species, wings are considerably shorter and more rounded, reaching only about midway down tail. Pauraque is larger and darker, with white restricted to tail-tips, and lacks the distinct collar; female White-tail is especially similar, but has almost square (not rounded) tail with no white tipping. See also Spot-tailed Nightjar (below).

Status and distribution: Uncommon and local (probably somewhat overlooked) in open rather dry grassy areas, bushy savannas, and rather barren hillsides in lowlands on Pacific slope from Chiriquí to western Darién (Santa Fé; seen in April 1967 by Eisenmann).

Habits: Nocturnal, resting by day on the ground. The call is a long high-pitched whistle, rising, then going down in pitch at the end, introduced by a short dry note (inaudible at a distance), *tk, chweeeeeeea* or *pick, speeeeeea,* slightly suggestive of a Pauraque but much higher and without burry quality.

Range: Costa Rica to the Guianas and extreme northern Brazil.

Note: Spot-tailed Nightjar (Pit-sweet) (*C. maculicaudus*) likely occurs at least as a migrant; it breeds in southern Mexico and probably also in eastern Nicaragua (where apparently absent in "winter"), has been taken calling near the Darién border in Colombia (J. Haffer), and is recorded widely in South America. In size (7½–8″) and pattern it resembles female White-tailed Nightjar, but has rounded tail and no pale wing-band. Both sexes have blackish crown and cheeks, buff superciliary, and blackish breast heavily spotted with buff; male's tail largely blackish with white spots near base (visible only in specimens) and white corners, female's tail browner without white. Its call is a thin high-pitched *pit-sweet* or *spit-sweet,* rather insect-like (D. Zimmerman); favors grassy savannas, pastures, scrub.

SWIFTS: Apodidae (11)

The swifts are a distinct group of superficially swallow-like birds, having long very narrow stiff wings, compact bodies, and generally dark plumage (in some species patterned with white or rufous). They are worldwide in distribution, but most species occur in the tropics. True swifts are pre-eminently birds of the air, not perching "normally," usually roosting and nesting on vertical surfaces such as cliffs or the inside of hollow trees (or chimneys); some even copulate in the air (the only birds known to do so), and some species are known to sleep on the wing (D. Lack). All swifts are totally insectivorous, catching insects in their wide-opening mouths during very swift flight. The nest is usually constructed against a vertical surface, its components being held together by a glue-like salivary excretion, in most species a simple cup or half-cup, in some (e.g. Lesser Swallow-tailed Swift) more elaborate. Of the two most diverse genera in Panama, *Cypseloides* differs from *Chaetura* in its narrower more swept-back wings, longer tail (some *Chaetura* appear virtually tail-less in the field), and in having rump same color as back (in *Chaetura* rump is paler than back), and throat (above collar when present) same color as breast (in *Chaetura* throat is often contrastingly paler than remainder of underparts). The status of many Panamanian swifts is still very inadequately known. Collection of swifts, while difficult, is still desirable, for field identification of many species is often dubious. Not only does variation in appearance occur because of wear on feathers and dirt accumulated from their roosting sites, but the exact status and distribution of many species is still so uncertain that one can often not safely identify by range.

WHITE-COLLARED SWIFT

(*Streptoprocne zonaris*) *page 148*

Description: 7½–8½. A *very large* blackish swift with *prominent white collar completely encircling neck;* tail distinctly forked (though often not noticeable). Immature has narrower collar, sometimes reduced to patches or entirely lacking.

Similar species: Much larger than any other Panama swift, with unmistakable white collar.

Status and distribution: Fairly common in foothills and highlands, ranging regularly down to coastal lowlands on Caribbean slope, less often to Pacific lowlands (recorded only Chiriquí, Coiba Island, eastern Panama province, and Darién).

Habits: Usually seen flying in fair-sized groups, occasionally in flocks of several hundred or more. They can fly at terrific speeds, and apparently range over great distances in their daily foraging. They alone among Panama swifts regularly soar on stiff outstretched wings. Often given is a thin hissing screech, quite loud and piercing at close range.

Range: Mexico to northern Argentina and southern Brazil; Greater Antilles.

CHESTNUT-COLLARED SWIFT

(*Cypseloides rutilus*)

Description: 4½–5. Sooty black with *broad rufous-chestnut collar encircling neck* in adult male (usually lacking in female); tail almost square, rather short for this genus.

Similar species: No other Panama swift has a chestnut collar, but this is difficult to see

Upper left, two Band-rumped Swifts; lower left, Vaux's Swift; middle, two Short-tailed Swifts; upper right, Lesser Swallow-tailed Swift; lower right, White-collared Swift

unless the bird chances to fly against a dark background or is seen from above. Overhead, with backlighting from the sky, it becomes almost impossible. Female and immature are similar to White-chinned Swift.

Status and distribution: Uncertain; very few records. Apparently rare, perhaps somewhat overlooked, in foothills and highlands; two specimens each from Chiriquí and Los Santos (Cerro Hoya), and one taken at Calobre, Veraguas, on June 2, 1969 (specimen in Gorgas coll.). Three sightings: at least 20 above Boquete (El Salto), Chiriquí on February 21, 1960 (Eisenmann and J. Linford); a small flock on Cerro Azul on March 21, 1968 (Ridgely); and 2 at Cerro Jefe, eastern Panama province (with *Chaetura* swifts) on July 17, 1973 (D. Hill). Whether a breeder in Panama uncertain, but believed to nest in southwestern Costa Rica (L. Kiff).

Range: Central Mexico south locally to Guyana and Bolivia.

WHITE-CHINNED SWIFT
(*Cypseloides cryptus*)

Description: 5½–5¾. Very rare. *Sooty black above* with some paler edging on forehead; dark grayish brown below, usually with a small whitish patch on chin (but not a field mark); tail very short. Female often has feathers on belly tipped white. In the hand, distinguished from other *Cypseloides* swifts by its short tail (41–48 mm) and relatively long tarsus (15–16 mm).

Similar species: Considerably larger than most *Chaetura* swifts and without contrasting paler rump. Chimney Swift has pale throat and dark olive upperparts; Chapman's Swift is similar but has slightly contrasting rump. Especially easily confused with female Chestnut-collared Swift and two other unrecorded, though possible, *Cypseloides* swifts (see below).

Status and distribution: Uncertain. Only two records: one taken at Armila, San Blas, on July 4, 1932; another taken off

Coiba Island on March 23, 1957. Perhaps only a visitant from South America, as practically all Middle American records are from austral winter months.

Range: Recorded from Belize to Guyana and Peru, but everywhere apparently scarce and local; breeding area unknown.

Note: Two other *Cypseloides* swifts may occur; specimens of both would be required due to great difficulty in field identification. Black Swift (*C. niger*), 6″ (tail 48–58 mm), is sooty black with whitish frosting on forecrown, sometimes with whitish marks on belly, and slightly forked tail. Spot-fronted Swift (*C. cherriei*), 5″ (tail 46–47 mm; tarsus 12–13 mm), is sooty black with white spots on forehead and a small whitish spot behind eye. Both these swifts have been recorded recently from as close as southwestern Costa Rica, where Black Swift is believed to be breeding (L. Kiff).

CHAPMAN'S (DARK-BREASTED) SWIFT

(*Chaetura chapmani*)

Description: 5–5½. A fairly large *Chaetura*. Looks mostly blackish in the field. Black above; *grayish brown on rump and upper tail-coverts,* tail slightly darker; *deep sooty below, including throat* (which, though slightly paler, shows no contrast); tail rather short.

Similar species: Fairly large size, dark color, and lack of contrast between throat and underparts will distinguish this species from other *Chaetura* swifts under favorable circumstances. In size nearest to Chimney and Ashy-tailed Swifts, but they have shorter tails and are not as dark, with throat distinctly paler than breast. Larger than Vaux's Swift, which has distinctly pale throat. *Cypseloides* swifts have rump and upper tail-coverts same color as back.

Status and distribution: Uncertain, perhaps breeding, though possibly only a wanderer from South America. Only two definite records: two taken at Gatun in Canal Zone on July 9, 1911; and two taken at Mandinga, San Blas on January 30, 1957. All sight reports are less than satisfactory. Panama specimens have been assigned to the northern South America race, so not likely to be migrants. Collection of large *Chaetura* swifts is needed when Chimney Swift is absent.

Range: Local or little known in lowlands of northern and central South America; Panama.

CHIMNEY SWIFT

(*Chaetura pelagica*)

Description: 5¼–5¾. Fairly large. *Dark sooty olive above* with slightly paler rump and upper tail-coverts (but little contrast); grayish brown below, *noticeably paler on throat;* tail short.

Similar Species: Most likely to be confused with Chapman's Swift, but not as black above, and with contrasting whitish to pale gray throat (wear and soiling may alter these distinctions in some birds, however, so caution is advised). Vaux's Swift is also very similar but local race is much smaller and blacker above.

Status and distribution: Probably a regular (perhaps common?) transient (October–November; March–May), but specimen records very few. Records are mostly from Caribbean slope, on Pacific slope from Canal Zone east to Darién, with no reports from Pacific western Panama; one reported sighting from Taboga Island.

Range: Breeds in eastern and central North America; winters mostly in western Amazonia, also apparently in western Peru; migrates through Colombia and Venezuela, Middle America, and in West Indies.

VAUX'S SWIFT

(*Chaetura vauxi*)

Description: 4. *Small.* Sooty black above, rump and upper tail-coverts dark gray (but *not strongly contrasting*); sooty gray below with *distinctly paler gray throat;* tail short (but relatively longer than in Short-tailed and Ashy-tailed Swifts).

Similar species: The other two *Chaetura* swifts that show only a little contrast between rump and upperparts, Chapman's and Chimney, are both notably larger than this species. Gray-rumped and Band-rumped Swifts have rump strongly contrasting with back and have longer tails. Short-tailed and Ashy-tailed Swifts look almost tail-less with *very* pale rump and upper tail coverts; Short-tailed is almost black below (including throat).

Status and distribution: Common (breeding) in highlands of western Chiriquí; probably breeding (numerous specimens) in southern Veraguas lowlands and foothills (including western side of Azuero Peninsula), on Coiba Island, and on Pearl Islands. Sight reports from drier eastern side of Azuero Peninsula, hill country of Coclé, and less surely from Pacific slope of Canal Zone and Panama city (these before Short-tailed Swift was known to breed commonly). Specimen confirmation needed from central Panama mainland.

Range: Western North America to Panama; northern Venezuela.

Note: Southern races from southern Mexico to Panama are by some authors considered a distinct species, *C. richmondi* (Dusky-backed Swift).

GRAY-RUMPED SWIFT
(*Chaetura cinereiventris*)

Description: 4–4¼. So far only recorded from western Bocas del Toro. Fairly small. Glossy black above with *contrasting gray triangular patch on rump and upper tail-coverts;* dark gray below, paler on throat; tail relatively long for a *Chaetura.*

Similar species: Very like Band-rumped Swift and often inseparable in the field. Band-rump has much paler (almost white) *band* across rump only (not including upper tail-coverts) and is blacker below with more contrasting whitish throat. Vaux's Swift shows much less contrast on rump and has a shorter tail but can be confused, though in Panama not known to overlap.

Status and distribution: Fairly common in lowlands of western Bocas del Toro, presumably breeding.

Range: Nicaragua to Caribbean western Panama; Colombia to Guyana and western Brazil; coastal Brazil, eastern Paraguay, and northeastern Argentina.

BAND-RUMPED SWIFT
(*Chaetura spinicauda*) *page 148*

Description: 4–4¼. Fairly small. Glossy black above with *strongly contrasting whitish band across rump;* upper tail-coverts and rather long tail blackish; throat whitish, remaining underparts dark gray, becoming blackish on belly.

Similar species: Very like Gray-rumped Swift (the two are not known from the same Panama locality), but that species has a triangular patch on rump *and* upper tail-coverts (not just rump); there is some variation due to feather wear and molt, so one must be cautious. Vaux's Swift shows much less contrast on rump.

Status and distribution: Common in lowlands and foothills on both slopes from Canal Zone and vicinity eastward, recorded also in western Chiriquí (where ranges up into lower highlands). The most numerous *Chaetura* on Caribbean side of Canal Zone.

Range: Costa Rica to Colombia and northern Brazil.

ASHY-TAILED SWIFT
(*Chaetura andrei*)

Description: 5¼–5½. Very rare. Fairly large, almost size of Chimney Swift. Deep sooty brown above with *contrasting pale ashy gray rump and upper tail-coverts;* sooty brown below with *contrasting pale gray throat;* tail gray and very short (usually covered by upper tail-coverts).

Similar species: Combination of large size and short tail, pale gray rump and upper tail-coverts, and pale gray throat will identify this rare species under *very* favorable circumstances. Short-tailed Swift has similar pale hind end but is much smaller and blacker generally with very dark throat. Also resembles Chimney Swift but has much more contrasting pale gray rump and upper tail-coverts.

Status and distribution: Only one record, a bird collected from a flock of swifts near Juan Diaz (just east of Panama city) on August 4, 1923. Apparently a migrant from southern South America; the single specimen was assigned to the migratory southern race (*meridionalis*) breeding from southeastern Brazil southward. Collection may prove it a regular migrant during southern winter months.

Range: Venezuela, Surinam; eastern and southern Brazil, eastern Paraguay, northeastern Argentina; northern Colombia and central Panama (once each, August migrants).

Note: Wetmore calls it André's Swift.

SHORT-TAILED SWIFT
(*Chaetura brachyura*) *page 148*

Description: 4–4¼. *Fairly small.* Black above with *very contrasting ashy gray rump and upper tail-coverts* (tail covered by upper tail-coverts); sooty black below, throat very slightly paler (no contrast), with under tail-coverts gray; tail very short, *appearing virtually tail-less in the field.*

Similar species: A small, very short-tailed swift that can be known by its overall black plumage and contrasting pale rump and hind end. The rare migrant Ashy-tailed Swift is rather similar but is much larger and has contrasting pale gray throat.

Vaux's Swift has darker, visible tail, pale grayish throat. Chapman's Swift is also generally blackish, but is larger with longer tail and has much less contrasting hind end.
Status and distribution: Recently (1970) discovered by E. S. Morton to be a locally common breeder in fairly open areas on Pacific slope of Canal Zone and vicinity; on Caribbean slope so far found mostly in middle Chagres River valley (especially Summit Gardens) but has also been seen on Galeta Island (Ridgely). Previously known only from a bird found dead in 1960. So far not seen elsewhere in Panama, but to be watched for. Had apparently been overlooked, as the Panama birds represent a new and rather distinct race (Eisenmann, pers. comm.). Easily seen at Balboa and Ancon Heights.
Habits: Similar to other *Chaetura* swifts. Found breeding in a woodpecker hole in trunk of dead palm on Chiva Chiva Road (E. S. Morton).
Range: Central Panama; Colombia to Peru, central Brazil, and the Guianas.

LESSER SWALLOW TAILED SWIFT
(*Panyptila cayennensis*) *page 148*

Description: 5. A distinctively patterned small swift. Mostly deep black with *white collar around hindneck connecting with white throat and chest* and *white patch on flanks;* tail very long and deeply forked, though usually held closed in a point.
Similar species: White-collared Swift is much larger, without white throat and flank patches.
Status and distribution: Locally fairly common in more humid lowlands on both slopes, with most records from Canal Zone and vicinity.
Habits: Attaches its conspicuous, usually tubular felt-like nest on the trunk of a tree or the side of a building (sometimes hung free from a branch or structure); these can be seen at Ancon Heights and at Summit Gardens. Nests are used both for reproduction and for roosting; birds are not often seen near the nests during daylight. Usually observed flying very high, singly or in pairs (not in flocks), occasionally with other swifts. For nesting seems to prefer towns or inhabited areas, though often observed flying over forest.
Range: Southern Mexico to Amazonian and coastal Brazil.
Note: Wetmore calls it Cayenne Swift.

HUMMINGBIRDS: Trochilidae (52)

Within this large family are found the smallest of birds (a few weigh no more than a dime) and perhaps the most brilliantly colored. Found exclusively in the Americas, they reach their highest development in northern South America; the family is well represented in all habitats in Panama, though the more spectacularly ornamented species are lacking. Hummingbirds are renowned for a number of things besides their size. Perhaps most remarkable is their power of flight: the wing is rotated through an angle of 180°, allowing a much greater measure of control, including perfectly stationary hovering and backward flight (of which no other birds are capable). The wings also beat incredibly rapidly, in some species at rates up to 80 beats per second, though notably slower in the larger species; the speed of flight can also be very great, with extraordinarily abrupt starting and stopping. Hummingbirds are most famous for their brilliant iridescent coloring; these brilliant areas are colorful only when bird, observer, and the sun are in perfect juxtaposition, and often change in hue depending on the angle of light (at other times they appear blackish). In many species, a glittering area is found on the throat, which is then termed a *gorget.* Males are almost always more brightly colored than females except in those species in which both sexes are dull (e.g. the hermits). Hummingbirds feed on nectar, tiny insects, and spiders in varying proportions; many are exceedingly belligerent in the defense of their feeding areas. A number of species apparently engage in seasonal movements, the details of which are as yet poorly understood and documented. Males of some species gather to display in communal leks in forest undergrowth where they "sing" interminably. In many other species, males simply select a prominent perch and emit their insignificant "songs," while in some others males have spectacular aerial display flights (especially in the genus *Selasphorous*). The nest is an attractive structure of plant down and spider webs, placed in the fork of a branch or underneath a large leaf; males play no role in the rearing process. Identification of many species is tricky: they are often seen only briefly and the salient characters not observed, and the light may be poor and the iridescent areas may not show up. Females are especially difficult. Bill length and shape are often particularly useful characters. Though, to my knowledge, they have not been tried on a large scale in Panama, hummingbird feeders would certainly attract numerous species to within easily identifiable range; they would be especially useful in the Chiriquí highlands.

BRONZY HERMIT
(*Glaucis aenea*) Pl.7

Description: 4. Known only from western Panama. Bill long (1¼″), decurved. Resembles the following species and possibly only subspecifically distinct. *Coppery bronze above* with dusky crown and sides of head; *rusty-cinnamon below,* paler on chin and duller on lower belly; tail rounded, *chestnut,* with broad black subterminal band and whitish tip. Female similar but more uniformly rufous and slightly brighter below.

Similar species: Rufous-breasted Hermit has different range, is larger, less bronzy or coppery above (more green), and not as bright rufous below. Band-tailed Barbthroat has white instead of chestnut in tail, and is larger, greener above, and much duller below.

Status and distribution: Uncommon and local in undergrowth of humid forest and forest borders in lowlands of western Chiriquí and western Veraguas (Zapotillo); fairly common in western Bocas del Toro (Almirante).

Habits: Usually found in heavily overgrown border growth, not inside forest, favoring *Heliconia* thickets and banana plantations.

Range: Nicaragua to western Panama; western Colombia to northwestern Ecuador.

Note: By some authors regarded as conspecific with *G. hirsuta.*

RUFOUS-BREASTED HERMIT
(*Glaucis hirsuta*) Pl.7

Description: 4½. Long, decurved bill (1¼″). Metallic to bronzy green above; *mostly dull rufous below,* whiter or grayer on throat and belly, with some green on sides; *tail rounded, mostly chestnut,* with black subterminal band and white tip. Female similar but with *underparts more uniform dull rufous.* Immature more bronzy above with buff edging, duller below.

Similar species: In western Panama see Bronzy Hermit. Band-tailed Barbthroat is rather similar but is more grayish white below (not so rufous) and lacks chestnut in tail. *Phaethornis* hermits have elongated central tail feathers.

Status and distribution: Uncommon to fairly common in undergrowth of humid forest, woodland clearings, and borders in lowlands and foothills on Caribbean slope from Coclé east through San Blas; on Pacific slope from western Panama province (Cerro Campana) east through Darién. In Canal Zone more numerous on Caribbean side.

Habits: Favors *Heliconia* thickets and banana plantations, usually remaining low in dense vegetation and not often seen, though regularly caught in mist-nets. In Trinidad 1 to 3 females nest in an area along a stream defended by a single male (which does not directly assist in rearing the young, however); the nest is attached to the underside of a *Heliconia* leaf, often directly over the stream (B. Snow).

Range: Central Panama to northern Bolivia and southern Brazil; Grenada.

Note: Wetmore calls it Hairy Hermit.

BAND-TAILED BARBTHROAT
(*Threnetes ruckeri*) Pl.7

Description: 6–7. Long, decurved bill (1½″), Bronzy green above with dull black patch behind eye bordered above and below by buffy stripes; *throat blackish,* feathers lightly edged with buff; remaining underparts mostly buffy grayish, with patch of cinnamon-rufous on chest and cinnamon-rufous flanks; *tail rounded, basal half white with broad black subterminal band* and white tip. Immature has dull buffy gray throat.

Similar species: The superficially similar Rufous-breasted Hermit lacks the blackish throat, has more uniform rufous underparts, and has mostly chestnut tail. *Phaethornis* hermits have similar facial pattern but have long pointed tails without white basal half. In western Panama see also Bronzy Hermit.

Status and distribution: Uncommon in humid forest and forest borders in lowlands and foothills on entire Caribbean slope; on Pacific slope recorded from Chiriquí, Veraguas foothills (above Santa Fé; Ridgely), Cerro Campana, and Canal Zone east through Darién. In Canal Zone, considerably more numerous on Caribbean side.

Habits: Like Rufous-breasted Hermit favors *Heliconia* thickets and banana plantations at edge of forest, but also regularly found within forest. Males display in loose groups (mostly May–July), perching on low branches and "singing" with a series of short, squeaky notes, while vibrating their partly fanned tails. Generally less numerous than Rufous-breasted Hermit in the Canal Zone, and more restricted to humid areas.

Range: Guatemala and Belize to western Venezuela and northwestern Ecuador

Note: Wetmore calls it Rucker's Hermit.

GREEN HERMIT
(*Phaethornis guy*) Pl.7

Description: 6–7. Long, decurved bill (1½″), most of lower mandible reddish. Male *mostly metallic bluish green,* with buffy throat, more slaty on center of breast and belly; tail long and graduated with central pair of feathers somewhat elongated. Female similar but with blackish patch behind eye bordered above and below by buffy stripes, and mostly slaty gray below; central tail feathers considerably more elongated than in male.

Similar species: Long-tailed Hermit is obviously browner above and below.

Status and distribution: Common in undergrowth of humid forest and forest borders in foothills and highlands (mostly 2000–5500 feet) on entire Pacific slope; on Caribbean slope known primarily from foothills and highlands of Bocas del Toro and Veraguas, also recorded from Coclé (Tigre on Río Coclé del Norte) and eastern Colon province (Cerro Santa Rita, Cerro Bruja), though not from San Blas. Status in Canal Zone unclear, with a few reports from Caribbean slope but no definite specimens, perhaps post-breeding wanderers. Numerous on Cerro Campana and in the Cerro Azul/Jefe area.

Habits: Usually seen singly inside forest. A sharp squeak is frequently heard, especially in flight. Males gather in loose groups to display during the breeding season; they then interminably utter short snappy noises (some almost manakin-like), accompanied by moving their tails, and are often frustratingly difficult to see as they perch low in the dense forest undergrowth.

Range: Costa Rica to northern Venezuela and southern Peru.

LONG-TAILED HERMIT
(*Phaethornis superciliosus*) Pl.7

Description: 6–7. Long, decurved bill (1½″), lower mandible yellow. *Mostly brownish;* more bronzy green on back with *rump cinnamon* barred with black; blackish mask through and behind eye, bordered below by a whitish streak; underparts mostly buffy whitish, the throat more brownish with a whitish central streak; tail long and graduated, mostly black with sides edged cinnamon, *central pair of feathers greatly elongated and tipped white.*

Similar species: Both sexes of Green Hermit are distinctly bluish green above. Pale-bellied Hermit is more uniformly green above and whiter below.

Status and distribution: Very common in undergrowth of forest, second-growth woodland, and borders in lowlands and lower foothills (to about 3000 feet) on both slopes, but absent from dry Pacific lowlands from eastern side of Azuero Peninsula to extreme western Panama province.

Habits: One of the characteristic birds of Panama's lowland forests. Most often seen as it dashes by, uttering a sharp squeak; like the other hermits, often seems almost curious, pausing abruptly to hover in front of the observer for a few seconds, then darting off. Groups of males, often large, perform at their "singing" assemblies in forest undergrowth through much of the year, interminably giving a short squeaky note to the accompaniment of tail wagging. The nest, shaped like an inverted cone, is attached to the underside of the tip of a palm or *Heliconia* leaf.

Range: Central Mexico to northern Bolivia and Amazonian Brazil.

PALE-BELLIED (BLACK-CHEEKED) HERMIT
(*Phaethornis anthophilus*) Pl.7

Description: 6–6½. Only hermit on *Pearl Islands.* Bill long (1¼″), but less decurved than in other Panama hermits. Dull bronzy green above, blackish on crown; blackish patch behind eye bordered above and below by whitish stripes; *mostly white below,* throat streaked with dusky, tinged with gray on breast and with buffy on flanks; tail long and graduated with central pair of feathers protruding (but not as far as in Long-tailed Hermit) and white-tipped.

Similar species: Long-tailed Hermit is more brownish above and below with cinnamon rump, more decurved bill, and longer tail.

Status and distribution: Fairly common in woodland undergrowth on larger Pearl Islands; on mainland recorded only from eastern Panama province (between Pacora and Chico) and once from eastern San Blas (Puerto Obaldía). To be looked for elsewhere in eastern Panama.

Habits: Seems to forage more in the open

and in clearings adjacent to woodland than do the other Panama hermits.

Range: Central Panama through northern Colombia to northern Venezuela.

LITTLE HERMIT
(*Phaethornis longuemareus*) Pl.7

Description: 3½. *Very small;* much of the given length is bill and tail. Bill long (1″) and moderately decurved. Bronzy green above shading to brownish on crown and chestnut on rump; blackish mask behind eyes, bordered above and below by whitish stripes; *mostly cinnamon below;* tail bronzy tipped with buff, *sharply graduated, but with central pair of feathers not excessively elongated.*

Similar species: Much larger Long-tailed Hermit has greatly elongated white-tipped central tail feathers. Rufous-breasted Hermit and Band-tailed Barbthroat have rounded tails with black subterminal bands.

Status and distribution: Fairly common to common in undergrowth of forest borders, second-growth woodland, and adjacent clearings in more humid lowlands and foothills on both slopes, less numerous or lacking in dry Pacific lowlands from eastern side of Azuero Peninsula to western Panama province. Widespread in the Canal Zone.

Habits: Usually seen singly, within a few feet of the ground. This species and a few other small hummingbirds regularly fly *through* mist-nets. When perched, often wags tail up and down. Males form "singing" assemblies during the breeding season, perching very low in dense undergrowth where they emit a series of insignificant squeaks.

Range: Southern Mexico to Peru, Amazonian Brazil, and the Guianas.

TOOTH-BILLED HUMMINGBIRD
(*Androdon aequatorialis*)

Description: 5¼. Known only from Darién highlands. *Bill very long (1½″), straight.* Forecrown metallic reddish copper, otherwise bronzy green above with *prominent white band across rump;* grayish white below *streaked with blackish,* especially on throat and breast; tail rounded, gray with broad dark green band and white tip. Female similar but with duller crown and less heavily streaked underparts. Immature male like female but with bluish nape. In the hand, minute serrations on the cutting edge of the outer half of the bill are prominent.

Similar species: No other Panama hummer has such a long bill and the streaked underparts.

Status and distribution: Recorded from for-

Upper, Tooth-Billed Hummingbird,
lower, White-Tipped Sicklebill

est in foothills and highlands of eastern Darién (2400–5200 feet).

Habits: Little known. Feeds at flowers near ground inside forest and at openings and borders.

Range: Eastern Panama to western Ecuador.

WHITE-TIPPED SICKLEBILL
(*Eutoxeres aquila*)

Description: 5½. *Very sharply decurved bill,* bent almost into a right angle, makes this species unmistakable. Bronzy green above; *sooty below streaked with whitish;* tail graduated, bronzy green tipped white.

Status and distribution: Rare to locally uncommon in undergrowth of humid forest in foothills (a few lowland records) locally on Caribbean slope in Bocas del Toro, eastern Colon province, and San Blas (where perhaps more numerous); on Pacific slope in foothills of western Chiriquí, Veraguas, Cerro Campana, Cerro Azul/Jefe area, and Darién.

Habits: A heavy-bodied hummingbird with slow audible wingbeats. Like a hermit, will often pause to briefly inspect the observer, hovering at eye-level a few yards away. Often feeds in *Heliconia,* clinging awkwardly to the flowers and probing their blossoms with its curious bill.

Range: Costa Rica to northern Peru.

GREEN-FRONTED LANCEBILL
(*Doryfera ludoviciae*) Pl.7

Description: 4½. Known only from highlands of west and east. *Bill very long (1½"), essentially straight,* black. *Forehead glittering bluish green, crown reddish coppery,* small white spot behind eye; otherwise dark metallic green above, glossed bluer on upper tail-coverts, with wings and tail blacker; throat sooty, remaining underparts dull grayish green. Female similar but duller, usually lacking glittering forehead; crown bronzy.

Similar species: A dark hummingbird, readily known by its striking long bill. Tooth-billed Hummingbird of Darién highlands has equally long bill, but has streaked underparts.

Status and distribution: Apparently rare in forest and forest borders in highlands of Chiriquí (5400–7500 feet), Veraguas (Chitra), and eastern Darién (Cerro Pirre and Cerro Tacarcuna, 3500–5000 feet). Little known in Panama.

Habits: Usually seen singly, feeding low at flowering shrubs in forest openings and borders.

Range: Costa Rica to western Venezuela and northern Bolivia.

SCALY-BREASTED HUMMINGBIRD
(*Phaeochroa cuvierii*) Pl.7

Description: 4½–5. Bill straight and *rather short* (¾"), base of lower mandible pink to whitish. Rather large. Dull bronzy green above; mostly grayish buffy below, *chest and breast with greenish spots giving scaly effect;* tail bronzy green, *outer feathers broadly tipped white* (giving effect of white corners to tail).

Similar species: A rather dull, good-sized, often confused hummingbird. Most likely to be mistaken for female White-necked Jacobin (which is even more scaly on throat and chest than this species) but jacobin has wholly white (not buffy) belly and lacks white tail corners. White-vented Plumeleteer is brighter green generally, without scaly effect, has prominent white vent, and lacks white tail-tips.

Status and distribution: Fairly common locally in clearings, gardens, and woodland borders in lowlands on Pacific slope in Chiriquí, Veraguas, and Los Santos, and in Canal Zone and eastern Panama province; on Caribbean slope locally from around Canal Zone east through San Blas; found also on Coiba Island.

Habits: One of the more accomplished "singers" in its family, uttering an endlessly repeated series of various chips (*tsup, sst-sst-sst*) from an exposed, usually low, perch, often emphasizing each note with a twist of its head.

Range: Guatemala to northern Colombia.

Note: Wetmore calls it Cuvier's Hummingbird.

VIOLET SABREWING
(*Campylopterus hemileucurus*) Pl.8

Description: 5½. Found only in western highlands. Bill fairly long (1¼"), *decurved.* Male *mostly brilliant dark violet;* inconspicuous white leg tufts; tail mostly black with *three outer feathers very broadly tipped white* so that when closed from below tail seems white on terminal half. Female metallic green above; mostly gray below, paler on belly, with *patch of violet on throat* and some green on sides; *tail as in male.*

Similar species: Male is spectacular, especially in flight when the white on the tail flashes out conspicuously. Female is best known by its large size and prominent white in tail; female Magnificent Hummingbird has long straight bill and lacks white in tail.

Status and distribution: Fairly common in forest and forest borders in highlands of Chiriquí and Veraguas, mostly above 4000 feet; single records from near Concepción, western Chiriquí (1500 feet) and near Cerro Viejo on western side of Azuero Peninsula (3000 feet).

Habits: Encountered singly or in pairs, feeding in the forest understory or in small openings. Often hovers before the observer like a hermit. Sometimes "sings" rhythmically and interminably, the voice suggestive of that of the Green Violetear but thinner.

Range: Southern Mexico to western Panama.

WHITE-NECKED JACOBIN
(*Florisuga mellivora*) Pl.7

Description: 4½–4¾. Bill straight and rather short (¾″), all black. Fairly large. Male has *entire head and chest dark blue* (bright cornflower blue in perfect light) and *white patch on hindneck;* otherwise shining green above; breast and belly white, contrasting strongly with blue chest; *tail mostly white,* tipped black. Female green above; throat and chest dusky, feathers edged with white, giving *scaly effect;* lower underparts white; tail dark green with broad black subterminal band, sometimes tipped with white. Some females assume varying degrees of male's plumage, especially the blue head and white tail.

Similar species: Most females are more conspicuously scaly below than Scaly-breasted Hummingbird but lack prominent white tail corners of that species.

Status and distribution: Fairly common to common in clearings and borders of forest and second-growth woodland in humid lowlands on both slopes, ranging in reduced number up into the lower highlands to about 5000 feet; more local on Pacific slope and largely absent from dry Pacific lowlands from eastern side of Azuero Peninsula to western Panama province. Apparently moves about seasonally, being mostly absent from Pacific slope of Canal Zone during dry season,

Habits: Usually seen singly, though small groups may gather around flowering trees. Birds in male plumage (some no doubt actually females) are noted much more often than the rather drab females. During breeding season, males have an attractive territorial display in which they swoop about and hover at considerable heights, fanning their mostly white tails into a semicircle.

Range: Southern Mexico to Bolivia and central Brazil.

GREEN VIOLETEAR
(*Colibri thalassinus*) Pl.8

Description: 4½. Found only in western highlands. Bill straight (1″). Sexes similar. Mostly shining green with a *long violet ear-patch* and some violet gloss on chest; tail greenish blue with broad black subterminal band.

Similar species: The violet ear-patch, usually quite conspicuous, distinguishes this hummer from all others in Panama except the otherwise very different Brown Violetear.

Status and distribution: Common in forest borders and clearings in highlands of Chiriquí (mostly above 5000 feet, sometimes down to around 4000 feet); recorded also from foothills of Veraguas (Chitra, Calovévora).

Habits: One of the most numerous hummingbirds in the western Chiriquí highlands. Its voice attracts attention, but the calling bird can be hard to see as it often sits high in a tall tree. The "song" is endlessly repeated, normally two-noted but with some variation, *tsip-tsup,* or *tsut-tsip,* given as the bird perches motionless on a bare twig, often rather ventriloquial.

Range: Central Mexico to western Panama: Colombia and northern Venezuela to northwestern Argentina.

BROWN VIOLETEAR
(*Colibri delphinae*) Pl.7

Description: 4¼. Bill straight, fairly short (¾″). *Mostly dull brownish,* somewhat streaked with whitish below; *long violet-blue ear-tuft;* upper throat green, becoming violet-blue on lower throat, *bordered by white moustachial streak;* rump mostly tawny, under tail-coverts rusty. Sexes similar. Immature lacks violet ear-tuft and has rusty tipping on back.

Similar species: A drab hummingbird, best known by the violet ear-patch (though it may be hard to see in poor light), a mark shared only by the otherwise very different Green Violetear. Most like Long-billed Starthroat, but without that species' very long bill.

Status and distribution: Apparently rare; known from highlands of Chiriquí (5000–5400 feet) and foothills of Veraguas (Calovévora; also one seen above Santa Fé on

January 5, 1974 by G. Stiles) and eastern Darién (Cana and Cerro Quía); one recent sighting of several birds on Cerro Campana on July 20, 1969 (J. Karr and H. Hespenheide).

Habits: Little known. Reported to favor woodland borders and small clearings and openings. Seasonally more numerous in some areas.

Range: Guatemala to Bolivia and northern and eastern Brazil.

GREEN-BREASTED MANGO
(*Anthracothorax prevostii*)

Description: 4½. Bill slightly decurved (1″). Male metallic green above; *brilliant green below,* more bluish on breast and center of belly; *tail mostly purplish maroon* with narrow black tip. Female metallic green above; mostly white below with *broad median stripe of greenish blue;* tail mostly blackish with outer feathers tipped white. Immature like female but with underparts adjacent to median stripe (which is more blackish) rufous.

Similar species: Much like Black-throated Mango but male largely green without Black-throat's broad black stripe on underparts; female Green-breast's median stripe is greenish blue (not black).

Status and distribution: Uncommon and local in open areas with trees, shrubby clearings, and along tree-bordered streams in lowlands on Pacific slope from Chiriquí to southern Coclé (Aguadulce). Two immature specimens from Gatun on Caribbean slope of Canal Zone are attributed to this species by Wetmore (the only ones from so far east or from the Caribbean slope).

Habits: Seems generally a scarce bird, found in open areas with bushes and low trees, particularly near water.

Range: Eastern Mexico to central Costa Rica; western and central Panama; Colombia and northern Venezuela; western Ecuador and northwestern Peru.

Note: Wetmore calls it Prevost's Mango. Birds from Panama have been considered a distinct species, *A. veraguensis* (Veraguan Mango).

BLACK-THROATED MANGO
(*Anthracothorax nigricollis*) Pl.7

Description: 4½. Bill slightly decurved (1″). Male green with *black throat continuing as broad black stripe down center of underparts; tail maroon-chestnut.* Female metallic green above; white below, with *black stripe down center of underparts* and green on sides; tail as in male but with broad blackish subterminal band and white tip. Immature like female but with some brownish edging above.

Similar species: Female more striking than male as its black median stripe contrasts more strongly with remainder of underparts; male somewhat tricky until seen in good light, but maroon tail usually evident. In Pacific western Panama see Green-breasted Mango.

Status and distribution: Uncommon to locally fairly common in woodland and forest borders, clearings, and around habitations in lowlands on Pacific slope from southern Veraguas (Santiago) and southern Coclé (Aguadulce) east through Darién; on Caribbean slope from Canal Zone east through San Blas. Old specimens attributed to "Chiriquí" are dubious.

Habits: Generally favors trees and shrubby areas near water. Female-plumaged birds outnumber adult males.

Range: Western Panama to Bolivia, northern Argentina, and southern Brazil.

VIOLET-HEADED HUMMINGBIRD
(*Klais guimeti*) Pl.7

Description: 3. Bill straight, short (½″). Male with *entire head (including throat) violet-blue* and *conspicuous white spot behind eye* (often giving effect of white eye); otherwise bright green above; grayish below flecked with green on breast; tail bluish green tipped whitish. Female similar but with only forecrown blue, pale gray below with some green on sides, broader whitish tail tipping.

Similar species: No other small Panamanian hummingbird has so prominent a white spot behind the eye.

Status and distribution: Uncommon to locally common in humid forest borders and second-growth woodland in foothills on both slopes (mostly 1000–4000 feet), ranging down occasionally to the lowlands, especially on Caribbean slope and in Chiriquí and Veraguas; not recorded from San Blas but probably present. Scarce in Canal Zone, reported only from Caribbean side, perhaps only a seasonal wanderer from hill country; fairly common on Cerro Campana and in the Cerro Azul/Jefe area.

Habits: Usually found singly, feeding low in shrubbery at edge of forest. Males gather in small loose groups to "sing" during the breeding season.

Range: Honduras to western Venezuela and Bolivia.

Note: Wetmore calls it Violet-crowned Hummingbird (which name is also in current use for a species of extreme southwestern United States and Mexico, *Amazilia violiceps*).

RUFOUS-CRESTED COQUETTE
(*Lophornis delattrei*) Pl.7

Description: 2¾. Bill short (⅓"), straight. *Minute.* Male with *crown and long bushy crest rufous;* otherwise bronzy green above with *conspicuous white or buff band across rump* and mostly rufous tail; throat glittering green, remaining underparts bronzy green. Female lacks crest, has *dull rufous forecrown;* otherwise bronzy green above with *band across rump as in male;* throat light cinnamon, upper chest dusky bronze, remaining underparts dull bronzy green; *tail cinnamon* with broad black subterminal band.

Similar species: Tiny rufous-crested males are unmistakable; females are best known by their size, rufous forecrown, and pale rump band (a mark shared by all the coquettes). In western Chiriquí see White-crested Coquette; see also Black-crested Coquette (below).

Status and distribution: Rare to uncommon and local in forest and woodland clearings and borders in lowlands and foothills; on Caribbean slope recorded from central Bocas del Toro (Cocoplum) and Canal Zone and vicinity; on Pacific slope from Chiriquí (Bugaba), Veraguas, Cerro Campana, and Canal Zone east through Darién (Cana). Not numerous anywhere, and seemingly very irregular; most records are from central Panama.

Habits: Usually seen perched on an exposed branch or twig, often at moderate heights. Usually feeds in low flowers and shrubbery. In flight, the tail is slowly waved up and down and the pale rump band is conspicuous; often looks strikingly bee-like.

Range: Southwestern Mexico; southwestern Costa Rica south locally to northern Bolivia.

Note: Black-crested Coquette (*L. helenae*) of Caribbean slope from southern Mexico to Costa Rica is possible in western Bocas del Toro. Male has greenish black crown and long narrow crest, black "beard" beneath brilliant green throat patch, and buff ear-tufts; female is uncrested, lacks rufous forecrown, has mottled dark spots on breast and sides.

WHITE-CRESTED COQUETTE
(*Lophornis adorabilis*) Pl.8

Description: 3. Known only from western Chiriquí. Bill short (½"), straight. Male with rufous forecrown, *pointed white crest,* and *very elongated pointed green ear-tufts* (extending out over back); otherwise mostly bronzy green above with white to buffy band across rump; throat glittering green, chest white, lower underparts cinnamon-rufous; tail rufous. Female lacks ornamental head plumes, has rufous forecrown and bronzy green upperparts with *white or buffy band across rump; throat and chest white* flecked with dusky on throat, lower underparts cinnamon-rufous; tail mostly rufous with broad black subterminal band.

Similar species: The beautiful males cannot be confused; females rather resemble female Rufous-crested Coquette (both have distinctive rump band) but are slightly larger and have white throat and chest (not cinnamon and bronzy).

Status and distribution: Apparently rare in clearings and woodland borders in lowlands of western Chiriquí; one specimen taken by Batty in 1902 and labeled Cébaco Island, off Veraguas, is disregarded by Wetmore, who considers it mislabeled.

Habits: Very little known in Panama; apparently more numerous in Costa Rica. Most likely to be seen where there is a local abundance of flowers; often very unsuspicious (A. Skutch).

Range: Costa Rica and Pacific western Panama.

Note: Wetmore calls it Adorable Coquette.

GREEN THORNTAIL
(*Popelairia conversii*) Pl.7

Description: ♂4; ♀3. Bill short, straight. Male mostly green with *white band across rump* and white leg tufts; *tail bluish black, extremely long and deeply forked,* with three outer pairs of feathers greatly elongated and very narrow (essentially reduced to the shaft), *the outermost pair curving inward and crossing.* Female notably smaller, green above with *white rump band;* throat black bordered by white stripes, *median underparts black bordered with white,* sides and flanks greenish; tail bluish black, forked (but without male's elongation), outer feathers tipped white.

Similar species: Male's tail is as long or even longer than his body; it is virtually unmistakable. Female's pattern is vaguely reminiscent of a female mango but is *much* smaller with white rump band.

Status and distribution: Rare and very local, with almost all records from humid foothills, 2000–4000 feet; recorded from eastern Chiriquí (Cerro Chame), Veraguas (Calovévora, Santa Fé, Cordillera del Chucú), and eastern Darién (Cerro Pirre); one nineteenth-century specimen from Caribbean side of Canal Zone. One recent sighting of a pair at El Valle, Coclé on February 19, 1960 (Eisenmann).

Habits: Favors humid forest borders and adjacent clearings, usually feeding high in trees. May engage in seasonal altitudinal movements (G. Stiles, oral comm.).

Range: Costa Rica to western Ecuador.

FORK-TAILED EMERALD

(*Chlorostilbon canivetii*) Pl.7

Description: 3. Bill short (½″), straight, blackish. Small. Male *entirely green,* glittering underparts, with white leg-tufts (usually not apparent); tail blue-black, *forked.* Female green above with *dusky mask bordered above by whitish streak behind eye;* pale gray below with some green on sides; tail not forked, mainly blue-black, outer feathers tipped pale gray.

Similar species: Male best known by its small size, all green plumage, and noticeably forked tail. Female best known by its mask, a field mark shared by no other similar Panama hummer.

Status and distribution: Fairly common to common in open areas, gardens, and clearings in lowlands and lower foothills on Pacific slope from Chiriquí to western Darién; on Caribbean slope known only from Bocas del Toro (where records few) and Canal Zone and vicinity; common also on Pearl Islands, Taboga Island, Coiba Island, and many other smaller islands off Pacific coast.

Habits: Primarily a flower feeder, and often attracted to gardens.

Range: Central Mexico to Colombia and Venezuela.

Note: Birds from southwestern Costa Rica and all of Panama, *C. assimilis* (Garden Emerald), are by some authors considered a distinct species. Others unite *assimilis* with *C. mellisugus* (Blue-tailed Emerald) of northern and central South America. Still others combine the *canivetii* group and *assimilis* in *C. mellisugus* as one species. Here Peters and Eisenmann are followed in tentatively merging the northern forms in one species. Wetmore treats *assimilis* as distinct, calling it Allied Emerald.

CROWNED WOODNYMPH

(*Thalurania colombica*) Pl.7

Description: ♂4; ♀3½. Bill fairly long (1″), slightly decurved at tip. Male has *crown glittering violet-blue* (glittering green in birds from Darién and eastern San Blas); otherwise bluish green above with bright violet patch on back (lacking or almost lacking in birds from eastern Panama); *throat and chest glittering green, contrasting with glittering violet-blue breast and belly;* tail blue-back, rather deeply forked. Female smaller, green above with bronzy crown; throat and chest pale brownish gray, ***breast and belly distinctly darker gray,*** some green on sides; tail less deeply forked than male's, outer feathers tipped white.

Similar species: Male in good light is one of Panama's most beautiful hummers; most likely to be confused with male of smaller Violet-belly, which lacks glittering crown, has only throat green, rounded tail. Female Violet-belly has uniform pale gray underparts (not distinctly two-toned).

Status and distribution: Fairly common in forest, second-growth woodland, and adjacent clearings in lowlands and foothills on both slopes, but absent from dry, open Pacific lowlands from Azuero Peninsula to western Panama province. In Canal Zone, much more numerous on Caribbean slope; regularly found at clearing on Barro Colorado Island.

Habits: Regularly found inside forest, foraging in lower growth, but more often seen along edge of forest clearings and openings, also in *Heliconia* thickets.

Range: Western Mexico; Guatemala to western Venezuela and Ecuador.

Note: Some authors separate green-crowned birds, *T. fannyi* (Green-crowned Woodnymph) of eastern Panama to western Ecuador, from blue-crowned birds, true *T. colombica* (Blue-crowned Woodnymph) of Mexico to central Panama and northern Colombia and western Venezuela. Others (including, with reservations, Wetmore) unite the broad *colombica* group with the dull-crowned *T. furcata* complex of much of South America, and call the whole Fork-tailed or Common Woodnymph. Here Eisenmann is followed in including in *colombica* all the glittering crowned birds.

FIERY-THROATED HUMMINGBIRD

(*Panterpe insignis*) Pl.8

Description: 4¼. Known only from western mountains. Bill straight (¾″), black above, pinkish below except for black tip. Sexes similar. *Crown blue,* line from lores and around nape velvety black, small white spot behind eye; otherwise metallic green above, tail blue-black; *throat golden orange becoming scarlet in center, chest blue becoming violet in center,* remaining underparts bluish green.

Similar species: A highly colored hummingbird, not likely to be confused, though the bright underparts are often hard to see.

Status and distribution: Uncommon in clearings and open areas in mountains of western Chiriquí and adjacent western Bocas del Toro, mostly above 7000 feet, sometimes down to around 6000 feet.

Habits: Relatively little known in Panama, perhaps more numerous in Costa Rica. Usually seen foraging in flowers at low heights.

Range: Costa Rica and western Panama.

VIOLET-BELLIED HUMMINGBIRD
(*Damophila julie*) Pl.7

Description: 3–3¼. Short straight bill (½"). Male shining green above; throat glittering green, *remaining underparts dark violet-blue; tail blue-black, graduated,* with pointed tips. Female averages a little smaller, is green above; *pale gray below,* fading to whitish on lower belly, sides of throat sometimes spotted with green; tail as in male but outer feathers tipped grayish.

Similar species: Somewhat resembles larger Crowned Woodnymph, particularly in poor light. Male woodnymph has forked tail, brilliant green chest, and glittering violet or green crown; female woodnymph has two-toned gray underparts (darker on belly instead of paler). Other similar small female hummers have green on sides and flanks and forked (not graduated) tails.

Status and distribution: Common in forest borders, second-growth woodland, and clearings in lowlands on both slopes from northern Coclé and western Panama province east through San Blas and Darién; ranges locally in small numbers up into lower foothills (Cerro Campana); one specimen in AMNH labeled Taboga Island. Common in much of Canal Zone, though on Pacific slope may be at least partly seasonal.

Habits: A widespread and usually numerous little hummingbird, but not often found around habitations.

Range: Central Panama to western Ecuador.

Note: Wetmore rejects the locality of two old specimens in AMNH labeled as from Costa Rica. He calls it Violet-breasted Hummingbird.

SAPPHIRE-THROATED HUMMINGBIRD
(*Lepidopyga coeruleogularis*) Pl.7

Description: 3½. Bill virtually straight (¾"), base of lower mandible often reddish. Male metallic green above; *throat and chest glittering violet-blue,* remaining underparts bright green; tail blue-black, *distinctly forked.* Female metallic green above; *white below with green sides;* tail as in male but with outer feathers tipped whitish and central feathers green.

Similar species: Male Blue-chested Hummingbird is duller, with only center of throat and chest blue, and with only slightly forked tail. Female like female Blue-chest but whiter below, without Blue-chest's green spotting on throat or blue spotting on chest.

Status and distribution: Locally fairly common to common in clearings, brushy areas, and near mangroves in lowlands on Pacific slope from Chiriquí to western Darién; on Caribbean slope locally from Canal Zone area east through San Blas; fairly common also on Coiba Island. Numerous in gardens in Panama city, and also at Coco Solo on Caribbean coast (J. Pujals).

Habits: Most numerous on or within a few miles of either coast. Forages rather low, at or below eye level.

Range: Western Panama to northern Colombia.

BLUE-THROATED GOLDENTAIL
(*Hylocharis eliciae*) Pl.7

Description: 3½. Bill almost straight, broad at base, *mostly coral red with black tip* (¾"). Green above, becoming *coppery bronze on rump and bright metallic golden bronze to golden green on tail; throat and upper chest violet-blue;* center of remaining underparts dull buff; breast, sides, and flanks bronzy green. Female similar, with dusky margins on throat feathers and more dusky on bill.

Similar species: The much more numerous Rufous-tailed Hummingbird can look quite similar, but has only base of lower mandible pink (not most of bill bright red), nonmetallic rufous-chestnut rump and tail, and lacks blue gorget (though throat can look bluish at certain angles). Male Sapphire-throated Hummingbird also has blue throat and chest, but has blue-black forked tail.

Status and distribution: Rare to uncommon and local (somewhat more numerous westward) in second-growth woodland, borders, and clearings in lowlands on Pacific slope, ranging up in smaller numbers into lower foothills; absent from eastern side of Azuero Peninsula to western Panama province; on Caribbean slope known only from Chagres River valley in Canal Zone; found also on Coiba Island, where apparently more numerous. Very scarce in Canal Zone, only recent report being a sighting of one near Summit Gardens on July 1, 1964 (Eisenmann).

Habits: Usually seen fairly low in shady areas, not often in the open.

Range: Southern Mexico to eastern Panama.

BLUE-HEADED SAPPHIRE
(*Hylocharis grayi*)

Description: 3¾. Known only from Darién. Bill almost straight, broad at base, *red to reddish* (brighter in male) *with black tip* (¾"). Male with *entire head bluish* (more violet-blue on crown and throat); otherwise metallic green above; chest bluish green, center of breast and belly white, sides mostly green; tail dark green, blackish toward tip. Female metallic green above; *mostly white below,* with green spotting on throat and chest and green sides; tail as in male but tipped whitish.

Similar species: Male Violet-headed Hummingbird has conspicuous white spot behind eye, lacks red bill. Female resembles female of several other species, notably female of foothill-inhabiting Violet-capped (which has mostly chestnut tail), and female Sapphire-throated (which lacks green on throat and chest and has forked tail); most other similar female hummers are grayish (not white) below.

Status and distribution: Known only from four specimens taken in 1946 near Jaqué in lowlands of southern Darién. They were feeding individually "at the border of the mangrove swamps or closely adjacent" (Wetmore).

Range: Eastern Panama to northwestern Ecuador.

VIOLET-CAPPED HUMMINGBIRD
(*Goldmania violiceps*) Pl.7

Description: 3½. Bill almost straight (½"). Male has *bright violet-blue crown;* otherwise bright metallic green above and below; under tail-coverts with small tuft of stiffened white feathers; *tail forked, rich chestnut, broadly tipped with bronze.* Female green above; mostly white below, with grayish spots on throat and green spotting on sides; under tail-coverts green with white tuft; *tail as in male,* but feathers tipped whitish.

Similar species: Violet-headed Hummingbird has conspicuous white spot behind eye and blue-black tail. See also male Crowned Woodnymph. No similar female hummingbird has deep chestnut on tail.

Status and distribution: Locally fairly common in humid forest and forest borders in hill country of eastern Colon province (Cerro Bruja), eastern Panama province (Cerro Azul/Jefe area), and eastern Darién (Cerro Tacarcuna, Cerro Malí). Quite easily seen in the Cerro Azul/Jefe area, particularly in the elfin cloud forest on Cerro Jefe.

Habits: Usually found singly, feeding low in forest undergrowth or at borders.

Range: Central Panama to extreme northwestern Colombia.

Note: Wetmore calls it Goldman's Hummingbird.

PIRRE (RUFOUS-CHEEKED) HUMMINGBIRD
(*Goethalsia bella*) Pl.32

Description: 3½. Known only from eastern Darién. Bill almost straight (½"). Male with *rufous-chestnut forehead, lores, and lower cheeks;* otherwise metallic green above; mostly green below with cinnamon-buff chin and flanks; under tail-coverts with *stiff tuft of recurved white feathers; patch of cinnamon-rufous at base of inner secondaries;* tail reddish buff. Female with green forehead, otherwise like male above; *mostly cinnamon-buff below,* fading to whitish on chest, with green confined to sides; *wings and tail as in male.*

Similar species: The only Darién hummingbird with rufous patch on wings, visible even in poor light.

Status and distribution: A species with an extremely limited distribution, known only from foothills and highlands (2000–5500 feet) of eastern Darién (Cerro Sapo and Cerro Pirre area) and adjacent northwestern Chocó, Colombia (Alturas de Nique).

BLUE-CHESTED HUMMINGBIRD
(*Amazilia amabilis*) Pl.7

Description: 3½. Bill straight (½"). Male has glittering green crown; otherwise bronzy green above; upper throat dull blackish, *center of lower throat and chest* *violet-blue* (often with duller edging), sides of chest and breast dull green, lower underparts brownish gray; tail blue-black, *slightly forked.* Female green above; grayish below *with green spotting* (*more bluish on center of chest*); tail as in male but tipped grayish. Birds from western Chiriquí (by some, including Wetmore, considered a distinct species, *A. decora,* Charming Hummingbird, also ranging in southwestern Costa Rica) have tail dull bronzy to bronzy blackish, and glittering crown of male extending over nape.

Similar species: Males are duller than other similar male hummingbirds and often give the impression of being a female or immature. Male Sapphire-throated has throat and chest entirely glittering blue (much more prominent than the blue in this species), and a more deeply forked tail. Female Blue-chests can be told by their conspicuous spotting below (including throat) and the blue on the chest.

Status and distribution: Fairly common in forest borders, second-growth woodland, and clearings in lowlands on entire Caribbean slope; on Pacific slope found in lowlands and foothills of western Chiriquí, and in lowlands from around Canal Zone east through Darién. In Canal Zone more numerous on Caribbean slope; usually common in the clearing on Barro Colorado Island.

Habits: Generally found individually, feeding in flowers fairly close to the ground.

Range: Nicaragua to western Ecuador.

SNOWY-BREASTED HUMMINGBIRD
(*Amazilia edward*) Pl.7

Description: 3½. Bill straight (¾″). Sexes similar. Metallic green above, becoming *coppery bronze on lower back, rump, and tail;* throat and chest glittering green *contrasting sharply with white breast and belly.* Birds from Chiriquí to eastern side of Azuero Peninsula and western Coclé (formerly considered a distinct species, *A. niveoventer,* also ranging in southwestern Costa Rica) have blue-black tail and less coppery (more green) lower back.

Status and distribution: Common in open woodland, clearings, and gardens in lowlands and foothills from western Chiriquí (where it ranges up in highlands to over 6000 feet) to Darién (Tuira River valley); on Caribbean slope known only from Canal Zone area and eastern Colon province (east to Portobelo), with one record from Bocas del Toro; found also on Pearl Islands, Coiba Island, and Taboga Island.

Habits: One of the more frequently seen hummingbirds of much of the Canal Zone. Often gathers in rather large concentrations at flowering trees, notably at Summit Gardens.

Range: Southwestern Costa Rica to eastern Panama.

Note: Mangrove Hummingbird (*A. boucardi*), known only from Pacific coast mangroves of Costa Rica, is possible in western Chiriquí, especially on the Burica Peninsula. Male is dull dark green above, throat and chest brilliant green, lower underparts white spotted with green on sides, tail dark green becoming blackish on outer half; female similar, but underparts entirely white, with throat sometimes spotted with green and sides washed with green, tail tipped grayish.

RUFOUS-TAILED HUMMINGBIRD
(*Amazilia tzacatl*) Pl.7

Description: 3½. Bill almost straight, usually black above with *basal half of lower mandible pinkish* (sometimes upper mandible as well) (¾″). Green above with *tail rufous-chestnut,* slightly forked; throat and chest glittering green (throat may look quite bluish at some light angles), breast and belly grayish. Female similar but feathers of throat and chest with buffy margins.

Similar species: Much less numerous Blue-throated Goldentail is brighter overall, with metallic golden bronzy tail and obviously blue throat and upper chest. Snowy-breasted Hummingbird has pure white breast and belly.

Status and distribution: Very common to abundant in open woodland, clearings, and around habitations in lowlands and foothills on both slopes, but not recorded from San Blas or Darién, and less numerous in drier more open areas on Pacific slope; found also on Isla Escudo de Veraguas (see below), Coiba Island, Taboga Island, and other small islands off Pacific coast, but not on Pearl Islands. In Canal Zone area the most numerous and familiar hummingbird, found everywhere except inside heavy forest.

Habits: Perhaps even more active and pugnacious than most members of its family.

Range: Eastern Mexico to western Venezuela and western Ecuador.

Note: Wetmore calls it Rieffer's Hummingbird. Included is *A. handleyi* (Escudo Hummingbird), restricted to Escudo de

Veraguas off coast of Bocas del Toro, recently described by Wetmore; it is larger and darker.

STRIPE-TAILED HUMMINGBIRD
(*Eupherusa eximia*) Pl.8

Description: 3½. Found only in western highlands. Bill straight (¾"). Male mostly green with white under tail-coverts; wings with *prominent patch of cinnamon-rufous on secondaries and base of inner primaries; tail mostly white, tipped black,* with two central pairs of feathers and outer web of outer pair black. Female like male but with underparts grayish white and green spotting on sides; cinnamon-rufous wing-patch smaller; outer tail feathers without black outer edge.

Similar species: The cinnamon wing-patch (easily visible at rest and in flight) and the mostly white tail are prominent in both sexes. Male Black-bellied Hummingbird (which also has a cinnamon wing-patch), is black below and on crown; female Black-belly closely resembles this species but is smaller with less conspicuous cinnamon wing-patch. White-tailed Emerald, also with mostly white tail, is smaller and lacks cinnamon in wings.

Status and distribution: Fairly common in forest, forest borders, and small clearings in highlands of Chiriquí and Veraguas (both slopes), recorded mostly above 5000 feet in western Chiriquí, lower in Veraguas; recorded also from adjacent highlands of Bocas del Toro (upper Río Changuena). Best known from western Chiriquí highlands.

Habits: Regularly forages within forest, in lower growth, but most often seen in shrubbery and low trees at forest edge.

Range: Southern Mexico to western Panama.

BLACK-BELLIED HUMMINGBIRD
(*Eupherusa nigriventris*) Pl.8

Description: 3¼. Known definitely only from Caribbean western highlands. Bill straight (½"). Male bronzy green above with crown edged with black; *mostly black below and on sides of head and forecrown,* with green sides and white under tail-coverts; somewhat concealed patch of cinnamon-rufous on secondaries; *tail mostly white,* only central pair of feathers black. Female has underparts grayish, patch of cinnamon on wings more restricted, and upper tail-coverts more bronzy; otherwise like male.

Similar species: Male, with its velvety black underparts, should not be confused. Female very difficult to distinguish from female Stripe-tailed but has notably less conspicuous cinnamon wing-patch, often not visible at all.

Status and distribution: Recorded from humid forest in highlands on Caribbean slope in Bocas del Toro and Veraguas (4500–6500 feet). Wetmore treats specimens labeled "Caribbean slope of Volcán de Chiriquí" as taken in Bocas del Toro; Eisenmann considers it possible that this refers to the north slope of the volcano itself (thus still on the Pacific side of the Continental Divide), and believes he once saw a male at Finca Lerida above Boquete, Chiriquí. Little known.

Range: Costa Rica and western Panama.

WHITE-TAILED EMERALD
(*Elvira chionura*) Pl.8

Description: 3¼. Found only in western highlands. Bill straight (½"). Male all metallic green except for *white center of belly; tail mostly white, broadly tipped black,* with central pair of feathers bronzy green. Female green above; *white below with green sides and flanks,* throat sometimes flecked with green; *tail similar to male's* but feathers narrowly tipped white.

Similar species: Lacks the cinnamon wing-patch so prominent in the otherwise somewhat similar Stripe-tailed Hummingbird. See also Black-bellied Hummingbird, the female of which is grayish (not mostly white) below. Female Snowcap is notably smaller, with underparts entirely grayish white (no green on sides).

Status and distribution: Uncommon to fairly common in forest and forest borders in foothills and lower highlands from western Chiriquí east through Veraguas (both slopes) to eastern Coclé (above El Valle, one specimen), mostly 2500–6500 feet.

Habits: Usually seen singly, foraging inside forest in lower growth, often drawing attention to itself by flashing its largely white tail open and shut.

Range: Southwestern Costa Rica to central Panama.

SNOWCAP
(*Microchera albocoronata*) Pl.7

Description: 2½. Known only from western Panama, mostly Caribbean slope. *Tiny.* Bill short and straight (⅓"). Male has *white crown; upperparts otherwise dark reddish* *purple,* brightest on rump; *underparts black glossed with purple; tail mostly white* with outer third black, central pair of feathers bronzy. Female green above; *uniform grayish white below; tail as in male* but feathers narrowly tipped white.

Similar species: The spectacular male is unmistakable. Female is best known by combination of diminutive size, mainly white tail, and lack of green spotting on underparts (present in female White-tailed Emerald, which is otherwise very similar except for its larger size).

Status and distribution: Known from nineteenth-century specimens taken in foothills on Caribbean slope of Veraguas (Cordillera del Chucú) and extreme western Colon province (Belém), and from a male seen in humid forest on Pacific side of Continental Divide above Santa Fé, Veraguas, on January 4, 1974 (Ridgely).

Habits: In Costa Rica, where apparently more numerous, ranges primarily in undergrowth of forest borders as well as inside forest; reported to engage in seasonal altitudinal movements (G. Stiles, oral comm.). Male's white cap and tail render it very conspicuous in the forest shade; both sexes frequently flick their tails.

Range: Southeastern Honduras to western Panama.

WHITE-VENTED PLUMELETEER
(*Chalybura buffoni*) Pl.7

Description: ♂4¾; ♀4¼. *Bill black,* almost straight, rather long (1″). Male metallic green with *conspicuous silky white feathers on under tail-coverts; tail blue-black.* Female similar but smaller, with grayish underparts and outer tail feathers tipped whitish.

Similar species: The enlarged white under tail-coverts are the characteristic of the plumeleteers, but distinguishing between the two species is not always easy. Bronze-tail has pale base to lower mandible (not all black), pinkish feet, and a purplish or golden bronzy tail (not steely blue-black), but to be certain, the bird must be seen closely and in good light. Scaly-breasted Hummingbird and female White-necked Jacobin are also generally similar, but neither shows the white vent, and both have scaly underparts (more obvious than in this species, which does sometimes look somewhat scaly below).

Status and distribution: Fairly common in second-growth and lighter woodland in lowlands on Pacific slope from western Panama province east through Darién; on Caribbean slope known mostly from middle Chagres River valley in Canal Zone, with one bird recently photographed at Fort Sherman on November 10, 1974 (J. Pujals). Widespread in woodland on Pacific slope of Canal Zone.

Habits: Forages primarily in woodland lower growth, only occasionally coming out into adjacent clearings. Usually found singly or in pairs.

Range: Central Panama to northern Venezuela and western Ecuador.

Note: Wetmore calls it Black-billed Plumeleteer.

BRONZE-TAILED PLUMELETEER
(*Chalybura urochrysia*) Pl.7

Description: ♂4½; ♀4. Bill almost straight, rather long (1″), with *base of lower mandible pale reddish brown to pinkish white,* remainder black. *Feet red to pinkish,* duller in female (black in White-vented), this often quite obvious in the field. Resembles White-vented Plumeleteer. Male bronzy green above; mostly blue to bluish green below (green in Darién), becoming grayish on lower belly; *under tail-coverts enlarged and white* (but often mixed with black in western Bocas del Toro); rump and tail purplish bronzy (rump green and tail more golden bronzy in San Blas and Darién). Female similar but mostly pale grayish below with bronzy green on sides of neck and whitish vent; *tail more greenish bronze* with dusky subterminal band and outer feathers tipped pale grayish.

Similar species: See the similar White-vented Plumeleteer.

Status and distribution: Rare to locally uncommon in undergrowth of humid forest in lowlands on Caribbean slope (recorded western Bocas del Toro, northern Veraguas, and Colon province east through San Blas); on Pacific slope known only from Veraguas foothills (above Santa Fé; Ridgely, G. Stiles), Cerro Campana, and eastern Darién. In Canal Zone known only from recent sight reports from the Achiote/Escobal Road area (Eisenmann, Ridgely).

Habits: Regularly forages within heavy forest, but also in shrubbery (e.g. *Heliconia* thickets) at forest borders.

Range: Nicaragua to northwestern Ecuador.

Note: Included is *C. melanorrhoa* (Dusky Plumeleteer) of eastern Nicaragua to extreme western Panama near Costa Rica border, with green throat and dusky under tail-coverts; it was formerly regarded as a distinct species, but intergradation with another race of this species (*isaurae*) has been shown in Bocas del Toro.

WHITE-BELLIED MOUNTAINGEM
(*Lampornis hemileucus*)

Description: 4. Known only from western Panama; rare. Bill straight (¾″). Male metallic green above with *prominent white stripe behind eye; throat shining violet-purple, remaining underparts white,* spotted with green on sides; tail bronzy green. Female similar but without gorget, throat white spotted with green.
Similar species: Male is not likely to be confused, but see Long-billed Starthroat. Female can be known by combination of mostly white underparts and bold white streak behind eye.
Status and distribution: Two nineteenth-century specimens merely labeled "Chiriqui" were until recently the only evidence this species occurred in Panama, and some doubt had been cast upon their validity; then a male was well observed in humid forest on Pacific side of Continental Divide above Santa Fé, Veraguas, on January 4, 1974 (Ridgely and G. Stiles). Probably the species occurs in Bocas del Toro foothills as well.
Habits: Usually seen foraging singly in lower growth at edge of forest, along roads.
Range: Costa Rica and western Panama.

VARIABLE (CHESTNUT-BELLIED) MOUNTAINGEM
(*Lampornis castaneoventris*) Pl.8

Description: 4. Found only in western highlands. Bill straight (¾″). Male has shining green crown, remaining upperparts bronzy green; ear-coverts and sides of head dusky, *bordered above and behind by a prominent white stripe; throat white,* chest bright green, lower underparts brownish gray; tail black. Female metallic green above, sides of head blackish bordered above by a whitish or buff streak; *entire underparts rufous-tawny;* outer tail feathers tipped white. Males from eastern Chiriquí, Veraguas, and Coclé have *throat violet-purple* (not white); a few males from western Chiriquí have purple throats (but white in vast majority).
Similar species: White-throated male can be instantly recognized, and purple-throated male in good light is also easily identified. No other similar Panama hummer has female's rich uniform tawny underparts.
Status and distribution: Common in forest, borders, and shrubby clearings in highlands of western Chiriquí (mostly 4000–10,000 feet); recorded also from highlands of eastern Chiriquí, Veraguas, and once in western Coclé (Alto Carvallo).
Habits: One of the most numerous hummingbirds of the western Chiriquí highlands, a number often gathering around a single flowering shrub or small tree. Males are outnumbered by female-plumaged birds (many doubtless immatures).
Range: Nicaragua to western Panama.
Note: The taxonomy of this group has been much disputed; Wetmore's recent treatment, combining all the allied forms into one species, is followed here. Because of the peculiar distribution of males with different throat and tail colors, many authors have recognized 2 or 3 species: the white-throated, black-tailed *L. castaneoventris* (White-throated Mountaingem) of western Chiriquí; the white-throated, gray-tailed *L. cinereicauda* (Gray-tailed Mountaingem) of southwestern Costa Rica (reported from Chiriquí without satisfactory proof); and the purple-throated, black-tailed *L. calolaema* (Purple-throated Mountaingem) of Nicaragua and most of Costa Rica, then skipping to west-central Panama. In western Chiriquí and southwestern Costa Rica, where the prevailing population is white-throated, rarely a male has a purple throat, and more often purple edging on the white feathers; in Costa Rica, where the range of birds with black tails meets that of those with gray tails, the tail may be of intermediate color.

White-bellied Mountaingem (male)

GREEN-CROWNED BRILLIANT
(*Heliodoxa jacula*) Pl.7

Description: 5¼. *Large.* Bill straight (1″). Male has *brilliant green crown,* otherwise metallic green above; *throat and chest brilliant green, with spot of brilliant violet on center of lower throat;* lower underparts metallic green; *tail rather long, forked,* blue-black. Female metallic green above with long white spot behind eye; *white below, throat and breast with large green spots.*

Similar species: Male is a large, mostly green hummingbird, best known by the violet spot on lower throat and the rather deeply forked tail. Female is easily distinguished by combination of large size and conspicuous green spotting below; female Violet Sabrewing and Magnificent Hummingbird are both plain grayish below. See also both plumeleteers.

Status and distribution: Uncommon in forest, forest borders, and adjacent clearings in highlands of Chiriquí, adjacent Bocas del Toro (upper Río Changuena), and both slopes of Veraguas (Calovévora, Santa Fé, Calobre, and Chitra), recorded mostly 2700–7000 feet; also recorded from foothills and lower highlands of eastern Darién (Cerro Pirre and Río Tacarcuna, 1750–4000 feet); only report from central Panama is a sighting of a male in forest near Cerro Jefe (2800 feet) on January 11, 1974 (Ridgely).

Habits: Seen foraging singly or in pairs, both in forest lower growth and in shrubby growth at forest borders and in clearings.

Range: Costa Rica to western Ecuador.

MAGNIFICENT HUMMINGBIRD

(*Eugenes fulgens*) Pl.8

Description: 5½. Found only in western Chiriquí highlands. *Bill long and straight* (1¼"). *Large.* Male has *violet-blue to purple crown* and *white spot behind eye;* forehead, sides of head, nape, and upper back varying from black to dark green; lower back and rump bronzy green; throat brilliant green, breast and sides dark bronzy green, lower belly grayish brown; tail forked, bronzy green, dusky toward tip. Female has crown and side of head dull black, upperparts otherwise as in male; throat buffy gray edged with paler, remaining underparts brownish gray washed with green on sides; tail as in male but with outer feathers tipped light grayish.

Similar species: Among other Chiriquí hummers, only the Violet Sabrewing bulks as large as this species. Male often appears mostly blackish. Female Green-crowned Brilliant has conspicuous green spotting below; female sabrewing has distinctly decurved bill and prominent white in tail.

Status and distribution: Fairly common in forest borders and clearings in highlands of western Chiriquí around Volcán Barú massif, usually above 5500 feet.

Habits: Most often seen singly, feeding at flowering shrubs and trees, also in gardens. Like many large hummingbirds, has relatively slow wingbeats.

Range: Southwestern United States to western Panama.

Note: Birds from Costa Rica and Panama (*spectabilis*) are sometimes considered specifically distinct from the *E. fulgens* group (Rivoli's Hummingbird) of United States to northern Nicaragua; surprisingly, the more tropical form is larger, and females especially have a longer bill.

GREENISH PUFFLEG

(*Haplophaedia aureliae*) Pl.32

Description: 4. Found only in eastern Darién. Bill straight (¾"). Male mostly green, becoming more coppery bronze on head and *bright golden bronze on upper tail-coverts;* faintly scaled with whitish below, becoming grayish white on lower belly; *large prominent whitish buff powder-puff-like tufts on legs;* tail slightly forked, blue-black. Female similar but feathers of underparts edged whitish giving more scaled or spotted effect; tail tipped whitish.

Similar species: The bronzy tail-coverts and conspicuous leg-tufts are conspicuous in both sexes and make the species relatively easy to recognize in its Panama range. Many Panama hummers have small white or buff leg tufts, but none is nearly as prominent as this species'.

Status and distribution: Common in undergrowth of humid forest in foothills and highlands of eastern Darién; recorded 1700 feet upwards.

Range: Eastern Panama to Bolivia.

PURPLE-CROWNED FAIRY

(*Heliothryx barroti*) Pl.7

Description: ♂4½; ♀4¾. Bill straight, quite short (⅔"). Male has *violet-purple crown and black mask* (ending in violet tuft) bordered below by brilliant green cheek stripe; otherwise shining green above; *immaculate white below; tail long and graduated, mostly white,* central feathers blue-black. Female similar but with green crown and without green cheek stripe. Immature has gray spotting on breast.

Status and distribution: Uncommon to fairly common in forest, second-growth woodland, and borders on both slopes but absent from dry and open Pacific lowlands from eastern side of Azuero Peninsula to southern Coclé;

ranges up into highlands to about 6000 feet in western Chiriquí.

Habits: This beautiful hummingbird generally keeps to middle and upper levels of forest and woodland, but sometimes comes lower. The wings beat relatively slowly, and the tail (notably longer in female than in male) moves from side to side and fans open and shut. Like the hermits, this species often seems somewhat curious, flying in to hover erratically in front of the observer, a lovely picture of flashing green and white.

Range: Southeastern Mexico to western Ecuador.

Note: Wetmore calls it Violet-crowned Fairy.

LONG-BILLED STARTHROAT

(*Heliomaster longirostris*) Pl.7

Description: 4½. *Bill very long, straight (1½")*. Male has light blue crown, otherwise bronzy green above; *throat glittering reddish purple bordered on either side by whitish streak;* remaining underparts brownish white; tail bronzy green, outer feathers sometimes tipped white. Female resembles male but lacks blue crown, has duller throat with wider streaks on either side, and outer tail feathers tipped whitish.

Similar species: Among Panama hummers, only the otherwise very different Green-fronted Lancebill and Tooth-billed Hummingbird have such a long straight bill. Somewhat resembles the Brown Violetear but lacks that species' violet ear patch, is less brownish generally, and has a much longer bill.

Status and distribution: Uncommon to fairly common in borders of second-growth and open woodland and shrubby clearings in lowlands and foothills on entire Pacific slope; on Caribbean slope more local and uncommon, recorded mostly from Canal Zone and vicinity, but also from Bocas del Toro and San Blas; ranges up to around 5000 feet in western Chiriquí highlands; found also on Taboga Island.

Habits: Not especially numerous in any locality and seemingly erratic in its appearances. Usually forages at middle and upper levels, singly or in pairs.

Range: Southern Mexico to Bolivia and southern Brazil.

MAGENTA-THROATED WOODSTAR

(*Philodice bryantae*) Pl.8

Description: 3½. Found only in western highlands. Bill straight, rather short (½"). Male metallic green above with *white spot behind eye; glittering reddish purple throat,* bordered below by a whitish band across chest; lower underparts mostly bronzy greenish with white lower belly and cinnamon-rufous flanks; *whitish tufts on either side of rump; tail black, rather long, narrow, and deeply forked.* Female like male above; cinnamon-buffy to whitish below, flanks more rufous; tail short and not forked, with broad black subterminal band and buff tips.

Similar species: Male Scintillant and Glow-throated Hummingbirds lack white eye-spot, white on rump, and the long deeply forked tail. Female resembles females of the same two species but also has small eye-spot and rump tufts, lacks throat speckling. See also female Ruby-throated Hummingbird.

Status and distribution: Uncommon and local in forest borders and shrubby clearings in highlands of Chiriquí and Veraguas, mostly 4000–6000 feet.

Habits: Relatively little known in Panama. Usually forages near the ground, but also perches high.

Range: Costa Rica and western Panama.

Note: Wetmore calls it Costa Rican Wood-Star.

RUBY-THROATED HUMMINGBIRD

(*Archilochus colubris*)

Description: 3½. Bill straight (¾"). Male green above with small white spot behind eye; *gorget bright ruby-red,* remaining underparts mostly white washed with grayish on sides and flanks; *tail black, forked.* Female lacks gorget, is green above with small white spot behind eye; *whitish below* with buffy flanks; tail unforked, *outer feathers tipped white.*

Similar species: Female Volcano and Scintillant Hummingbirds are smaller and have mainly rufous tails. Female Magenta-throated Woodstar lacks white tail-tips and is buffier below.

Status and distribution: Apparently a rare winter visitant; recorded only from lowlands on Pacific slope, with a few century-old specimens from western Chiriquí, and a recent sight report of 4 or 5 (including one adult male) at Playa Coronado, western Panama province on November 25, 1962 (Eisenmann).

Habits: In its winter quarters favors light (often scrubby) woodland, borders, and semi-open areas.

Range: Breeds in eastern and central North America; winters in southern Florida and from Mexico to Costa Rica, rarely to Panama.

GORGETED WOODSTAR

(*Acestrura heliodor*)

Description: 2½. Known only from eastern Darién. *Tiny*. Bill straight (½"). Male dark shining green above with small white spot behind eye and blackish ear-coverts; white spot on each side of rump; *gorget rose-red or purplish red and elongated to a point at sides,* bordered below by a narrow band of white; chest gray, lower underparts dark bluish green; *tail black, deeply forked, with outer feathers very narrow and pointed,* the outermost shorter and narrower. Female bronzy green above with blackish cheeks and small white spot behind eye; rump cinnamon, with white spots on either side; *cinnamon-buff below;* tail not deeply forked, feathers normal, cinnamon with broad black subterminal band.

Similar species: Except for the Rufous-crested Coquette, this species is easily the smallest hummingbird known from Darién.

Status and distribution: Known only from one specimen taken at Cana, at base of Cerro Pirre, in eastern Darién highlands on April 13, 1938.

Range: Eastern Panama to northwestern Venezuela and northwestern Ecuador.

VOLCANO HUMMINGBIRD

(*Selasphorus flammula*) Pl.8

Description: 2¾. Found only in western Chiriquí mountains. Bill straight (½"). Male bronzy green above; *gorget dull grayish purple to grayish green and elongated at sides;* chest and middle of breast and belly white, sides and flanks cinnamon; *tail mostly black.* Female like male but without gorget; *throat white with small dusky spots; tail mostly rufous* with broad black subterminal band and *white tip.*

Similar species: Rather closely resembles partly sympatric Scintillant Hummingbird; male Scintillant has bright orange-red (not grayish purple or greenish) gorget and has mostly rufous (not largely black) tail; female Scintillant very similar but has tail tipped with buff (not white) and usually is buffier below.

Status and distribution: Fairly common in forest borders and shrubby clearings in mountains of western Chiriquí on Volcán Barú massif, mostly above 6500 feet. Most readily seen along Boquete Trail above Cerro Punta.

Habits: Often allows a remarkably close approach as it sits on a twig in a bush or low tree.

Range: Costa Rica and western Panama.

Note: Some authors recognize Chiriquí birds as a separate species, *S. torridus* (Heliotrope-throated Hummingbird), because most Costa Rica birds have purplish red throats. Others regard the two as partly localized color phases; Wetmore treats them as subspecies.

GLOW-THROATED HUMMINGBIRD

(*Selasphorus ardens*) Pl.8

Description: 2¾. Known only from eastern Chiriquí and Veraguas highlands. Bill straight (½"). Male bronzy green above; *gorget bright rose-red to purplish red and elongated on sides;* chest white, lower underparts bronzy green, becoming grayish white on lower belly; tail graduated, black, with rufous inner web of most feathers. Female bronzy green above; throat pale buff finely dotted with dusky; remaining underparts mainly whitish, tinged buff on chest, and buffy on flanks and lower belly; tail mostly rufous, crossed by black band.

Similar species: Closely resembles Scintillant Hummingbird (not known to occur together). Males differ in color of gorget (reddish orange in Scintillant, rose-red in Glow-throat); female Glow-throat differs from female Scintillant in having rufous edging to middle (green) tail feathers for only basal half, and is usually paler below.

Status and distribution: Definitely known only from highlands of eastern Chiriquí (Cerro Flores) and century-old specimens from Veraguas (Santa Fé, Castillo, and Calovévora). Wetmore rejects several old specimens labeled as from Chiriquí and Costa Rica.

Range: Western Panama.

Note: Some authors consider *S. simoni* (Cerise-throated Hummingbird) of central Costa Rica as a race of this species.

SCINTILLANT HUMMINGBIRD

(*Selasphorus scintilla*) Pl.8

Description: 2¾. Found only in western Chiriquí highlands. Bill straight (½"). Male bronzy green above, more rufous on rump; *gorget brilliant reddish orange to orange-red* (in some lights pure red or even golden green) *and elongated at sides;* chest and center of breast white, sides and belly cinnamon-rufous; *tail rufous.* Female bronzy green above; throat buffy with tiny dusky dots; chest and middle of breast white, sides and belly cinnamon; tail mostly rufous with broad black subterminal band and *buff tip.*

Similar species: Resembles Volcano Hummingbird. Male has bright gorget (not grayish purple or green) and mostly rufous (not black) tail; female has tail tipped buff (not white). Male Magenta-throated Woodstar is larger, with long deeply forked tail; female woodstar lacks throat spots, and has small white spot behind eye. See also Glow-throated Hummingbird.

Status and distribution: Common in forest borders, clearings, and gardens in highlands of western Chiriquí, mostly above 4000 feet.

Habits: Often perches beside the flower blossom they are probing. Seasonally numerous in the Volcán and Cerro Punta area.

Range: Costa Rica and western Panama.

TROGONS: Trogonidae (11)

Trogons are widely distributed in forested areas in the neotropics, Africa, and southern Asia. They reach their highest diversity and abundance in Middle and South America, and are well represented in Panama. Trogons are among the most beautiful of birds: most males are largely metallic green or blue above with contrasting red, orange, or yellow lower underparts; females are duller, usually brown or slaty above. Despite their bright coloration, trogons are often difficult to see because they perch quietly for long periods; their posture is erect, with the tail hanging straight down. All have loud resonant calls that are characteristic forest sounds, but are often difficult to track down to their source. Trogons eat fruit and insects, procuring both on the wing in spectacular, fluttering flights. The nest is in a tree cavity or in a hole dug out of an arboreal termite or wasp nest. Several Panamanian species resemble each other closely, and care must be taken in distinguishing especially the females. The pattern on the underside of the tail is often the key mark; other important points are the color of the bill, eye-ring, and lower underparts. Most Panamanian species are reasonably numerous in suitable habitat; however the gorgeous Resplendent Quetzal of the western highlands is becoming increasingly scarce in accessible areas due to forest destruction and persecution.

RESPLENDENT QUETZAL
(*Pharomachrus mocinno*) Pl.9

Description: 14–15; male's plumes add 15–30″. Found only in western highlands. Male unmistakable, *mostly glittering golden green* with rounded and laterally flattened crest and *extraordinary train* consisting of lengthened feathers of upper tail-coverts; *breast and belly scarlet;* tail white from below. Female duller green, with upper tail-coverts usually not extending beyond tip of tail and with bushy crest; green above with head more bronzy; mostly brownish gray below with metallic green chest and red belly; tail slaty, outer feathers barred and tipped with white.

Similar species: Female might possibly be confused with considerably smaller Collared Trogon; male Collared has white band across breast separating green chest from red belly, female Collared is brown above and on throat and chest.

Status and distribution: Uncommon to locally fairly common (in less disturbed areas) in highlands of western Chiriquí, now primarily above 5000 feet (formerly lower); recorded also in highlands of adjacent Bocas del Toro, eastern Chiriquí, and Veraguas, but present status in these areas unknown. Inhabits humid mountain forests, but regularly comes to clearings and park-like pastures. Still locally fairly numerous in western Chiriquí but decreasing in numbers, in part because of persecution for their plumes and for the cagebird traffic (though now protected by law), but mainly because of felling of mountain forests. Can usually be seen along the Boquete Trail and in surviving forest areas above Cerro Punta, and also at Finca Lerida above Boquete. Panamanians in Chiriquí know the bird well (known locally as "guaco," but "quetzal" is usually understood) and can often direct one to it.

Habits: Considered by many to be the most beautiful bird in the world—the sight of a male, particularly in flight with its incredible train curving gracefully, is unforgettable. Often difficult to spot in dense foliage as it sits motionless, usually rather high in a tree. Has a variety of calls, the most characteristic being a loud *hwaao* or *hwaco,* or sometimes *wek-wek-wecko* or *wek-wek;* also has a very different throaty whistle, *keeeoo-keeeoo.* Nests in holes in

trees excavated by large woodpeckers or by the birds themselves; during breeding season (February to at least May), local residents often know their location. A magnificent bird that fully deserves all the protection and encouragement it can get.
Range: Southern Mexico to western Panama.

GOLDEN-HEADED QUETZAL
(*Pharomachrus auriceps*) Pl.9

Description: 13–14; male's tail plumes add 3–4″. Found only in eastern Darién highlands. Male *metallic golden green above* and on throat and chest; breast and belly red; *elongated upper tail-coverts extending slightly beyond tip of tail;* wings largely black except for elongated green coverts; tail black. Female like male but head and breast bronzy brown, upper tail-coverts shorter than tail, outer tail feathers tipped white.
Similar species: Slaty-tailed Trogon lacks the train and has wing coverts vermiculated black and white.
Status and distribution: Known only from forest of highlands (4000–5000 feet) on Cerro Pirre in eastern Darién.
Range: Eastern Panama to northwestern Venezuela and northern Bolivia.

SLATY-TAILED (MASSENA) TROGON
(*Trogon massena*) Pl.9

Description: 12–13. Male has *orange-red bill* and eye-ring; in female only lower mandible and base of bill are reddish. Male mostly metallic green above with area of black and white vermiculations (appearing gray at a distance) on wing-coverts; facial area and throat black, chest metallic green, *breast and belly bright red; underside of tail slaty, with no white.* Female has slaty replacing male's green.
Similar species: Only other Panama trogon with red belly and wholly dark underside of tail is Black-tailed Trogon; male Black-tail has yellow bill (not orange-red or salmon), and narrow white band separating green and red of underparts; female Black-tail differs from this species in having lower mandible yellow (not dull reddish). See also Lattice-tailed Trogon.
Status and distribution: Common in forest and second-growth woodland and borders in lowlands and foothills on both slopes, but absent from drier Pacific lowlands. The common red-bellied trogon of the Canal Zone area; especially widespread and numerous on the Caribbean side.
Habits: Like other trogons, often phlegmatic, perching motionless for considerable periods and then difficult to locate. Though basically a forest bird, it regularly comes to clearings and borders (where it is more easily seen), and also inhabits mangroves. Usually found singly or in pairs, occasionally in small groups. The call is a series of loud *cuh's,* sometimes 20 or more, usually with a steady tempo and often with a ventriloquial effect.
Range: Southern Mexico to western Ecuador.

BLACK-TAILED TROGON
(*Trogon melanurus*) Pl.9

Description: 12–13. Found only from Canal Zone east. Very like better known Slaty-tailed Trogon. Male has *yellow bill* and orange-red eye-ring; female has only *lower mandible yellow* and inconspicuous blackish eye-ring marked with red. Male like male Slaty-tail but with *narrow white band separating green chest from red breast and belly.* Female like Slaty-tailed Trogon except for yellowish lower mandible.
Similar species: See Slaty-tailed Trogon.
Status and distribution: Uncommon and local in humid forest and second-growth woodland and borders in Canal Zone area, but becomes commoner eastward in lowlands on both slopes through San Blas and Darién. Can often be seen in gallery woodland between Tocumen and Chepo; recently (April–May 1971) found breeding at Summit Gardens (E. S. Morton).
Habits: Similar to Slaty-tailed Trogon. The call also is similar, but the notes seem louder, more resonant, *kwo-kwo-kwo . . .*
Range: Central Panama to northern Bolivia and Amazonian Brazil.
Note: Wetmore calls it Long-tailed Trogon.

LATTICE-TAILED TROGON
(*Trogon clathratus*) Pl.9

Description: 11–12. Known primarily from western Caribbean slope. *Iris yellow or cream-colored* (rarely pale blue). *Bill yellow in male,* upper mandible dusky and *lower mandible yellow in female.* Male resembles male Slaty-tailed Trogon, is metallic green above and on throat and chest, wing-coverts finely vermiculated black and white; breast and belly red; *underside of tail black with widely spaced very narrow white bars.* Female like female Slaty-tail, slaty above and on throat and chest, becoming brown on breast, red on belly; *underside of tail as in male.*

Similar species: The tail barring is not very prominent in the field. The very similar Slaty-tailed Trogon has dark eye, reddish bill and eye-ring, and all dark underside of tail. Collared Trogon has dark eye, more conspicuous barring on underside of tail, and white band separating green and red on underparts; female Collared is brown (not slaty) above.

Status and distribution: Recorded only from humid forest in lowlands and foothills on Caribbean slope in Bocas del Toro, Veraguas, and Coclé (Río Cascajal; not mentioned by Wetmore though listed by Ridgway), spilling over onto Pacific slope foothills in Veraguas (one specimen from Santa Fé); apparently not recorded above 2400 feet in Panama, though in Costa Rica reported up to about 4500 feet (Slud).

Habits: Little known in Panama. Very similar to Slaty-tailed Trogon in appearance and behavior. The call is higher-pitched and not as steady or as long as Slaty-tail's; it starts slowly, speeds up in the middle, and then trails off (Ridgely, in Costa Rica).

Range: Caribbean Costa Rica and western Panama.

WHITE-TAILED TROGON

(*Trogon viridis*) Pl.9

Description: 10–11. Bill bluish gray in male, as is lower mandible in female (upper mandible black); *pale blue eye-ring in both sexes.* Male has upperparts, throat, and chest metallic blue-black with strong violet gloss on head, neck, and chest; *breast and belly orange-yellow; underside of tail essentially white.* Female *slaty above and on throat and chest;* breast and belly orange-yellow; *underside of tail mostly white* but with some irregular black barring or blotching on inner webs and near base of feathers.

Similar species: Males of all other "yellow-bellied" trogons have prominent black and white barring on underside of tail. Female resembles female Violaceous Trogon but has blue (not yellow) eye-ring and mostly white underside of tail (not prominently barred with black).

Status and distribution: Locally fairly common in humid forest, second-growth woodland, and borders in lowlands on Caribbean slope from central Bocas del Toro (Chiriquicito Grande) east through San Blas; on Pacific slope known from eastern Panama province (where evidently rare or local: one old Panama city record and seen in hills east of Chepo, on road from Platanares to Jesús María—Ridgely and Eisenmann) and from Darién (where more numerous). In Canal Zone quite common on Barro Colorado Island and in the Fort Sherman/San Lorenzo area.

Habits: Similar to other trogons; often perches rather high in forest trees. The call is a series of rather soft *coo's,* repeated slowly at first, then accelerated into a roll, sometimes ending with several slower notes. Occasionally the call will be varied with 3 or 4 *kuh*'s. Also calls *chuck, chuck, chuck,* and twitches spread tail from side to side.

Range: Western Panama to northern Bolivia and central Brazil.

BAIRD'S TROGON

(*Trogon bairdii*) Pl.9

Description: 10–11. Known only from western Chiriquí. A close ally of the White-tailed Trogon. Both sexes have bluish bill and pale blue eye-ring. Male like male White-tailed but with *orange-red breast and belly.* Female resembles female White-tailed but has *orange-red lower underparts* and is paler slaty above; *underside of tail look essentially barred,* with white bars much narrower (half the width) than slaty bars.

Similar species: Male Collared and Orange-bellied Trogons have underside of tail black with numerous white bars (not essentially white) and have narrow white band separating green chest from red or orange (respectively) lower underparts; females of the two species are brown above and on breast (not slaty). White-tailed Trogon has entirely different range and is orange-yellow (not orange-red) below; underside of tail of female White-tailed is mostly white (not barred).

Status and distribution: Known only from forest and forest borders in lowlands and foothills (to about 4000 feet) of western Chiriquí; becoming rare due to clearing of most forest.

Habits: Little known in Panama. In Costa Rica reported to be sympatric with Slaty-tailed Trogon, and to occur more often in small groups than other trogons. The call is similar to the White-tail's, starting slowly with an accelerating roll (Slud).

Range: Southwestern Costa Rica and Pacific western Panama.

Note: By some authors considered a race of the White-tailed Trogon.

COLLARED TROGON
(*Trogon collaris*) Pl.9

Description: 10. Known only from highlands of extreme west and east. Both sexes have mostly yellow or greenish yellow bill and inconspicuous bare brown eye-ring. Male metallic green above and on chest, sides of head and throat black; *white band across upper breast, lower underparts pure red; underside of tail black with numerous narrow white bars* (about half as wide as the black interspaces). Female has *brown* replacing male's green upperparts, and has *prominent broken white eye-ring* (feathered), broader to rear; throat slaty, chest brown; *lower underparts as in male* (though red somewhat paler); underside of tail mostly pale gray with dusky flecking, crossed by three white "bands" bordered by black (formed by feather tips).

Similar species: Both sexes resemble respective sexes of Orange-bellied Trogon but have underparts red (not reddish orange to orange-red). Male Baird's Trogon has mostly white underside of tail; female Baird's is slaty (not brown) above and on chest.

Status and distribution: Fairly common in forest and forest borders in highlands of western Chiriquí (mostly 4000–8000 feet, occasionally down to 2300 feet) and eastern Darién (Cerro Malí, Cerro Tacarcuna, and Cerro Pirre), spilling over divide into highlands of western Bocas del Toro. Wetmore believes that all published records from eastern Chiriquí and Veraguas are erroneous; fresh specimens of the complex from this area are needed.

Habits: Usually found singly or in pairs. The typical call is a slow and steady *cow* or *caow,* repeated a number of times; also gives a churring note, often uttered as it slowly lowers its tail.

Range: Eastern Mexico to nothern Bolivia and Amazonian and eastern Brazil.

ORANGE-BELLIED TROGON
(*Trogon aurantiiventris*) Pl.9

Description: 10. Closely resembles Collared Trogon. Male differs only in having *lower underparts orange, reddish orange, or orange-red* (never true red). Female likewise differs only in having lower underparts orange to reddish orange.

Similar species: See Collared Trogon. Some males in western Chiriquí are so orange-red that field separation from Collared is difficult; birds on Cerro Campana are definitely orange. Black-throated Trogon is somewhat similar but has bright yellow lower underparts, evenly banded black and white tail (not black with narrow white bands), and blue eye-ring.

Status and distribution: Fairly common in forest and forest borders in foothills and highlands of Chiriquí and Veraguas (recorded 1300 to at least 6000 feet), chiefly on Pacific slope but spilling over onto Caribbean slope in highlands of adjacent Bocas del Toro; fairly common also on Cerro Campana.

Habits: Much like Collared Trogon, though found more commonly at somewhat lower elevations. Probably the most numerous trogon on Cerro Campana (where Collared does not occur). May possibly be a partly localized color phase of Collared Trogon; studies are needed of its behavior and to determine whether there is interbreeding in areas of overlap. E. S. Morton considers its vocalization to be like that of Black-throated Trogon.

Range: Costa Rica to central Panama.

BLACK-THROATED TROGON
(*Trogon rufus*) Pl.9

Description: 9½–10. Greenish bill and *light blue eye-ring in both sexes.* Male metallic green above and on chest, throat black; *breast and belly bright yellow; underside of tail evenly barred black and white,* with three broader white "bars" (formed by tips of outer feathers). Female *brown above and on throat and chest* with incomplete but prominent white orbital area (feathered); *breast and belly bright yellow;* underside of tail as in male.

Similar species: Male resembles male Violaceous Trogon but has blue (not yellow) eye-ring and strong green tones on head and neck (not violet-blue). Female is only brown trogon with yellow underparts. Both sexes resemble Orange-bellied Trogon but have yellow underparts (not orange) and show light blue eye-ring.

Status and distribution: Fairly common in forest and shady second-growth woodland in more humid lowlands on both slopes, ranging regularly up into lower foothills (to over 2500 feet on Cerro Campana); more numerous and widespread on Caribbean side; not reported from Azuero Peninsula nor lowlands of southern Coclé.

Habits: Generally found at low heights within forest and often very tame. The typical call consists usually of 2 to 4 well separated *cow's* (sometimes with rhythm of Chestnut-backed Antbird); also has a sharp *chirr,* often given in alarm and as the bird, having raised its tail, slowly lowers it.

Range: Honduras to eastern Peru, Paraguay, northeastern Argentina, and southern Brazil.

Note: Wetmore calls it Graceful Trogon.

VIOLACEOUS TROGON
(*Trogon violaceus*) Pl.9

Description: 9. Male has *orange-yellow eye-ring;* black head and throat, *hindneck and chest violet-blue;* upperparts otherwise metallic green; *breast and belly orange-yellow;* underside of tail evenly barred black and white with three broader white "bars" (formed by feather tips). Female *slaty above* and on throat and chest with incomplete white (feathered) orbital area; breast and belly yellow; underside of tail much like male except inner webs are slaty with white tips.

Similar species: Male readily confused with male Black-throated Trogon but has strong violet-blue tone to neck and chest (not green) and a yellow (not pale blue) eye-ring. Female White-tailed Trogon is also slaty above but has mostly white underside of tail and a blue eye-ring. Female Baird's Trogon has orange-red belly.

Status and distribution: Fairly common in forest borders, lighter woodland, and clearings with large trees in lowlands on both slopes, ranging regularly up into foothills in Chiriquí, Cerro Azul, and elsewhere; not reported from Azuero Peninsula.

Habits: Not a bird of forest interior. Usually found singly or in pairs, occasionally in small groups. The call is a series of soft *cow's* or sometimes *kyoo's,* repeated steadily 10 to 15 times, somewhat higher in pitch and usually faster than Slaty-tailed Trogon's.

Range: Eastern Mexico to northern Bolivia and Amazonian Brazil.

Note: Wetmore calls it Gartered Trogon.

KINGFISHERS: Alcedinidae (6)

The kingfishers are a large and cosmopolitan group of birds that reach their highest development in tropical Africa and Asia. Only six species are found in the Western Hemisphere, all of which occur in Panama. Many African and Asian species are brightly colored, but the New World kingfishers are relatively somberly clad in blue-gray or metallic green and white and rufous. In the Old World, kingfishers occupy a variety of niches; however all six American kingfishers are found only near water, where they feed primarily on fish. They are solitary birds, usually seen perched on a branch overlooking some body of water. The nest is frequently in a hole burrowed into a bank.

RINGED KINGFISHER
(*Ceryle torquata*) Pl.10

Description: 15–16. *Panama's largest kingfisher.* Bushy crest. *Bluish gray above,* throat and collar around hindneck white; *underparts mostly chestnut-rufous.* Female similar but with bluish gray band across chest, bordered below by narrow white band; lower underparts chestnut-rufous.

Similar species: Belted Kingfisher is smaller and mostly white below with band of bluish gray (male) or bands of bluish gray and chestnut (female).

Status and distribution: Fairly common along both coasts and on lakes, rivers, and streams in lowlands on both slopes, ranging occasionally into lower highlands of western Chiriquí; found also on Coiba Island and larger Pearl Islands. Widespread in Canal Zone.

Habits: Usually seen singly or in pairs, often perched on horizontal branches above water. Frequently flies high overhead between feeding areas, then giving a harsh *keerrek.* Also has a rattle much like Belted Kingfisher's but louder.

Range: Southern Texas and Mexico to Tierra del Fuego.

BELTED KINGFISHER
(*Ceryle alcyon*)

Description: 12–13. Bushy crest. *Bluish gray above* with white collar on hindneck; *mostly white below,* chest crossed by bluish gray band. Female has an added band of rufous across breast and extending over flanks.

Similar species: Ringed Kingfisher is considerably larger with mostly chestnut-rufous underparts (not mostly white). Amazon Kingfisher is green above (as are all other Panama kingfishers).

Status and distribution: Uncommon but widely distributed winter resident in lowlands on both slopes along either coast (primarily) and on lakes and larger rivers, ranging into lower highlands in western Chiriquí; recorded also from Taboga Island, Pearl Islands, and other smaller Pacific coastal islands. Recorded in Panama mid-September–early April; two late stragglers, probably "summering": one in Pearl Islands (Pedro Gonzalez) on May 30, 1969 (Ridgely and R. Sharp), and one at Miraflores Locks in Canal Zone on June 23, 1970 (Ridgely and J. Gwynne). Usually found singly in Panama.

Range: Breeds in North America; winters from United States to Panama and in West Indies, rarely to Colombia, Venezuela, and the Guianas.

AMAZON KINGFISHER

(*Chloroceryle amazona*) Pl.10

Description: 11–12. *Largest of the "green" kingfishers.* Somewhat crested. Dark metallic green above with narrow white collar on hindneck and a few white spots on wings (occasionally forming a narrow band); white below with broad rufous chest band (male) or green spotting on sides of chest, sometimes forming a narrow broken band (female).

Similar species: Green Kingfisher is much smaller and has more white in wings and tail. Green-and-rufous Kingfisher is rich rufous below.

Status and distribution: Fairly common to locally common along larger streams, rivers, and shores of lakes in lowlands on both slopes, ranging up into lower foothills in Darién. In Canal Zone area more numerous on Caribbean slope; easily seen at Río Piedras, eastern Colon province.

Habits: Usually not found on coast but may occur in brackish lagoons or tidal rivers and river mouths. Favors wider watercourses, not shady streams (though present in small numbers in such situations as well). Has a loud harsh *cack* and a higher rapidly repeated note approaching a rattle.

Range: Mexico to central Argentina.

GREEN KINGFISHER

(*Chloroceryle americana*) Pl.10

Description: 7–8. The commonest Panama kingfisher. Dark metallic green above with narrow white collar and *numerous small white spots on wings* and *patch of white on each side of tail* (flashes conspicuously in flight); *white below* with broad chestnut band across chest and green spotting on flanks (male), or with two narrow green bands across chest and green spotting on flanks (female).

Similar species: Amazon Kingfisher is much larger, without conspicuous white on tail and less on wings; female has only one green chest band (not two). Green-and-rufous Kingfisher is rich rufous below and has less white on tail.

Status and distribution: Common along streams and rivers and along shores of lakes in lowlands on both slopes, found also in mangroves and locally on rocky coasts; ranges in reduced numbers up into highlands of western Chiriquí (to about 5300 feet) and foothills of southern Azuero Peninsula (Cerro Hoya) and Darién; found also on Coiba Island and other Pacific coastal islands, but not recorded from islands in Gulf of Panama (Taboga, Pearl Islands, etc.).

Habits: Found singly or in pairs. Often raises its head and jerks its tail. Regularly perches on rocks in streambeds. Gives a clicking *trit-trit-trit* in flight, much like two pebbles being struck together.

Range: Extreme southwestern United States to northern Chile and central Argentina.

GREEN-AND-RUFOUS KINGFISHER

(*Chloroceryle inda*) Pl.10

Description: 8–9. Dark metallic bronzy green above; *rich orange-rufous below,* fading to buff on throat; tail with a little white barring. Female like male but with broad, greenish black band (edged with whitish) across chest.

Similar species: Pygmy Kingfisher is much smaller and white on lower belly. Green Kingfisher is mostly white below, with more white on tail.

Status and distribution: Rare to locally uncommon along small forest streams and in swampy forest and mangroves in lowlands on entire Caribbean slope; on Pacific slope recorded from eastern Panama province (just east of Panama city) east through Darién; found also on larger Pearl Islands. Scarce in Canal Zone but more numerous locally in Bocas del Toro and Darién.

Habits: Unobtrusive and the least often encountered kingfisher in Panama. This and the Pygmy Kingfisher prefer shady backwaters and swampy areas and only rarely perch in the open, usually remaining hidden from view by a screen of leaves. Has a crackling *trit-trit-trit,* most often tripled.

Range: Nicaragua to northern Bolivia and southern Brazil.

PLATES

PLATE 1

RAILS, QUAIL, TINAMOUS, HERONS, ETC.

1. COLOMBIAN CRAKE (*Neocrex columbianus*). Red legs, gray underparts with no barring. Rare. *p. 90*
2. SPOTTED RAIL (*Pardirallus maculatus*). Barred, streaked, and spotted black and white. Rare. *p. 87*
3. UNIFORM CRAKE (*Amaurolimnas concolor*). Uniform brown, short greenish bill. Local. *p. 88*
4. GRAY-BREASTED CRAKE (*Laterallus exilis*). Small size, gray head and breast, chestnut nape. Rare. *p. 89*
5. YELLOW-BREASTED CRAKE (*Porzana flaviventris*). Small size, buffyish underparts, yellow legs. Local. *p. 89*
6. WHITE-THROATED CRAKE (*Laterallus albigularis*). Rufous and brown generally, bold belly barring. *p. 89*
7. GRAY-NECKED WOOD-RAIL (*Aramides cajanea*). Large size, gray head and neck (outer half of bill greener than portrayed). *p. 87*
8. RUFOUS-NECKED WOOD-RAIL (*Aramides axillaris*). Fairly large size, rufous head and neck, black lower underparts. Local, mangroves. *p. 88*
9. SUNBITTERN (*Eurypyga helias*). Intricate variegated pattern, orange wing flashes, short legs and long tail. Forest streams. *p. 92*
10. SUNGREBE (*Heliornis fulica*) male. Striped head and neck, slender form. Aquatic. *p. 91*
11. NORTHERN JACANA (*Jacana spinosa*). 3-lobed yellow frontal shield. W. Panama. *p. 92*
12. WATTLED JACANA (*Jacana jacana*). 2-lobed purplish frontal shield, yellow on wings, long toes. *p. 93*
13. RUFOUS-FRONTED WOOD-QUAIL (*Odontophorus erythrops*) male. Rufous forecrown and underparts (female lacks black face and throat), purplish or blackish orbital skin. Local, foothills. *p. 85*
14. BLACK-BREASTED WOOD-QUAIL (*Odontophorus leucolaemus*). Mostly black head and underparts, usually white throat. Local, w. highlands. *p. 85*
15. TACARCUNA WOOD-QUAIL (*Odontophorus dialeucos*). White on face, throat, and chest, blackish crown. Darién highlands. *p. 86*
16. SPOTTED WOOD-QUAIL (*Odontophorus guttatus*). Black throat, spotted underparts. Chiriquí highlands. *p. 86*
17. MARBLED WOOD-QUAIL (*Odontophorus gujanensis*). Lacking bold pattern, reddish orbital skin. *p. 85*
18. TAWNY-FACED QUAIL (*Rhynchortyx cinctus*). *Male*: tawny face, gray underparts. *Female*: narrow eyestripe, light barring below. *p. 86*
19. HIGHLAND TINAMOU (*Nothocercus bonapartei*). Blackish head, rufous underparts, large size. Chiriquí highlands. *p. 28*
20. GREAT TINAMOU (*Tinamus major*). Large size, olive brown plumage (crested in e. Panama). *p. 27*
21. LITTLE TINAMOU (*Crypturellus soui*) female. Small size, uniform brown plumage, tinamou shape. *p. 28*
22. CAPPED HERON (*Pilherodius pileatus*). Black crown, blue bill and facial area. E. Panama. *p. 43*
23. WHITE-NECKED HERON (*Ardea cocoi*). Like a white Great Blue Heron, black crown. E. Panama. *p. 41*
24. CHESTNUT-BELLIED HERON (*Agamia agami*). Long slender bill, chestnut neck and belly, green upperparts. Forest streams. *p. 43*
25. STRIATED HERON (*Butorides striatus*). Gray (or grayish brown) neck and chest, small size. *p. 42*
26. GREEN HERON (*Butorides virescens*). Chestnut neck and chest. *p. 42*
27. RUFESCENT TIGER-HERON (*Tigrisoma lineatum*). *Adult*: rufous head and neck, large size. *Juvenal*: coarse black barring, feathered white throat. *p. 44*
28. BARE-THROATED TIGER-HERON (*Tigrisoma mexicanum*). *Adult*: bare yellow throat, gray sides of head. *Juvenal*: coarse black barring, bare yellow throat. *p. 45*
29. FASCIATED TIGER-HERON (*Tigrisoma fasciatum*). *Adult*: looks very dark, slaty sides of head, heavily barred neck and sides of chest. *p. 45*

1
2
3
4
5
6
7
8
9
10
11
12
13
14
15
16
17
18
♂
♀
19
20
21
22
23
24
25
26
27
28
29

PLATE 2

BIRDS OF PREY I

1. Bat Falcon (*Falco rufigularis*). Small size and long pointed wings, white throat, very dark underparts. *p. 81*
2. Plumbeous Hawk (*Leucopternis plumbea*). All slaty gray, orange cere and legs, single tail-band. Rare. *p. 70*
3. Semiplumbeous Hawk (*Leucopternis semiplumbea*). Orange cere and legs, white underparts, single tail-band. *p. 70*
4. Roadside Hawk (*Buteo magnirostris*). Small size, gray head and chest, rufous wing-patch. Clearings and savannas. *p. 68*
5. Collared Forest-Falcon (*Micrastur semitorquatus*). Lanky shape with long graduated tail, black facial crescent and white (or buffy) collar. *p. 77*
6. Slaty-backed Forest-Falcon (*Micrastur mirandollei*). Slaty upperparts, yellow cere and legs, tail-bands (see text). Rare. *p. 78*
7. Barred Forest-Falcon (*Micrastur ruficollis*). Small size, even barring below, yellow orbital area. *p. 78*
8. Tiny Hawk (*Accipiter superciliosus*). Very small size, barred underparts. Rare. *p. 63*
9. Bicolored Hawk (*Accipiter bicolor*). Two-toned gray plumage, chestnut thighs. Rare. *p. 63*
10. Gray-headed Kite (*Leptodon cayanensis*). *Adult*: gray head, blackish upperparts, white underparts. *Light-phase immature*: white head, black crown patch (see text). *p. 58*
11. Hook-billed Kite (*Chondrohierax uncinatus*). *Male*: strongly hooked bill, mostly gray plumage, indistinct barring below, usually greenish cere. *Female*: tawny collar, coarse barring below. *p. 60*
12. Double-toothed Kite (*Harpagus bidentatus*) male. Dusky throat stripe, more or less rufous underparts. *p. 61*

1
2
3
4
5
6
7
8
9
10
11
♂
♀
12

PLATE 3

BIRDS OF PREY II

1. Gray Hawk (*Buteo nitidus*). Mostly pearly gray, narrow barring below, white tail-bands. *p. 66*

2. Black-chested Hawk (*Leucopternis princeps*). Dark throat and chest contrasting with light lower underparts, large size. Highlands. *p. 69*

3. Great Black-Hawk (*Buteogallus urubitinga*). Much like Common Black, but larger with slaty lores, two white tail-bands, and whitish upper tail-coverts, white thigh barring (usually). In e. Panama (see text). *p. 71*

4. Common Black-Hawk (*Buteogallus anthracinus*). *Adult*: yellow lores and cere, single tail-band. *Immature*: heavy streaking below, numerous tail-bands (see text). *p. 71*

5. Ornate Hawk-Eagle (*Spizaetus ornatus*). Tawny sides of head and neck, long crest, barred underparts. *p. 74*

6. Red-throated Caracara (*Daptrius americanus*). Bare red face and throat, white belly. Local. *p. 79*

7. Crane Hawk (*Geranospiza caerulescens*). All slaty, dark cere and lores, long orange reddish legs. *p. 75*

8. Yellow-headed Caracara (*Milvago chimachima*). Buffy head and underparts, black eye-streak. *p. 79*

9. Crested Caracara (*Polyborus plancus*). Red facial skin, black crown, white sides of head and throat. *p. 80*

10. Savanna Hawk (*Heterospizias meridionalis*). Large size, long legs, mostly tawny-rufous plumage, tail-band. *p. 71*

11. Black-collared Hawk (*Busarellus nigricollis*). Mostly rufous, whitish head, black patch on foreneck. Local in marshes. *p. 70*

1
2
3
4
5
6
7
8
9
10
11

PLATE 4

PIGEONS

1. Band-tailed Pigeon (*Columba fasciata*). White crescent on nape, two-toned gray tail. W. highlands. *p. 118*
2. Scaled Pigeon (*Columba speciosa*). Scaly underparts, red bill. *p. 119*
3. Pale-vented Pigeon (*Columba cayennensis*). Whitish lower belly and vent. *p. 118*
4. Short-billed Pigeon (*Columba nigrirostris*). All ruddy brown (see Ruddy Pigeon). *p. 119*
5. Maroon-chested Ground-Dove (*Claravis mondetoura*). *Male*: gray, purplish chest, white on tail. W. highlands, local. *p. 121*
6. Plain-breasted Ground-Dove (*Columbina minuta*). *Male*: mostly grayish, conspicuous chestnut primaries in flight. *Female*: duller (see text). *p. 120*
7. Ruddy Ground-Dove (*Columbina talpacoti*). *Male*: ruddy brown, gray head. *Female*: duller, but still brown above. *p. 121*
8. Gray-headed Dove (*Leptotila plumbeiceps*). Gray crown and nape, pinkish underparts. W. Panama. Local. *p. 122*
9. Gray-chested Dove (*Leptotila cassinii*). Gray head, foreneck, and breast; narrow white tail-tipping; red orbital skin. *p. 122*
10. White-tipped Dove (*Leptotila verreauxi*). Broad white tail-tipping, pinkish brown underparts. *p. 122*
11. Blue Ground-Dove (*Claravis pretiosa*). *Male*: all bluish gray. *Female*: chestnut wing-spots, black and rufous tail. *p. 121*
12. Ruddy Quail-Dove (*Geotrygon montana*). *Male*: rufous upperparts, cinnamon facial stripe and underparts, chestnut moustache. *Female*: much duller, brown and cinnamon-buffy. *p. 124*
13. Violaceous Quail-Dove (*Geotrygon violacea*) male. Largely whitish underparts, purplish back, no moustache or facial stripes. Local. *p. 124*
14. Rufous-breasted Quail-Dove (*Geotrygon chiriquensis*). Gray crown and nape, rufous and cinnamon underparts. W. highlands. *p. 123*
15. Purplish-backed Quail-Dove (*Geotrygon lawrencii*). Purplish back, white facial stripe and black moustache (see Russet-crowned Quail-Dove). Foothills. *p. 123*
16. Buff-fronted Quail-Dove (*Geotrygon costaricensis*). Buff forehead, green crown and nape, purplish back, mostly gray underparts. W. highlands. *p. 124*
17. Olive-backed Quail-Dove (*Geotrygon veraguensis*). Conspicuous white facial stripe and forehead. *p. 123*

1
2
3
4
5
♀
6
♂
7
♀
♂
8
9
10
11
♀
♂
♀
12
♂
13
14
15
16
17

PLATE 5

PARROTS

1. Chestnut-fronted Macaw (*Ara severa*). Large size (but see other macaws), long tail, reddish under wings and tail. E. Panama. *p. 127*
2. Barred Parakeet (*Bolborhynchus lineola*). Small size, barred with black, wedge-shaped tail. W. highlands. *p. 128*
3. Orange-chinned Parakeet (*Brotogeris jugularis*). Small size, wedge-shaped tail, brown shoulders. *p. 129*
4. Brown-throated Parakeet (*Aratinga pertinax*). Brownish throat and chest, long pointed tail, orange ocular area. Pac. w. Panama. *p. 127*
5. Sulphur-winged Parakeet (*Pyrrhura hoffmanni*). Red ear-patch, conspicuous yellow on wing in flight. W. highlands. *p. 128*
6. Crimson-fronted Parakeet (*Aratinga finschi*). Red forecrown, long pointed tail. W. Panama. *p. 127*
7. Red-fronted Parrotlet (*Touit costaricensis*) male. Small size, short square tail, red forecrown and on wings. W. Panama, very rare. *p. 129*
8. Blue-headed Parrot (*Pionus menstruus*). Blue head, neck, and chest. *p. 130*
9. Brown-hooded Parrot (*Pionopsitta haematotis*) male. Rather small size, brownish head, red axillars (in flight). *p. 129*
10. Red-lored Amazon (*Amazona autumnalis*). Red lores and part of forehead. *p. 130*
11. Mealy Amazon (*Amazona farinosa*). Prominent eye-ring, no red or yellow on head. *p. 131*
12. Yellow-headed Amazon (*Amazona ochrocephala*). Yellow forecrown. *p. 131*

1
2
3
4
5
6
7
8
9
10
11
12

PLATE 6

OWLS AND CUCKOOS

1. Bare-shanked Screech-Owl (*Otus clarkii*). Ear-tufts, tawny facial area, reddish brown upperparts. Highlands. *p. 137*
2. Tropical Screech-Owl (*Otus choliba*). Ear-tufts, whitish superciliary, black facial rim, herring-bone pattern below. *p. 137*
3. Vermiculated Screech-Owl (*Otus guatemalae*). Ear-tufts, no facial rim, barred and mottled underparts. *p. 136*
4. Mottled Owl (*Ciccaba virgata*). No ear-tufts; mostly brown, mottled, barred, and streaked. *p. 140*
5. Black-and-white Owl (*Ciccaba nigrolineata*). No ear-tufts; narrow black barring below. *p. 140*
6. Striped Owl (*Rhynoptynx clamator*). Prominent ear-tufts, streaked underparts. *p. 141*
7. Spectacled Owl (*Pulsatrix perspicillata*). Large size, no ear-tufts, white spectacles, black chest. *p. 138*
8. Crested Owl (*Lophostrix cristata*). Conspicuous long pale ear-tufts and eyestripe. *p. 137*
9. Mangrove Cuckoo (*Coccyzus minor*). Black mask, buffy underparts (see other *Coccyzus* cuckoos). *p. 132*
10. Striped Cuckoo (*Tapera naevia*). Short bushy crest, streaked brown upperparts, whitish underparts. *p. 135*
11. Pheasant Cuckoo (*Dromococcyx phasianellus*). Long graduated tail, elongated upper tail-coverts, chest streaking. *p. 135*
12. Little Cuckoo (*Piaya minuta*). Smaller than Squirrel Cuckoo; red orbital ring, no gray below. *p. 133*
13. Squirrel Cuckoo (*Piaya cayana*). Mostly chestnut, gray breast and belly, very long tail. *p. 133*
14. Rufous-vented Ground-Cuckoo (*Neomorphus geoffroyi*). Large size; crest, bronzy upperparts, very long tail. Rare. *p. 135*

1
2
3
4
5
6
7
8
9
10
11
12
13
14

PLATE 7

HUMMINGBIRDS

1. Violet-headed Hummingbird (*Klais guimeti*). *Male*: violet-blue head and throat, white spot behind eye. *Female*: white spot behind eye. Especially foothills. *p. 157*
2. Violet-capped Hummingbird (*Goldmania violiceps*). *Male*: violet-blue crown, chestnut tail. E. Panama foothills. *p. 161*
3. Blue-throated Goldentail (*Hylocharis eliciae*). *Male*: mostly red bill, bright golden bronzy tail, violet-blue throat. Local, Pac. slope. *p. 160*
4. Sapphire-throated Hummingbird (*Lepidopyga coeruleogularis*). *Male*: blue throat and chest, forked tail. *Female*: mostly white underparts. *p. 160*
5. Crowned Woodnymph (*Thalurania colombica*). *Male*: blue crown (green in e. Panama), forked tail, green throat and chest. *Female*: two-toned grayish underparts. *p. 159*
6. Fork-tailed Emerald (*Chlorostilbon canivetii*). *Male*: all green, forked tail. *Female*: blackish mask, white streak behind eye. *p. 159*
7. White-necked Jacobin (*Florisuga mellivora*). *Male*: bright blue head, white nape patch, white tail. *Female*: very scaly underparts. *p. 156*
8. Scaly-breasted Hummingbird (*Phaeochroa cuvierii*). Large whitish tail corners, overall dull greenish plumage. *p. 155*
9. Blue-chested Hummingbird (*Amazilia amabilis*). *Male*: violet-blue patch on lower throat, notched tail. *Female*: much green spotting below. *p. 161*
10. Violet-bellied Hummingbird (*Damophila julie*). *Male*: mostly violet-blue underparts, graduated tail. *Female*: uniform pale grayish underparts. *p. 160*
11. White-vented Plumeleteer (*Chalybura buffoni*). *Male*: prominent white vent, blue-black tail. Cen. and e. Panama. *p. 164*
12. Bronze-tailed Plumeleteer (*Chalybura urochrysia*). *Male*: white vent, purplish bronzy tail (more golden in e. Panama), pinkish feet and bill. *p. 164*
13. Rufous-tailed Hummingbird (*Amazilia tzacatl*). Rufous-chestnut tail, pinkish base of bill. *p. 162*
14. Snowy-breasted Hummingbird (*Amazilia edward*). Sharp green-white contrast on underparts. *p. 162*
15. Purple-crowned Fairy (*Heliothryx barroti*). *Male*: pure white underparts, much white in long tail. *Female*: similar, with green crown. *p. 166*
16. Black-throated Mango (*Anthracothorax nigricollis*). *Male*: maroon-purple tail, black throat and center of underparts. *Female*: black stripe down underparts. *p. 157*
17. Rufous-crested Coquette (*Lophornis delattrei*). *Male*: rufous crest, pale rump band. *Female*: pale rump band, rufous forecrown. *p. 158*
18. Snowcap (*Microchera albocoronata*). *Male*: white crown, mostly white tail, otherwise very dark. W. Carib. slope, rare. *p. 163*
19. Long-billed Starthroat (*Heliomaster longirostris*). *Male*: very long bill, reddish gorget bordered by whitish streak. *p. 167*
20. Green-fronted Lancebill (*Doryfera ludovicae*). *Male*: very long bill, green frontlet, otherwise quite dark. Highlands, scarce. *p. 155*
21. Green Thorntail (*Popelairia conversii*). *Male*: extremely long slender tail, whitish rump band. *Female*: rump band, black and white underparts. Foothills. *p. 158*
22. Green-crowned Brilliant (*Heliodoxa jacula*). *Male*: mostly green, violet spot on lower throat, deeply forked tail. *Female*: underparts with large green spots. Foothills and highlands. *p. 165*
23. Brown Violetear (*Colibri delphinae*). Mostly dull brownish, green gorget bordered by whitish streak, purple ear-tuft. Rare, highlands. *p. 156*
24. Little Hermit (*Phaethornis longuemareus*). Long graduated tail, small size, *p. 154*
25. Green Hermit (*Phaethornis guy*). *Female*: bluish green upperparts, slaty underparts. Foothills and highlands. *p. 153*
26. Long-tailed Hermit (*Phaethornis superciliosus*). Mostly brownish, cinnamon rump, long white-tipped central tail feathers. *p. 153*
27. Pale-bellied Hermit (*Phaethornis anthophilus*). Mostly white underparts, rather green upperparts. Pearl Ids., locally in e. Panama. *p. 153*
28. Band-tailed Barbthroat (*Threnetes ruckeri*). Blackish throat, rounded tail with no chestnut. *p. 152*
29. Rufous-breasted Hermit (*Glaucis hirsuta*). *Female*: much chestnut in rounded tail, dull rufous underparts. Cen. and e. Panama. *p. 152*
30. Bronzy Hermit (*Glaucis aenea*). Coppery bronzy upperparts. W. Panama. *p. 152*

7

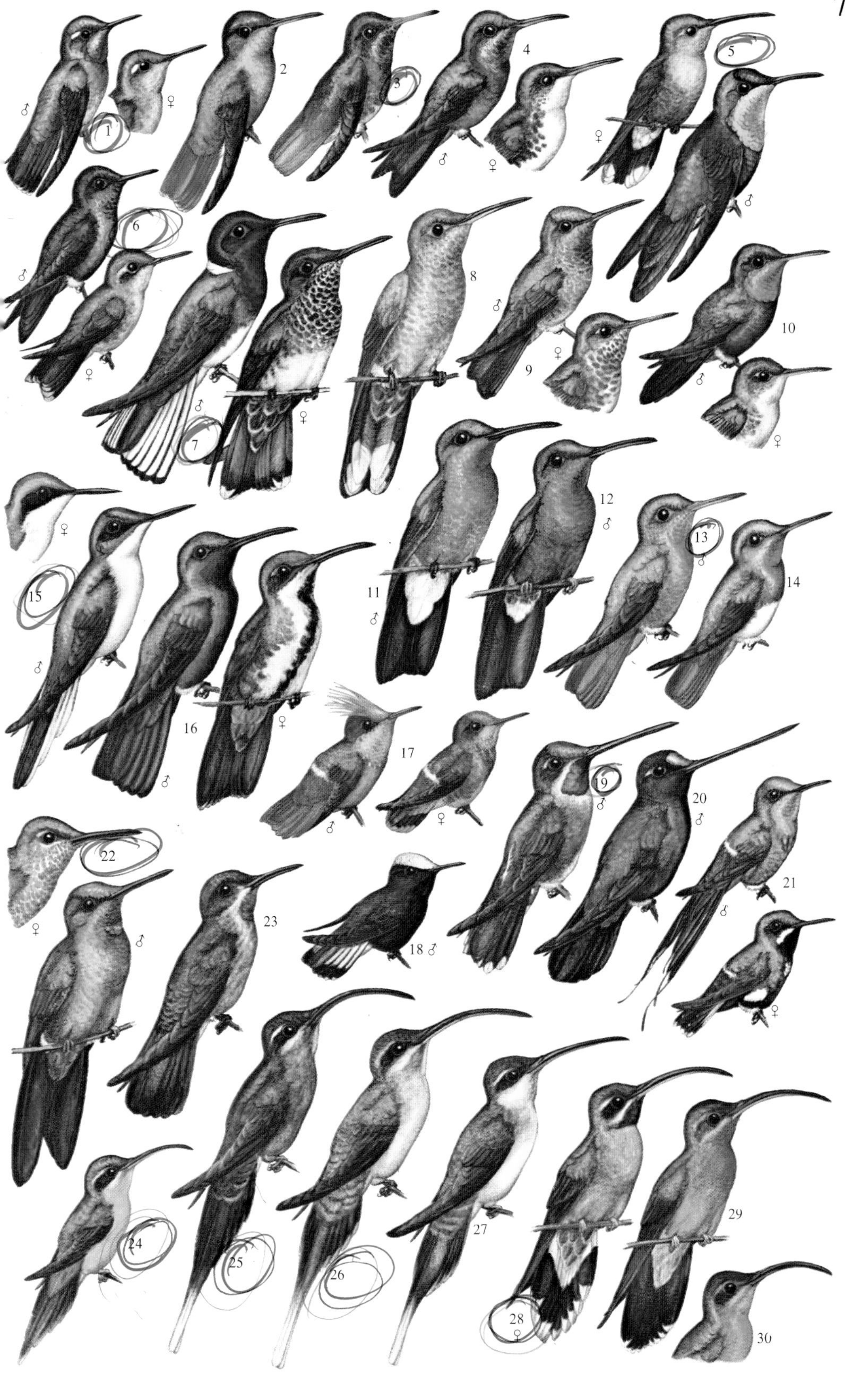

1 ♂ ♀
2
3
4 ♂ ♀
5 ♀ ♂
6 ♂ ♀
7 ♂ ♀
8
9 ♂
10 ♂ ♀
11 ♂
12 ♂
13 ♂
14
15 ♀ ♂
16 ♂ ♀
17 ♂ ♀
18 ♂
19 ♂
20 ♂
21 ♂ ♀
22 ♀ ♂
23
24
25
26
27
28 ♀
29
30

PLATE 8

CHIRIQUÍ HUMMINGBIRDS AND FURNARIIDS

All of the following are found primarily in the western highlands, with a few also ranging into the highlands of Darién.

1. SCINTILLANT HUMMINGBIRD (*Selasphorus scintilla*). *Male*: small size, bright red gorget, rufous tail. *Female*: spotted throat, mostly rufous tail. Chiriquí only. *p. 168*
2. VOLCANO HUMMINGBIRD (*Selasphorus flammula*). *Male*: dull-colored gorget, mostly black tail. Chiriquí only. *p. 168*
3. GLOW-THROATED HUMMINGBIRD (*Selasphorus ardens*). *Male*: bright rose red gorget. E. Chiriquí and Veraguas only. *p. 168*
4. MAGENTA-THROATED WOODSTAR (*Philodice bryantae*). *Male*: long deeply forked black tail. *Female*: unspotted throat, whitish tufts on sides of rump. *p. 167*
5. ~~VARIABLE~~ WHITE-THROATED MOUNTAINGEM (*Lampornis castaneoventris*). *Male*: throat white (w. Chiriquí) or purple (e. Chiriquí and Veraguas), white post-ocular streak. *Female*: uniform rufous-tawny underparts. *p. 165*
6. WHITE-CRESTED COQUETTE (*Lophornis adorabilis*). *Male*: white crest, green ear-tufts, pale rump band. *Female*: pale rump band, blackish forecrown, white throat. Chiriquí lowlands and foothills. *p. 158*
7. FIERY-THROATED HUMMINGBIRD (*Panterpe insignis*). Orange and red throat, violet-blue chest, blue crown. Chiriquí only. *p. 159*
8. BLACK-BELLIED HUMMINGBIRD (*Eupherusa nigriventris*). *Male*: black underparts. Carib. slope. *p. 163*
9. MAGNIFICENT HUMMINGBIRD (*Eugenes fulgens*). *Male*: large size, overall dark appearance, purple crown. *Female*: white post-ocular streak, grayish underparts. Chiriquí only. *p. 166*
10. VIOLET SABREWING (*Campylopterus hemileucurus*). *Male*: mostly dark violet, much white in tail. *Female*: large size, decurved bill, violet throat patch, white on tail. *p. 155*
11. GREEN VIOLETEAR (*Colibri thalassinus*). Violet ear-patch, otherwise mostly green. *p. 156*
12. WHITE-TAILED EMERALD (*Elvira chionura*). *Male*: much white in tail, no cinnamon wing-patch. *p. 163*
13. STRIPE-TAILED HUMMINGBIRD (*Eupherusa eximia*). *Male*: conspicuous cinnamon wing-patch, much white in tail. *Female*: cinnamon wing-patch, grayish underparts. *p. 163*
14. LINEATED FOLIAGE-GLEANER (*Syndactyla subalaris*). *Adult*: narrow streaks on back and underparts (eyestripe not as conspicuous as portrayed). See Striped Foliage-gleaner of lowlands (Plate 14). *Immature*: orange-tawny sides of neck, throat, and chest. W. and e. highlands. *p. 198*
15. RED-FACED SPINETAIL (*Cranioleuca erythrops*). Rufous head, rufous wings and tail. W. and e. highlands. *p. 196*
16. BUFF-FRONTED FOLIAGE-GLEANER (*Philydor rufus*). Buffy forehead and eyestripe, plain ochraceous underparts, rufous wings. *p. 199*
17. GRAY-THROATED LEAFTOSSER (*Sclerurus albigularis*). Pale gray throat. See other leaf-tossers (Plate 14). Chiriquí only. *p. 201*
18. SPECTACLED FOLIAGE-GLEANER (*Anabacerthia variegaticeps*). Conspicuous eye-ring and eyestripe, no streaking. Chiriquí only. *p. 199*
19. RUDDY TREERUNNER (*Margarornis rubiginosus*). Mostly rufous, white superciliary and throat (breast not as white as portrayed). *p. 197*
20. STREAK-BREASTED TREEHUNTER (*Thripadectes rufobrunneus*). Large size, tawny streaks below. *p. 200*
21. BUFFY TUFTEDCHEEK (*Pseudocolaptes lawrencii*). Large size, conspicuous tuft on sides of neck. *p. 198*
22. SPOTTED BARBTAIL (*Premnoplex rubescens*). Small size, prominent spots below, creeping behavior. Foothills and highlands. *p. 197*

1
♀
♂
2 ♂
3 ♂
4
♀
♂
5
♀
♂
♂
6
♀
♂
♂
7
8
9
♀
♀
10
♂
11
12
♂
13
♀
♂
14
15
16
17
18
19
20
21
22

PLATE 9

TROGONS

1. RESPLENDENT QUETZAL (*Pharomachrus mocinno*). *Male*: spectacular long train. *Female*: large size, bushy crest, red belly. W. highlands. *p. 169*

2. GOLDEN-HEADED QUETZAL (*Pharomachrus auriceps*). *Male*: mostly golden green, train slightly longer than tail, dark underside of tail. Darién highlands. *p. 170*

3. BLACK-TAILED TROGON (*Trogon melanurus*). *Male*: like Slaty-tail, but bill yellow, white band across chest. C.Z. east. *p. 170*

4. SLATY-TAILED TROGON (*Trogon massena*). *Male*: orange-red bill, red belly, black underside of tail. *Female*: reddish on bill, red belly. *p. 170*

5. LATTICE-TAILED TROGON (*Trogon clathratus*). *Male*: like Slaty-tail, but with pale eye, yellow bill, very narrow bars on underside of tail. *Female*: yellow on bill, pale eye, tail as in male. W. Carib. slope. *p. 170*

6. COLLARED TROGON (*Trogon collaris*). *Male*: white chest band, red belly, white bars on underside of tail. *Female*: brown, white eye-ring, pale red belly. Highlands. *p. 172*

7. ORANGE-BELLIED TROGON (*Trogon aurantiiventris*). *Male*: like Collared, but belly orange or orange-red. *Female*: orange belly, white eye-ring. *p. 172*

8. BLACK-THROATED TROGON (*Trogon rufus*). *Male*: blue eye-ring, yellow belly. *Female*: brown upperparts and chest, yellow belly. *p. 172*

9. BAIRD'S TROGON (*Trogon bairdii*). *Male*: blue eye-ring, orange-red belly, white underside of tail. *Female*: blue eye-ring, slaty upperparts, orange-red belly, barred underside of tail. Chiriquí. *p. 171*

10. WHITE-TAILED TROGON (*Trogon viridis*). *Male*: blue eye-ring, orange-yellow belly, white underside of tail. *Female*: blue eye-ring, slaty upperparts and chest, mostly white underside of tail. *p. 171*

11. VIOLACEOUS TROGON (*Trogon violaceus*). *Male*: yellow eye-ring, orange-yellow belly. *Female*: slaty upperparts and chest, barred underside of tail. *p. 173*

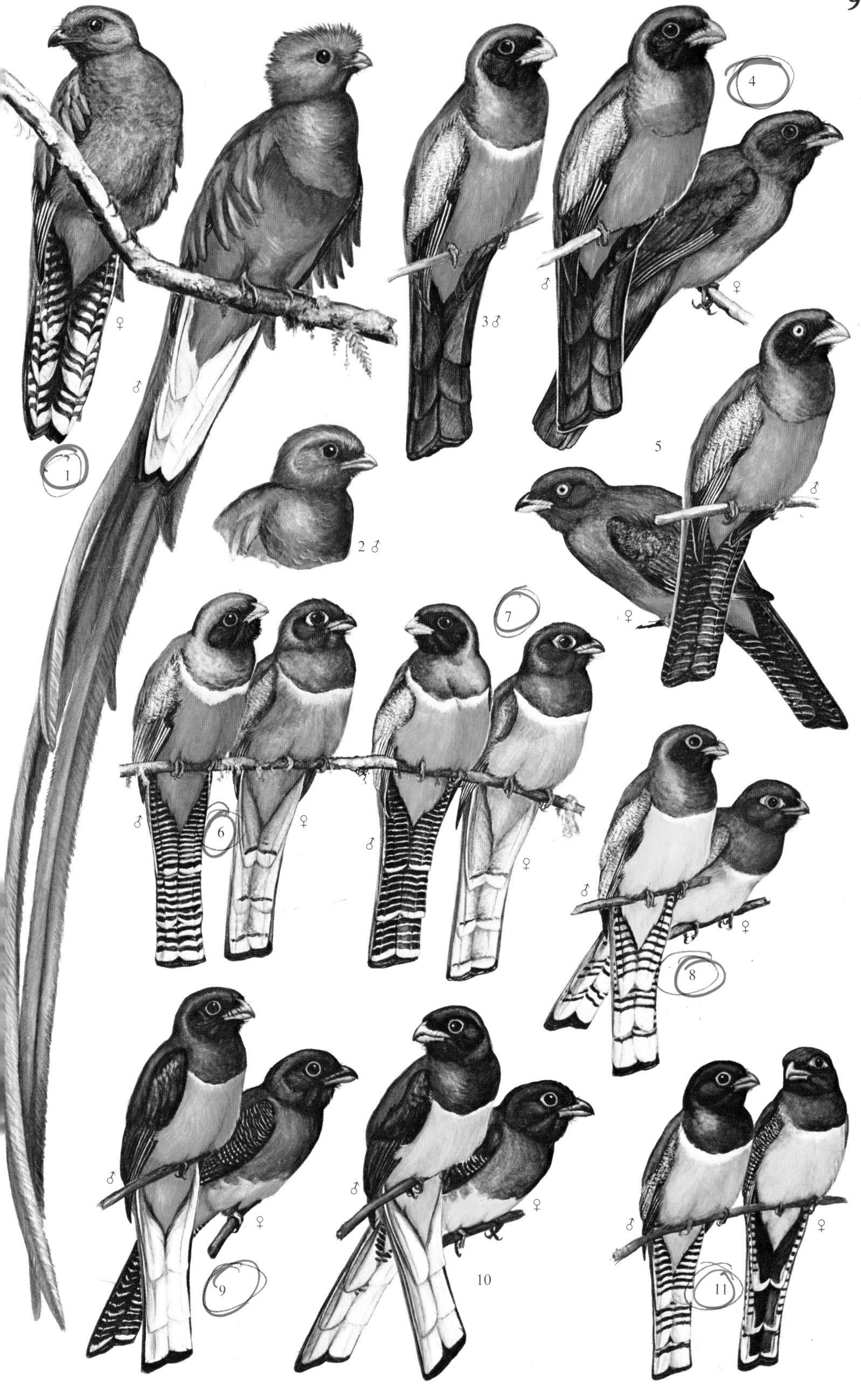

♀
♂
1
2 ♂
3 ♂
4
♂
♀
5
♂
♀
7
♂
6
♀
♂
♀
♂
♀
8
♂
♀
9
♂
♀
10
♂
♀
11

PLATE 10

MOTMOTS, JACAMARS, AND KINGFISHERS

1. BROAD-BILLED MOTMOT (*Electron platyrhynchum*). Like Rufous Motmot, but smaller, with green on underparts extending farther up. *p. 175*

2. RUFOUS MOTMOT (*Baryphthengus martii*). Large size; rufous head, neck, and most of underparts. *p. 176*

3. BLUE-CROWNED MOTMOT (*Momotus momota*). Conspicuous blue eyestripe, large size; underparts greener in w. Panama. *p. 176*

4. TODY MOTMOT (*Hylomanes momotula*). Buffy head stripes, small size, no racquet tail-tips. Local. *p. 175*

5. BLACK-CHINNED JACAMAR (*Galbula melanogenia*) male. Long slender bill, rufous underside of tail, glittering green upperparts. W. Panama. *p. 177*

6. GREAT JACAMAR (*Jacamerops aurea*) female. Heavy bill, rufous underparts. *p. 178*

7. AMAZON KINGFISHER (*Chloroceryle amazona*) female. Fairly large size, green upperparts, little white in wings and tail. *p. 174*

8. PYGMY KINGFISHER (*Chloroceryle aenea*) male. Very small size, oily green upperparts, rich rufous underparts. *p. 175*

9. GREEN-AND-RUFOUS KINGFISHER (*Chloroceryle inda*) male. Essentially a larger version of Pygmy Kingfisher, but no white below. *p. 174*

10. RINGED KINGFISHER (*Ceryle torquata*) male. Large size, blue-gray upperparts, mostly rufous underparts. *p. 173*

11. GREEN KINGFISHER (*Chloroceryle americana*). Small size, white spots on wings and tail. *p. 174*

1
2
3
4
5
6
7
8
9
10
11
♀
♂

PLATE 11

PUFFBIRDS, BARBETS, TOUCANS, AND JAYS

1. WHITE-WHISKERED PUFFBIRD (*Malacoptila panamensis*) male. Puffy and brown, white "whiskers." *p. 180*

2. GRAY-CHEEKED NUNLET (*Nonnula frontalis*). Slender decurved bill, gray face, rusty breast. *p. 180*

3. RED-HEADED BARBET (*Eubucco bourcierii*). *Male*: bright red head and neck. *Female*: bluish sides of head, yellowish breast. Highlands. *p. 181*

4. SPOT-CROWNED BARBET (*Capito maculicoronatus*). *Male*: glossy black upperparts, yellow chest band, black and orange flanks. *Female*: similar to male, throat and chest also black. *p. 181*

5. PRONG-BILLED BARBET (*Semnornis frantzii*). Thick grayish bill, ochraceous head and breast. W. highlands. *p. 181*

6. EMERALD TOUCANET (*Aulacorhynchus prasinus*). Mostly green plumage, blue throat. Highlands. *p. 182*

7. YELLOW-EARED TOUCANET (*Selenidera spectabilis*). *Male*: yellow ear-patch, black underparts. *p. 183*

8. CHESTNUT-MANDIBLED TOUCAN (*Ramphastos swainsonii*). Bicolored bill, yellow bib. *p. 184*

9. KEEL-BILLED TOUCAN (*Ramphastos sulfuratus*). Multicolored bill, yellow bib. *p. 183*

10. COLLARED ARACARI (*Pteroglossus torquatus*). Black head and neck, yellow underparts with red and black. *p. 183*

11. SILVER-THROATED JAY (*Cyanolyca argentifrons*). White throat. Chiriquí highlands. *p. 264*

12. AZURE-HOODED JAY (*Cyanolyca cucullata*). Light blue crown and nape. W. highlands, mostly Carib. slope. *p. 265*

13. BLACK-CHESTED JAY (*Cyanocorax affinis*). Black throat and chest, white underparts and tail-tipping. *p. 265*

FIERY-BILLED ARACARI
p. 183

1
2
3
♂
♀
4
♀
♂
5
6
7 ♂
8
9
10
11
12
13

PLATE 12

WOODPECKERS

1. SPOT-BREASTED WOODPECKER (*Chrysoptilus punctigula*). Spotted underparts, barred back, white sides of head. E. Panama, rare. *p. 185*
2. RUFOUS-WINGED WOODPECKER (*Piculus simplex*). Plain olive throat, no cheek stripe, rufous on wings. W. Panama. *p. 186*
3. STRIPE-CHEEKED WOODPECKER (*Piculus callopterus*). Whitish cheek stripe, spotted throat. Foothills. *p. 186*
4. GOLDEN-GREEN WOODPECKER (*Piculus chrysochloros*). Yellow cheek stripe, boldly barred underparts, unspotted throat. E. Panama, rare. *p. 186*
5. GOLDEN-OLIVE WOODPECKER (*Piculus rubiginosus*). Gray on crown, whitish sides of head, wings edged with yellow. W. foothills and highlands. *p. 185*
6. GOLDEN-NAPED WOODPECKER (*Melanerpes chrysauchen*) male. Yellow forecrown and nape. Pac. w. Panama. *p. 188*
7. BLACK-CHEEKED WOODPECKER (*Melanerpes pucherani*) male. Black sides of head and neck, black barring on lower underparts. *p. 188*
8. RED-CROWNED WOODPECKER (*Melanerpes rubricapillus*) male. Evenly barred upper parts, whitish sides of head and underparts. *p. 187*
9. ACORN WOODPECKER (*Melanerpes formicivorus*) male. Clown-like facial pattern, streaked underparts. W. highlands. *p. 187*
10. HAIRY WOODPECKER (*Dendrocopus villosus*) male. White back stripe, dull brownish underparts. W. highlands. *p. 189*
11. RED-RUMPED WOODPECKER (*Veniliornis kirkii*) male. Small size, red rump, barred underparts. Local. *p. 189*
12. SMOKY-BROWN WOODPECKER (*Veniliornis fumigatus*). All olive brownish, small size. Foothills and highlands. *p. 189*
13. CINNAMON WOODPECKER (*Celeus loricatus*). Short bushy crest, rufous plumage, heavy black barring. *p. 186*
14. CHESTNUT-COLORED WOODPECKER (*Celeus castaneus*) male. Long pointed crest, pale head, little black barring. Bocas del Toro. *p. 186*
15. LINEATED WOODPECKER (*Dryocopus lineatus*). Large size, parallel white back stripes. *p. 187*
16. CRIMSON-CRESTED WOODPECKER (*Campephilus melanoleucos*). Large size, white back stripes converging in "V," blackish bill. *p. 190*
17. PALE-BILLED WOODPECKER (*Campephilus guatemalensis*). Large size, whitish bill, white back stripes almost converging in "V." *p. 189*
18. CRIMSON-BELLIED WOODPECKER (*Campephilus haematogaster*) male. Large size, mostly crimson underparts, buff facial stripe. Rare. *p. 190*

1 ♂
♀
2 ♂
♀
3 ♂
♀
4 ♂
♀
5 ♂
♀
6 ♂
7 ♂
8 ♂
9 ♂
10 ♂
11 ♂
12 ♂
♀
13 ♂
♀
14 ♂
15 ♂
♀
16 ♂
♀
17 ♂
♀
18 ♂

PLATE 13

WOODCREEPERS, PICULET

1. Olivaceous Piculet (*Picumnus olivaceus*) male. Tiny size, spotted crown. *p. 185*
2. Ruddy Woodcreeper (*Dendrocincla homochroa*). Uniform rufous brown, brightest on crown. *p. 191*
3. Tawny-winged Woodcreeper (*Dendrocincla anabatina*). Dull olive brown generally, contrasting tawny flight feathers. Chiriquí. *p. 191*
4. Plain-brown Woodcreeper (*Dendrocincla fuliginosa*). Dull brown overall with no spotting or streaking, dusky moustache. *p. 191*
5. Olivaceous Woodcreeper (*Sittasomus griseicapillus*). Grayish head and underparts. *p. 192*
6. Wedge-billed Woodcreeper (*Glyphorynchus spirurus*). Small size, short wedge-shaped bill. *p. 192*
7. Spot-crowned Woodcreeper (*Lepidocolaptes affinis*). Spotted crown, slender decurved bill. Chiriquí highlands. *p. 194*
8. Streak-headed Woodcreeper (*Lepidocolaptes souleyetii*). Streaked crown, pale slender decurved bill. *p. 194*
9. Buff-throated Woodcreeper (*Xiphorhynchus guttatus*). Rather long straight dark bill, buffy throat. Most widespread and frequently encountered woodcreeper. *p. 193*
10. Long-tailed Woodcreeper (*Deconychura longicauda*). Long tail, eyestripe and eyering. (See text.) *p. 191*
11. Spotted Woodcreeper (*Xiphorhynchus erythropygius*). Spotted underparts. Foothills and lower highlands. *p. 194*
12. Straight-billed Woodcreeper (*Xiphorhynchus picus*). Straight whitish bill, white sides of head and throat. Mangroves, mostly Pac. slope. *p. 193*
13. Strong-billed Woodcreeper (*Xiphocolaptes promeropirhynchus*). Very large size, heavy bill. W. foothills, rare. *p. 192*
14. Black-banded Woodcreeper (*Dendrocolaptes picumnus*). Large size, barred lower underparts. W. highlands, rare. *p. 194*
15. Barred Woodcreeper (*Dendrocolaptes certhia*). Large size, generally barred appearance. *p. 192*
16. Black-striped Woodcreeper (*Xiphorhynchus lachrymosus*). Boldly striped appearance. *p. 194*
17. Red-billed Scythebill (*Campylorhamphus trochilirostris*). Very long decurved reddish bill. Cen. and e. Panama. *p. 195*
18. Brown-billed Scythebill (*Campylorhamphus pusillus*). Very long decurved dark bill, blackish head. Foothills, lower highlands. *p. 195*

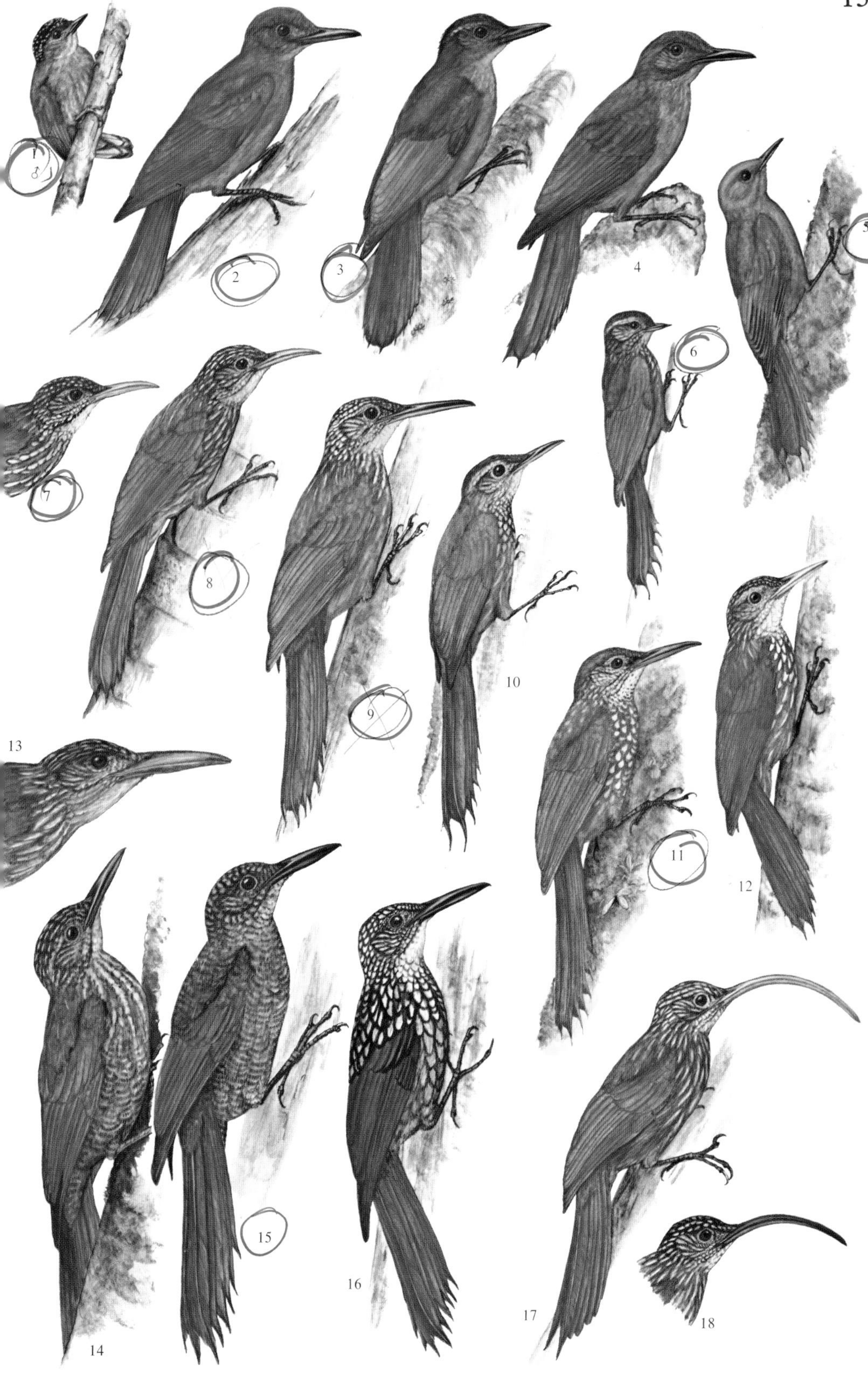
1
♂
2
3
4
5
6
7
8
9
10
11
12
13
14
15
16
17
18

PLATE 14

LOWLAND FURNARIIDS, ANTSHRIKES

1. Pale-breasted Spinetail (*Synallaxis albescens*). Long pointed tail, rufous hindcrown and wing-coverts, whitish underparts. Pac. savannas. *p. 196*
2. Slaty Spinetail (*Synallaxis brachyura*). Very dark overall, with slaty underparts; rufous hindcrown and wing-coverts; long pointed tail. Local. *p. 196*
3. Rusty-backed Spinetail (*Cranioleuca vulpina*). Coiba Id. only. Rufous upperparts, buffy eyestripe. *p. 196*
4. Plain Xenops (*Xenops minutus*). Short upturned bill, silvery cheek stripe. *p. 201*
5. Striped Foliage-gleaner (*Hyloctistes subulatus*). Streaked upper back and breast, buffy throat, chestnut wings and tail (see text). Local. *p. 198*
6. Rufous-rumped Foliage-gleaner (*Philydor erythrocercus*). Tawny eyestripe and underparts, contrasting dusky wings. Especially foothills. *p. 199*
7. Buff-throated Foliage-gleaner (*Automolus ochrolaemus*). Buff eyestripe and narrow eye-ring, pale throat, no streaking. *p. 200*
8. Scaly-throated Leaftosser (*Sclerurus guatemalensis*). Mostly dark brown, whitish scaly-looking throat. *p. 202*
9. Tawny-throated Leaftosser (*Sclerurus mexicanus*). Tawny throat and chest, rufous rump. *p. 201*
10. Russet Antshrike (*Thamnistes anabatinus*). Heavy hooked bill, buffy eyestripe and underparts, rufous wings and tail. Especially foothills. *p. 205*
11. Black-hooded Antshrike (*Thamnophilus bridgesi*). *Male*: mostly black, slaty belly, white on wing-coverts. *Female*: lightly streaked head and throat, brown upperparts, Pac. w. Panama. *p. 204*
12. Barred Antshrike (*Thamnophilus doliatus*). *Male*: broad black and white barring, yellow eye. *Female*: rufous upperparts, buffy underparts, yellow eye. *p. 203*
13. Slaty Antshrike (*Thamnophilus punctatus*). *Male*: mostly slaty gray, black crown, much white on wing. *Female*: olive brown upperparts, much buff on wing. *p. 204*
14. Great Antshrike (*Taraba major*). *Male*: black and white, red eye. *Female*: rufous brown and white, red eye. *p. 203*
15. Fasciated Antshrike (*Cymbilaimus lineatus*). *Male*: narrow black and white barring, red eye. *Female*: narrow buff and dark brown barring, red eye. *p. 203*

1
5
2
4
6
3
8
7
9
10
11
12
13
♀
♀
♀
♂
♂
♂
14
15
♂
♀
♂
♀

PLATE 15

ANTWRENS, ANTBIRDS

1. RUFOUS-RUMPED ANTWREN (*Terenura callinota*). Rufous rump, gray sides of head and throat, yellow lower underparts. Foothills and highlands, rare. *p. 209*

2. PLAIN ANTVIREO (*Dysithamnus mentalis*). *Male*: chunky, big-headed, mostly gray, yellowish belly. *Female*: russet crown. Foothills and lower highlands. *p. 205*

3. SPOT-CROWNED ANTVIREO (*Dysithamnus puncticeps*). Resembles Plain Antvireo, crown with white (male) or tawny (female) spots. Especially lowlands. *p. 205*

4. STREAKED ANTWREN (*Myrmotherula surinamensis*). *Male*: streaked black and white. *Female*: bright tawny head and underparts. *p. 206*

5. PYGMY ANTWREN (*Myrmotherula brachyura*). Tiny size, streaked upperparts, pale yellow underparts. C.Z. east. *p. 206*

6. SLATY ANTWREN (*Myrmotherula schisticolor*). *Male*: slaty, black throat. *Female*: dull tawny underparts, no wing-spotting. Especially foothills. *p. 207*

7. CHECKER-THROATED ANTWREN (*Myrmotherula fulviventris*). *Male*: checkered throat. *Female*: uniform buffy underparts, pale eye. *p. 206*

8. WHITE-FLANKED ANTWREN (*Myrmotherula axillaris*). *Male*: black, white flank tuft. *Female*: whitish throat and flanks, dark eye. *p. 207*

9. DOT-WINGED ANTWREN (*Microrhopias quixensis*). *Male*: white on wing, tipping on rather long tail. *Female*: rufous underparts, wings and tail as in male. *p. 208*

10. DUSKY ANTBIRD (*Cercomacra tyrannina*). *Male*: uniform gray (blacker in w. Panama). *Female*: uniform tawny underparts. *p. 209*

11. IMMACULATE ANTBIRD (*Myrmeciza immaculata*). *Female*: chocolate brown, blackish cheeks, pale blue orbital area (see text). Mostly foothills, rare. *p. 211*

12. BARE-CROWNED ANTBIRD (*Gymnocichla nudiceps*). *Male*: bare bright blue crown and orbital area. *Female*: bright rufous underparts, bare blue orbital skin. *p. 209*

13. JET ANTBIRD (*Cercomacra nigricans*). *Male*: black, much white on wings and tail (see text). *Female*: streaking on throat and chest (variable in extent). *p. 209*

15

PLATE 16

ANTBIRDS, ANTTHRUSHES, ANTPITTAS

1. Dull-mantled Antbird (*Myrmeciza laemosticta*). *Male*: no blue orbital skin, olive brown upperparts, white spots on wing-coverts (see text). Rare. *p. 210*

2. Chestnut-backed Antbird (*Myrmeciza exsul*). *Male*: chestnut upperparts, bare blue orbital area, black head and underparts. *p. 210*

3. Spotted Antbird (*Hylophylax naevioides*). *Male*: black-spotted breast. *Female*: duller and buffier, wing-bands. *p. 212*

4. White-bellied Antbird (*Myrmeciza longipes*). *Male*: black throat and chest, white belly, chestnut upperparts. *Female*: like male, but throat and chest buffyish. *p. 210*

5. Bicolored Antbird (*Gymnopithys leucaspis*). Brown and white, black cheeks. *p. 212*

6. Ocellated Antbird (*Phaenostictus mcleannani*). Generally spotted appearance, bright blue around eye. *p. 212*

7. Streak-chested Antpitta (*Hylopezus perspicillatus*). Plump tail-less shape, streaked underparts, buffy eye-ring and wing-bars. *p. 215*

8. Black-crowned Antpitta (*Pittasoma michleri*). Boldly scalloped underparts. Rare. *p. 214*

9. Ochre-breasted Antpitta (*Grallaricula flavirostris*). Very small size, buffy underparts, eye-ring. Highlands. *p. 215*

10. Black-faced Antthrush (*Formicarius analis*). Rail-like shape, black throat and cheeks (see other antthrushes). *p. 213*

11. Wing-banded Antbird (*Myrmornis torquata*) male. Three tawny wing-bands, short tail, dark underparts. *p. 212*

1 ♂
2 ♂
♂
3
♀
♀
4
5
♂
6
7
8
9
10
11 ♂

PLATE 17

MANAKINS, TAPACULO

1. BLUE-CROWNED MANAKIN (*Pipra coronata*). *Male*: blue crown. *Female*: mostly green (not olive). *p. 217*

2. RED-CAPPED MANAKIN (*Pipra mentalis*). *Male*: red head. *Female*: olive, brownish legs. *p. 217*

3. GOLDEN-HEADED MANAKIN (*Pipra erythrocephala*). *Male*: yellow-orange head. E. Panama. *p. 218*

4. GOLDEN-COLLARED MANAKIN (*Manacus vitellinus*). *Male*: bright yellow collar and throat (a), extending to upper back in Bocas del Toro race (b). *Female*: orange-red legs. *p. 219*

5. ORANGE-COLLARED MANAKIN (*Manacus aurantiacus*). *Male*: orange collar and throat. Pac. w. Panama. *p. 220*

6. LANCE-TAILED MANAKIN (*Chiroxiphia lanceolata*). *Male*: blue black, red crown. *Female*: projecting central tail feathers, orange-red legs. Mostly Pac. slope. *p. 218*

7. WHITE-CROWNED MANAKIN (*Pipra pipra*). *Male*: white crown and hindneck. *Female*: bluish gray cap and hindneck. W. foothills, rare. *p. 218*

8. WHITE-RUFFED MANAKIN (*Corapipo altera*). *Male*: white bib. *Female*: grayish throat. Foothills and lower highlands. *p. 219*

9. BROAD-BILLED MANAKIN (*Sapayoa aenigma*) male. Yellowish underparts, broad bill, yellow crown patch in male (see text). Cen. and e. Panama. *p. 221*

10. THRUSHLIKE MANAKIN (*Schiffornis turdinus*). *dumicola* (a): uniform dark olive brown. *panamensis* (b): more rufescent, grayish olive lower underparts. See text. *p. 220*

11. SILVERY-FRONTED TAPACULO (*Scytalopus argentifrons*). *Male*: dark slaty gray, silvery forehead and eyestripe (sometimes reduced or lacking). *Female*: browner, no silvery (see text). W. highlands; other tapaculos in Darién highlands (see text). *p. 216*

♂ 1
♀
2
♀
♂
3 ♂
4
♀
♂ a
4 ♂ b
5 ♂
6
♀
♂
♂
7
♀
♂
8
♀
9 ♂
a 10
b
♀
♂
11

PLATE 18

COTINGAS

1. White-winged Becard (*Pachyramphus polychopterus*). *Male*: black back, broad white scapular stripe, dark gray underparts. *Female*: buffy wing-bars and edging, brownish crown. *p. 225*

2. Black-and-white Becard (*Pachyramphus albogriseus*). *Male*: gray back contrasting with black cap, white supraloral stripe, pale gray underparts. *Female*: chestnut cap, white eyestripe. W. Panama, rare. *p. 226*

3. One-colored Becard (*Platypsaris homochrous*). *Male*: uniform slaty gray. *Female*: no supraloral stripe, upperparts rufous-tawny (including crown), pale buffy underparts (see text). E. Panama. *p. 226*

4. Barred Becard (*Pachyramphus versicolor*). *Male*: yellowish sides of head and throat, lightly barred underparts. *Female*: much rufous edging on wings, barring below. Chiriquí highlands. *p. 225*

5. Cinereous Becard (*Pachyramphus rufus*). *Male*: light gray back, rather white underparts. *Female*: crown darker than back (see text). C.Z. east, rare. *p. 225*

6. Cinnamon Becard (*Pachyramphus cinnamomeus*). Pale supraloral stripe, grayish lores (sexes similar). *p. 224*

7. Bright-rumped Attila (*Attila spadiceus*). Bull-headed look, hooked bill, yellow rump (usually), streaked underparts. *p. 223*

8. Purple-throated Fruitcrow (*Querula purpurata*) male. Purple throat (lacking in female), otherwise black. *p. 227*

9. Speckled Mourner (*Laniocera rufescens*). Spotted and edged wing-coverts, faintly scalloped breast (see text). *p. 223*

10. Rufous Mourner (*Rhytipterna holerythra*). Uniform rufous brown; smaller than Rufous Piha. *p. 224*

11. Rufous Piha (*Lipaugus unirufus*). Uniform rufous brown; larger than Rufous Mourner. *p. 224*

12. Blue Cotinga (*Cotinga nattererii*). *Male*: shining turquoise blue, distinctive shape. *Female*: generally scaled and spotted. Cen. and e. Panama (in Chiriquí see very similar Turquoise Cotinga). *p. 221*

13. Three-wattled Bellbird (*Procnias tricarunculata*). *Male*: three hanging wattles, white head and neck. *Female*: streaked underparts, olive appearance, fairly large size. W. highlands. *p. 228*

14. Masked Tityra (*Tityra semifasciata*). Bare red ocular area and bill. Male mostly white, female with brown on upperparts. *p. 226*

15. Black-crowned Tityra (*Tityra inquisitor*). Black crown, female with chestnut sides of head. *p. 227*

1
♂
♀
2
♂
♀
3
♂
♀
4
♂
♀
5
♂
♀
6
9
17
8
10
11
12
♀
♂
13
♂
♀
14
♂
♀
15
♂
♀

PLATE 19

LARGE TYRANT FLYCATCHERS

1. SIRYSTES (*Sirystes sibilator*). Blackish head, white rump, white-tipped blackish tail. Cen. and e. Panama. *p. 230*
2. GOLDEN-BELLIED FLYCATCHER (*Myiodynastes hemichrysus*). Dusky moustache, yellow underparts with no prominent streaking. W. highlands. *p. 234*
3. STREAKED FLYCATCHER (*Myiodynastes maculatus*). Generally streaked brown appearance, rufous tail (see Sulphur-bellied Flycatcher). *p. 234*
4. PIRATIC FLYCATCHER (*Legatus leucophaius*). Short bill, breast streaking, long white eyestripe, no rufous in tail. *p. 233*
5. TROPICAL KINGBIRD (*Tyrannus melancholicus*). Notched tail, gray head, olive chest. *p. 233*
6. GRAY-CAPPED FLYCATCHER (*Myiozetetes granadensis*). Gray crown, short white superciliary. *p. 236*
7. WHITE-RINGED FLYCATCHER (*Conopias parva*). Broad white superciliary extending around hindneck. Forest canopy and borders, cen. and e. Panama. *p. 235*
8. SOCIAL FLYCATCHER (*Myiozetetes similis*). Indistinct wing-bars, olive upperparts, dusky ear-coverts. *p. 235*
9. BOAT-BILLED FLYCATCHER (*Megarhynchus pitangua*). Large size, heavy broad bill, olive upperparts (with no rufous). *p. 235*
10. GREAT KISKADEE (*Pitangus sulphuratus*). Large size, brown upperparts with rufous in wings and tail. Bocas del Toro and cen. Panama, spreading. *p. 237*
11. LESSER KISKADEE (*Pitangus lictor*). Like Great Kiskadee, but smaller, with more slender bill, less rusty in wings and tail. Cen. and e. Panama, near water. *p. 237*
12. RUSTY-MARGINED FLYCATCHER (*Myiozetetes cayanensis*). Rusty brown primary edging, rather brown upperparts, blackish ear-coverts (see text). Especially near water, more numerous eastward. *p. 236*

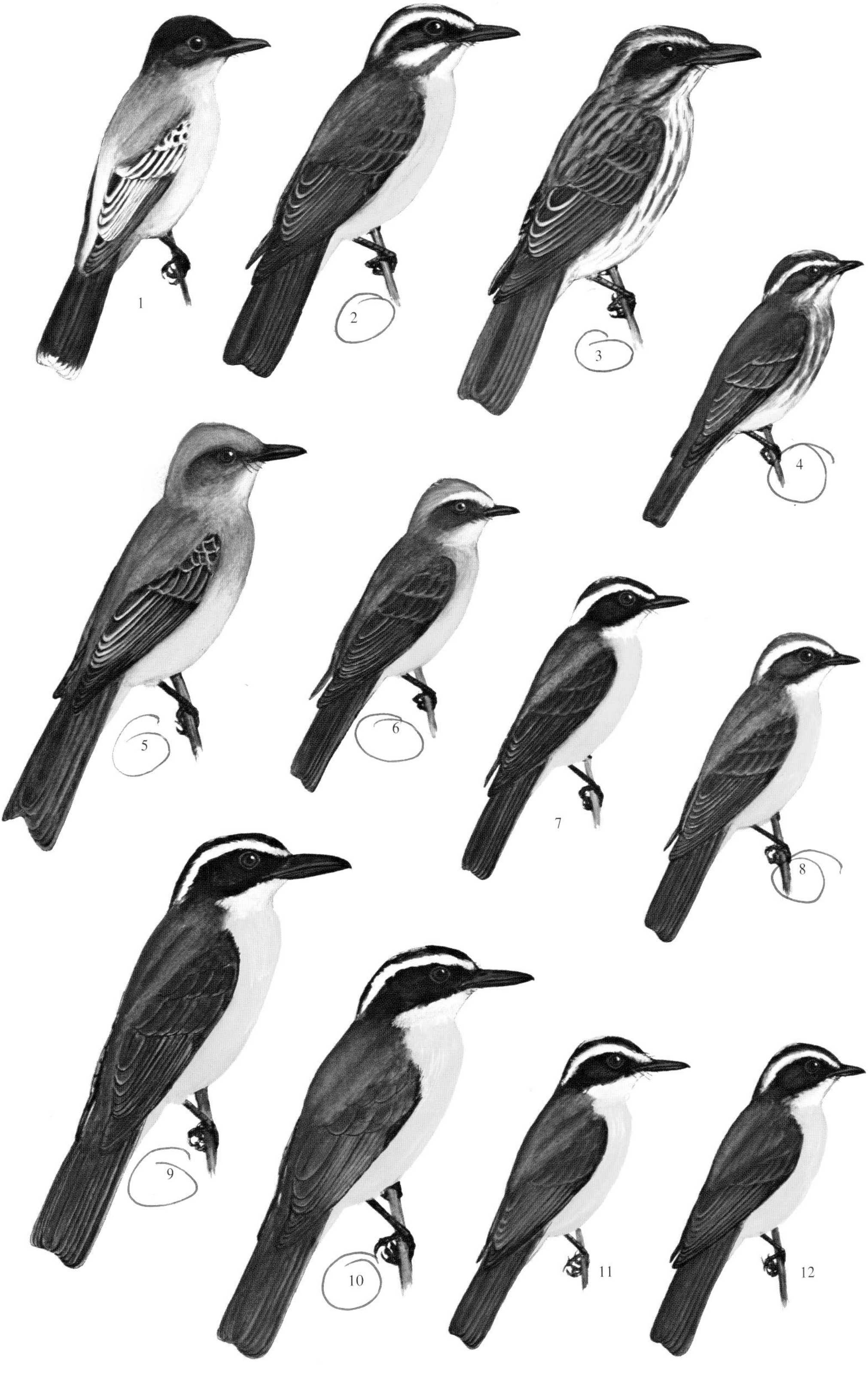
1
2
3
4
5
6
7
8
9
10
11
12

PLATE 20

MEDIUM-SIZED TYRANT FLYCATCHERS

1. BLACK-TAILED FLYCATCHER (*Myiobius atricaudus*). Conspicuous yellow rump, mostly yellowish underparts. *p. 244*

2. SULPHUR-RUMPED FLYCATCHER (*Myiobius sulphureipygius*). Conspicuous yellow rump, tawny chest and sides. *p. 244*

3. YELLOW-MARGINED FLYCATCHER (*Tolmomyias assimilis*). White eye-ring and short supraloral stripe, prominent wing-edging (but no bars), fairly broad bill. *p. 246*

4. YELLOW-OLIVE FLYCATCHER (*Tolmomyias sulphurescens*). Resembles preceding, but no eye-ring and with yellowish wing-bars (see text). *p. 246*

5. FOREST ELAENIA (*Myiopagis gaimardii*). Yellow crown patch, prominent wing-bars and edging, short bill. Cen. and e. Panama. *p. 253*

6. GREENISH ELAENIA (*Myiopagis viridicata*). Very like preceding, but lacks wing-bars (see text). *p. 253*

7. TROPICAL PEWEE (*Contopus cinereus*). Rather dark appearance, vague wing-bars, belly often yellowish (see text, as it closely resembles the two wood-pewees). *p. 240*

8. YELLOW-BELLIED ELAENIA (*Elaenia flavogaster*). Upstanding crest showing white, yellow lower underparts. *p. 252*

9. LESSER ELAENIA (*Elaenia chiriquensis*). Resembles preceding, but only slight crest shows (with only a little white), less contrast on underparts (see text). *p. 252*

10. MOUNTAIN ELAENIA (*Elaenia frantzii*). Very like Lesser Elaenia, but usually showing eye-ring and with rounded head (white not showing), underparts quite uniform (see text). W. highlands. *p. 253*

11. SCRUB FLYCATCHER (*Sublegatus arenarum*). Short bill, supraloral stripe, contrast on underparts. *p. 254*

12. DUSKY-CAPPED FLYCATCHER (*Myiarchus tuberculifer*). Contrasting blackish cap. *p. 238*

13. PANAMA FLYCATCHER (*Myiarchus panamensis*). No rufous in wings or tail (except immatures), gray throat and chest. See Great Crested Flycatcher. *p. 237*

14. NORTHERN ROYAL-FLYCATCHER (*Onychorhynchus mexicanus*). Hammerhead effect (bright-colored fan-shaped crest rarely showing), ochraceous rump and basal half of tail. *p. 244*

15. BROWNISH FLYCATCHER (*Cnipodectes subbrunneus*). Overall brown appearance, rump and tail more rufous (see text). Wing-lifts. Cen. and e. Panama. *p. 246*

16. OLIVE-STRIPED FLYCATCHER (*Mionectes olivaceus*). Dark appearance, conspicuous light eye-spot, streaked underparts. *p. 257*

17. OLIVACEOUS FLATBILL (*Rhynchocyclus olivaceus*). Broad flat bill, yellowish wing-bars and edging. Cen. and e. Panama. *p. 247*

18. EYE-RINGED FLATBILL (*Rhynchocyclus brevirostris*). Resembles previous species, but with more conspicuous eye-ring, no wing-bars, darker olive throat and chest. *p. 247*

1
2
3
4
5
6
7
8
9
10
11
12
13
14
♂
♀
15
16
17
18

PLATE 21

SMALL TYRANT FLYCATCHERS

1. RUDDY-TAILED FLYCATCHER (*Terenotriccus erythrurus*). Very small size; cinnamon-rufous underparts, wings, and tail. *p. 243*
2. NORTHERN BENTBILL (*Oncostoma cinereigulare*). Like next species, but throat and chest grayish white. W. Panama. *p. 249*
3. SOUTHERN BENTBILL (*Oncostoma olivaceum*). Bent downward bill, yellowish olive underparts. Cen. and e. Panama. *p. 249*
4. MOUSE-COLORED TYRANNULET (*Phaeomyias murina*). Drab appearance, pale lower mandible, buffyish wing-bars (see text). Pac. w. Panama. *p. 254*
5. BLACK-CAPPED PYGMY-TYRANT (*Myiornis atricapillus*). Minute with very short tail, black cap, mostly whitish underparts. *p. 250*
6. BROWN-CAPPED TYRANNULET (*Ornithion brunneicapillum*). Very small size, brown cap, conspicuous white eyestripe. *p. 256*
7. PALE-EYED PYGMY-TYRANT (*Atalotriccus pilaris*). Pale eye, whitish underparts, slender bill (see text). *p. 249*
8. OCHRE-BELLIED FLYCATCHER (*Pipromorpha oleaginea*). Uniform olive upperparts, mostly ochraceous below. Wing-lifts. *p. 257*
9. PALTRY TYRANNULET (*Tyranniscus vilissimus*). Slaty cap, conspicuous yellow wing-edging (but no bars), pale grayish underparts. *p. 255*
10. BLACK-HEADED TODY-FLYCATCHER (*Todirostrum nigriceps*). Very small size with short tail, black head contrasting with green back, white throat. *p. 248*
11. COMMON TODY-FLYCATCHER (*Todirostrum cinereum*). Broad bill, slaty head with no contrast, pale eye, all yellow underparts. *p. 248*
12. SLATE-HEADED TODY-FLYCATCHER (*Todirostrum sylvia*). Slaty head and nape, white supraloral stripe, yellow wing-bars and edging, pale grayish underparts (see text). *p. 248*
13. WHITE-FRONTED TYRANNULET (*Acrochordopus zeledoni*). White forehead and eyestripe, prominent wing-bars. Chiriquí highlands. *p. 256*
14. SOUTHERN BEARDLESS TYRANNULET (*Camptostoma obsoletum*). Brownish crown, narrow whitish eyestripe, mostly yellow underparts (see text). *p. 255*
15. YELLOW-GREEN TYRANNULET (*Phylloscartes flavovirens*). White eye-ring, yellow wing-bars, all yellow underparts. Local, cen. and e. Panama. *p. 250*
16. SEPIA-CAPPED FLYCATCHER (*Leptopogon amaurocephalus*). Brownish cap, dusky patch on ear-coverts (see text). Local, mostly Pac. slope. *p. 257*
17. BRAN-COLORED FLYCATCHER (*Myiophobus fasciatus*). Brown upperparts, blurry breast streaking, *Empidonax* size and shape. *p. 244*
18. TUFTED FLYCATCHER (*Mitrephanes phaeocercus*). Pointed crest. Foothills and highlands. *p. 243*
19. SCALE-CRESTED PYGMY-TYRANT (*Lophotriccus pileatus*). Black and rufous crest (usually laid flat). Foothills and lower highlands. *p. 249*
20. GOLDEN-CROWNED SPADEBILL (*Platyrinchus coronatus*). Very small and stubby, very broad flat bill, cinnamon-rufous crown, black patches on face. *p. 245*
21. YELLOW-CROWNED TYRANNULET (*Tyrannulus elatus*). Slaty crown, yellow crown patch (often visible), grayish sides of head and throat (see text). *p. 256*
22. YELLOW TYRANNULET (*Capsiempsis flaveola*). Overall yellow appearance. *p. 251*
23. YELLOWISH FLYCATCHER (*Empidonax flavescens*). Mostly rich yellow underparts, conspicuous yellow eye-ring. W. highlands. *p. 242*
24. BLACK-CAPPED FLYCATCHER (*Empidonax atriceps*). Contrasting black cap. Chiriquí highlands. *p. 242*

1
2
3
4
5
6
7
8
9
10
11
12
13
14
15
16
17
18
19
20
21
22
23
24

PLATE 22

WRENS

1. Plain Wren (*Thryothorus modestus*). Mostly whitish underparts, indistinct wing and tail barring. W. and cen. Panama. *p. 267*

2. Buff-breasted Wren (*Thryothorus leucotis*). Rather buffy underparts, prominent wing and tail barring. Cen. and e. Panama. *p. 266*

3. Southern House-Wren (*Troglodytes musculus*). Dull brownish, no distinctive markings. *p. 270*

4. Ochraceous Wren (*Troglodytes ochraceus*). Bright brown, buffy eyestripe and underparts. Highlands. *p. 270*

5. Timberline Wren (*Thryorchilus browni*). White eyestripe, white on wings. High altitudes on Volcán Barú, Chiriquí. *p. 270*

6. Rufous-and-white Wren (*Thryothorus rufalbus*). Bright rufous upperparts, white underparts. Mostly Pac. slope. *p. 267*

7. Rufous-breasted Wren (*Thryothorus rutilus*). Streaked sides of head and throat, bright rufous breast. *p. 269*

8. Bay Wren (*Thryothorus nigricapillus castaneus*). Black crown and nape, chestnut underparts. W. and cen. Panama (in e. Panama see Plate 32). *p. 268*

9. Black-bellied Wren (*Thryothorus fasciatoventris*). White throat and breast, contrasting black belly. *p. 269*

10. White-breasted Wood-Wren (*Henicorhina leucosticta*). Small size with very short tail, mostly white underparts. *p. 270*

11. Gray-breasted Wood-Wren (*Henicorhina leucophrys*). Mostly gray underparts. Highlands. *p. 271*

12. Stripe-breasted Wren (*Thryothorus thoracicus*). Streaked underparts. W. Carib. slope. *p. 267*

13. Black-throated Wren (*Thryothorus atrogularis*). Black throat and chest, otherwise mostly chestnut. Bocas del Toro. *p. 269*

14. Riverside Wren (*Thryothorus semibadius*). Chestnut upperparts, barred underparts. Chiriquí. *p. 268*

15. Nightingale Wren (*Microcerculus marginatus*). Dark and unpatterned, quite variable (see text). *p. 272*

16. Song Wren (*Cyporhinus phaeocephalus*). Chestnut sides of head, throat, and chest; bare blue ocular area. *p. 271*

17. White-headed Wren (*Campylorhynchus albobrunneus*). Large size, white head and underparts. Cen. and e. Panama. *p. 266*

18. Band-backed Wren (*Campylorhynchus zonatus*). Banded upperparts, mostly spotted underparts, large size. W. Carib slope. *p. 266*

1
2
3
4
5
6
7
8
9
10
11
12
13
14
15
16
17
18

PLATE 23

THRUSHES, WRENTHRUSH, SILKY-FLYCATCHERS

1. Wrenthrush (*Zeledonia coronata*). Plump with short tail, tawny crown, gray underparts. W. highlands. *p. 305*
2. Black-and-yellow Phainoptila (*Phainoptila melanoxantha*). *Male*: black head and upperparts, yellow sides. *Female*: black cap, yellow sides. W. highlands. *p. 281*
3. Long-tailed Silky-Flycatcher (*Ptilogonys caudatus*) male. Sleek and bluish gray, yellowish crest, long tail. *p. 281*
4. Black-faced Solitaire (*Myadestes melanops*). Slaty gray overall, white wing-band, orange bill and legs. W. highlands. *p. 274*
5. Orange-billed Nightingale-Thrush (*Catharus aurantiirostris*). Gray head, brown back, orange bill and legs. W. foothills and lower highlands. *p. 276*
6. Ruddy-capped Nightingale-Thrush (*Catharus frantzii*). Ruddy cap, brown upperparts. Chiriquí highlands. *p. 276*
7. Black-billed Nightingale-Thrush (*Catharus gracilirostris*). Dark bill and legs, mostly gray head and underparts. Chiriquí mountains. *p. 276*
8. Slaty-backed Nightingale-Thrush (*Catharus fuscater*). Mostly slaty, white eye, orange bill and legs. Foothills and lower highlands. *p. 276*
9. Black-headed Nightingale-Thrush (*Catharus mexicanus*). Black head, brownish olive upperparts, dark eye. W. foothills, mostly Carib. slope. *p. 276*
10. Pale-vented Robin (*Turdus obsoletus*). Dark bill, white lower belly and vent. Foothills and lower highlands. *p. 275*
11. Sooty Robin (*Turdus nigrescens*). Sooty brown and blackish, white eye, orange bill and legs. Chiriquí mountains. *p. 276*
12. Mountain Robin (*Turdus plebejus*). Dull uniform brown, dark bill. W. highlands. *p. 275*
13. White-throated Robin (*Turdus assimilis*). White throat (with dusky streaks) and upper chest. Foothills and lower highlands. *p. 274*
14. Clay-colored Robin (*Turdus grayi*). Light-colored bill, sandy brown overall. *p. 275*

1
2
♀
3
♂
4
6
5
7
10
8
9
12
11
13
14

PLATE 24

GNATCATCHERS, VIREOS, ETC.

1. TROPICAL GNATCATCHER (*Polioptila plumbea*). Slender and long-tailed; bluish gray upperparts with black crown in male, all-white underparts. *p. 279*
2. SLATE-THROATED GNATCATCHER (*Polioptila schistaceigula*). Dark slaty throat, chest, and upperparts. E. Panama, rare. *p. 279*
3. TAWNY-FACED GNATWREN (*Microbates cinereiventris*). Tawny face, black streaks across chest, short tail. *p. 280*
4. LONG-BILLED GNATWREN (*Ramphocaenus rufiventris*). Long straight bill, long tail often cocked, cinnamon-buffy sides of head and underparts. *p. 279*
5. RUFOUS-BROWED PEPPERSHRIKE (*Cyclarhis gujanensis*). Heavy hooked bill, rufous eyestripe (Chiriquí birds duller). *p. 282*
6. YELLOW-BROWED SHRIKE-VIREO (*Smaragdolanius eximius*). Like next species, but with yellow eyestripe, entire crown and nape blue. Darién. *p. 283*
7. GREEN SHRIKE-VIREO (*Smaragdolanius pulchellus*). Stout hooked bill, brilliant green upperparts, yellow throat. *p. 283*
8. YELLOW-GREEN VIREO (*Vireo flavoviridis*). Yellow sides and vent; gray cap, white eyestripe (see Red-eyed Vireo). *p. 284*
9. YELLOW-WINGED VIREO (*Vireo carmioli*). Yellow spectacles, broad yellow wing-bars. Chiriquí highlands. *p. 284*
10. BROWN-CAPPED VIREO (*Vireo leucophrys*). Brown cap, vireo (not greenlet) shape (see Philadelphia Vireo). W. highlands. *p. 286*
11. SCRUB GREENLET (*Hylophilus flavipes*). Pale eye, pinkish bill, olive upperparts (see text). *p. 287*
12. TAWNY-CROWNED GREENLET (*Hylophilus ochraceiceps*). Brown wings and tail, tawny crown, gray throat. *p. 286*
13. GOLDEN-FRONTED GREENLET (*Hylophilus aurantiifrons*). Orangey forehead, brown cap, mostly yellow underparts. Cen. and e. Panama. *p. 286*
14. LESSER GREENLET (*Hylophilus decurtatus*). Puffy-headed, short-tailed, whitish underparts; gray head in w. and cen. Panama, olive in e. Panama (see text). *p. 286*
15. SWALLOW-TANAGER (*Tersina viridis*). *Male*: mostly turquoise blue, black face and throat. *Female*: bright green overall, barring on lower underparts. E. Panama, rare. *p. 313*
16. YELLOWISH PIPIT (*Anthus lutescens*). Slender, brown, streaked, white outer tail feathers. Pac. savannas. *p. 280*

1
♂
♀
2
3
4
5
6
7
8
9
10
11
12
13
14
15
♂
♀
16

PLATE 25

HONEYCREEPERS, WOOD-WARBLERS

1. Green Honeycreeper (*Chlorophanes spiza*). *Male*: bright green plumage, black head, yellow bill. *Female*: uniform paler green, only slightly decurved bill (see text). *p. 289*

2. Blue Dacnis (*Dacnis cayana*). *Male*: mostly bright blue, short bill. *Female*: bluish head, short pointed bill. *p. 289*

3. Scarlet-thighed Dacnis (*Dacnis venusta*). *Male*: bright blue head and neck, black underparts. *Female*: buffy underparts. *p. 290*

4. Shining Honeycreeper (*Cyanerpes lucidus*). *Male*: yellow legs, black throat and chest, long decurved bill. *Female*: blue chest streaking, decurved bill, short tail. *p. 288*

5. Red-legged Honeycreeper (*Cyanerpes cyaneus*). *Male*: pale blue crown, red legs, decurved bill. *Female*: reddish legs, streaked chest, decurved bill. *p. 289*

6. Bananaquit (*Coereba flaveola*). White eyestripe, gray throat, short decurved bill. *p. 287*

7. Tropical Parula (*Parula pitiayumi*). Grayish blue upperparts, yellow underparts, wing-bars. *p. 291*

8. Flame-throated Warbler (*Vermivora gutturalis*). Slaty gray upperparts with black back, bright orange throat and chest. Chiriquí highlands. *p. 292*

9. Mangrove Warbler (*Dendroica erithachorides*). *Male*: rufous-chestnut head. Mangroves, islands. *p. 293*

10. Chestnut-capped Warbler (*Basileuterus delatrii*). Chestnut crown and ear-patch, long white eyestripe. *p. 304*

11. Three-striped Warbler (*Basileuterus tristriatus*). Crown stripes, black ear-coverts (much less in e. Panama), dull yellow underparts. Local, foothills and highlands. *p. 303*

12. Golden-crowned Warbler (*Basileuterus culicivorus*). Orange crown stripe (sometimes yellow), bright yellow underparts. W. foothills and highlands. *p. 303*

13. Black-cheeked Warbler (*Basileuterus melanogenys*). Chestnut crown, long white eyestripe, black sides of head. W. highlands. *p. 304*

14. Collared Redstart (*Myioborus torquatus*). Yellow face and underparts, black chest band. W. highlands. *p. 303*

15. Slate-throated Redstart (*Myioborus miniatus*). Slaty throat and upperparts. Highlands. *p. 303*

16. Buff-rumped Warbler (*Basileuterus fulvicauda*). Buff rump and basal two-thirds of tail (usually fanned). Watercourses. *p. 304*

1
♂
♀
2
♀
♂
3
♂
♀
4
♂
♀
5
♂
♀
6
7
8
9
10
11
12
13
14
15
16

PLATE 26

ICTERIDS

1. Yellow-tailed Oriole (*Icterus mesomelas*). Black back, yellow on tail and wing-coverts. *p. 310*
2. Yellow-backed Oriole (*Icterus chrysater*). Rich orange-yellow (including back), all black wings and tail. *p. 310*
3. Orange-crowned Oriole (*Icterus auricapillus*). Contrasting orange crown and nape. E. Panama. *p. 310*
4. Black-cowled Oriole (*Icterus prosthemelas*). Largely black, yellow lower underparts. Carib. w. Panama. *p. 310*
5. Yellow-billed Cacique (*Amblycercus holosericeus*). All black, yellowish bill. *p. 307*
6. Scarlet-rumped Cacique (*Cacicus uropygialis*). Scarlet rump, blue eye. *p. 307*
7. Yellow-rumped Cacique (*Cacicus cela*). Yellow rump and basal half of tail. *p. 307*
8. Chestnut-headed Oropendola (*Zarhynchus wagleri*). Chestnut head and neck, yellow tail. *p. 306*
9. Black Oropendola (*Gymnostinops guatimozinus*). Large size, yellow-tipped black bill. E. Panama. *p. 306*
10. Montezuma Oropendola (*Gymnostinops montezuma*). Large size, mostly chestnut plumage, blue and pink facial skin. W. Carib. slope to C.Z. *p. 306*
11. Crested Oropendola (*Psarocolius decumanus*). Mostly black, all yellowish bill. Local. *p. 306*
12. Red-breasted Blackbird (*Leistes militaris*). *Male*: red underparts. *Female*: pink-tinged breast (usually). Pac. slope (mostly) savannas. *p. 312*
13. Great-tailed Grackle (*Cassidix mexicanus*). *Male*: long creased tail. *Female*: buffy brown eyestripe and underparts. *p. 309*
14. Shiny Cowbird (*Molothrus bonariensis*). *Male*: small size, all glossy blue-black plumage. E. Panama. *p. 308*
15. Bronzed Cowbird (*Molothrus aeneus*) male. Ruff (more conspicuous in male), mostly bronzy plumage, red eye. *p. 308*
16. Giant Cowbird (*Scaphidura oryzivora*). *Male*: large size, conspicuous ruff, black bill and frontal shield. *Female*: smaller, with less prominent ruff. *p. 308*

1
2
3
4
5
6
7
8
9
10
11
12
♂
♀
13
♀
♂
14 ♂
15 ♂
16
♂
♀

PLATE 27

TANAGERS I

1. GOLDEN-BROWED CHLOROPHONIA (*Chlorophonia callophrys*). *Male*: very gaudy, bright green and yellow. W. highlands. *p. 314*

2. WHITE-VENTED EUPHONIA (*Euphonia minuta*). *Male*: white lower belly and vent. Especially foothills. *p. 315*

3. FULVOUS-VENTED EUPHONIA (*Euphonia fulvicrissa*). *Male*: tawny center of belly and vent. *Female*: tawny lower belly, rufous forecrown. Cen. and e. Panama. *p. 315*

4. BLUE-HOODED EUPHONIA (*Euphonia elegantissima*). *Male*: blue crown and nape. W. highlands. *p. 314*

5. YELLOW-THROATED EUPHONIA (*Euphonia hirundinacea*). *Male*: very like next species, but smaller yellow area on forecrown. Chiriquí. *p. 316*

6. THICK-BILLED EUPHONIA (*Euphonia laniirostris*). *Male*: underparts entirely yellow (including throat). *Female*: yellowish underparts, olive wash on chest. *p. 316*

7. SPOT-CROWNED EUPHONIA (*Euphonia imitans*). *Male*: yellow forecrown with dusky spots (see text). Chiriquí. *p. 316*

8. YELLOW-CROWNED EUPHONIA (*Euphonia luteicapilla*). *Male*: entire cap yellow, lower underparts all yellow. *Female*: uniform dull yellow underparts. *p. 315*

9. OLIVE-BACKED EUPHONIA (*Euphonia gouldi*). *Male*: glossy green upperparts, yellow forecrown, tawny center of breast and belly (see text). W. Carib. lowlands. *p. 316*

10. TAWNY-CAPPED EUPHONIA (*Euphonia anneae*). *Male*: tawny crown. Foothills. *p. 314*

11. PLAIN-COLORED TANAGER (*Tangara inornata*). Mostly gray, small mask and wings black. *p. 318*

12. GOLDEN-HOODED TANAGER (*Tangara larvata*). Golden head with black mask, black breast, blue on wings and sides. *p. 317*

13. EMERALD TANAGER (*Tangara florida*). Mostly bright green, black cheek-patch. Foothills. *p. 317*

14. BAY-HEADED TANAGER (*Tangara gyrola*). Chestnut head, blue underparts. *p. 318*

15. RUFOUS-WINGED TANAGER (*Tangara lavinia*). *Male*: chestnut head, rufous wings, yellow hindneck, green underparts. Foothills. *p. 318*

16. SILVER-THROATED TANAGER (*Tangara icterocephala*). Mostly bright yellow, whitish throat. Foothills and highlands. *p. 317*

17. SPANGLE-CHEEKED TANAGER (*Tangara dowii*). Mostly black, green and buff spangling, cinnamon lower underparts. W. highlands. *p. 319*

18. SPECKLED TANAGER (*Tangara guttata*). Spotted above and below. Foothills. *p. 317*

1 ♂
2 ♂
3
♂
♀
4 ♂
5 ♂
6
♀
♂
7 ♂
8
♀
♂
9 ♂
10 ♂
11
12
13
14
15
16
17
18

PLATE 28

TANAGERS II

1. GREEN-NAPED TANAGER (*Tangara fucosa*). Mostly black, green and blue spangling, cinnamon lower underparts; see Spangle-cheeked Tanager (Plate 27). Darién highlands. *p. 319*

2. BLUE-AND-GOLD TANAGER (*Bangsia arcaei*). Blue upperparts, rich yellow underparts, red eye. Foothills, local. *p. 319*

3. GRAY-AND-GOLD TANAGER (*Tangara palmeri*). Mostly bluish gray and whitish, yellow band across chest (sometimes indistinct). Darién. *p. 318*

4. PALM TANAGER (*Thraupis palmarum*). Olive, black rear half of wing. *p. 320*

5. BLUE-GRAY TANAGER (*Thraupis episcopus*). All pale grayish blue. *p. 319*

6. CRIMSON-COLLARED TANAGER (*Phlogothraupis sanguinolenta*). Brilliant red collar, bluish bill. Carib. w. Panama. *p. 321*

7. YELLOW-RUMPED TANAGER (*Ramphocelus icteronotus*). *Male*: black, yellow lower back and rump. *Female*: yellow lower back and rump, mostly yellow underparts, bluish bill. *p. 320*

8. SCARLET-RUMPED TANAGER (*Ramphocelus passerinii*). *Male*: black, scarlet lower back and rump. *Female*: bluish bill, rump and chest orange (Chiriquí) or more yellow (Bocas del Toro). W. Panama. *p. 320*

9. CRIMSON-BACKED TANAGER (*Ramphocelus dimidiatus*). *Male*: red lower back and rump, lower underparts; silvery on bill. *Female*: duller, still with red rump and belly. *p. 320*

10. FLAME-COLORED TANAGER (*Piranga bidentata*). *Male*: mostly orange-red, streaked back. *Female*: yellowish head and underparts, streaked back. Chiriquí highlands. *p. 322*

11. WHITE-WINGED TANAGER (*Piranga leucoptera*). *Male*: mostly rose red, broad white wing-bars, black mask. *Female*: yellowish, bold wing-bars. W. highlands. *p. 322*

12. RED-CROWNED ANT-TANAGER (*Habia rubica*). *Male*: scarlet crown with narrow black border. *Female*: yellow crown with narrow black border. Closely resembles next species (see text). *p. 323*

13. RED-THROATED ANT-TANAGER (*Habia fuscicauda*). *Male*: mostly dull carmine, bright red throat. *Female*: brownish olive, contrasting yellow throat. *p. 323*

14. CARMIOL'S TANAGER (*Chlorothraupis carmioli*). Mostly olive green, yellow throat (see text). Especially foothills. *p. 322*

15. LEMON-BROWED TANAGER (*Chlorothraupis olivacea*). Like preceding, but with yellow eye-ring and short eyestripe. Darién. *p. 323*

16. HEPATIC TANAGER (*Piranga flava*). *Male*: all brick red, blackish bill. *Female*: bright yellowish underparts, blackish bill (see text). Foothills. *p. 321*

1
2
3
4
5
♀ b
♀ a
6
7
♀
8
♂
♂
9
♂
♀
10
♂
♀
11
♀
♂
12
♀
♂
13
♀
♂
14
15
16
♀
♂

PLATE 29

TANAGERS III

1. WHITE-THROATED SHRIKE-TANAGER (*Lanio leucothorax*). *Male*: heavy hooked bill, black head, white throat. *Female*: heavy hooked bill, grayish head, brown upperparts (see text). W. Panama, local. *p. 323*

2. WHITE-SHOULDERED TANAGER (*Tachyphonus luctuosus*). *Male*: (a) conspicuous white shoulder patch, (b) tawny crown patch (in Chiriquí). *Female*: (a) contrasting gray head (cen. and e. Panama), or (b) pale area on bill (Chiriquí); see text. *p. 324*

3. YELLOW-BACKED TANAGER (*Hemithraupis flavicollis*). *Male*: yellow throat and rump, white lower underparts. *Female*: dull yellow underparts, narrow eye-ring (see text). Darién. *p. 326*

4. BLACK-AND-YELLOW TANAGER (*Chrysothlypis chrysomelas*). *Male*: bright yellow, black wings and tail. *Female*: bright yellow underparts (see text). Foothills. *p. 326*

5. TAWNY-CRESTED TANAGER (*Tachyphonus delatrii*). *Male*: orange-tawny crest. *Female*: all dark brown. *p. 325*

6. SULPHUR-RUMPED TANAGER (*Heterospingus rubrifrons*). Gray generally, yellow rump, white tuft on sides of breast. *p. 325*

7. SCARLET-BROWED TANAGER (*Heterospingus xanthopygius*). *Male*: glossy black generally, scarlet post-ocular stripe, yellow rump (female resembles previous species). Darién. *p. 325*

8. GRAY-HEADED TANAGER (*Eucometis penicillata*). Gray head and neck, bright yellow underparts. *p. 325*

9. WHITE-LINED TANAGER (*Tachyphonus rufus*). *Male*: all black, bluish bill, white under wing-linings. *Female*: rufous brown and tawny, bluish bill (see text). *p. 324*

10. DUSKY-FACED TANAGER (*Mitrospingus cassinii*). Blackish sides of head and throat, yellowish crown, pale eye. *p. 325*

11. ROSY THRUSH-TANAGER (*Rhodinocichla rosea*). *Male*: rosy red underparts. *Female*: tawny underparts. *p. 326*

12. SOOTY-CAPPED BUSH-TANAGER (*Chlorospingus pileatus*). Sooty black head, broad white eyestripe. W. highlands. *p. 328*

13. COMMON BUSH-TANAGER (*Chlorospingus ophthalmicus*). White spot behind eye, (a) head brownish (Chiriquí and Bocas del Toro) or (b) blackish (Veraguas and Coclé). W. highlands. *p. 326*

14. PIRRE BUSH-TANAGER (*Chlorospingus inornatus*). Blackish head, yellow underparts. Darién highlands. *p. 327*

15. YELLOW-THROATED BUSH-TANAGER (*Chlorospingus flavigularis*). Dull, with no white markings on head; throat yellow, whitish lower underparts. Carib. w. foothills. *p. 327*

16. TACARCUNA BUSH-TANAGER (*Chlorospingus tacarcunae*). Olive green, no white head markings but with pale eye; yellow throat and chest. E. Panama, local. *p. 327*

1
♀
♂
♂ a
♀ a
2
♂ b
4
♀
♀
3
♂
♀ b
♂
5
♂
♀
6
7 ♂
8
9
♀
♂
12
13 b
10
13 a
16
11
♂
♀
15
14

PLATE 30

FINCHES I

1. YELLOW-THIGHED FINCH (*Pselliophorus tibialis*). Dark slaty, conspicuous yellow thighs. Chiriquí highlands. *p. 337*

2. YELLOW-GREEN FINCH (*Pselliophorus luteoviridis*). Like preceding, but underparts mostly bright olive green. Highlands e. Chiriquí and Veraguas. *p. 337*

3. BLACK-FACED GROSBEAK (*Caryothraustes poliogaster*). Mostly yellowish olive, black face and throat, grayish belly. W. Carib. slope (in Darién see Yellow-green Grosbeak). *p. 329*

4. SOOTY-FACED FINCH (*Lysurus crassirostris*). Chestnut cap, white moustache, yellow lower underparts. Foothills and highlands locally. *p. 338*

5. SLATE-COLORED GROSBEAK (*Pitylus grossus*). All slaty, heavy bright red bill. *p. 329*

6. BLACK-THIGHED GROSBEAK (*Pheucticus tibialis*). Very heavy blackish bill, mostly yellow head and underparts (mottled with blackish to varying degrees). W. highlands. *p. 330*

7. STREAKED SALTATOR (*Saltator albicollis*). Streaked underparts, no throat patch. *p. 329*

8. BLACK-HEADED SALTATOR (*Saltator atriceps*). Large size, black crown and nape, white throat. W. and cen. Panama. *p. 328*

9. BUFF-THROATED SALTATOR (*Saltator maximus*). Mostly dark gray head, buffy throat patch. *p. 328*

10. LARGE-FOOTED FINCH (*Pezopetes capitalis*). Mostly unpatterned olive green, slaty head. Chiriquí highlands. *p. 336*

11. YELLOW-THROATED BRUSH-FINCH (*Atlapetes gutturalis*). Yellow throat, white underparts, black head. W. highlands. *p. 337*

12. BLACK-HEADED BRUSH-FINCH (*Atlapetes atricapillus tacarcunae*). Mostly white underparts, black head with narrow gray median stripe and superciliary. Foothills and lower highlands, e. Panama (Chiriquí birds have broader gray head stripes and grayer underparts). *p. 337*

13. CHESTNUT-CAPPED BRUSH-FINCH (*Atlapetes brunneinucha*). Chestnut crown, black chest band. Foothills and highlands. *p. 338*

14. BLACK-STRIPED SPARROW (*Arremonops conirostris*). Gray head with black stripes, grayish underparts. *p. 338*

15. ORANGE-BILLED SPARROW (*Arremon aurantiirostris*). Bright orange bill, black chest band. *p. 338*

1
2
3
4
5
6
7
8
9
10
11
12
13
14
15

PLATE 31

FINCHES II

1. BLUE SEEDEATER (*Amaurospiza concolor*). *Male*: all dark blue (see text). *Female*: all tawny brown (see text). Very local. *p. 334*

2. BLUE-BLACK GROSBEAK (*Cyanocompsa cyanoides*). *Male*: all blackish blue, very stout bill. *Female*: all rich brown, very stout bill. *p. 330*

3. THICK-BILLED SEED-FINCH (*Oryzoborus funereus*). *Male*: almost grotesque bill, all black, white wing-spot. *Female*: almost grotesque bill, mostly rich brown. *p. 335*

4. SLATY FINCH (*Spodiornis rusticus*). *Male*: rather slender bill, uniform slaty gray. *Female*: rather slender bill, brownish, lightly streaked underparts (see text). Chiriquí highlands. *p. 335*

5. BLUE-BLACK GRASSQUIT (*Volatinia jacarina*). *Male*: all glossy blue-black. *Female*: brownish, streaked underparts. *p. 332*

6. RUDDY-BREASTED SEEDEATER (*Sporophila minuta*). *Male*: gray upperparts, cinnamon-rufous underparts. *Female*: buffy to dull cinnamon underparts. Pac. savannas. *p. 334*

7. SLATE-COLORED SEEDEATER (*Sporophila schistacea*). *Male*: yellow bill, mostly gray plumage, white wing-spot. Very local. *p. 332*

8. YELLOW-BELLIED SEEDEATER (*Sporophila nigricollis*). *Male*: pale yellow or whitish lower underparts. *p. 334*

9. VARIABLE SEEDEATER (*Sporophila aurita*). *Male*: basically black above and white below (but variable; see text). *Female*: dull brown to buffyish (see text). *p. 333*

10. YELLOW-BELLIED SISKIN (*Spinus xanthogaster*). *Male*: mostly black, yellow belly and band on wings. *Female*: olive, conspicuous yellow wing-band, whitish lower belly. Chiriquí highlands. *p. 340*

11. YELLOW-FACED GRASSQUIT (*Tiaris olivacea*). *Male*: yellow eyestripe, eye-ring, and throat. *Female*: echoes facial pattern of male. *p. 332*

12. WEDGE-TAILED GRASS-FINCH (*Emberizoides herbicola*). Streaked and buffy brownish, long pointed tail, whitish eye-ring. Local, Pac. grasslands. *p. 340*

13. SAFFRON FINCH (*Sicalis flaveola*). *Male*: bright yellow, orange on head (variable in extent). Carib. slope C.Z. *p. 336*

14. GRASSLAND YELLOW-FINCH (*Sicalis luteola*). *Male*: facial area, underparts, and rump yellow. Very local, Pac. grasslands. *p. 336*

15. RUFOUS-COLLARED SPARROW (*Zonotrichia capensis*). Rufous collar, striped head. W. highlands. *p. 339*

16. VOLCANO JUNCO (*Junco vulcani*). Pink bill, yellow eye, streaked back. Above timberline on Volcán Barú, Chiriquí. *p. 339*

1
2
3
4
5
6
7
8
9
10
11
12
13
14
15
16

PLATE 32

SOME DARIÉN SPECIALTIES

All of the following are known only from eastern Panama, with most being found only in Darién.

1. PURPLE HONEYCREEPER (*Cyanerpes caeruleus*). *Male*: like Shining Honeycreeper (Plate 25), but more purple (less blue), with smaller black throat patch. *p. 289*
2. WHITE-EARED CONEBILL (*Conirostrum leucogenys*). *Male*: small size, short tail, gray plumage, white ear-patch. *Female*: grayish, rather undistinctive (see text). *p. 288*
3. VIRIDIAN DACNIS (*Dacnis viguieri*). *Male*: mostly opalescent green to bluish green. *Female*: mostly greenish, undistinctive (see text). *p. 290*
4. PIRRE HUMMINGBIRD (*Goethalsia bella*). *Male*: cinnamon wing-patch, white vent. Highlands. *p. 161*
5. GREENISH PUFFLEG (*Haplophaedia aureliae*) male. Conspicuous whitish leg-tufts. Highlands. *p. 166*
6. DOUBLE-BANDED GRAYTAIL (*Xenerpestes minlosi*). Small size, whitish underparts, wing-bars, and eyestripe. *p. 197*
7. BRONZE-OLIVE PYGMY-TYRANT (*Pseudotriccus pelzelni*). Overall dark appearance, slight crest (see text). Highlands. *p. 250*
8. SOOTY-CRESTED TYRANNULET (*Phyllomyias griseiceps*). Brownish cap, no wing-bars, mostly yellow underparts (see text). *p. 255*
9. GOLDEN-CROWNED FLYCATCHER (*Myiodynastes chrysocephalus*). Dusky moustache, light chest streaking. Highlands. *p. 235*
10. GRAY ELAENIA (*Myiopagis caniceps*). *Male*: bluish gray appearance, much white on wing. *p. 254*
11. BLACK-BILLED FLYCATCHER (*Aphanotriccus audax*). Slender and long-tailed, mostly yellow underparts, white supraloral stripe. *p. 243*
12. TAWNY-BREASTED FLYCATCHER (*Myiobius villosus*). Like Sulphur-rumped Flycatcher (Plate 20), but more tawny below, darker above, larger. Highlands. *p. 243*
13. VARIED SOLITAIRE (*Myadestes coloratus*). Tawny back and wings, slaty head and underparts, orange bill and legs. Highlands. *p. 274*
14. SPECTACLED PARROTLET (*Forpus conspicillatus*) male. Very small size, short tail, blue rump. *p. 128*
15. SAFFRON-HEADED PARROT (*Pionopsitta pyrilia*). Yellow head and neck. *p. 130*
16. DUSKY-BACKED JACAMAR (*Brachygalba salmoni*). Long slender bill, dark green upperparts, black chest and sides. *p. 177*
17. STRIPE-THROATED WREN (*Thryothorus leucopogon*). Brownish underparts, striped sides of head and throat. *p. 268*
18. SOOTY-HEADED WREN (*Thryothorus spadix*). Mostly chestnut; gray and black head and throat. *p. 269*
19. BAY WREN (*Thryothorus n. nigricapillus*). Barred underparts, black cap (not barred in cen. and w. Panama; see Plate 22). *p. 268*
20. RUFOUS-WINGED ANTWREN (*Herpsilochmus rufimarginatus*) male. Rufous wing-edging, pale yellow underparts, long white superciliary. *p. 207*
21. BLACK ANTSHRIKE (*Thamnophilus nigriceps*). *Male*: all black, no white showing on wings or tail (except under wing). *Female*: streaked head and underparts. *p. 204*
22. SPECKLED ANTSHRIKE (*Xenornis setifrons*). *Male*: streaked upperparts, slaty gray underparts. *Female*: streaked underparts. *p. 204*
23. PIRRE WARBLER (*Basileuterus ignotus*). Greenish yellow eyestripe (see text). Highlands. *p. 304*
24. GREEN MANAKIN (*Chloropipo holochlora*). Yellow belly, bright green plumage. *p. 220*
25. SHARP-TAILED STREAMCREEPER (*Lochmias nematura*). Leaftosser-like, conspicuous white spotting below. *p. 202*

1 ♂
2
♀
♂
3
♀
♂
4
5
6
7
8
9
10
11
12
13
14
15
16 ♂
17
18
19
20
21
♀
22
♀
♂
23
24
25

PYGMY KINGFISHER
(*Chloroceryle aenea*) Pl.10

Description: 5½. *Panama's smallest kingfisher.* Dark metallic bronzy green above; *rich rufous below,* buffier on throat, becoming *white on lower belly;* no white on tail. Female like male but with band of greenish black (edged with white) across chest.

Similar species: Not likely to be confused because of its small size. Much larger Green-and-rufous Kingfisher is similarly plumaged but is rufous to the vent and has some white barring on tail.

Status and distribution: Uncommon to locally fairly common along small streams in woodland and forest and in mangroves in lowlands on both slopes, including Azuero Peninsula, but apparently absent from drier areas on Pacific slope from eastern Coclé to Canal Zone; also found on Coiba Island, but not on islands in Gulf of Panama.

Habits: Shy and unobtrusive, perching very low over water under cover of vegetation. Sometimes found perched over a small forest puddle no more than an inch deep; occasionally seen sallying out after low-flying insects like a flycatcher. The call is a sharp *tyeet.*

Range: Southern Mexico to northern Bolivia and southern Brazil.

MOTMOTS: Momotidae (4)

The motmots are a small, neotropical family, with the greatest number of species being found in Middle America. Most species inhabit lower and middle growth of forest and woodland, though a few are found in more open situations. Despite their fairly large size, they are not conspicuous birds, being active mostly in the early morning and late afternoon, usually resting the remainder of the day. The three large Panama motmots are most often recorded from their far-carrying hooting or nasal calls. Motmots feed mostly on large insects, to a lesser extent on fruit and even small vertebrates. The nest is a burrow dug into an earth bank. The racquet tail tips of the central pair of tail feathers of three of the four Panamanian species are produced as a result of preening (and to some extent perhaps also abrasion), so that the barbs just above the feather tips fall off, leaving only the shaft exposed. Birds with new central tail feathers (and no, or only one, racquet) are regularly seen.

TODY MOTMOT
(*Hylomanes momotula*) Pl.10

Description: 6½–7. *A small motmot with no racquet tips on short tail.* Crown mixed greenish and rusty, *short turquoise blue eyestripe;* ear-coverts black *bordered below by buffy-white stripe;* otherwise dull green above; *throat buffy bordered by stripe-like tuft of buffy-white feathers;* remaining underparts dull brownish, more greenish on sides, fading to whitish on lower belly.

Similar species: Much smaller and proportionately shorter-tailed than other Panama motmots and the only one without black patch on chest and racquet tail-tips (at times absent in the others too). A rather dull and unobtrusive bird, best known by its distinctive facial pattern.

Status and distribution: Apparently rare; known only from humid forest in hill country of Veraguas (Chitra, specimen AMNH), eastern Colon province (Cerro Bruja), and from eastern Panama province (Cerro Azul) east through Darién; recorded in Panama 300–3000 feet. Though found locally in Costa Rica, so far unrecorded from Bocas del Toro.

Habits: Little known in Panama. Found singly or in pairs, sitting quietly in undergrowth where their dull plumage makes them inconspicuous. Call is a far-carrying resonant *kwa-kwa-kwa-kwa . . . ,* reminiscent of Prong-billed Barbet.

Range: Southeastern Mexico to western Colombia.

BROAD-BILLED MOTMOT
(*Electron platyrhynchum*) Pl.10

Description: 13. Tail long, usually with *racquet tips. Head, neck, and chest rufous* with broad black mask through eyes, green chin, and black spot on chest; otherwise green above; *breast and belly bluish green.*

Similar speies: Rufous Motmot is larger with rufous of underparts extending lower, onto breast and belly (bluish green only on lower belly); it has violet on wings.

Status and distribution: Fairly common in forest and second-growth woodland in lowlands and lower foothills on entire Caribbean slope; on Pacific slope found in eastern Chiriquí (San Félix), Veraguas foothills (Santa Fé, Chitra), El Valle and Cerro Campana, and in eastern Panama province and Darién. Widespread in forested areas on Caribbean side of Canal Zone, though not as numerous as Rufous Motmot.

Habits: Found singly or in pairs, sitting quietly on a horizontal branch or liana. Forages at all levels, but most often in middle or even upper strata. The call is very distinctive, a loud and resonant, somewhat nasal *aahnk* or *cwahnk,* usually given singly, but sometimes repeated rapidly in a series.

Range: Honduras to Bolivia and central Brazil.

Note: Keel-billed Motmot (*E. carinatum*) of southern Mexico to Costa Rica has been reported within 10 miles of Panama border on both Pacific (near Cañas Gordas) and Caribbean (headwaters of Río Coén) slopes in lower highlands of Costa Rica (*fide* G. Stiles). It somewhat resembles Blue-crowned Motmot but is considerably smaller (13″) with broader bill, green (not black) crown, and only a short blue superciliary; it inhabits humid forest, where one would not expect a Blue-crown.

RUFOUS MOTMOT

(*Baryphthengus martii*) Pl.10

Description: 18. Tail long, usually with *racquet tips. Head, neck, and underparts rufous* with broad black mask through eyes and black spot on chest; otherwise green above with violet-blue on wings; *lower belly bluish green.*

Similar species: Broad-billed Motmot is smaller with bluish green breast and belly (rufous down only to chest), has green chin, lacks violet in wings.

Status and distribution: Fairly common to common in forest and second-growth woodland in lowlands and lower foothills on entire Caribbean slope; on Pacific slope known from hill country of Veraguas and Coclé, in lowlands and lower foothills from western Panama province east through Darién. In Canal Zone widespread and common in forest on Caribbean side, less numerous on Pacific.

Habits: Found singly or in pairs in lower growth of forest or woodland. Frequently, especially when disturbed, swings its tail back and forth like a pendulum. Often executes an abrupt about-face on its perch. The call, heard most often in the early morning just before dawn, is a loud resonant rhythmic hooting, *hó-hoo-hoo* or *hoó-too-too,* often repeated and echoed by other individuals, sometimes varied and accelerated into a roll; the effect is almost owl-like. Another common call is a *hoórro.*

Range: Nicaragua to western Ecuador and western Amazonia.

Note: Often regarded as conspecific with *B. ruficapillus* of eastern Brazil to Paraguay and northwestern Argentina.

BLUE-CROWNED MOTMOT

(*Momotus momota*) Pl.10

Description: 16. Tail long, usually with *racquet tips. Crown and sides of head black* with *blue forehead and superciliary;* upperparts otherwise green; underparts mostly dull tawny, washed with olive on breast, with black spot on chest. Birds from western Panama east at least to Herrera (*lessonii*) have underparts mostly light olive green.

Similar species: Broad-billed and Rufous Motmots have rufous heads; Tody Motmot is much smaller and lacks tail racquets.

Status and distribution: Fairly common in forest borders, second-growth and gallery woodland, and clearings with dense undergrowth in lowlands and especially in foothills on much of Pacific slope (absent from the most open areas), including Azuero Peninsula, ranging in small numbers up into lower highlands (to about 6000 feet) in western Chiriquí; on Caribbean slope known only from Canal Zone area and extreme eastern San Blas. In Canal Zone more numerous on Pacific side, where widespread in wooded areas and the commonest motmot.

Habits: Unlike other Panama motmots, not a true forest bird, and especially in the west often found in thickets and hedgerows in pastures. Usually seen in pairs, resting quietly in the lower growth and not very conspicuous, often passed by unnoticed. Dustbathes regularly, and at dusk quite often seen sitting on little-traveled dirt roads. Canal Zone birds give a rather dove-like single *hoo-oo* (sometimes doubled), somewhat hoarser or more tremulous than the usually tripled hoot of the Rufous Motmot; also has a very tremulous *hoorr* or *hrrroo,* softer than corresponding call of Rufous Motmot. Chiriquí birds seem to have a somewhat different vocalization, a *woot* or *woop* repeated 2 to 6 or more times.

Range: Eastern Mexico to northern Argentina and southern Brazil.

Note: More than one species may be involved. Birds from Mexico to western Panama, *M. lessonii* (Lesson's Motmot), have been considered a distinct species; intergradation has not yet been shown between *lessonii* and *conexus* (the race found in central and eastern Panama), with specimens from the geographically intermediate area (Pacific slope Coclé) not having been taken. Central and eastern Panama birds (ranging west at least to western Panama province) have sometimes been considered a race of *M. subrufescens* (Tawny-bellied Motmot), ranging through Colombia to Venezuela, when that form is separated from the *momotus* group of most of South America.

JACAMARS: Galbulidae (4)

The jacamars form an exclusively neotropical family of slender very attractive birds, most species with very long thin bills. Four species are found in Panama, none of which is particularly numerous or widespread. Especially puzzling is the absence from most of Panama of a jacamar of the genus *Galbula,* at least one of which is found virtually everywhere else in tropical Middle and South America in forested areas. Rather active and conspicuous arboreal birds, they usually perch not too high above the ground, with the bill characteristically angled upward. Jacamars are primarily insectivorous, capturing their prey entirely on the wing; they consume many large butterflies. Their nest is a burrow dug into an earth bank, or sometimes a termitary.

DUSKY-BACKED JACAMAR
(*Brachygalba salmoni*) Pl.32

Description: 7. Known only from eastern Darién. Bill very long (2″) and slender. *Dark oily green to greenish black above,* browner on crown; throat and sides of neck buffy white, *chest and sides black glossed with green,* center of breast and belly cinnamon.

Similar species: Not likely to be confused; much smaller and duller than the brilliant green Rufous-tailed Jacamar.

Status and distribution: Known only from lowlands of eastern Darién (mostly the Tuira River valley, also Cana).

Habits: Inhabits forest and forest borders. Often seen perched along streams, sallying out after passing insects (Wetmore).

Range: Eastern Panama and northwestern Colombia.

Note: Wetmore calls it Salmon's Jacamar.

BLACK-CHINNED JACAMAR
(*Galbula melanogenia*) Pl.10

Description: 9. Known only from western Panama. Bill very long (2″) and slender. *Glittering golden green above and on chest; chin black,* throat white in male, tawny in female; breast and belly rufous; *underside of tail looks rufous* (though two middle pairs of feathers are green).

Similar species: Great Jacamar is larger, with heavy somewhat decurved bill and with no green on chest or rufous on tail. Rufous-tailed Jacamar of eastern Darién (of which Black-chinned is perhaps only a race) is very similar but lacks black chin and has more of tail rufous.

Status and distribution: Uncommon in forest and forest borders in lowlands of western Chiriquí and western Bocas del Toro, ranging occasionally up into lower highlands of western Chiriquí to over 4000 feet. Not known from eastern Panama, though possible as it occurs in adjacent Colombia.

Habits: Usually seen in pairs, perching alertly in lower growth of trees. Makes long sallies after flying insects, even butterflies. The call is a loud *peek.* The song is variable, often "drawn out peeps and squeaks followed by a laughing trill that speeds up" (Slud).

Range: Southern Mexico to western Panama; western Colombia and western Ecuador.

Note: Often considered conspecific with *G. ruficauda,* which it overlaps and with which it hybridizes in northwestern Colombia (J. Haffer).

RUFOUS-TAILED JACAMAR
(*Galbula ruficauda*)

Description: 9. Known only from eastern Darién. Bill very long (2″) and slender. Like Black-chinned Jacamar but *lacks black chin* and has more of tail rufous (only middle pair of feathers, instead of two pairs, green).

Similar species: See Black-chinned Jacamar.

Status and distribution: Known only from four specimens (all in AMNH, including two young taken from nest burrow) from near El Real in eastern Darién lowlands.

Habits: Favors more open, and generally drier, thickety areas than Black-chinned Jacamar. In Venezuela noted singing *wheéoo, wheeoo, wheee, wheeu, wheeárree-*

rreeree or *pheeo, pheeoo, pheee, pheee-pheee* (Eisenmann).
Range: Eastern Panama to northern Bolivia, northern Argentina, and southern Brazil.

GREAT JACAMAR
(*Jacamerops aurea*) Pl.10

Description: 11–12. *Bill broad and heavy, somewhat decurved* (1¾"). *Brilliant metallic golden green above;* upper throat golden green, lower throat white in male (tawny in female); remaining underparts rich tawny.
Similar species: Other jacamars have very different long, slender, straight bills.
Status and distribution: Rare to uncommon and rather local in humid forest and (to a lesser extent) second-growth woodland in lowlands and lower foothills on Caribbean slope; on Pacific slope known from Canal Zone (sighting of 1 at Fort Clayton on October 6, 1968—Ridgely and J. Karr), eastern Panama province (Río Pacora, Bayano River valley), and Darién. In Canal Zone, as elsewhere, scarce and infrequently encountered, though it has been reported from a number of forested localities on the Caribbean side.
Habits: Generally perches quietly on a branch at lower or middle levels in forest interior, and easily overlooked unless one catches a glimpse of its shimmering golden green upperparts. Occasionally utters a long hawk-like *kee-eeeeeeew,* and has other whistled calls (Slud).
Range: Costa Rica to northern Bolivia and central Brazil.

PUFFBIRDS: Bucconidae (8)

The puffbirds are a rather heterogenous group of exclusively neotropical birds found chiefly in forest and woodland. Most species are characterized by their somber plumage, large heads and short necks, and short tails; many (a striking exception being the nunbirds) are rather inactive. Most puffbirds (nunbirds excepted) are relatively silent, though *Notharchus* puffbirds especially do have loud vocalizations, usually given with long pauses between utterances. They feed on large insects and also small lizards and frogs (and some fruit), often captured in flight. The nest is a burrow in a bank or on level ground, or a cavity in an arboreal termite nest.

Left to right, WHITE-NECKED PUFFBIRD, BLACK-BREASTED PUFFBIRD, PIED PUFFBIRD, BARRED PUFFBIRD, LANCEOLATED MONKLET, WHITE-FRONTED NUNBIRD

WHITE-NECKED PUFFBIRD
(*Notharchus macrorhynchus*)

Description: 9½. Mostly black above with *white forecrown* and broad white collar; mostly white below with *broad black band across breast* and black barring on flanks.

Similar species: See Black-breasted Puffbird.

Status and distribution: Fairly common in forest borders and second-growth and lighter woodland on both slopes, but unrecorded from dry Pacific lowlands from eastern side of Azuero Peninsula to extreme western Panama province. The most widespread and generally the most numerous puffbird in the Canal Zone.

Habits: Usually seen perched rather high on an exposed branch. Often remains motionless for long periods, then flying off in pursuit of a large insect, which it captures with an audible snap, frequently then returning to its original perch where it kills its prey by beating it vigorously against the branch. Generally silent, but has a thin high twittery song, surprisingly weak considering the size of the bird.

Range: Southern Mexico to Bolivia, northeastern Argentina, and southern Brazil.

BLACK-BREASTED PUFFBIRD
(*Notharchus pectoralis*)

Description: 8. Mostly glossy blue-black above with *white patch on ear-coverts* and a narrow white collar; center of throat white, with very broad black band across lower chest and breast; lower underparts white with blackish barring on flanks.

Similar species: White-necked Puffbird is somewhat larger, with white forecrown and considerably more white on sides of head and neck. Pied Puffbird is much smaller.

Status and distribution: Local; fairly common in humid forest and forest borders on Caribbean slope of Canal Zone; on Pacific slope found in lowlands from Canal Zone (where rare) east through Darién. Apparently unrecorded from eastern Colon province or San Blas, but should occur. Quite easily seen on Pipeline Road, also found regularly on Barro Colorado Island.

Habits: Usually perches high, frequently within the concealing foliage of the forest canopy, doubtless often escaping observation. Sometimes, however, comes out into small trees in forest clearings. Its presence is often made known by its distinctive loud song, an often long series of whistles usually ending with three drawling and descending couplets, *kweee-kweee-kweee-kweee-kweee, kweee-a, kwey-a, kyoo-a;* there may be as many as 30 *kweee*'s before the falling notes.

Range: Central Panama to northwestern Ecuador.

PIED PUFFBIRD
(*Notharchus tectus*)

Description: 6. *Obviously smaller than other Notharchus puffbirds.* Black above with white spotting on forecrown, white superciliary, *white patch on scapulars,* and white spotting on tail; white below with *breast crossed by narrow black band* and blackish barring on flanks.

Similar species: White-necked and Black-breasted Puffbirds are larger with broad black breast bands and no white on wings or tail.

Status and distribution: Uncommon to fairly common in humid forest canopy and borders in lowlands on entire Caribbean slope (unrecorded from northern Coclé and western Colon province though doubtless occurs); on Pacific slope from eastern Panama province (Bayano River) and Darién. In central Panama most easily found along road to Portobelo (especially at Río Piedras) and on Achiote Road.

Habits: Usually found in pairs; most likely to be seen perched at low and middle levels at edge of forest (difficult to see when high in forest canopy). More active than other *Notharchus* puffbirds, though it too will perch for long periods without moving. The song is a high, thin, weak whistle, rapidly given though slowing at end, *wee-weeda-weeda-weeda, weee-a weee-a, weee-a,* the slow terminal couplets sometimes replaced by *wheeeer.*

Range: Costa Rica to Peru and Amazonian Brazil.

BARRED PUFFBIRD
(*Nystalus radiatus*)

Description: 8½. *Tawny to cinnamon-buff above barred with black* and with *broad buff collar;* buff below narrowly barred with black.

Similar species: Female Fasciated Antshrike is smaller, black above barred with brown, has wholly rufous cap and no buff collar.

Status and distribution: Rare to uncommon (becoming more numerous eastward) in humid forest and forest borders in lowlands and lower foothills on Caribbean slope from northern Coclé (possibly Veraguas) east through San Blas; on

Pacific slope reported mostly from Darién (where fairly common) with one old record from western Panama province (Capira, probably in humid foothills). In Canal Zone known only from a nineteenth-century report of a pair collected; not recorded since.

Habits: Perches quietly, often hidden by leaves; the usual call is a two-noted whistle, given slowly, a perfect imitation of the "wolf whistle" (Wetmore).

Range: Central Panama to western Ecuador.

WHITE-WHISKERED PUFFBIRD

(*Malacoptila panamensis*) Pl.11

Description: 8. *"Puffy" looking.* Iris red. Rufous brown above lightly spotted with buff and with *prominent white "whiskers" and forehead;* throat and chest tawny, lower underparts pale buff *streaked with dusky.* Female more grayish to olive brown above, less streaked below.

Similar species: Overall puffy and brown appearance, conspicuous white about bill, and streaked lower underparts are characteristic.

Status and distribution: Fairly common in undergrowth of forest, second-growth woodland, and borders in lowlands and foothills (to about 4000 feet) on both slopes, but absent from dry Pacific lowlands from eastern side of Azuero Peninsula to extreme western Panama province. Widespread in forested and wooded areas of Canal Zone.

Habits: Most often found in pairs, perching lethargically in the undergrowth, and doubtless often overlooked. Once discovered very unsuspicious, almost "stupid," allowing a close approach. Captured quite regularly in mist-nets, and when handled sometimes lives up to its name, fluffing out its feathers until it becomes a veritable puffball. Rather silent birds, occasionally uttering a very thin high *tseet,* and other thin high-pitched whistles.

Range: Southern Mexico to western Ecuador.

LANCEOLATED MONKLET

(*Micromonacha lanceolata*) *page 178*

Description: 5½. Very rare. Heavy bill. Short tail. Rufous brown above and on sides of head, with forehead and area around bill white, tail with black spots; *white below heavily streaked with black,* under tail-coverts rufous.

Similar species: Small size and boldly streaked underparts should preclude confusion.

Status and distribution: Only record is a bird collected at Guaval on Río Calovévora (at 1800 feet), Caribbean slope of Veraguas on border with Bocas del Toro, on September 6, 1926.

Habits: Nothing seems to be recorded. Presumably a humid forest bird, rare throughout its range.

Range: Costa Rica to Peru and western Amazonian Brazil.

GRAY-CHEEKED NUNLET

(*Nonnula frontalis*) Pl.11

Description: 6. *Bill rather long, slender, and slightly decurved.* Plain brown above, ruddier on forecrown; *sides of head contrastingly gray; bright tawny below,* fading to buffy whitish on belly.

Status and distribution: Rare in humid forest, second-growth woodland, and borders in lowlands on Caribbean slope in northern Coclé and the Canal Zone; uncommon in gallery and second-growth woodland in lowlands on Pacific slope in eastern Panama province (Tocumen/Chepo area, Bayano River valley) and Darién. Scarce in Canal Zone, with several old specimens, a couple sightings from Barro Colorado Island, one collected at Juan Mina on January 16, 1961, and two recent sightings from Achiote Road (Ridgely). Unrecorded from eastern Colon province or San Blas, but should occur.

Habits: Generally seen in lower growth of trees, perching inactively with an upright posture, occasionally flying out to pick up an insect off a leaf or branch. Sometimes joins mixed foraging flocks of antwrens, small flycatchers, etc.

Range: Central Panama to northern Colombia.

Note: Some authors consider *frontalis* a race of *N. ruficapilla* of western Amazonia.

WHITE-FRONTED NUNBIRD

(*Monasa morphoeus*) *page 178*

Description: 11. Unmistakable. *Bill bright red,* rather long, slender and somewhat decurved. *Mostly dark slaty* with white forehead; head and neck blacker. Birds from Bocas del Toro (*grandior*) also have chin white, as do some birds from central Panama. Birds from eastern Panama (*pallescens*) are somewhat paler gray, especially on wing-coverts, and black of head extends down over chest.

Status and distribution: Uncommon to locally fairly common in humid forest and forest borders in lowlands and foothills (to about 3000 feet) on Caribbean slope in western Bocas del Toro, eastern Colon province (Chilar; Cerro Santa Rita—N. G. Smith), and eastern San Blas; on Pacific slope found in eastern Panama province (Cerro Azul, Bayano River valley) and Darién. Becomes more numerous in eastern Panama, with an apparent gap in its range through west-central Panama. Only report from Canal Zone is a sighting of at least 2 on Barro Colorado Island on April 6, 1950 (Wetmore).

Habits: Most often seen in small groups, usually noisy. Nunbirds give a variety of loud whistles and gabbles, and groups often call together excitedly with their bills pointing upward. The nest in Costa Rica is in a burrow in level ground (A. Skutch).

Range: Southeastern Honduras to northern Bolivia and southeastern Brazil.

BARBETS: Capitonidae (3)

Barbets are found in the tropical parts of America, Africa, and southern Asia; three very distinctive species are found in Panama. They are heavy-bodied birds with stout bills. Basically forest birds, barbets are usually found in pairs or small groups, often gathering to feed with other birds in fruit laden trees. They nest in holes hollowed out in dead trees.

SPOT-CROWNED BARBET
(*Capito maculicoronatus*) Pl.11

Description: 6¾. Stout, grayish bill. Male *glossy blue-black above,* the crown brownish with whitish spots; mostly white below with *band of yellow across breast* (orange in center), *large blue-black spots on sides and flanks,* and *streaked with orange* (red in eastern birds, *rubrilateralis*) *on flanks.* Female like male above but with *throat, chest, and breast blue-black;* lower underparts white with a large orange (red in eastern birds) patch and black spots on flanks.

Status and distribution: Uncommon to locally fairly common in humid forest and borders in lowlands and lower foothills on Caribbean slope from Veraguas (several seen above Santa Fé, on Caribbean side of Divide, on April 8, 1975; N. G. Smith) and northern Coclé east through Canal Zone to San Blas; on Pacific slope from eastern Panama province (Cerro Azul) east through Darién where more numerous. In Canal Zone most easily seen in Achiote/Escobal Road area.

Habits: Usually seen in pairs or small groups, often perching in dead trees. The call is a loud croaking; male also gives a harsh two-syllabled "throat-clearing" call. Nests in holes dug into dead trees; a nest with fledged young was seen on Escobal Road on June 2, 1971 (J. Pujals and Eisenmann).

Range: Central Panama to western Colombia.

RED-HEADED BARBET
(*Eubucco bourcierii*) Pl.11

Description: 6¼. Found only in highlands of west and east. Bill stout, greenish yellow. Male unmistakable: *head and neck bright red* with black around eye and narrow bluish white bar across hindneck; otherwise dull green above; *red of throat passing into orange on chest and yellow on breast and center of belly,* flanks whitish streaked with greenish. Female very different: forehead and area around eyes black, crown olive green washed with yellow, *sides of head grayish blue bordered behind by a yellow bar;* otherwise dull green above; throat grayish yellow, chest orange-yellow, *lower underparts yellowish streaked with greenish.*

Status and distribution: Fairly common in forest and forest borders in highlands of western Chiriquí and adjacent Bocas del Toro (mostly 3000–6000 feet); recorded also from foothills of Veraguas (Santa Fé, Chitra, Calobre) and from foothills and lower highlands of eastern Darién (about 1500–4500 feet); reported seen near La Bonga at about 500 feet, back of Puerto Obaldía, San Blas, on June 18, 1965 (D. R. Sheets).

Habits: Forages at all levels, usually at medium heights and lower. Often feeds in dead leaf clusters. Most often found singly, frequently accompanying mixed flocks of other highland birds. Although usually silent, Eisenmann has heard it utter a soft *wrrrrr.*

Range: Costa Rica to northern Peru.

PRONG-BILLED BARBET
(*Semnornis frantzii*) Pl.11

Description: 7. Found only in western highlands. *Very heavy bluish gray bill,* tip of lower mandible pronged, upper mandible notched. Yellowish olive above, more tawny on crown; black tuft on nape (absent in female) and black around base of bill; *sides of head, throat, and breast ochraceous-tawny,* with patch of bluish gray on sides of breast; flanks grayish, center of belly light yellow.

Similar species: Though without a strong pattern or bright colors, this species should be easily recognized by its thick-set appearance, very stout bill, and the yellowish tawny head and breast. The male's black tuft normally lies flat. Female Red-headed Barbet has blue cheeks, streaks on belly, greenish yellow bill. See also Black-faced Grosbeak.

Status and distribution: Rare to uncommon in forest and forest borders in highlands of western Chiriquí (4000–7000 feet); recorded also from adjacent Bocas del Toro, eastern Chiriquí (Cerro Flores), and Veraguas (Chitra). More numerous above Boquete than on the Cerro Punta side of Volcán Barú, but not a common bird in Panama, seemingly more numerous in Costa Rica.

Habits: Usually seen in small groups at low and middle tree levels. Often very unsuspicious, especially when feeding in a fruit-laden tree or bush. Has a very distinctive, deep far-carrying call, *cwa-cwa-cwa-cwa* . . . , repeated many times, which has been compared to the "Indian yell in which the palm of the hand is rapidly and repeatedly pressed against and removed from the mouth" (Slud).

Range: Costa Rica and western Panama.

TOUCANS: Ramphastidae (6)

The toucans are a characteristic group of neotropical birds found in forest and woodland. They are best known for their enormously enlarged and multicolored bills (superficially similar to those of the Old World hornbills, Bucerotidae, though the two groups are not closely related). Though the bill makes the birds look awkward, it actually is very light, being largely hollow. Toucans are gregarious birds, usually seen in small flocks, especially at fruiting trees. Though their food is primarily fruit and berries, that diet is supplemented with large insects and small reptiles and amphibians, as well as the eggs and young of other birds. They nest in hollows in trees, the smaller species often roosting as a group in a disused woodpecker hole. The larger toucans are shot for food in some parts of Panama, but are numerous and easily observed in the Canal Zone. The continued existence in Panama of one species, the Fiery-billed Araçari, is threatened by the continuing clearing of forest and woodland in Chiriquí.

EMERALD TOUCANET

(*Aulacorhynchus prasinus*) Pl.11

Description: 12–13. Bill proportionately smaller than in other Panama toucans, mostly black with upper half of upper mandible yellow, base sharply outlined with vertical stripe of white. *Mostly bright green,* paler below, with brownish crown; *throat blue,* under tail-coverts and tail tipping (from below) chestnut.

Similar species: The only all green toucan in Panama. Yellow-eared Toucanet has olive green mantle but is largely black on head and below.

Status and distribution: Common in forest, forest borders, and clearings with trees in highlands of Chiriquí and Veraguas (mostly 4000–8000 feet in western Chiriquí, down locally to 2000 feet in Veraguas); rare in isolated patches of cloud forest in Coclé (Río Cascajal) and western Panama province (Cerro Campana); found also in highlands of eastern Darién.

Habits: Found in pairs or small groups, foraging at all levels. Omnivorous, regularly taking eggs and nestlings of other birds. Quite noisy, repeating a variety of loud, harsh, often hoarse *kwack* or *kweck* notes in a series, rising to *queerk* when excited; also a *kee-kee-krrr,* and a repeated *krik,* which can suggest call of Keel-billed Toucan.

Range: Central Mexico to western Venezuela and southern Peru.

Note: The blue-throated Costa Rica and Panama birds are sometimes considered distinct from other green toucanets, *A. caeruleogularis* (Blue-throated Toucanet).

COLLARED ARAÇARI (TOUCANET)

(*Pteroglossus torquatus*) Pl.11

Description: 15–16. *Upper mandible mostly ivory whitish,* shading to brown near base, with black tip and keel stripe; lower mandible black; base sharply outlined with vertical stripe of white. *Head and neck* *black,* with bare skin around eye reddish, and inconspicuous chestnut collar; otherwise dull olive above with red rump; throat black, *remaining underparts mostly yellow* more or less stained with red and black; spot of black on center of breast and *band of mixed black and red across upper belly.*

Similar species: Fiery-billed Araçari of Pacific western Panama has upper mandible mostly reddish orange and solid red band across upper belly (not mixed red and black). See Stripe-billed Araçari (below).

Status and distribution: Common in forest, second-growth woodland, and borders in lowlands on entire Caribbean slope; on Pacific slope in lowlands and lower foothills from Canal Zone east through Darién. Some form of araçari (probably this) occurs at Cerro Campana and El Valle, but its exact identity has not been determined. Common and widespread on both sides of Canal Zone.

Habits: Travels about in groups of up to about a dozen individuals, generally keeping in close contact; they "follow the leader," one by one, flying on a straight line with fluttering wing-beats and short glides. The usual call is a distinctive high squeaky or sneezy *ksíyik, ksíyik;* also a *kecheéf.*

Range: Southern Mexico to northern Colombia and northwestern Venezuela.

Note: Stripe-billed Araçari (*P. sanguineus*) of western Colombia and northwestern Ecuador may occur in extreme eastern Darién as it has been taken in immediately adjacent Colombia. It closely resembles Collared Araçari, but differs in having black stripe on side as well as keel of upper mandible, yellow (not black) bill tip, and lacks chestnut collar.

FIERY-BILLED ARAÇARI (TOUCANET)

(*Pteroglossus frantzii*)

Description: 15–16. Known only from Chiriquí and southwestern Veraguas. Similar to Collared Araçari. Differs in having *upper mandible mostly orange-red* with more dusky "teeth" marks on cutting edge; *band across upper belly broader and more solidly red,* with black restricted to a narrow broken line at upper edge.

Similar species: See Collared Araçari.

Status and distribution: Locally still uncommon to fairly common in forest, second-growth woodland, and borders in lowlands and foothills on Pacific slope in Chiriquí and southwestern Veraguas (Río San Lorenzo), mostly below 5000 feet, occasionally up to 6000 feet. A few can sometimes still be found in surviving patches of woodland around Volcán; decreasing rapidly with destruction of forest.

Habits: Similar to Collared Araçari. The usual call is a *kachíf,* varied to *ksichík* and *weechíf.*

Range: Southwestern Costa Rica and Pacific western Panama.

Note: Sometimes considered conspecific with Collared Araçari. Wetmore calls it Frantz's (= Frantzius') Araçari.

YELLOW-EARED TOUCANET

(*Selenidera spectabilis*) Pl.11

Decription: 14–15. Bill mostly brownish black, with upper part of upper mandible yellowish green. Sexes differ slightly. Male has *head, neck, and underparts black;* bare skin around eye green and yellow, *tuft of yellow feathers on ear-coverts;* patch of yellow on flanks, red under tail-coverts; back and wings olive. Female similar but has *chestnut crown and hindneck* and lacks yellow ear tufts.

Similar species: Emerald Toucanet can look very dark in poor light.

Status and distribution: Uncommon and local in very humid forest and forest borders in lowlands and (mostly) foothills (rarely to 4800 feet) on entire Caribbean slope; on Pacific slope recorded in humid hill country of eastern Chiriquí (Cordillera de Tolé) and Veraguas, Cerro Campana, and from eastern Panama province (Cerro Azul/Jefe area) east through Darién. Rather rare in Canal Zone; in recent years reported most often but irregularly (though probably breeding) in the Achiote Road/Piña area and on Pipeline Road.

Habits: Seen in pairs or small groups, foraging at all levels of trees. The call is a dry rhythmic repeated *t-krrrk, t-krrrk . . .* or *ak-tkrrrk, ak-tkrrrk . . . ,* easily confused with typical call of Keel-billed Toucan but drier and more rhythmic, less loud, usually with a two-syllabled effect.

Range: Honduras to western Colombia.

Note: Wetmore calls it Cassin's Araçari.

KEEL-BILLED TOUCAN

(*Ramphastos sulfuratus*) Pl.11

Description: 18–20. *Bill multicolored,* mostly yellowish green with dark red tip, light orange-red area on upper mandible, and light blue area on lower mandible. *Mostly black* with *bright yellow throat and chest,* bordered below by a narrow red band; rump white, under tail-coverts red, bare skin around eye yellowish green.

Similar species: Chestnut-mandibled Toucan is larger with a bicolored yellow and chestnut bill.

Status and distribution: Common in forest, second-growth woodland, and borders in lowlands and lower foothills (to about 3000 feet) on entire Caribbean slope; on Pacific slope less numerous and more local except in eastern Panama province (Cerro Azul/Jefe area, Bayano River valley) and Darién, ranging in forested foothills from Veraguas eastward and on Azuero Peninsula; absent from dry open lowlands from eastern side of Azuero Peninsula to extreme western Panama province. Conspicuous in forested areas on Caribbean side of Canal Zone; more local, perhaps irregular, on Pacific side.

Habits: Most often seen in small groups in the treetops, sometimes accompanied by Chestnut-mandibled Toucans. Their flight is deeply undulating, with several rapid wing-beats followed by a descending glide on set wings, then more wing-beats to regain altitude—unmistakably a toucan, at any distance. The typical call is an endlessly repeated, grunting or croaking *kre-ék, kre-ék, kre-ék . . .* , the calling bird often bobbing its head or turning from side to side with each note. Also has other croaking and guttural calls.

Range: Eastern Mexico to northern Colombia and northwestern Venezuela.

CHESTNUT-MANDIBLED (SWAINSON'S) TOUCAN
(*Ramphastos swainsonii*) Pl.11

Description: 21–23. *Bill bicolored,* most of upper mandible yellow, lower mandible and wedge-shaped area at base of upper mandible dark maroon-chestnut. In plumage like Keel-billed Toucan, but sometimes shows a narrow white line at lower edge of yellow bib.

Similar species: Easily distinguished from Keel-billed Toucan by its larger size and differently colored and longer bill. See Black-mandibled, or Chocó, Toucan (below).

Status and distribution: Fairly common to locally common in forest and forest borders in lowlands and foothills on entire Caribbean slope; on Pacific slope known only from western Chiriquí (in past recorded up to 5500 feet, but has greatly decreased in recent years due to forest destruction) and from western Panama province (Chorrera) and southwestern Canal Zone (occasional) east through Darién. Widespread in forest on Caribbean side of Canal Zone, perhaps most numerous in Fort Sherman/San Lorenzo area.

Habits: Similar to and often occurring with Keel-billed Toucan. The call is, however, entirely different, an almost gull-like repeated yelping *kee-yoo, tedick-tedick-tedick,* the rhythm of the basic phrase being well expressed by the Spanish vernacular name of "Dios-te-dé."

Range: Honduras to western Ecuador.

Note: Black-mandibled Toucan (*R. ambiguus*) of northern South America has long been credited to Panama on the basis of "an ancient specimen of uncertain history" (Wetmore); it had been assumed that the small form *brevis* occurred in Darién (it is known from near the Panama border in northwestern Colombia south to western Ecuador), but as yet there are no definite records. Some recent authors have elevated *R. brevis* to species rank (Chocó Toucan). It closely resembles Chestnut-mandibled in bill pattern (differing in that black replaces chestnut), but is smaller (19″) and has bill shape more like Keel-billed Toucan, which it replaces in its range; the croaking voice is also similar to the Keel-bill's (E. O. Willis). Recently it has been suggested that *swainsonii* be treated as a race of *ambiguus* (calling the enlarged species Yellow-breasted Toucan), retaining *brevis* as a full species (J. Haffer).

WOODPECKERS: Picidae (20)

The woodpeckers are a virtually cosmopolitan and well known group of birds, living wherever there are trees (except on oceanic islands), specializing in clinging to trunks and branches. They are heavy-bodied birds with strong, straight, pointed bills and stiffened tail feathers (except in the piculets and Old World wrynecks) used to brace themselves against the trunk. They are widely distributed in Panama, though in most areas the number of species is not large. Most species are sexually dimorphic, males usually with more red on head. Woodpeckers are primarily insectivorous, drawing their prey out of bark or wood with their long sticky tongue, but some species also eat fruit, some go to the ground for ants, and a few capture insects on the wing. They nest in holes dug into trunks and branches (usually dead wood); their nests are much used by other birds after the woodpeckers have abandoned them.

OLIVACEOUS PICULET

(*Picumnus olivaceus*) Pl.13

Description: 3½. A *tiny* woodpecker, by far Panama's smallest. *Crown and hindneck black, spotted with orange in front and with white to the rear* (spots all white in female); otherwise dull yellowish olive above with yellowish wing-edging; tail black; buffy yellowish below, indistinctly streaked with brownish olive.

Status and distribution: Uncommon and rather local in lighter woodland and shrubby woodland borders and clearings in more humid lowlands on Pacific slope in Chiriquí (where recorded up to 5400 feet), western Veraguas, and southern Los Santos, and on both slopes from about the Canal Zone east through San Blas and Darién. Scarce in Canal Zone proper; in central Panama most readily found at Río Piedras.

Habits: Forages actively at lower and middle heights, creeping up and down trunks and branches, much like a nuthatch (*Sitta sp.*), not using its tail for support. Often perches normally like a songbird. Usually found in pairs or small family groups.

Range: Guatemala to northwestern Venezuela and western Ecuador.

SPOT-BREASTED WOODPECKER

(*Chrysoptilus punctigula*) Pl.12

Description: 7½–8. *Crown black;* hindcrown, nape, and moustachial streak red; *sides of head white;* upperparts otherwise golden olive barred with black; throat white checkered with black, remaining underparts yellowish olive *spotted with black,* chest sometimes tinged orange-red. Female similar but with black moustachial stripe and only nape red.

Similar species: The combination of the black crown and spotted underparts is diagnostic.

Status and distribution: Rare; known only from open woodland and mangroves in coastal lowlands on Pacific slope from eastern Panama province (Juan Diaz) east to Darién (El Real). Perhaps more numerous than the few (5) records would indicate; much of its recorded Panama range is difficult of access.

Habits: In Panama known from mangroves and adjacent second-growth; elsewhere a bird of open palm savannas and borders of deciduous woodland. The usual call in Venezuela is a high, sharp, whistled *week-week-week,* somewhat reminiscent of a flicker (*Colaptes*) (Eisenmann).

Range: Central Panama to northern Bolivia, western Brazil, and the Guianas.

GOLDEN-OLIVE WOODPECKER

(*Piculus rubiginosus*) Pl.12

Description: 8–8½. Known only from western Panama. *Crown gray;* narrow line on either side, nape, and moustachial streak red; *sides of head grayish white;* upperparts otherwise golden olive with dull yellow rump, the wings edged with yellow; throat blackish, streaked with whitish, remaining underparts brownish olive barred with yellowish. Female similar but with only nape red.

Similar species: See other *Piculus* woodpeckers.

Status and distribution: Fairly common in second-growth woodland, forest borders, and clearings in foothills and highlands on Pacific slope in Chiriquí, Veraguas, and the Azuero Peninsula, mostly 2000–5000 feet (occasionally recorded near sea level but not recently); one recent specimen taken in a heavily forested area on Caribbean slope of Coclé (Río Guabal, at about 1400 feet).

Habits: Found singly or in pairs, usually at middle and upper levels. Its calls are somewhat kiskadee or flicker-like, a loud *geep* or *keer;* also has a peculiar *utzia-deek.*

Range: Southern Mexico to western Panama; Colombia to northwestern Argentina and Guyana.

STRIPE-CHEEKED WOODPECKER

(*Piculus callopterus*) Pl.12

Description: 7. Crown and moustachial streak red; *a whitish stripe across lower cheeks;* upperparts otherwise orange-brown or brassy olive with rump pale olive barred with yellowish and flight feathers rufous barred with black; *throat and chest olive spotted with whitish,* remaining underparts dull yellowish barred with dusky olive. Female similar but with crown and moustachial region dark grey, only nape red.

Similar species: Rufous-winged Woodpecker is similar but lacks whitish cheek stripe and has plain olive (unspotted) throat. Golden-green Woodpecker has a yellow cheek stripe and is brighter green above and brighter yellow below.

Status and distribution: Uncommon and local in humid forest and forest borders in foothills on Caribbean slope from Veraguas eastward; on Pacific slope from eastern Panama province (Cerro Azul/Jefe area) east through Darién. Apart from one nineteenth-century specimen, not known from Canal Zone.

Habits: Rather quiet and inconspicuous; usually found singly or in pairs on lower or middle part of trees.

Range: Panama.

Note: By some authors merged with *P. leucolaemus* (White-throated Woodpecker) of western Colombia to western Amazonia. Eisenmann believes it more closely allied to *P. simplex*.

RUFOUS-WINGED WOODPECKER

(*Piculus simplex*) Pl.12

Decription: 7–7¼. Known only from western Panama lowlands. Crown, nape, and moustachial streak red; *sides of head dull olive green;* upperparts otherwise dull yellowish olive with *flight feathers barred rufous and black* (all rufous below); *throat and chest olive,* latter sparingly spotted with buffy yellow; lower underparts buffy yellow barred with dark olive. Female similar but with crown and moustachial region dull olive, only nape red, sometimes with some red around eyes.

Similar species: Rather like Stripe-cheeked Woodpecker but without that species' whitish cheek stripe and with plain olive throat (not spotted with whitish). Golden-olive Woodpecker has a gray crown and barred underparts.

Status and distribution: Rare; known from two nineteenth-century specimens from Chiriquí lowlands (where quite possibly extirpated with felling of most forest), from lowlands of Bocas del Toro and from hill country of Carribbean slope Veraguas (Calovévora). Not recorded in Panama since the 1920's.

Habits: Slud notes that in Costa Rica it is "a forest-based species seen singly or in pairs . . . at or below medium heights in trees."

Range: Honduras to western Panama.

GOLDEN-GREEN WOODPECKER

(*Piculus chrysochloros*) Pl.12

Description: 8¼–8¾. Known only from eastern Panama. Crown, nape, and moustachial streak red; *broad yellow streak above red moustache;* upperparts otherwise olive green; *throat golden buff, remaining underparts golden yellow barred with blackish.* Female similar but with crown and moustachial region golden yellow.

Similar species: The brightest of Panama's green woodpeckers. Stripe-cheeked Woodpecker is smaller and has a whitish (not yellow) cheek stripe, a spotted throat, and rufous and black barred wings.

Status and distribution: Evidently rare, known in Panama from only three specimens: two from the Tuira/Chucunaque River valley of eastern Darién, and one collected on the Bayano River at Majé, eastern Panama province, on May 5, 1973 (R. Hinds, specimen in Gorgas Lab collection).

Habits: Unknown in Panama apart from the specimens taken. In Brazil, seen to forage singly rather high in trees in swampy forest and open woodland (Ridgely).

Range: Eastern Panama to northern Argentina, Paraguay, and southeastern Brazil.

CHESTNUT-COLORED WOODPECKER

(*Celeus castaneus*) Pl.12

Description: 9. Known only from western Bocas del Toro. Bill yellowish with bluish base. *Long pointed crest. Mostly chestnut, shading to paler dull tawny on head;* sparsely barred with black above and below except on head and wings; rump sometimes yellowish; moustachial streak and area below eyes red in male.

Similar species: Cinnamon Woodpecker is smaller, with a shorter bushier crest and with head same color as back (not paler); its black barring is much more noticeable, especially below.

Status and distribution: Uncommon in humid forest and forest borders in lowlands of western Bocas del Toro.

Habits: Less conspicuous and quieter than Cinnamon Woodpecker; like that species forages at all levels. Usually found singly or in pairs.

Range: Southeastern Mexico to Caribbean western Panama.

CINNAMON WOODPECKER

(*Celeus loricatus*) Pl.12

Description: 8. *Distinct but short bushy crest.* Bill greenish. *Mostly rufous, heavily* *barred with black especially on tail and underparts;* moustachial streak and throat red in male.

Similar species: In Bocas del Toro see Chestnut-colored Woodpecker.

Status and distribution: Uncommon in humid forest and forest borders in lowlands of western Bocas del Toro and from Caribbean slope Veraguas and eastern Panama province east through San Blas and Darién; ranges locally into hill country in the Cerro Azul/Jefe area. Local in Canal Zone, where most easily found on Pipeline Road.

Habits: Usually seen foraging singly high in forest trees, though occasionally met much lower inside forest. More readily found once its distinctive call is learned: a loud, clear, semi-whistled and rhythmic *wheeeet, wheet-wheet,* sometimes with an introductory *chuweéoo;* somewhat reminiscent of call of Black-striped Woodcreeper, but with notes not as run together.

Range: Nicaragua to western Ecuador.

LINEATED WOODPECKER

(*Dryocopus lineatus*) Pl.12

Description: 13–14. *Large.* Mostly black above with crown, *conspicuous pointed crest,* and moustachial stripe bright red; *two virtually parallel white stripes down back* and another from bill to behind eye and down sides of neck; throat and chest black, lower underparts barred buff and blackish. Female similar but with forecrown and moustache black.

Similar species: Superficially much like a Crimson-crested Woodpecker but with white back stripes not converging and different facial pattern. In extreme western Panama see also Pale-billed Woodpecker.

Status and distribution: Common in forest borders, second-growth woodland, and clearings with a few large trees left standing in fairly humid lowlands on both slopes, ranging in smaller numbers up into foothills to over 4000 feet.

Habits: Found singly or in pairs, climbing up trunks and larger branches at all heights. Usually slightly more numerous than the Crimson-crested Woodpecker. Its call is a loud flicker-like *wícka-wícka-wícka;* also has a *keep, grrrrr* or *tic-wurr.*

Range: Mexico to northern Argentina, Paraguay, and southeastern Brazil.

ACORN WOODPECKER

(*Melanerpes formicivorus*) Pl.12

Description: 8–9. Found only in western highlands. The "clown face." Mostly glossy black above with red crown and *pale yellow forecrown, the latter extending down in front of eye and connecting with pale yellow band across upper chest;* white rump; throat black, remaining underparts white *streaked with black on breast and sides.* Female similar but only nape red. Small white patch on wings and white rump conspicuous in flight.

Similar species: The unusual facial pattern renders this species virtually unmistakable; no other Panama woodpecker has streaked underparts.

Status and distribution: Common in forest, forest borders, and clearings with large trees in highlands of western Chiriquí, mostly above 4000 feet; recorded also from highlands of Veraguas. One sighting of 4 birds on Cerro Campana, western Panama province on September 7, 1968 (N. G. Smith) is the sole report away from the western highlands.

Habits: A characteristic and conspicuous species in the western Chiriquí highlands, especially favoring the many clearings with large dead trees left standing. Usually seen in groups, foraging actively, sometimes even flycatching for insects. Also eats many acorns (which it may store), as well as some fruit. A rather noisy species, with a variety of loud throaty calls.

Range: Western United States to western Panama; Colombia.

Note: By some authors placed in the genus *Balanosphyra.*

RED-CROWNED WOODPECKER

(*Melanerpes rubricapillus*) Pl.12

Description: 7–7½. Crown and nape red; *remaining upperparts barred black and white,* with white rump; *forehead and sides of head whitish;* grayish white below, tinged with red on center of lower belly. Female similar but with crown grayish buff, only nape red. Immature has yellowish forehead.

Similar species: Likely to be confused only with Black-cheeked Woodpecker but is evenly barred black and white above and lacks black on sides of head.

Status and distribution: Very common in lighter woodland, shrubby clearings, mangroves, and residential areas in lowlands on Pacific slope from western Chiriquí to central Darién (Punta La Sabana); on Caribbean slope found in cleared areas from Coclé east through San Blas; ranges in smaller numbers up into foothills; found also on Coiba and Cébaco Islands and on the Pearl Islands (but not on Taboga).

Habits: The most familiar and numerous woodpecker on most of the Pacific slope and throughout the Canal Zone except in heavy forest. Found singly or in pairs. Rather noisy, the typical calls being a *churr, churr,* rather like the call of its North American congener *M. carolinus* (Red-bellied Woodpecker), and a *wícka, wícka.* Eats fruit as well as insects.

Range: Southwestern Costa Rica through Panama, northern Colombia and Venezuela, and the Guianas.

Note: By some authors placed in the genus *Centurus.* Wetmore calls it Wagler's Woodpecker.

BLACK-CHEEKED WOODPECKER

(*Melanerpes pucherani*) Pl.12

Description: 7½–8. Forehead yellow, crown and nape red, *cheeks and sides of neck black; upperparts otherwise black,* narrowly barred on back and spotted on wings with white, and with white rump; throat and breast olive grayish, *lower underparts buffy whitish barred with black,* with red on center of belly. Female has crown black, only nape red.

Similar species: A much darker bird overall than the Red-crowned Woodpecker, blacker above, with black on sides of head, and black on lower underparts. In Pacific western Panama see also Golden-naped Woodpecker.

Status and distribution: Common in forest, forest borders, and second-growth woodland in lowlands on entire Caribbean slope; on Pacific slope found in humid areas from foothills of Veraguas eastward, in lowlands from around Canal Zone eastward. Replaces the better known Red-crowned Woodpecker in more wooded areas of Canal Zone, more numerous and widespread on Caribbean side.

Habits: Usually forages rather high in the trees. The calls are similar to but higher pitched than those of the Red-crowned Woodpecker, a *churrr* and a *chirririree.*

Range: Southern Mexico to western Ecuador.

Note: By some authors placed in the genus *Tripsurus,* by others in *Centurus,* as is the following species.

GOLDEN-NAPED WOODPECKER

(*Melanerpes chrysauchen*) Pl.12

Description: 7½–8. Found only in Chiriquí and Veraguas. Crown red, forehead and *hindneck yellow;* cheeks and sides of neck black; otherwise black above with *broad white stripe down center of back* and white rump; mostly olive grayish below, paler on throat, barred with black on sides and flanks, red on center of belly. Female similar but has black crown.

Similar species: Recalls better known Black-cheeked Woodpecker, though always to be known by its prominent golden nape. Hairy Woodpecker also has a whitish back stripe.

Status and distribution: Uncommon in lowlands and to a lesser extent in foothills (to about 4000 feet) of Chiriquí; recorded also from coastal lowlands of Pacific slope Veraguas.

Habits: Favors forest and forest borders. An attractively patterned woodpecker that recalls both Red-crowned and Black-cheeked Woodpeckers, with similar churring calls.

Range: Southwestern Costa Rica and Pacific western Panama.

Note: By some authors *M. pulcher* (Beautiful Woodpecker) of northern Colombia is considered conspecific.

YELLOW-BELLIED SAPSUCKER

(*Sphyrapicus varius*)

Decsription: 7–8. Male mostly black above white rump and barring on back; *wings with elongated white stripe* (conspicuous at rest); crown and nape patch red, white striped behind eye and back from bill; throat red, patch on chest black, remaining underparts yellowish white with dusky barring on sides. Female has white throat and mostly black crown. Immature quite different, *mostly brownish,* but already with the *characteristic white wing-stripe.*

Similar species: This scarce northern migrant is most likely to be seen in dull immature plumage. No resident woodpecker has a similar wing-stripe.

Status and distribution: Rare and irregular winter visitant to western and central Panama, especially in the foothills and highlands (November–March). Very rare in Canal Zone, with a sighting of 1 at Summit Gardens on December 17, 1950 (R. Scholes), and several seen near Caribbean coast in December 1974, including 1 at Fort Randolph on December 28 (S. West *et al.*).

Habits: Favors light woodland, borders, and clearings with large trees. Rather inconspicuous on its wintering grounds, but sometimes draws attention to itself by its distinctive slurred squealing call.

Range: Breeds in North America (more

than one species may be involved), wintering south to Honduras and the Greater Antilles, rarely to Panama and the Lesser Antilles. Birds wintering in Middle America and the West Indies belong to the nominate race, breeding in eastern North America.

SMOKY-BROWN WOODPECKER
(*Veniliornis fumigatus*) Pl.12

Description: 6–6¾. Known only from highlands of west and east. *Small. Entirely smoky brown to tawny-olive,* male with red crown. Female has dusky crown, immature male has only rearcrown red.

Similar species: The plain, essentially unmarked brownish plumage is characteristic. Red-rumped Woodpecker is somewhat similar but has red rump and barred underparts. Ruddy Woodcreeper is differently shaped and more brightly colored.

Status and distribution: Uncommon and rather local in second-growth woodland and borders in foothills and highlands of Chiriquí (where also one old record from lowlands), Bocas del Toro, Veraguas (Santa Fé), and eastern Darién (Cerro Tacarcuna).

Habits: Inconspicuous and not often seen, though regularly encountered in patches of woodland below Volcán in western Chiriquí. Found singly or in pairs, usually foraging at lower levels in lighter shady growth and borders.

Range: Eastern Mexico to Venezuela and northwestern Argentina.

RED-RUMPED WOODPECKER
(*Veniliornis kirkii*) Pl.12

Description: 6–6½. Known only from western and eastern Panama. *Small.* Crown blackish speckled more or less with red, band of yellow across nape; *upperparts otherwise tawny-olive,* often tinged with red, *rump bright red; underparts narrowly and evenly barred with buff and dark brown.* Female similar but without red on crown.

Similar species: Smoky-brown Woodpecker lacks red rump, barring below.

Status and distribution: Rather rare in forest, forest borders, and overgrown clearings in humid lowlands; apparently very local, recorded only from western Chiriquí (where decreasing rapidly with clearing of most forest), Veraguas (nineteenth-century specimens from Calobre and the Cordillera del Chucú), eastern San Blas (Permé, Puerto Obaldia), eastern Panama province (Bayano River valley at and above Majé, where not uncommon—Ridgely, Eisenmann, J. Gwynne *et al.*), and eastern Darién; found also on Coiba Island.

Habits: Inconspicuous, foraging on smaller branches at all levels, both inside forest and at borders.

Range: Costa Rica to Venezuela and western Ecuador.

HAIRY WOODPECKER
(*Dendrocopus villosus*) Pl.12

Description: 7–7½. Found only in western highlands. Mostly black above with *brownish white stripe down center of back* and whitish line behind eye and on sides of head; *grayish brown below.* Male has red nape patch; immature male has more red on crown (red sometimes replaced with yellow).

Similar species: Considerably smaller than the North American races of the Hairy Woodpecker (actually about the size of the Downy Woodpecker, *D. pubescens*), and with its uniform brownish underparts rather different in appearance. The otherwise very different Golden-naped Woodpecker also has a white stripe down the back.

Status and distribution: Fairly common in forest, forest borders, and clearings with large trees in highlands of western Chiriquí, mostly above 5000 feet (less often down to 4000 feet); recorded also from adjacent Bocas del Toro and highlands of eastern Chiriquí (Cerro Flores).

Habits: Found singly or in pairs, foraging at all heights but generally rather high. Not as conspicuous or noisy as the Acorn Woodpecker, with which it is often found; the calls are reminiscent of those of the North American races, though higher-pitched and more subdued. Drums fairly often.

Range: North American to western Panama.

PALE-BILLED (FLINT-BILLED) WOODPECKER
(*Campephilus guatemalensis*) Pl.12

Description: 13–14. Found only in extreme western Panama. *Large. Bill yellowish white. Conspicuous crest, entire head, and throat bright red;* otherwise mostly black with long white stripes extending down sides of neck onto back and *almost converging in a "V" on lower back;* breast and belly buffy barred with black. Female similar but with only face and crest red, crown and throat black.

Similar species: Best told from similar Crimson-crested Woodpecker by its pale (not blackish) bill; the two allied species are apparently not sympatric. Lineated Woodpecker has parallel white back stripes and black on face.

Status and distribution: Fairly common in forest, second-growth woodland, and borders in western Chiriquí (ranging up to about 5000 feet) and lowlands of western Bocas del Toro.

Habits: Though basically a forest bird, it often forages in largely cleared areas. Found singly or in pairs, feeding at all heights. Has a characteristic double drumming, the second stroke not so loud; also gives a nasal *nyuck, nyuck*.

Range: Mexico to western Panama.

Note: By some authors placed in the genus *Phloeoceastes*.

CRIMSON-CRESTED WOODPECKER
(*Campephilus melanoleucos*) Pl.12

Description: 14–15. A *large* woodpecker. *Bill blackish. Conspicuous pointed crest and head largely bright red,* with white spot at base of bill and another small black and white spot on ear-coverts; otherwise mostly black with long white stripes extending down sides of neck and *almost converging in a "V" on lower back;* lower breast and belly barred buffy white and black. Female similar but crown black with white neck stripe starting broadly at base of bill and extending through face.

Similar species: Lineated Woodpecker has almost parallel white stripes down back; female Lineated has white facial stripe narrowing in front of eye. In extreme western Panama see Pale-billed Woodpecker.

Status and distribution: Fairly common to common in forest, second-growth woodland, and borders in lowlands on both slopes from central Bocas del Toro and eastern Chiriquí east through San Blas and Darién, ranging in reduced numbers up into lower foothills.

Habits: Typically forages in pairs, feeding at all levels, sometimes in isolated trees a considerable distance from actual forest or woodland. Drums loudly (including a double drum like Pale-billed) but does not have an equivalent to flicker-like call of Lineated Woodpecker. Like other large woodpeckers, has a deeply undulating flight with deep wing-strokes.

Range: Western Panama to northern Argentina and southeastern Brazil.

Note: By some authors placed in the genus *Phloeoceastes*. Wetmore calls it Malherbe's Woodpecker.

CRIMSON-BELLIED WOODPECKER
(*Campephilus haematogaster*) Pl.12

Description: 13½–14½. *Large. Crown, crest, and neck red;* broad black band across sides of head *bordered above by narrow buff line and below by a broader one;* otherwise mostly black above with lower back and rump crimson; throat black, *remaining underparts crimson.* Female similar but with broad buff band on head extending down sides of neck, and with breast and belly mixed dull crimson and blackish, sometimes barred with buffy.

Similar species: No other Panama woodpecker has crimson underparts.

Status and distribution: Rare and local in humid forest and forest borders in lowlands and foothills on Caribbean slope from Bocas del Toro east through San Blas; on Pacific slope from eastern Panama province (sighting on Cerro Azul; Eisenmann) east through Darién. Only recently (1968) found in Canal Zone; now known to be a rare resident on Pipeline Road (numerous sightings, one shot bird photographed; E. O. Willis, J. Karr *et al.*).

Habits: This spectacular species is most often found inside tall forest, foraging at low levels, especially on trunks of large trees. Often encountered in pairs. Loud double drumming as in other members of genus.

Range: Western Panama to eastern Peru.

Note: The form from Panama to western Ecuador, *C. splendens* (Splendid Woodpecker), is sometimes regarded as specifically distinct. By some authors placed in the genus *Phloeoceastes*.

WOODCREEPERS: Dendrocolaptidae (17)

The woodcreepers are a widespread neotropical family that superficially resembles the smaller brown or tree creepers (Certhiidae) of the Northern Hemisphere. In Panama most inhabit forest; several species are quite rare, thinly spread, and little known. They climb trees and branches at varying heights, always clinging closely, probing for insects in bark, crevices, and epiphytes. Stiffened tails, usually with protruding central shafts, help support them in the manner of woodpeckers. The nests of a number of species remain undescribed; those that are known are in crevices and crannies on tree trunks and branches, often behind a piece of dead bark. All are easily recognized as woodcreepers (though some Furnariids look and act like them), but many are similar in appearance and often confused. The key points to watch for are: 1) total length; 2) shape, length, and color of bill; 3) presence or absence of streaking or spotting on crown and back and/or underparts; and 4) degree of ruddiness on head and upper back.

PLAIN-BROWN WOODCREEPER

(*Dendrocincla fuliginosa*) Pl.13

Description: 8. Bill straight, blackish. *Cap and back plain dull brown,* duller on crown and wing-coverts, wings slightly more rufous with dusky tips, with *no buff spotting or streaking;* sides of head more grayish, usually showing a *dusky moustachial stripe;* dull brown below with a few inconspicuous buffy streaks on breast; tail rufous.

Similar species: Within its range, the lack of any spotting or streaking above will distinguish it from all similar species except the rather rare Ruddy Woodcreeper, which is uniform rufous (not plain brown), especially bright on crown. In Chiriquí see Tawny-winged Woodcreeper.

Status and distribution: Fairly common in humid forest and second-growth woodland in lowlands and foothills on entire Caribbean slope; on Pacific slope known from foothills of Veraguas (Chitra), Cerro Campana, and eastern Panama province (Cerro Azul/Jefe area, Bayano River) east through Darién.

Habits: A regular army ant follower (half a dozen or more sometimes gathering), it is also found foraging singly or in pairs at low and middle heights. Unlike most woodcreepers, it often perches "normally," across a branch. Its usual call is a loud squeaky *sweeach* or *scheeah.*

Range: Honduras to northeastern Argentina and southeastern Brazil.

Note: Wetmore calls it Brown Woodcreeper.

TAWNY-WINGED WOODCREEPER

(*Dendrocincla anabatina*) Pl.13

Description: 7–7½. Found only in Chiriquí. Bill straight, blackish. *Olive brown above,* sometimes with indistinct, fine streaks on crown, darker on wing-coverts; *tawny streak behind eye;* throat buff, remaining underparts olive brown with indistinct, narrow buff streaks on chest; *flight feathers mainly tawny,* wing-tips dusky; tail rufous. Feathers of nape often look ragged (G. Stiles).

Similar species: Resembles Plain-brown Woodcreeper but somewhat smaller, more olive brown generally, with contrasting tawny area on wings; the two do not occur together in Panama. Olivaceous Woodcreeper is considerably smaller and is uniform grayish olive on head and underparts.

Status and distribution: Uncommon in forest in western Chiriquí, mostly in lowlands but rising in smaller numbers to about 4000 feet; decreasing due to forest destruction.

Habits: Similar to Plain-brown Woodcreeper. Like that species a regular army ant follower. A notably pugnacious bird (A. Skutch). Often flicks its wings.

Range: Southern Mexico to Pacific western Panama.

RUDDY WOODCREEPER

(*Dendrocincla homochroa*) Pl.13

Description: 7½. Bill straight, pale brownish to dull flesh, often with blackish tip. *Uniform deep rufous, brightest on crown* and wing-coverts, somewhat duller below.

Similar species: Many other woodcreepers have rufous wings and tails, but this is the only one that is bright rufous all over. The brown Plain-brown Woodcreeper can be confused, however, especially in the dull light inside forest: note that Ruddy's crown is markedly brighter than rest of its head.

Status and distribution: Uncommon in forest in lowlands and foothills on Pacific slope (absent in lowlands west of Canal Zone except in western Chiriquí); on Caribbean slope known only from a few records from foothills of Bocas del Toro and lowlands of Canal Zone. Apparently most numerous in eastern Panama province.

Habits: Rather furtive and easily overlooked. A regular army ant follower. Constantly flicks its wings.

Range: Southeastern Mexico to northern Colombia and northwestern Venezuela.

LONG-TAILED WOODCREEPER

(*Deconychura longicauda*) Pl.13

Description: 7½. Bill straight and rather slender, dusky above, paler below. Dull brown above with buffy superciliary and very indistinct buffy streaking on crown; dull brown below with large buffy spots on chest, becoming narrow buffy streaks below; wings and tail chestnut, the *tail noticeably longer than in other woodcreepers.*

Similar species: Often not recognized, though the longer tail is quite apparent when the bird is seen well. Buff-throated Woodcreeper is larger with longer bill and conspicuous buff streaking on head and upper back. The little Wedge-billed Woodcreeper has a distinctive short, wedge-shaped bill. See also Spotted Woodcreeper.

Status and distribution: Uncommon and local in humid forest in lowlands and foothills on Caribbean slope; on Pacific slope known from two old specimens from lowlands of western Chiriquí, and from Cerro Campana and eastern Panama province (Cerro Azul/Jefe area, Bayano River) east through Darién. In central Panama most easily found on Pipeline Road.

Habits: Forages at all levels, usually singly, sometimes in pairs, often accompanying mixed flocks of forest birds.

Range: Honduras to eastern Peru and Amazonian Brazil.

OLIVACEOUS WOODCREEPER

(*Sittasomus griseicapillus*) Pl.13

Description: 6–6½. A small woodcreeper with straight, slender, mostly blackish bill. *Grayish olive head, neck, and entire underparts contrasting with ruddy back;* buff wing-band conspicuous in flight; tail rufous.

Similar species: No other Panamanian woodcreeper has the *mostly grayish plumage* of this species. In Chiriquí, see Tawny-winged Woodcreeper.

Status and distribution: Local, known primarily from lowlands and (especially) foothills (to about 5000 feet) on Pacific slope but apparently not common anywhere in Panama; on Caribbean slope known from a few records from Veraguas (Calovévora) east to western San Blas (Mandinga). Apparently most numerous and widespread in lower highlands of Chiriquí and on Azuero Peninsula.

Habits: Usually found singly, foraging rather in the open at medium heights. An active feeder, occasionally even sallying out after passing insects. The usual call is a thin high trill.

Range: Central Mexico to northern Argentina and southeastern Brazil.

WEDGE-BILLED WOODCREEPER

(*Glyphorynchus spirurus*) Pl.13

Description: 5¾–6. *Panama's smallest woodcreeper. Bill short, wedge-shaped.* Generally dull brown with *buffy whitish superciliary;* throat buffy and with small, wedge-shaped buffy spots on breast; buff wing-band conspicuous in flight; tail chestnut.

Similar species: Small size and oddly shaped bill should easily distinguish it from other Panamanian woodcreepers; see especially Long-tailed. Plain Xenops is smaller, has a silvery stripe on sides of head, and does not creep up trunks and branches.

Status and distribution: Fairly common locally in humid forest and second-growth woodland in lowlands on entire Caribbean slope, ranging in smaller numbers well up into foothills; on Pacific slope found in western Chiriquí (to about 4000 feet), humid hill country of Veraguas, and from eastern Panama province (Cerro Azul/Jefe area, Bayano River) east through Darién.

Habits: Usually found singly, sometimes in pairs, generally low on trunks of larger trees.

Range: Southeastern Mexico to northern Bolivia and central Brazil.

STRONG-BILLED WOODCREEPER

(*Xiphocolaptes promeropirhynchus*) Pl.13

Description: 12–12½. Known only from western foothills. *Panama's largest woodcreeper. Bill heavy and long* (2"), slightly decurved, blackish. Brown above, narrowly streaked with buff on head and upper back; mostly dull brown below with buffy throat and buff streaking on breast and sides; wings and tail rufous.

Similar species: In plumage rather like Buff-throated Woodcreeper but *much* larger with stouter bill.

Status and distribution: Apparently rare; known only from humid forest in foothills of western Chiriquí (one record) and Veraguas (Chitra); recorded in Panama 3000–4000 feet.

Habits: Unknown in Panama apart from the few specimens taken. Elsewhere has been recorded accompanying army ant swarms.

Range: Central Mexico to western Panama; Colombia to Guyana, Amazonian Brazil, and northern Bolivia.

BARRED WOODCREEPER

(*Dendrocolaptes certhia*) Pl.13

Description: 10–11. Bill heavy, nearly straight (1½"), pale dusky, blackish at tip. *Head, back, and underparts brown barred with dusky,* finer on head and neck, coarser below, fainter on back; wings and tail rufous, unbarred.

Similar species: The only Panama woodcreeper that is barred above; see Black-banded Woodcreeper.

Status and distribution: Uncommon in forest and second-growth woodland in lowlands on both slopes, ranging up in diminished numbers into foothills; absent from drier lowlands on Pacific slope. Scarce in Canal Zone, perhaps most numerous in Madden Forest and the Madden Dam area.

Habits: Usually solitary and rather lethargic, often clinging motionless to a trunk, hence probably often overlooked. Sometimes found at army ant swarms, but not a persistent follower. The call in Nicaragua is a loud *téw-wee, téw-wee, téw-wee* (T. Howell).

Range: Southeastern Mexico to Bolivia and central Brazil.

BLACK-BANDED WOODCREEPER
(*Dendrocolaptes picumnus*) Pl.13

Description: 10½–11. Bill heavy, almost straight (1½"), dusky, paler toward tip. Olive brown above with fine buff streaks on head, neck, and back; throat whitish, chest brown streaked with buffy, *lower underparts buffy brown barred narrowly with black;* wings and tail rufous.

Similar species: The combination of large size and rather prominent black banding on lower underparts readily distinguishes this rare species.

Status and distribution: Apparently rare; known only from humid forest in highlands of western Chiriquí (6000–7000 feet) and Veraguas (3500–4000 feet); one nineteenth-century specimen from Capira, western Panama province which Wetmore regards as "questionable."

Habits: Forages at all heights in trees. A pair in Costa Rica gave a rather soft nasal *wrenh* with an upward inflection (Ridgely).

Range: Southern Mexico to western (central?) Panama; Colombia to the Guianas, Amazonian Brazil, Paraguay, and northwestern Argentina.

STRAIGHT-BILLED WOODCREEPER
(*Xiphorhynchus picus*) Pl.13

Description: 8–8½. Found locally in or near mangroves. *Bill straight, dull whitish or pinkish.* Rufous brown above, duller on crown which is also streaked with buffy; whitish superciliary; *most of sides of head, throat, and large spots on chest whitish;* lower underparts brown with buffy white spots on breast that become streaks on belly.

Similar species: The only woodcreeper that usually occurs in mangroves, though Buff-throated and Streak-headed often occur in adjacent areas. Distinguished from Buff-throat by its smaller size, pale straight bill, and prominent whitish (not buffy) throat and sides of head; from Streak-head by its straight (not slightly decurved) bill and the whitish sides of head and throat.

Status and distribution: Uncommon in mangroves (especially) and open woodland adjacent to Pacific coast from eastern side of Azuero Peninsula to Darién (Garachiné); recently (1972) found to occur locally in mangroves on Caribbean coast of Canal Zone at Galeta Island and Fort Randolph (J. Pujals *et al.*). Quite local and easily missed in its largely inaccessible habitat.

Habits: Usually found singly, sometimes in pairs, feeding at lower and middle heights. Rather quiet, but has a soft trill somewhat like Streak-headed Woodcreeper's.

Range: Western Panama to northern Bolivia and Amazonian Brazil.

Note: Sometimes separated in the genus *Dendroplex.*

BUFF-THROATED WOODCREEPER
(*Xiphorhynchus guttatus*) Pl.13

Description: 8½–9½. The most numerous and widespread Panamanian woodcreeper. *Bill fairly heavy, almost straight, rather long, blackish.* Dull brown above, the *head and upper back with buff streaks* margined with black; *throat buffy,* remaining underparts brown, breast with buff streaks somewhat edged with black; wings and tail rufous.

Similar species: Often confused with Streak-headed Woodcreeper, though that species is considerably smaller and has pale and differently shaped bill (slender and distinctly decurved). Long-tailed Woodcreeper is smaller, lacks distinct streaking on head and neck, and has notably long tail. Straight-billed Woodcreeper has shorter pale bill and whitish sides of head and throat.

Status and distribution: Very common and widespread in lowlands and lower foothills (to just over 2000 feet) throughout, occurring virtually wherever there are trees, though normally not within extensive heavy forest except at borders or clearings.

Habits: Usually forages at low levels, often in pairs. Rather noisy, calling, especially in early morning and late afternoon, a series of clear whistles that starts fast, then slows down and drops at the end, *pee-pee-pee-pee-pee-pew-pew-pew.*

Range: Guatemala to northern Bolivia and Amazonian and southeastern Brazil.

BLACK-STRIPED WOODCREEPER
(*Xiphorhynchus lachrymosus*) Pl.13

Description: 9½. Bill slightly decurved, dusky. *Blackish above with conspicuous broad streaks of buffy white;* throat buffy, *remaining underparts buffy whitish streaked with black* and with buffy feathers edged with black; wings and tail rufous.

Similar species: No other Panama woodcreeper is so brightly patterned.

Status and distribution: Fairly common in humid forest and forest borders in lowlands and foothills on entire Caribbean slope; on Pacific slope found in lowlands of western Chiriquí, hill country of Veraguas (Santa Fé), and from eastern Panama province (Cerro Azul, Bayano River) east through Darién. In central Panama most easily seen on Pipeline Road.

Habits: Usually forages higher than other woodcreepers, often in or near the forest canopy. The usual call is very distinctive, a series of 3 or 4 very loud descending whistles, *whee, hew, hew,* reminiscent of call of Cinnamon Woodpecker, but with notes more rapidly given.

Range: Nicaragua to northwestern Ecuador.

SPOTTED WOODCREEPER
(*Xiphorhynchus erythropygius*) Pl.13

Description: 8½. Bill almost straight, dusky. Olive brown above usually with a few buffy streaks on nape; throat buffy, *remaining underparts olive brown with tear-shaped buffy spots;* wings and tail rufous.

Similar species: Best distinguished by its rather olive overall plumage and the distinct spotting below. Long-tailed Woodcreeper is smaller with buffy superciliary, streaking (not spotting) on belly, with long tail. See Buff-throated Woodcreeper.

Status and distribution: Uncommon to fairly common in humid forest chiefly in foothills on both slopes (recorded mostly 1000–4500 feet); a few records from Caribbean lowlands in west and extreme east; one old specimen from Canal Zone (the La Jagua specimen mentioned by Wetmore was a pen-slip). Quite easily seen on Cerro Campana and in the Cerro Jefe area.

Habits: Usually found singly, often accompanying mixed flocks of insectivorous birds. The call is a nasal descending *ddrreew, ddrreew, ddrreew,* sometimes only doubled.

Range: Central Mexico to western Ecuador.

STREAK-HEADED WOODCREEPER
(*Lepidocolaptes souleyetii*) Pl.13

Description: 7½. *Bill slender and distinctly decurved, pale brownish or flesh.* Warm brown above with *distinct narrow buff streaks on head* (also on upper back in birds from western Panama, *compressus*); throat buffy whitish streaked dusky on sides, remaining underparts dull brown streaked with buffy; wings and tail rufous.

Similar species: Inhabits relatively open areas, not the forests preferred by most other woodcreepers. Frequently confused with Buff-throated Woodcreeper but smaller with a more slender and decurved, paler bill. Straight-billed Woodcreeper is slightly larger with straight whitish bill and whitish sides of head and throat. In western Panama see also the very similar montane Spot-crowned Woodcreeper.

Status and distribution: Locally fairly common in open and gallery woodland and in trees and shrubby clearings and largely cleared areas in lowlands and in smaller numbers in foothills (to about 5000 feet) on Pacific slope (specimens in AMNH from Pacific slope Veraguas; also seen in western Panama province by Eisenmann); on Caribbean slope known from western Bocas del Toro and from Canal Zone east through San Blas. Regularly seen at Summit Gardens.

Habits: Usually found singly, foraging actively at all heights. Frequently gives a rather musical trill or chirring of variable intensity.

Range: Southern Mexico to northwestern Peru, extreme northern Brazil, and Guyana.

SPOT-CROWNED WOODCREEPER
(*Lepidocolaptes affinis*) Pl.13

Description: 7½–8. Found only in Chiriquí highlands. *Bill slender and distinctly decurved,* pale. Warm brown above with *small diamond-shaped buffy spots on crown* and nape (looking more streaky on nape) but *essentially unstreaked on back;* throat buffy, remaining underparts dull brown with conspicuous buffy streaks; wings and tail rufous.

Similar species: Very like Streak-headed Woodcreeper; however, the two species are not normally found together. Spot-crowned is spotted (not streaked) on crown and is unstreaked on back (or has at most only a few very narrow streaks; Streak-head in western Panama is distinctly streaked on upper back); its throat is deeper buff (not whitish), extending further onto sides of head (in Streak-head, throat bordered with dusky streaking).

Status and distribution: Common in forest and forest borders in highlands of western Chiriquí, mostly above 4000 feet; only record from eastern Chiriquí is a specimen in AMNH taken on Cerro Flores (3600 feet) by L. Griscom.

Habits: Forages actively at all heights, often joining mixed flocks of insectivorous birds. One of the more numerous forest birds in the western Chiriquí highlands.

Range: Central Mexico to western Panama; Colombia and northern Venezuela to northern Bolivia.

Note: South American birds (*L. lachrymiger*, Montane Woodcreeper) are sometimes considered specifically distinct from Middle American form.

RED-BILLED SCYTHEBILL
(*Campylorhamphus trochilirostris*) Pl.13

Description: 9–10. *Bill enormously long (3") and very decurved, reddish.* Brown above streaked with buffy on head and back; throat buffy whitish, remaining underparts brown streaked with buffy; wings and tail rufous. Bill of juvenal browner.

Similar species: Though resembling several other woodcreepers in plumage, will at once be known by its unmistakable bill. Brown-billed Scythebill has a brown bill, blackish crown, and is a foothill or highland bird.

Status and distribution: Rare in forest borders and open second-growth woodland in lowlands on Caribbean slope from northern Coclé (El Uracillo) east through San Blas; on Pacific slope from eastern Panama province (Bayano River) east through Darién. In central Panama most likely to be seen along road to Portobelo.

Habits: Normally *not* found within forest. Usually forages singly, often in semi-open, occasionally accompanying mixed flocks of insectivorous birds.

Range: Central Panama to northern Argentina and southern Brazil.

BROWN-BILLED SCYTHEBILL
(*Campylorhamphus pusillus*) Pl.13

Description: 10. *Bill as in preceding species but not quite as long (2½") and dull brown. Head blackish* and back brown, both narrowly streaked with buffy; throat buffy, remaining underparts brown streaked with buffy; wings and tail rufous.

Similar species: Red-billed Scythebill has red (not brown) bill, lacks blackish head, and inhabits lowlands (not foothills and highlands).

Status and distribution: Rare in humid forest and forest borders in foothills and lower highlands on both slopes in western Bocas del Toro, western Chiriquí, and Veraguas (mostly 1000–5500 feet, rarely lower); rare also in hill country of eastern Panama province (one specimen from Cerro Azul, with several recent sightings from the Cerro Jefe area that probably refer to this species) and highlands of eastern Darién (Cerro Pirre, Cerro Tacarcuna, Cerro Quía).

Habits: More of a true forest bird than Red-billed Scythebill. Has a fine song, consisting of a clear ascending trill to which is then added (simultaneously) a loud ringing *tewe tewe tewe tewe tewe we we we we we we* (A. Skutch).

Range: Costa Rica to western Ecuador and Guyana.

OVENBIRDS AND ALLIES: Furnariidae (23)

The ovenbirds or horneros (no group name is especially fitting) are a diverse group of neotropical sub-oscines allied to the woodcreepers, best developed in temperate and montane South America, with only a few species reaching the lowlands of Panama (more in mountain areas of east and west). They are essentially insectivorous, but occupy a great variety of niches. All the Panamanian species have rather dull plumage, mostly in tones of brown, some with buff spotting and streaking. Most of the Panamanian representatives are forest birds; the exception, the two *Synallaxis* spinetails, are found in bushes in open country or border growth. The variety of nests of members of this family is remarkable. The "ovenbirds," or "horneros" as the Argentinians call them, for which the family is named, are found only in South America and get their name from their large domed nests which resemble a Dutch oven. Among Panama representatives, the *Synallaxis* spinetails construct large twig nests with a narrow tubular entrance, the Red-faced Spinetail builds a pendant, coconut-shaped globe, and a number of genera construct nests in holes in banks. The nests of a number of species are still unknown.

PALE-BREASTED SPINETAIL
(*Synallaxis albescens*) Pl.14

Description: 5½. Grayish brown above with gray forehead and *rufous crown and hindneck* and *rufous wing-coverts; white below,* tinged with brownish gray on chest and sides, and with sometimes concealed dusky patch on lower throat; *tail long and graduated.* Immatures lack rufous and are browner below.

Similar species: No similar bird is found with it in most of its Panama range; locally occurs with the much darker Slaty Spinetail. Wedge-tailed Grass-Finch is larger and buffier, without rufous on crown and wings.

Status and distribution: Common in open grassy areas with scattered bushes, scrubby areas, and sedgy or wet meadows in lowlands on Pacific slope from Chiriquí to eastern Panama province (lower Bayano River); in Chiriquí ranges up in cleared pastures to around 4000 feet; not known from Darién. Very local in Canal Zone due to absence of much suitable habitat, but common and easily found in the Tocumen/Chepo area.

Habits: Unless singing, usually rather unobtrusive, creeping about in tangles near ground. The song is distinctive, two-noted, *wee-bzü* or *fee-bü,* reminiscent of the *fitzbew* song of the Willow Flycatcher.

Range: Southwestern Costa Rica to central Argentina.

SLATY SPINETAIL
(*Synallaxis brachyura*) Pl.14

Description: 6. Dark grayish brown above with *crown and hindneck rufous* and *mostly rufous wings; sides of head and underparts slaty* with a few whitish streaks on throat; tail long and graduated.

Similar species: Likely to be confused only with Pale-breasted Spinetail, but much darker overall with uniform slaty (not mostly white) underparts.

Status and distribution: Local. Fairly common in lowlands and foothills of western Bocas del Toro and western Chiriquí (where recorded up to around 4000 feet in partly cleared areas); recorded also from Caribbean slope of Veraguas (Calovévora) and Canal Zone area (where now evidently very rare, with only recent report a sighting of one at Río Piedras, eastern Colon province on January 17, 1968; Ridgely); fairly common again in western San Blas (Mandinga) and eastern Darién.

Habits: Favors shrubby clearings and woodland borders in more humid areas. More skulking than Pale-breasted Spinetail, but presence often given away by its calls, a broken, sometimes prolonged, *ch-ch-chirrrrr* or *brrrrr.*

Range: Honduras to western Ecuador.

RED-FACED SPINETAIL
(*Cranioleuca erythrops*) Pl.8

Description: 5½. Found only in highlands of west and east. *Front half of head rufous,* hindneck and most of upperparts olive brown except for mostly rufous wings and tail; underparts somewhat paler olive brown, lightest on throat; tail long and graduated. Immature very similar but with olive brown crown, only sides of head rufous.

Similar species: *Synallaxis* spinetails are not arboreal forest birds; foliage-gleaners are considerably larger. In any case, none has the contrasting rufous face.

Status and distribution: Fairly common in forest and forest borders in highlands of western Chiriquí, mostly above 4000 feet; recorded also from highlands of Veraguas (Chitra, Santa Fé) and eastern Darién (Cerro Pirre, Cerro Malí).

Habits: Usually forages slightly above eye-level, gleaning in dead-leaf clusters, epiphytes, and among twigs. Found singly or in pairs, frequently in flocks of other highland birds.

Range: Costa Rica to western Ecuador.

RUSTY-BACKED SPINETAIL
(*Cranioleuca vulpina*) Pl.14

Description: 5¾. *Found only on Coiba Island.* In form resembles Red-faced Spinetail but not found with it. *Rusty brown above with rufous crown and narrow buff superciliary;* sides of head brownish lightly streaked with grayish; throat whitish, remaining underparts light olive brown; wings and tail rufous, tail long and graduated.

Similar species: Unlike any other bird on Coiba.

Status and distribution: Fairly common in open woodland on Coiba Island; not known from mainland. A most peculiar distribution.

Habits: Arboreal, but usually keeps fairly low, creeping among epiphytes and in dense foliage; also ascends vertically up a tree trunk, occasionally using tail for support.

Range: Coiba Island; South America east of

the Andes south to northern Bolivia and southeastern Brazil.

DOUBLE-BANDED GRAYTAIL (SOFTTAIL)
(*Xenerpestes minlosi*) Pl.32

Description: 4. Known only from Darién. Dark olive gray above with blackish crown, *yellowish white superciliary,* and *two white wing-bars; yellowish white below;* tail dark gray, graduated. Immature similar but with blackish streaks on throat and breast.

Similar species: Unlike any other Panama Furnariid. Most resembles an antwren or antvireo, particularly Rufous-winged Antwren. Its inclusion in the Furnariidae has been questioned.

Status and distribution: Apparently rare in forest and forest borders in lowlands of Darién (Río Cupe at Cituro, Río Sambú, and Garachiné).

Habits: Little known. Reported to be arboreal, occurring with mixed insectivorous birds. The two birds collected on the lower Río Sambú "were acting and feeding just like warblers" (L. Griscom).

Range: Eastern Panama and western Colombia.

BEAUTIFUL TREERUNNER
(*Margarornis bellulus*)

Description: 6. Found only in eastern Darién highlands. In form like Ruddy Treerunner.

Beautiful Treerunner

Dull brown above with rufous wing-coverts and tail; *prominent creamy white eye-ring, superciliary, and streaks on sides of head;* throat white, remaining underparts brown with *conspicuous pale yellowish black-edged tear-shaped spots.*

Similar species: A brightly marked species of very limited known range which should be easily identified. Not found with the uniform rufous Ruddy Treerunner. See also Spotted Barbtail.

Status and distribution: Apparently rare in forest in highlands of eastern Darién (Cerro Pirre, Cerro Malí).

Range: Eastern Panama. Perhaps occurs in adjacent Colombia, but not yet recorded.

Note: Wetmore calls it Beautiful Margarornis.

RUDDY TREERUNNER
(*Margarornis rubiginosus*) Pl.8

Description: 6. Found only in western highlands. *Almost entirely rufous, paler below;* buffy superciliary, *whitish throat,* and a few very small buffy dusky-margined spots on chest; buffy wing-band noticeable in flight.

Similar species: Somewhat resembles a woodcreeper as it creeps up branches and trunks often using its tail for support, but small with a short bill and more uniform rufous than any except the Ruddy (with no obvious streaking or spotting). Foliage-gleaners only rarely use their tails for support, and they normally do not creep up branches.

Status and distribution: Uncommon in forest and forest borders in highlands of western Chiriquí (mostly above 6000 feet); found also in eastern Chiriquí (Cerro Flores) and Veraguas (Chitra, where recorded down to 4000 feet).

Habits: Forages at all levels, hitching itself up tree trunks and branches like a woodcreeper, sometimes also feeding in dead leaf clusters. Found singly or in pairs, often with flocks of other highlands Furnariids, warblers, etc.

Range: Costa Rica and western Panama.

Note: Wetmore calls it Ruddy Margarornis.

SPOTTED BARBTAIL
(*Premnoplex brunnescens*) Pl.8

Description: 5½. Dark brown above, more grayish on crown, with buff superciliary; throat buffy, *remaining underparts dark brown profusely marked with large oval buff black-outlined spots;* tail dusky brown.

Similar species: An obscure dark brown bird

with conspicuous spotting below. Foliage-gleaners are larger with longer bills and lack spots. Streaked Xenops is smaller, not so dark, with up-turned lower mandible and crescentic silvery patch on sides of head. In Darién see also Beautiful Tree-runner.

Status and distribution: Uncommon to fairly common in humid forest and forest borders in foothills and highlands on both slopes in Bocas del Toro, Chiriquí, Veraguas, Cerro Campana, and eastern Darién (where apparently less numerous); recorded mostly from 2500 feet upward.

Habits: Very inconspicuous and not often seen, its true abundance better reflected by its often frequent mist-net captures. Favors wet wooded ravines and hillsides. Forages mostly at low levels, usually alone or in pairs, sometimes associating with mixed flocks. Creeps over mossy branches and trunks, only occasionally using its tail for support, almost recalling a nuthatch.

Range: Costa Rica to northern Venezuela and Bolivia.

BUFFY TUFTEDCHEEK

(*Pseudocolaptes lawrencii*) Pl.8

Description: 8. Found only in western mountains. Ruddy brown above, more rufous on rump and tail, with cap dusky streaked with buff; wings mostly blackish, edged buff on wing-coverts; *throat pale buff extending over sides of neck into conspicuous tuft;* buffy below, mottled with dusky on chest and becoming rufous on sides.

Similar species: A rather robust bird whose broad moustache-like tufts easily distinguish it. See Streak-breasted Treehunter.

Status and distribution: Rare in forest in Chiriquí and Veraguas, recorded as low as 4000 feet, but in western Chiriquí now rarely seen below 6000 feet; one specimen from highlands of adjacent western Bocas del Toro (Camp Cylindro).

Habits: Perhaps sometimes overlooked due to its habit of foraging at high levels in tall forest trees. Feeds especially in epiphytes, sometimes using its tail as a lever on horizontal branches as it probes for insects and invertebrates. Often sits normally on a large branch.

Range: Costa Rica and western Panama; western Colombia and northwestern Ecuador.

Note: Wetmore calls it Lawrence's Tufted-cheek.

STRIPED FOLIAGE-GLEANER (WOODHAUNTER)

(*Hyloctistes subulatus*) Pl.14

Description: 6¼. Bill rather long, slender, and straight. Brown above with *fine buffy streaks on head and somewhat broader streaks on hindneck and upper back; wings, rump, and tail chestnut;* throat buff, edged with olive, *remaining underparts buffy olive with buff streaks on breast.* Birds from eastern Panama (*cordobae*) are grayer above with less distinct streaks on crown, no streaks on back; wings are duller brown; breast is less sharply streaked.

Similar species: A confusing bird, which inhabits humid lowland and foothill forest; most similar species are mountain birds, though there is some overlap. Lineated Foliage-gleaner (a highland bird) is very similar but larger with browner underparts and brown (not chestnut) wings. Buff-throated Foliage-gleaner is unstreaked and has buff superciliary and eye-ring. In pattern resembles many woodcreepers, but does not creep up trunks and branches using its tail for support.

Status and distribution: Apparently rare and local in humid forest; on Caribbean slope recorded in lowlands and foothills from Bocas del Toro to Coclé, on Pacific slope in lowlands (probably only formerly) of western Chiriquí (Bugaba) and foothills of Chiriquí and Veraguas; eastern race recorded from hill country of eastern Colon province (Cerro Bruja), eastern San Blas (Ranchón), and eastern Darién. Several birds believed this species were seen near Cerro Jefe, eastern Panama province on June 25–26, 1970 (Ridgely).

Habits: Found singly or in pairs, rummaging about in dense vegetation and epiphytes at low and middle levels.

Range: Nicaragua to southern Peru and western Brazil.

Note: Wetmore calls all the foliage-gleaners (genera *Hyloctistes, Syndactyla, Anabacerthia, Philydor,* and *Automolus*) leaf-gleaners.

LINEATED FOLIAGE-GLEANER

(*Syndactyla subalaris*) Pl.8

Description: 7½. Found only in highlands. Warm brown above, *streaked narrowly with buff, most prominent on hindneck;* rump and tail rufous; throat pale buff, remaining underparts dull brown *streaked narrowly with buff,* becoming tawny-olive on flanks. Immature much more brightly colored, darker on crown and hindneck with conspicuous orange-tawny streaks on latter; more reddish brown above; *throat, sides of neck, and breast orange-tawny* with paler streaks; belly dull brown.

Similar species: Note the *buff streaking above and below;* the large Streak-breasted Treehunter lacks streaks above. Spectacled Foliage-gleaner has a conspicuous ochre eye-ring and superciliary. See also Striped Foliage-gleaner.

Status and distribution: Fairly common in forest and forest borders in highlands of western Chiriquí, Veraguas (on both slopes), and eastern Darién; in Chiriquí mostly above 5000 feet, but in Veraguas recorded 2500–4300 feet.

Habits: Forages mostly at low and middle levels, gleaning among twigs and in dead leaf clusters. Usually met with singly or in pairs, sometimes accompanying mixed flocks of other highland birds.

Range: Costa Rica to northwestern Venezuela and southern Peru.

SPECTACLED (SCALY-THROATED) FOLIAGE-GLEANER

(*Anabacerthia variegaticeps*) Pl.8

Description: 6¼. Known only from Chiriquí highlands. Bill rather short. *Crown grayish olive contrasting with ruddy back* (only indistinct buff streaks on crown); *conspicuous ochre eye-ring and superciliary;* throat yellowish white, feathers of lower throat margined with dusky; remaining underparts light brown, darker on flanks; wings and tail ruddy brown.

Similar species: The contrasting crown and prominent eye-ring and eyestripe make this species relatively easy to identify. Lineated Foliage-gleaner is markedly streaked on crown and hindneck, while the Buff-fronted Foliage-gleaner has cinnamon-buff forehead. Both lack the eye-ring and are larger.

Status and distribution: Fairly common in forest in highlands of western Chiriquí, from about 4000 feet up; only record from eastern Chiriquí is a specimen in AMNH taken on Cerro Flores (4000 feet) by L. Griscom.

Habits: Much like Lineated Foliage-gleaner, foraging actively at all levels among epiphytes and foliage and along branches. A frequent member of mixed bird flocks.

Range: Southern Mexico to western Panama; western Colombia and western Ecuador.

RUFOUS-RUMPED FOLIAGE-GLEANER

(*Philydor erythrocercus*) Pl.14

Description: 6¼. *Mostly plain chestnut above,* more grayish on crown, with rump and tail brighter rufous-chestnut; ear-coverts grayish with *conspicuous long narrow tawny stripe extending back from eye; wings dusky contrasting strongly with back;* throat buffy, remaining underparts tawny-buff.

Similar species: An unusually strongly patterned and attractive member of the family. The bold eyestripe and dark grayish wings are the points to watch for.

Status and distribution: Uncommon and local (becoming more numerous in eastern Panama, especially in eastern Darién) in lower growth of humid forest; recorded on Caribbean slope in Veraguas (where also spills over onto Pacific slope foothills) and Coclé, lowlands of Canal Zone (three records: a nineteenth-century specimen; 1 specimen taken at Pipeline Road on January 25, 1964 by E. Tyson and F. L. Chapman; and 4 seen farther out on Pipeline Road on January 5, 1975 by Ridgely and S. West), hill country of eastern Colon province (Cerro Santa Rita; Ridgely, J. Karr), and lowlands of eastern San Blas; on Pacific slope known from the Cerro Azul/Jefe area in eastern Panama province and lowlands and foothills of Darién.

Habits: A very active feeder, often probing in dead leaf clusters. Usually in pairs or small groups, sometimes with flocks of other species but also by itself.

Range: Western Panama to Bolivia and Amazonian Brazil.

BUFF-FRONTED FOLIAGE-GLEANER

(*Philydor rufus*) Pl.8

Description: 7½. Known only from western highlands. *Forehead cinnamon-buff,* crown and hindneck brownish gray; *superciliary and cheeks ochre;* back grayish brown; wings and tail rufous; *underparts uniform ochraceous.*

Similar species: The smaller Spectacled Foliage-gleaner has an ochre eye-ring and eyestripe and lacks the buff forehead. Rufous-rumped Foliage-gleaner has contrasting dark grayish or dusky wings.

Status and distribution: Rare in forest and forest borders in highlands of western Chiriquí and adjacent Bocas del Toro (4000–7000 feet); one old specimen labeled as from "Veragua" probably was taken in Chiriquí; not known from Darién, but possible. In recent years, most frequently noted at Finca Lerida above Boquete.

Habits: Not well known in Panama. Usually feeds well above the ground, foraging in typical foliage-gleaner fashion, mostly along horizontal branches; one or two will sometimes accompany a mixed flock.

Range: Costa Rica and western Panama; Colombia and Venezuela to Bolivia, Paraguay, northeastern Argentina, and southeastern Brazil.

RUDDY FOLIAGE-GLEANER
(*Automolus rubiginosus*)

Description: 7¾. Known definitely only from foothills of west and east. *Very dark, warm brown above;* rufous on rump, tail, and under tail-coverts; *throat and chest cinnamon-rufous;* lower underparts cinnamon-tawny. Immature less richly colored below. Darién birds (*saturatus*) are even darker, with black tail.

Similar species: A very dark brown and essentially unpatterned species. See Ruddy Woodcreeper.

Status and distribution: Rare; known only from forest in foothills and lower highlands (2000–4500 feet) of western Chiriquí and eastern Darién (Cana on Cerro Pirre, La Laguna on Cerro Tacarcuna). A bird believed this species was mist-netted and released on Cerro Jefe, eastern Panama province (3300 feet) on July 17, 1973 (D. Hill); specimen confirmation desirable.

Habits: Little known in Panama. Favors thick undergrowth, especially in humid ravines, and usually very difficult to see; the call is a distinctive whistled *ka-kweek* (Wetmore).

Range: Central Mexico south locally to northern Bolivia, extreme northern Brazil, and the Guianas.

BUFF-THROATED FOLIAGE-GLEANER
(*Automolus ochrolaemus*) Pl.14

Description: 7. Olive brown above with *narrow buff eye-ring and superciliary;* wings somewhat browner, rump and tail chestnut; *throat mostly white,* remaining underparts pale dull brown. Birds from Chiriquí and Pacific slope Veraguas (*exsertus*) have throat pale buff; birds from Bocas del Toro and Caribbean slope Veraguas (*hypophaeus*) have throat deeper buff, and remaining underparts darker olive brown.

Similar species: The only numerous foliage-gleaner-like bird in most of the lowlands; see Striped Foliage-gleaner. See also Plain-brown Woodcreeper, which is also unstreaked.

Status and distribution: Fairly common but inconspicuous in humid forest in lowlands and foothills (to about 3000 feet) on entire Caribbean slope; on Pacific slope known from Chiriquí lowlands, humid hill country of Veraguas, and from eastern Panama province (Cerro Azul/Jefe area, Bayano River) east through Darién. In Canal Zone most readily seen on Pipeline Road; also numerous in Cerro Azul/Jefe area.

Habits: Usually forages in dense vegetation and dead leaf clusters in lower and middle growth; despite its active and even acrobatic feeding habits, not often seen, mist-netting better revealing its true abundance. One or two often accompany a mixed flock of antwrens and other birds. Its call is a nasal unmusical descending trill, distinctive once learned; it calls especially in the early morning.

Range: Southeastern Mexico to northern Bolivia and Amazonian Brazil.

STREAK-BREASTED TREEHUNTER
(*Thripadectes rufobrunneus*) Pl.8

Description: 8¼. Found only in western highlands. Rather heavy bill. *Dark warm brown above,* duller on head; rump and tail chestnut; sides of head and throat rufous with dusky scaling, remaining underparts olive brown, *streaked with ochraceous on breast* and with rufescent on under tail-coverts.

Similar species: The largest Furnariid of the western highlands; *has no buff streaks on upperparts.* Lineated Foliage-gleaner is smaller and is streaked with buff on head, hindneck, and upper back. Buffy Tufted-cheek is arboreal and has conspicuous buffy tuft on sides of head.

Status and distribution: Uncommon to locally fairly common in undergrowth of forest in highlands of Chiriquí, adjacent Bocas del Toro, and Veraguas, ranging mostly 4000–8000 feet, in Veraguas recorded as low as 2500 feet.

Habits: An active bird that usually remains in dense undergrowth (though sometimes rising into low tree branches) and hence is not often seen clearly. Favors vicinity of mountain streams where there are high banks for nesting. Its typical call is a harsh sharp *tseeyk.*

Range: Costa Rica and western Panama.

Note: Wetmore calls it Streak-breasted Leaf-gleaner.

STREAKED XENOPS
(*Xenops rutilans*)

Description: 4½. Found only in highlands, replacing the more common lowland Plain Xenops. Resembles that species but has *cap, hindneck, and upper back streaked with buff;* throat white, remaining underparts brown *streaked with white, most broadly on breast.*

Similar species: See Plain Xenops (*unstreaked*); the two only rarely overlap. Spotted Barbtail is a little larger, lacks cheek stripe, and is spotted (not streaked) below.

Status and distribution: Rare in forest in highlands of western Chiriquí and eastern Darién (Cerro Pirre), mostly 4000–6000 feet.

Habits: Similar to Plain Xenops, usually found singly or in pairs, often accompanying mixed flocks.

Range: Costa Rica to northern Argentina and southeastern Brazil.

PLAIN XENOPS
(*Xenops minutus*) Pl.14

Description: 4½. *Bill short and wedge-shaped,* the lower mandible conspicuously upturned. Brown above with indistinct whitish eyestripe and *prominent silvery crescentic stripe on cheeks;* rump, tail, and wing-band (visible in flight) rufous; throat whitish, remaining underparts dull brown.

Similar species: Wedge-billed Woodcreeper is larger with buff throat and buff spots on breast, lacks silvery cheek stripe, and creeps up trees. See also Streaked Xenops.

Status and distribution: Common in forest and second-growth woodland in lowlands on both slopes, ranging regularly in smaller numbers well up into the foothills to over 3000 feet, and recorded once at 6200 feet in western Chiriquí; not recorded from dry Pacific lowlands on eastern side of Azuero Peninsula and southern Coclé.

Habits: Gleans over small branches and twigs, usually at middle and upper heights, often hanging upside-down like a chickadee. Almost always accompanies mixed feeding flocks of antwrens, greenlets, etc.

Range: Southeastern Mexico to northern Bolivia, Paraguay, northeastern Argentina, and southeastern Brazil.

STREAKED XENOPS

GRAY-THROATED LEAFTOSSER (LEAFSCRAPER)
(*Sclerurus albigularis*) Pl.8

Description: 6¼. Known only from western Chiriquí highlands. Dark rich brown above with *rufous rump* and wing edging; *throat pale gray,* chest tawny-chestnut, lower underparts dull dark brown.

Similar species: Tawny-throated Leaftosser is very similar but has tawny (not gray) throat. Scaly-throated Leaftosser has white throat with feathers edged black giving scaly appearance and lacks the rufous rump.

Status and distribution: Rare in humid forest in lower highlands of western Chiriquí, recorded mostly 4000–6000 feet.

Habits: See Tawny-throated Leaftosser.

Range: Costa Rica and western Panama; Colombia and northern Venezuela to northern Bolivia.

TAWNY-THROATED LEAFTOSSER (LEAFSCRAPER)
(*Sclerurus mexicanus*) Pl.14

Description: 6. Dark rich brown above with rufous rump; *throat and chest tawny-rufous,* lower underparts dark brown.

Similar species: Scaly-throated Leaftosser has white throat with feathers edged black giving scaly appearance, and lacks rufous rump; it too has a tawny chest. Often confused with the much more numerous Song Wren; the wren is best known by the pale blue spot behind its eye, barred wings and tail, and almost constant churring notes. See also Gray-throated Leaftosser.

Status and distribution: Generally rare and local in humid forest in lowlands and foothills on entire Caribbean slope; on Pacific slope known from foothills and lower highlands (2400–5000 feet) of Chiriquí, Veraguas, eastern Panama province, and Darién. In Canal Zone apparently most numerous at Achiote Road.

Habits: Leaftossers are furtive, mostly terrestrial, forest birds, not often seen but frequently captured in mist-nets. They feed on the ground, usually in moist areas, flicking leaves aside with their bills and probing the soil. When disturbed, they usually fly up with a loud and harsh squeak and perch a short distance away on a low and open branch; there they remain motionless for several minutes before flying off, again with a squeak. The nest is in holes burrowed in banks.

Range: Southern Mexico to northern Bolivia and central Brazil.

SCALY-THROATED LEAFTOSSER (LEAFSCRAPER)

(*Sclerurus guatemalensis*) Pl.14

Description: 6. Dark rich brown above (*no rufous rump*); *throat white with feathers outlined in black giving scaly effect;* chest tawny, lower underparts dark brown.

Similar species: Both other Panama leaftossers have rufous rumps.

Status and distribution: Uncommon to locally fairly common in humid forest in lowlands and (in smaller numbers) foothills on entire Caribbean slope; on Pacific slope known from lowlands of western Chiriquí, western side of Azuero Peninsula (Cerro Hoya, 2600 feet), Cerro Campana, and from Canal Zone east through Darién. Generally the most numerous Panamanian leaftosser. In Canal Zone most easily found on Pipeline Road, but there as elsewhere inconspicuous and recorded largely from mist-net captures.

Habits: See Tawny-throated Leaftosser.

Range: Southeastern Mexico to northern Colombia.

SHARP-TAILED STREAMCREEPER

(*Lochmias nematura*) Pl.32

Description: 6. Known only from eastern Darién highlands. Bill long and narrow, slightly decurved; rather short tail. Uniform dark warm brown, *spotted conspicuously with white on sides of head and entire underparts.*

Similar species: The habitat and bold white spotting below should make this species easy to recognize. Rather like a leaftosser in shape and posture.

Status and distribution: Apparently rare; recorded from undergrowth bordering forested streams in highlands of eastern Darién (Cerro Pirre, Cerro Malí, Cerro Quía).

Habits: Largely terrestrial and usually difficult to see in the dense undergrowth. Hops along the edges of streams.

Range: Eastern Panama and locally in Colombia and South America east of the Andes south to Bolivia, Paraguay, northeastern Argentina, and Uruguay.

Note: Wetmore calls it Sharp-tailed Creeper.

ANTBIRDS: Formicariidae (38)

The antbirds are a large and diverse family of exclusively neotropical birds, well represented in Panama, where there are many species in lowland forests and woodlands, fewer at higher elevations. The term "antbird" is something of a misnomer as very few species are known to feed on ants; the name is derived from the habit of several species of following swarms of army ants (especially *Eciton burchelli*) and feeding on the insects and other arthropods disturbed by them. A majority of antbirds, however, pay scant attention to the swarms, feeding at various strata from the ground to the canopy. Antbirds are not brightly colored, but many are attractively or contrastingly patterned in black, gray, white, and various shades of brown. The sexes differ in most species, females frequently tending to be more rufescent than males. A number have an area of bare blue skin around the eyes, the function of which is unknown. Antshrikes resemble the true shrikes (Laniidae) only in their heavy hooked bills. Antvireos resemble the true vireos in their heavy-headed dull-colored appearance and their relatively lethargic behavior. Antwrens are small spritely birds that roam about forest and woodland usually in mixed flocks; they behave more like wood-warblers than wrens. Antthrushes are plump, terrestrial forest birds that unlike the thrushes usually carry their tails cocked up; they walk rather than hop. Antpittas are remarkably like the Old World pittas (Pittidae) in shape though not with the latter's gorgeous coloration; they are plump, almost "tail-less," very long-legged, terrestrial or almost terrestrial forest birds. Many antbirds (in the broad sense) are shy and difficult to see, but most have distinctive calls that frequently are the best indication of the species' presence. All members of the family are apparently almost exclusively insectivorous. Breeding habits for many species are unknown, but most of those known construct an open cup nest, rather vireo-like, while some nest in small tree cavities or holes in stubs (e.g. Black-faced Antthrush, Bicolored Antbird).

FASCIATED ANTSHRIKE
(*Cymbilaimus lineatus*) Pl.14

Description: 6½–6¾. Heavy hooked bill. *Iris red.* Male *black narrowly barred with white* except on crown. Female dark brown above *narrowly barred with buff,* with chestnut crown; buff below *narrowly barred with brown.*

Similar species: The more familiar Barred Antshrike has male *broadly* barred black and white, female very different and bright rufous above and buffy below with no barring; both have yellow (not red) eyes. Female has pattern somewhat reminiscent of the considerably larger Barred Puffbird.

Status and distribution: Uncommon to fairly common in dense lower growth of forest borders and second-growth woodland in lowlands and lower foothills on entire Caribbean slope; on Pacific slope recorded in more humid lowlands and foothills from Chiriquí to Coclé (but reported recently only from Veraguas foothills above Santa Fé; Ridgely and G. Stiles), and from Canal Zone east through Darién. No reports from Azuero Peninsula. Widespread but never especially numerous in wooded areas on both slopes of Canal Zone.

Habits: Especially partial to thickets not far from water. Usually in pairs. Not very active and generally rather inconspicuous unless calling, and even then often not easy to see. The call is a repetition of one note, rather musical, steady in pace and pitch, *cü, cü, cü, cü, cu . . . .*

Range: Southeastern Honduras to northern Bolivia and Amazonian Brazil.

GREAT ANTSHRIKE
(*Taraba major*) Pl.14

Description: 7½–8. Heavy, hooked bill. *Red iris.* Sometimes shows a loose crest. Male *black above* with white edging on wing-coverts forming two white bars; *white below,* tinged gray on flanks and under tail-coverts. Female *rufous brown above; white below,* tinged buff on flanks and under tail-coverts.

Similar species: Large size, prominent red eye, and two-toned color pattern are diagnostic. Bicolored Antbird is smaller, with dark eye and black on face, and is a bird of forest interior (not clearings or borders).

Status and distribution: Fairly common in dense undergrowth and thickets of clearings and forest and woodland borders in more humid lowlands on both slopes, less numerous and more local on Pacific slope west of Canal Zone and absent from drier areas and Azuero Peninsula; ranges up in smaller numbers into lower foothills. Seems especially numerous at Río Piedras.

Habits: Usually in pairs and difficult to see as it remains concealed in dense tangles even when calling. The call is a series of fairly loud hoots, usually increasing in tempo, sometimes ending in a snorting or whining nasal *nyaaha;* the total effect is quite trogon-like except for the contrasting ending.

Range: Southeastern Mexico to northern Argentina and Uruguay.

BARRED ANTSHRIKE
(*Thamnophilus doliatus*) Pl.14

Description: 6–6¼. Fairly thick, hooked bill. *Iris yellow or white.* Loose crest elevated especially when excited. Male *black broadly barred with white* throughout except for wholly black crown (white bases of feathers sometimes showing). Female very different, *bright rufous above,* hindneck and sides of head deep buff streaked with black; *buffy below.* Immature male barred dark brown and buff.

Similar species: Male Fasciated Antshrike is *narrowly* barred with white and has a red (not yellow) eye.

Status and distribution: Common in thickets and dense undergrowth in savanna areas, shrubby clearings, gardens, and lighter woodland in lowlands on Pacific slope from Chiriquí to eastern Panama province (Bayano River); not reported from Darién; on Caribbean slope known only from northern Coclé (El Uracillo) east to eastern Colon province (Río Guanche); ranges in reduced numbers up into lower foothills; common also on Coiba Island and most of larger Pearl Islands (not San José).

Habits: Usually in pairs; often the bright female is easier to see than the barred male. Heard much more often than seen, the call being a series of rapidly accelerating notes giving a whinnying effect, but ending with a lengthened emphasized nasal note on a rising inflection, *heh-heh-heh-heh-heh-heh-heh-heh-weng;* also has a growling *ahrrrr* and a repeated *enk.*

Range: Eastern Mexico to Bolivia, northern Argentina, and southern Brazil.

BLACK ANTSHRIKE
(*Thamnophilus nigriceps*) Pl.32

Description: 5¾. Known only from eastern Panama. Fairly thick hooked bill. Male *entirely black* with white under wing-coverts. Female has *black head streaked with buffy whitish; back, wings, and tail chestnut;* slaty below, *broadly streaked with buffy whitish;* thighs and under tail-coverts cinnamon.

Similar species: Male Slaty Antshrike is slaty (not black), has white spotting and edging on wings, and tail tipped white. Male Immaculate Antbird has bare pale blue to whitish orbital skin. Male Jet Antbird has much white on wings and tail; female is slaty (not chestnut) above and also has white on wings and tail.

Status and distribution: Uncommon in shrubby undergrowth of clearings and lighter woodland in lowlands of eastern Panama province (Cañita and Majé on Bayano River) and Darién.

Habits: Favors somewhat taller growth than Barred Antshrike in areas where the two overlap. Apparently replaces that species in Darién.

Range: Eastern Panama and northern Colombia.

BLACK-HOODED ANTSHRIKE
(*Thamnophilus bridgesi*) Pl.14

Description: 6–6¼. Found only in Pacific western Panama. Fairly thick, hooked bill. Male *mostly black,* slaty on lower underparts; *wing-coverts lightly spotted with white.* Female similar to male but *head, throat, and breast narrowly streaked with white;* back brown; lower underparts tinged with olive.

Similar species: Slaty Antshrike is not found in this species' range. The smaller Jet Antbird has male with much more white on wing and also on tail, female with white streaking only on underparts (not on head) and brown (not slaty black) back.

Status and distribution: Fairly common in undergrowth of forest and second-growth and gallery woodland in lowlands on Pacific slope in Chiriquí, Veraguas, and both sides of Azuero Peninsula; ranges up in smaller numbers into foothills to about 3700 feet.

Habits: Generally replacing the Slaty Antshrike in its range, this species is also usually found in pairs. Its typical hooting call is similar but with a less vigorous ending; also gives a *cooa, cooa, cooa.*

Range: Costa Rica and Pacific western Panama.

Note: Wetmore calls it Bridges' Antshrike.

SLATY ANTSHRIKE
(*Thamnophilus punctatus*) Pl.14

Description: 5¾–6. Fairly thick, hooked bill. Male *slaty gray above with black crown,* wings, and tail; *much white spotting and edging on wings* and tail tipped white; slaty gray below. Female *olive brown above with dull chestnut crown; wings with much buff spotting and edging* and tail tipped buff; dull brownish olive below.

Similar species: Male Dusky Antbird is smaller and more uniform slaty gray, and has more slender bill and less white on wing; female Dusky has uniform tawny underparts. In eastern Panama see also Black Antshrike.

Status and distribution: Very common in lower growth of forest and second-growth woodland in lowlands and lower foothills on entire Caribbean slope; on Pacific slope found from Cerro Campana and Canal Zone east through Darién. Wetmore believes an old record from Santiago, Veraguas (on Pacific slope), is in error.

Habits: Normally occurring in relatively open undergrowth within forest and often bold and inquisitive, this species is much easier to observe than other Panama antshrikes. Usually in pairs, often on the periphery of a mixed foraging flock of antwrens, etc. Its call is one of the characteristic sounds of the Panamanian forest, an accelerating roll, the last note accented and with an upward inflection; rather like Barred Antshrike's call but more nasal.

Range: Guatemala and Belize to Bolivia and southern Brazil.

SPECKLED (SPECKLE-BREASTED) ANTSHRIKE
(*Xenornis setifrons*) Pl.32

Description: 6¼–6½. Known only from eastern Panama. Bill heavy and hooked. Male has *crown and upperparts dark brown with short tawny streaks; wings with two* *prominent deep buff wing-bars;* tail dark gray, outer feathers tipped whitish; *sides of head and entire underparts dark slaty gray.* Female *like male above;* upper throat whitish edged with buff, remaining underparts brown, deepest on belly, mottled with buff on breast.

Similar species: The dark brown and gray male is unlike any other Panama antbird. Female resembles female Slaty Antshrike except for streaking on upperparts.

Status and distribution: Apparently rare; recorded in humid forest of eastern San Blas (Armila) and foothills of eastern Darién (Tacarcuna ridge).

Habits: Little known. Favors heavy undergrowth in forest where usually difficult to see; usually in pairs (Wetmore).

Range: Eastern Panama and northwestern Colombia.

Note: Wetmore calls it Spiny-faced Antshrike.

RUSSET ANTSHRIKE

(*Thamnistes anabatinus*) Pl.14

Description 5½. *Bill stout and hooked. Brown above,* more rufous on crown and particularly on wings and tail, with *buffy eyestripe;* concealed patch of orange-buff on back (absent in female); *yellowish buffy-brown below,* tinged grayish on sides.

Similar species: A rather confusing bird. Note the stout bill and buffy superciliary and underparts. Female Slaty Antshrike is more olive brown, with buff spots on wings. Somewhat resembles several Furnariids (e.g., Buff-throated Foliage-gleaner). Thrushlike Manakin is more uniform and darker brown, lacks the eyestripe, and has much less heavy bill. See also Cinnamon and female Cinereous and One-colored Becards (none of which has such a heavy, hooked bill).

Status and distribution: Uncommon to locally fairly common in forest in foothills on entire Caribbean slope (recorded mostly 1000–3000 feet), in lowlands in Canal Zone (especially on Pipeline Road) and San Blas; on Pacific slope found in Chiriquí foothills (where rare; also one old specimen from Bugaba in lowlands), hill country of Veraguas, Cerro Campana, and from eastern Panama province (Cerro Azul/Jefe area) east through Darién.

Habits: Often forages considerably higher than other antshrikes, frequently in association with a mixed flock of insectivorous birds. Quite active, gleaning in the foliage. The usual call is a *wee-tsip,* often repeated.

Range: Southeastern Mexico to western Venezuela and Bolivia.

PLAIN ANTVIREO

(*Dysithamnus mentalis*) Pl.15

Description: 4¼–4½. Bill heavy. Male *mostly dark olive gray,* darkest on crown and cheeks; two narrow white wing-bars; somewhat paler olive gray below (palest on throat), fading to *buffy yellowish on belly.* Female more olive above with *distinct russet crown* and a whitish eye-ring; two narrow buff wing-bars; throat whitish, breast and sides grayish olive, lower belly yellowish.

Similar species: Note thick-set, heavy-headed appearance with short tail and stout slightly hooked bill; reminiscent of a manakin except for the bill. Antwrens are smaller and slighter with narrower bills and more active behavior. Spot-crowned Antvireo of lowland forests is similar but both sexes have spots on crown. See also Tawny-crowned Greenlet (which lacks wing-bars).

Status and distribution: Uncommon to fairly common in lower growth of humid forest in foothills and lower highlands on both slopes, mostly 2000–5000 feet, occasionally somewhat lower or higher. In central Panama known only from Cerro Campana and the Cerro Azul/Jefe area and uncommon at both localities.

Habits: Usually in pairs, foraging independently of mixed flocks, normally within a few meters of the ground. Their deliberate behavior is somewhat reminiscent of the larger vireos. Has an accelerating call similar in pattern to those of the *Thamnophilus* antshrikes but higher; also has a nasal but rather soft *nyoot, nyoot* and a *choot-nyoo.*

Range: Southeastern Mexico to northern Bolivia, Paraguay, northeastern Argentina, and southern Brazil.

SPOT-CROWNED ANTVIREO

(*Dysithamnus puncticeps*) Pl.15

Description: 4¼–4½. Bill heavy. Rather like Plain Antvireo. Male *mostly slaty olive,* the *crown black with small white spots;* two narrow white wing-bars; somewhat paler gray below, breast narrowly streaked with dusky, fading to buffy on belly. Female brownish above with *bright tawny crown streaked and spotted with black;* two narrow buff wing-bars; buffy below, with narrow black streaks on throat and breast.

Similar species: Plain Antvireo lacks crown

spots and occurs in foothills and highlands (not mostly lowlands). Antwrens, with which this species often occurs, are smaller and more active. See also Streak-crowned Antvireo (below).

Status and distribution: Uncommon to locally fairly common in lower growth of humid forest in lowlands and lower foothills on entire Caribbean slope (to about 2000 feet); on Pacific slope found only in Darién (especially in foothills to about 2500 feet). In Canal Zone most numerous well out on Pipeline Road.

Habits: Rather sluggish inconspicuous forest birds, usually seen foraging at lower levels. A pair or two often joins a mixed flock of antwrens.

Range: Southeastern Costa Rica to western Ecuador.

Note: Streak-crowned Antvireo (*D. striaticeps*), often incorrectly attributed to Panama (the specimen from Río Sixaola mentioned by Carriker was actually *D. puncticeps*), might occur in lowlands and foothills of western Bocas del Toro. It is very similar to Spot-crowned but male lacks white crown spots (has faint gray streaks), has throat and chest broadly streaked with slaty gray, and is more olive above; female is paler below with less streaking, whitish throat and lower belly.

PYGMY ANTWREN
(*Myrmotherula brachyura*) Pl.15

Description: 2¾. *Tiny and virtually tail-less.* Male *black above, streaked with white,* rump pale gray; two white wing-bars; black line through eye and another on cheeks; throat white, *cheeks and remaining underparts pale lemon yellow.* Female very similar but crown sometimes streaked with buff, not white.

Similar species: Combination of streaked upperparts and pale yellow underparts make identification of this minute but very attractive bird easy. Only possible confusion is with considerably larger male Streaked Antwren (which is streaked below); see also the equally small, Black-headed Tody-Flycatcher (unstreaked above).

Status and distribution: Apparently rare or local; on Caribbean slope known only from Canal Zone and western San Blas (Mandinga), on Pacific slope from eastern Panama province (Bayano River valley at and above Majé, where apparently fairly common; Ridgely, J. Gwynne *et al.*) and Darién. Recorded in small numbers on Achiote Road and Pipeline Road (especially around Limbo Hunt Club).

Habits: Favors forest borders and small clearings rather than forest interior. Sometimes joins mixed flocks of other antwrens but also regularly forages alone or in pairs at middle levels. The song is a repetition of a single note, which increases in rapidity and ends in a trill, *tree-tree-tree-tree-ee-ee-ee* (Wetmore).

Range: Central Panama to northern Bolivia and Amazonian Brazil.

Note: Birds from Panama and western Colombia (*ignota*) may represent a distinct species, or possibly are allied to *M. obscura* (Short-billed Antwren) of western Amazonia.

STREAKED ANTWREN
(*Myrmotherula surinamensis*) Pl.15

Description: 3½. Male *black above streaked with white;* two white wing-bars; *white below streaked with black.* Female with *head bright orange-rufous* lightly streaked with black; remaining upperparts black streaked white, two white wing-bars; *pale orange-buffy below,* unstreaked.

Similar species: Color pattern of male is reminiscent of Black-and-white Warbler though it is very different in shape and behavior. The pretty female should be easily recognized. Pygmy Antwren is smaller, with shorter tail and pale yellow underparts.

Status and distribution: Locally fairly common in shrubby clearings and woodland and forest borders in lowlands on entire Caribbean slope; on Pacific slope in lowlands from eastern Panama province (La Jagua) east through Darién. In central Panama, most easily seen on Achiote Road; also numerous at Río Piedras, eastern Colon province.

Habits: Not a forest bird, rarely if ever associating with other antwrens. Usually found in pairs, foraging in tangled vines and foliage at low and middle levels, often near water. The call is a fast, accelerating chipper, rising slightly as it goes along, *chee-chee-chee-chee-chee-chee;* also has a nasal *nyee deea.*

Range: Western Panama to eastern Peru and Amazonian Brazil.

CHECKER-THROATED (FULVOUS-BELLIED) ANTWREN
(*Myrmotherula fulviventris*) Pl.15

Description: 4. *Iris pale in both sexes.* Male olive brown above with blackish wing-coverts and two buffy wing-bars; *white* *throat, feathers edged with black, giving checkered appearance;* remaining underparts brownish buffy. Female similar but lacks checkered throat; *uniform plain brownish buffy below.*

Similar species: Male easily recognized by checkered throat. Female closely resembles female White-flanked Antwren, but has pale (not dark) eye (this usually not too prominent in the field) and uniform buffy underparts (no whitish throat and flank tufts). Female Slaty Antwren is more tawny below; it is more of a foothill bird (not lowlands), though there is some overlap.

Status and distribution: Common in lower growth of forest and second-growth woodland in lowlands and in smaller numbers in lower foothills on entire Caribbean slope; on Pacific slope in Veraguas foothills (above Santa Fé; Ridgely and G. Stiles) and from western Panama province (Cerro Campana, Chorrera) east through Darién. In Canal Zone and vicinity more numerous on Caribbean side.

Habits: Usually in small groups, frequently associating with mixed foraging flocks, and very often with White-flanked Antwrens, though usually feeding rather lower than that species. A very active feeder, often probing into dead leaf clusters. The song is a series of high-pitched whistles gradually going up-scale, *pe-peh-pey-pü-pih-pee-pyee;* its calls are variable, usually single-noted and harsh and squeaky.

Range: Honduras to western Ecuador.

Note: Wetmore calls it Fulvous Ant-wren.

WHITE-FLANKED ANTWREN
(*Myrmotherula axillaris*) Pl.15

Description: 3½. Iris dark. Male mostly *black;* wing-coverts spotted lightly with white, tail (usually) tipped white; *long silky white tuft on flanks* (sometimes partly concealed under wings); under wing-coverts also white. Female grayish brown to grayish olive above with some buff spots on wing-coverts; *throat whitish,* remaining underparts buffy, with buffy whitish flanks.

Similar species: Female Checker-throated Antwren has pale (not dark) eye and is deeper buff below with no white on throat or flanks. Female Slaty Antwren is tawny below and lacks spots on wings.

Status and distribution: Very common in lower and middle growth of forest and second-growth woodland in lowlands on entire Caribbean slope; on Pacific slope found from western Panama province (Cerro Campana) and Canal Zone east through Darién; ranges in reduced numbers into lower foothills. On Pacific side of Canal Zone and vicinity even less numerous and more local than Checker-throated Antwren.

Habits: Almost invariably found in a mixed foraging flock, and often the numerically dominant species in such flocks. Tends to forage higher than the Checker-throat and even more active. The most frequent call is a high piping on a descending scale, *peea, püa, peha;* also has others, such as *pip-pip,* and a *weechip.*

Range: Honduras to northern Bolivia and southeastern Brazil.

Note: Wetmore calls it Black Ant-wren.

SLATY ANTWREN
(*Myrmotherula schisticolor*) Pl.15

Description: 3¾. Male *slaty with black throat and chest;* wing-coverts and tail tipped white. Female olive brown above; *sides of head and throat buff, remaining underparts dull tawny.*

Similar species: In most areas where it occurs, the only antwren present. Male White-flank is black (not slaty) with white tuft on flanks (always at least partially visible). Female Checker-throats and White-flanks have buff spots on wings (lacking in Slaty) and buff (not tawny) underparts.

Status and distribution: Uncommon to fairly common in undergrowth of forest and forest borders in foothills and lower highlands on Pacific slope (mostly 2000–5500 feet), spilling over onto Caribbean slope in Veraguas (Río Calovévora); in western Chiriquí and on western side of Azuero Peninsula also reported near sea level. In central Panama, found readily only on Cerro Campana; not recorded from Canal Zone and rare in the Cerro Azul/Jefe area.

Habits: Usually in pairs, generally not joining in mixed flocks. Forages lower than other Panama antwrens. The calls are a nasal *nyeeah* scold, and a *pseeyt.*

Range: Southern Mexico to northern Venezuela and southern Peru.

RUFOUS-WINGED ANTWREN
(*Herpsilochmus rufimarginatus*) Pl.32

Description: 4¼. Known only from eastern Panama. Male bluish gray above with *black crown and white superciliary; black wings margined with rufous* and with two white wing-bars; black tail tipped white; throat white, *remaining underparts pale yellow.* Female similar but with rufous cap, back more brownish, chest tinged buff.

Similar species: Only other Panamanian antwren with mostly yellow underparts is the tiny, dissimilar Pygmy Antwren. Rufous-rumped Antwren is mostly olive above with rufous lower back, has no rufous in wings, and has gray throat and breast. See also Double-banded Graytail.

Status and distribution: Apparently rare or local; recorded from forest and second-growth woodland in lowlands of eastern Panama province (Bayano River valley at and above Majé, where seems fairly common; J. Gwynne, Ridgely, Eisenmann *et al.*) and lowlands and foothills of Darién (to about 3000 feet).

Habits: Usually found in pairs, foraging in middle levels of trees, most often independently of mixed flocks. The most frequent call is a nasal *ahrr,* sometimes repeated.

Range: Eastern Panama to northern Bolivia, Paraguay, northeastern Argentina, and southern Brazil.

DOT-WINGED ANTWREN

(*Microrhopias quixensis*) Pl.15

Description: 4½. Tail proportionately longer than in *Myrmotherula* antwrens, *often held somewhat cocked and fanned.* Male *glossy black,* with white spots and *broad white bar on wing* and *broad white tipping on tail;* usually concealed white dorsal patch revealed when excited. Female slaty or black above, *rich rufous below,* with wings and tail and white dorsal patch as in male.

Similar species: Female easily recognized. Male White-flanked Antwren is smaller, with white tuft on flanks and less white on wings and tail. Male Jet Antbird is larger with heavier build and lacks white spots on wing (has only two, broad white bars).

Status and distribution: Common in forest and second-growth woodland in lowlands on entire Caribbean slope; on Pacific slope known from lowlands of western Chiriquí and western Veraguas (where now scarce due to forest destruction) and from Canal Zone area east through eastern Panama province and Darién; ranges in small numbers into lower foothills. In Canal Zone considerably more numerous on Caribbean side.

Habits: Very active and spritely, gleaning among foliage at lower and middle levels. Though often found in mixed flocks of *Myrmotherula* antwrens and other birds, also regularly forages in pairs and small groups of exclusively its own species. Its calls are similar to those of other antwrens, though some are more musical.

Range: Southeastern Mexico to Bolivia and Amazonian Brazil.

WHITE-FRINGED (BLACK-BREASTED) ANTWREN

(*Formicivora grisea*)

Description: 4½. *Found only on Pearl Islands.* Male dull slaty above, wings with white spots and one white band; black below with *long white stripe extending from forehead over eye, down side of head and neck and along sides, widening on flanks.* Female grayish brown above with whitish eyebrow and two white wing-bars; buffy below, deeper on chest, whiter on throat.

Similar species: One of just three antbirds on the Pearl Islands (others being Barred Antshrike and Jet Antbird); there should be no problem in recognition. Recalls Dot-winged Antwren in shape and behavior.

Status and distribution: Fairly common in lower growth of woodland and borders on larger Pearl Islands; not found on mainland.

Habits: Usually found singly or in pairs, feeding in bushes and low branches of trees, often fanning their tails from side to side, and drooping their wings. Has fast semi-whistled calls, also a musical *chirp.*

Range: Pearl Islands; Colombia to the Guianas and Amazonian and southeastern Brazil.

WHITE-FRINGED ANTWREN
(male above, female below)

RUFOUS-RUMPED ANTWREN
(*Terenura callinota*) Pl.15

Description: 4½. Very rare. Male has black crown, narrow whitish superciliary, and pale grayish sides of head; otherwise olive green above with *rufous lower back and rump;* wings black with *yellow on shoulder* and two white wing-bars; throat and chest pale gray, lower underparts greenish yellow, becoming brighter yellow on lower belly. Female similar but duller with crown grayish brown.

Similar species: Antvireos lack rufous lower back and rump and yellow on bend of wing; their bills are shorter and stouter. Rufous-winged Antwren has prominent rufous in wing, is mostly pale yellow below, has conspicuous white tail tips.

Status and distribution: Apparently very rare in forest of foothills and lower highlands; known from only four specimens, one from "Chiriquí" (no definite locality), one from Veraguas (Calobre), and two from eastern Darién (Cerro Malí, Cerro de Nique).

Habits: Little known. Reported to occur in lower tree growth of humid forest, foraging among leaves at tips of branches (*fide* Wetmore).

Range: Western Panama to northwestern Venezuela and central Peru; Guyana.

Note: Wetmore calls it Rufous-backed Antwren.

DUSKY ANTBIRD
(*Cercomacra tyrannina*) Pl.15

Description 5½. Male *uniform slaty gray* (*blackish slate* in birds from western Panama east to northern Veraguas, *crepera*); wing-coverts and tail tipped white; usually concealed white dorsal patch. Female olive above with some buffy tipping on wing-coverts; *sides of head and underparts tawny,* tinged olive on flanks.

Similar species: Male most likely to be confused with male Slaty Antshrike, which is larger with heavier bill, black crown, and more white spotting on wings. Male Jet Antbird is uniform glossy black (in area of overlap, Dusky is slaty gray). Female Slaty Antshrike has brownish olive (not tawny) underparts; female Bare-crowned Antbird has brighter orange-rufous underparts and bare blue orbital area.

Status and distribution: Common in thickets and undergrowth of shrubby clearings, second-growth woodland, and forest borders in lowlands and lower foothills on both slopes; absent from drier Pacific slope lowlands.

Habits: Almost always in pairs, usually rather difficult to see clearly. The call is distinctive and frequently heard, a series of whistled notes, the first two given slowly, the remaining three to five fast and rhythmic, usually on a rising scale, *pü, pü, pí-pipi.* Also has a *dididit,* and a *wheeerrr.*

Range: Southeastern Mexico to western Ecuador and northern and eastern Brazil.

Note: Wetmore calls it Tyrannine Antbird.

JET ANTBIRD
(*Cercomacra nigricans*) Pl.15

Description: 5½. Male *glossy black* with *two broad white wing-bars* and broad white tip to tail; usually concealed white dorsal patch. Female slaty above with wings and tail as in male; *throat and chest slaty prominently streaked with white,* remaining underparts slaty gray (in some females white streaks extend to belly).

Similar species: Male Dusky Antbird in central and eastern Panama is slaty gray and has very little white on wing. Male Dot-winged Antwren is smaller and has prominent white spots on wings (as well as bars) and is more active. Male Immaculate Antbird has bare blue orbital skin and white only on shoulder. Female's white-streaked throat and chest distinguishes her from other Panama antbirds except female Black Antshrike (which is chestnut above) and female Black-hooded Antshrike (which is brown above).

Status and distribution: Uncommon and rather local in thickets and undergrowth in shrubby clearings and woodland borders in lowlands on Pacific slope from Veraguas east through Darién; on Caribbean slope recorded locally from western Colon province (Río Indio) east to western San Blas (Mandinga); more numerous on some of larger Pearl Islands (Rey, Cañas, Viveros).

Habits: Usually in pairs, often along streams or in damp areas. Like so many other antbirds, often difficult to see, though the bird's presence is frequently revealed by its distinctive call, a repeated *tch-ker, tch-ker, tch-ker, tch-ker.*

Range: Western Panama to southern Peru and extreme northern Brazil.

BARE-CROWNED ANTBIRD
(*Gymnocichla nudiceps*) Pl.15

Description: 6. Male *black* with *bare, bright blue crown and orbital area;* white spotting on wing-coverts and white tip on tail. Female has *only orbital area bright blue* (crown is feathered); olive brown above with some buff spotting on wing-coverts; *bright rufous below.*

Similar species: Male Immaculate Antbird lacks blue crown; female Immaculate is brown (not rufous) below. Female Chestnut-backed Antbird is also brown below.

Status and distribution: Uncommon in undergrowth of second-growth woodland and forest borders in lowlands on entire Caribbean slope; on Pacific slope found locally in lowlands and lower foothills in Chiriquí, Veraguas, eastern Panama province (Bayano River), and Darién. In central Panama scarce and local, reported mostly from areas near Caribbean coast, especially along Achiote and Escobal Roads.

Habits: A confirmed army ant follower, in central Panama at least rarely noted away from them. Not a true forest bird.

Range: Guatemala and Belize to northern Colombia.

WHITE-BELLIED ANTBIRD

(*Myrmeciza longipes*) Pl.16

Description: 5¾. Male *bright chestnut above* with gray cap; *sides of head, throat, and chest black; lower underparts white,* sides washed with pale tawny. Female similar but duller, with browner cap and dusky sides of head; throat and chest buffy.

Similar species: Chestnut-backed Antbird has bare blue orbital skin and all dark underparts (no white or whitish belly). Bicolored Antbird has only cheeks black (underparts mostly white) and likewise has blue orbital area.

Status and distribution: Common in undergrowth of second-growth and gallery woodland, dry woodland, and borders in lowlands and (in smaller numbers) in lower foothills on Pacific slope from southern Coclé (El Valle) and western Panama province (base of Cerro Campana) east to Darién (specimens in AMNH from Capetí, also a recent one in AMNH taken at Santa Fé on June 20, 1966 by E. S. Morton); old specimens labeled "Veragua" require modern confirmation; on Caribbean slope found locally in middle Chagres River valley. Numerous in virtually any woodland on Pacific slope of Canal Zone, though usually hard to see.

Habits: Feeds almost entirely on or very near the ground. The call is loud and distinctive, often given as the bird perches on a fallen log, a fast accelerating crescendo, tailing off markedly at the end, typically, *cheer, cheer, cheer-cheer-cheercheercheecheer, chew, chew, chew.*

Range: Central Panama to northern Colombia, Venezuela, Guyana, and northeastern Brazil.

CHESTNUT-BACKED ANTBIRD

(*Myrmeciza exsul*) Pl.16

Description: 5½. Male has *head, neck, and underparts slaty black; back, wings, and tail chestnut;* bare orbital skin pale blue; flanks and (sometimes) lower belly dull brown. Female like male above but duller; sides of head and throat slaty black, remaining underparts brown. Birds from eastern Darién (*cassini*) have conspicuous white spots on wing-coverts and are duller chestnut above.

Similar species: Rare Dull-mantled Antbird lacks blue orbital skin, has red eye (not brown), and has upper back olive brown. See also White-bellied Antbird.

Status and distribution: Common in undergrowth of forest and second-growth woodland in lowlands and lower foothills on entire Caribbean slope; on Pacific slope found from Chiriquí to western side of Azuero Peninsula and from Canal Zone area (where uncommon and local) east through Darién. Widespread and numerous in forest and woodland on Caribbean side of Canal Zone.

Habits: Typically seen alone or in pairs low in forest undergrowth, but usually not on ground itself, often perching sideways on small vertical saplings. Does not regularly follow army ant swarms, but is sometimes attracted to them. The call is a series of two or three emphatic whistles, easily imitated, *peh, peh, peeéa,* or *peh, peeea;* Chapman paraphrases it as "come-right-heŕe" or "come-here." Black-faced Antthrush's call is similar but more hesitant and less emphatic. Also has a soft *chirr.*

Range: Nicaragua to western Ecuador.

Note: Birds from eastern Darién to western Ecuador (*maculifer* complex) were formerly regarded as a distinct species (Wing-spotted Antbird) but there are intermediates in western Darién, and wing spotting occasionally occurs further west.

DULL-MANTLED ANTBIRD

(*Myrmeciza laemosticta*) Pl.16

Description: 5½. Iris red in adults of both sexes. Rather like Chestnut-backed Antbird. Male has slaty gray head and neck and *dull olive brown upper back and wings;*

Left, CHESTNUT-BACKED ANTBIRD (top to bottom, male *M.e. cassini,* male *M.e. exsul,* female *M. e. exsul*); center, DULL-MANTLED ANTBIRD (male above, female below); right, above IMMACULATE ANTBIRD (male)

lower back, rump, and tail chestnut; *quite noticeable white spots on black wing-coverts;* throat black, remaining underparts slaty, becoming brown on flanks and lower belly. Female similar but has browner head and *white spots on black throat.*

Similar species: Chestnut-backed Antbird has bare blue orbital skin and entire back chestnut.

Status and distribution: Apparently rare, with records scattered in humid forest in lowlands and foothills on Caribbean slope (not reported from Bocas del Toro); on Pacific slope known from hill country of Veraguas (Santa Fé), Cerro Campana, and from eastern Panama province (Cerro Azul, Chepo) east through Darién. Recently (1969) found in small numbers on Pipeline and Achiote Roads in Canal Zone (J. Karr *et al.*).

Habits: Seems partial to shady streamsides and ravines. Found singly or in pairs; more terrestrial than Chestnut-backed Antbird. Sometimes attracted to army ant swarms (Wetmore).

Range: Costa Rica to northwestern Venezuela and northwestern Ecuador.

Note: Wetmore calls it Salvin's Ant-bird.

IMMACULATE ANTBIRD

(*Myrmeciza immaculata*) Pl.15

Description: 6½. Male *black* with white at bend of wing; *bare orbital skin pale blue to whitish.* Female *uniform chocolate brown* with blackish cheeks and throat and white at bend of wing; bare orbital skin as in male.

Similar species: Male Bare-crowned Antbird has bright blue crown; male Jet Antbird has much white on wings and lacks bare orbital skin; male Black Antshrike has heavier hooked bill and lacks bare orbital skin. Female resembles female Chestnut-backed Antbird but is larger with longer, more blackish tail and is brown (not dull chestnut) above.

Status and distribution: Rare to uncommon in undergrowth of humid forest in foothills and lower highlands (mostly 1000–4000 feet, occasionally to 5000 feet) on Caribbean slope in Bocas del Toro and Veraguas (where crosses to Pacific slope at Santa Fé); on Pacific slope in foothills of eastern Darién (Cana, Río Tacarcuna); one old "Volcán de Chiriquí" record. Not known from central Panama.

Habits: In Costa Rica, reported to occur in noisy active groups of its own species and to follow army ant swarms. Its tail is constantly raised slowly and lowered rapidly. The call is a series of 6 to 8 resonant, musical, excited *beep's* (Slud).

Range: Costa Rica to northwestern Venezuela and western Ecuador.

BICOLORED ANTBIRD
(*Gymnopithys leucaspis*) Pl.16

Description: 5½. Sexes similar. *Chestnut brown above* with *black cheeks* and narrow area of bare bluish gray skin before and behind eye; *white below* with brown sides.

Similar species: Basically two-toned brown and white plumage is distinctive among forest antbirds. Female Great Antshrike is also brown above and white below but is larger, with prominent red eye, and lacks black cheeks. Black-bellied Wren is also superficially similar but has black across all of lower underparts.

Status and distribution: Fairly common in undergrowth of forest in lowlands and foothills on both slopes, ranging rather high into Chiriquí highlands (to 6000 feet); absent from drier Pacific slope lowlands from eastern side of Azuero Peninsula to Canal Zone.

Habits: An inveterate follower of army ants and rarely seen away from them; in such assemblages, it is usually the most numerous of the several attendant species. A distinctive whining *chirrrr* is the most frequently given call; also has a nasal *nyap-nyap*.

Range: Honduras to northern Peru and northern Brazil.

Note: Some authors use specific name *G. bicolor* for birds from Honduras to western Ecuador, considering them not conspecific with true *G. leucaspis* (White-cheeked Antbird) of western Amazonia.

SPOTTED ANTBIRD
(*Hylophylax naevioides*) Pl.16

Description: 4¼. Tail short and often fanned. Male *reddish brown above with head and nape ashy gray;* wings with chestnut and black bars and white spots; throat black, remaining underparts white, *breast crossed by band of large black spots.* Female echoes pattern of male but is duller and buffier, head brownish, mostly whitish below with breast crossed by band of less distinct brownish spots.

Similar species: Small size and bright coloration facilitate recognition of this common species. Only possible confusion is with larger Wing-banded Antbird, which has black and gray (in male), or rufous and gray (female), underparts.

Status and distribution: Common in undergrowth of forest and second-growth woodland in lowlands and foothills on entire Caribbean slope; on Pacific slope in foothills from Veraguas eastward, in lowlands from just west of Canal Zone east through Darién. In Canal Zone more numerous and widespread on Caribbean slope; on Pacific side local in areas of more humid forest.

Habits: A faithful attendant at army ant swarms but also often found foraging independently, alone or in pairs. Its most distinctive call is a series of soft, deliberate notes, falling slightly in pitch, *peedee, pihdee, püdee, pödee;* also has a *chit-chit-chit-chit.*

Range: Honduras to western Ecuador.

OCELLATED ANTBIRD
(*Phaenostictus mcleannani*) Pl.16

Description: 7½–7¾. Rather long-tailed. *Large area of bare bright blue skin around eyes* and *generally spotted appearance* preclude confusion. Sexes similar. Olive brown above with large black spots; ear-coverts, throat, and chest black; remaining underparts chestnut with large black spots.

Status and distribution: Uncommon in undergrowth of forest in lowlands and foothills on Caribbean slope; on Pacific slope found in humid foothills from Veraguas eastward (including Cerro Campana and Cerro Azul/Jefe area), in lowlands in eastern Panama province (Chepo, Bayano River) and Darién.

Habits: The least numerous of central Panama's faithful trio of regular army ant followers, and rarely seen away from ants. Often raises and lowers its tail in the manner of a Hermit Thrush (*Catharus guttatus*). Has a very fast series of soft whistles going upscale, *puhpüpehpeypihpee;* also gives a sharp *dzeerrr.*

Range: Southeastern Honduras to northwestern Ecuador.

WING-BANDED ANTBIRD
(*Myrmornis torquata*) Pl.16

Description: 5½. *Looks virtually tail-less.* Bill rather long. Bare pale blue orbital area. Male dull chestnut above with black area on center of back; *wings slaty crossed by three distinct tawny bands; throat and upper chest black, margined irregularly by a stripe of white barred with black;* remaining underparts slaty gray with rufous under tail-coverts. Female similar but with throat and upper chest tawny, cheeks black.

Similar species: Antthrushes are larger, with visible tails, and lack bands on wings. See also Spotted Antbird.

Status and distribution: Apparently rare and

local; known only from humid forest in lowlands on Caribbean slope in Canal Zone and eastern San Blas, on Pacific slope in eastern Panama province (Cerro Chucantí) and lowlands and foothills (to about 3500 feet) of Darién (where more numerous). In Canal Zone, found recently in small numbers on Pipeline Road, but unrecorded elsewhere in central Panama.

Habits: Almost entirely terrestrial, hopping (not walking as in antthrushes) about on forest floor, probing in ground litter and flicking aside leaves with its bill. Often gives a nasal whining *chirrrr,* similar to call of Bicolored Antbird.

Range: Southeastern Nicaragua; central Panama to eastern Ecuador and central Brazil.

Note: Birds from Middle America and northern and western Colombia are sometimes considered a distinct species, *M. stictoptera* (Buff-banded Antbird).

BLACK-FACED ANTTHRUSH
(*Formicarius analis*) Pl.16

Description: 6½–7. Short tail, usually cocked. Sexes similar. Bare blue skin before and behind eye. *Olive brown above,* more rufous on sides of head and neck; *cheeks and throat black,* chest slaty gray, remaining underparts paler gray with tawny under tail-coverts.

Similar species: The most numerous and widespread antthrush in Panama. Black-headed Antthrush has entirely black head and neck; Rufous-breasted Antthrush has crown, nape, and chest obviously chestnut.

Status and distribution: Common in forest and second-growth woodland in lowlands and foothills on both slopes; absent from drier Pacific lowlands from Veraguas to western Panama province. In Canal Zone more numerous on Caribbean side.

Habits: An almost completely terrestrial bird that walks slowly and deliberately (almost like a little rail) over the forest floor, often with its tail cocked practically straight up in the air. Regularly found at the periphery of army ant swarms. Not easy to see, but its call is a characteristic sound of the Panamanian forest, a series of three (sometimes many more) plaintive and deliberate whistles, the first longer and a little higher in pitch, followed after a hesitation by the next two (or more) slightly lower pitched notes, *pee; pü, pü, ...* Sometimes the last note is repeated (occasionally as many as 10–15 times), giving a very different effect. The three-noted call resembles call of Chestnut-backed Antbird but is unemphatic and hesitant, with accent on first note (not last). A calling bird can often be drawn in very close by a whistled imitation of its call.

Range: Southeastern Mexico to northern Bolivia and Amazonian Brazil.

BLACK-HEADED ANTTHRUSH
(*Formicarius nigricapillus*)

Description: 6–6½. Rather like Black-faced Antthrush but darker. *Entire head, neck, throat, and chest black,* merging into dark slaty gray on lower underparts; upperparts dark brown; bare skin behind eye whitish (faintly blue). Female similar but tinged olive below.

Similar species: Black-faced Antthrush has brown crown and nape and is not as dark

Left to right, BLACK-HEADED ANTTHRUSH, RUFOUS-BREASTED ANTTHRUSH, BLACK-FACED ANTTHRUSH

below. Looks very dark in the field, virtually black below.

Status and distribution: Rare to locally uncommon in humid forest in foothills and lower highlands on both slopes; recorded from Bocas del Toro (1500–5000 feet), Veraguas, and Cerro Campana. Not recorded from eastern half of Panama. On Cerro Campana, essentially sympatric (but much less numerous) with Black-faced Antthrush; found higher up, near 3000 feet.

Habits: Similar to Black-faced Antthrush. The call is a series of slightly accelerating short whistles, becoming a little louder, then stopping suddenly, *hü-hü-hü-hü* . . . , repeated about ten times (lasting about five seconds), followed by a pause of about ten seconds, then another repetition.

Range: Costa Rica to western Ecuador.

RUFOUS-BREASTED ANTTHRUSH
(*Formicarius rufipectus*) *page 213*

Description: 7–7½. Resembles Black-faced Antthrush. *Crown, nape, sides of neck, and chest chestnut;* cheeks and throat black; otherwise dark olive brown above; remaining underparts dark olive with chestnut under tail-coverts.

Similar species: Black-faced Antthrush has brown crown and nape and slaty gray chest.

Status and distribution: Rare in foothills on Pacific slope in Chiriquí and Veraguas (two nineteenth-century specimens; no recent records) and in highlands of eastern Darién (Cerro Pirre, Cerro Tacarcuna, Cerro Malí).

Habits: Similar to Black-faced Antthrush but favors second-growth on very humid hillsides (E. O. Willis). The call in Colombia consists of two deliberate whistled notes, described as being on near the same pitch (E. O. Willis) or with second a semitone above first (L. A. Fuertes).

Range: Costa Rica to eastern Peru.

BLACK-CROWNED ANTPITTA
(*Pittasoma michleri*) Pl.16

Description: 6¾–7½. Panama's most spectacular antbird, large and essentially tailless, with *very long legs.* Crown and nape glossy black, cheeks and upperparts brown; *white below, feathers broadly edged with black giving striking scalloped effect.*

Status and distribution: Rare and local (more numerous in eastern Panama) in humid forest in lowlands and lower foothills on Caribbean slope; on Pacific slope in hill country of eastern Veraguas (Santa Fé), Cerro Campana, and from eastern Panama province (Cerro Azul, Bayano River) east through Darién. In Canal Zone found recently only on Pipeline Road.

Habits: A regular follower of army ant swarms. Though mostly terrestrial, also perches on horizontal branches, particularly when disturbed. Hops rather than walks and can move rapidly, bounding along almost like a tiny kangaroo. Its most

Left to right, SCALED ANTPITTA, STREAK-CHESTED ANTPITTA, FULVOUS-BELLIED ANTPITTA

frequent call is a loud harsh grating *qua, qua, qua,* rather squirrel-like.

Range: Costa Rica to northwestern Colombia.

SCALED ANTPITTA
(*Grallaria guatimalensis*)

Description: 7. Found only in highlands of west and east. Plump, short-tailed, very long-legged. Crown and nape slaty, otherwise olive above, *all of upperparts scaled with black;* tawny below with indistinct blackish mottling on chest.

Similar species: Large size and scaly upperparts should make recognition of this highland species easy.

Status and distribution: Apparently rare in forest in foothills and highlands of Bocas del Toro, Chiriquí, Veraguas, and eastern Darién; in Chiriquí recorded mostly above 5000 feet, though considerably lower elsewhere (1900–4300 feet).

Habits: Mostly terrestrial, hopping over the forest floor and rarely flying; favors steep slopes and ravines.

Range: Central Mexico to southern Peru and extreme northern Brazil.

STREAK-CHESTED (SPECTACLED) ANTPITTA
(*Hylopezus perspicillatus*) Pl.16

Description: 5–5½. *A plump, short-tailed, very long-legged terrestrial forest bird.* Cap gray, otherwise olive brown above with *buff spots on wings* (forming two buffy wing-bars) and *prominent buffy eye-ring;* whitish below, chest tinged buffy, with *chest, breast, and sides streaked blackish.*

Similar species: The only numerous antpitta in the lowlands. Only likely confusion is with the much rarer Fulvous-bellied Antpitta, which see.

Status and distribution: Fairly common in humid forest in lowlands and lower foothills on entire Caribbean slope; on Pacific slope in lowlands and foothills (to about 4000 feet) in western Chiriquí, foothills of Veraguas, western Panama province (one nineteenth-century specimen from Capira), and from Canal Zone (one specimen in National Museum taken at Pedro Miguel) east through Darién. Especially numerous in forest along Achiote Road.

Habits: Generally keeps to areas of forest with little undergrowth; terrestrial, walking quietly and sedately on the forest floor, usually escaping observation. Heard *far* more often than seen, the usual call being a far-carrying series of clear melancholy whistles, rising slightly at first, then falling off in the last three couplets, *deh, dee, dee, dee, dee, deé-eh, déh-oh, dóh-a.* Usually calls from a slightly elevated perch, such as a fallen log.

Range: Nicaragua to western Ecuador.

Note: Sometimes placed in the genus *Grallaria.*

FULVOUS-BELLIED ANTPITTA
(*Hylopezus fulviventris*)

Description 5–5½. Recalls Streak-chested Antpitta. *Slaty above,* wings olive brown edged with rufous (*but with no spots*); throat white, *remaining underparts ochre,* streaked dusky on chest and sides. *No eye-ring.*

Similar species: Streak-chested Antpitta is olive brown above (not mostly slaty) with buff spots on wings and prominent buffy eye-ring, whiter below.

Status and distribution: Apparently very rare and local; known only from lowlands of western Bocas del Toro (Almirante) and lower foothills of eastern Darién (Cerro Pirre, Cerro Tacarcuna). Possibly more numerous than the few records would indicate.

Habits: In Costa Rica prefers dense undergrowth in humid second-growth woodland and forest borders. A calling bird can often be decoyed in by imitating its call, but will usually remain hidden. The call (in Costa Rica) resembles the Streak-chest's, a series of 6 to 8 whistled notes of similar quality, but more rapidly given, and ending abruptly (not trailing off as in Streak-chest); the first 4 or 5 notes rise slightly in pitch (Ridgely).

Range: Nicaragua to Ecuador.

Note: Sometimes placed in the genus *Grallaria.*

OCHRE-BREASTED ANTPITTA
(*Grallaricula flavirostris*) Pl.16

Description: 4–4¼. Known only from highlands of west and east. *Tiny, almost tailless.* Olive brown above with *tawny eye-ring; sides of head and underparts buffy,* fading to whitish on belly, usually with a few blackish streaks on breast and sides.

Similar species: Rather like Streak-chested and Fulvous-bellied Antpittas but much smaller.

Status and distribution: Apparently rare and local in humid forest in lower highlands (mostly 3000–4500 feet) of Bocas del

Toro, Chiriquí, both slopes of Veraguas, and eastern Darién (Cerro Pirre).

Habits: Little known in Panama; very hard to see and likely more numerous than the few records would indicate. Reported to keep low in forest undergrowth, not on ground (Slud).

Range: Costa Rica to northern Bolivia.

Note: Wetmore calls it Ochraceous Pygmy Ant-pitta.

TAPACULOS: Rhinocryptidae (3)

The tapaculos are a small family of neotropical birds, allied to the antbirds, found mostly in temperate areas of South America (especially Chile) and in the Andes, with only one species ranging as far north as Costa Rica. Four forms of one genus (*Scytalopus*) occur in the highlands of Panama, each in a different area, and their relationship to each other has been disputed (depending on the author, from two to four species being recognized). Most tapaculos are terrestrial or semi-terrestrial, the Panama species occurring in dense thickets in humid forest. Many are fast runners but fly poorly. They tend to carry their tails cocked up over their backs. Tapaculos are insectivorous. Their nesting situation is varied, though always well hidden: in burrows, in banks, in hollows or crevices of trees, or in dense tangled vegetation on or near the ground. The nesting of the Panama species is unknown, however. The name "tapaculo," according to Darwin (*Voyage of the Beagle*), refers to the birds' habit of exposing their rear end, but according to Johnson (*Birds of Chile,* Vol. II: 212, 1967), is an onomatopoeic version of the call of one Chilean species.

SILVERY-FRONTED TAPACULO

(*Scytalopus argentifrons*) Pl.17

Description: 4¼. Found only in western highlands. Male *sooty black above* with rump feathers tinged rusty and *silvery forehead and superciliary* (often absent; present only on older birds); *throat dark slaty, remaining underparts slaty gray,* becoming silvery on belly, with flanks tipped rusty. Female lacks the silvery, and has feathers margined with brown above and below. Juvenal dark brown above narrowly margined with black (giving barred effect), dark brown below margined with tawny. Males from eastern Chiriquí and Veraguas (*chiriquensis*), formerly considered a distinct species, have only forehead silvery (no superciliary behind eye) and are uniformly blackish slate below.

Similar species: An obscure little bird of forest undergrowth, somewhat wren-like but without wing and tail barring, and mostly gray and black (not brown). Like a wren, it often carries its tail cocked. See also Wrenthrush.

Status and distribution: Local and apparently uncommon in undergrowth of humid forest in highlands of western Chiriquí (mostly 5000–7500 feet, recorded as low as 4000 feet) and eastern Chiriquí (Cerro Flores, 5500 feet) and Veraguas (Chitra, 3600–4000 feet).

Habits: Prefers shady, dark thickets on forested hillsides and in ravines. Very secretive and difficult to observe, creeping about in dense tangles near the ground. Has a sharp chirring rattle suggestive of an antbird or perhaps a wren.

Range: Costa Rica and western Panama.

PALE-THROATED TAPACULO

(*Scytalopus panamensis*)

Description: 4¼. Known only from Tacarcuna range in eastern Darién highlands. Closely resembles Silvery-fronted Tapaculo of western highlands. Males differ in having forehead black, *broad silvery superciliary* (above and behind eye), and pale gray throat.

Similar species: Nariño Tapaculo is found only on Cerro Pirre; males lack the silvery superciliary. See also Silvery-fronted Tapaculo.

Status and distribution: Common in forest in highlands of eastern Darién (Cerro Tacarcuna, Cerro Malí); recorded 3400–4600 feet.

Habits: Usually in pairs, low down or on the forest floor, often around fallen tree trunks; a piping song, a repetition of a single note, *tseety, seety seety seety,* is occasionally given (Wetmore).

Range: Eastern Panama and adjacent northwestern Colombia.

Note: *S. vicinior* (Nariño Tapaculo) is often regarded as conspecific with this species, but Wetmore regards them as distinct.

NARIÑO TAPACULO
(*Scytalopus vicinior*)

Description: 4¼. Known only from Cerro Pirre in eastern Darién highlands. Resembles Pale-throated Tapaculo of Tacarcuna range. Males differ in lacking the silvery superciliary (have some gray on forehead) and being slightly grayer above.

Similar species: See Pale-throated Tapaculo.

Status and distribution: Known only from two specimens taken on Cerro Pirre in highlands of eastern Darién; recorded 4400–4800 feet.

Range: Eastern Panama to western Ecuador.

Note: Often treated as conspecific with *S. panamensis* (Pale-throated Tapaculo).

MANAKINS: Pipridae (11)

Manakins are small, strictly neotropical birds found in forests and woodland, mostly at low elevations with a few species higher. Typical manakins are plump birds with short bills and short tails (though several species have lengthened tail feathers); most males are brightly or contrastingly colored, while females usually are drab olive green. Several aberrant genera (represented in Panama by *Sapayoa* and *Schiffornis*), at present generally placed in the Pipridae, may not actually belong here. Typical manakins are best known for their elaborate courtship behavior in which males gather to display in groups; here they perform a variety of stereotyped actions, and emit an astonishing array of loud, often cracking or whirring, noises, in some species made mechanically. In typical manakins, so far as known, females build the nest and rear the young alone, constructing a small shallow cup nest in a tree fork, usually not far above the ground. Manakins feed primarily on fruit, to a lesser degree on insects.

BLUE-CROWNED MANAKIN
(*Pipra coronata*) Pl.17

Description: 3½. Legs dark. Male black with *bright blue crown.* Female *dark green above,* paler olive green below.

Similar species: Female is distinctly greener above, less olive, than other female manakins. In eastern Panama, see the larger Green Manakin.

Status and distribution: Locally fairly common in humid forest and second-growth woodland in western Chiriquí (ranging up to about 4200 feet) and in lowlands of central Bocas del Toro (Cricamola), foothills of Veraguas (AMNH specimens from Santa Fé), and locally in lowlands on both slopes from Canal Zone vicinity eastward. In Canal Zone most readily found on Pipeline Road.

Habits: Seems to favor forested areas with relatively sparse undergrowth, often near streams. Not as noisy as most other typical manakins, though both sexes often give a semimusical trill *treereereeree.* At their display grounds, located in forest lower growth, males also utter several harsher vocalizations, but do not give loud wing-produced snapping noises like the Red-capped Manakin. Their courtship behavior is not nearly as complex as in that species, consisting mostly of back and forth flights over a relatively wide area (A. Skutch).

Range: Costa Rica to northern Bolivia and Amazonian Brazil.

RED-CAPPED MANAKIN
(*Pipra mentalis*) Pl.17

Description: 3¾–4. *Legs brownish;* iris white in adult male, dark brown in female and immatures. Male black with *glistening red head* (base of feathers yellow, showing through at times) and yellow thighs (usually hidden except in display). Female olive green above, paler yellowish olive below.

Similar species: Female Golden-collared Manakin is similar but has reddish orange (not dark) legs; female Blue-crowned Manakin is smaller with distinctly green (not olive) upperparts. In eastern Panama see also Golden-headed Manakin.

Status and distribution: Very common in forest and second-growth woodland in lowlands on both slopes (rare above 2000 feet), east on Caribbean slope to western San Blas (Mandinga), and on Pacific slope to eastern Panama province, where it overlaps with Golden-headed Manakin from near Chepo (Río Mamoní) east through Bayano River drainage to at least Cerro Chucantí; absent from drier Pacific lowlands from eastern side of Azuero Peninsula to southern Coclé. Widespread in forested areas of Canal Zone, especially numerous on Caribbean side.

Habits: Often one of the most abundant forest birds on the Caribbean slope, though usually not very conspicuous, flying rapidly from perch to perch, then remaining motionless, their black or olive plumage blending into the shadows and foliage. Especially during the dry season, males gather to display in small loose groups, and at such times the forest may resound with their long-drawn rising *sick-seeeeeee* and other loud snapping and clicking noises (the latter made mostly with the wings, perhaps also with the bill). Each male has its own display perch, located 15 to 50 or more feet above the ground, which is the center of its activity. On and around it, the male performs a variety of stereotyped actions, including rapid to-and-fro flights to a nearby branch, sidling quickly up and down the display branch, abrupt "about-faces," and wing quivering, all the while accompanied by a variety of loud noises, both vocal and mechanical.

Range: Southeastern Mexico to northwestern Ecuador.

GOLDEN-HEADED MANAKIN

(*Pipra erythrocephala*) Pl.17

Description: 3½–3¾. Found only in eastern Panama. *Bill whitish; legs pinkish to whitish;* iris white in adult male, yellowish in female, darker in immatures. Male black with *glistening yellow-orange head,* and red and white thighs (usually hidden). Female olive green above, paler yellowish olive below.

Similar species: Male Red-capped Manakin has red head and yellow thighs; female Red-cap closely resembles female Golden-head but has dark bill and legs, somewhat longer tail. See also female Golden-collared Manakin.

Status and distribution: Common in forest and second-growth woodland in lowlands (up to about 2000 feet) of eastern San Blas and from eastern Panama province (Río Mamoní near Chepo, and Puerto San Antonio near mouth of Bayano River) east through Darién. On Pacific slope there is a zone of overlap with Red-capped Manakin in eastern Panama province, with both occurring at Majé on Bayano River but with Red-cap much more numerous (P. Galindo). On Caribbean slope, area of overlap or replacement unknown. At least one hybrid is known (J. Strauch).

Habits: Similar to Red-capped Manakin in habitat and behavior. The voice, however, is rather different, with a variety of whirring, buzzy, and humming sounds, but without the loud snaps (D. Snow).

Range: Eastern Panama to eastern Peru, northern Brazil, and the Guianas.

Note: Some authors include in this species the red-headed species *P. rubrocapilla,* found south of the Amazon River, in which case the enlarged species is called Flame-headed Manakin.

WHITE-CROWNED MANAKIN

(*Pipra pipra*) Pl.17

Description: 3½–3¾. Known only from western foothills and lower highlands. Male velvety black with striking *white crown and hindneck.* Female olive green above with *cap and hindneck slaty gray;* mostly olive green below, more yellowish on belly. Immature male is like female but with white crown.

Similar species: Female's distinctly gray cap (often looking quite bluish) distinguishes her from other female manakins (see especially female White-ruffed, with grayish throat).

Status and distribution: Rare; known only from humid forest in foothills and lower highlands of eastern Chiriquí (Cordillera de Tolé), both slopes of Veraguas, and Caribbean slope of Coclé (Río Guabal); recorded mostly 2000–4000 feet. Not recorded from Bocas del Toro but to be expected there; also not definitely known from central or eastern Panama.

Habits: Little known in Panama. In Guyana, males are thinly dispersed through the forest (not gathering in groups as do the Red-capped and Golden-headed Manakins), and display in a less ritualized and less noisy manner (D. Snow).

Range: Costa Rica and western Panama; Colombia to eastern Peru, Amazonian and eastern Brazil, and the Guianas.

LANCE-TAILED MANAKIN

(*Chiroxiphia lanceolata*) Pl.17

Description: 5–5¼. *Orange-red legs; projecting, pointed central tail feathers,* somewhat longer in male. Male black with *red crown* and *sky blue back.* Female olive green above, sometimes with some red on crown; somewhat paler olive green below, fading to whitish on belly. Immature male is like female but with red crown.

Similar species: Female larger than female Golden- and Orange-collared Manakins, with protruding central tail feathers.

Status and distribution: Common in thick scrub and lower growth of dry and second-growth woodland in lowlands on Pacific slope from western Chiriquí (ranging up to about 4000 feet, rarely to 5300 feet) to western Darién (Garachiné); on Caribbean slope known only from middle Chagres River valley (Gamboa, Madden Dam area, near Summit Gardens); found also on Coiba Island and Cébaco Island.

Habits: Even the lovely males are often frustratingly difficult to see in the dense undergrowth this species favors. The vocalizations are very unlike those of other Panama manakins, most characteristic being a mellow semi-whistled *doh* or *tee-o,* often repeated and sometimes accelerated into a roll, *dowee-oh;* also gives a very different nasal snarl, *nyaah.* As with many other manakins, males gather to display in courtship assemblies during the breeding season; two males often perch side by side on the same branch, calling steadily and occasionally jumping up and down in alternation.

Range: Southwestern Costa Rica to northern Venezuela.

WHITE-RUFFED MANAKIN
(*Corapipo altera*) Pl.17

Description: 3½–3¾. Legs dark. Male *mostly shiny blue-black; throat white,* feathers lengthened at the sides to form a ruff. Female mostly bright olive green with *grayish throat* and pale yellowish belly.

Similar species: Female resembles female Red-capped Manakin but is brighter green above and has distinctly grayish throat. Female White-crowned Manakin has mostly gray head.

Status and distribution: Fairly common to common in undergrowth of forest in foothills and lower highlands on both slopes, recorded mostly 1500–4000 feet, occasionally as high as 5700 feet (in Chiriquí) or as low as sea level (in Bocas del Toro and San Blas). May engage in altitudinal movements, ranging lower after the breeding season. Not definitely recorded from the Canal Zone, but common on Cerro Campana and in the Cerro Azul/Jefe area.

Habits: Similar to other manakins, like them often seen at fruiting trees with other birds. The usual call is a sharp *prrrrreep.* Small groups of males gather to display on and around mossy fallen logs in the forest, either flying silently toward the log in a striking slow bouncing manner with ruff fully spread, or flying more rapidly and directly, giving a dull snap with the wings as the log is neared, sometimes uttering several harsh vocalizations as well (A. Skutch).

Range: Honduras to northwestern Colombia.

Note: By some authors considered a race of *C. leucorrhoa* (White-bibbed Manakin) of eastern Colombia and northwestern Venezuela.

GOLDEN-COLLARED MANAKIN
(*Manacus vitellinus*) Pl.17

Description: 4–4¼. *Reddish orange legs.* Male has *bright golden yellow collar and throat,* the feathers lengthened and stiffened; otherwise mostly black above with center of back and rump olive; lower underparts olive. Female dull olive green above, paler and more yellowish olive green below. Males from western Bocas del Toro, formerly often regarded as a distinct species (*M. cerritus,* Almirante Manakin), have a more lemon yellow collar and throat, and this extends to upper back and lower on underparts.

Similar species: See Orange-collared Manakin of western Pacific slope. Female Golden-collar resembles several other female manakins, but can be known by its reddish orange legs; female Lance-tail also has orange-red legs but is larger with projecting central tail feathers.

Status and distribution: Common in forest borders and second-growth woodland in lowlands and lower foothills on entire Caribbean slope; on Pacific slope known from more humid areas in lowlands and foothills from eastern Veraguas east through Darién; common also on Escudo de Veraguas. A common woodland bird on both sides of Canal Zone.

Habits: The noisiest Panama manakin, the males producing a variety of sounds. The most striking is an almost firecracker-like snap produced by the wings; also has a softer *chee-póo* or *pee-yóo,* and a ripping sound like cloth tearing. Small groups of males display in woodland undergrowth throughout the prolonged breeding season; each male has its own "court," a small area where the ground is cleared of leaves and other debris. Calling and wing-snapping is especially intense at the approach of a female; often the lengthened throat feathers are puffed out away from the body to form a "beard."

Range: Western Panama (probably also adjacent Caribbean Costa Rica) to Colombia.

ORANGE-COLLARED MANAKIN
(*Manacus aurantiacus*) Pl.17

Description: 3¾–4. Found only on Pacific western slope. *Orange legs.* Similar to Golden-collared Manakin, replacing it in its range, and by some considered conspecific. Male has *more orange collar and throat,* extending over upper back, with lower underparts yellow (not olive) and tail olive (not black); otherwise as in Golden-collar. Female more golden olive green above, more yellowish below.

Similar species: See Golden-collared Manakin.

Status and distribution: Fairly common in undergrowth of second-growth woodland and gallery woodland in lowlands and lower foothills of Chiriquí, southern Veraguas, and both sides of Azuero Peninsula.

Habits: Similar to Golden-collared Manakin, but seems somewhat less noisy. Has a repeated clicking *tick,* a *chewp,* and a "Bronx-cheer"-like *prrr.*

Range: Southwestern Costa Rica and Pacific western Panama.

GREEN MANAKIN
(*Chloropipo holochlora*) Pl.32

Description: 4½–4¾. Found only in eastern Panama. Bill black above, bluish gray below; legs brown to bluish gray. *Bright olive green above;* throat and breast dark grayish olive green, *belly contrastingly yellowish.* Sexes similar.

Similar species: Distinguished from females of other typical manakins by its large size (only Lance-tail is as large), brighter greenish coloration above (only female Blue-crown is brighter green), and relatively longer tail. Female Lance-tailed Manakin lacks contrasting yellow belly and has protruding central tail feathers. Broad-billed Manakin is larger with broad and flat bill, and is mostly yellow below (not just on belly).

Status and distribution: Known only from undergrowth of forest in lowlands and foothills (to about 4000 feet) in eastern San Blas and eastern Darién. Little known in Panama, though apparently not uncommon in Darién (P. Galindo).

Range: Eastern Panama to southern Peru.

THRUSHLIKE MANAKIN
(*Schiffornis turdinus*) Pl.17

Description: 6½. Sexes similar. *Essentially brown or olive brown,* without distinctive markings. In lowlands of central and eastern Panama (*panamensis*) lighter, with brighter brown cap, wings, and tail; *throat and chest light cinnamon-rufous contrasting with grayish olive breast and belly.* In lowlands and foothills of western Panama (*dumicola*) and in highlands of eastern Darién (*acrolophites*) darker, more olive brown, more uniformly colored above and below.

Similar species: Broad-billed Manakin is basically a yellowish green (not brownish) bird, and has a broad flat bill; it tends to feed more actively and higher. Brownish Flycatcher has more slender build with relatively longer tail, has buffy wing-edging and fairly distinct wing-bars, brighter brown tail; it has wing-lifting habit.

Status and distribution: Fairly common, but infrequently seen, in lower growth of forest and shady second-growth woodland in more humid areas on both slopes (usually not above 5000 feet); not recorded from Bocas del Toro (except at Guaval on Veraguas border), nor from drier Pacific slope lowlands from eastern side of Azuero Peninsula to western Panama province. Occurs on Cerro Campana and in Cerro Azul/Jefe area, but form not determined definitely, though certainly not *panamensis.* The lighter and brighter Canal Zone form (*panamensis*) occurs eastward on both slopes up to about 2500 feet; higher in the Tacarcuna range of eastern Darién (4300 feet) the dark form (*acrolophites*) occurs. This distribution, apparently accompanied by voice differences, suggests that two species (rather than altitudinal races) are involved, represented in Panama, on the one hand, by the darker western *dumicola* (sometimes merged in the Central American *veraepacis*) and the Darién montane *acrolophites* (sometimes called *furvus*), and on the other by the lighter *panamensis* of lowlands.

Habits: Not often seen except when caught in mist-nets. Perches rather low, sometimes clinging to upright stems, peering about with a wide-eyed look. Frequently utters loud, deliberate, musical whistles. In the Canal Zone *panamensis* gives a phrase of four rhythmic whistles, the first and last long-drawn, *weyoo, weet-weet, weeeeoo,* sometimes *weeeeyoo, whit-whit, wheeeet.* In the foothills (Santa Fé, Veraguas; Cerro Campana) *dumicola* gives a plaintive whistled phrase of recognizably similar quality, *wheeoowee, tü* or *teeooee-tü.* The voice of the Darién highland *acrolophites* is described by Wetmore as a slow three-noted *tsick-sweet-tsee*. The nest (in Central America) is bulky, often placed in hollow of a rotten stub.

Range: Southeastern Mexico to Bolivia and southeastern Brazil.

Note: As suggested above, more than one species is likely involved. The genus *Schiffornis* is only dubiously allocated to the Pipridae: in appearance, voice, and general behavior it suggests the mourners, usually placed in the Cotingidae but recently assigned by some authors to the Tyrannidae.

BROAD-BILLED MANAKIN
(*Sapayoa aenigma*) Pl.17

Description: 6–6¼. Broad, flat bill noticeable only at close range. Olive green above, wings duskier edged with olive green; *mostly yellowish below* with sides and flanks olive green. Male has partly concealed golden yellow crown patch.

Similar species: A confusing bird, probably often overlooked. Like many female manakins in coloration but much larger and with longer tail and different bill. Thrush-like Manakin is basically brown, not olive green. Olivaceous Flatbill is similar in color and proportions, but has broad, yellowish margins on wings, an eye-ring, and indistinct dusky streaking on chest. Carmiol's Tanager has different bill and rather contrasting yellow throat; it troops about in noisy, active flocks.

Status and distribution: Uncommon to rare and local in humid forest in lowlands on Caribbean slope from Canal Zone eastward; on Pacific slope, known from one specimen taken on Cerro Azul and from lowlands and foothills of Darién. In Canal Zone, known only from Pipeline Road, where it can occasionally be seen within forest.

Habits: Found singly or in pairs, often near streams, foraging in a manner reminiscent of a flatbill at low and middle levels inside forest, sallying out after insects. Often joins mixed foraging flocks of antwrens, small flycatchers, etc.

Range: Central Panama to northwestern Ecuador.

Note: Probably belongs in the Tyrannidae or the Cotingidae; if so, may be called Broad-billed Sapayoa.

COTINGAS: Cotingidae (20)

The cotingas are a very diverse group of neotropical birds that reach their highest development in tropical South America, but are well represented in Panama. They are most closely allied to the Tyrannidae, and some recent authors have placed the Panamanian genera *Attila, Laniocera, Rhytipterna,* and sometimes *Lipaugus,* in that family (chiefly on the basis of the anatomy of the syrinx). The variety in vocalization effort matches the variety in appearance, ranging from virtual silence in the typical cotingas to attractive melodic songs in some of the becards. Cotingas are apparently largely frugivorous. The nest is placed in a variety of situations: the becards building large domed nests with a side entrance, the typical cotingas and the fruitcrow a shallow cup in a fork of a branch, the tityras and attila in tree holes, but the nesting of many species is as yet unknown. Some species do not form any pair bond, and females exclusively care for the young.

BLUE COTINGA
(*Cotinga nattererii*) Pl.18

Description: 7½. Rather short bill and small head give somewhat dove-like expression. Male unmistakable in its range, *mostly shining blue* with black patch (faintly tinged purple) on throat and upper chest and rounded purple patch on center of belly; black eye-ring; wings and tail black broadly edged with blue. Female very different, dark brown above with buff edging, lighter brown below with buff edging, giving *overall scaly effect*.

Similar species: Even the gorgeous males can look dull when seen against the light. Females are best known by their distinctive silhouette and scaly appearance. Turquoise Cotinga is very similar but has different range.

Status and distribution: Uncommon to locally fairly common in humid forest and second-growth woodland in lowlands on both slopes from just west of Canal Zone east through San Blas and Darién, ranging up at least locally into foothills (Cerro Azul/Jefe area). No member of this genus is known from western Caribbean slope, but see Lovely Cotinga (below). In Canal Zone usually most easily seen along Pipeline Road; also frequently noted at clearing on Barro Colorado Island.

Habits: Usually seen high on trees, often on

an exposed perch; usually solitary except when small groups gather at fruiting trees. Widespread but never very numerous.

Range: Central Panama to northwestern Venezuela and northwestern Ecuador.

Note: Wetmore calls it Natterer's Cotinga. Lovely Cotinga (*C. amabilis*), of southern Mexico to Costa Rica, is possible in western Bocas del Toro, especially in foothills. It closely resembles Blue Cotinga but male differs in lacking black eye-ring and having throat patch more purple; female differs in being more spotted (not so scaly) below.

TURQUOISE COTINGA
(*Cotinga ridgwayi*)

Description: 7½. Found only in western Chiriquí. Very like the Blue Cotinga. Male differs in having patch on throat and upper chest more purple (less black) and larger patch of purple on center of lower breast and belly. Female very similar to female Blue Cotinga but somewhat paler, margined with buffy whitish above, generally buff below with dark brown spots.

Similar species: See Blue Cotinga.

Status and distribution: Rare in forest and second-growth woodland in western Chiriquí, ranging up to about 4000 feet; becoming increasingly scarce with destruction of most forest. In recent years recorded primarily from area around Volcán and Volcán Lakes.

Habits: As in Blue Cotinga.

Range: Southwestern Costa Rica and Pacific western Panama.

Note: Perhaps conspecific with *C. nattererii* (Blue Cotinga). Wetmore calls it Ridgway's Cotinga.

SNOWY COTINGA
(*Carpodectes nitidus*)

Description: 8. Found only in western Bocas del Toro. *Bill bluish gray. Male looks pure white,* but is tinged with very pale bluish gray above. Female brownish gray above with white eye-ring, wings grayer edged with white; grayish white below, whitest on throat and belly.

Similar species: Almost identical to (and possibly conspecific with) Yellow-billed Cotinga of Chiriquí but with bluish gray bill. Female might be confused with the two tityras but has different bill and no black or brown on head.

Status and distribution: Uncommon in forest and forest borders in lowlands and lower foothills (about 1000 feet) of western Bocas del Toro.

Habits: Most reports are of birds perching

Left to right, SNOWY COTINGA (male, immature male, and female); YELLOWED-BILLED COTINGA (male); BLACK-TIPPED COTINGA (male)

high in tall trees just back from the coast. Possibly its appearances on the coast represent post-breeding wandering.

Range: Honduras to Caribbean western Panama.

YELLOW-BILLED COTINGA
(*Carpodectes antoniae*)

Description: 8. Known only from coast of western Chiriquí. Like Snowy Cotinga but has *yellow bill.* Male *almost pure white.* Female similar to female Snowy Cotinga, mostly brownish gray above, grayish white below, but with *yellow bill.*

Similar species: Male unmistakable in its range; female could only be confused with the two tityras, but yellow bill is diagnostic.

Status and distribution: Apparently very rare in coastal mangroves and adjacent forest in western Chiriquí. Possibly occurs in mangroves farther east as R. Benson reported (to Eisenmann) having collected one almost forty years before (in the 1920's) in mangroves near Aguadulce, Coclé, but specimen lost. Only recent report is a pair seen near Puerto Armuelles on February 10, 1966 (Wetmore).

Habits: In Costa Rica usually found in small groups high in trees. Courtship display observed by Skutch in forest at 2500 feet suggests possible inland breeding.

Range: Southwestern Costa Rica and Pacific western Panama.

Note: By some authors considered conspecific with *C. nitidus* (Snowy Cotinga). Wetmore calls it Antonia's Cotinga.

BLACK-TIPPED (WHITE) COTINGA
(*Carpodectes hopkei*)

Description: 9–10. Known only from eastern Darién. Male *white,* tinged very pale gray above; outer primaries very narrowly tipped black, and (in younger birds) central tail feathers tipped black, in neither case very noticeable in the field; bill black. Female brownish gray above; wings and tail black, former with broad white edging; throat and breast pale gray, belly white.

Status and distribution: Apparently locally not uncommon in forest in lowlands and lower foothills of eastern Darién. First reported near Cerro Sapo in April 1922 (T. Barbour); one pair was seen along forested shore at Piñas Bay on June 20–21, 1969 (Ridgely and E. Tyson); a male was collected at Cerro de Nique on March 25, 1972 (R. Hinds and P. Galindo), with a number of others seen.

Habits: Usually seen perching high in forest trees.

Range: Eastern Panama to northwestern Ecuador.

BRIGHT-RUMPED ATTILA
(*Attila spadiceus*) Pl.18

Description: 7¾. *Bill heavy and prominently hooked,* pinkish basally; *rather bull-headed.* Variable in color. Olive green to brownish olive above (rarely grayish) with *yellow rump* (sometimes buffy yellow or even bright tawny); wings and tail brownish edged with buff; olive yellow below, fading to whitish on lower belly, *streaked with dusky on throat and breast.*

Similar species: When the yellow rump cannot be seen, this can be a confusing bird. Its very upright posture suggests a flycatcher and it may belong in that family. Panama mourners and piha are more uniform brown. Olivaceous Flatbill has broad flat bill and an eye-ring, lacks the bright rump. See also Broad-billed Manakin.

Status and distribution: Fairly common in forest, second-growth woodland, and borders in lowlands and foothills on both slopes; ranges in reduced numbers well up into highlands; absent from drier scrubbier lowlands on Pacific slope; found also on Coiba Island.

Habits: Usually found singly at low and middle levels, both inside forest and at borders. Often lifts its tail slowly and about-faces abruptly. The call is a series of loud and emphatic whistles, down-sliding at the end, *wheédip, wheédip, wheédip, whéedip, wheedip, wheeeeer,* or *whit, whit, weeda, weeda, weedoo;* very distinctive but also quite ventriloquial.

Range: Western and southern Mexico to northern Bolivia and southeastern Brazil.

SPECKLED MOURNER
(*Laniocera rufescens*) Pl.18

Description: 8. Mostly rufous brown, somewhat paler and more tawny below; *wing-coverts dusky with buff spots; breast finely* (often very indistinctly) *scalloped with dull grayish; patch of elongated yellow feathers on either side of breast* (often hidden by wing). Female sometimes has patch on sides of breast tawny-orange. Immature like female but with more distinct dark markings on wings and underparts.

Similar species: Not always easy to identify. Rufous Mourner is more uniformly rufous brown, lacks contrasting spots on wing, vague barring on breast, and yellow side patches. See also larger Rufous Piha and smaller Cinnamon Becard.

Status and distribution: Rather rare to locally fairly common in forest and second-growth woodland in lowlands on Caribbean slope from Veraguas (Río Calovévora, Santa Fé) east through San Blas; on Pacific slope in lowlands and foothills from Canal Zone east through Darién (to about 4500 feet on Cerro Tacarcuna). Not known from Bocas del Toro though probable, as it has been recorded in adjacent Costa Rica. Becomes fairly common in Darién.

Habits: Usually seen singly, perching quietly in trees at middle levels inside forest, sometimes at borders. Seems to favor vicinity of swampy places or streams. The call is a loud clear *teé; dĕh,* with long pause of about half a second between notes; sometimes a note of very different metallic quality is interposed, *teé-clee-dĕh.*

Range: Southeastern Mexico to northwestern Ecuador.

RUFOUS MOURNER
(*Rhytipterna holerythra*) Pl.18

Description: 8. *Uniform plain rufous brown,* paler and more tawny below.

Similar species: Easily confused. Speckled Mourner has quite conspicuous rufous spots on dusky wing-coverts. Often difficult to distinguish from Rufous Piha: the mourner is smaller and has crown and wings (especially primary coverts) duller and darker than back, has wings edged with rufous (lacking in piha), and is more uniform rufous brown below. Cinnamon Becard is smaller and stouter with buffy supraloral stripe and is paler below; see also female One-colored Becard. Thrushlike Manakin favors forest undergrowth, is considerably smaller, has crown, wings and tail somewhat brighter brown than back, and birds of lowlands of central and eastern Panama have grayish olive breast and belly.

Status and distribution: Uncommon and rather local in humid forest and second-growth woodland in lowlands and foothills on entire Caribbean slope; on Pacific slope known from foothills from Chiriquí (where also ranges sparingly to about 6000 feet) to Darién, recorded in lowlands only in Chiriquí (perhaps only formerly) and from eastern Panama province to Darién; not reported from Azuero Peninsula.

Habits: Usually encountered singly, perched on a branch inside forest at almost any height though often rather high. Has an infrequently given, clear, mournful whistle, *whip, wheeeer,* or "so dear," which Slud likens to a minor-keyed "wolf-whistle."

Range: Southeastern Mexico to northwestern Ecuador.

RUFOUS PIHA
(*Lipaugus unirufus*) Pl.18

Description: 9–9½. *Uniform rufous brown,* brightest on crown, palest on throat.

Similar species: Not always easy to distinguish from somewhat smaller Rufous Mourner but is larger with crown brighter than back (not duller) and wings uniform with back (not duller). Might also bring to mind a robin, but of different proportions, with smaller head, and more uniform rufous in coloration.

Status and distribution: Uncommon to fairly common but usually inconspicuous in humid forest and second-growth woodland in lowlands on entire Caribbean slope (but less numerous westward); uncommon and local in lowlands on Pacific slope in western Chiriquí, Veraguas (Santiago), and from eastern Panama province (Panama city area) east through Darién, where more numerous and ranging well up into foothills (Cerro Pirre).

Habits: Active at times, but also sits quietly for long periods, often hunched forward, on a branch within forest, usually rather high. The call is a loud explosive whistled *peeeéa* or *wheéoo;* also has a *chooweeéoo,* sometimes the two combined. It is very difficult to track down, for not only does it have a ventriloquial quality but the calls are given at very long intervals, frequently in response to another abrupt noise such as a shout, handclap, or the slamming of a car door.

Range: Southeastern Mexico to western Ecuador.

CINNAMON BECARD
(*Pachyramphus cinnamomeus*) Pl.18

Description: 5½. Rufous brown above, *darkest on crown,* with *grayish lores* and *buffy supraloral stripe; tawny-buff below.*

Similar species: Resembles females of several other less numerous becards. Female One-colored is slightly larger, paler above and particularly below, with cap same color as back and no distinct supraloral stripe. Female Cinereous is slightly smaller and has whitish lores; it also has less distinct supraloral stripe. Rufous Mourner is considerably larger and more uniformly rufous brown. Female White-lined Tanager is superficially similar but is larger with differently shaped bill, head same color as back, no supraloral stripe, and is not arboreal.

Status and distribution: Fairly common but somewhat local in clearings with trees and woodland and forest borders in lowlands and lower foothills on entire Caribbean slope; on Pacific slope found very locally from eastern Chiriquí (Las Lajas) eastward, more numerous in eastern Panama province (Cerro Azul, Bayano River) and Darién (where ranges to over 4000 feet on Cerro Malí).

Habits: Favors trees in partly cleared areas, often near water. Its song is a loud fast series of musical notes, typically *teedeedeedeedeedee*, sometimes shorter and slower; occasionally begins or ends with a downsliding *tew* and at times given so fast as to become a musical trill.

Range: Southeastern Mexico to northwestern Venezuela and northwestern Ecuador.

BARRED BECARD

(*Pachyramphus versicolor*) Pl.18

Description: 4¾. Known only from western Chiriquí highlands. Male glossy black above with gray rump; wings spotted and edged with white, tail tipped white; *throat and sides of head and neck greenish yellow, remaining underparts whitish, entire underparts lightly barred with slaty gray.* Female has crown and hindneck gray, remaining upperparts olive; wings duskier, *edged broadly with cinnamon and rufous; underparts dull yellowish with indistinct slaty barring.*

Similar species: Smaller and chunkier than any other Panama becard, and *the only one with barred underparts.*

Status and distribution: Uncommon in forest, lighter woodland, and borders in highlands of western Chiriquí, mostly above 5000 feet.

Habits: Seems to prefer wooded ravines and hillsides; found singly or in pairs, usually not too high up except in tall forest. More active than other becards, frequently joining mixed foraging flocks. Utters a thin *tseet-tseet-tseet-tseet.*

Range: Costa Rica and western Panama; Colombia to northwestern Venezuela and northern Bolivia.

CINEREOUS BECARD

(*Pachyramphus rufus*) Pl.18

Description: 5. Apparently rare. Male *mostly gray above* with *black crown and white forehead and lores;* wings blackish *narrowly* edged with white, usually forming one or two indistinct bands; *white below,* tinged gray on breast and sides; tail slaty gray very narrowly (if at all) tipped with white. Female tawny above, darker and grayer on crown, with *whitish lores and forehead;* cinnamon-buffy below, deepest on chest.

Similar species: Male White-winged Becard is black above with much more white in wings than this species, has black tail broadly tipped white, and is much darker uniform gray below. More closely resembles male Black-and-white Becard but has gray tail (not black tipped white), less white on wing, is whiter below, and has paler gray back. Females present even more of a problem: Cinnamon Becard is somewhat larger and has grayish (not white) lores; female One-colored is distinctly larger.

Status and distribution: Uncertain. Recorded from both slopes of Canal Zone and in eastern Panama province (Chepo, Puerto San Antonio); also one specimen labeled only "Veragua." Only recent records are two specimens from Bayano River valley taken (male) near Majé on May 10, 1973, and (female) near Aguas Claras on Feb. 18, 1974 (R. Hinds, P. Galindo, both specimens in Gorgas lab coll.). Should occur in Darién.

Habits: In South America favors groves of trees, woodland borders, and second-growth woodland.

Range: Central Panama to northern Peru, Amazonian Brazil, and the Guianas.

WHITE-WINGED BECARD

(*Pachyramphus polychopterus*) Pl.18

Description: 6. Male *mostly black above* with slaty rump and rarely a gray collar on hindneck; wings with *broad white stripe on scapulars* and broad white edging and tipping, usually forming two wing-bars; *uniform gray below.* Female olive above, somewhat browner on crown; wings duskier *with broad buff bars and edging; pale yellowish below,* tinged olive on breast and sides.

Similar species: By far the most numerous and widespread Panama becard. Male Cinereous Becard is largely gray above and white below. See also Black-and-white Becard.

Status and distribution: Fairly common in clearings with trees, lighter woodland, and forest borders in lowlands on both slopes; in Chiriquí ranges up to about 4000 feet.

Habits: Found singly or in pairs, foraging at low and middle levels. One vocalization is a rhythmic tittering with some musical quality *tut-tut-tut-tut-tut-tut;* male also has a pretty, mellow song consisting of three slow-paced introductory notes followed by 3 or 4 shorter and faster ones, slightly higher in pitch.

Range: Guatemala and Belize to Bolivia and northern Argentina.

BLACK-AND-WHITE BECARD

(*Pachyramphus albogriseus*) Pl.18

Description: 5½. Known definitely only from western Panama. Male has *white supraloral stripe* extending narrowly over forehead and *black cap contrasting strongly with gray back;* wings black with broad white edging and tipping, forming one or two wing-bars; tail black broadly tipped white; *pale gray below, becoming whitish on throat and pure white on belly.* Female has *striking chestnut cap margined below and behind by a black line, and narrow white eyestripe;* otherwise olive above, wings duskier with broad buff bands; tail dusky tipped buff; pale yellow below, tinged olive on chest.

Similar species: Male best distinguished from male of much more numerous White-winged Becard by its white supraloral stripe, black cap contrasting with gray back (not uniform black above), and pale gray (not uniform slaty gray) underparts, becoming white on belly. See also the smaller Cinereous Becard. Pattern of male also suggests Sirystes, but latter is larger with duller black cap (less contrast), white rump, and longer tail. Female like female White-winged Becard except for diagnostic chestnut cap.

Status and distribution: Rare in forest in Pacific western Panama; recorded from Chiriquí (sea level to 6500 feet) and from humid foothills of Veraguas (Chitra, Calovévora); a reported specimen from Puerto San Antonio, eastern Panama province was a misidentified female Cinereous Becard (*fide* Wetmore); Wetmore also doubts the identification of another female taken at Punta de Sabana, Darién. Little known in Panama.

Range: Western Nicaragua to western Panama; Colombia to northern Venezuela and northwestern Peru.

ONE-COLORED BECARD

(*Platypsaris homochrous*) Pl.18

Description: 6–6¼. Male *mostly slaty gray,* somewhat paler below, darker on wings and tail, with black cap. Female *uniform rufous-tawny above,* often rather pale about head, primaries dusky edged with cinnamon; buffy below, paler (sometimes almost white) on throat and center of belly.

Similar species: Male's dark slaty plumage is unlike that of any other Panama becard. More numerous Cinnamon Becard resembles female but is smaller with cap darker than back and with distinct buffy supraloral stripe. Female Cinereous Becard is also similar but notably smaller. See also Rufous Mourner.

Status and distribution: Rare to locally uncommon in forest and forest borders; recorded from Caribbean slope of Canal Zone (no recent reports) and from Río Pequení above Madden Lake in eastern Panama province; on Pacific slope known from lowlands of eastern Panama province (Puerto San Antonio and Majé on Bayano River) and Darién (where ranges up into lower foothills). Apparently fairly common around and above Majé in Bayano River valley (Ridgely, Eisenmann, *et al.*).

Habits: Usually seen in pairs, foraging rather high in trees, sometimes accompanying mixed flocks of insectivorous birds.

Range: Central Panama to northwestern Venezuela and northwestern Peru.

MASKED TITYRA

(*Tityra semifasciata*) Pl.18

Description: 7¾. Male *mostly white,* tinged pearly gray above, with wings and basal half of tail black; forehead and facial area black with *bare skin around eye and bill red.* Female similar, *retaining red bill and bare skin around eyes* but with head brown and back tinged brownish.

Similar species: Both sexes of Black-crowned Tityra lack red on face and bill and have black crowns. See also female Snowy and Yellow-billed Cotingas.

Status and distribution: Common and widespread in wooded lowlands and foothills (in Chiriquí small numbers to over 6000 feet) on both slopes except in dry scrubby lowlands of southern Coclé and adjacent western Panama province; found also on Coiba and Cébaco Islands.

Habits: Can occur almost anywhere in wooded or forested areas, but prefers clearings and borders with tall dead trees for perching and nesting places. Usually in pairs, quite high up, gathering in small groups at fruiting trees. Has an odd, grunting, almost pig-like call, *querp,* sometimes doubled.

Range: Northern Mexico to Bolivia and Amazonian Brazil.

BLACK-CROWNED TITYRA
(*Tityra inquisitor*) Pl.18

Description: 7¼. *Bill black above, bluish gray below.* Male *mostly white* with *black crown,* more pearly gray on back; wings and terminal half of tail black. Female similar, *retaining black crown* but with buffy whitish or rusty forehead, *chestnut sides of head,* and brownish nape and hindneck; back grayish brown.

Similar species: Both sexes of Masked Tityra have bill and bare orbital skin red, have only forehead black (male) or crown brown (female). See also female Snowy and Yellow-billed Cotingas.

Status and distribution: Uncommon to locally fairly common in forest and second-growth woodland in lowlands and foothills (to about 4000 feet) on both slopes, but absent from Azuero Peninsula and drier scrubby lowlands on Pacific slope. Almost everywhere outnumbered by the Masked Tityra.

Habits: Similar to the Masked Tityra, the two occasionally nesting in the same dead tree. Its call is drier and less grunty, *zick-zick-zick.*

Range: Eastern Mexico to Bolivia and northeastern Argentina.

Note: By some authors separated in the genus *Erator.* Wetmore calls it Black-crowned Becard.

PURPLE-THROATED FRUITCROW
(*Querula purpurata*) Pl.18

Description: ♂ 11½; ♀ 10½. *Black* with *reddish purple throat.* Females and immatures lack the purple throat. Broad wings and short tail very evident in flight.

Status and distribution: Common in forest and second-growth woodland in lowlands on entire Caribbean slope; on Pacific slope found from Canal Zone eastward, though less numerous except in Darién; also recorded from humid Pacific slope foothills of Veraguas; rare above 1000 feet. Widespread in wooded areas of Canal Zone but considerably more numerous on Caribbean side.

Habits: A noisy and conspicuous bird, generally trooping about in small groups of its own species, but sometimes joining oropendolas and toucans in fruiting trees. Has a variety of loud calls, some harsh, others quacking, still others almost whistled: *wak-wak-wheéawoo; cher-kaw* on different pitches; and *kwick-oo, oooo-waa,* and simply *oo.*

Range: Costa Rica to northern Bolivia and Amazonian Brazil.

BARE-NECKED UMBRELLABIRD
(*Cephalopterus glabricollis*)

Description: ♂ 18; ♀ 15. Found only in west, mostly in highlands. Male unmistakable, *black with upstanding umbrella-shaped crest over head and bill; throat and neck bare, vivid scarlet when expanded,* with short narrow wattle hanging from neck (usually not too prominent). Female less spectacular, blackish above with much smaller crest, neck feathered and no wattle; brownish black below.

Similar species: Even female should be easily identified; only possible confusion lies with much smaller Purple-throated Fruitcrow of lowlands.

Status and distribution: Apparently rare, recorded in highlands of Chiriquí (4000–8000 feet), Bocas del Toro, and Veraguas; descends lower after breeding, especially on Caribbean slope, where occasionally found at sea level at least in Bocas del Toro.

BARE-NECKED UMBRELLABIRD

Probably more numerous on Caribbean side of mountains; at any rate, very rare in western Chiriquí highlands.

Habits: Not very well known in Panama. Usually seen perched high in forest trees. Mostly quiet. Males in display often perch much lower, spread crest, and distend their scarlet air sac on upper chest and emit a booming sound. Males also chase each other with chuckling sounds and a throaty *oooah* (C. Cordier).

Range: Costa Rica and western Panama.

THREE-WATTLED BELLBIRD

(*Procnias tricarunculata*) Pl.18

Description: ♂ 12; ♀ 10½. Found only in west, mostly in highlands. Male unmistakable, *mostly bright chestnut-rufous,* with *striking white head and neck; three wormlike wattles hang limply from base of bill.* Female olive green above, feathers margined with yellowish; *yellow below streaked with olive green;* no wattles. Immature males have short wattles with plumage of female.

Status and distribution: Breeding status in much of its range uncertain. Undoubtedly breeds in highlands of western Chiriquí and recorded through western highlands (mostly 5000–7000 feet) to eastern Veraguas (where mostly 2000–3000 feet) and in adjacent Bocas del Toro; possibly also breeds in hill country on Azuero Peninsula (2000–3000 feet); disperses after breeding season, when recorded regularly at sea level during dry season in Bocas del Toro, Chiriquí, and Veraguas. In highlands mostly March–September, in lowlands mostly October–March, though notably irregular in its appearances; can be common locally. In western Chiriquí highlands, seems more numerous on Boquete side of Volcán Barú than around Cerro Punta.

Habits: Its presence in an area will usually be obvious from the male's unmistakable and far-carrying call. The bird hunches forward and opens its cavernous mouth so that lower mandible practically touches breast and emits a harsh resonant grunt (not at all bell-like), *ihrk,* then pauses for about a second (mouth still wide open) before giving a louder sharper croak, *kyahrrk* or *krreeak.* Either note may be given alone. At the conclusion, he often jumps a short distance into the air and then returns to his perch with a reversed orientation. Males may be calling from all around but can often be frustratingly difficult to see as they perch high in the canopy often hidden from the ground. Females are, not unexpectedly, less conspicuous and are much less often observed. Chiriquí residents know the bird by the inappropriate name of "calandria," the Spanish name for lark!

Range: Honduras to western Panama.

SHARPBILLS: Oxyruncidae (1)

The one species in this family has a very discontinuous range, being found very locally in highland forests of southern Middle America and eastern South America. Its exact taxonomic position is unclear; it has been regarded as an aberrant member of the Tyrannidae, but in habits seems more like a Cotingid. Little is known of it in life: it is reported to be largely frugivorous; its nesting habits remain unknown.

SHARPBILL

(*Oxyruncus cristatus*)

Description: 6–6½. Known only from highlands of west and east. *Short sharply pointed bill.* Mostly olive green above with *forehead and sides of crown blackish,* a usually concealed scarlet crown patch, and sides of head whitish narrowly banded with black; two narrow yellowish wing-bars; *pale yellow below, profusely spotted with black,* especially on breast. Darién birds (*brooksi*) are whiter below.

Similar species: Speckled Tanager is spotted above as well as below and has different bill and facial pattern. Female Blue and

SHARPBILL

Turquoise Cotingas are larger and mostly brown, with very different bills.

Status and distribution: Apparently very rare in humid forest and forest borders in lower highlands of western Chiriquí (one old specimen from Boquete), Veraguas, and eastern Darién; recorded 2400–4000 feet. Only recent report from western Panama is a sighting of one in cloud forest above Santa Fé, Veraguas on Cerro Tute (3500 feet) on Jan. 5, 1974 (Ridgely).

Habits: Little known. Rather heavy-bodied and short-legged, superficially resembling several medium-sized Cotingidae (Wetmore). Perches high in canopy where it may be overlooked. In southeastern Brazil has a long-drawn thin high whistle that very gradually slides down in pitch (Eisenmann).

Range: Locally in Costa Rica, Panama, southern Venezuela, Guyana, eastern Peru, Amazonian and southeastern Brazil, and eastern Paraguay.

TYRANT-FLYCATCHERS: Tyrannidae (85)

There are more species of flycatchers in Panama than in any other family, and several of them are among the most conspicuous of Panama's birds. The family is strictly American in distribution, and is most diverse in tropical areas, though a number of species nest in temperate North and South America, most migrating to the tropics during their nonbreeding seasons. The family exhibits great variation in size and form, and it is difficult to generalize about it. Many species have rather dull plumage, others are boldly patterned with striped heads and bright yellow underparts; in only two Panamanian species (the accidental Vermilion Flycatcher and the rare Gray Elaenia) do the sexes differ markedly. Many genera have a usually concealed crown patch of a bright color, often larger in the male, the function of which is uncertain. Identification in this family is often difficult, and some members of two genera (the migrant species of *Empidonax* and *Contopus*) are impossible to distinguish in the field unless singing (and are difficult in the hand). Most Panamanian species are essentially arboreal, though they differ greatly in the degree to which they expose themselves: some are very conspicuous and cannot be missed (e.g. Tropical Kingbird and Social Flycatcher), while many others are obscure, often skulking in undergrowth (e.g. Slate-headed Tody-Flycatcher), or remaining hidden in foliage high in trees (e.g. Black-capped Pygmy-Tyrant). The food of the group as a whole consists chiefly of insects and other arthropods, but unlike the situation in temperate North America many are not sallying flycatchers, rather gleaning more like wood-warblers or vireos in the foliage. A number of species (including some migrants such as the Eastern Kingbird and Great Crested Flycatcher) also eat a large amount of fruit, and a few may have an almost total fruit diet as adults (e.g. Piratic Flycatcher; *fide* E. S. Morton); several other species (notably the Great Kiskadee) also take small reptiles and amphibians, even fish and small birds. The nesting situation is varied, with many species building a simple cup nest; a number build distinctive pensile nests, with entrance on the side, often hung over a shaded stream; *Myiarchus* flycatchers nest in holes. Many species remain poorly known, and would repay investigation.

BLACK PHOEBE
(*Sayornis nigricans*)

Description: 6–6½. *River and stream borders. Slaty black with contrasting white belly.* Western Panama birds have wings margined with gray; eastern Panama birds have conspicuous white wing edging, two white wing-bars, and less white on belly.

Similar species: Torrent Tyrannulet is smaller and mostly pale gray. Dark Pewee is slaty gray (not black), conspicuously crested, lacks the white belly, and perches high on dead branches.

Status and distribution: Fairly common along streams and rivers in highlands of western Chiriquí (above 3500 feet) and adjacent Bocas del Toro (one record from Río Changuinola in foothills); also in hill country of eastern Colon province (Cerro Bruja, Río Boqueron above Madden Lake), eastern Panama province (Cerro Chucantí), and foothills and highlands of Darién. A pair was photographed in lowlands of eastern Panama province on Bayano River a few miles above dam site on Aug. 4, 1972 (Ridgely and J. Pujals).

Habits: Often sits on a rock out in the middle of the torrent, flying out after passing in-

BLACK PHOEBE (eastern Panama race)

sects. Jerks up its tail like the well known Eastern Phoebe (*S. phoebe*) of temperate eastern North America. Nests in rock crevices and under bridges and eaves. The song in Chiriquí is a *peep-feebreew*.

Range: Southwestern United States to northern Venezuela and northwestern Argentina.

Note: Birds from eastern Panama and South America have been considered a distinct species, *S. latirostris* (White-winged Phoebe).

SIRYSTES

(*Sirystes sibilator*) Pl.19

Description: 7–7½. A distinctive white, gray, and black flycatcher of the forest canopy. *Cap black, shading to slaty gray on sides of head;* back light gray, *rump white;* wings black with white edging and two broad, white wing-bars; *rather long, square-tipped tail black tipped whitish;* pale gray below, becoming whitish on belly.

Similar species: In pattern rather resembles male of Black-and-white Becard, which is smaller, has a glossier black cap, darker gray back, and no white rump. Vaguely recalls a tityra but much more slender and not as white; also somewhat resembles an immature Fork-tailed Flycatcher lacking lengthened central tail feathers.

Status and distribution: Uncommon locally in humid forest in lowlands and foothills (to about 2600 feet) from Veraguas (early specimens) and Canal Zone area east through San Blas and Darién. In Canal Zone seems most numerous on Pipeline Road; more common eastward.

Habits: Often in pairs, sometimes accompanying mixed foraging flocks high in forest trees. In shape and actions rather like a *Myiarchus* flycatcher. Frequently utters a rather loud *chup-chup-chup . . .* or *prip-prip-prip. . . .*

Range: Panama to northern Bolivia, Paraguay, northeastern Argentina, and southeastern Brazil.

Note: Perhaps belongs in the Cotingidae.

LONG-TAILED TYRANT

(*Colonia colonus*)

Description: ♂ 9–10; ♀ 7–8. Unmistakable. *Mostly black* with *white forehead and superciliary;* whitish streaking on lower back and rump (often concealed); *central pair of tail feathers greatly elongated* (up to 4″ beyond rest of tail) in males, somewhat shorter in females and molting males.

Similar species: Fork-tailed Flycatcher is larger, has white underparts, and has *outer* tail feathers elongated; it is an open country (not a forest-based) bird.

Status and distribution: Fairly common in forest borders and small clearings in humid forest in lowlands and foothills (to about 3000 feet) on entire Caribbean slope; on Pacific slope found in foothills of Veraguas (fairly common above Santa Fé January 2–6, 1974; Ridgely and G. Stiles) and from eastern Panama province (Cerro Azul, Bayano River) east through Darién. In Canal Zone most numerous on Pipeline Road and in Fort Sherman/San Lorenzo area.

Habits: Generally perches conspicuously on an exposed stub or dead branch, sallying out after passing insects, usually returning

LONG-TAILED TYRANT

to its original perch. Seen singly or in pairs. Nests in tree holes, typically in a dead, burned tree in a clearing. The calls are a distinctive soft *twee* or *chweet;* also has a musical humming *drüü,* accompanied by whipping the long tail.

Range: Honduras to Bolivia, Paraguay, northeastern Argentina, and southeastern Brazil.

PIED WATER-TYRANT
(*Fluvicola pica*)

Description: 5. *A small black and white flycatcher,* unmistakable in the marshy areas where it occurs. Mostly white, with black nape and center of back, black wings margined with white, and black tail tipped white.

Status and distribution: Locally common in fresh water marshes and ponds and adjacent brushy areas in lowlands near coast on Pacific slope in eastern Panama province (Juan Diaz eastward); no satisfactory reports from Canal Zone or points west; not recorded from Darién. Easily seen in the Tocumen/La Jagua area.

Habits: An attractive and unsuspicious bird, usually seen feeding on or near the ground, on emergent vegetation, or in shrubs; gleans rather than flycatches. Its call is a nasal *zhweeoo.*

Range: Central Panama to northern Argentina.

PIED WATER-TYRANT

VERMILION FLYCATCHER
(*Pyrocephalus rubinus*)

Description: 5½. Accidental. Male has *head* (somewhat crested) *and entire underparts flaming vermilion;* stripe through eye and upperparts blackish. Female brownish gray above; whitish below, *narrowly streaked with dusky,* becoming *pale salmon on flanks and lower belly.* Immature resembles female but has lower belly often yellowish, not salmon.

Status and distribution: Two records: an adult male photographed at Playa Coronado, western Panama province on August 19, 1947 (Eisenmann); and an apparently subadult male (with whitish throat) seen repeatedly and photographed at Gatun Dam spillway, Canal Zone January 16–March 20, 1974 (D. Engleman, Mrs. Kani Myers *et al.*). Neither bird's origin could be determined. A species of semi-open country and savannas.

Range: Southwestern United States to Nicaragua; Colombia to northern Chile and central Argentina.

SCISSOR-TAILED FLYCATCHER
(*Muscivora forficata*)

Description: ♂ 12–14; ♀ 10–11½. A beautiful, *silvery gray* bird with a *very long and deeply forked tail* (longer in male). Pale gray above, wings black, edged with whitish and with orange-red to salmon patch under wing; white below, becoming *pale salmon on belly.* Immatures have red replaced with creamy buff; they and molting adults lack the very long outer tail feathers.

Similar species: The far more numerous Fork-tailed Flycatcher lacks the red or salmon, has a distinct black cap, and is darker gray above.

Status and distribution: An apparently irregular winter visitor (November–March) to open country in lowlands on Pacific slope, most numerous in western Panama, with only a very few records from Canal Zone and none from farther east; one specimen taken at Almirante, Bocas del Toro on October 31, 1962 (several others seen), is only record from Caribbean slope.

Habits: Often associates with Fork-tailed Flycatcher.

Range: Breeds in south-central United States; winters from southern Mexico (a few also in southern Florida) to central Panama.

Note: Sometimes included in the genus *Tyrannus.*

FORK-TAILED FLYCATCHER
(*Muscivora tyrannus*)

Description: ♂ 13–16; ♀ 10½–12½. *Very long deeply forked tail* (longer in male). *Head and nape black* with usually concealed yellow crown patch; back pale gray, wings darker gray, tail black; *white below*. Immatures (with more brownish caps) and molting adults lack the very long outer tail feathers.

Similar species: See Scissor-tailed Flycatcher.

Status and distribution: Common in lowlands on Pacific slope (numbers fluctuating seasonally and locally) in savannas and dry scrubby areas, extensive lawns, and residential areas from Chiriquí (where ranges up to about 4500 feet) to eastern Panama province (lower Bayano River around El Llano); not recorded from Darién. On Caribbean slope reported only from Canal Zone and vicinity, where usually uncommon and probably not breeding; one also seen at Puerto Obaldía, San Blas in mid-June 1965 (D. Sheets). Also once reported (January) from Coiba Island (Wetmore), and once (July) from Taboga Island (Eisenmann). Birds nesting on Pacific slope (*monachus*) gather in post-breeding flocks, and apparently engage in some movement away from nesting areas, but whether in true migration uncertain. Birds of the same race which breed farther north in Middle America probably occur in Panama as migrants. On Caribbean coast of Canal Zone birds seeming to be migrants have been seen in late August and September. The highly migratory southern South America race (nominate *tyrannus*) may also reach Panama, though as yet no specimen has been taken (perhaps the San Blas sighting was of a bird of this race); it regularly migrates to northern South America during the austral autumn and winter (March–October), and individuals casually even reach the United States. In the hand this race can be known by its much darker gray back than *monachus*.

Habits: Often occurs in sizable flocks, at times gathering in large numbers to roost. Usually seen perched on low bushes or trees, sometimes on the ground. Most of its food, insects, is obtained by flycatching; also eats royal palm fruit taken in flight. At its best in the air, when the long tail is spread and whipped around to aid in maneuverability.

Range: Southern Mexico to central Argentina.

Note: Sometimes called *Muscivora savana*, or (when included in the genus *Tyrannus*), *Tyrannus savana*.

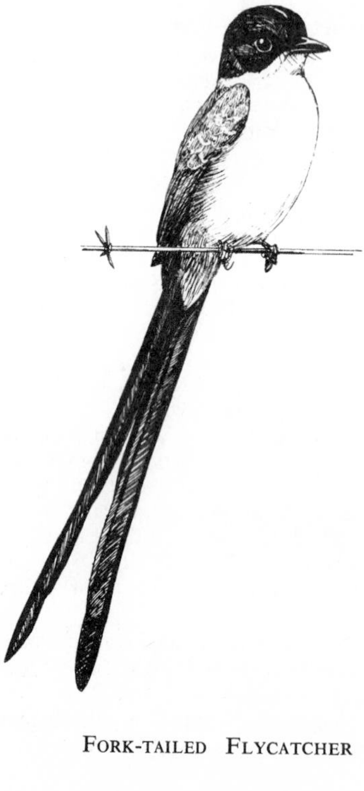

FORK-TAILED FLYCATCHER

EASTERN KINGBIRD
(*Tyrannus tyrannus*)

Description: 8–9. *Blackish above* with usually concealed orange-red crown patch; white below; rather rounded *tail tipped conspicuously with white*. Immature is duller above with less white in tail.

Similar species: Gray Kingbird is gray (not blackish) above and has forked tail without any white. Tropical Kingbird shows much yellow on underparts.

Status and distribution: Common transient in lowlands (to about 2500 feet) on entire Caribbean slope (sometimes abundant on northward migration) and common transient on Pacific slope from Canal Zone eastward, apparently less numerous westward with only a few reports from Veraguas and Chiriquí (where perhaps irregular); a few may winter on Pacific slope; recorded also from Pearl Islands (especially on northward migration) and Taboga and Taboguilla Islands; recorded in Panama mostly early September–late November and late March–mid-May.

Habits: Sometimes occurs in large flocks of many hundreds, occasionally even more, especially on spring migration. On its breeding grounds found in open country, but in Panama more often in border growth. While migrating, often occurs in flocks in the forest canopy, feeding on fruit; often flies in compact groups, like waxwings. Usually silent in Panama.

Range: Breeds chiefly east of the Rockies in North America; winters in Peru and Bolivia, possibly northward to Costa Rica (wintering north of Peru uncertain).

TROPICAL KINGBIRD

(*Tyrannus melancholicus*) Pl.19

Description: 8½–9½. Head gray with dusky ear-coverts and usually concealed reddish orange crown patch; *otherwise grayish olive above* with dull brown wings and *slightly forked tail;* throat whitish, *remaining underparts yellow,* chest tinged with olive.

Similar species: Both other kingbirds known from Panama have white underparts. Great Crested and Panama Flycatchers both have wing-bars and distinctly gray throats and breasts. See also the possible Western Kingbird (below).

Status and distribution: An abundant and widespread bird, most common in open and semi-open country, but also in residential areas, roadsides, and clearings in generally forested areas; occurs virtually wherever there is adequate habitat, even ranging well into highlands (to about 6200 feet) in clearings; occurs on all large and most small islands off both coasts.

Habits: One of the most conspicuous Panama birds, often sitting on wires and other exposed perches. Like the other kingbirds, a typical sallying flycatcher, sometimes following an insect in almost swallow-like pursuit. Its dawn song, a couple short *pip*'s followed by a rising twitter, *píririree,* is often the first bird sound heard in the morning, frequently being given well before first light. Also gives a *feet-feet-feet.*

Range: Extreme southwestern United States to central Argentina. More than one species is likely involved.

Note: Western Kingbird (*T. verticalis*), breeding in western temperate North America, wintering from southern Mexico to Nicaragua, casually to Costa Rica, is possible during winter months, especially in western Panama. Western would be easily overlooked as it is similar to the omnipresent Tropical, but has gray chest and black (not dusky brown) unforked tail with narrow white edging on sides (Tropicals in fresh plumage sometimes show narrow whitish edging and tipping, and worn Westerns often lack them).

GRAY KINGBIRD

(*Tyrannus dominicensis*)

Description: 9–9½. Thick bill and heavy head and body give characteristic *bull-headed effect. Gray above* with dusky ear-coverts and usually concealed orange crown patch; wings and tail more brownish, *tail slightly forked;* white below with gray wash on chest.

Similar species: Eastern Kingbird is smaller and slenderer, blacker above, with tail tipped white. Tropical Kingbird also has forked tail, but shows much yellow below, is more olive above, and is smaller with less heavy bill.

Status and distribution: Uncommon to locally fairly common winter resident (late August–late April) in open and residential areas on both slopes of central Panama; recorded also in San Blas (specimens from Permé and Puerto Obaldía) and lowlands on Pacific slope in southern Coclé and Herrera; on Pacific side they appear later and leave earlier than on Caribbean, and they seem irregular west of the Canal Zone.

Habits: Usually seen perched on fences or telephone wires, often with the much more numerous Tropical Kingbird. The call is a rolling throaty *pe-cheer-ry* (R. T. Peterson).

Range: Breeds in coastal southeastern United States, West Indies, islands off Venezuela and also in Venezuelan llanos; winters in southern West Indies, Panama, and northern South America.

PIRATIC FLYCATCHER

(*Legatus leucophaius*) Pl.19

Description: 6–6¼. *Bill rather short.* Olive brown above with usually concealed yellow crown patch, *whitish superciliary,* dusky ear-coverts, a whitish submalar streak, and a dusky moustachial stripe; throat white, remaining underparts pale yellow, brightest on belly, with *dusky streaking on breast.*

Similar species: In pattern and colors much like Streaked and Sulphur-bellied Flycatchers, but much smaller with stubbier bill and no rufous in tail.

Status and distribution: A common breeding bird in clearings and forest and woodland borders in lowlands on both slopes, ranging up to about 5000 feet in Chiriquí highlands; apparently migrates to South America during the late rainy season: no Panama records from November or December and very few for October.

Habits: Appropriates domed or closed nests of various species (oropendolas, caciques, becards, some other flycatchers, etc.) for its own use, driving away the rightful owners by its constant pestering; virtually every oropendola or cacique colony has a pair of these birds. The call consists of a whining *weé-yee,* often followed, after a pause, by a rising *pírrirriree,* and is endlessly repeated from late January through September, even in the heat of the day. It usually calls while sitting on a bare twig at the top of a leafy tree, where often hard to see from below.

Range: Eastern Mexico to northern Argentina and southeastern Brazil; Middle American birds evidently migrate to South America during non-breeding season.

SULPHUR-BELLIED FLYCATCHER
(*Myiodynastes luteiventris*)

Description: 8. Closely resembles much more numerous Streaked Flycatcher. Differs in having lower mandible flesh only at base (in Streaked pinkish except for black tip), crown brownish gray or olive (not tawny brown), *superciliary white* (not dull yellowish), chin dusky, and *underparts distinctly clear sulphur yellow* (in Streaked whitish, or at most tinged dingy yellowish).

Similar species: See Streaked Flycatcher.

Status and distribution: Uncommon transient throughout (September–October; once November 20; March–April), most numerous in western highlands.

Habits: Similar to Streaked Flycatcher. The call in Costa Rica is totally unlike Streaked's (but rather like Golden-belly's), "an angry-sounding *squisser* or *squí-ick*" (Slud).

Range: Breeds from southeastern Arizona and Mexico to Costa Rica; winters in Peru and Bolivia.

STREAKED FLYCATCHER
(*Myiodynastes maculatus*) Pl.19

Description: 8. Bill long. Lower mandible pinkish except for black tip. *Mostly brown above streaked with dusky* and with *rufous rump and tail;* usually concealed yellow crown patch, pale yellowish superciliary, dusky ear-coverts, yellowish submalar stripe, and dusky moustachial stripe; *whitish or dingy yellowish below streaked with dusky.*

Similar species: Of Panama flycatchers only the Piratic and Sulphur-bellied are so conspicuously streaked and brownish. The Streaked is the most numerous and widespread of the three.

Status and distribution: Apparently permanent resident, common in clearings, open second-growth woodland, and forest borders in lowlands and foothills on both slopes but especially in fairly humid regions; ranges up into highlands (to about 5500 feet) in Chiriquí; found also on Pearl Islands and Coiba and Cébaco Islands.

Habits: Noisy and conspicuous birds, often around habitations. The calls are harsh and nasal, *chup* and *eéchup,* but also has an unexpectedly musical but still squeaky song, *weéarooweép.* Nests in natural cavities, under eaves of buildings, on window ledges, etc.

Range: Eastern Mexico to Bolivia, northern Argentina, and southeastern Brazil; northern Middle American birds move southward during non-breeding season to winter in South America and Panama.

GOLDEN-BELLIED FLYCATCHER
(*Myiodynastes hemichrysus*) Pl.19

Description: 7¾–8. Found only in western highlands. Looks rather like a cross between Streaked and Boat-billed Flycatchers. Bill somewhat broader than in Streaked. *Olive brown above* with blackish crown and usually concealed yellow crown patch; white superciliary, blackish ear-coverts, white submalar stripe, and *prominent dusky moustache stripe;* wings edged inconspicuously with rufous; throat white, *remaining underparts yellow* (immature has buffy tinge) with indistinct light olive streaking on sides of breast.

Similar species: Boat-billed Flycatcher is larger, with broader bill, lacks the moustachial stripe and streaking below. Golden-crowned Flycatcher is found only in Darién highlands.

Status and distribution: Uncommon in clearings and forest borders, often along streams, in highlands of western Chiriquí, mostly above 5000 feet; recorded also from adjacent Bocas del Toro and Veraguas (where recorded as low as 3500 feet). Can be regularly seen along Río Chiriquí Viejo in the Nueva Suiza and Bambito area.

Habits: Much like the Streaked Flycatcher, noisy and conspicuous, though never as numerous. The voice is a peculiar *skee-eey* or *skweey.*

Range: Costa Rica and western Panama.

Note: Treated by some authors as a race of

the mainly South American *M. chrysocephalus* (Golden-crowned Flycatcher).

GOLDEN-CROWNED FLYCATCHER
(*Myiodynastes chrysocephalus*) Pl.32

Description: 8. Found only in eastern Darién highlands. Resembles Golden-bellied Flycatcher of western highlands but has *distinctly buff throat and chest* (adults as well as immatures) and is more *definitely streaked with olive on breast.*

Similar species: See Golden-bellied Flycatcher. Streaked and Sulphur-bellied Flycatchers are brown and heavily streaked above. Boat-billed Flycatcher is larger with broader bill, lacks the moustache stripe, buff throat and chest, and streaking below.

Status and distribution: Rare in highlands of eastern Darién above 4500 feet (single specimens from Cerro Pirre and Cerro Malí).

Habits: Elsewhere a bird of forest borders and woodland, often near streams. In Venezuela the call is a *kseeyoo* (Eisenmann).

Range: Eastern Panama to northern Venezuela and southern Peru.

BOAT-BILLED FLYCATCHER
(*Megarhynchus pitangua*) Pl.19

Description: 9–9¼. A *large* flycatcher with a *heavy, broad bill. Olive above* with black crown and usually concealed orange-yellow crown patch, white superciliary, and black ear-coverts; throat white, remaining underparts yellow. Immature has some rufous edging on wings.

Similar species: Much like a Great Kiskadee in size and pattern, but olive (not more or less rufous) above, with wider bill. Social Flycatcher is also olive above but is much smaller with shorter and narrower bill and shows indistinct wing-bars.

Status and distribution: Common in clearings, second-growth woodland, and forest borders in lowlands and foothills on both slopes, ranging up to over 6000 feet in Chiriquí highlands; found also on Cébaco Island.

Habits: Very noisy, with a variety of harsh grating vocalizations, typical being a rattling *keerrrrrr-eék;* also has shorter calls such as *kirr-wick* and *krrrrreek*. Usually found singly or in pairs, often foraging high in trees. Builds a cup nest on a branch, unlike most flycatchers with its color pattern.

Range: Mexico to Bolivia, Paraguay, northeastern Argentina, and southeastern Brazil.

WHITE-RINGED FLYCATCHER
(*Conopias parva*) Pl.19

Description: 6. Olive above; crown sooty brown with usually concealed yellow crown patch, bordered below by *broad white superciliary that extends around nape,* ear-coverts blackish; throat white, remaining underparts yellow.

Similar species: Strongly resembles Social Flycatcher but has distinctly longer bill, lacks even indistinct wing-bars, and always shows broader white eyestripe meeting at back of head. Both kiskadees also have white eyestripes meeting at back of head, but they have longer and more pointed bills, are markedly rufescent above, and usually occur in a different habitat.

Status and distribution: Uncommon to locally fairly common in humid forest canopy and forest borders in lowlands and lower foothills on Caribbean slope from Canal Zone eastward and on Pacific slope from eastern Panama province (Tocumen, Cerro Azul, Bayano River) eastward; not reported from western Caribbean slope but should occur as known from Costa Rica. In central Panama, most easily seen on Pipeline Road.

Habits: Usually found in pairs high in forest trees. The common call is a whirring trill *wherr-r-r,* with several variations. Nests in holes or crevices in trees.

Range: Costa Rica to northwestern Ecuador, extreme northern Brazil, and the Guianas.

Note: Sometimes placed in the genus *Coryphotriccus.* Birds from Costa Rica to western Ecuador (*albovitattus*) are sometimes considered distinct from yellow-throated birds from east of the Andes in South America.

SOCIAL (VERMILION-CROWNED) FLYCATCHER
(*Myiozetetes similis*) Pl.19

Description: 6–6½. *Olive above* with *indistinct, pale wing-bars;* crown brownish gray with usually concealed vermilion (sometimes orange-red) crown patch, prominent white superciliary, and *dark brownish gray ear-coverts;* throat white, remaining underparts yellow. Immature lacks crown patch, has grayish brown upperparts, and shows pale rusty edging on wings and tail.

Similar species: Rather resembles the less numerous White-ringed and Rusty-margined Flycatchers; see both species for distinctions. See also Gray-capped Flycatcher.

Status and distribution: Abundant around houses, in shrubby areas and clearings, and in lighter woodland and forest borders in lowlands and foothills on both slopes east to eastern Colon province (Río Guanche) and eastern Panama province (Bayano River); not recorded from Darién and only sightings from San Blas (at Puerto Obaldía on June 16–18, 1965; D. Sheets), which require confirmation; also ranges well up into western highlands; not recorded from offshore islands.

Habits: This species, the Yellow-bellied Elaenia, and the Tropical Kingbird are the three most widespread and numerous flycatchers in the open and semi-open parts of Panama. Often forages on lawns, though usually at middle heights and occasionally in forest canopy. At times it is distinctly "social," usually where there is a good supply of food. Eats much fruit as well as the more standard flycatcher fare of insects. The nest is a rather untidy large, domed ball with the entrance on one side near the top, often in a thorn tree or near a bee or wasp nest, occasionally using the nest of another bird as a foundation. A very noisy bird, with a variety of loud and harsh calls, most commonly *kree-yoo;* also *tsiyoo* and *kree-kree-kree-kree.* This species and the many other fairly large flycatchers with mostly yellow underparts are called "pechi-amarillo" by Panamanians.

Range: Northern Mexico to Bolivia, Paraguay, northeastern Argentina, and southeastern Brazil.

RUSTY-MARGINED FLYCATCHER

(*Myiozetetes cayanensis*) Pl.19

Description: 6–6¼. *Olive brown above* with *rusty edging on flight feathers;* crown blackish or sooty with usually concealed orange crown patch, prominent white superciliary, *blackish ear-coverts;* white throat, remaining underparts yellow. Immature lacks crown patch, has more rusty edging on wing and rusty edging on tail.

Similar species: Often difficult to distinguish from Social Flycatcher (immature Socials show some rusty on wings and tail). Best told by its brown (not greenish olive) tone above, lack of indistinct wing-bars, blacker crown and ear-coverts, and (usually most useful of all) its different calls (see below). Lesser Kiskadee is somewhat larger, brighter rufous brown above, has distinctly longer and slenderer bill, and also has different calls.

Status and distribution: Rare (west of Canal Zone) to locally common eastward in clearings and shrubby areas, usually near water, in lowlands on Pacific slope from eastern Chiriquí (Río Dupí west of San Félix) east through Darién; on Caribbean slope known only from just west of Canal Zone east through San Blas. Widespread in waterside habitat in Canal Zone; common in the Tocumen/La Jagua area.

Habits: Generally not as familiar as the abundant Social Flycatcher, and usually not around houses. Much less vocal than the Social, its most characteristic and frequent call being a high thin whining long-drawn *feeeee* or *wheeeeeee,* lasting 2–3 seconds, often repeated several times. Some other calls are more like Social's, a *cheepcheeree-chew* and a rapid, repeated *keéwit.*

Range: Western Panama to northern Bolivia and southern Brazil.

GRAY-CAPPED FLYCATCHER

(*Myiozetetes granadensis*) Pl.19

Description: 6¼. Recalls Social Flycatcher. Mostly olive above and yellow below (throat whitish), but with different pattern on head: instead of Social's broad white superciliary, has *gray crown with white restricted to forehead and short, narrow superciliary extending slightly behind eye;* ear-coverts blackish; only adult males have usually concealed orange-yellow crown patch (greatly reduced when present in females). Immature has more olive crown and pale tawny edging on wings and tail.

Similar species: Tropical Kingbird is larger with no white on head, and has pale gray throat and chest.

Status and distribution: Fairly common to common in lowlands on most of Caribbean slope, though rare and local in Canal Zone; on Pacific slope found in western Chiriquí (where ranges fairly commonly up to 4000 feet, rarely to 5000 feet), less commonly in drier lowlands from eastern Chiriquí to southern Coclé, and again in eastern Panama province (Río Chico eastward; common on Bayano River above Majé) and Darién. Near Canal Zone can be seen regularly only at Río Piedras and Río Guanche, eastern Colon province; also readily found at Boquete.

Habits: Favors cut-over shrubby areas and clearings with scattered larger trees, in most areas especially near water. Often occurs with Social Flycatcher, which it resembles in actions. Gray-cap's calls somewhat suggest Social's but are sharper and usually shorter, as *keep, geer-geer* (much like Great Kiskadee) or *kip-kee-kew,* with variations.

Range: Honduras to northern Bolivia and western Brazil.

GREAT KISKADEE

(*Pitangus sulphuratus*) Pl.19

Description: 8½–8¾. A *large* flycatcher, almost the size of a Boat-bill, and like that species with a *heavy* (but not as broad) *bill. Brown above with much rufous on wings and tail;* crown black with usually concealed yellow-orange crown patch, broad white superciliary that just meets at nape, and black ear-coverts; throat white, remaining underparts yellow.

Similar species: Best told from Boat-billed Flycatcher by its brown (not olive) upperparts with prominent rufous in wings and tail. Lesser Kiskadee is considerably smaller with more slender bill.

Status and distribution: Fairly common around habitations and in clearings and shrubby areas, especially near water, in lowlands on Caribbean slope in western Bocas del Toro, Canal Zone, and eastern Colon province (east to Portobelo); on Pacific slope uncommon in Canal Zone and Panama city area, and has recently spread west to Playa Coronado, western Panama province (1971, Eisenmann) and east to Tocumen, eastern Panama province (1973, Ridgely and Eisenmann). One recent sighting of one near the Volcán Lakes in lower highlands of western Chiriquí on February 15, 1973 (C. Leahy and A. Morgan). Has been spreading in recent years and probably will continue to do so; a post-World War II arrival in Canal Zone area, presumably from Bocas del Toro, where it has long been common.

Habits: An adaptable and agressive bird that will eat almost anything. Has a variety of loud characteristic calls, some of them buzzy. One of the most distinctive is reflected in its common name, *kisk-a-deé;* others include a *geep* and a *cheekaw* (the last resembling a call of the Squirrel Cuckoo).

Range: Southern Texas and Mexico to central Argentina.

LESSER KISKADEE

(*Pitangus lictor*) Pl.19

Description: 6½. *Bill long and slender.* Like Great Kiskadee in plumage except for somewhat less rich rufous on wings and less rufous in tail.

Similar species: Best distinguished from Great Kiskadee by its smaller size and different calls (see below). Also resembles the somewhat smaller Rusty-margined Flycatcher but has long slender (not stubby) bill.

Status and distribution: Locally fairly common in shrubby growth and low trees, invariably near water (especially in marshy areas) on Caribbean slope from around Canal Zone east through San Blas, on Pacific slope from Canal Zone (where scarce) east through Darién; only record from west of Zone is a specimen taken at Water Valley, western Bocas del Toro (N. G. Smith). Rather numerous around marshes in Tocumen/La Jagua area.

Habits: Usually in pairs, often in the same areas as the Rusty-margined Flycatcher; rather retiring. Its usual calls are vigorous and rather nasal, often a buzzy *dzay, drwey* or *dzai-dey-dzéy-dah;* sometimes a *keekzideeée* suggesting Great Kiskadee.

Range: Panama to northern Bolivia and southern Brazil.

GREAT CRESTED FLYCATCHER

(*Myiarchus crinitus*)

Description: 8. Plain olive above, head browner and often appearing distinctly crested; wings with indistinct whitish wing-bars and with *rufous edging on primaries; tail with much rufous edging* (*whole underside looks rufous*); throat and chest gray, lower underparts light yellow.

Similar species: See Panama Flycatcher.

Status and distribution: Fairly common transient and somewhat less numerous winter resident in lowlands on both slopes (late September–May, mostly October–April); recorded also on Pearl Islands (Saboga) and Coiba and Cébaco Islands.

Habits: Favors second-growth woodland and forest canopy, sometimes clearings. Often eats small fruit in Panama. Its most distinctive call, a whistled *wheeeep,* is often heard; also gives a throaty rolling *prrrrreet* (R. T. Peterson).

Range: Breeds in eastern North America; winters in southern Florida and from Texas to Colombia (casually to Venezuela).

PANAMA FLYCATCHER

(*Myiarchus panamensis*) Pl.20

Description: 7½. Very like Great Crested Flycatcher and often confused with it, but *adults lack rufous in wings and tail.* Grayish olive above, the head usually *not* giving a crested appearance, wings with pale grayish wing-bars; throat and chest pale gray, lower underparts light yellow. Immature shows some narrow rufous edging on wings and tail.

Similar species: Immature Panama Flycatcher is very like Great Crest but underside of tail is dusky (not rufous). See also Dusky-capped Flycatcher. Scrub Flycatcher resembles adult of this species in pattern but it is markedly smaller with a shorter bill. Tropical Kingbird lacks gray on underparts and has slightly forked tail.

Status and distribution: Fairly common in semi-open and scrubby areas, clearings, light woodland, and coastal growth and mangroves in lowlands and foothills (to about 4500 feet) on entire Pacific slope (local and uncommon in Darién); on Caribbean slope found in western Bocas del Toro (Almirante, Cocoplum) and from northern Coclé east through San Blas; found also on the Pearl Islands, Coiba Island, Taboga Island, and many other smaller islands off the Pacific coast.

Habits: Similar to Great Crested Flycatcher, but much more a bird of semi-open situations. Its vocalizations are softer and less arresting than the Great Crest's: the dawn song is a fast whistled *tseeédew* or *wheédeedew;* another call is a semi-whistled twittering *tee, deedeedeedeedeedee* with variations; also has a soft clear whistled *wheee* and a *prrrt.*

Range: Southwestern Costa Rica to northern Venezuela.

Note: Often considered a race of the South American *M. ferox* (Short-crested Flycatcher) and so designated in much literature. W. Lanyon (oral comm.) believes it represents a distinct species (vocalizations quite different).

DUSKY-CAPPED (OLIVACEOUS) FLYCATCHER

(*Myiarchus tuberculifer*) Pl.20

Description: 6. Mostly greenish olive above with *contrasting blackish cap;* throat and chest pale gray, lower underparts light yellow. Birds from western Panama east to Veraguas (*bangsi*) have narrow cinnamon edging on wings and tail. Immatures throughout show this cinnamon edging, and have dusky cap.

Similar species: The sooty black cap sets it apart from other similar flycatchers; noticeably smaller than other Panama *Myiarchus.*

Status and distribution: Common in forest borders and second-growth woodland in more humid areas on both slopes, ranging up to about 6000 feet in highlands; absent from dry Pacific lowlands from eastern side of Azuero Peninsula to western Panama province. In Canal Zone more numerous on Caribbean side.

Habits: Characteristic and often heard is a whistled, long-drawn, plaintive *whee-eew,* often slightly burred or throaty in quality; also gives a thin *pheeeee* or *seeeee* (suggestive of Rusty-margined Flycatcher) and an unmusical *wheerrrrp.*

Range: Extreme southwestern United States to northwestern Argentina, Paraguay, and southern Brazil.

OLIVE-SIDED FLYCATCHER

(*Nuttallornis borealis*)

Description: 7–7½. A rather large, *dark* flycatcher with a *short tail* and *bull-headed look.* Grayish olive above with indistinct whitish wing-bars; *mostly grayish below* with throat, narrow stripe down center of breast, and belly whitish (suggesting a "dark unbuttoned vest over a white shirt"); *tuft of white feathers* sometimes protrudes (but is often hidden) from under wings onto flanks.

Similar species: Most easily confused with the wood-pewees but larger, darker below, with relatively shorter tail and less distinct wing-bars. See also Dark Pewee (almost uniformly dark).

Status and distribution: Uncommon transient throughout except in very open areas (late August–mid-November; mid-March–late May); a few individuals winter in foothills and highlands.

Habits: Typically seen perched on a high, exposed, dead branch or tall stub, flying out for long distances after passing insects, usually returning to its original perch. Its unmistakable loud whistled *hic-three-beers* is occasionally heard, especially on spring migration; also gives a *whip-whip-whip,* like Dark Pewee.

Range: Breeds in northern and western North America; winters from Venezuela and Colombia to southern Peru, a few in southern Middle America.

DARK PEWEE

(*Contopus lugubris*)

Description: 6½–6¾. Known only from western Chiriquí highlands. *Distinctly crested. Uniform dark olive slate* relieved only by whitish chin and lower belly.

Similar species: Readily recognized by its

Dark Pewee

prominent crest and dark coloration. See especially Olive-sided Flycatcher (lacking crest and not as dark) and Black Phoebe.

Status and distribution: Fairly common in forest and forest borders in highlands of western Chiriquí above 4000 feet, most numerous 6000–8000 feet.

Habits: Reminiscent of an Olive-sided Flycatcher, perching high on dead branches, making long sallies, shivering tail on return to perch. Has several short calls, most frequent a *pip-pip-pip.*

Range: Costa Rica and western Panama.

Note: By some authors considered conspecific with *C. pertinax* (Greater Pewee or Coues' Flycatcher) of extreme southwestern United States to Nicaragua, including also as conspecific *C. fumigatus* (Smoke-colored Pewee) of South American mountains.

[OCHRACEOUS PEWEE]

(*Contopus ochraceus*)

Description: 6½. Perhaps found in western Chiriquí mountains. *Ochraceous olive above* with duskier cap, wings, and tail; *wings with two buff bars; mostly yellow below* tinged with ochraceous olive on chest and neck.

Similar species: In color resembles the much smaller Tufted Flycatcher except for the yellower underparts.

Status and distribution: Known only from one nineteenth-century specimen labeled as from "Chiriquí" in AMNH; also one brief sighting of a bird that may have been this species on the Boquete Trail above Cerro Punta (about 7000 feet) on February 29, 1960 (Eisenmann). Possibly a rare resident on the high slopes of Volcán Barú; has been recorded from the Talamanca Cordillera of Costa Rica (Empalme), which stretches southward virtually to Panama.

Range: Costa Rica, possibly western Panama.

EASTERN WOOD-PEWEE

(*Contopus virens*)

Description: 5½–6. Dark olive to grayish olive above with two distinct whitish wingbars; whitish below, washed with olive gray on sides of throat and breast. Some birds, especially fall immatures, are tinged yellowish below.

Similar species: A drab flycatcher, easily confused; its voice is generally the best clue (see below). Often cannot be safely distinguished in the field from Western Wood-Pewee and Tropical Pewee; see respective species for distinctions. *Empidonax* flycatchers are smaller than wood-pewees, usually have a complete eye-ring (sometimes faintly indicated in wood-pewees, especially in front of eye), and have shorter wings in proportion to tail (in wood-pewees, wings usually extend more than halfway down tail), but longer tarsus (14.5–17.5 mm in *Empidonax,* 12.0–14.5 in wood-pewees). Olive-sided Flycatcher is larger with short tail, darker below.

Status and distribution: Common to very common transient throughout, mostly in lowlands (September–November; March–May); recorded also from Pearl Islands, Taboguilla Island, and Escudo de Veraguas; a few may possibly winter, but no definite records December–February.

Habits: Usually seen perched at low and medium heights in clearings, second-growth woodland, and forest borders. Often heard on both migrations is its characteristic sweet plaintive whistle *pee-a-wee,* sometimes shortened to *pee-weé,* or slurred downward and burred to *pee-ur.*

Range: Breeds in eastern North America; winters in northern and western South

America, possibly in southern Middle America.

WESTERN WOOD-PEWEE
(*Contopus sordidulus*)

Description: 5½–6. Very similar to Eastern Wood-Pewee and, unless calling, usually not safely distinguished in the field (nor sometimes in the hand). Averages grayer or browner above and more extensively dark below (often without white on center of breast); *bill sometimes entirely or almost entirely dark* (in Eastern, lower mandible always largely yellowish or pinkish except at tip); wing formula similar.

Status and distribution: Transient and perhaps occasional winter resident (early August–late November; early March–May; one specimen from February 15); exact status and abundance uncertain due to identification problem. Specimens chiefly from western foothills and highlands, where on migration it generally outnumbers Eastern Wood-Pewee and where Tropical Pewee does not usually occur.

Habits: Like Eastern Wood-Pewee. Its common call is a harsh or hoarse, nasal *peeyee* or *peeeer* (R. T. Peterson) or *phreeer* (A. Phillips), which is quite distinctive but is not often heard away from its breeding grounds; might be confused with the burred but sweet *pee-ur* of Eastern Wood-Pewee.

Range: Breeds from western North America to Honduras (possibly to Costa Rica); winters in northern and western South America, a few occasionally in Panama.

Note: By some authors considered conspecific with *C. virens,* the English name of the entire complex then being simply Wood Pewee.

TROPICAL PEWEE
(*Contopus cinereus*) Pl.20

Description: 5–5½. Closely resembles both Eastern and Western Wood-Pewees, some individuals not safely distinguishable in the field unless calling. Somewhat smaller and more slender, with relatively longer tail; rather dark above, especially on crown; belly often tinged yellowish. None of these characters is diagnostic in the field. In the hand note that Tropical's 10th (outermost) primary is shorter than 6th and about same length as 5th (in Eastern and Western, 10th is distinctly longer than 6th), and that Tropical's wing is shorter (65–77 mm) than Eastern's or Western's (77–91 mm).

Status and distribution: Locally fairly common in shrubby areas and overgrown pastures with scattered trees or small shrubs in lowlands (occasionally to 3000 feet) on both slopes east to eastern Colon province and western Darién (Garachiné); more widespread on Pacific slope, though apparently absent from driest areas in eastern Herrera, southern Coclé, and western Panama province; on Caribbean slope only where clearings are fairly extensive; found also on Coiba Island.

Habits: Similar to those of the two wood-pewees, but tends to perch lower. Makes short sallies and often quivers its tail upon alighting. The call is a rapid *sreerrip* or variants, often repeated, very different from the wood-pewees.

Range: Southeastern Mexico to northern Argentina and southern Brazil.

YELLOW-BELLIED FLYCATCHER
(*Empidonax flaviventris*)

Description: 4¾–5. Greenish olive above with pale yellowish eye-ring and wing-bars; yellowish olive below, fading to *dull yellow on throat* and pale yellow on belly. Immature is duller above and below, with buffier wing-bars.

Similar species: Easily confused with Acadian Flycatcher, which can be very yellow below (even on throat), especially in fall. Yellow-bellied usually has difference between longest and 6th primary of 5 mm or less (in Acadian usually 6 mm or more) and has 10th (outer) primary usually equal to or longer than 5th; outer web of 6th primary sometimes slightly emarginate (cut out or narrowed toward tip); total wing length 62–70 mm. See also Yellowish, Yellow-olive, and Yellow-margined Flycatchers.

Status and distribution: Fairly common winter resident (early September–mid-April) in western Panama (especially in Chiriquí highlands), becoming rare in central and eastern Panama, with only two specimens (in AMNH) from Canal Zone and one from Darién (Cana).

Habits: Favors woodland and woodland borders. All of the migrant *Empidonax* tend to be solitary (though often appearing in "waves" on migration) and forage at low and middle heights, making short sallies after passing insects, often quivering their tails upon returning to their perch. The Yellow-belly's most characteristic call is a spirit-less whistle *chu-wee* or *per-wee* with a rising inflection (R. T. Peterson), somewhat suggestive of a shortened call of the Eastern Wood-Pewee; it is occasionally heard in Panama.

Range: Breeds in northern North America; winters from eastern Mexico to Panama.

ACADIAN FLYCATCHER
(*Empidonax virescens*)

Description: 5½–6¾. Olive green above with whitish eye-ring and wing-bars; mostly whitish below, tinged olive on breast and (especially in fall) yellowish on belly. *Throat usually whitish,* but some birds (especially in fall) have clear yellow throat and predominantly yellow underparts. Immatures have buffier wing-bars.

Similar species: Yellower fall individuals are very easily taken for a Yellow-bellied Flycatcher (see in hand characteristics, some given under that species). Duller individuals are sometimes very hard to separate from Traill's Flycatcher but are usually greener above and yellower below, slightly larger, and have slightly differing wing formula. Acadian usually has difference between longest and 6th primary of 6 mm or more (in Yellow-belly usually 5 mm or less; in Traill's usually less than 6 mm), and has 10th (outer) primary usually equal to or longer than 5th; total wing length 67–81 mm.

Status and distribution: Probably a fairly common transient and winter resident in wooded areas throughout (September–late April); recorded from Pearl Islands and Taboguilla Island. Exact status uncertain due to field identification problems.

Habits: Tends to be found in woodland and woodland borders (Traill's favors more open, shrubbier areas). The song is a sharp explosive *spit-chee!* (R. T. Peterson) or *ka-zeép* (Saunders), with a sharp upward inflection, but not likely to be heard in Panama; the usual call is a *peet* or *wheep,* snappier and less dry than the similar call of the Traill's.

Range: Breeds in eastern United States; winters from Costa Rica to Venezuela and western Ecuador.

TRAILL'S FLYCATCHER
(*Empidonax traillii*)

(Includes Alder (*E. alnorum*) and Willow (*E. traillii*) Flycatchers.)

Description: 5¼–6½. Plain to brownish olive above (*E. t. brewsteri* of western North America is more brownish) with whitish eye-ring (often incomplete) and wing-bars; whitish below, washed with grayish olive on breast, and pale yellowish on flanks and often on lower belly. Immature browner with buffy wing-bars, sometimes with buff on under wing-coverts and thighs.

Similar species: Immatures resemble dull examples of White-throated Flycatcher, and adults can be easily confused with Acadian Flycatcher or even a wood-pewee. Traill's usually has difference between 6th and longest primary of 6 mm or less, and has 10th primary usually equal to or longer than 5th in eastern birds (usually equal to or a little shorter in western birds); total wing length 64–78 mm. The differences between this species and the Acadian are thus very subtle, even in the hand and especially in fall. In general the best policy in Panama is not to attempt to distinguish between the Acadian and Traill's Flycatchers unless the bird sings, or unless one has the bird in hand and carefully checks wing measurements and primary formula. The whole situation is further complicated by the until recently unsuspected presence of two kinds of "Traill's" Flycatchers, indistinguishable in the field on morphological characters, separable only by vocalizations.

Status and distribution: Fairly common to common transient and winter resident throughout (early September–mid May); recorded also on Pearl Islands (Saboga).

Habits: Tends to remain more in the open than other migrant *Empidonax,* usually perching low in shrubby areas, often near water. The two song types represent the two species mentioned above; the more northern, semi-whistled, burry *fee-zwee-o* or *wee-bzee-o* birds are *E. alnorum* (Alder Flycatcher), which probably winter mainly or entirely in South America, occurring in Panama as transients; while the more southern and western *fitz-bew* birds are *E. traillii* (Willow Flycatcher), including nominate *traillii* and the western *brewsteri,* which appear to be the kinds wintering in Panama. The usual calls heard in Panama are a short dry *whit* or *kit;* occasionally a bird may sing its song.

Range: Breeds in North America; winters from Guatemala to northern Argentina.

Note: The A.O.U. Check-list Committee now recognizes the two species, but in the field, unless the diagnostic calls are heard, it is best to refer to the birds as Traill's Flycatchers.

LEAST FLYCATCHER
(*Empidonax minimus*)

Description: 4¾–5¼. Very rare. Brownish to grayish olive above, the crown somewhat grayer, with conspicuous whitish eye-ring and wing-bars; mostly whitish below, tinged grayish on throat and chest, with yellowish tinge chiefly on flanks. Immature has buffy wing-bars and is more brownish on chest and yellowish below.

Similar species: Closely resembles Traill's and Acadian Flycatchers, but smaller and tends to be more grayish olive above and more uniformly dull whitish below, without the usual contrast between white throat and olive-tinged chest. Least has notched tail and 10th (outer) primary equal to or shorter than 5th; outer web of 6th primary is distinctly emarginate; total wing length 57–68 mm.

Status and distribution: Very rare winter visitant, with only a few scattered records: one specimen from Chiriquí (October 16, 1900, at David); one from western Bocas del Toro (a bird mist-netted, measured by Eisenmann, and released on October 19, 1965, at Almirante); three old McLeannan specimens from Canal Zone; and one recent Canal Zone specimen (October 5, 1953, at Farfan Beach).

Habits: Prefers woodland borders and shrubby areas. Its well-known song, an emphatic *chebéc,* is not likely to be heard on its winter quarters; its call, a dry *whit,* resembles Traill's.

Range: Breeds in eastern North America; winters from Mexico (a few in extreme southern United States) to Panama.

WHITE-THROATED FLYCATCHER
(*Empidonax albigularis*)

Description: 4¾–5. *Olive brown above* with indistinct or partial yellowish buffy eye-ring and *buffy wing-bars;* throat whitish, breast and sides brownish olive, belly buffy yellowish, deepening to buff on under tail-coverts; under wing-coverts and thighs buffy brown. Immature has wing-bars broader and more cinnamon.

Similar species: The brown upperparts, buffy wing-bars, and buff tone to lower underparts should set it apart from all the migrant *Empidonax* except immatures of the larger Traill's Flycatcher, which are often brown above with brownish buffy wing-bars. White-throated's 10th primary is distinctly (3–5 mm) shorter than 5th (in Traill's at most only slightly shorter); inner web of 6th primary slightly emarginate; total wing length 55–63 mm. See also Bran-colored Flycatcher.

Status and distribution: Apparently a rare resident in highlands of western Chiriquí, mostly 4000–6000 feet. Two specimens from lowlands (one taken at Chiriquicito, Bocas del Toro, on March 26, 1926; one nineteenth-century McLeannan specimen from Canal Zone) represent either wanderers from highlands or possibly migrants from farther north in Middle America.

Habits: Favors rather open shrubby areas. Its song is an explosive, but not loud, buzzy *pseeyp* or *kseeyip.*

Range: Mexico to western (casually central) Panama.

YELLOWISH FLYCATCHER
(*Empidonax flavescens*) Pl.21

Description: 4¾. Found only in western highlands. *Yellowish olive green above* with *very prominent yellowish eye-ring,* broader to the rear; two buffy wing-bars; *rich yellow below* (with an almost brassy tone), tinged with olive on chest and sides. Immature is browner above with cinnamon wing-bars, buffier on chest, but becoming almost whitish on belly.

Similar species: Much yellower than any other *Empidonax,* including the Yellow-bellied, and with more prominent eye-ring. Immature might be confused with Bran-colored Flycatcher but is much yellower and lacks Bran-color's breast streaking.

Status and distribution: Fairly common in forest borders and clearings with trees in highlands of Chiriquí and Veraguas, mostly 3500–7000 feet.

Habits: Generally stays fairly low in shrubs and small trees, usually within ten feet of ground. Very unsuspicious. The common call is a simple *seee* (A. Skutch); generally a rather quiet bird.

Range: Southern Mexico to western Panama.

Note: By some authors considered conspecific with *E. difficilis* (Western Flycatcher) of western United States and Mexico.

BLACK-CAPPED FLYCATCHER
(*Empidonax atriceps*) Pl.21

Description: 4½. Found only in western mountains. *Cap black* contrasting with otherwise olive upperparts; prominent white eye-ring and indistinct grayish wing-bars; throat white, chest and sides brownish, fading to pale yellow on flanks; outer web of outer pair of tail feathers white. Immature has cap more sooty but it still contrasts with back.

Similar species: No other similar flycatcher has the contrasting black or sooty cap.

Status and distribution: Fairly common in brushy clearings in mountains of western Chiriquí and adjacent Bocas del Toro, mostly above 7000 feet.

Habits: Usually stays at or below eye-level, perching conspicuously on the top of a small bush, fence post, or low tree. Often shivers tail sideways. Very unsuspicious. The call is a simple *tsip*.

Range: Costa Rica and western Panama.

BLACK-BILLED FLYCATCHER
(*Aphanotriccus audax*) Pl.32

Description: 5. Found only in eastern Panama. Bill blackish. Olive green above with white eye-ring and *narrow white supraloral stripe;* wings with two buffy yellowish bars; mostly light yellow below with whitish throat and *broad olive green band across breast.*

Similar species: In plumage, somewhat like an *Empidonax,* but they never show a supraloral stripe and none has mostly yellow underparts crossed by olive breast band. See also *Leptopogon sp.*

Status and distribution: Little known. Recorded in lowlands of eastern Panama province on Bayano River at Puerto San Antonio and at Majé (where uncommon, with a specimen taken on January 25, 1973 by P. Galindo, and others seen nearby by Ridgely, Eisenmann, and J. Gwynne) and foothills of eastern Darién (near Cana and on Cerro Pirre).

Habits: Favors undergrowth in forest. Looks very slender in the field, with very much less upright posture than an *Empidonax.*

Range: Eastern Panama and northwestern Colombia.

Note: By some placed in the genus *Praedo.*

TUFTED FLYCATCHER
(*Mitrephanes phaeocercus*) Pl.21

Description: 4½–4¾. *Conspicuous pointed crest* is unique among small Panama flycatchers. Olive green above with tawny sides of head; *tawny below,* becoming yellow on lower belly. Birds from Darién (*eminulus*) are paler below, more buff on throat and breast, and yellow on belly.

Status and distribution: Common in clearings and forest borders in highlands of Chiriquí (mostly above 4000 feet) and Veraguas (where ranges lower, to 2500 feet); uncommon in hill country of Coclé and on Cerro Campana (2500–3000 feet); found also in foothills and highlands of eastern Darién.

Habits: Acts like a diminutive wood-pewee. Perches conspicuously at low and middle heights, sallying out after passing insects, often returning to its original perch, and characteristically shivering its tail sideways upon alighting. Frequently gives a piping whistle, *pee-pee-pee-pee . . .* (up to 8 notes).

Range: Northern Mexico to Bolivia.

RUDDY-TAILED FLYCATCHER
(*Terenotriccus erythrurus*) Pl.21

Description: 3½–3¾. *Small.* Short rather stubby bill. Head and back grayish olive; *rump and tail cinnamon-rufous; most of wings and entire underparts ochraceous.*

Similar species: Likely to be confused only with the larger Ochre-bellied Flycatcher, which is mostly olive green above and on throat, with rather long and slender bill.

Status and distribution: Common in second-growth woodland and forest in lowlands and in smaller numbers up into lower foothills (to about 2600 feet) on both slopes; absent from dry Pacific lowlands from eastern side of Azuero Peninsula to western Panama province.

Habits: Forages at low and middle levels, often perching in the open and not difficult to see. Sometimes twitches wings rapidly up over its back, both going up simultaneously. Its calls are a thin *pseeoo-see* and a *seeoo-bzeew.*

Range: Southeastern Mexico to northern Bolivia and central Brazil.

TAWNY-BREASTED FLYCATCHER
(*Myiobius villosus*) Pl.32

Description: 5½–6. Known only from eastern Darién highlands. *Conspicuous yellow rump;* graduated tail. *Dark olive green above* with usually concealed yellow crown patch (dull cinnamon in female); throat whitish, *most of underparts tawny brown,* center of belly pale yellow.

Similar species: Sulphur-rumped Flycatcher is smaller, shows much more yellow on underparts (including throat), with only chest and sides suffused with brighter tawny, and is not as dark above. Black-tailed Flycatcher lacks tawny altogether; both species are essentially lowland birds.

Status and distribution: Recorded from two specimens taken in forest in highlands of eastern Darién (Cerro Tacarcuna, 4000–4800 feet).

Range: Eastern Panama to northwestern Venezuela and northern Bolivia.

Note: Wetmore calls it Greater Black-tailed Flycatcher.

SULPHUR-RUMPED FLYCATCHER

(*Myiobius sulphureipygius*) Pl.20

Description: 4¾–5. *Conspicuous yellow rump;* graduated tail. Olive above with usually concealed yellow crown patch in male; tail black; yellow below *suffused with bright tawny on chest and sides.*

Similar species: Black-tailed Flycatcher has buffy-olive instead of bright tawny on underparts. In eastern Darién see also Tawny-breasted Flycatcher.

Status and distribution: Locally fairly common in lower growth of humid forest in lowlands and lower foothills on entire Caribbean slope; on Pacific slope in lowlands and foothills in western Chiriquí, hill country of Veraguas (Calobre, Santa Fé), Cerro Campana, and eastern Panama province (vicinity of Panama city, Cerro Azul/Jefe area) east through Darién. In Canal Zone, most readily seen on Pipeline Road.

Habits: Always seems to be showing off its yellow rump by drooping its wings and fanning its tail. Usually found singly, often accompanying a mixed foraging flock moving through the lower growth of the forest. The nest is an irregular, closed structure attached to the end of a slender branch, the entrance on the side; it often hangs over a small stream.

Range: Southeastern Mexico to western Ecuador.

Note: By some authors considered conspecific with *M. barbatus* (Whiskered Flycatcher) of South America east of the Andes to Peru and southern Brazil, the English name of the entire complex then being Sulphur-rumped Flycatcher.

BLACK-TAILED FLYCATCHER

(*Myiobius atricaudus*) Pl.20

Description: 4¾–5. Resembles Sulphur-rumped Flycatcher but has *chest washed with buffy-olive* (not suffused with bright tawny on chest and sides).

Similar species: See Sulphur-rumped Flycatcher.

Status and distribution: Fairly common in lower growth of second-growth woodland and forest borders in lowlands on both slopes, though absent from drier parts of eastern side of Azuero Peninsula to western Panama province. Normally not found *within* humid forest where the Sulphur-rump takes over.

Habits: Very active and spritely, moving about restlessly, displaying its yellow rump and fanning its tail. Found especially near streams.

Range: Southwestern Costa Rica to Peru and southern Brazil.

Note: Wetmore calls it Lesser Black-tailed Flycatcher.

BRAN-COLORED FLYCATCHER

(*Myiophobus fasciatus*) Pl.21

Description: 4½–4¾. Suggests an *Empidonax* in size and shape. *Brown above* with usually concealed yellow crown patch (smaller in female; absent in immature); wings and tail dusky with *two broad buffy whitish wing-bars;* buffy yellowish below with *indistinct brownish streaks on breast.*

Similar species: Superficially resembles White-throated Flycatcher except for the blurry breast streaking and concealed crown patch, and lack of an eye-ring.

Status and distribution: Uncommon to fairly common but local in overgrown fields and pastures and shrubby areas in lowlands on Pacific slope from Chiriquí to eastern Panama province (lower Bayano River at Puerto San Antonio), ranging up sparingly to about 4000 feet in western Chiriquí; on Caribbean slope known only (and in small numbers) from Canal Zone and adjacent Colon province; not recorded from Azuero Peninsula or Darién; found also on some of Pearl Islands.

Habits: Perches low on fences and bushes, often in pairs. Usually rather inconspicuous. Its song is a loud but unemphatic, monotonous *weeb, weeb, weeb, weeb . . .,* sometimes sounding like *weeup* or *tweep.*

Range: Southwestern Costa Rica to northern Chile and northern Argentina.

NORTHERN ROYAL-FLYCATCHER

(*Onychorhynchus mexicanus*) Pl.20

Description: 6½–7. The remarkable *fan-shaped crest* for which this bird is famous is unfortunately not often seen. Bill long and broad. Brown above with *small buffy spots on wing-coverts; rump and tail tawny-ochraceous,* becoming brown toward tip of tail; yellowish buffy below with indistinct olive mottling or barring on chest (more obvious in immatures). When closed (almost always), the crest lies flat but protrudes to the rear, giving a *distinct hammerhead effect;* when spread, the crest is a full semi-circle of scarlet (yellow-orange in female) with black spots and steel blue tips, held perpendicular to axis of body; only rarely does any color show through when crest is folded.

Similar species: No other similar bird has the hammerhead effect. Might be confused with Brownish Flycatcher or a *Myiarchus.*

Status and distribution: Uncommon in lower growth of forest borders and second-growth woodland, usually near streams, in lowlands and (in smaller numbers) foothills on both slopes, recorded up to 3700 feet in western Chiriquí; more numerous on Pacific slope but absent from driest areas on eastern side of Azuero Peninsula to western Panama province.

Habits: Rather an inconspicuous bird generally. When handled (as after capture in a mist-net), the bird raises its crest to its fullest glory and twists its head rhythmically from side to side, at the same time opening its bill and exposing the orange gape. This display has so rarely been noted under natural conditions that its function remains uncertain, most probably a threat. The nest is very long and slender (2–6 feet), loosely constructed with entrance on the side, and hung from the tip of a drooping branch usually over a small shady stream.

Range: Southern Mexico to western Colombia.

Note: Possibly conspecific with *O. coronatus* (Amazonian Royal-Flycatcher) and other members of the genus found in South America.

WHITE-THROATED SPADEBILL
(*Platyrinchus mystaceus*)

Description: 3½–3¾. *Tiny* and stubby, with *broad flat bill* and short tail. Olive brown above with usually concealed yellow crown patch (small or absent in female and immature), *buffy supraloral stripe and eye-ring,* and a patch of dusky with buff center on ear-coverts; *throat white,* chest and sides buffy brownish, remaining underparts pale yellow.

Similar species: No highland species at all resembles it. Golden-crowned Spadebill has more strongly marked facial pattern, golden-rufous crown, and lacks the con-

WHITE-THROATED SPADEBILL

spicuous white throat; the two are found together only very locally.

Status and distribution: Uncommon to fairly common in undergrowth of humid forest in foothills and highlands of Chiriquí, adjacent Bocas del Toro, Veraguas (both slopes), Cerro Campana, and eastern Darién; recorded in Panama mostly 2000–7500 feet, but one specimen from Water Valley in coastal lowlands of western Bocas del Toro was taken on January 22, 1958. Mist-netting indicates it is fairly common in western Chiriquí above 5000 feet.

Habits: Seems even harder to see than Golden-crowned Spadebill. Usually remains motionless for long periods in dense undergrowth, then darts off abruptly to a new perch. The call is a single sharp *wheek.*

Range: Costa Rica to northern Bolivia, Paraguay, northeastern Argentina, and southeastern Brazil.

Note: Some authors include in this species *P. cancrominus* (Stub-tailed Spadebill) of southern Mexico to northwestern Costa Rica.

GOLDEN-CROWNED SPADEBILL
(*Platyrinchus coronatus*) Pl.21

Description: 3½–3¾. A *tiny,* stubby flycatcher with a *broad, flat bill* and a *very short tail. Crown cinnamon-rufous* bordered with black, superciliary yellowish, *a black spot in front of eye and another on ear-coverts;* otherwise olive above; pale yellow below, tinged with olive on breast and sides.

Similar species: In shape, not unlike a manakin. The bright facial pattern and very broad bill should preclude confusion.

Status and distribution: Uncommon to fairly common in undergrowth of humid forest in lowlands (up to about 2800 feet locally) on entire Caribbean slope; on Pacific slope recorded in lowlands of western Chiriquí (old specimen from Bugaba), hill country of Veraguas, on Cerro Campana, and from eastern Panama province (Panama city vicinity) east through Darién. More numerous from Canal Zone eastward.

Habits: Inconspicuous, remaining motionless for long periods of time; mist-netting better reveals its true numbers. Frequently gives a weak buzzy trill, almost insect-like, *bzzp,* often doubled.

Range: Honduras to Peru and Amazonian Brazil.

BROWNISH FLYCATCHER

(*Cnipodectes subbrunneus*) Pl.20

Description: ♂ 7; ♀ 6. *Mostly olive brown, more rufous on tail,* paler on throat and breast, becoming pale buffy yellowish on belly; wings dusky with *buffy edging and buffy brown wing-bars.* Adult male has stiffened and peculiarly twisted outer primaries (function unknown).

Similar species: Bran-colored Flycatcher is smaller, has blurry breast streaking and more conspicuous buffy wing-bars, and is a bird of more open habitats (not forest interior). More likely to be confused with Thrushlike Manakin, with which it regularly occurs: the manakin is not as bright brown on tail, lacks the buffy wing-edging and the longish tail, and in central and eastern Panama lowlands has breast and belly grayish olive. The flycatcher can often easily be known by its wing-lifting habit (see below).

Status and distribution: Uncommon in undergrowth of humid forest and second-growth woodland in lowlands on Caribbean slope from Coclé (Río Cascajal, El Uracillo) eastward, and on Pacific slope from Canal Zone eastward.

Habits: Favors areas where the forest floor is open and dark, and, for a bird of the forest interior, not too hard to see. Shares with Ochre-bellied and *Leptopogon* flycatchers the habit of frequently lifting wings above body, one at a time; in this species the movement is so leisurely that it seems as if the bird is stretching its wing. The call is a distinctive sharp and emphatic whistle, usually doubled (sometimes single or triple), *keeew, keeee* or *wheea-wheea.*

Range: Central Panama to northern Peru and western Amazonian Brazil.

YELLOW-OLIVE FLYCATCHER

(*Tolmomyias sulphurescens*) Pl.20

Description: 5. Rather heavy-headed, with *fairly broad, somewhat flattened bill.* Bright olive green above, grayer on cap with short white supraloral stripe (but *no eye-ring*); wings and tail dusky, *wings with narrow yellow edging and more or less distinct yellow wing-bars;* throat grayish tinged with yellow, becoming yellowish olive green on chest and sides, and clear yellow below.

Similar species: Yellow-margined Flycatcher is very similar but has dark gray cap contrasting with back, white eye-ring (as well as a supraloral stripe), broader and more conspicuous yellow wing-edging (but lacking wing-bars), and grayer throat and chest. Forest Elaenia differs in having short unflattened bill, less bright yellow wing-edging, and a yellow-orange crown patch (usually concealed). See also Yellow-green Tyrannulet.

Status and distribution: Uncommon to fairly common in second-growth and open woodland, woodland borders, and clearings with many scattered trees in lowlands on entire Pacific slope, ranging up to about 5500 feet in Chiriquí highlands; on Caribbean slope known only from northern Coclé (El Uracillo) and western Colon province (Chilar) east through Canal Zone to western San Blas (Mandinga).

Habits: Usually forages at middle heights, gleaning in the foliage and often difficult to see clearly. The call is somewhat similar to the Yellow-margined's but is thinner and not as penetrating, usually of only one or two notes, a high sibilant *dzz, dzz* or *tsit, tsit,* sometimes followed by a fast musical rattle. The foot-long, hanging, purse-shaped nest with a downward extending tube, made of fine hair-like fibers, is conspicuous (rarely more than 20 feet above ground) and can be regularly seen at Summit Gardens.

Range: Southern Mexico to northern Argentina and southeastern Brazil.

YELLOW-MARGINED FLYCATCHER

(*Tolmomyias assimilis*) Pl.20

Description: 4¾. Very like Yellow-olive Flycatcher. Bright olive green above with *contrasting gray cap* and *white supraloral stripe* *and eye-ring* (interrupted in front); wings dusky with *broad, yellow edging but no distinct wing-bars;* throat and chest pale grayish, *contrasting with yellow lower underparts.*

Similar species: Best distinguished from Yellow-olive Flycatcher by the eye-ring, contrasting gray cap, broad yellow wing-edging and no bars, and greater contrast on underparts; the Yellow-margined is a brighter, cleaner-cut bird. Also resembles Greenish Elaenia but is smaller with broader flatter bill, and different voice and habitat. See also Yellow-green Tyrannulet.

Status and distribution: Common in forest and forest borders in lowlands on entire Caribbean slope; on Pacific slope known from one specimen from western Chiriquí (Cerro Pando), Cerro Campana, and from Canal Zone east through Darién. In Canal Zone, widespread and numerous in forested areas on Caribbean side, more local and uncommon on Pacific side.

Habits: Forages at middle and upper levels, often joining mixed flocks of insectivorous birds. Gleans from foliage, often carrying tail partly cocked up. The frequently heard call is a series of 3 to 5 (usually 4) identical notes, rather harsh and buzzy, given deliberately, *zhweek, zhweek, zhweek, zhweek* or *tsish, tsish, tsish, tsish,* with pause of several minutes before being uttered again.

Range: Costa Rica to northern Bolivia and Amazonian Brazil.

OLIVACEOUS FLATBILL

(*Rhynchocyclus olivaceus*) Pl.20

Description: 6. Heavy-headed, with *very broad, flat bill.* Mostly olive green above with an *indistinct whitish eye-ring; wings broadly margined with yellowish and with yellow wing-bars;* throat and chest olive green, indistinctly streaked with pale yellow, lower underparts pale yellow.

Similar species: See Eye-ringed Flatbill of highlands. The fairly large size, broad flat bill, and generally dull olive green plumage set it apart from other flycatchers; see the smaller slender-billed Olive-striped Flycatcher. Broad-billed Manakin lacks the eye-ring, wing-bars, and wing-edging, and is yellower on chest with no streaking.

Status and distribution: Uncommon to fairly common in forest and second-growth woodland in lowlands on Caribbean slope from western Colon province (Chilar) east through San Blas, and on Pacific slope from Canal Zone east through Darién (where ranges up to at least 2000 feet at Cana and Cerro Sapo); one old record from "Veragua" is only report from western Panama. In central Panama more numerous on Caribbean slope.

Habits: Somewhat phlegmatic, usually seen sitting quietly inside forest at low and middle heights. Sometimes joins mixed foraging flocks of insectivorous birds. Its characteristic call is a loud harsh *tsheet* or *bzeeyp;* the song is a very thin, high, but musical *tee-tee-tee-tee.* The nest is a very bulky pear-shaped structure with projecting spout entrance at bottom on side, similar in shape to those of *Tolmomyias* but larger and covered with coarse (not fine) plant material.

Range: Central Panama to northern Bolivia and Amazonian and eastern Brazil.

EYE-RINGED FLATBILL

(*Rhynchocyclus brevirostris*) Pl.20

Description: 6. Found chiefly in highlands. Very like Olivaceous Flatbill. Heavy-headed, with *very broad flat bill.* Olive green above with *fairly conspicuous whitish eye-ring;* wings without yellowish edging (except in Darién) and wing-bars; *throat, chest, and breast olive,* lightly streaked with yellow on breast and sides, lower underparts pale yellow.

Similar species: Best told from Olivaceous Flatbill by its more prominent eye-ring, darker and more uniform olive throat and chest, and lack of wing-bars. No other similar flycatcher is found in the highlands.

Status and distribution: Uncommon to fairly common in forest and forest borders (especially in ravines) in foothills and highlands on Pacific slope in western Chiriquí, Veraguas (common at Santa Fé and Chitra, spilling over onto Caribbean side at Calovévora), western side of Azuero Peninsula (Río Mariato) and Herrera (Cerro Montoso), on Cerro Campana (the only known locality in central Panama), and in eastern Darién; recorded mostly 1300–7500 feet, but there are lowland records from Chiriquí (Bugaba, Divala) and southern Veraguas (Río San Lorenzo, Arena), possibly representing post-breeding descent; not recorded from Bocas del Toro though probably occurs.

Habits: Much like Olivaceous Flatbill.

Range: Southern Mexico to northwestern Ecuador.

BLACK-HEADED TODY-FLYCATCHER
(*Todirostrum nigriceps*) Pl.21

Description: 3. *Tiny,* with *short tail.* Bill rather long and flat. *Iris dark. Cap and sides of head glossy black, contrasting sharply with bright olive green back;* wings black with yellowish green edging and two yellow wing-bars; *throat white,* remaining underparts yellow.

Similar species: Common Tody-Flycatcher is notably larger and has prominent pale eye, black of forecrown merging into gray on nape and upper back (without contrast), and entirely yellow underparts (no white throat). Black-capped Pygmy-Tyrant is even smaller, also has contrasting black head but with conspicuous white supraloral spot and eye-ring, and with mostly white (not yellow) underparts.

Status and distribution: Rare to locally uncommon (perhaps somewhat overlooked) in humid forest borders, second-growth woodland, and clearings with trees in lowlands on Caribbean slope (but unreported from Veraguas and San Blas); on Pacific slope from Canal Zone (southwestern sector) east through Darién. In central Panama seems most numerous near Caribbean coast.

Habits: Small size and habit of foraging in dense foliage, often rather high up, make observation difficult. Its distinctive call is a series of fast high *chip*'s or *cheep*'s, gradually falling off in intensity.

Range: Costa Rica to western Venezuela and western Ecuador.

Note: By some considered a race of *T. chrysocrotaphum* (Painted Tody-Flycatcher) of northern South America east of the Andes.

COMMON TODY-FLYCATCHER
(*Todirostrum cinereum*) Pl.21

Description: 3¾. Bill flat and rather long. *Conspicuous pale iris. Forecrown and face black shading to slaty on nape and grayish olive on back;* wings black edged with yellow, tail black tipped white; *entire underparts yellow.*

Similar species: See Black-headed Tody-Flycatcher.

Status and distribution: Common in clearings, shrubby areas, woodland borders, and gardens in lowlands on both slopes, ranging up in reduced numbers in suitable habitat into the foothills, and to about 5000 feet in Chiriquí; found also on Coiba Island.

Habits: A droll little bird, usually found in pairs, foraging in foliage at low and middle levels in shrubs and smaller trees. Its tail is constantly in motion, often held flopped to one side, sometimes flipped around in an almost circular manner. Active and not at all hard to see, unlike Panama's other tody-flycatchers. The pear-shaped pendant nest is generally in plain sight. The usual calls are a short unmusical trill, *srrrr,* and a repeated ticking note.

Range: Southeastern Mexico to Bolivia and southeastern Brazil.

SLATE-HEADED TODY-FLYCATCHER
(*Todirostrum sylvia*) Pl.21

Description: 3¾. Bill flat and rather long. *Crown and nape slaty* with *narrow whitish line from lores to over eyes* and grayish ear-coverts; otherwise bright olive green above, wings blackish with bright yellowish edging and two yellow wing-bars; *pale grayish below,* throat indistinctly streaked with whitish, sides and belly tinged with pale yellow. Immature has cap and nape olive green like back, throat and chest tinged olive.

Similar species: Other Panama tody-flycatchers have bright yellow underparts. Paltry Tyrannulet is similar but has differently shaped bill and lacks yellow wing-bars; they occupy different habitats. Most closely resembles Pale-eyed Pygmy-Tyrant but usually lacks pale eye; adult has distinctly slaty crown (lacking in pygmy-tyrant), brighter back, prominent wing-edging (lacking in pygmy-tyrant), and differently shaped bill (pygmy-tyrant's is slender and quite short).

Status and distribution: Uncommon to locally fairly common in dense brush and thickets in clearings and overgrown pastures in lowlands on Pacific slope from Chiriquí east to eastern Panama province (Río Pacora and La Jagua), recorded up to about 2700 feet in foothills of western Chiriquí, but unreported from most of Azuero Peninsula and Darién; on Caribbean slope known only from western Bocas del Toro and western Colon province (Río Indio) to Canal Zone.

Habits: A very difficult bird to observe clearly, usually remaining inside dense thickets within 10 or 15 feet of the ground, moving restlessly. Its calls, a rather soft croaking *trrp* (often doubled), a *thaa-trrrr,* and a trill *trrrreee,* often reveal the bird's presence but are rather similar to calls of the Pale-eyed Pygmy-Tyrant.

Range: Southeastern Mexico to the Guianas and northeastern Brazil.

NORTHERN BENTBILL
(*Oncostoma cinereigulare*) Pl.21

Description: 3¾. Known only from western Panama lowlands. Rather like the more widespread Southern Bentbill, with the same *peculiar bent downward bill.* Iris pale. Olive above, adults usually (but not always) with grayish cap, wings edged with grayish though usually (but not always) without wing-bars; *throat and chest grayish white streaked with gray;* lower underparts pale yellow tinged with olive on flanks. Immature has olive cap and narrow wing-bars.
Similar species: Resembles Southern Bentbill (the two are not known to occur together); best distinguished by the grayish throat and chest (in Southern olive yellowish like rest of underparts). Otherwise easily known by the unusual bill.
Status and distribution: Uncommon in undergrowth of second-growth woodland and forest borders in lowlands of western Bocas del Toro and western Chiriquí; one nineteenth-century specimen from Canal Zone was probably mislabeled.
Habits: Apparently similar to Southern Bentbill. The call in Costa Rica is a guttural *ahrrp* or *awrrr* (Slud).
Range: Southern Mexico to western Panama.
Note: *O. olivaceum* may prove to be conspecific; collecting is needed in eastern Bocas del Toro and Caribbean slope Veraguas.

SOUTHERN BENTBILL
(*Oncostoma olivaceum*) Pl.21

Description: 3½. The odd, rather thick, *distinctly bent downward bill* prevents confusion with all except the previous species. Iris color variable, usually pale. Olive green above with narrow yellowish wing-bars; *yellowish olive below,* sometimes indistinctly streaked with olive on breast.
Similar species: See Northern Bentbill of western Panama.
Status and distribution: Common in thickets and undergrowth in second-growth woodland and forest borders in lowlands on Caribbean slope from Coclé (Río Indio) east through San Blas and on Pacific slope from Canal Zone east through Darién. Widespread in wooded areas throughout Canal Zone.
Habits: Usually hard to see, sitting quietly in dense low cover, then darting off to a new perch. Its guttural, rather toad-like trill, *grrrr* or *chiurrrrrrr,* is given more or less continuously. The nest is a small rounded structure of light-colored fibers, the entrance on the side, suspended from a small branch within 15 feet of the ground.
Range: Central Panama to northern Colombia.
Note: By some authors considered a race of *O. cinereigulare;* on this treatment, English name would be simply Bentbill.

SCALE-CRESTED PYGMY-TYRANT
(*Lophotriccus pileatus*) Pl.21

Description: 3½. A very small flycatcher with a *transverse crest of black rufous-tipped feathers;* the crest is usually not carried erect, but even when laid flat, the color pattern is apparent and a small tuft extends on back of head. Olive green above with brownish forehead and rusty-tinged ear-coverts; wings with two narrow yellowish bars; yellowish below, indistinctly streaked with grayish olive on throat and chest. Females and immatures have reduced crest, more brownish head.
Similar species: The unusual head markings should preclude confusion.
Status and distribution: Fairly common to common in lower growth of forest and second-growth woodland in foothills and lower highlands on both slopes, recorded 1500–5000 feet but most numerous 2000–4000 feet. In central Panama most easily seen on Cerro Campana and in Cerro Azul/Jefe area.
Habits: As with royal-flycatcher, the crest is most likely to be seen erect when the bird is handled after being mist-netted. The calls are astonishingly loud for so small a bird, and include a harsh sharp note, *kreek,* repeated interminably, and also a *trit,* likewise endlessly repeated.
Range: Costa Rica to northern Venezuela, extreme western Brazil, and southern Peru.

PALE-EYED PYGMY-TYRANT
(*Atalotriccus pilaris*) Pl.21

Description: 3½. Very small. *Conspicuous pale iris* (whitish or yellowish). Olive green above with two yellowish wing-bars; *mostly whitish below,* tinged with light brownish gray on sides of head and chest, faintly streaked brownish on throat, tinged with yellow only on flanks.
Similar species: This slender and fairly long-tailed bird is rather like Slate-headed Tody-Flycatcher except for the differing bills (in

this species fairly short and slender, in tody-flycatcher long and flat), olive (not slaty) head, and lack of wing-edging in the pygmy-tyrant; tody-flycatcher's eye color is variable (sometimes pale), hence that character alone is not diagnostic. Mouse-colored Tyrannulet is considerably larger, with a dark eye, is browner above with buffy wing-bars, and is more yellow below, especially on belly. Paltry Tyrannulet also has whitish eye but has slaty cap and whitish superciliary, bright yellow wing-edging (but no bars).

Status and distribution: Uncommon to fairly common in dry scrub and shrubby areas in lowlands on Pacific slope from western Chiriquí (Alanje, David) east to eastern Panama province, most numerous near coast but recorded up to 3600 feet in Veraguas (Chitra).

Habits: An active little bird, gleaning in foliage of low trees and shrubbery. The usual calls are fairly long dry trills, *trrrrr* and *trrreeet,* sometimes *tit, tit, trrrrrtreeeeet.*

Range: Western Panama to Colombia, Venezuela, and Guyana.

Note: Wetmore calls it Light-eyed Pygmy-Tyrant.

BLACK-CAPPED PYGMY-TYRANT

(*Myiornis atricapillus*) Pl.21

Description: 2¾. *Tiny* and *looks virtually tail-less;* the smallest Panamanian passerine. *Cap black* with *prominent white supraloral spot and eye-ring,* the black shading to slaty gray on hindneck and sides of head; otherwise bright olive green above, wings blackish edged with yellowish; mostly white below, with gray on sides and yellow lower belly. Most of female's cap is dark slaty, only forehead black. Immature has entire cap slaty.

Similar species: Minute size and black cap distinguish it from all but the Black-headed Tody-Flycatcher, which has mostly yellow underparts and lacks white on face.

Status and distribution: Apparently uncommon or very local in forest, forest borders, and second-growth woodland in lowlands on Caribbean slope (recorded from Bocas del Toro, Canal Zone, eastern Colon province, and San Blas); on Pacific slope known from eastern Panama province (several sightings on Bayano River at Majé—J. Gwynne and Ridgely, D. Hill) and eastern Darién; ranges up at least locally into lower foothills (Cerro Santa Rita; Ridgely *et al.*). Probably more numerous than the relatively few records indicate; E. O. Willis considers it common within forest on Barro Colorado Island.

Habits: The combination of its tiny size and habit of generally remaining rather high in trees makes it difficult to observe and recognize. Also occurs lower, both within forest and at forest borders. The call is a high-pitched sharp *tseek* (E. O. Willis) or *tseeyp,* repeated several or many times, quite distinctive but easily passed by as a cricket or tree frog.

Range: Costa Rica to western Ecuador.

Note: By some authors considered a race of *M. ecaudatus* (Short-tailed Pygmy-Tyrant) of South America east of the Andes. Sometimes placed in the genus *Perissotriccus.*

BRONZE-OLIVE PYGMY-TYRANT

(*Pseudotriccus pelzelni*) Pl.32

Description: 4½. Found only in eastern Darién highlands. Somewhat crested. *Mostly dark brownish olive above,* crown dusky streaked inconspicuously with olive; wings and tail dusky *edged with dark rufous brown; mostly dull olive below,* throat and center of belly pale yellow. Immature is browner above and below.

Similar species: A dull, rather dark, almost uniformly colored flycatcher. Other small Panama tyrannids are more extensively yellow or whitish below.

Status and distribution: Recorded from forest in highlands of eastern Darién (Cerro Pirre and Cerro Tacarcuna, 4300–4800 feet). Little known, but apparently a bird of forest undergrowth (Wetmore).

Range: Eastern Panama to southern Peru.

Note: Wetmore calls it Olive-crowned Pygmy-Tyrant.

YELLOW-GREEN TYRANNULET

(*Phylloscartes flavovirens*) Pl.21

Description: 4¼. Slender, longish bill; rather long tail. Olive green above with *conspicuous white eye-ring* (but no superciliary); wings dusky edged with yellow and with *two bright yellow wing-bars; entire underparts (including throat) yellow,* slightly tinged olive on chest.

Similar species: Readily confused with a number of species. Southern Beardless Tyrannulet is similar but has short bill, brownish cap (not same color as back), and whitish throat. Yellow-crowned Tyrannulet differs in having distinctly slaty cap (when crown patch not exposed), narrow yellowish wing-bars, and grayish throat. Yellow-olive and Yellow-margined Flycatchers are larger, stouter birds with fairly broad bills; the former has no eye-ring and is rather olive on chest, the latter lacks bright wing-bars and is quite gray on chest. Forest Elaenia is larger with whitish superciliary (but no eye-ring) and pale gray throat; Greenish Elaenia is a little larger still, lacks wing-bars, and is olive gray on throat and chest; both have usually concealed crown patches.

Status and distribution: Uncommon locally in second-growth woodland in lowlands on Pacific slope from Canal Zone (Curundu, Chiva Chiva, Fort Clayton) east to western Darién (Garachiné); on Caribbean slope known only from middle Chagres River valley (first part of Pipeline Road, near Summit Gardens, Madden Forest, Madden Lake area).

Habits: Spritely and active, foraging like a warbler in foliage at middle and upper levels in trees. Frequently droops its wings, both lowered at the same time, often a useful aid in identification. Regularly found with mixed foraging flocks of insectivorous birds. The calls are a *peeewit* or *ptweet,* less stacatto than call of Forest Elaenia.

Range: Central and eastern Panama.

Note: A bird of very limited range, by some authors considered conspecific with *P. ventralis* (Mottle-cheeked Tyrannulet) of South America east of the Andes.

RUFOUS-BROWED TYRANNULET
(*Phylloscartes superciliaris*)

Description: 4. Known only from Veraguas and Darién highlands. Slender longish bill; rather long tail. *Crown slaty* with *narrow rufous forehead and superciliary;* cheeks white, with dusky patch on ear-coverts; otherwise bright olive green above, wings dusky edged with green; *white below* with short but distinct *narrow dusky "moustachial" streak,* chest tinged with pale gray, belly tinged with pale yellow.

Similar species: The rufous eyestripe sets it apart from all other Panama flycatchers.

Status and distribution: Records few in Panama. Known from humid forest and forest borders in foothills and lower highlands on both slopes of Veraguas and in eastern Darién (Cerro Tacarcuna, Cerro Malí). Only recent report from Veraguas is sighting of one on Pacific side of Continental Divide above Santa Fé on January 4, 1974 (Ridgely and G. Stiles).

Habits: Little known. Forages actively like a wood warbler, often with mixed flocks. The Santa Fé bird uttered a short sharp *screech.*

Range: Very locally from Costa Rica to northwestern Venezuela.

YELLOW TYRANNULET
(*Capsiempis flaveola*) Pl.21

Description: 4. Slender and rather long-tailed. *Yellowish olive above* with two yellow wing-bars; *forehead, superciliary, and entire underparts yellow.*

Similar species: No other Panama tyrannulet is so yellow overall.

Status and distribution: Fairly common to locally common in thickets in clearings and overgrown pastures and in woodland borders in lowlands on Pacific slope from Chiriquí to eastern Panama province (lower Bayano River near Chepo; not reported from Darién); ranges sparingly up to about 3800 feet in lower highlands of western Chiriquí; on Caribbean slope found locally in western Bocas del Toro (one specimen from Almirante) and from Coclé (El Uracillo) east through Canal Zone to eastern Colon province (Río Piedras); found also on Coiba Island.

Habits: Generally found in small groups of 2–4 birds, usually foraging within 10 feet of the ground. Gleans like a warbler or vireo, only when quiet perching upright in typical flycatcher posture. Has a variety of conversational notes, such as an oft-repeated sweet *weéteetee,* and a *deéoo, deé-oo.*

Range: Nicaragua to Bolivia, Paraguay, northeastern Argentina, and southeastern Brazil.

TORRENT TYRANNULET
(*Serpophaga cinerea*)

Description: 4. Found only in western highlands *along rivers and streams. Mostly gray,* whiter below; *crown black* with small,

Torrent Tyrannulet

usually concealed white crown patch; wings and tail blackish.

Similiar species: Black Phoebe is also found along highland streams; it is considerably larger and predominantly black, not gray.

Status and distribution: Common along rocky torrents in highlands of Chiriquí and adjacent Bocas del Toro, and in foothills and highlands of Veraguas (both slopes); in Chiriquí mostly 4000–6500 feet, but lower in Veraguas. Common along Chiriquí Viejo River between Volcán and Cerro Punta.

Habits: A perky little bird, usually seen perched on a rock out in the middle of the stream or on a twig over the water. Often very tame. Jerks its tail up and down like so many other river-haunting passerines. The common call is a repeated *tsip.*

Range: Costa Rica and western Panama; Colombia and northwestern Venezuela to northern Bolivia.

YELLOW-BELLIED ELAENIA

(*Elaenia flavogaster*) Pl.20

Description: 6–6¼. Bill quite short; tail rather long and slender. Usually shows a *distinct, upstanding* (bifurcate) *crest,* often revealing partly concealed white center. Olive or olive brown above with narrow white eye-ring and two yellowish to whitish wing-bars; pale gray throat merging into grayish olive on chest and sides; *lower underparts yellow, usually contrasting with grayish chest.* Immature browner above with buff wing-bars, no white in crown.

Similar species: Lesser Elaenia lacks the conspicuous crest (though it can show some) and is more uniform and darker grayish olive below. Scrub Flycatcher has no crest at all and has gray throat and chest with no tinge of olive. Panama Flycatcher is considerably larger with longer heavier bill, lacks the prominent crest, and also has distinctly gray throat and chest with no olive.

Status and distribution: Very common, sometimes abundant, in clearings, shrubby areas, and gardens in lowlands and foothills on entire Pacific slope, following clearings and roadsides well up into highlands (very sparingly to about 6300 feet in western Chiriquí); on Caribbean slope, found only from northern Coclé (El Uracillo) east through Canal Zone to western San Blas (Mandinga); common also on larger Pearl Islands, Coiba Island, Taboga Island, and other smaller islands off Pacific coast.

Habits: Noisy and conspicuous wherever found, one of the most numerous birds in open areas on Pacific slope. Usually seen singly or in pairs, but sometimes gathers in larger groups at fruiting trees. When excited, the crest is especially noticeable. The calls are varied, but usually rather hoarse, typically a *week-krreeup,* second syllable sometimes repeated; also a *freeee* and a *wrrreee.* The nest is an open cup placed in the fork of a branch.

Range: Eastern Mexico to northern Argentina and southeastern Brazil; Lesser Antilles.

LESSER ELAENIA

(*Elaenia chiriquensis*) Pl.20

Description: 5¼–5½. Much like Yellow-bellied Elaenia, but shows *only a slight crest* (at times giving back of head a squared-off appearance) that sometimes reveals a *partly concealed white center.* Often has pinkish or flesh base of lower mandible. Grayish olive above with narrow whitish eye-ring and two whitish wing-bars; throat gray, somewhat tinged with yellowish, *blending into olive on chest, sides, and flanks,* and pale yellow on center of breast and belly. Immature browner above with brownish wing-bars, no white in crown.

Similar species: Yellow-bellied Elaenia is larger with more conspicuous crest, and has more contrast in coloration below. Mountain Elaenia has a rounded head with no visible white in center of crown, lacks the grayish effect on the throat, and is more uniformly yellowish below. Scrub Flycatcher has sharply contrasting gray and yellow underparts, lacks white in crown.

Status and distribution: Fairly common in scrubby and shrubby areas, and open fields and pastures with small trees in lowlands and foothills on Pacific slope from Chiriquí to eastern Panama province (lower Bayano River; not reported from Darién), ranging up to at least 5000 (rarely 6000) feet in Chiriquí highlands; on Caribbean slope uncommon and found only in more open parts of Canal Zone and adjacent Colon province; found also on Coiba and Cébaco Islands and some of the Pearl Islands. Especially numerous on the open eroded hillsides of Cerro Campana.

Habits: Has a variety of calls, all lacking the raucous quality of the Yellow-bellied Elaenia, a buzzy *dzbew* or *peb-zü,* a soft *weeb* or *beebzb* repeated at intervals, and a burry *freeee* or sweeter *feeee.*

Range: Costa Rica to northern Bolivia and southern Brazil.

MOUNTAIN ELAENIA

(*Elaenia frantzii*) Pl.20

Description: 5½–5¾. Found only in western highlands. Very like Lesser Elaenia, but ranges overlap only in part. Often has pinkish or flesh base of lower mandible. Greenish to brownish olive above with narrow yellowish eye-ring, wings with broad white edging and two pale yellowish or whitish wing-bars; *practically uniform light yellowish olive below* (*with no grayish throat*), passing to pale yellow (sometimes whitish) on belly. Immature browner above with buffy wing-bars, and often whiter on breast and belly.

Similar species: Lesser Elaenia sometimes shows a slight crest revealing white in center (Mountain Elaenia's head usually looks rounded and never shows white); Lesser is also grayer above and on throat, and not so uniformly yellowish below. Yellow-bellied Elaenia is larger, distinctly crested, and shows more contrast in color below.

Status and distribution: Very common in farmland, clearings, and forest borders in highlands of Chiriquí (mostly 4000–11,000 feet); less common in Veraguas and western Herrera (Cerro Montoso), where ranges lower (to 2500 feet on Cerro Montoso). The most numerous tyrannid in the Chiriquí highlands.

Habits: The usual calls are a whistled *peeee-oo* or *twee-oo* and a drawn out *peeee-err,* the latter suggestive of call of Western Wood-Pewee.

Range: Guatemala to western Panama; Colombia and western Venezuela.

Note: The South American population may be specifically distinct.

FOREST ELAENIA

(*Myiopagis gaimardii*) Pl.20

Description: 5. Bill short. Greenish olive above, crown darker and browner with usually concealed *canary yellow crown patch;* indistinct whitish superciliary and finely streaked ear-coverts; *wings with yellowish olive edging and two conspicuous yellowish wing-bars;* throat pale gray, remaining underparts pale yellow, strongly tinged olive on chest.

Similar species: Easily confused. Greenish Elaenia has an orange-yellow crown patch and lacks wing-bars (at most indistinct); it is also grayer (less olive) on chest, contrasting more with yellow on belly. Yellow-margined Flycatcher has broader more flattened bill (not short and quite slender), lacks crown patch, and shows a whitish eye-ring, brighter and broader wing-edging (but no distinct wing-bars), and more gray on underparts. See also Yellow-olive Flycatcher and Yellow-green Tyrannulet.

Status and distribution: Fairly common in humid forest, forest borders, and (locally) second-growth woodland in lowlands on Caribbean slope from Coclé (El Uracillo) east through San Blas, and on Pacific slope from Canal Zone (one specimen from Chiva Chiva) east through Darién. In Canal Zone most numerous on Pipeline Road.

Habits: A hard bird to see, usually remaining in upper parts of trees, gleaning in foliage or among twigs. Most often recorded by voice; its frequently heard call is a sharp and emphatic *pitchweét* or *pitchéw,* usually with a long pause between repetitions.

Range: Central Panama to northern Bolivia and southern Brazil.

GREENISH ELAENIA

(*Myiopagis viridicata*) Pl.20

Description: 5¼. Bill short. Olive green above, crown grayish brown with usually concealed *orange-yellow crown patch;* indistinct whitish superciliary and ear-coverts finely streaked grayish; wings with light yellow edging but *no* (or very indistinct) *wing-bars*; throat pale gray deepening to olive gray on chest, *contrasting with light yellow lower underparts.* Juvenal brown above with no crown patch.

Similar species: Easily confused. Forest Elaenia has paler yellow crown patch and conspicuous yellow wing-bars, lacks the contrast below; they normally occur in different habitats. Lesser and Mountain Elaenias occur in more open habitats, lack contrast below, and show olive wash on sides and flanks. Yellow-olive Flycatcher is very similar and occurs in same habitats as this species; it has a broader more flattened bill, lacks the crown patch, and has yellow wing-bars. See also Yellow-margined Flycatcher.

Status and distribution: Uncommon to locally fairly common in second-growth woodland and woodland borders, gallery woodland, and clearings with trees in lowlands on Pacific slope from Chiriquí (where ranges up sparingly to 4000 feet) east to western Darién (Garachiné); on Caribbean slope found only in Canal Zone and adjacent Colon province; found also on Coiba Island and some of the Pearl Islands.

Habits: Usually inconspicuous, gleaning in foliage at low and middle levels, normally not perching vertically in the open. Its usual call is a buzzy *cheerip* (Ridgely) or *screechit* (E. S. Morton), more slurred and less emphatic than call of Forest Elaenia (which sounds distinctly two-noted).

Range: Mexico to northern Argentina and southeastern Brazil.

GRAY ELAENIA
(*Myiopagis caniceps*) Pl.32

Description: 4¾. Known definitely only from eastern Darién. Sexes differ. Male *bluish gray above* with usually concealed white crown patch; *wings black with prominent white edging and two white wing-bars;* mostly whitish below, breast tinged with gray. Some South American males have back bright olive green and lower belly often yellowish (this plumage not recorded from Panama). Female has gray cap with pale yellow crown patch; remaining upperparts olive green; *throat and chest gray,* lower underparts yellow.

Similar species: No other similar Panama flycatcher is so gray. One Darién specimen was long identified as a Torrent Tyrannulet (not known away from western highlands). Male also superficially resembles a male becard (especially Cinereous).

Status and distribution: Apparently rare in forest in foothills (1800–3200 feet) of eastern Darién (Cana, Cerro Malí). Recent reports of birds believed this species on Pipeline Road (E. O. Willis, J. Karr, Ridgely) require confirmation (preferably specimen). A little known bird throughout its range.

Range: Eastern Panama to northern Argentina, Paraguay, and southern Brazil.

SCRUB FLYCATCHER
(*Sublegatus arenarum*) Pl.20

Description: 5½. *Bill short, blackish.* Brownish gray above with *whitish supraloral stripe* and a narrow, broken, grayish eye-ring; wings with two whitish bars (sometimes a third visible); *throat and chest gray contrasting with light yellow lower underparts.*

Similar species: In pattern, similar to Panama Flycatcher but much smaller with short bill and whitish supraloral stripe. Yellow-bellied Elaenia is smaller-headed with conspicuous crest and is more olive on chest (not pure gray); Lesser Elaenia has mostly grayish olive underparts with little contrast. Mouse-colored Tyrannulet is smaller and more slender, with brownish wings and buffy wing-bars, and shows less contrast on underparts.

Status and distribution: Uncommon to locally fairly common in scrub, dry woodland, and mangroves in lowlands on Pacific slope from Chiriquí to western Darién (Garachiné), especially in more arid areas and most numerous near coast; possibly reaches drier parts of middle Chagres River valley in Canal Zone; also found on Coiba and Cébaco Islands, Taboga Island, the Pearl Islands (where more common than on mainland), and some other smaller islands off Pacific coast. In Canal Zone most readily found around Farfan Beach and on Fortified Islands at Fort Amador.

Habits: An unobtrusive and quiet bird, generally remaining in thickets and shrubs. Perches quite upright. The call is a soft clear whistled *peep,* often doubled.

Range: Costa Rica to Peru and Amazonian Brazil.

Note: Some authors merge this species in *S. modestus* (Short-billed Flycatcher) of eastern and southern South America, the English name of the complex then being Scrub Flycatcher.

MOUSE-COLORED TYRANNULET
(*Phaeomyias murina*) Pl.21

Description: 4¼–4¾. *Lower mandible pinkish or yellowish;* iris dark. Rather long tail. Grayish brown or brownish olive above with dull whitish superciliary (narrower in front) and *two buffy wing-bars;* throat whitish, *chest pale gray* tinged with yellow, lower underparts olive yellow. Immature duller with paler, almost white, lower belly.

Similar species: A very drab bird. Southern Beardless Tyrannulet is smaller (and relatively shorter tailed), less brownish olive above with whitish (not buffy) wing-bars, and clearer yellow below (less olive and no gray), and has all black bill. Pale-eyed Pygmy-Tyrant is smaller with prominent pale eye.

Status and distribution: Locally fairly common in dry scrub and thickets in lowlands near Pacific coast from Veraguas (Soná) and eastern side of Azuero Peninsula through southern Coclé to western Panama province (Nueva Gorgona, Campana). Not reported from Canal Zone area, but to be watched for, especially in scrub near coast.

Habits: An inconspicuous bird, keeping rather low in smaller trees and tall shrubbery. The call is a fast unmusical rhythmic tittering, *tsit-te-reéreet* and *ta-teé-tit-tahtoó*.

Range: Western and central Panama; Colombia to northwestern Argentina, Paraguay, and southern Brazil.

SOUTHERN BEARDLESS TYRANNULET

(*Camptostoma obsoletum*) Pl.21

Description: 3¾. Very small. Short black bill; dark iris. Greenish olive above with *fairly distinct, dark, dull brownish cap* and *narrow whitish superciliary;* wings with two whitish to yellowish bars (cinnamon in younger birds) and some edging on secondaries; *clear yellow below except for white upper throat* and a faint tinge of olive on chest. Juvenal duller and browner above, paler below.

Similar species: Yellow-crowned Tyrannulet has slaty cap with yellow in crown, gray superciliary, and yellow restricted to lower underparts (entire throat whitish, chest distinctly olive). Mouse-colored Tyrannulet is larger and longer-tailed, dull brownish on back with buffy wing-bars, and has mostly pinkish lower mandible. See also Yellow-green Tyrannulet.

Status and distribution: Fairly common to common in scrubby and shrubby areas, second-growth woodland, and borders in lowlands on entire Pacific slope (less numerous and more local in Darién); on Caribbean slope known only from Canal Zone and adjacent Colon province and San Blas (Permé, Puerto Obaldía); found also on Coiba and Cébaco Islands and the Pearl Islands.

Habits: Forages actively like a warbler among outer twigs and foliage, occasionally making aerial sallies. Often cocks tail well above horizontal. The usual call is a very distinctive, rather melancholy series of 3–5 (most often 4) *pee* or *twee*'s, sometimes dropping slightly in pitch and varying in speed; also gives a *tooreé tooreé*.

Range: Costa Rica to northern Argentina and southeastern Brazil.

Note: Wetmore calls it Southern Beardless Flycatcher.

SOOTY-CRESTED (SOOTY-HEADED) TYRANNULET

(*Phyllomyias griseiceps*) Pl.32

Description: 4. Known only from eastern Darién. Slightly crested. *Cap brownish becoming gray on sides of head and neck,* short whitish supraloral stripe and narrow superciliary, and fine whitish streaks on ear-coverts; otherwise greenish olive above, wings duskier with *narrow* paler edging (*no wing-bars*); throat white, *remaining underparts pale yellow,* breast washed with olive.

Similar species: Paltry Tyrannulet has pale grayish underparts (no yellow), conspicuous yellow wing-edging, slaty cap. See also Southern Beardless and Yellow-crowned Tyrannulets, both of which have wing-bars.

Status and distribution: Only one specimen from Panama, that a bird taken at Cana (1800 feet) in foothills of eastern Darién; one recent sighting of 2 birds believed this species east of Bayano River bridge, eastern Panama province on January 1, 1975 (Ridgely).

Range: Eastern Panama to central Peru, extreme northern Brazil, and Guyana.

Note: Wetmore calls it Crested Tyrannulet.

PALTRY TYRANNULET

(*Tyranniscus vilissimus*) Pl.21

Description: 4. Short blackish bill; pale iris. Slaty cap and whitish superciliary contrasting with olive back; *wings conspicuously edged with yellow* (*but no wing-bars*); *pale grayish below,* slightly tinged yellowish olive on sides.

Similar species: All other forest-based tyrannulets have predominantly yellow underparts; see especially Yellow-crowned and White-fronted Tyrannulets. Slate-headed Tody-Flycatcher is also pale grayish below but has very different fairly long flat bill, and yellow wing-bars as well as wing-edging; it inhabits thickets.

Status and distribution: Common in second-growth woodland, forest, and borders on both slopes, ranging up in highlands to at least 8000 feet; more widespread on Caribbean side, at least in central Panama, but not recorded from San Blas; absent from drier Pacific lowlands from eastern side of Azuero Peninsula to southern Coclé. Especially numerous in the Chiriquí highlands.

Habits: Not always easy to see, as it often forages high in trees, but also comes low. Tail is often carried "half-cocked," well above horizontal. The call is frequently heard, a semi-whistled *peeayik* or *peee-yip,* rather similar to a call sometimes given by the Thick-billed Euphonia.

Range: Southern Mexico to northern Venezuela.

YELLOW-CROWNED TYRANNULET
(*Tyrannulus elatus*) Pl.21

Description: 4. Bill short. Olive above with *slaty cap* and *often revealed yellow crown patch* (very rarely tawny) and *grayish superciliary* above darker line through eye; wings edged with yellow and with two yellowish wing-bars; *pale yellow below* except for *grayish throat* and tinge of olive on chest. Juvenal lacks crown patch.

Similar species: Easily and frequently confused with Southern Beardless Tyrannulet, which lacks yellow crown patch and has brownish cap and mainly yellow throat. Paltry Tyrannulet also lacks the crown patch and the wing-bars and has grayish (not mostly yellow) underparts. See also Yellow-green Tyrannulet.

Status and distribution: Fairly common to common in gardens, clearings, lighter woodland, and forest borders in lowlands on entire Pacific slope; on Caribbean slope known from northern Coclé (El Uracillo) east through Canal Zone (where common) to western San Blas (Mandinga).

Habits: Does not seem to carry its tail "half-cocked" as do the Southern Beardless and Paltry Tyrannulets. Usually forages at low and middle levels in trees and taller shrubbery. The call is a distinctive clear whistle *pray teér* (Wetmore); usually reveals its yellow crown when vocalizing.

Range: Western Panama (should spread to southwestern Costa Rica) to northern Bolivia and Amazonian Brazil.

WHITE-FRONTED TYRANNULET
(*Acrochordopus zeledoni*) Pl.21

Description: 4¼. Known only from western Chiriquí highlands. Olive above with slaty cap and *white superciliary distinctly broader in front of eye and on forehead;* cheeks flecked with slaty and white; dusky wings edged with yellowish and with *two yellowish wing-bars; mostly pale yellow below,* with whitish throat and chest mottled with olive.

Similar species: Somewhat resembles Yellow-crowned Tyrannulet (of lowlands) except for the broader white eyestripe and lack of a yellow crown patch. Paltry Tyrannulet lacks wing-bars and has grayish (not pale yellow) underparts.

Status and distribution: Rare in forest borders and clearings in highlands of western Chiriquí, mostly above 4000 feet.

Habits: Not very well known, probably often overlooked. A bird may occasionally lift its wing up over back much like an Ochre-bellied Flycatcher. In Costa Rica reported to give an excited-sounding insistent *psss psss psss* (Slud).

Range: Costa Rica and western Panama; locally from Colombia and Venezuela to southern Peru.

Note: By some authors considered conspecific with *A. burmeisteri* (Rough-legged Tyrannulet) of Bolivia to southeastern Brazil. Costa Rican and Panamanian birds have also been considered distinct from those of northern South America (*leucogenys*).

BROWN-CAPPED TYRANNULET
(*Ornithion brunneicapillum*) Pl.21

Description: 3. *Tiny,* with very short tail. Olive green above with *dark brown cap* and *prominent short white superciliary;* wings duskier with indistinct olive green edging; *entirely bright yellow below.*

Status and distribution: Rare in forest borders and second-growth woodland in lowlands on Caribbean slope from Bocas del Toro (Cocoplum) to western Colon province, becoming fairly common on both slopes from Canal Zone and western Panama province east through San Blas and Darién; ranges up into foothills locally on Cerro Campana and Cerro Azul. In Canal Zone more numerous on Caribbean side.

Habits: Usually forages at middle and upper levels, often joining mixed flocks of insectivorous birds. Has a very distinctive fast high piping whistle of 4–6 notes, *pee-pih-pey-peh-püh,* going down the scale, rapidly uttered; also has a single high *peep.*

Range: Costa Rica to northern Venezuela and northwestern Ecuador.

Note: By some authors considered conspecific with *O. semiflavum* (Yellow-bellied Tyrannulet) of southern Mexico to Costa Rica. Sometimes placed in the genus *Microtriccus.*

SLATY-CAPPED FLYCATCHER
(*Leptopogon superciliaris*)

Description: 5. Known only from foothills and highlands of west and east. Rather long, narrow bill; fairly long tail. Olive green above with *slaty cap,* whitish areas (flecked with dusky) in front of and below eye, and *blackish crescentic patch on ear-coverts;* wings edged with yellowish buffy and with *yellowish buffy spots forming two broad but broken wing-bars;* throat grayish, becoming yellowish olive on chest and sides, and light yellow on belly.

Similar species: Sepia-capped Flycatcher has brownish (not slaty) cap.

Status and distribution: Apparently rare in forest and forest borders in foothills and lower highlands of western Chiriquí (site of most Panamanian records), Veraguas (Calovévora), and eastern Darién (Cerro Pirre, Cerro Malí); recorded in Panama at 2000–4500 feet, with one wanderer near sea level at Bugaba, western Chiriquí.

Habits: Usually seen foraging singly in lower growth of forest, though in eastern Darién it ranges rather high "mainly in and immediately below the tree crown" (Wetmore). Sometimes accompanies mixed flocks of forest birds (A. Skutch). Elsewhere observed to lift one wing at a time up over back much like an Ochre-bellied Flycatcher.

Range: Costa Rica to Venezuela and northern Bolivia.

SEPIA-CAPPED FLYCATCHER

(*Leptopogon amaurocephalus*) Pl.21

Description: 5. Rather long slender bill; fairly long tail. *Brownish cap* contrasting with otherwise mostly olive green upperparts; *dusky patch on ear-coverts;* wings with buffy edging and *two broad buffy wing-bars;* tail brown; throat pale grayish, deepening to olive on chest and faintly streaked with paler; breast and belly pale yellow. Coiba Island birds (*idius*) are duller, with less distinct patch on ear-coverts.

Similar species: Slaty-capped Flycatcher has dark gray (not brown) cap, and inhabits mainly foothills and highlands (though there is some overlap with this species). The duller Coiba Island form can be confused with Greenish Elaenia.

Status and distribution: Rare and local in undergrowth of light and second-growth woodland in lowlands on Pacific slope from Chiriquí to eastern Panama province (east of Panama city; not reported from farther east in Panama province or Darién, though probable); absent from eastern side of Azuero Peninsula to western Panama province; ranges up to about 2200 feet (Cerro Montoso in Herrera); one old record from Caribbean slope of Canal Zone (between Gamboa and Frijoles); found also on Coiba Island. Only recent reports from Canal Zone are from near Chiva Chiva Road (J. Karr, Ridgely).

Habits: Both *Leptopogon* flycatchers are so scarce in Panama that little is known about their behavior there. Usually seen perched quietly in undergrowth inside woodland. Twitches up one wing at a time like Slaty-capped Flycatcher. On Coiba Island a male uttered a low *pree-ee-ee-ee* (Wetmore).

Range: Southern Mexico to northern Argentina and southeastern Brazil.

OLIVE-STRIPED FLYCATCHER

(*Mionectes olivaceus*) Pl.20

Description: ♂5; ♀4½. Rather long, slender bill; fairly long tail; slim appearance with smallish head. Dark greenish olive above with *usually prominent short whitish streak behind eye;* lighter olive below, *finely streaked with yellowish on throat, breast, and flanks,* becoming uniform light yellow on center of belly. Adult male has 9th primary shortened and very narrowed terminally.

Similar species: Looks dark in the field, but easily recognized by the light post-ocular streak and the yellowish streaking below. The larger flatbills are also mostly dark olive, but have much broader flat bills, and are large-headed and heavy-bodied.

Status and distribution: Fairly common to locally common in lower growth of humid forest and second-growth woodland on both slopes, most numerous in foothills and lower highlands (1000–4000 feet), ranging up in diminishing numbers to almost 6000 feet in Chiriquí highlands; on Pacific slope unknown from lowlands west of Canal Zone. In Canal Zone, known chiefly from Caribbean slope.

Habits: Favors shady ravines with heavy thickety growth. Quiet and inconspicuous, its true abundance is revealed by the frequency with which it is caught in mist-nets. Infrequently flicks up one wing at a time like Ochre-bellied Flycatcher.

Range: Costa Rica to northern Venezuela and southern Peru.

OCHRE-BELLIED FLYCATCHER

(*Pipromorpha oleaginea*) Pl.21

Description: 4½. Fairly long slender bill; rather slim, small-headed appearance. Olive green above with ochraceous upper tail-coverts, wings narrowly edged with yellowish buff and with inconspicuous buffy wing-bars; tail grayish brown; *sides of head and* *throat grayish olive, becoming yellowish ochre on remaining underparts.* Birds from west of Canal Zone are duller, with grayer throat, and lack wing-bars and have reduced wing-edging. Most easily recognized by its *frequent habit of briefly lifting up its wings over its back,* one after the other (seen more often in this species than in others with the habit).

Similar species: Combination of uniform upperparts, "tarnished brass" tone of most of underparts, and the wing-lifting is characteristic. Ruddy-tailed Flycatcher is smaller with short stubby bill, has largely rufous wings and tail.

Status and distribution: Common in lower growth of forest, second-growth woodland, borders, and adjacent clearings in lowlands on both slopes, ranging in reduced numbers into foothills to about 3500 feet; absent from dry Pacific lowlands from eastern side of Azuero Peninsula to western Panama province; found also on Coiba and Cébaco Islands and the larger Pearl Islands.

Habits: Usually seen singly, though often accompanying a mixed flock. Pipromorphas eat a combination of insects, obtained by gleaning, and fruits, especially mistletoe. Males during the breeding season sing interminably from perches in their small territories, *twich, twich, twich . . . ,* with variations, sometimes bisyllabic, *tit-twich* or *tsyick,* all the while flicking their wings. The nest is ball-shaped with a side entrance and is usually covered with moss; it is suspended from a slender vine or root, hung over a stream or from the side of a bank or tree trunk. The female alone raises the young.

Range: Southern Mexico to Bolivia and Amazonian and eastern Brazil.

SWALLOWS: Hirundinidae (13)

The swallows are a familiar group of highly aerial birds found virtually throughout the world, with many highly migratory species (including over half the recorded Panama species). With long pointed wings and rapid graceful flight, they differ most obviously from the swifts in their frequent perching on exposed branches and wires and their more maneuverable flight. Most species are dark above and light below, many with notched or forked tails. All but a few are gregarious, some gathering in large flocks (in Panama especially the martins); a number are colonial breeders as well. Swallows are essentially insectivorous, capturing prey in flight in their wide gape. Nesting sites are rather varied, with many favoring man-made structures: several species (non-Panamanian breeders) nest on cliff ledges, but most nest in holes or crevices, either in trees, on buildings, or in banks.

BANK SWALLOW
(*Riparia riparia*)

Description: 5. Rather small. *Grayish brown above;* white below, *including throat,* with *grayish brown band across chest.*

Similar species: Very like Brown-chested Martin in pattern but much smaller. Rough-winged Swallow is also brown above, but lacks distinct chest band and is not white on throat.

Status and distribution: Fairly common fall and uncommon spring transient (early September–late October; early March–early May; once on August 26 and stragglers later in May and once on June 3) in lowlands on both slopes, including Pearl Islands; no definite evidence of wintering (records on November 30 and February 22 were probably only transients).

Habits: Usually seen flying low over open country, particularly near coast; frequently accompanies Barn Swallows.

Range: Breeds in North America, Europe, northern Africa, and southern Asia; in New World winters in South America.

TREE SWALLOW
(*Tachycineta bicolor*)

Description: 5–6. Rare. *Steely blue-black or green-black above;* immaculate white below. Immature dusky brown above; whitish below, with indistinct and incomplete dusky band on sides of chest.

Similar species: Mangrove Swallow is smaller with prominent white rump. Blue-and-white Swallow is very similar but has prominent black under tail-coverts (white in Tree). Immature Trees can be confused with Rough-winged and Bank Swallows. See also Violet-green Swallow.

Status and distribution: Apparently a rare and irregular winter visitant. Few records, most from Caribbean slope near coast: a flock of about 100 seen on January 17 and several on March 4, 1958, at Changuinola, Bocas del Toro (Wetmore; on the latter date one collected); a flock of about 225 seen and photographed at Gatun Dam, Canal Zone on February 16, 1969 (Ridgely); and a group of 12 seen at Gamboa, Canal Zone, on February 1, 1973 (Eisenmann, Ridgely *et al.*), with another large flock of 200–300 at Gatun Dam on February 4, 1973 (Eisenmann and C. Leahy). Evidently flocks occasionally wander south from their normal wintering grounds further north.

Range: Breeds in North America; winters from southern United States to Nicaragua and in Greater Antilles, casually or irregularly to Costa Rica, Panama, Colombia, and Guyana.

Note: Sometimes placed in the genus *Iridoprocne.*

MANGROVE SWALLOW
(*Tachycineta albilinea*)

Description: 4½. *Glossy greenish to steel blue above* (greener in fresh plumage, becoming bluer with wear) with narrow white supraloral stripe and *white rump; immaculate white below.* Immature more grayish above except for white rump, tinged with brownish on sides of chest.

Similar species: Blue-and-white Swallow lacks white rump and has black under tail-coverts. See very rare Tree and Violet-green Swallows. See also White-winged Swallow (below).

Status and distribution: Common locally, almost always near water, in lowlands on Caribbean slope east to eastern Colon province (Portobelo); somewhat less numerous on Pacific slope east to eastern Darién (Tuira River valley); found also on Coiba Island.

Habits: Usually seen in small groups skimming low over the water of lakes, ponds, rivers, and in mangroves, sometimes over damp fields and meadows, even over salt water just beyond the shoreline. Perches low on snags and dead branches. Its call is a *dzreet, dzreet,* often given in flight.

Upper row, left to right, WHITE-THIGHED SWALLOW, ROUGH-WINGED SWALLOW, GRAY-BREASTED MARTIN; lower row, MANGROVE SWALLOW, BLUE-AND-WHITE SWALLOW, BROWN-CHESTED MARTIN

Range: Mexico to eastern Panama; northwestern Peru.

Note: Sometimes placed in the genus *Iridoprocne.* White-winged Swallow (*T. albiventer*) of South America (occurring as close as northwestern Colombia) is possible in San Blas; it resembles Mangrove Swallow but has large white patches on wings (visible at rest, very prominent in flight) and lacks white supra-loral stripe.

[VIOLET-GREEN SWALLOW]
(*Tachycineta thalassina*)

Description: 5–5½. Very rare. Steely green above, glossed with violet and with *white of underparts extending up and behind eyes; broad white patch on each side of rump* (leaving only a narrow dark central stripe); immaculate white below.

Similar species: Tree Swallow lacks white on face and the white rump patches. Mangrove Swallow also lacks white on face and has an all-white rump.

Status and distribution: Very rare or irregular; reported only during winter of 1960, when it was apparently widespread at least for a time in the highlands of western Chiriquí. At least 50 were seen at El Salto above Boquete (4500 feet) on February 20–21 (Eisenmann and J. Linford); the same observers then observed between 70 and 100 every afternoon in the Volcán/Cerro Punta area February 23–27. No records before or since; no Panama specimen. Like the Tree Swallow evidently very erratic in Panama, well south of its normal wintering range.

Range: Breeds in western North America; winters from Mexico to Honduras, casually to Costa Rica and Panama.

Note: Sometimes placed in the genus *Iridoprocne.*

BARN SWALLOW
(*Hirundo rustica*)

Description: 6–7½. *Long deeply forked tail.* Steely blue-black above with chestnut forehead; throat chestnut, remaining underparts cinnamon-buff; tail blue-black with band of white spots on inner webs. Immature and molting adult may lack the long outer tail feathers.

Similar species: The only Panama swallow with a deeply forked tail. Cliff Swallow is superficially similar (especially to Barns without the long tail streamers) but has buffy rump.

Status and distribution: Very common to occasionally abundant transient (late August–late November; early March–mid-May; a few as early as late July and as late as May) virtually throughout (less numerous in highlands above 6000 feet) but especially in coastal lowlands; rare to locally fairly common winter resident in more open areas, most numerous in Pacific western Panama; a few scattered individuals occasionally spend the summer. By far the most numerous migrant swallow in Panama.

Habits: During migration, small groups are almost constantly visible in open country, flying swiftly and steadily low over the ground. Often flies directly over Panama Bay. Can be seen anywhere, but in greatest numbers along either coast, flying generally eastward in fall, westward in spring.

Range: Breeds in North America, Europe, northern Africa, and Asia; in New World winters primarily in South America, in small numbers in southern Middle America.

CLIFF SWALLOW
(*Petrochelidon pyrrhonota*)

Description: 5–5¾. Mostly dull, steely blue-black above, with *buff to whitish forehead,* buffy grayish collar on hindneck, and narrow white streaks on back; *rump buffy brown; cheeks and throat chestnut,* with black patch on center of lower throat; remaining underparts grayish buff, fading to whitish on lower belly; *tail almost square-tipped.* One race has forehead chestnut like throat. Immature duller above, but often with deep rufous forehead; throat dull grayish buffy, usually lacking black patch on lower throat.

Similar species: Barn Swallow lacks this species' conspicuous pale buffy rump, and most have tail deeply forked (lacking in immature and molting winter adult). See Cave Swallow (below).

Status and distribution: Uncommon to fairly common transient (late August–late October; early March–early May) throughout, but especially in coastal lowlands; one sighting of two as early as July 29 (Ridgely and J. Karr); small numbers apparently winter at least occasionally, usually among the flocks of Barn Swallows in Pacific slope lowlands.

Habits: Most often seen migrating, often with Barn Swallows, low over the ground in open areas.

Range: Breeds in North America; winters mostly in southern South America.

Note: The very similar Cave Swallow (*P.*

fulva), breeding locally in West Indies, southwestern United States, Mexico, and western Ecuador and Peru (winter range of northern birds unknown), is unrecorded in Panama though possible. Adults resemble Cliff but have chestnut forehead, cinnamon cheeks and throat and also chest and sides of breast, lack black on throat, and have remaining underparts white; immature like adult but duller, less glossy black above.

GRAY-BREASTED MARTIN

(*Progne chalybea*) *page 259*

Description: 6¼–7¼. A *large* swallow. Male *steely blue-black above* (*including forehead*); throat, breast, and sides grayish brown, lower underparts white. Female similar but duller with less glossy upperparts and sooty forehead, paler gray throat. Immature like female but more sooty brown above, with grayish of breast blending into white of lower underparts.

Similar species: The commonest martin in Panama; see other martins for distinctions. Immature Gray-breast can be confused with Brown-chested Martin but lacks clearly marked chest band and white throat.

Status and distribution: Very common to locally abundant in flocks that gather after breeding season in lowlands on both slopes, more numerous and widespread on Pacific side; ranges up in smaller numbers into foothills and where widely cleared into lower highlands (to about 5000 feet); found also on Coiba Island. Numbers seem much larger after breeding season—the local population is probably augmented by migrating birds from further north in Middle America.

Habits: Not found in extensively forested areas, this species appears soon after clearings are made. It favors towns and habitations, especially near water. Nests in crevices and under eaves of houses and in hollow trees; colonial martin houses like those used in the United States would probably also be suitable, but seem not to have been tried in Panama.

Range: Mexico (casually southern Texas) to central Argentina; birds from northern Middle America are at least in part migratory but their winter range is unknown.

PURPLE MARTIN

(*Progne subis*)

Description: 7–8. Male *entirely glossy blue-black*. Female and immature sooty brown above with *forecrown usually gray margined with whitish, giving a hoary effect;* sooty brown below, fading to white on breast and belly (which are usually streaked, sometimes heavily, with dusky), with *patches of whitish to dull buff on sides of neck,* sometimes extending around hindneck to form a narrow whitish collar.

Similar species: Female-plumaged bird resembles Gray-breasted Martin but has gray forehead (sometimes absent), pale areas on sides of neck, darker underparts, and usually streaked lower underparts (in Gray-breasted at most faint shaft streaks). Adult male easily distinguished from Gray-breasted Martin, but cannot be separated in field from adult male Southern Martin. Female Southern Martin resembles a very dark female Purple, but lacks grayish forehead and pale sides to neck, and has entire underparts dusky, usually with pale edging (the effect being more like scaling than streaking). See also Snowy-bellied Martin (below).

Status and distribution: Uncommon to locally common fall transient along immediate Caribbean coast (mostly early August–late September), with most reports from Canal Zone and immediately adjacent Colon province (also two specimens from Bocas del Toro); uncommon but possibly regular on Gatun Lake; rare on Pacific slope, with only reports being an adult male in southwestern Canal Zone on September 12, 1961 (R. Ryan), and four between Antón and Penonomé, Coclé, on September 18, 1965 (Eisenmann). Rare spring transient, reported only from Caribbean coast of Bocas del Toro and Canal Zone, and from Tocumen, eastern Panama province (mid-February–mid-March).

Habits: Usually in small flocks, feeding over open areas, often with other martins or migrating swallows.

Range: Breeds in North America; winters in South America; recorded spottily as a transient from Middle America and West Indies.

Note: Snowy-bellied or Caribbean Martin (*P. dominicensis*), breeding in West Indies and western Mexico (*sinaloae*), winter range unknown, is possible in Panama. It resembles Gray-breasted Martin, but adult male has blue-black throat, chest, and sides *sharply demarcated* from white on central lower underparts; female and immature similar to Gray-breasted Martin, but also showing sharp demarcation of white lower underparts.

SOUTHERN MARTIN
(*Progne modesta*)

Description: 7–8. Apparently very rare, though quite possibly overlooked. A *large* swallow. Male *entirely glossy blue-black* (tail more deeply forked than in Purple Martin). Female and immature blackish above; *sooty brown to dusky below (including belly) with pale edging* (some adult females look almost uniformly dark below).

Similar species: Adult male cannot be distinguished in the field from adult male Purple Martin. Female-plumaged Southern Martin can be distinguished from Gray-breasted and female-plumaged Purple Martin by its lack of white lower underparts.

Status and distribution: Only one definite record, an immature taken at Puerto Obaldía, San Blas on July 14, 1931; most likely during austral winter (April–September), thus with some overlap with period of transience of Purple Martin. An all blue-black martin was seen on June 20, 1958, at Coco Solo, Canal Zone (J. Ambrose), and on the basis of date was probably this species; another all dark martin near Gamboa, Canal Zone, on July 15, 1970 (Eisenmann and E. S. Morton) may also have been this species.

Range: Breeds in Galapagos Islands (*modesta*), coastal Peru and northern Chile (*murphyi*), and from Bolivia and Paraguay to southern Argentina (*elegans*); southern birds (*elegans*) winter to northern South America, casually to Panama, accidentally to Florida. The three forms may possibly be distinct species.

BROWN-CHESTED MARTIN
(*Phaeoprogne tapera*) *page 259*

Description: 6½–7½. A *large* swallow. *Grayish brown above;* white below with *distinct grayish brown band across chest* and a line of small brownish spots below the chest band.

Similar species: Almost a replica of the Bank Swallow, but much larger. Other adult Panama martins are blue-black or blackish above (not brown), and even the more brownish immatures never show a distinct chest band contrasting with white throat.

Status and distribution: Variable in numbers and rather local. Uncommon to (in some years) abundant austral winter visitant from southern South America (mid-April–late September, most numerous May–August; 4 presumed stragglers seen near Antón, Coclé, on January 2, 1974; Ridgely) in lowlands on both slopes, recorded west to western Bocas del Toro (where irregular) and western Chiriquí. Seems much more numerous in some years than others, sometimes noted in very large flocks of hundreds of birds. Found in open areas, often in association with smaller numbers of Gray-breasted Martins.

Range: Colombia and the Guianas to central Argentina; southern birds (*fusca*) winter in northern South America and Panama.

Note: Sometimes included in the genus *Progne.*

WHITE-THIGHED SWALLOW
(*Neochelidon tibialis*) *page 259*

Description: 4–4½. *Small. Sooty black above, paler grayish brown below;* thighs white (difficult to see).

Similar species: No other Panamanian swallow is so uniformly dusky. Superficially suggests a *Chaetura* swift but note different shape, flight, and perching habit.

Status and distribution: Uncommon to locally fairly common in small clearings and along borders and roads in humid forest in lowlands and foothills (to about 3000 feet) from Caribbean slope of Canal Zone and eastern Panama province (Cerro Azul) east through San Blas and Darién; one sighting of a flock of 6 at El Valle, Coclé, on April 27, 1969 (Ridgely), is the westernmost record. In Canal Zone, readily seen on Pipeline Road and in Fort Sherman/San Lorenzo area.

Habits: Usually in small groups flying about in small forest clearings or over streams or perched on dead branches. Nests in holes in dead trees.

Range: Central Panama to southern Peru and Amazonian and eastern Brazil.

BLUE-AND-WHITE SWALLOW
(*Pygochelidon cyanoleuca*) *page 259*

Description: 4¾–5. Glossy, steely blue above; white below, usually with a few small blackish spots on chest, with *black under tail-coverts.* Migrants from southern South America (*patagonica*) are larger and have gray under wing-coverts (not blackish) and black on under tail-coverts not extending so far up.

Similar species: Tree Swallow has white under tail-coverts; Mangrove Swallow has white rump.

Status and distribution: Common breeder in open areas in foothills and highlands (2000 to over 10,000 feet) on Pacific slope in Chiriquí and Veraguas; also breeds on Cerro Campana, western Panama province, to which it has apparently only recently (1967) spread, and has also been seen in recent years at El Valle, Coclé. Birds from southern South America (*patagonica*) have been recorded as a scarce austral winter visitant to central Panama, with a few nineteenth-century specimens (McLeannan), three July specimens from the Canal Zone taken in different years (Juan Mina and Gatun), and three recent (1971–1972) sight reports of small flocks in eastern Panama province and Pacific slope of Canal Zone (Eisenmann, J. Pujals, Ridgely) in mid-June and early August.

Habits: A common and familiar bird in the western highlands, often around towns and habitations. Can also be seen regularly flying over the open, grassy hillsides of Cerro Campana.

Range: Costa Rica to central Panama; Colombia to Guyana, Brazil, and Tierra del Fuego; southern birds (*patagonica,* Patagonian Swallow, possibly a distinct species) winter in northern South America and Panama, casually reaching Nicaragua, Honduras, and southern Mexico.

Note: Sometimes placed in the genera *Atticora* or *Notiochelidon.*

ROUGH-WINGED SWALLOW

(*Stelgidopteryx ruficollis*) *page 259*

Description: 4½–5½. *Grayish brown above,* duskier on cap, with *rump whitish to pale buffy* (rump dark like rest of upperparts in Chiriquí breeding birds, *fulvipennis*); *throat and upper chest cinnamon,* breast and sides pale grayish brown, fading to whitish on belly. North American migrants (*serripennis*) also lack the whitish rump, and have throat and upper chest dingy grayish brown (like breast).

Similar species: Breeding race of most of Panama (*uropygialis*) is the only brown swallow with a whitish rump; immature Mangroves are grayer above and pure white below. Northern migrants can be confused with the smaller Bank Swallow, but lack that species' white throat and distinct brown chest band. White-thighed Swallow is dusky above and below.

Status and distribution: Fairly common to common breeder in open areas and clearings in lowlands and foothills on both slopes, ranging up into highlands (to about 6500 feet) in western Chiriquí; northern birds are also fairly common as transients and winter residents (early September–mid-March), apparently migrating mostly through the foothills, though wintering in the lowlands as well, particularly near water.

Habits: Resident birds are usually found in pairs or small family groups, though there is a tendency to some flocking after the breeding season; northern birds generally occur in flocks. Usually the two do not mingle.

Range: Southern Canada to northern Argentina and Uruguay; northern birds winter in the West Indies and from southern United States south at least to Panama; southern breeders also winter northward.

CROWS AND JAYS: Corvidae (4)

Of this varied and widespread family, only jays are found in Panama (and South America), typical crows not occurring south of Nicaragua. Only one of the four Panamanian species, the Black-chested Jay, is at all widespread in the country. Jays are typically found in small often noisy groups, moving through the trees at all heights. They are virtually omnivorous. Jay nests are usually large open structures of twigs, lined with finer material, generally well hidden in bushes and trees; however, virtually nothing seems to have been recorded about nesting in Panama.

BROWN JAY

(*Psilhorinus morio*)

Description: 15–16. Regular only in Bocas del Toro lowlands. Considerably larger than other Panama jays, with long tail. Bill black in adult, with yellow base in immature (some variation). *Uniform brown above; somewhat paler brown on throat and chest;* breast and belly white; tail brown with broad white tips to outer feathers, very prominent in flight.

Similar species: Panama's other jays are largely blue above, not brown.

Status and distribution: Uncommon in forest borders, lighter woodland, and shrubby clearings in lowlands of western and central

Brown Jay

Bocas del Toro; two recent sightings of a group of about 6 individuals one mile north of Achiote, western Colon province (just over Canal Zone border), the first on January 21, 1969, and again in early 1970 (both N. G. Smith).

Habits: A noisy and conspicuous bird, trooping about in groups of half a dozen or more. Often heard is its loud raucous call, *keeyah, keeyah,* sometimes given at the approach of a human.

Range: Southern Texas and eastern Mexico to Caribbean western (casually central) Panama.

BLACK-CHESTED JAY

(*Cyanocorax affinis*) Pl.11

Description: 12½–14½. Panama's only widespread jay. *Head, throat, and chest black* with small bright blue patches above and below eye and on cheeks; otherwise blue above, more brownish violet-blue on back; *breast and belly creamy white; tail broadly tipped creamy white.*

Similar species: The only jay in most of its Panama range. Brown Jay of Bocas del Toro is mostly brown.

Status and distribution: Locally uncommon to fairly common in forest and forest borders, second-growth woodland, gallery woodland, and even dry deciduous woodland in lowlands on both slopes including Azuero Peninsula and up into foothills at El Valle in Coclé, ranging into lower highlands in western Chiriquí (sparingly to 5400 feet). In Canal Zone, appears to be rare or irregular in middle Chagres River valley, but numerous near Caribbean coast (e.g., Achiote and Escobal Roads, Fort Sherman/San Lorenzo).

Habits: Travels about in small active groups, usually of no more than half a dozen individuals. Calls frequently, a loud and distinctive *chowng, chowng* or *kyoo-kyoo,* with a ringing metallic quality.

Range: Costa Rica to northern Colombia and Venezuela.

SILVERY-THROATED JAY

(*Cyanolyca argentigula*) Pl.11

Description: 10. Found only in western Chiriquí highlands. Head and neck black with *bluish white forecrown extending as narrow stripe over eye;* remaining upperparts purplish blue; *throat pale silvery blue,* chest black, shading into dusky purplish blue on lower underparts. Juvenal lacks blue stripe on head and has bluish dusky crown.

Similar species: See Azure-hooded Jay.

Status and distribution: Uncommon in forest and forest borders in highlands of western Chiriquí, recorded 5000–10,000 feet.

Habits: Usually rather inconspicuous, in pairs or small groups. The call is a moderately loud, nasal *chaak, cheuk, cheh.*

Range: Costa Rica and western Panama.

AZURE-HOODED JAY
(*Cyanolyca cucullata*) Pl.11

Description: 11. Known only from highlands of Bocas del Toro and Veraguas. *Mostly dull dark blue; rearcrown and nape contrasting pale blue;* forecrown and sides of head and neck black.

Similar species: See Silvery-throated Jay.

Status and distribution: Known only from humid forest and forest borders in upper foothills and highlands on Caribbean slope of Bocas del Toro (3000–7000 feet), crossing to Pacific slope in Veraguas (Chitra, 3500 feet). No fully authenticated records from Chiriquí.

Habits: This beautiful jay is little known in Panama. In Costa Rica (where perhaps more numerous) generally found in groups of from 2 to 8 individuals, moving about actively in middle and upper tree levels; its call is an arresting, rather nasal *renk* or *renk-ee-renk* (Ridgely).

Range: Central Mexico to western Panama.

Note: The genus *Cyanolyca* is sometimes merged into the genus *Aphelocoma.*

DIPPERS: Cinclidae (1)

The dippers are remarkable in their aquatic habits, being the only truly aquatic passerine. The family is small and has a discontinuous distribution: two species are found in the Old World, two or three in the New, all similar except in color pattern. Dippers are restricted to clear, rapid, rocky streams. They are chunky, short-tailed, rather wren-like birds, fully capable of swimming underwater in even very fast currents and of walking on the bottom of the stream or river. Dippers feed on a variety of small aquatic life, mostly procured underwater. The nest is a large, domed structure placed on a ledge on a rock or steep bank or cliff along the watercourse; it is sometimes placed behind a waterfall.

AMERICAN DIPPER
(*Cinclus mexicanus*)

Description: 6½. Found only *along streams in western highlands.* Chunky and short-tailed. *Entirely slaty gray.* Juvenal has pale gray underparts and narrow white wing-bars.

Status and distribution: Uncommon along clear rocky streams in highlands of Chiriquí and Veraguas, chiefly 4000–7000 feet, though occurs lower in Veraguas (to 2500 feet). Most readily seen along Chiriquí Viejo River between Cerro Punta and Bambito, but even there pairs are widely spaced and can be difficult to locate.

Habits: Usually seen singly, perched on a rock in the middle of the torrent, bobbing up and down, or flying rapidly low over the water. Utters a sharp *bzeet,* frequently in flight.

Range: Western North America to western Panama.

Note: A dipper may occur in eastern Darién; Dr. C. R. Schneider (a chemist) believes he saw one on the Cana River near Cana, Darién (at over 3000 feet), in July 1965 (*fide* Eisenmann). If any dipper does occur in Darién, it might be either this species, or the allied White-capped Dipper (*C. leucocephalus*) of South American Andes, or possibly an undescribed intermediate form.

WRENS: Troglodytidae (21)

The wrens are an essentially American family, with only one species having spread into the Old World via Alaska; the family is most abundant and diverse in the neotropics. Most wrens are rather small, compact birds, largely brown with paler underparts, often with a short tail, in most species with wings and tail conspicuously barred with blackish. Many species are skulking, rarely coming into the open, though most are curious and the patient observer will usually eventually be rewarded with at least a brief view. Most wrens have well developed and often very attractive songs; many in the genus *Thryothorus* sing antiphonally, each member of the pair giving part of the total phrase. Wrens are essentially insectivorous; most species construct closed domed nests, while a few nest in cavities of some sort. In some species a number of individuals roost communally in a "dormitory," either another nest (often built specifically for the purpose) or a natural cavity; other species roost individually in a cavity.

WHITE-HEADED WREN
(*Campylorhynchus albobrunneus*) Pl.22

Description: 7½. Unmistakable. *Very large. Head and entire underparts white;* back, wings, and tail dark brown.

Status and distribution: Rather local. One old record from "Veraguas"; recorded from western Colon province (Río Indio); several old records from Chagres basin but in recent years recorded in Canal Zone only along Achiote Road where it can be regularly seen in small numbers; reported eastward in San Blas and in eastern Panama province (Bayano River valley) and Darién, where it becomes more numerous and widespread.

Habits: Favors forest borders, where it forages in small groups in lianas and epiphytes, mostly at middle levels. The call is a harsh *churk*, the song a *ch-ch-ch-ch-ch-kaw-kaw*, with last notes semi-musical.

Range: Central Panama to western Colombia.

Note: Allied to and apparently replaces Band-backed Wren (*C. zonatus*).

BAND-BACKED WREN
(*Campylorhynchus zonatus*) Pl.22

Description: 7½. Known only from western Panama. *Very large.* Crown black broadly edged with brownish gray, superciliary whitish; *upperparts otherwise boldly banded black and buffy whitish; throat, chest, and breast white conspicuously spotted with black;* belly tawny. Juvenal has plain black cap, back black spotted or streaked with brown (wings and tail banded as in adult), underparts mostly dull whitish mottled with gray.

Similar species: Large size and striking banded and spotted appearance render this species virtually unmistakable.

Status and distribution: Uncommon or local in forest borders and adjacent clearings with large trees in lowlands of western and central Bocas del Toro; also recorded from hill country on Pacific slope of Veraguas (Santa Fé), 2300–2800 feet.

Habits: Usually found in pairs or small groups that forage at all levels, often climbing about among vines and epiphytes. Has a variety of harsh scratchy rhythmical calls such as *zikarúk-tzíkadarik* and *zick-urr* and others (Slud).

Range: Eastern Mexico to western Panama; northern Colombia; northwestern Ecuador.

SHORT-BILLED MARSH-WREN (GRASS or SEDGE WREN)
(*Cistothorus platensis*)

Description: 4¼. Very rare; known only from western Chiriquí. Brown cap usually streaked with black and whitish; *back blackish streaked with white;* wings and tail barred buffy brown and blackish; whitish below, cinnamon on sides.

Similar species: Small size, streaked back, and habitat (see below) should distinguish this species from other Panama wrens.

Status and distribution: Very rare and local, seemingly erratic; known only from a few specimens from western Chiriquí, one from Bugaba in the lowlands, several from around Boquete (five different localities, 2000–5000 feet), and one on Volcán Barú (9000 feet). Curiously, unreported since 1902. To be looked for in grassy or sedgy marshes (even those that dry up seasonally) and wet meadows.

Habits: Elsewhere very secretive and difficult to observe unless singing. Generally creeps around in grasses or sedgy growth very near the ground, flushing only reluctantly. In Costa Rica the same race is reported to be found in numbers where it does occur; the call is described as a grasshopper-like *tzrrr* and the song as a *chyip-chyip-chyip-chyip-chyip,* sometimes with a gurgling quality (Slud).

Range: Eastern and central North America south very locally to Tierra del Fuego.

Note: More than one species may be involved.

BUFF-BREASTED WREN
(*Thryothorus leucotis*) Pl.22

Description: 5¼. Brown above with white superciliary and whitish cheeks streaked with dusky; *distinctly barred with black on wings and tail;* throat white, *remaining underparts buffy,* brightest on flanks and belly.

Similar species: Often confused with Plain Wren in central Panama. Plain Wren has less distinct barring on wings and tail (not sharply black) and is mostly white below (not mostly buff); in zone of overlap the two also tend to segregate out by habitat; the songs are also very different.

Status and distribution: Fairly common in thickets and dense undergrowth and woodland borders (usually near water) in lowlands on both slopes from at least Canal Zone eastward; fairly common also on some of the larger Pearl Islands (Rey, Víveros).

Habits: Rather shy and often hard to see well, but has a loud rich musical rollicking song with one phrase of one or two parts repeated over and over and then changed to another phrase, typically *choreéwee, choreéwee, choreéwee . . . wheeooreé-tickwheeoo, wheeooreé-tickweeoo* . . . and so on.

Range: Central Panama to Peru and central Brazil.

PLAIN WREN
(*Thryothorus modestus*) Pl.22

Description: 5¼. Rather like Buff-breasted Wren. Brown above, tinged slightly grayish especially on crown, with white superciliary; *wings and tail indistinctly barred with dusky; mostly white below,* tinged buffy brown on sides, becoming richer buff on flanks and lower belly. Birds from western Bocas del Toro (*zeledoni,* Canebrake Wren, sometimes considered a distinct species) have back and wings olive (not brown) and underparts tinged with grayish olive.

Similar species: See Buff-breasted Wren. Somewhat larger Rufous-and-white Wren is brighter rufous above and purer white below and has sharp barring on wings and tail. Southern House-Wren is smaller and less distinctly marked, with only vague buffy superciliary (not white) and buffy brownish underparts.

Status and distribution: Common in thickets and bushes in clearings and grassy areas and in gardens in lowlands and foothills on Pacific slope from western Chiriquí (where ranges up to over 6000 feet in suitable cleared habitat) through Azuero Peninsula to eastern Panama province (Cerro Azul and Bayano River); on Caribbean slope reported only from lowlands of western Bocas del Toro (*zeledoni*), and Canal Zone area east to eastern Colon province (Río Guanche).

Habits: Generally shy, remaining in thick cover. The song, though musical, lacks the rich mellow quality of the Buff-breasted Wren's, consisting of a variety of repeated phrases, the most common being variants of *cheéncheereegwee*. The *churr* call resembles that of other *Thryothorus* wrens but is exceptionally loud and sharp.

Range: Southern Mexico to central Panama.

Note: Included is *T. zeledoni* of Nicaragua to Caribbean western Panama.

RUFOUS-AND-WHITE WREN
(*Thryothorus rufalbus*) Pl.22

Description: 5¾. *Bright rufous above* with sharp white superciliary and white cheeks streaked with black; wings and tail prominently barred with dusky; *white below,* tinged with brown on sides and flanks.

Similar species: Note the striking contrast between rufous upperparts and white underparts. See Plain Wren.

Status and distribution: Fairly common in shrubby clearings and undergrowth of dry deciduous woodland in lowlands on Pacific slope from western Chiriquí to eastern Panama province (Bayano River), ranging up into foothills and even highlands (to about 5000 feet) where suitable semi-open habitat exists; on Caribbean slope known only from middle Chagres River valley in Canal Zone (Madden Dam area, Summit Gardens vicinity, Gamboa), and possibly rarely to clearings near Caribbean coast in Canal Zone area.

Habits: Very shy and furtive, heard far more often than seen. Its song is unmistakable, a series of very low-pitched "hooting" whistles, often with four or more notes on same pitch followed by another on a different pitch, sometimes with interposed trilling, exceptionally hard to describe but one recurring phrase is a *hoo, hoo-hoo-hoo-whít.*

Range: Southern Mexico to Colombia and northern Venezuela.

STRIPE-BREASTED WREN
(*Thryothorus thoracicus*) Pl.22

Description: 5. Plain brown above, more olive on head, with narrow white superciliary and black barring on wings and tail; *sides of head and most of underparts whitish conspicuously streaked with black,* dull brown on sides and flanks.

Similar species: No other Panama wren has such boldly *streaked* (not barred) underparts.

Status and distribution: Uncommon in humid forest and forest borders in lowlands on Caribbean slope from Bocas del Toro to Coclé, rarely to the Canal Zone, with one sighting of a pair near Gatun Dam in September 1963 (E. O. Willis), and recently (1974) reported from Achiote Road (J. Pujals); spills over Divide to Pacific slope in foothills of Santa Fé, Veraguas (recorded in March 1974; A. Skutch *et al.*).

Habits: Usually in pairs or small groups, foraging chiefly at low and middle tree levels, often among vines and lianas. Its call is a characteristic single whistled note, regularly repeated at short intervals, heard especially soon after dawn; the song resembles that of other *Thryothorus* wrens, consisting of a variety of rich phrases, each usually repeated several times before going on to another, often given antiphonally between members of a pair.

Range: Nicaragua to central Panama.

STRIPE-THROATED WREN
(*Thryothorus leucopogon*) Pl.32

Description: 5. Known only from extreme eastern Panama. Olive brown above with narrow white superciliary and *black barring on wings* and tail; *sides of head and throat white streaked with black; remaining underparts deep tawny brown.*

Similar species: Stripe-breasted Wren of Caribbean western Panama has most of underparts streaked with black (not merely throat). Rufous-breasted Wren is rather similar but has unbarred wings and is brighter rufous below, especially on chest; it is not known from Darién.

Status and distribution: Known only from lowlands of eastern San Blas and eastern Darién. Little known but probably a humid forest inhabitant.

Range: Eastern Panama to northwestern Ecuador.

Note: By some authors considered a race of the previous species, *T. thoracicus* (Stripe-breasted Wren).

BAY WREN
(*Thryothorus nigricapillus*) Pl.22, Pl.32

Description: 5½. *Bright chestnut above* with *black crown and nape,* white spot on ear-coverts, and black and white stripes on sides of head, wings and tail boldly barred chestnut and black; birds from western Caribbean slope east to eastern Colon province (formerly considered a distinct species, the *T. castaneus* group) have white throat, remaining underparts tawny rufous with a little black barring on sides and flanks; birds from San Blas and Darién (the *nigricapillus* group, formerly called Black-capped Wren) are *mostly white below boldly barred with black,* tinged chestnut on flanks and under tail-coverts. Intermediates between the two occur in eastern Colon and Panama provinces (Portobelo, Cerro Jefe area, Bayano River) with mostly rufous underparts and black barring.

Similar species: The main divisions of this species are very different looking below, but both should be easily recognized. Riverside Wren of Chiriquí rather resembles eastern populations of this species but has chestnut crown and nape (like back) and narrower barring below.

Status and distribution: Common in rank undergrowth near streams and roadsides through forest and in overgrown clearings in humid lowlands on entire Caribbean slope; on Pacific slope found in humid foothills from Veraguas (Santa Fé), Coclé (El Valle), and eastern Panama province (Cerro Jefe area) eastward, in lowlands from southwestern Canal Zone (scarce) and eastern Panama province (Bayano River) eastward; found also on Escudo de Veraguas.

Habits: Seems especially fond of *Heliconia* thickets. Usually remains hidden from view, but often inquisitive and will regularly come out to look over the patient observer. A very vocal bird, with a variety of calls and rich musical songs, one of the best singing wrens; the song consists of loud ringing whistled phrases, each phrase repeated many times, then switched to another often very different phrase.

Range: Nicaragua to western Ecuador.

Note: Sometimes split into two species, Bay Wren (*T. castaneus*) of Nicaragua to central Panama, and Black-capped Wren (*T. nigricapillus*) of eastern Panama to Ecuador.

RIVERSIDE WREN
(*Thryothorus semibadius*) Pl.22

Description: 5½. Found only in western Chiriquí. *Bright chestnut above* with white superciliary and sides of head streaked black and white, wings and tail prominently barred pale rusty and black; throat white, *remaining underparts conspicuously barred black and white.*

Similar species: Eastern races of Bay Wren have black crown and nape and coarser black barring below; they have an entirely different range. Otherwise unmistakable.

Status and distribution: Local and uncommon in thickets and undergrowth along rapid streams in lowlands of western Chiriquí, ranging up in reduced numbers to about 4000 feet below Volcán.

Habits: Like other members of the genus, usually hard to glimpse. Has a variety of two or three-syllabled sweet ringing songs (Skutch); one in Chiriquí sounded like *tsring, tseweé, tsereeweé*; in Costa Rica, believed to have perhaps the greatest variety of songs of its genus (Slud).

Range: Costa Rica and Pacific western Panama.

Note: By some authors considered a race of *T. nigricapillus* (Bay Wren).

BLACK-THROATED WREN
(*Thryothorus atrogularis*) Pl.22

Description: 5½. Found only in western Bocas del Toro. Chestnut above, dull brown below, with *sides of head, throat, and upper chest black;* wings barred with black; tail black, faintly barred with brown. Juvenal entirely dull brown with some dusky on sides of head and throat, tail as in adult.

Similar species: Sooty-headed Wren of Darién has entire head dark sooty gray and lower underparts mostly rufous (not dull brown). Superficially rather antbird-like.

Status and distribution: Fairly common locally in tangled second-growth woodland, shrubby overgrown clearings, and swampy woodland in lowlands of western Bocas del Toro.

Habits: Usually found singly or in pairs, in dense undergrowth. The song is a short and sweet *twee-teeo, tew-tew* ending with a trill *trererererereree* somewhat like trill in song of Rufous-sided Towhee (*Pipilo e. erythropthalmus*) of northeastern United States.

Range: Nicaragua to Caribbean western Panama.

SOOTY-HEADED WREN
(*Thryothorus spadix*) Pl.32

Description: 5½. Known only from eastern Darién foothills. *Crown sooty gray, becoming black on sides of head, throat, and upper chest;* narrow white superciliary and ear-coverts lightly streaked white; *otherwise rufous,* becoming duller brown below; wings and tail barred with black. Juvenal duller with face and throat more slaty.

Similar species: Black-throated Wren of Bocas del Toro has crown chestnut brown and lower underparts mostly dull brown (breast not rufous).

Status and distribution: Recorded only from foothills of eastern Darién (Cerro Tacarcuna, Cerro Quía, Cana), 1800–4000 feet. Little known; apparently a bird of humid forest undergrowth (R. de Schauensee).

Range: Eastern Panama to western Colombia.

Note: By some authors considered a race of *T. atrogularis* (Black-throated Wren).

BLACK-BELLIED WREN
(*Thryothorus fasciatoventris*) Pl.22

Description: 6. Chestnut brown above with narrow white superciliary and dusky ear-coverts; *throat and chest white contrasting with black breast and belly,* belly more or less barred with white; tail barred brown and black. Juvenal much duller with throat and chest gray, lower underparts brownish somewhat barred with dusky.

Similar species: Note sharp contrast between upper and lower underparts. In pattern somewhat antbird-like.

Status and distribution: Fairly common in thickets and dense undergrowth of woodland and forest borders and lighter woodland in lowlands of western Chiriquí and in lowlands on both slopes from Canal Zone eastward; one old specimen labeled only "Veragua."

Habits: Quite partial to the vicinity of water. Usually the most difficult *Thryothorus* wren to observe. Its song is very fine, rich and mellow, rather low-pitched and slow-paced, often ending with a characteristic *wheeowheét* or "cream of wheat" (F. O. Chapelle) with an upward inflection; it has a large repertory of phrases, which it repeats many times before changing.

Range: Costa Rica to Colombia.

RUFOUS-BREASTED WREN
(*Thryothorus rutilus*) Pl.22

Description: 5. Plain brown above (*wings unbarred*), more rufous on crown, with white superciliary; *sides of head and throat black speckled with white; remaining underparts tawny-rufous, brightest (almost orange) on chest;* tail grayish brown barred with black.

Similar species: No other Panama wren shows such a contrast between the speckled throat and the bright orange-rufous chest. In extreme eastern Panama see Stripe-throated Wren.

Status and distribution: Fairly common in dense thickets and undergrowth of lighter and drier second-growth woodland in lowlands and (especially) foothills on Pacific slope from western Chiriquí (where ranges up in smaller numbers to about 5500 feet) to eastern Panama province (Bayano River; not reported from Darién); not reported from drier lowlands from eastern side of Azuero Peninsula to extreme western Panama province, but occurs in hill country at El Valle and Cerro Campana.

Habits: Often found with Rufous-and-white

Wren but usually in somewhat less dense areas. Normally not as difficult to see as most other *Thryothorus* wrens. The song is rollicking and musical (though less rich than that of most other species), very variable, typically a five or six-syllabled phrase repeated rapidly over and over, often with a slurred downward ending, such as *whee-ha-chweéoo* and *weeper-cheepeereéyoo.* Like most other *Thryothorus* wrens, frequently sings antiphonally.

Range: Costa Rica to central Panama; northeastern Colombia to northern Venezuela.

Note: Possibly conspecific with *T. maculipectus* (Spot-breasted Wren) of Mexico to Costa Rica and central Colombia to northern Peru.

SOUTHERN HOUSE-WREN
(*Troglodytes musculus*) Pl.22

Description: 4½. *Mostly brown,* somewhat paler and buffier below, becoming buffy whitish on throat; indistinct buffy brown superciliary; some indistinct dusky barring on wings and tail.

Similar species: Among Panamanian wrens only the very dark Nightingale Wren of humid forest is quite so devoid of distinctive markings. Most likely to be confused with larger Plain Wren, which has more prominent white eyestripe and contrastingly whitish underparts. See also Ochraceous Wren.

Status and distribution: Common in open country, clearings, and especially around habitations in lowlands and foothills on both slopes, ranging into highlands where there are suitable clearings (to at least 7000 feet in western Chiriquí); common also on Coiba Island and some of the larger Pearl Islands (San José, Pedro Gonzalez; not Rey).

Habits: An unsuspicious and friendly bird, often nesting in crannies of buildings. The energetic and gurgling song will at once be recognized as similar to that of the eastern race of Northern House-Wren (*T. aedon*) but is perhaps even more pleasing and musical, less raspy; also gives a musical *chew-chew-chew. . . .*

Range: Southeastern Mexico to Tierra del Fuego; Lesser Antilles.

Note: Probably conspecific with *T. aedon* (Northern House-Wren) of North America.

OCHRACEOUS WREN
(*Troglodytes ochraceus*) Pl.22

Description: 4. A highland bird. Small and rather short-tailed. Tawny brown above with *conspicuous ochre superciliary* above brown eye-streak; *buffy-ochre below,* fading to whitish on belly.

Similar species: Small size and bright brown coloration with prominent superciliary simplify identification. Southern House-Wren is duller brown with indistinct superciliary.

Status and distribution: Fairly common in forest and forest borders in highlands of western Chiriquí (mostly above 5000 feet); found also in foothills and highlands in eastern Chiriquí and Veraguas (2500–6000 feet) and in highlands of eastern Darién (Cerro Pirre); one sight report of two birds on Cerro Campana (at about 3000 feet) on September 7, 1968 (N. G. Smith).

Habits: Generally forages well up in the trees, feeding among the epiphytes and other air plants so numerous on larger branches and trunks. The song is a fairly musical trilling *seerrrrrrr,* sometimes introduced by a more musical *tswee-tswee,* at times somewhat reminiscent of the Winter Wren (*T. troglodytes*).

Range: Costa Rica to eastern Panama.

TIMBERLINE WREN
(*Thryorchilus browni*) Pl.22

Description: 4. Found only above 9000 feet on Volcán Barú. Rather short-tailed. Tawny brown above with *broad white superciliary; primaries edged with white; mostly white below,* chest flecked with brown, flanks tinged with tawny-olive.

Similar species: Ochraceous Wren has an ochre superciliary and is buffy-ochre below. The only Panama wren with white on the wings. See also immature Nightingale Wren.

Status and distribution: Found above 9000 feet on Volcán Barú, chiefly around timberline (10,000–11,000 feet), also on summit of Barú's spur, Cerro Copete, at about 10,000 feet.

Habits: Found in bamboo thickets near timberline, in low bushes above timberline. The song in Costa Rica is a rather thin repeated phrase *chee·tee·wee tit tit tit* (Slud).

Range: Costa Rica and western Panama.

WHITE-BREASTED (LOWLAND) WOOD-WREN
(*Henicorhina leucosticta*) Pl.22

Description: 4. Small with *very short tail,* usually cocked up. Brown above with *prominent white superciliary;* sides of head and neck streaked black and white; wings and tail barred with black; *mostly white below,* grayish on sides, brownish on lower belly.

Similar species: Very like Gray-breasted Wood-Wren except for white (not gray) underparts and shorter tail.

Status and distribution: Locally common in undergrowth of forest in lowlands and foothills on Caribbean slope from Bocas del Toro to eastern Colon province (not yet reported from San Blas); on Pacific slope found mostly in foothills (but reaching lower highlands in small numbers) from western Chiriquí east through Darién, in lowlands known only from old records from western Chiriquí and from Canal Zone to Darién. In Canal Zone most numerous in Fort Sherman/San Lorenzo area; common also on Cerro Campana and in Cerro Azul/Jefe area.

Habits: Particularly fond of steep, forested hillsides and ravines and the tangled undergrowth that springs up after the fall of a forest tree creates an opening in the canopy. Usually in pairs, keeping very low in undergrowth; often curious so normally not too hard to observe. The song is variable, quite rich and melodic, with short repeated whistled phrases; characteristic is a "pretty pretty-bird" (F. O. Chapelle) or *churry-churry-cheer;* others include a somewhat shrike-vireo—like *teea-teea-teeoo,* and a *wheé-tew-tew.* The call is a peculiar *bweeer,* somewhat reminiscent of call of Swainson's Thrush.

Range: Mexico to central Peru, northern Brazil, and the Guianas.

GRAY-BREASTED (HIGHLAND) WOOD-WREN

(*Henicorhina leucophrys*) Pl.22

Description: 4½. *Highlands.* Small and short-tailed (but tail longer than in White-breasted Wood-Wren). Rather like White-breasted Wood-Wren and in a few areas found with it. Brown above with white superciliary; wings and tail lightly barred with black; sides of head and neck streaked black and white; *underparts slaty gray,* tinged with brown on flanks and belly.

Similar species: White-breasted Wood-Wren has mostly white underparts, is a lowland bird.

Status and distribution: Very common in undergrowth of forest and forest borders, coffee plantations, and even heavily overgrown clearings in highlands of Chiriquí and Veraguas, mostly above 4000 feet in western Chiriquí, as low as 2500 feet in Veraguas; occurs in small numbers on summits of Cerro Campana (c. 3000 feet) and Cerro Jefe (c. 3300 feet; D. Hill, Ridgely), Panama province; found also in highlands of eastern Darién.

Habits: Like the White-breast an inquisitive little bird that often will come out to look over the patient observer. The song has much longer phrases but is not as rich as that of the White-breasted Wood-Wren's; a typical example is *cheerooeecheé-cheeweé-cheerooeéchee,* and variations, repeated over and over; the call is a mild *chirrrr.*

Range: Mexico to northern Venezuela and northern Bolivia.

SONG WREN

(*Cyphorhinus phaeocephalus*) Pl.22

Description: 5. Bill rather long and ridged. Mostly warm brown with *sides of head and neck, throat, and chest bright chestnut; patch of pale blue bare skin around eye;* wings and tail barred with black. Female more grayish on lower belly.

Similar species: The pale blue skin around the eye brings to mind several antbirds, but none has barred wings and tail; see especially female Bare-crowned Antbird. Tawny-throated Leaftosser almost duplicates this species in general pattern but lacks the pale blue skin and the wing and tail barring.

Status and distribution: Fairly common to common in undergrowth of forest and second-growth woodland in lowlands on entire Caribbean slope; on Pacific slope known from more humid lowlands and lower foothills (to about 3000 feet) from Cerro Campana and Canal Zone east through Darién. In Canal Zone more numerous and widespread on Caribbean side.

Habits: Usually seen in pairs or small groups, on or near the ground, individuals often pausing briefly on a stump or low branch to look over the observer, then moving on, all the while "churring" distinctively. Sometimes follows army ants. The song is a characteristic and far-carrying mixture of harsh *churr*'s and other guttural notes, interspersed with clear musical whistles of varying pitches; some songs consist of three pure musical whistles that may leap or fall a full octave.

Range: Honduras to western Ecuador.

Note: By some authors merged with *C. arada* (Musician Wren) of Amazonia and the Guianas.

NIGHTINGALE WREN
(*Microcerculus marginatus*) Pl.22

Description: 4¼. Bill rather long and slender; *tail very short. Mostly dark brown above and below,* paler brown (sometimes whitish) on throat, brownish gray on breast; wings and tail blackish brown, unbarred. Some birds, believed immatures, are more or less speckled with dusky below and are duller brown above; others have white throat and grayish breast with varying amounts of brown markings below. Molts are little understood in this species.

Similar species: A dark, essentially unpatterned little wren of forest undergrowth.

Status and distribution: Locally fairly common, but rarely seen, in undergrowth of humid forest in lowlands and foothills on entire Caribbean slope; on Pacific slope not reported from lowlands west of eastern Panama province (Bayano River above Majé; Ridgely and J. Pujals) but fairly common in foothills and highlands from western Chiriquí (where once recorded at over 10,000 feet) to Darién. In Canal Zone, most readily recorded (by voice) from Pipeline Road.

Habits: Prefers steep, forested hillsides, ravines, and dense undergrowth near streams. Very furtive and inconspicuous: when glimpsed, its never ceasing habit of bobbing its hind end up and down like a waterthrush will at once be apparent. The unmistakable song is the usual indication of this species' presence; after a rather short, fairly rapid, and irregular opening phrase (often not heard at a distance), it consists of a long series (usually 10 or more) of almost sibilant single long-drawn whistles (each lasting about a second), progressively very slightly lower in pitch and less loud, with even longer pauses between notes (almost tantalizing toward end when each pause may last more than 10 seconds); not forgotten once recognized.

Range: Southeastern Mexico to northern Bolivia and Amazonian Brazil.

Note: Birds from Mexico to central Costa Rica (*philomela*) sing very differently from birds of southern Costa Rica, Panama, and northwestern South America, and are probably a distinct species. Birds from east of the Andes in South America (*marginatus*) have also been considered a separate species

MOCKINGBIRDS AND THRASHERS: Mimidae (3)

This family of rather slender, long-tailed birds is found only in the New World; the typical thrashers are found mostly in southwestern United States and Mexico and none occurs in Panama. Mimids are usually dull in color, shades of brown and gray predominating; most have loud and vigorous songs of repeated phrases. The group is mostly insectivorous, some fruit also being taken; species whose nesting is known build an open, often bulky, cup nest in a dense bush or tree.

GRAY CATBIRD
(*Dumetella carolinensis*)

Description: 8. Slender, with rather long blackish tail. *Mostly slaty gray* with black cap and *chestnut under tail-coverts.*

Status and distribution: Uncommon to locally common transient and winter resident (mostly early October–late April) in lowlands and foothills (rarely to about 5000 feet) on both slopes in western Panama, most common in Bocas del Toro lowlands, becoming less numerous eastward; scarce in Canal Zone and Panama city and unreported east of Canal Zone area; one record from Taboga Island.

Habits: Often skulks in thickets and shrubbery; its characteristic cat-like mewing note will often reveal its presence.

Range: Breeds in North America; winters from southern United States to central Panama (accidentally to Colombia) and in West Indies.

TROPICAL MOCKINGBIRD
(*Mimus gilvus*)

Description: 10. Rather slender, with long blackish tail. *Pale brownish gray above* with dusky patch through eye; wings blackish with two white bars; tail blackish tipped white; *whitish below.* Immature browner above and buffier below but still easily recognizable.

Status and distribution: Apparently introduced from Colombia, first reported around Balboa in 1932 (H. Deignan); now common in cleared and residential areas on both slopes of Canal Zone and in Panama city and Colon; has spread as far east as Tocumen and Portobelo (Ridgely) and as

Left, TROPICAL MOCKINGBIRD;
right, BLACK-CAPPED DONACOBIUS

far west as Chorrera and Boca del Río Indio (a bird taken above Boquete and another seen at David airport were both probably isolated cage bird escapes).

Habits: Like its northern relative, noisy, conspicuous, and aggressive. Especially fond of areas where extensive lawns are maintained. The song is a series of various notes and phrases, reminiscent of the Northern Mockingbird (*M. polyglottos*) but less rich, without tendency to repeat a phrase several times, and with more churring notes; there seems to be no tendency to imitate other birds.

Range: Southern Mexico to El Salvador and Honduras; Colombia to the Guianas and northern Brazil and south along Brazilian coast; Lesser Antilles; introduced in central Panama.

BLACK-CAPPED DONACOBIUS (MOCKINGTHRUSH)

(*Donacobius atricapillus*)

Description: 8. Known only from eastern Darién. Slender and sleek in appearance. *Iris conspicuously yellow. Head black; upperparts otherwise dark chocolate brown;* wings black with white patch in primaries; tail black tipped white; *buffy below,* sometimes with fine black barring on sides; a bare orange area on sides of neck is usually concealed but can be expanded.

Status and distribution: Locally fairly common in marshes and canal borders around El Real and the lower Tuira River in lowlands of eastern Darién. Not definitely recorded elsewhere but to be watched for in suitable marshy habitat.

Habits: Usually seen in pairs or small groups, often perching in the open and not difficult to observe. In display one bird perches a few inches above another and gives a *whirrr,* flashing (and partly spreading) tail from side to side; the lower bird then answers with a louder semi-whistled *kweéa, kweéa, kweéa;* both birds also sometimes expose the orange skin on the neck.

Range: Eastern Panama to Bolivia and northern Argentina.

THRUSHES: Turdidae (16)

The thrushes are a large and widespread group of birds, most diverse in the Old World, though there are many familiar American species. Most American species are rather subdued in color, though many are handsome birds; a number are, however, exceptionally fine songsters. Three genera are especially important in Panama. Robins of the genus

Turdus are especially well represented from the foothills to above timberline with one species, the Clay-colored Robin, being widespread in the lowlands. The genus *Catharus* contains three temperate North American breeding migrants and five species resident in the highlands (mostly in the west); several members of this genus are among the finest singing birds in the world, with hauntingly beautiful clear whistled phrases. The solitaires (genus *Myadestes*) are also excellent songsters; they differ from *Catharus* in their broader bill, and in other respects, and are perhaps more closely allied to the silky-flycatchers. Many Panama thrushes are primarily terrestrial feeders, though their open-cup nests are placed in a tree or bush; solitaires, however, are mainly arboreal but like *Catharus* nest on or near the ground. Thrushes have a varied diet, some species taking mainly fruit, others mostly animal matter.

BLACK-FACED SOLITAIRE
(*Myadestes melanops*) Pl.23

Description: 7. Found only in western highlands. *Rather broad bill and legs bright orange. Mostly slaty gray* with forehead and face black; *white wing band conspicuous in flight.* Juvenal prominently spotted with buff.

Similar species: Slaty-backed Nightingale-Thrush is blacker generally (not so gray) and has pale eye with orange eye-ring and whitish belly. Sooty Robin is much larger and blacker (not so gray) with prominent whitish eye.

Status and distribution: Common in forest and forest borders in highlands of western Chiriquí (4000–9700 feet); found also in foothills and highlands of eastern Chiriquí and Veraguas (above 2500 feet) and in highlands of Bocas del Toro (above 3200 feet), with one wandering individual collected at Almirante on October 28, 1963.

Habits: Often sits rather upright, almost like a trogon. Generally sluggish, remaining motionless for some time and allowing a close approach, then flying off abruptly with a flash of white in the wings. The song is a series of loud, very clear, liquid whistles, given deliberately with rather long pauses between phrases, *teedleedleé . . . tleedleeé . . . lee-dah . . . lee-doo,* with variations; also has a liquid *tlee-loo,* and other two- and three-note phrases given alone. Though often sharply brassy in quality and generally with an inconclusive ending, the best songs have a beautiful ethereal quality that is difficult to describe.

Range: Costa Rica and western Panama.

Note: By some authors considered a race of *M. ralloides* (Andean Solitaire) of Venezuela to Bolivia.

VARIED SOLITAIRE
(*Myadestes coloratus*) Pl.32

Description: 7. Found only in Darién highlands. Resembles Black-faced Solitaire, with which it is often considered conspecific. Bill and legs orange. *Head, neck, and underparts slaty gray; back and wings tawny,* wings with white band conspicuous in flight; tail gray.

Status and distribution: Recorded from forest and forest borders in foothills and highlands of eastern Darién (Cerro Tacarcuna, Cerro Pirre, and Cerro Quía; recorded from 2600 feet up). Little known.

Range: Eastern Panama and extreme northwestern Colombia.

Note: Often considered a race of the Andean *M. ralloides.*

WHITE-THROATED ROBIN (THRUSH)
(*Turdus assimilis*) Pl.23

Description: 9. Bill and narrow eye-ring yellow. Mostly dark brownish olive to grayish olive above; *throat white boldly streaked with dusky, white continuing below as a white patch on upper chest* contrasting strongly with dull brown of adjacent underparts; lower belly white. Darién (*daguae*) and Coiba Island (*coibensis*) birds have blackish bill, are ruddier above.

Similar species: No other Panama thrush has contrasting white throat.

Status and distribution: Fairly common in forest and forest borders in foothills and lower highlands (mostly 2000–5500 feet) on Pacific slope in Chiriquí, Veraguas, western side of Azuero Peninsula, El Valle and Cerro Campana, and eastern Darién; an isolated population at sea level on Coiba Island. Several recent sightings after nesting season on Barro Colorado Island (single individuals following army ants October 28, 1960 to January 14, 1961; September 16, 1961; and January 2, 1971—all E. O. Willis) and another from Fort Sherman on November 15, 1973 (J. Pujals) may indicate descent or wandering from breeding areas. Fairly common on Cerro Campana, but has not been reported from the Cerro Azul/Jefe area.

Habits: Mostly arboreal, often in small groups, with occasionally a larger number gathering to feed in a fruiting tree. Western mainland birds have a good, typical robin-like song, and another of loud and rich repeated phrases, somewhat thrasher-like. Also has a characteristic peculiar short guttural or nasal *enk* or *urrrk,* almost frog-like in quality, and a screechy *dzee-yoo.* Song of Coiba Island birds suggestive of Clay-colored Robin's, but higher and slower (Wetmore).

Range: Northern Mexico to northwestern Ecuador.

Note: By some authors merged with *T. albicollis* (White-necked Robin, or Thrush) of South America east of the Andes. Darién to western Ecuador birds, *T. daguae* (Dagua Robin), to which the Coiba Island birds seem most closely allied, also have sometimes been considered specifically distinct.

PALE-VENTED ROBIN (THRUSH)

(*Turdus obsoletus*) Pl.23

Description: 9. *Bill blackish. Almost uniform, warm reddish brown,* somewhat streaked with dusky on throat and duller below, with *contrasting white belly and under tail-coverts.*

Similar species: Much more numerous Clay-colored Robin has pale greenish bill and lacks white belly. Mountain Robin is duller and also lacks white belly.

Status and distribution: Uncommon and local in humid forest and forest borders in foothills on Caribbean slope in Bocas del Toro (3000–4500 feet) and probably eastward (but no records), crossing to Pacific slope in humid hill country of Veraguas and hill country eastward on Cerro Campana (scarce), Cerro Azul/Jefe area, and in eastern Darién (1400–4500 feet); one nineteenth-century specimen from Canal Zone but no records since.

Habits: A rather shy, essentially arboreal bird. The song is somewhat like Clay-colored Robin's but is faster and less rich and is interspersed with *chrrrr*'s and squeaky notes.

Range: Costa Rica to western Brazil and northern Bolivia.

Note: By some authors merged with *T. fumigatus* (Cocoa Robin, or Thrush) of northern and eastern South America and Lesser Antilles.

CLAY-COLORED ROBIN (THRUSH)

(*Turdus grayi*) Pl.23

Description: 9–10. *Bill greenish yellow or olive* (dusky in immature). Brownish olive above; *dull light buffy brown below,* inconspicuously streaked with dusky on throat.

Similar species: Mountain Robin of western highlands has blackish bill and is darker and duller throughout than the Clay-color. See also Pale-vented Robin.

Status and distribution: Very common to locally abundant in clearings, gardens, lighter woodland, and generally more open areas in lowlands and foothills on both slopes, in western Chiriquí following clearings up to about 6000 feet; not recorded from Darién; most numerous in Canal Zone with its many extensive lawns and well tended gardens.

Habits: A very familiar and conspicuous bird, the Panamanian replacement for the well known American Robin (*T. migratorius*) of temperate North America. The song is a whistled caroling, reminiscent of the northern bird but clearer and more melodic; in addition to typically robin-like cackles, it also utters a characteristic long-drawn, nasal, whining *wee-eé-gwa,* and a querulous *keyaah.*

Range: Central Mexico (casually southern Texas) to northern Colombia.

MOUNTAIN ROBIN (THRUSH)

(*Turdus plebejus*) Pl.23

Description: 10. Found only in western highlands. *Bill blackish.* Dark dull olive brown above; dark dull brownish gray below, throat inconspicuously streaked with dusky.

Similar species: *Nondescript.* Clay-colored Robin is smaller, paler and sandier with greenish bill. Sooty Robin has bright orange bill, legs, and eye-ring, and is dark sooty brown. Pale-vented Robin is brighter brown with white belly.

Status and distribution: Common in forest, forest borders, and small clearings in highlands of western Chiriquí (4000–8000 feet); recorded also from adjacent Bocas del Toro and eastern Chiriquí (where ranges down to 3500 feet).

Habits: Found singly or in small groups, usually well up in the trees. Sings very little, and its song is inferior to that of its allies, being faster, more repetitious and monotonous, with few pitch changes; its calls are a repeated *cack* or *kick* and a mournful *oóoooreee.*

Range: Southern Mexico to western Panama.

Note: By some authors merged with *T. ignobilis* (Black-billed Robin, or Thrush) of northern South America.

SOOTY ROBIN (THRUSH)
(*Turdus nigrescens*) Pl.23

Description: 10. Found only in western Chiriquí mountains. *Bill, legs, and eye-ring bright orange. Whitish iris. Dark sooty brown all over,* blackest on head, wings, and tail.

Similar species: Panama's only "black" robin. Mountain Robin is duller and more olive, with dark eye, bill, and legs. Slaty-backed Nightingale-Thrush is rather similar but is notably smaller and has white belly. See also Black-faced Solitaire.

Status and distribution: Uncommon to fairly common on volcanic lava fields and high clearings in mountains of western Chiriquí, mostly from 7500 feet to above timberline, but also occurring on rocky Llanos del Volcán as low as 6100 feet. Can be regularly seen in small numbers in the little clearings near the crest of the Boquete Trail above Cerro Punta at 7500–8000 feet.

Habits: Usually seen on or near the ground in pairs or small groups. It is reported to have a poor but still somewhat robin-like song (Slud); the calls are a *trrrr* and a harsh *tchweerp, tchweerp.*

Range: Costa Rica and western Panama.

WOOD THRUSH
(*Hylocichla mustelina*)

Description: 7½. Brown above shading to *rufous on crown and nape;* white below with *numerous large black spots.*

Similar species: No other adult thrush has such conspicuous spotting below. Veery is uniform tawny above; Swainson's and Gray-cheeked Thrushes are uniform olive brown above.

Status and distribution: Uncommon to rare winter resident in western and central Panama, most numerous in Bocas del Toro (early October–mid April) and in western Chiriquí highlands; rare in Canal Zone and not reported from farther east.

Habits: Usually seen singly on or near the ground in forest or second-growth woodland. Its distinctive call is a rapid *whip-whip-whip.*

Range: Breeds in eastern North America; winters from Mexico to Panama; a rare transient in West Indies; accidental in Guyana.

SWAINSON'S THRUSH
(*Catharus ustulatus*)

Description: 7. Brownish olive to rather russet brown above with *buffy brown cheeks* and a *usually prominent buffy eye-ring and supraloral stripe;* white below, throat and chest tinged buffy and lightly spotted with dusky.

Similar species: Gray-cheeked Thrush is very similar but has grayish cheeks and lacks the eye-ring; one population of Swainson's is rather grayish with eye-ring less distinct or even (in fall) absent, so caution is required in identification. For in-hand characters, see under that species.

Status and distribution: Common to sometimes locally abundant fall (mostly October–November, a few late September) and fairly common to common spring (March–April, with stragglers into May) transient throughout, including Chiriquí highlands to at least 6000 feet and Pearl Islands; uncommon to rare winter resident in lowlands and foothills. On migration widespread in forest borders, second-growth woodland, and shrubby areas; apparently most numerous on Caribbean slope, especially in Bocas del Toro.

Habits: Like other migrant thrushes, usually keeps to rather dense cover and shy, so not visible in large numbers; at times, however, the number mist-netted is staggering. Easily the most numerous migrant thrush in Panama. During April can sometimes be heard to sing.

Range: Breeds in North America; winters from southern Mexico to northern Argentina.

GRAY-CHEEKED THRUSH
(*Catharus minimus*)

Description: 7. Dull olive brown above with *grayish cheeks* and *no distinct eye-ring;* white below, washed with buffy grayish on chest and spotted lightly with dusky on chest and breast.

Similar species: Often very difficult to distinguish from Swainson's Thrush. Gray-cheeks tend to be duller above than most (but not all) Swainson's and have grayish (not buffy) cheeks and show no distinct buffy eye-ring or loral stripe. In the hand, Gray-cheek's tail (except in immature) is longer than bend of wing to tip of secondaries (not longer in Swainson's), and Gray-cheek's 6th, 7th, and 8th primaries are sinuate on inner web (in Swainson's usually only 7th and 8th primaries have inner web sinuate).

Status and distribution: Somewhat uncertain. Until recently considered to be very rare in Panama. Recent mist-netting data have seemingly changed this, though whether the identification of all birds was correct cannot be known because the wing characters were not checked. Mist-netting identifications were based on an absence of a buffy eye-ring, and apparently one race of the Swainson's lacks a buffy eye-ring in the fall (*fide* Eisenmann). In any case, the Gray-cheek is probably an uncommon fall transient (late September–early November), a rare or occasional winter resident (records few and scattered, possibly more numerous in Darién), and an even rarer spring transient (April); records are concentrated along Caribbean coast, especially in Bocas del Toro and Canal Zone. Definite specimens include an old one from Volcán de Chiriquí; one at Almirante, Bocas del Toro on October 12, 1962 (Gorgas Laboratory, *fide* Wetmore); two on Cerro Campana on November 2 and 8, 1966 out of many netted (G. V. N. Powell and S. G. Martin); one at base of Cerro Malí, Darién on March 5, 1964 (Wetmore); and one at Cerro Quía, Darién on February 20, 1971 (P. Galindo).

Habits: Similar to Swainson's Thrush, but observed even less often relative to the number mist-netted, possibly keeping to thicker cover.

Range: Breeds in northern North America and northeastern Siberia; winters mostly in northern South America, rarely in Middle America.

VEERY
(*Catharus fuscescens*)

Description: 7. *Uniform tawny brown above;* white below, washed with buff on throat and chest and *very indistinctly spotted with dusky on chest.*

Similar species: Wood Thrush is much more prominently spotted below and is rufous only on crown and nape. Swainson's and Gray-cheeked Thrushes are usually olive brown above (but some Swainson's are almost as russet above) and are more distinctly spotted below. See also Ruddy-capped Nightingale-Thrush.

Status and distribution: Uncommon fall transient along immediate Caribbean coast (late September–late October), recorded only in Bocas del Toro and Canal Zone; rare fall transient elsewhere, with only three reports from Pacific slope, one from Chiriquí highlands, two from Fort Clayton in Canal Zone; a few stragglers remain into November but evidently does not winter in Panama; very rare spring transient, with only two reports (early March and early April), both from Bocas del Toro. The least numerous migrant thrush in Panama.

Range: Breeds in North America; winters in northern South America; a scarce transient, apparently, in both Middle America and West Indies.

BLACK-HEADED NIGHTINGALE-THRUSH
(*Catharus mexicanus*) Pl.23

Description: 6. Known only from western foothills. *Bill orange;* legs orange-yellow. *Iris dark. Head black* with prominent narrow orange eye-ring; otherwise *brownish olive above;* whitish below with grayish chest and sides.

Similar species: Note black head contrasting with olive back and dark eye. Slaty-backed Nightingale-Thrush is all dark slaty gray above and has prominent pale eye. Black-billed Nightingale-Thrush has dark bill and legs, and gray head.

Status and distribution: Known only from undergrowth of humid forest in foothills of Bocas del Toro and both slopes of Veraguas; recorded mostly 2500–3500 feet.

Habits: Little known in Panama. Reported to have a mediocre variable song, usually one or two short phrases with an extra note or two at the beginning or end, sometimes including a sharp *sreek*; one call is a dry rattle like stones being knocked together (Slud).

Range: Eastern Mexico to western Panama.

SLATY-BACKED NIGHTINGALE-THRUSH
(*Catharus fuscater*) Pl.23

Description: 6½. *Bill and legs orange. Iris whitish. Slaty blackish above,* blackest on head with narrow orange eye-ring; *mostly slaty gray below,* fading to white on center of breast and belly. Darién birds have yellower legs, and throat, breast, and sides rather olive, with center of belly pale yellow (olive and yellow fading to grayish and whitish, respectively, in old specimens).

Similar species: The only nightingale-thrush known from central or eastern Panama. Black-headed Nightingale-Thrush has dark eye and black head contrasting with olive upperparts; Orange-billed Nightingale-Thrush is brown above (no slaty) with gray head, dark eye. Black-faced Solitaire has broader bill and more upright posture, is uniform gray below. See also the larger Sooty Robin.

Status and distribution: Now apparently rare to uncommon in undergrowth of forest in lower highlands of western Chiriquí (4000–7500 feet), eastern Chiriquí, and Veraguas; also occurs (race uncertain) in cloud forest on Cerro Jefe, eastern Panama province (recent sightings by E. S. Morton and E. O. Willis, D. Hill, and Ridgely); known also from highlands of eastern Darién (3600–5200 feet). Formerly more numerous in lower highlands (especially 4000–5000 feet) of western Chiriquí (W. W. Brown collected 21 specimens); these areas are now mostly cleared or have been converted to coffee plantations.

Habits: Not well known in Panama. The song of a bird on Cerro Jefe was a series of very pure clear whistles (somewhat suggesting a solitaire) in a minor key, first 3 notes, then 2 more, the whole repeated after a pause of about 3 seconds, *to tee too, too tee* (E. S. Morton). In Costa Rica, the two-note phrase sometimes comes first, and birds also give a different sort of song, *eeay eeooleéee*, suggesting quality of solitaire (Slud).

Range: Costa Rica to northwestern Venezuela and northern Bolivia.

RUDDY-CAPPED NIGHTINGALE-THRUSH

(*Catharus frantzii*) Pl.23

Description: 6½. Found only in western Chiriquí highlands. Bill dusky above, pale salmon below; legs brown. Brown above with *russet cap*; pale grayish below, fading to whitish on throat and belly.

Similar species: The only Panama nightingale-thrush with a russet cap (others are gray or black). Veery is slightly spotted on chest and is more uniform tawny above.

Status and distribution: Common in undergrowth of forest and forest borders in highlands of western Chiriquí, recorded 4000–8000 feet but mostly 5000–7000 feet. The most numerous nightingale-thrush in the Bambito and Cerro Punta area.

Habits: Usually on or near the ground, sometimes hopping out into clearings but never far from cover. Has a beautiful far-carrying ethereal song consisting of many phrases and sometimes very long, in quality rather like a Hermit Thrush (*C. guttatus*) but in phrasing like a Wood Thrush (C. Hartshorne). The solitaire's song has a somewhat similar liquid quality but it is richer, louder, less varied, and is usually much shorter in duration and with longer pauses between phrases. A distinctive call is a sweet long-drawn burred *ooeerrrp*.

Range: Central Mexico to western Panama.

ORANGE-BILLED NIGHTINGALE-THRUSH

(*Catharus aurantiirostris*) Pl.23

Description: 6½. Found only in western foothills and highlands. *Bill and legs orange.* Brown above with *gray head* and narrow orange eye-ring; light gray below, fading to whitish on throat, middle of breast, and belly.

Similar species: Ruddy-capped and Black-billed Nightingale-Thrushes have dark bills and legs. Black-headed Nightingale-Thrush has obviously black (not gray) head.

Status and distribution: Fairly common to common in forest borders, lighter woodland, and gardens with dense shrubbery in foothills and lower highlands of Chiriquí (mostly 3000–5500 feet) and both slopes of Veraguas (where ranges lower, to about 1300 feet). In western Chiriquí, numerous around Boquete and fairly common in the town itself.

Habits: Usually hard to see, keeping to dense low vegetation. For a nightingale-thrush, its song is poor and unmusical with varied phrases, some twangy, others squeaky; a short *tsip, wee-ee, tsirrip-tsip* is one of several.

Range: Northern Mexico to western Panama; Colombia and Venezuela.

Note: Gray-headed birds of southwestern Costa Rica, western Panama, and western Colombia were formerly regarded as specifically distinct from brown-headed races of the rest of the range and were called *C. griseiceps* (Gray-headed Nightingale-Thrush).

BLACK-BILLED NIGHTINGALE-THRUSH

(*Catharus gracilirostris*) Pl.23

Description: 6. Found only in Chiriquí mountains. *Bill and legs blackish.* Plain brown above, grayer on head; *gray below* with band of tawny-olive across chest.

Similar species: The only nightingale-thrush with an all-dark bill.

Status and distribution: Fairly common in undergrowth of forest in mountains of western Chiriquí, mostly 7000 to over 10,000 feet, but occasionally ranging lower at least locally to 5000 feet. In Panama most easily seen along the Boquete Trail above Cerro Punta.

Habits: A bird of higher elevations, though found locally with Ruddy-capped Nightingale-Thrush. Often quite unsuspicious. The song suggests that of the Ruddy-capped, but is thinner, higher and distinctly inferior.

Range: Costa Rica and western Panama.

GNATCATCHERS, GNATWRENS, AND OLD WORLD WARBLERS: Sylviidae (4)

The taxonomic position of the two exclusively American groups placed in this family is unclear (especially in the case of the gnatwrens); they are usually placed with the Sylviidae, almost all of which are Old World in distribution. Others place the solely American genera in a family Polioptilidae or in a subfamily Polioptilinae of the broad family Muscicapidae (treating the Old World Warblers as a separate subfamily). Gnatcatchers are tiny, slender, mainly gray birds whose long tails constantly flip around in an animated fashion; arboreal birds, they favor forest borders and woodland. Gnatwrens inhabit forest and woodland undergrowth and borders, where due to their small size, rather dull brown plumage, and retiring behavior they are difficult to see. Both groups are insectivorous, and construct a pretty open-cup nest in a bush or tree (the nest of *Microbates* seems to be unrecorded).

TROPICAL GNATCATCHER

(*Polioptila plumbea*) Pl.24

Description: 4. A slender little bird with a rather long tail, often cocked up. Male *bluish gray above* with *glossy black crown and hindneck*; superciliary, sides of head, and entire underparts white; tail black with outer feathers white. Female similar but without black cap.

Similar species: Warbler-like in its spritely behavior. See Slate-throated Gnatcatcher.

Status and distribution: Fairly common and widespread in forest canopy and borders, second-growth woodland, shrubby clearings, and locally even in scrubby areas in lowlands and foothills on both slopes, ranging up to around 4000 feet, occasionally higher; found also on Coiba Island; recent sight report of a pair on Pearl Islands (Rey) on February 11, 1970 (Ridgely).

Habits: Seen singly or in pairs, often with mixed foraging flocks of insectivorous birds. Very active, constantly moving its tail about. Has a rather thin but musical song consisting of a series of simple notes with decreasing intensity, *sweet, weet, weet, weet, weet,* sometimes faster and more sibilant; the usual call is a *tzeet-tzeet.*

Range: Southeastern Mexico to central Peru and central Brazil.

SLATE-THROATED GNATCATCHER

(*Polioptila schistaceigula*) Pl.24

Description: 4. Very rare, known only from eastern Panama. Sexes are evidently similar. *Slaty gray above* with narrow white eye-ring and interrupted moustachial streak; *throat and chest slaty gray,* breast and belly white; tail black, outer feathers very narrowly tipped white.

Similar species: Tropical Gnatcatcher is paler more bluish gray above, and *entirely* white below; male has conspicuous black cap.

Status and distribution: Apparently very rare. Known in Panama only from an old specimen labeled "Gulf of Darién," and recent specimens taken on Río Boqueron above Madden Lake in eastern Panama province (Wetmore) and at Cerro Quía in southeastern Darién (P. Galindo).

Habits: Little known but seems similar to Tropical Gnatcatcher; a bird of humid forest and forest borders. Forages singly or in pairs, high in forest trees, often accompanying mixed flocks of tanagers, etc.

Range: Central Panama to northwestern Ecuador.

LONG-BILLED GNATWREN

(*Ramphocaenus rufiventris*) Pl.24

Description: 4¾. *Very long, slender, straight bill;* tail narrow and long, often cocked. Mostly grayish olive above with crown and hindneck brown; sides of head and neck cinnamon; *mostly buffy below,* throat whitish with indistinct dusky streaks; tail blackish with feathers tipped white. Immature brownish above.

Similar species: Somewhat wren-like but easily known by its very long bill. Tawny-faced Gnatwren is smaller with a shorter bill and is mostly gray below (except for white throat) with broad broken black stripe along sides of neck.

Status and distribution: Fairly common to

common in lower growth of forest borders, second-growth woodland, lighter scrubby woodland, and shrubby clearings in more humid lowlands on both slopes, ranging locally up to about 3500 feet in the foothills; apparently absent from drier areas on Pacific slope from eastern side of Azuero Peninsula to extreme western Panama province. Widespread in lighter woodland on both slopes of Canal Zone.

Habits: Rather skulking and often difficult to see. Usually in pairs, frequently calling back and forth to each other with a distinctive clear musical trill usually only on one pitch, sometimes rising in intensity and then softening toward end. At times joins mixed foraging flocks of insectivorous birds.

Range: Southeastern Mexico to Colombia.

Note: By some authors merged with *R. melanurus* (Straight-billed Gnatwren) of northern and central South America.

TAWNY-FACED (HALF-COLLARED) GNATWREN

(*Microbates cinereiventris*) Pl.24

Description: 4. Bill long but proportionately shorter than in Long-billed Gnatwren; tail short, usually cocked. Dark brown above with *sides of head and neck bright tawny*; throat white *bordered by broad broken black stripe; partial collar of black streaks across chest;* remaining underparts gray.

Similar species: Superficially like several wrens but without wing and tail barring; in dark light of forest undergrowth, the collar and bright sides of head can be hard to see, so might be confused with the unpatterned Nightingale Wren. See also Long-billed Gnatwren.

Status and distribution: Uncommon and inconspicuous in undergrowth of humid forest in lowlands on entire Caribbean slope, ranging at least locally up into lower foothills (Cerro Santa Rita); on Pacific slope found in foothills of Chiriquí, Veraguas, Cerro Campana, and Cerro Azul/Jefe area east through Darién, where also in lowlands.

Habits: Usually in pairs or small family groups, mostly near the ground. Not very often seen but regularly captured in mist-nets. The usual call is a fast chattering *chrichrichrichrichri.*

Range: Nicaragua to southern Peru.

PIPITS AND WAGTAILS: Motacillidae (1)

Only pipits occur in the New World, except in Alaska where two species of wagtails breed. Two species of pipits are found in North America and seven others in South America, with one of these extending to the Pacific slope of Panama. Pipits are slender terrestrial birds of open country, generally streaked in plumage, with slender bills and rather long dark tails with outer feathers white. Unlike most passerines, they usually walk rather than hop. Pipits are mainly insectivorous, and the Panama species, like most of the others, nests on the ground in grass.

YELLOWISH PIPIT

(*Anthus lutescens*) Pl.24

Description: 5. A small, slender bird of Pacific grasslands. Brown above streaked with buffy and black and with narrow pale buffy whitish eye-ring; *yellowish white below* streaked with dusky on chest; tail blackish with *outer feathers whitish,* prominent in flight.

Similar species: The only small brownish bird of Pacific grassland that walks on ground. Female seedeaters are not streaked; Grasshopper Sparrow is more furtive, never walking in open.

Status and distribution: Locally common in short grass savannas and fields in lowlands on Pacific slope from western Chiriquí through eastern side of Azuero Peninsula to eastern Panama province, less numerous westward. Rather local in Canal Zone but common wherever there is suitable habitat, e.g. Albrook AFB.

Habits: Found in well-scattered colonies, the birds blending into the ground and often difficult to spot until flushed. The male's song is distinctive and attractive, initially a series of *dzee*'s on a rising pitch, usually given as the bird ascends in a looping manner into the sky, then a long slurred *dzeeeeeeeeeeee* given as it slowly glides back to earth, often with a *dzip* at end. Also sings from ground, a shorter *tsitsirrit.*

Range: Western and central Panama; South America east of the Andes south to northern Argentina, west of them in coastal Peru and northern Chile.

WAXWINGS: Bombycillidae (1)

The waxwings are a small group of but three species breeding in temperate North America and Eurasia, with one species irregularly migrating to Panama. Their common name is derived from the wax-like red tips to the secondaries. They are gregarious, rather unsuspicious birds, feeding mostly on fruit and berries, with some insects captured in the air at least during the breeding season.

CEDAR WAXWING
(*Bombycilla cedrorum*)

Description: 7. Rare. A *sleek* brownish bird with a *conspicuous pointed crest. Mostly soft pinkish brown* with black around face, paler below fading to yellowish on belly; wings more grayish with *secondaries tipped waxy scarlet;* tail gray *tipped yellow.* Immature similar but duller and grayer, more whitish below with light brownish streaking, crest shorter, generally without waxy red wing tipping.

Similar species: Long-tailed Silky-Flycatcher has somewhat similar sleek and crested appearance but is distinctly gray in male (olive in female) with notably long tail.

Status and distribution: A rare and very irregular winter visitant (January–March), with records few and scattered; reported from Chiriquí highlands, western Panama province, both slopes of Canal Zone, and Pearl Islands. Not recorded during many winter seasons.

Habits: In its normal range, usually in compact flocks, often quite large, but has occurred in Panama as scattered individuals or in small groups. Has a very distinctive high thin sibilant *tseeee,* frequently given in flight.

Range: Breeds in North America; winters south increasingly irregularly to central Panama and in Greater Antilles, accidentally to Colombia and Venezuela.

SILKY-FLYCATCHERS: Ptilogonatidae (2)

The silky-flycatchers form a group of only four species found from southwestern United States to western Panama. They are usually considered most closely related to the waxwings, and are sometimes given only subfamily status in the Bombycillidae. Recently it has been suggested (C. G. Sibley, *Auk* 90: 394–410, 1973) that the solitaires (genus *Myadestes*), now generally placed in the Turdidae, actually belong in the Ptilogonatidae. The name "silky-flycatcher" is something of a misnomer, as they are not at all related to the Tyrannidae. Three of the four species are notably gregarious, the exception being the Black-and-yellow Phainoptila (which perhaps does not belong with this group). All apparently eat both berries and insects, and construct shallow nests placed in forks or on a branch in a bush or tree.

LONG-TAILED SILKY-FLYCATCHER (SILKY)
(*Ptilogonys caudatus*) Pl.23

Description: 9½. Found only in western Chiriquí highlands. *Sleek and slender,* with *prominent bushy crest* and *long, graduated tail.* Male *soft bluish gray above* with *crest and most of head olive yellowish;* wings and tail black, latter with white patch and central feathers somewhat elongated; throat yellowish olive, remaining underparts gray becoming yellow on lower belly and under tail-coverts. Female similar but with upperparts mostly olive green.

Status and distribution: Common in forest borders and clearings and pastures with large trees in highlands of western Chiriquí, mostly above 5000 feet.

Habits: Very attractive birds, somewhat variable in numbers but usually one of the more conspicuous birds in the western Chiriquí highlands. Generally in small groups perched high in the trees, sometimes lower in fruiting trees. The call is a frequently uttered dry *cheerink* varied to *seerip* or *chirrip.*

Range: Costa Rica and western Panama.

BLACK-AND-YELLOW PHAINOPTILA (SILKY-FLYCATCHER)
(*Phainoptila melanoxantha*) Pl.23

Description: 8½. Found only in western highlands. Male *mostly glossy black above* with yellow rump; *throat also black, contrasting with yellowish olive green chest;* lower underparts gray with *bright yellow* *sides and flanks*. Female olive green above, yellower on rump, with *glossy black cap;* throat grayish, chest olive green, *lower underparts as in male.*

Similar species: Does not at all resemble Long-tailed Silky-Flycatcher. Both sexes are best known by their characteristic yellow sides and glossy black on head (at least). Rather thrush-like in proportions and posture. See also Yellow-thighed Finch.

Status and distribution: Uncommon in forest and forest borders in highlands of western Chiriquí (5500–9800 feet), adjacent Bocas del Toro (one record, 5200 feet), and eastern Chiriquí and Veraguas (4500–6000 feet).

Habits: Not well known in Panama; evidently more numerous in Costa Rica. Usually seen singly or in pairs, feeding actively on fruit in dense foliage at low and middle levels. The call is a thin *tsip*.

Range: Costa Rica and western Panama.

PEPPERSHRIKES: Cyclarhidae (1)

The peppershrikes comprise a very small group of two species, found from Mexico to central Argentina, sometimes considered a subfamily of the Vireonidae. They resemble the vireos but are larger and have a heavy, strongly hooked bill. Like the vireos, they are arboreal and insectivorous, and sing constantly, well concealed in the foliage. The nest is a deep cup hung between two forking branches.

RUFOUS-BROWED PEPPERSHRIKE

(*Cyclarhis gujanensis*) Pl.24

Description: 5¾. Heavy-headed, with *stout, strongly hooked bill.* Olive green above with *brownish or gray cap, gray sides of head, and broad rufous superciliary;* mostly yellow below, in some regions paling to white on belly. Chiriquí birds (*subflavescens*) are duller above and below.

Similar species: In proportions like a shrike-vireo but with very different color pattern and habitat. Vireos are slimmer, have less heavy bill, lack rufous eyestripe.

Status and distribution: Fairly common in forest borders and clearings with trees in foothills and highlands of Chiriquí (3000–8200 feet) and in light and scrubby woodland in lowlands on Pacific slope locally from Veraguas and eastern side of Azuero Peninsula to western Panama province (Playa Coronado, Nueva Gorgona); recorded also in extreme eastern Panama province and western Darién (Garachiné); found also on Coiba Island. Only report from Canal Zone is a singing bird on Barro Colorado Island, May 9–10, 1950 (Wetmore), but to be watched for as it seems only recently to have spread to western Panama province (*fide* Eisenmann). A pair was also noted in mangroves near Tocumen, eastern Panama province on July 10, 1975 (Ridgely), further evidence of this species' slow spread into central Panama.

Habits: An arboreal and rather lethargic bird; when singing usually sits quietly in the foliage and often very hard to see. The song is monotonous, consisting of short but musical rather oriole or grosbeak-like whistled phrases, sometimes repeated without change for 5–10 minutes, then changed to a new phrase which is likewise repeated for a long period, and so on; characteristic phrases are *tootoo-wheétee, tooweeoo* and *chee-weech, awatweéa;* one bird may sing for hours, going through a repertory of numerous different phrases.

Range: Eastern Mexico to central Argentina.

SHRIKE-VIREOS: Vireolaniidae (2)

The shrike-vireos are a small, little known group of three or four neotropical species, like the peppershrikes sometimes considered a subfamily in the Vireonidae. They resemble the vireos except for their larger size and heavier appearance and much thicker, strongly hooked bill. The two Panama forms (by some considered one species) somewhat resemble peppershrikes except for their bright emerald green and blue plumage. Panamanian shrike-vireos forage high in trees in lowland forests, where they would go unnoticed except for their incessantly given song. Nothing seems to be recorded of the nesting of any species.

GREEN (EMERALD) SHRIKE-VIREO
(*Smaragdolanius pulchellus*) Pl.24

Description: 5½. Heavy-headed, with *stout, hooked bill. Brilliant grass green above* with pale blue band on hindneck (Bocas del Toro birds, *verticalis,* also have blue forehead); *throat bright yellow,* remaining underparts light yellowish green.

Similar species: Brilliantly colored but difficult to see. Golden-browed Chlorophonia of western highlands is generally similar in color but mostly bright yellow below with contrasting green throat (the reverse of this species) and has yellow eyestripe and short wide bill. Green Honeycreeper is also bright green but has slimmer proportions and slenderer, slightly decurved bill, lacks yellow on throat.

Status and distribution: Common but apparently rather local in forest and second-growth woodland; recorded from lowlands of eastern Bocas del Toro and Veraguas, foothills on both slopes of Veraguas, El Valle and Cerro Campana, both slopes of Canal Zone (where numerous and widespread in forested areas), and lowlands and foothills of eastern Panama province; probably occurs in lowlands of western Bocas del Toro and in Caribbean lowlands of Coclé and western Colon province but not yet recorded.

Habits: Deliberate behavior, green plumage blending into the foliage, and habit of usually remaining high in forest trees, all combine to make this beautiful bird exasperatingly difficult to see. Sometimes, however, joins a mixed flock of insectivorous birds and then may descend much lower. Heard far more often than it is seen, its true abundance is best indicated by its distinctive song consisting of a phrase of three whistles, tirelessly repeated, *peeea, peeea, peeea . . . ,* the notes sometimes lacking the downward slide (then *pee-pee-pee . . .*), reminiscent of song of Tufted Titmouse (*Parus bicolor*) of temperate North America.

Range: Southeastern Mexico to eastern Panama.

YELLOW-BROWED SHRIKE-VIREO
(*Smaragdolanius eximius*) Pl.24

Description: 5½. Known only from eastern Darién. Resembles Green Shrike-Vireo and often considered conspecific with it though there are no known intergrades and there is a considerable gap between the known ranges of the two forms. Has *entire crown and nape blue* (not merely band on hindneck) and *conspicuous yellow superciliary;* otherwise like Green Shrike-Vireo.

Status and distribution: Known only from foothills of eastern Darién (Cana, 3000 feet). Any shrike-vireo in San Blas, extreme eastern Panama province, or Darién should be carefully checked and if possible collected so as to determine whether there is intergradation.

Range: Eastern Panama to Colombia and northwestern Venezuela.

VIREOS: Vireonidae (13)

The vireos are a strictly American family of rather plain, arboreal, primarily (but not exclusively) insectivorous birds, represented in Panama by both migrant and resident species. Typical vireos of the genus *Vireo* are olive above, with or without wing-bars, and with either a superciliary (most Panama species) or an eye-ring. Greenlets of the genus *Hylophilus* (all of which are resident) are smaller, with more slender bills; they lack wing-bars and superciliary, though most have crown (at least) either tawny, brownish, or gray in contrast to remaining upperparts. Typical vireos differ from wood-warblers in their usually larger size, somewhat heavier bills, and less active behavior; greenlets are more warbler-like in size and actions, but resemble none in plumage details and are somewhat stockier larger-headed birds. Nests of the genus *Vireo* are rather deep cups suspended between two forking horizontal branches; little is recorded about the nesting of *Hylophilus,* though it appears to be similar to *Vireo.*

WHITE-EYED VIREO
(*Vireo griseus*)

Description: 4½–5. Accidental. *White iris* in adult only, dark in immature. Olive above with *yellow eye-ring and supraloral stripe,* wings dusky with two white wing-bars; whitish below *tinged with yellow on sides and flanks.*

Similar species: Yellow-throated Vireo has yellow spectacles but also has bright yellow throat. In color pattern somewhat like a number of small flycatchers but differs in bill shape, posture, and actions.

Status and distribution: Only one record, a bird collected at Almirante, Bocas del Toro on October 16, 1964 (D. Hicks).
Range: Breeds in eastern United States and northeastern Mexico; winters from southern United States to Nicaragua and in Cuba, once in western Panama.

YELLOW-WINGED VIREO
(*Vireo carmioli*) Pl.24

Description: 4½. Found only in Chiriquí highlands. Greenish olive above with *yellowish eye-ring and short superciliary,* and *broad yellow wing-bars* and wing-edging; *mostly yellow below,* whitish on throat, tinged olive on sides.
Similar species: No other Panamanian vireo has *yellow* wing-bars; Golden-winged and Chestnut-sided Warblers (in fall) do, but both are whitish below. Most resembles Yellow-throated Vireo.
Status and distribution: Fairly common in forest canopy and borders and large trees in clearings in highlands of western Chiriquí, mostly above 6000 feet.
Habits: Forages mostly at high levels, sometimes with mixed flocks. The song consists of short, leisurely phrases with a hoarse quality somewhat suggestive of a Solitary Vireo, often with distinctive, accented terminal phrase, *cheéyah . . . cheéyou . . . chipcheeweé,* or sometimes *chewit, chweéoo.*
Range: Costa Rica and western Panama.

YELLOW-THROATED VIREO
(*Vireo flavifrons*)

Description: 5¼–5½. Olive green above with *prominent yellow eye-ring* and two prominent white wing-bars; *throat and breast bright yellow,* belly white.
Similar species: The brightest and most clean-cut vireo. In pattern recalls several winter-plumaged wood warblers but can always be known by the combination of yellow spectacles and yellow throat and breast.
Status and distribution: Fairly common transient and winter resident (late October–early April) throughout.
Habits: Usually found singly, often in mixed flocks with wood-warblers. Lethargic and slow-moving even for a vireo. Its burry, phrased song is quite often heard, especially in spring.
Range: Breeds in eastern North America; winters from southern Mexico to Colombia and northern Venezuela, also in Cuba.

[SOLITARY VIREO]
(*Vireo solitarius*)

Description: 5–6. Two recent sightings. *Head blue-gray with conspicuous white "spectacles";* olive green back, wings duskier with *two whitish wing-bars; underparts white* with yellowish green sides and flanks.
Similar species: Only vireo with blue-gray head; note contrast of head with olive back and snowy white throat. Birds breeding in western United States have duller gray head and gray back, but are unlikely in Panama. See also the *Tolmomyias* flycatchers, both of which have contrasting gray heads.
Status and distribution: Two recent sight reports from Volcán in lower highlands of western Chiriquí: one on March 17, 1972 (C. Leahy and R. Forster), and one on January 16, 1974 (C. Leahy and Ridgely). Specimen or photographic confirmation desirable.
Range: Breeds in North America and south in highlands to El Salvador and Honduras; eastern North American birds winter south to Nicaragua and in Greater Antilles, casually to Costa Rica (one recent sighting) and western Panama.

RED-EYED VIREO
(*Vireo olivaceus*)

Description: 5½–6¼. Olive green above with *gray crown and white superciliary bordered above by thin black line and below by dusky streak;* whitish below, sometimes tinged yellowish on flanks (especially in fall and in immatures). Red iris visible only at close range.
Similar species: Very like Yellow-green Vireo but with a sharper, cleaner-cut facial pattern and at most only a little yellow below (Yellow-green has bright greenish yellow sides, flanks, and vent). In the hand, a helpful distinction is that the Red-eye's 9th primary is usually distinctly longer than its 6th and always distinctly longer than its 5th. See also Black-whiskered Vireo. Philadelphia and Brown-capped Vireos are smaller and duller, with less distinct white eyestripes and no bordering black lines.
Status and distribution: Very common spring and fall transient throughout (mostly September–October and March–April, occasionally August and May); a few may winter but definite proof is lacking (no specimens).
Habits: Frequents clearings, second-growth

woodland, and woodland borders throughout. Often occurs in marked waves on migration. Commonly sings on spring migration, the song with longer phrases than Yellow-green Vireo.

Range: Breeds in North America; winters mostly in the Amazon basin.

YELLOW-GREEN VIREO

(*Vireo flavoviridis*) Pl.24

Description: 5¼–6. Much like the Red-eyed Vireo, by some considered conspecific. Olive green above with gray crown and whitish or pale grayish superciliary, bordered above and below by thin dusky lines (sometimes absent); whitish below with *bright greenish yellow sides, flanks, and under tail-coverts.* Red iris visible only at close range.

Similar species: Closely resembles Red-eyed Vireo but brighter olive-green above, head stripes less distinct, and with much more yellow on sides and vent. In the hand can be told by its shorter wing: 9th (outer) primary usually distinctly shorter than 6th (occasionally equally as long), sometimes as short as 5th. See also Black-whiskered Vireo. Philadelphia Vireo also has considerable yellow below but is smaller with olive (not gray) crown and shorter less distinct eyestripe.

Status and distribution: A common to abundant breeder in gardens, clearings, coastal scrub and mangroves, and light second-growth woodland in lowlands on Pacific slope; on Caribbean slope known to breed only in cleared areas of Canal Zone and vicinity; ranges up into highlands in cleared areas to around 5500 feet; also very common on Pearl Islands and Coiba Island. Breeding status in Darién uncertain. Transients from farther north are common along Caribbean slope from late September–October and in March. Breeding birds apparently absent in South America from late September to early January (a few rarely arriving late December).

Habits: One of the most numerous and widespread birds in open and semi-open country on Pacific slope. Its song is much like the Red-eyed Vireo's, an endlessly repeated (even during the heat of the day) series of abrupt phrases, but slower and more monotonous with shorter individual phrases and longer intervening pauses.

Range: Breeds from southern Texas and Mexico to Panama, migrating to South America during nonbreeding season.

Note: Merged by some authors with the previous species, *V. olivaceus,* with *V. chivi* of South America included.

BLACK-WHISKERED VIREO

(*Vireo altiloquus*)

Description: 6. Very much like Red-eyed Vireo but with *dusky "whisker" stripe* on each side of throat. Olive green above, tinged with grayish or brownish gray on crown, white superciliary bordered below by blackish stripe; whitish below tinged with pale yellowish olive on flanks.

Similar species: The definite whisker is the diagnostic mark, but one must be very careful because some molting fall Red-eyed and Yellow-green Vireos may also *seem* to show a whisker.

Status and distribution: Uncertain, probably a rare fall transient or winter resident in lowlands on Caribbean slope. Three specimens: one nineteenth-century specimen taken at Lion Hill, Canal Zone; one taken at Guaval on Río Calovévora, Caribbean slope Veraguas on August 31, 1926; and one taken at Puerto Obaldía, San Blas on September 12, 1930. Several recent sightings in Canal Zone: one at Achiote Road on September 29, 1968 (Ridgely); and one at Gatun Dam on January 29, 1970 (E. S. Morton). Perhaps more regular than realized.

Range: Breeds in Florida, West Indies, and other Caribbean islands; winters in Lesser Antilles and northern South America; rare migrant or winter resident in Panama.

PHILADELPHIA VIREO

(*Vireo philadelphicus*)

Description: 4¾. Dull olive green above, grayer on head, with whitish superciliary; *dull pale yellow below,* somewhat brighter on chest.

Similar species: Lacks Brown-capped Vireo's brown cap though otherwise very similar. Yellow-green Vireo is larger, with more pronounced eyestripe, and with yellow restricted to sides and under tail-coverts. See also Tennessee Warbler.

Status and distribution: Fairly common winter resident in foothills and highlands of Chiriquí and Veraguas (October–early April); rare winter resident in lowlands of western and central Panama, with reports few and scattered (Bocas del Toro, Coiba Island, Cerro Campana, and Canal Zone). Perhaps overlooked until recently in the lowlands; recent Canal Zone reports (all E. S. Morton) are: one collected at Albrook

AFB on February 19, 1971; one seen at Madden Lake Scout Camp on February 26, 1971; one collected at Gatun Dam on April 4, 1971.

Habits: On its Chiriquí wintering grounds frequents brushy clearings and forest borders, often foraging at little more than eye-level.

Range: Breeds in northern North America; winters from southern Mexico to central Panama, casually to Colombia.

BROWN-CAPPED VIREO
(*Vireo leucophrys*) Pl.24

Description: 4½. Known only from western highlands. Dull olive green above with *brown cap* and whitish superciliary; pale dull yellow below.

Similar species: No other "vireo" has a brown cap; Philadelphia Vireo is otherwise very similar. Tawny-crowned Greenlet also has brown cap, but is smaller and essentially brown (not olive green) above; it is a slenderer, more active, warbler-like bird.

Status and distribution: Common in forest borders, more open woodland, and shrubby clearings in highlands of Chiriquí, western Bocas del Toro, and Veraguas, mostly above 4000 feet but somewhat lower in eastern Chiriquí and Veraguas.

Habits: Often in small groups, associating with other highland birds. The song, a fairly continuous warble, is reminiscent of the Warbling Vireo (*V. gilvus*) but is shorter and less varied.

Range: Costa Rica to northern Venezuela and Bolivia.

Note: Birds of this group breeding from southern Mexico to Nicaragua are probably closer to *V. gilvus* of temperate North America than to *V. leucophrys;* both are sometimes regarded as conspecific with *V. gilvus.*

LESSER GREENLET
(*Hylophilus decurtatus*) Pl.24

Description: 3¾–4. Two forms, *H. decurtatus* (Gray-headed Greenlet) and *H. minor* (Lesser Greenlet), often regarded as distinct species, are here merged; they apparently intergrade extensively in the Canal Zone and Cerro Azul area (E. S. Morton). A puffy-headed, very active little bird with a short tail. Birds from western Panama and most from Canal Zone area have *crown and nape gray with whitish eye-ring,* fading to pale grayish on sides of head; upperparts otherwise bright olive green; *grayish white below* with a little greenish yellow on sides. Immature tinged buffy below. Birds from eastern Panama have dull olive instead of gray head, but are otherwise very similar.

Similar species: Different shape (big head, short tail) from any wood warbler, many of which have superficially similar color patterns (see especially Tennessee Warbler). Other greenlets have yellow on underparts.

Status and distribution: Very common in forest and second-growth woodland in lowlands and foothills on both slopes, ranging up to around 5000 feet in Chiriquí highlands.

Habits: One of the most numerous birds of forested country. Usually seen at middle and upper levels, often in small groups and as one of the more abundant species in mixed foraging flocks of insectivorous birds. The call is a rapid, musical phrase suggestive of a single phrase of the Yellow-green Vireo but even more monotonous, constantly repeated, typically *deedereét* or *itsacheét.*

Range: Southern Mexico to western Ecuador.

GOLDEN-FRONTED GREENLET
(*Hylophilus aurantiifrons*) Pl.24

Description: 4¼. *Forehead orange-yellow; cap brown contrasting with olive green of remaining upperparts;* pale yellow below, tinged buffy on chest and olive on sides.

Similar species: Easily confused with Tawny-crowned Greenlet; note Golden-front's olive green (not brownish) upperparts and more uniform yellow underparts (not distinctly brown on chest). The two are not normally found together, and their vocalizations are very different.

Status and distribution: Common in dry scrubby areas and shrubby clearings in lowlands on Pacific slope from western Panama province east through Darién; on Caribbean slope occurs locally in middle Chagres River valley of Canal Zone.

Habits: Usually remains fairly low in bushes and small trees. The call resembles the Lesser Greenlet's, an often-heard, usually four-noted whistled phrase, *cheetsacheéyou,* sometimes shortened to three or lengthened to five notes.

Range: Central Panama to northern Colombia and Venezuela.

TAWNY-CROWNED GREENLET
(*Hylophilus ochraceiceps*) Pl.24

Description: 4½. *Crown tawny,* a little yellower on forehead; remaining upperparts brownish to olive, but *wings and tail* *always russet brown;* rump yellowish olive; throat grayish, chest and sides usually brownish, lower underparts olive yellow. Darién birds (*bulunensis*) are more olive, Chiriquí and Bocas del Toro birds (nominate *ochraceiceps*) browner.

Similar species: Golden-fronted Greenlet is olive green (not brownish) above and on wings and has mostly yellow underparts (lacking distinct brownish tones). See also female Plain Antvireo and Brown-capped Vireo.

Status and distribution: Uncommon in forest and second-growth woodland in lowlands and foothills on both slopes, to about 5000 feet in Chiriquí highlands, more numerous in foothills, less so in lowlands.

Habits: Usually occurs within forest, where it forages actively at low and middle levels, often accompanying mixed flocks of antwrens, etc. The call is very different from that of other greenlets, a harsh nasal note, constantly uttered, *nya, nya.* Also has a rather long, slightly descending whistle.

Range: Southeastern Mexico to northern Bolivia and Amazonian Brazil.

SCRUB GREENLET
(*Hylophilus flavipes*) Pl.24

Description: 4½–4¾. Heavier-bodied than other greenlets; more upright and flycatcher-like. *Bill pale pinkish* and *iris conspicuously whitish* in adult; both dark in immature. Olive green above, slightly more brownish on head; throat grayish, *remaining underparts yellow.*

Similar species: A confusing bird, it does not look like other Panama greenlets and often seems more like a little flycatcher. Best distinguished by the prominent white eye and characteristic song (see below).

Status and distribution: Common in scrubby areas and shrubby clearings in lowlands on entire Pacific slope, extending locally onto Caribbean slope in cleared areas of Canal Zone region; found also on Coiba Island (where more buffy below).

Habits: Less active than other greenlets, in this respect more resembling the true vireos. The call is easily recognized and often heard, a melancholy *tuweé, tuweé, tuweé . . . ,* often repeated up to twenty times without pausing.

Range: Southwestern Costa Rica to northern Colombia and Venezuela.

HONEYCREEPERS: Coerebidae (10)

The honeycreepers form a composite family, undoubtedly with most closely allied to the tanagers, while a few have been supposed related to the wood-warblers, with others having no evident close affinities. Recently they have been much discussed by taxonomists, and while many believe the family will have to be dismembered, there is still disagreement as to how various genera should be assigned. It is thus convenient meanwhile to continue to maintain them as a separate family. They are found only in the neotropics, chiefly in forested and wooded areas. While generally regarded as primarily nectar feeders, honeycreepers take a variety of food including fruit and insects (sometimes caught in flight). Many species are gregarious and often occur with mixed flocks of other birds, but several are seen only in pairs or family groups. Nests, so far as known, are placed in a tree or bush, and are rather varied in form but generally cup-shaped though sometimes very shallow; the Bananaquit, however, builds a globular nest with a side entrance. The nest of the White-eared Conebill and its immediate allies seems to be unrecorded.

BANANAQUIT
(*Coereba flaveola*) Pl.25

Description: 3¾. Rather short, slender, decurved bill. Sexes similar. Dark olive gray above with black crown and *prominent long white superciliary;* small white patch on primaries; *throat pale gray,* remaining underparts yellow. Pearl Islands birds (*cerinoclunis*) are *black above.*

Similar species: No other honeycreeper has the long white eyestripe.

Status and distribution: Locally common in gardens, shrubby clearings, lighter woodland, and forest borders in more humid areas of lowlands and foothills on both slopes; absent or in very small numbers (possibly seasonal) in dry Pacific slope lowlands from eastern side of Azuero Peninsula to Pacific side of Canal Zone and Panama city area; common on Coiba Island and the Pearl Islands.

Habits: A very active, tame little bird that will feed wherever there are flowers; also extremely fond of sugar. Has a high, sibilant song, rather warbler-like, *tsee, tsee, tsee, tsee. . . .*

Range: Southeastern Mexico to northern Bolivia, Paraguay, and northeastern Argentina; West Indies (except Cuba) and most Caribbean islands, rarely in southern Florida.

SLATY FLOWER-PIERCER
(*Diglossa plumbea*)

Description: 4¾. Found only in western highlands. Unusual bill with *lower mandible upturned and upper mandible hooked at tip.* Male *uniform dark bluish slate,* somewhat paler below. Female *deep olive gray,* becoming buffy on lower belly. Birds with partial albinistic tendencies are sometimes seen in Chiriquí.

Similar species: The curious bill is unlike that of any similar Panama bird. See Slaty Finch (largely terrestrial).

Status and distribution: Common in shrubby clearings and forest borders in highlands of western Chiriquí, mostly above 5000 feet; also known from highlands of Veraguas around Chitra (4600–5000 feet). Not found in highlands of eastern Panama, nor, curiously, is any *Diglossa.*

Habits: Very active, most often seen in pairs, usually remaining low. Punctures the corolla of certain flowers to obtain nectar; also flycatches. Has a weak, rapidly given warbler-like song.

SLATY FLOWER-PIERCER
(male above, female below)

Range: Costa Rica and western Panama.

Note: By some authors considered conspecific with *D. baritula* (Cinnamon Flower-piercer) of northern Middle America; others also include *D. sittoides* (Rusty Flower-piercer) of the Andes in the complex.

WHITE-EARED CONEBILL
(*Conirostrum leucogenys*) Pl.32

Description: 3½–3¾. Known only from eastern Panama. Conical pointed bill; short tail. Male *bluish slate above* with black cap, *conspicuous white ear-coverts,* and (usually) white patch on rump; wings and tail blackish edged with gray and with white speculum; *paler gray below* with rufous under tail-coverts. Female similar but duller, without black cap and with much less distinct white ear-patch; tinged olive above, paler gray tinged buffy below.

Similar species: See female Scarlet-thighed Dacnis.

Status and distribution: Fairly common and widespread in forest and woodland borders in lowlands of eastern Panama province (Bayano River valley at and above Majé; Ridgely *et al.*) and Darién.

Habits: Feeds fairly high, frequently in flowering trees with flocks of tanagers, orioles, etc.

Range: Eastern Panama to Colombia and northern Venezuela.

SHINING HONEYCREEPER
(*Cyanerpes lucidus*) Pl.25

Description: 4. *Bill long, slender, and decurved; legs bright yellow in male, greenish in female.* Male *mostly bright purplish blue,* paler on crown and sides of head; wings, tail, *throat, and chest black.* Female green above with head and nape sometimes tinged bluish, wings and tail duskier; buffy whitish below, *streaked with blue on chest,* sides and flanks greenish.

Similar species: Superficially like Red-legged Honeycreeper; male easily distinguished by its yellow (not red) legs and black patch on throat and chest; female's distinctly blue streaking below and greenish (not reddish) legs will identify her. In eastern Darién see also Purple Honeycreeper.

Status and distribution: Common in forest and forest borders in foothills on both slopes, regularly wandering into Caribbean lowlands at least locally but breeding status there uncertain. Usually fairly numerous well out on Pipeline Road.

Habits: Typically forages rather high in trees,

often in small groups and accompanying mixed flocks of tanagers, other honeycreepers, etc.

Range: Southeastern Mexico to northwestern Colombia.

Note: By some authors considered conspecific with *C. caeruleus* (Purple Honeycreeper), in which case the entire complex called Yellow-legged Honeycreeper.

PURPLE HONEYCREEPER
(*Cyanerpes caeruleus*) Pl.32

Description: 4. Known only from eastern Darién. Extremely similar to the more widespread (in Panama) Shining Honeycreeper. Male difficult to distinguish, but darker more uniformly purplish blue, with black of throat not extending over chest. Female somewhat easier, with buffy (not dusky) lores, deeper buffy throat (not buffy whitish), and *green* (not blue) *streaks on chest.*

Similar species: See Shining Honeycreeper.

Status and distribution: Known only from lowlands and lower foothills of eastern Darién (Jaqué, Cerro Quía). Reported to be sympatric with Shining Honeycreeper in immediately adjacent Colombia, and may be so in this area as well.

Habits: Much like Shining Honeycreeper.

Range: Eastern Panama to northern Bolivia and Amazonian Brazil.

RED-LEGGED HONEYCREEPER
(*Cyanerpes cyaneus*) Pl.25

Description: 4½. Bill long, slender, decurved; *legs bright red in male, reddish in female.* Male *mostly purplish blue* with *pale turquoise crown* and black back, wings, and tail. Female greenish above, yellowish green below, streaked with dusky on breast. Male has nonbreeding "eclipse" plumage (July–September) in which it resembles female except for black wings and tail.

Similar species: Male Shining Honeycreeper has yellow legs, lacks pale turquoise crown, has black throat and chest patch; female Shining has greenish (not reddish) legs and buffy underparts prominently streaked bluish on breast. Dacnises have short straight bills. Female Green Honeycreeper is larger, brighter green without streaks, and has less decurved bill.

Status and distribution: Very common in residential areas, clearings, shrubby areas, second-growth woodland, and forest borders in lowlands on both slopes, ranging up in somewhat smaller numbers in foothills to about 4000 feet; common also on Coiba Island and the Pearl Islands. Not yet recorded from western Bocas del Toro lowlands.

Habits: The most widespread and familiar of its family in Panama; comes to feeding trays. Often occurs in flocks of up to a dozen or more individuals, sometimes alone but frequently joining mixed groups of other birds.

Range: Southern Mexico to northern Bolivia and southern Brazil; Cuba.

GREEN HONEYCREEPER
(*Chlorophanes spiza*) Pl.25

Description: 5¼. *Bill stouter and less decurved than in other honeycreepers,* bright yellow in male, duller yellow in female. Male mostly *bright emerald green* with *black cap and sides of head.* Female bright grass green above, yellowish green below.

Similar species: Male is easily identified; female is brighter and more uniform green than other honeycreepers and has less decurved bill. Female Blue Dacnis is also mostly green, but has bluish head and short straight bill. Green Shrike-Vireo is also bright green but has different shape (heavy-bodied, with large head) with heavier hooked bill and yellow throat.

Status and distribution: Fairly common in forest, second-growth woodland, and borders in lowlands and foothills on both slopes; less numerous and more local on Pacific slope west of Canal Zone.

Habits: Usually seen singly or in pairs (not in groups), remaining quite high in the trees, often accompanying mixed flocks of tanagers, other honeycreepers, etc.

Range: Southeastern Mexico to northern Bolivia and southern Brazil.

BLUE DACNIS
(*Dacnis cayana*) Pl.25

Description: 4½. *Bill short, straight, and pointed;* legs dull reddish. Male *mostly bright blue* with *black throat,* upper back, wings, and tail. Female bright green, paler below, with *bluish head.*

Similar species: Honeycreepers have decurved bills. Female Scarlet-thighed Dacnis is buffy (not pale green) below. Female most resembles female White-shouldered Tanager but is a little smaller, brighter green (less olive) above, and not as yellow below, with bluish (not grayish) head. In Darién, see also female Viridian Dacnis.

Status and distribution: Common in second-growth woodland and forest borders in lowlands on both slopes, more numerous and widespread on Caribbean side, ranging in reduced numbers up into foothills to about 3000 feet.

Habits: Usually in pairs or small groups, foraging actively at all heights, often with mixed flocks of tanagers, other honeycreepers, etc.

Range: Nicaragua to Bolivia, north-eastern Argentina, and southern Brazil.

VIRIDIAN DACNIS

(*Dacnis viguieri*) Pl.32

Description: 4½. Known only from eastern Darién lowlands. *Bill short, straight, and pointed.* Male *rich green to bluish green* (depending on light) with black in front of eye, on upper back, wings, and tail; wing-coverts bright olive green. Female light greenish olive above; pale greenish yellow below, tinged olive on sides; *wings blackish* edged with olive.

Similar species: Male Blue Dacnis is obviously blue (not green or bluish green) and has black throat; female Blue Dacnis has bluish head. Female Green Honeycreeper is larger with somewhat decurved bill, lacks blackish wings.

Status and distribution: Known only from forest in lowlands of southeastern Darién at Jaqué. A rare bird of restricted range about which very little is known.

Range: Eastern Panama and adjacent northwestern Colombia.

SCARLET-THIGHED DACNIS

(*Dacnis venusta*) Pl.25

Description: 4½. Bill short, straight, and pointed. Male unmistakable with *bright blue head, neck,* lower back, and rump; *black underparts,* back, wings, and tail; the scarlet thighs are often hidden. Female dull bluish green above and on sides of head, somewhat tinged with dusky, especially on back; *mostly buffy brownish below.*

Similar species: No other female Coerebid has plain buffy underparts. See female White-eared Conebill.

Status and distribution: Fairly common in forest and forest borders in foothills on both slopes, ranging regularly to lower highlands (to about 5500 feet) in western Panama, and down into lowlands on Caribbean slope (where breeding not certain). In Canal Zone, most easily seen well out on Pipeline Road, where apparently occurs at all seasons.

Habits: Usually in small groups, with marked tendency not to associate with other species.

Range: Costa Rica to northwestern Ecuador.

WOOD-WARBLERS: Parulidae (48)

The wood-warblers are a rather large family of lively, and often very pretty chiefly insectivorous birds found only in the New World. Most of the species occurring in Panama are migrants from temperate North America, mainly from east of the Rockies; the resident species are found mostly in the highlands. Most of the migrants arrive in Panama in dull, often very confusing, nonbreeding or "fall" plumage. By the time they leave in the spring, however, adult males have usually attained full breeding plumage, though few species ever sing. They are most numerous during their periods of transience, mostly September–early November and March–April, less so during the intervening northern winter months. With few exceptions they shun the interior of forest in favor of second-growth woodland, borders, shrubby clearings, and even residential areas. In woodland they often join mixed foraging flocks of resident species. Identification is often a real challenge, for not only are many of the species easy to confuse with each other, but they also resemble some resident groups such as the greenlets, a few small tanagers, and certain small flycatchers. The resident warblers fall into three main groups. The three native species of yellowthroats resemble the familiar northern species in appearance and behavior. The two redstarts (genus *Myioborus*) are attractive birds of highland forests, reminiscent in their lively behavior of the American Redstart. The six species (as here treated) of *Basileuterus* warblers in Panama are rather plain birds of forest and woodland undergrowth, mostly in the highlands; one, the Buff-rumped Warbler, is very different, occupying a niche similar to that of the water-thrushes. Yellowthroats build open cup nests of grass on or near the ground; *Basileuterus* and *Myioborus* (so far as known) build domed nests with a side entrance, also on or near the ground.

BLACK-AND-WHITE WARBLER
(*Mniotilta varia*)

Description: 4¾–5¼. *Striped black and white all over,* center of belly white; male has black cheeks and throat; female has underparts whiter than male. *Creeps over tree branches* and even up tree trunks.
Similar species: No other warbler really resembles it, but see spring male of extremely rare Blackpoll Warbler, also black and white but with solid black (not striped) crown. See also male Streaked Antwren.
Status and distribution: Fairly common transient and winter resident (late August–early April, migration chiefly in September and March) throughout but primarily in lowlands (though ranging to 6000 feet in highlands); recorded also on Pearl Islands.
Habits: Generally found singly, often accompanying mixed foraging flocks, creeping over larger limbs and branches, the only Panama warbler to habitually do this.
Range: Breeds in eastern North America; winters from southern United States to northern Venezuela and Ecuador, and in West Indies.

PROTHONOTARY WARBLER
(*Protonotaria citrea*)

Description: 5–5½. Male has *head and underparts brilliant orange-yellow;* back olive; *wings and tail plain blue-gray.* Female similar but duller, less orange.
Similar species: Yellow Warbler also has head and underparts bright yellow but has yellowish (not blue-gray) wings. Male Black-and-yellow Tanager has vaguely similar pattern.
Status and distribution: Locally common transient and fairly common winter resident (early August–late March; main migration September–mid-October and early February–mid-March) throughout in lowlands near water, rarely in highlands during migration.
Habits: Almost invariably found low in shrubbery bordering water: in mangroves, near fresh water lakes and marshes, and along streams and rivers. Small groups are often noted during migration.
Range: Breeds in eastern United States; winters from southern Mexico to northern Colombia and Venezuela, casually to Ecuador and Surinam.

WORM-EATING WARBLER
(*Helmitheros vermivorus*)

Description: 5–5½. Sexes similar. Head pale buff with *broad black stripes on crown and narrow black line through eye;* otherwise brownish olive above; *plain buffy brownish below.*
Similar species: The striped head pattern and otherwise dull coloration sets it apart from other migrant warblers. Resembles several *Basileuterus* warblers, particularly the Three-striped, except for its buffy (not yellowish) underparts.
Status and distribution: Uncommon transient and winter resident in western Panama (chiefly in highlands), becoming rarer in central Panama and not recorded further east than the lower Bayano River in eastern Panama province (late September–late April).
Habits: Generally very unobtrusive, remaining near the ground in thick undergrowth.
Range: Breeds in eastern United States; winters from Mexico to Panama and in West Indies.

GOLDEN-WINGED WARBLER
(*Vermivora chrysoptera*)

Description: 4½–5. Male gray above with yellow forecrown and *large patch of yellow on wing;* sides of head and underparts white with *black patch through eye and black throat.* Female similar but with eyepatch and throat pale gray.
Similar species: Male is easily recognized; some females and immatures show only a trace of the characteristic facial pattern but always have prominent and characteristic yellow wing-patch.
Status and distribution: Fairly common transient (mid-September–early November; late March–mid-April) throughout and rare to uncommon winter resident (when mostly in foothills, but in smaller numbers elsewhere).
Habits: Forages at all levels, often with mixed flocks of various insectivorous birds. Frequently feeds in dead leaf clusters.
Range: Breeds in eastern North America; winters from Guatemala to Colombia and northern Venezuela.

BLUE-WINGED WARBLER
(*Vermivora pinus*)

Description: 4½–5. Male has yellow face and underparts with *narrow black line through eye;* hindneck and back olive green; *wings bluish gray with two white wing-bars.* Female similar but somewhat duller.
Similar species: Female and immature Yellow and Wilson's Warblers lack both the black eyeline and the white wing-bars.

Status and distribution: A rare and infrequently reported winter visitant in western and central Panama; in west known only from Caribbean lowlands, in Canal Zone area reported on both slopes, and once collected as far east as near Chepo, eastern Panama province; recorded in Panama mid-October–late March.

Range: Breeds in eastern United States; winters mostly from southern Mexico to Nicaragua, rarely to Costa Rica and Panama, casually to Colombia.

Note: Hybrids between this species and the Golden-wing regularly occur in North America; to date they have not been reported from Panama but they should be watched for. The "Brewster's" resembles a Blue-wing but has yellow wing-bars and mostly whitish underparts; the "Lawrence's" recalls a Golden-wing but has white wing-bars and wholly yellow underparts; females and immatures of the two forms are duller.

TENNESSEE WARBLER
(*Vermivora peregrina*)

Description: 4¼–4¾. Nonbreeding plumage: olive green above with *prominent whitish or yellowish superciliary;* sometimes a trace of a whitish wing-bar; dingy yellowish below, becoming whitish on lower belly. In breeding plumage, male's crown becomes gray, superciliary and underparts white; female becomes whiter below and has whiter eyestripe.

Similar species: In nonbreeding plumage can be confused with dull immature Yellow Warbler but invariably shows an eyestripe and lacks yellow on tail. Also resembles several vireos, particularly the Philadelphia, but can be known by its smaller size, more slender pointed bill, and more active behavior. Breeding plumage birds somewhat resemble the smaller Lesser (Gray-headed) Greenlet except for the conspicuous white eyestripe and lack of an eye-ring.

Status and distribution: Very common transient and winter resident throughout, from lowlands to mountains (mid-September–mid-April, usually arriving in numbers during October, most leaving by early April).

Habits: Very widespread and numerous, occurring wherever there are trees, and foraging at all levels, even on or near the ground.

Range: Breeds in northern North America; winters from southern Mexico to Colombia and northern Venezuela.

FLAME-THROATED WARBLER
(*Vermivora gutturalis*) Pl.25

Description: 4½. Found only in Chiriquí highlands. Sexes similar. *Slaty gray above* with black patch on cheeks and on back; *throat and chest bright orange,* lower underparts white. Immature similar but duller, throat and chest buffier.

Similar species: The smaller Tropical Parula is more bluish above with greenish patch on back and is mostly yellow (not orange) below; it also shows at least one white wing-bar.

Status and distribution: Fairly common in forest and forest borders in highlands of Chiriquí, mostly above 5000 feet.

Habits: A very active and pretty warbler, usually foraging quite high in trees but occasionally dropping low. Pairs or small groups often join mixed foraging flocks. Its song is a weak dry buzz, *zeeeeeoo* (R. Ward).

Range: Costa Rica and western Panama.

Note: By some authors placed in the genus *Parula.*

TROPICAL PARULA (OLIVE-BACKED WARBLER)
(*Parula pitiayumi*) Pl.25

Description: 4. Sexes similar. *Grayish blue above* with black facial area and *patch of olive green on back;* two white wing-bars, one sometimes indistinct; *yellow below,* somewhat tawnier on throat, becoming whitish on lower belly.

Similar species: Likely to be confused only with Flame-throated Warbler. See also Northern Parula (below).

Status and distribution: Local. Fairly common in lower highlands of Chiriquí (3000–6000 feet), foothills of Veraguas and Herrera (1500–3000 feet), lowlands and lower foothills of eastern Panama province (hills just east of Chepo, on road from Platanares to Jesús María, eastward; common in Bayano River valley) and Darién (to around 2000 feet), and also on Coiba Island.

Habits: Favors forest borders and woodland. Small size and habit of usually foraging at considerable heights sometimes make observation difficult, but readily attracted by squeaking. Its song is a buzzy trill, typically *tsip-tsip-tsip-tsip-tsip-tsrrrrrrrrrip,* with variations.

Range: Southern Texas and Mexico to Bolivia, northern Argentina, and Uruguay.

Note: Sometimes placed in the genus *Vermi-*

vora. Northern Parula (*P. americana*) is possible in Panama, especially on Caribbean slope; it breeds in eastern North America, wintering mostly in West Indies, also in Florida and from eastern Mexico to Guatemala (casually to Costa Rica and islands off north coast of South America). It resembles Tropical Parula but lacks black facial area, and chest of male is crossed by dark chestnut or orange-rufous band (reduced or absent in female).

YELLOW WARBLER
(*Dendroica aestiva*)

Description: 4–5. Male *mostly yellow* (in breeding plumage sometimes orange-yellow on forecrown), back more olive, wings and tail dusky with yellow edging; *varying amounts of chestnut-red streaking on breast.* Female and immature duller, more olive above, less bright yellow below.

Similar species: Though many other warblers appear mostly yellow, this and the Mangrove are the only ones with yellow tail edging. Most easily confused with immature Wilson's and Tennessee Warblers; see also Mangrove Warbler.

Status and distribution: Very common transient and winter resident in lowlands on both slopes, including Pearl Islands (mid-August–mid-May, most not arriving before late August and leaving by end of April).

Habits: Frequents open and semi-open areas, where in season it is often one of the most conspicuous birds. Very noisy, giving a constant repeated *tsip* or *chip.*

Range: Breeds in North America and Mexico; winters from Mexico to Peru, northern Brazil, and the Guianas.

Note: Many authors use the specific name *D. petechia,* merging the North American population with West Indian birds.

MANGROVE WARBLER
(*Dendroica erithachorides*) Pl.25

Description: 4–4½. Adult male has *entire head and chest rufous-chestnut* (only a wash in immature); upperparts otherwise olive; remaining underparts yellow, streaked rufous on breast. Female olive green above (*sometimes rather grayish*), brighter on rump; yellow edging on wings and tail; dull pale yellow below, tinged olive on sides. Immature even duller, *mainly grayish above* (only rump olive green), mostly whitish below.

Similar species: The striking male is unmistakable; female and immature are often difficult to distinguish from female and immature Yellows but tend to be grayer. The two occur together only in nonbreeding season in mangrove and adjacent habitats and on islands.

Status and distribution: Locally common in mangroves on both coasts, but apparently lacking from some mangrove areas that would appear suitable; also common on some of the Pearl Islands and on islands off Veraguas and Chiriquí and on Escudo de Veraguas, on some of which it is not restricted to mangroves. On the mainland it sometimes occurs a short distance away from mangroves but never away from salt water. Common around Miraflores Locks and on the Fortified Islands in the Canal Zone, also in mangroves near the Aguadulce salinas in Coclé.

Habits: Similar to the northern Yellow Warbler. The song is variable but will be easily recognized by one familiar with the northern Yellow's.

Range: Pacific coast from Mexico to Peru; Caribbean coast from Mexico to Venezuela.

Note: Many authors consider this form and the northern *D. aestiva* (Yellow Warbler), along with the "intermediate" *D. petechia* (Golden Warbler) of the West Indies, as conspecific under the specific name of *D. petechia* and the English name of Yellow Warbler.

MAGNOLIA WARBLER
(*Dendroica magnolia*)

Description: 4½–5. Nonbreeding plumage: olive green above with grayish head and white eye-ring, two white wing-bars, and *broad white band on tail,* rump patch yellow; mostly yellow below with a little black streaking on sides and flanks, and usually a *grayish band across chest.* Breeding plumage much brighter (especially in male): bluish gray above with black face patch and back (latter streaked with olive in female); bright yellow below with heavy black streaking except on throat.

Similar species: In any plumage the white tail band combined with the mostly yellow underparts is distinctive.

Status and distribution: Uncommon winter resident (mid-October–mid-April, one report from September 25), chiefly in Caribbean lowlands from Bocas del Toro to Canal Zone but with several recent sightings from eastern Panama province as far east as the Bayano River valley (Ridgely).

Habits: Usually seen singly, feeding at low levels, often with mixed foraging flocks in second-growth woodland. Sometimes fans its tail as if to display the characteristic white tail band.

Range: Breeds in northern North America; winters from Mexico to Panama and in West Indies (rarely Florida), casually in Colombia.

CAPE MAY WARBLER
(*Dendroica tigrina*)

Description: 4½–5. Very rare. Nonbreeding plumage: olive green above (sometimes more grayish), with dull yellowish rump and *small indistinct* (but nearly always visible) *yellowish patch behind ear;* wings duskier with two whitish wing-bars; whitish or pale yellowish below, *rather uniformly* (often heavily) *streaked with dusky*. Breeding plumage male very different and quite unmistakable, with *chestnut cheeks* and bright yellow underparts boldly streaked with black. Breeding plumage female resembles nonbreeders but is brighter with more distinct yellow neck-spot and yellower underparts.

Similar species: Though older males retain varying degrees of their spring pattern through the winter, many nonbreeding birds are dull, and are readily confused with several other warblers. These include the Yellow-rumped (Myrtle), which is larger and browner, distinctly streaked above, and with much more conspicuous clear yellow rump, and the Palm, which has distinctive yellow under tail-coverts and wags its tail almost incessantly.

Status and distribution: A very rare vagrant, possibly overlooked until recently. Five sight reports: one at Almirante, Bocas del Toro, on February 2 and 10, 1958 (Wetmore); one at Changuinola, Bocas del Toro, on December 7, 1962 (Eisenmann); one below Volcán, western Chiriquí, on January 20, 1970 (P. Alden); one bright male at Summit Gardens, Canal Zone, on February 2, 1973 (Ridgely, Eisenmann, C. Leahy, J. Gwynne); and one male at Volcán, Chiriquí, on January 15, 1974 (C. Leahy and Ridgely). Specimen or photographic confirmation desirable.

Habits: On its wintering grounds, found mostly at flowering trees.

Range: Breeds in northern North America; winters mostly in West Indies, rarely in Florida, Yucatan, and San Andres, casually in Middle America.

[BLACK-THROATED BLUE WARBLER]
(*Dendroica coerulescens*)

Description: 5–5½. One sight report. Male very clean cut, *dark grayish blue above* with prominent white spot at base of primaries; *sides of head, throat, and sides black;* breast and belly white. Female very dull, brownish olive above with narrow whitish superciliary and the *same prominent white wing-spot as in male;* dull pale brownish yellow below, sometimes buffier, sometimes more whitish.

Similar species: Dapper male is easily recognized; female is more difficult but can be known by the wing-spot, a mark shared by no other similar bird.

Status and distribution: Only report is of a male near Gatun Locks (beside the French Canal), Canal Zone on January 14, 1973 (D. Engleman, James Smith, N. Gale, and A. Ramirez). To be watched for during northern winter months, especially along Caribbean coast.

Range: Breeds in eastern North America; winters mostly in Greater Antilles, more rarely in Lesser Antilles, with a very few scattered records from Middle America and northern South America.

YELLOW-RUMPED (MYRTLE) WARBLER
(*Dendroica coronata*)

Description: 5–5½. Nonbreeding plumage: brownish above streaked with dusky; two white wing-bars and *conspicuous yellow rump; throat white, remaining underparts whitish* with grayish on chest and sides and *yellow patch on sides.* Breeding plumage male brighter, *bluish gray above* streaked with black and with *yellow crown patch;* white below with broad black band across chest and down sides, and yellow patch on sides; *conspicuous yellow rump.* Breeding plumage female similar but duller.

Similar species: The bright yellow rump will in any plumage distinguish this species from most other warblers; Magnolia and Cape May (both of which do show yellowish rumps) are mostly yellow (not whitish) below. Another good point is the Myrtle's frequently heard call, a loud *tchek.*

Status and distribution: A regular, but usually uncommon winter visitant in western Panama (at least in Chiriquí and Bocas del Toro), becoming highly irregular eastward to central Panama, where fairly common some years and almost absent in others, occurring especially on Pacific side of

Canal Zone and in Panama province; not reported east of Cerro Azul and Río Pacora in eastern Panama province; occasional on Pearl Islands; recorded in Panama early November–late March.

Habits: In Panama usually feeds on the ground in fairly open areas, flying up to trees when disturbed. Often occurs in small flocks of only its own species.

Range: Breeds in North America; winters from central United States to Panama and in West Indies, casually to Colombia.

Note: The forms breeding in western North America (*auduboni* complex), formerly considered a distinct species (Audubon's Warbler), but now regarded as conspecific with *D. coronata,* may occur casually in the western highlands (winters south regularly to Honduras, casually to Costa Rica). They resemble the Myrtle but have yellow (not white) throat and more white on wing (in dull nonbreeding plumage difficult to distinguish, especially as hybridization occurs where the breeding ranges of the two groups overlap).

[TOWNSEND'S WARBLER]

(*Dendroica townsendi*)

Description: 4½–5. One sighting. Nonbreeding plumage: olive above streaked with dusky, wings duskier with two white wing-bars; *cheek patch blackish or dusky-olive bordered above by broad yellow superciliary; throat and breast yellow;* throat (in males), chest, and sides flecked with blackish; lower underparts whitish. Breeding plumage male is brighter, with black crown, cheek patch, throat and chest; back streaked with black.

Similar species: Female and immature Black-throated Green Warblers lack black streaks on crown, show only a trace of an olive or dusky cheek patch (their entire face looks yellow), and usually have whitish throat and breast (male sometimes has some yellow on breast). Female and immature Blackburnian Warblers have striped back and less yellow on face.

Status and distribution: Only report is a male seen repeatedly at Nueva Suiza in highlands of western Chiriquí on November 19–30, 1967 (T. V. Heatley and V. M. Kleen). Specimen or photographic confirmation desirable.

Range: Breeds in northwestern North America; winters from western United States to Nicaragua, casually (sight reports only) to Costa Rica and western Panama.

BLACK-THROATED GREEN WARBLER

(*Dendroica virens*)

Description: 4½–5. Nonbreeding plumage: olive green above with *contrasting yellow sides of head;* wings duskier with two white wing-bars; whitish below with *varying amounts of blackish on throat and chest* and dusky streaking on sides. Breeding plumage male is brighter, with solid black throat and chest.

Similar species: Can be recognized in any plumage by its yellow cheeks. Some birds (especially immature) show little black on throat and chest and might be confused with an immature Blackburnian but have much more yellow on face and no streaking on back. See also Townsend's and Hermit Warblers.

Status and distribution: Common winter resident in foothills and highlands of western Panama, more irregular but at times still common in hill country of central Panama, occurring in lowlands only as transient; not reported east of Cerro Azul/Jefe area; reported in Panama mostly late September–late March, a few arriving by mid-September and lingering until mid-April. Rather rare in Canal Zone.

Habits: An arboreal warbler, usually occurring as a member of mixed foraging flocks in second-growth woodland, borders, and clearings.

Range: Breeds in eastern North America; winters from Mexico (rarely southern United States) to Panama and in West Indies, casually to Colombia and Venezuela.

[HERMIT WARBLER]

(*Dendroica occidentalis*)

Description: 4½–5. Sightings. Male has *bright golden yellow head; otherwise mostly gray above,* back streaked with black, wings duskier with two white wing-bars; throat black, *remaining underparts white,* with a little dusky streaking on sides. Female similar but duller, with black throat patch reduced. Immature resembles female but often has black throat patch entirely lacking.

Similar species: Male easily known by its all-yellow head; female and immature can be known from respective stages of Black-throated Green by their gray (not olive) back and less streaking on sides. Male's black throat patch is considerably smaller than that of male Black-throated Green.

Status and distribution: Only report is an

adult male seen at very close range at Nueva Suiza in highlands of western Chiriquí on December 22, 1973 (Dana Gardner), and almost certainly the same bird (at the exact same locality) again on January 15, 1974 (Ridgely and C. Leahy). Specimen or photographic confirmation desirable.

Range: Breeds in western United States; winters in highlands from Mexico (rarely southern California) to Nicaragua, casually to Costa Rica (one recent sighting) and western Panama (sightings).

CERULEAN WARBLER
(*Dendroica cerulea*)

Description: 4¼–4¾. Male *grayish blue above* streaked with black; wings blackish with two white wing-bars; *white below with narrow black band across chest* and black streaking on sides and flanks. Female and immature olive green above, sometimes tinged with bluish gray especially on crown, with *narrow whitish superciliary;* whitish below, sometimes tinged buffy or yellowish.

Similar species: The pretty male is easily recognized; duller female and immature are more difficult. They resemble a female Tennessee Warbler but have prominent white wing-bars; also resemble female Bay-breasted Warbler but are unstreaked above with more prominent eyestripe and are whiter below. See also the very rare Blackpoll Warbler.

Status and distribution: Uncommon fall and rare spring transient (late August–early October; mid- to late March; one report from November 4); not reported from western Pacific slope or extreme eastern Panama; a few reports from Pearl Islands; only winter report is a sighting of a male on Cerro Campana on January 1, 1969 (Ridgely).

Habits: Usually arrives in small "waves" in September when small groups may be encountered. Normally feeds rather high in trees.

Range: Breeds in eastern United States; winters from Colombia and Venezuela to northern Bolivia.

BLACKBURNIAN WARBLER
(*Dendroica fusca*)

Description: 4¾–5¼. Nonbreeding plumage: olive green above with *prominent whitish striping on back;* wings duskier with two white wing-bars; *narrow yellow superciliary and line on ear-coverts* outlining dark olive cheek; *throat and chest yellow,* lower underparts white, sides streaked with black. Breeding plumage male unmistakable: mostly black above with white striping on back and large white patch on wings; *flaming orange replacing yellow on head, throat, and chest.* Breeding plumage female similar to breeding male but much duller.

Similar species: Nonbreeding Black-throated Green Warbler has more or less solid yellow face and mostly white underparts (not yellow on throat and chest). See also Yellow-throated Warbler.

Status and distribution: Fairly common fall and spring transient throughout, including Pearl Islands; uncommon to rare winter resident mostly in foothills and highlands; recorded in Panama early September–late April.

Habits: Usually met singly in mixed foraging flocks. Feeds primarily at middle and high tree levels.

Range: Breeds in eastern North America; winters from Costa Rica to Venezuela and Peru.

YELLOW-THROATED WARBLER
(*Dendroica dominica*)

Description: 5–5½. Casual. Sexes similar. *Gray above* with *white stripe over eye and another on cheeks;* two prominent white wing-bars; *throat and upper chest yellow,* bordered with a black stripe; remaining underparts white, streaked with black on sides.

Similar species: Nonbreeding Blackburnian Warbler is less sharply patterned, has striped back and yellow stripes on head.

Status and distribution: Only two reports: one seen at Almirante, Bocas del Toro, on February 3, 1958 (Wetmore); and one seen and photographed at Summit Gardens, Canal Zone, on February 2, 1973 (C. Leahy, J. Gwynne, Ridgely, and Eisenmann). To be watched for in the Caribbean lowlands during winter months.

Range: Breeds in eastern United States and on several of the Bahamas; winters from Florida and Texas to Nicaragua and in the Greater Antilles, rarely to Costa Rica, casually to Panama, northern South America, and the Lesser Antilles.

CHESTNUT-SIDED WARBLER
(*Dendroica pensylvanica*)

Description: 4¼–4¾. Nonbreeding plumage: *yellowish olive green above,* somewhat grayer about head and with narrow white eye-ring; wings duskier with two yellowish wing-bars; *sides of head and underparts white,* adult usually with *some chestnut on* *sides.* Breeding plumage birds have *yellow crown,* black striping on back, a black stripe below eye, and *prominent chestnut sides and flanks* (less in females).

Similar species: Immature (most of which lack any chestnut on sides) can be known by its bright, unstreaked, lemon green upperparts in conjunction with the whitish underparts.

Status and distribution: Very common winter resident in western and central Panama but apparently less numerous in eastern Panama; recorded mid-September–late April. In Canal Zone, one of the most numerous wintering warblers, favoring second-growth woodland, clearings, and edge situations.

Habits: Often occurs in small groups in mixed foraging flocks. Unlike most other wintering warblers, males of this species regularly begin to sing before their departure in April.

Range: Breeds in eastern North America; winters from Guatemala to Panama, casually to Colombia and Venezuela.

BAY-BREASTED WARBLER
(*Dendroica castanea*)

Description: 5–5½. Nonbreeding plumage: olive green above *streaked with blackish on back;* wings dusky with two white wing-bars; *buffy whitish below* with at most very indistinct dusky streaking on breast (often lacking); most adults, particularly males, show *a trace of chestnut on flanks.* Breeding plumage male entirely different, looks very dark: *cap, throat, chest, and sides dark chestnut;* face black and *conspicuous pale buffy patch on sides of neck.* Breeding plumage female has same pattern but is duller.

Similar species: Except for the extremely rare Blackpoll Warbler, the only warbler with combination of streaked back and essentially unstreaked underparts. Look for the tinge of chestnut on flanks.

Status and distribution: Fairly common to common transient and winter resident in lowlands and foothills on entire Caribbean slope, on Pacific slope from eastern Veraguas eastward; not reported from Chiriquí or western Veraguas, nor from any of Pacific offshore islands; recorded mostly late September–mid-April, a few arriving in mid-September and lingering into early May; in winter, more numerous eastward.

Habits: Usually occurs in light woodland and borders or in clearings with trees, often foraging rather high.

Range: Breeds in northern North America; winters from Costa Rica (rare) to Colombia and western Venezuela.

BLACKPOLL WARBLER
(*Dendroica striata*)

Description: 5–5½. Very rare. Nonbreeding plumage: very similar to the much more numerous Bay-breasted Warbler but greener below (less buffy) with white under tail-coverts (buffy in Bay-breast); legs yellowish (blackish in Bay-breast). Unfortunately these points are somewhat variable so that sight reports of winter Blackpolls must be regarded with a little suspicion. Breeding plumage male very different (and easily identified), with black cap and grayish olive black-streaked upperparts, white cheeks and underparts with black streaking on sides; breeding female is duller and lacks the black cap.

Similar species: See Bay-breasted Warbler.

Status and distribution: One nineteenth-century specimen from Canal Zone is the only absolutely certain record from Middle America south of Mexico. There have been a couple of fairly recent, not fully satisfactory, sight reports from "fall" in the Canal Zone; on October 19 and 29, 1964, individuals identified as this species were banded and released at Almirante, Bocas del Toro (D. L. Hicks). Specimen confirmation highly desirable.

Range: Breeds in northern North America; winters from eastern Colombia to eastern Peru, northern Brazil, and the Guianas (accidental in northern Argentina and central Chile); migrates through West Indies; casual in Mexico and Panama.

PALM WARBLER
(*Dendroica palmarum*)

Description: 5–5½. Nonbreeding plumage: brownish above indistinctly streaked with dusky; wings with two indistinct whitish or yellowish wing-bars; whitish or pale yellowish below, indistinctly streaked with dusky; *lower belly and under tail-coverts yellow.* Breeding plumage birds have chestnut cap, and some races become quite bright yellow below. Often first recognized by its *almost constant tail-wagging.*

Status and distribution: A rare but probably regular winter visitant in small numbers to Caribbean slope of Canal Zone and savannas of eastern Panama province; first recorded only in 1965 (mid-November–mid-March). To be watched for elsewhere in open or semi-open areas.

Habits: Usually on or very near the ground. In Canal Zone, prefers lawns in residential areas. Shows no preference for palms!

Range: Breeds in northern North America; winters from central United States to Honduras and in Greater Antilles; rarely to northern Costa Rica and central Panama; accidental on Cocos Island.

Note: Prairie Warbler (*D. discolor*) is possible in Panama; it breeds in eastern North America, wintering mostly in Florida and West Indies, in small numbers from Yucatan to Nicaragua (mostly on islands off Caribbean coast), casually to Costa Rica (recent sightings) and islands off north coast of South America. It is olive above, yellow below, with prominent black streaking on face and sides; also has chestnut streaks on back, two whitish wing-bars; females and (especially) immatures are duller, most resembling immature Magnolia but lacking white tail band; like Palm, often wags tail.

OVENBIRD
(*Seiurus aurocapillus*)

Description: 5½–6. This species and the waterthrushes have a more horizontal posture than most other warblers. Olive above with *white eye-ring* and *orange crown bordered by narrow black stripe;* white below streaked with black on breast and sides. Crown of immature is less bright orange.

Similar species: Waterthrushes have eyestripes (not eye-rings), lack the orange crown, and bob up and down when walking. Vaguely reminiscent of several of the migrant thrushes.

Status and distribution: Fairly common transient and winter resident in Bocas del Toro; less numerous elsewhere, becoming rather rare in central Panama and only one record from Darién; recorded in Panama late September–late April.

Habits: Solitary and quite unobtrusive. Usually seen walking sedately on the ground inside forest or woodland; readily attracted by squeaking.

Range: Breeds in eastern and central North America; winters in Florida and the West Indies, and from Mexico to Panama, rarely to Colombia and Venezuela.

NORTHERN WATERTHRUSH
(*Seiurus noveboracensis*)

Description: 5½–6. Olive brown above with *prominent buffy or yellowish superciliary;* whitish to pale yellowish below streaked with dusky.

Similar species: The less numerous Louisiana Waterthrush is very similar; see under that species for the distinctions between the two. The Ovenbird has the same shape but has prominent orange crown and white eyering instead of a superciliary.

Status and distribution: Very common transient and common winter resident in lowlands on both slopes, including Pearl Islands; in highlands occurs mostly on migration (late September–late April, a few arriving in mid-September and lingering into May).

Habits: Usually in mangroves or along streams, but on migration may appear almost anywhere. Near water it is a common sight, walking with a teetering gait much like a Spotted Sandpiper. Its loud and easily recognized metallic call, *tchink,* is often heard, especially when the bird is alarmed.

Range: Breeds in northern North America; winters in Florida and the West Indies and from Mexico to northern Peru, Venezuela, and the Guianas.

LOUISIANA WATERTHRUSH
(*Seiurus motacilla*)

Description: 5¾–6¼. Very similar to Northern Waterthrush. Averages a little larger and is grayer above; bill somewhat heavier. Louisiana always has a *pure white eyestripe* (Northern's is usually yellowish but can be dull whitish) and is *essentially white below* (sometimes tinged with pale buff), *often contrastingly buffy brownish on flanks;* central area of *throat white without dusky streaks* (Northern's is flecked with dusky).

Similar species: See Northern Waterthrush.

Status and distribution: Uncommon transient throughout (mostly mid-August to September and in March, a few arriving by early August and lingering into early April) and rather rare winter resident (when recorded mostly from Chiriquí highlands). At all times in the lowlands the Northern is much the commoner of the two waterthrushes.

Habits: Very like the Northern Waterthrush but prefers running streams to quiet water.

Range: Breeds in eastern United States; winters from Mexico to northern Colombia and Venezuela and in West Indies.

KENTUCKY WARBLER
(*Oporornis formosus*)

Description: 4¾–5¼. Olive green above with black forecrown, *prominent yellow eye-ring* and loral stripe, and *black "sideburns" extending down sides of neck;* bright yellow below. Female has less extensive black on head, immature virtually none, but both are otherwise very like male.

Similar species: Male yellowthroats (except Gray-crowned) have black masks and both sexes lack the yellow "spectacles" of both sexes of Kentucky; the yellowthroats favor shrubbry in semi-open areas, not forest undergrowth as does Kentucky. Immature Kentucky can also be confused with immature Canada Warbler (which may show little if any chest streaking), but Canada is gray (not olive) above.

Status and distribution: Fairly common but inconspicuous transient and winter resident in suitable forested habitat throughout (early September–late April), wintering primarily in the lowlands.

Habits: A skulker, favoring undergrowth in forest or well-shaded second-growth woodland. The species is one of the few northern migrants that regularly inhabits the interior of mature forest on its wintering grounds (the only other migrant warbler to do so is the Ovenbird).

Range: Breeds in eastern United States; winters from southern Mexico to northern Colombia and Venezuela.

Note: Some authors merge the genus *Oporornis* in *Geothlypis.*

CONNECTICUT WARBLER
(*Oporornis agilis*)

Description: 5¼–5¾. Very rare. In all plumages has a *complete whitish eye-ring* (but this is not absolutely diagnostic, as a few adult female and immature Mourning and MacGillivray's Warblers also have complete yellowish eye-rings). Breeding plumage male olive green above; *sides of head, throat, and chest gray* contrasting with dull yellow lower underparts. Female and immature more difficult, with gray hood duller and washed with brownish; see below.

Similar species: In the field, probably only adult male Connecticut, Mourning, and MacGillivray's Warblers can be distinguished with certainty. Mournings are *easily* the most numerous of the three in Panama. Browner hood, under tail-coverts almost reaching to tip of tail, and complete eye-ring will usually identify Connecticuts. In the hand (data from W. Lanyon and J. Bull, *Bird Banding,* 38: 187–194, 1967) wing of Connecticut is longest of the three (64–74 mm, av. 70), wing minus tail equals 19 mm or more.

Status and distribution: Recently recorded as a rare fall and spring transient in western Bocas del Toro lowlands (late September–late October; late March–early April). Three specimens have been taken, all in fall; spring specimens would be desirable. Mist-netting may reveal that it also occurs as a rare transient elsewhere in Panama.

Range: Breeds in north-central North America; winters in Venezuela, eastern Colombia, and northern Brazil; migrates through (or over) West Indies, with a few records from Panama.

MOURNING WARBLER
(*Oporornis philadelphia*)

Description: 5–5½. Adult male has gray head and olive green upperparts; *throat and chest black* (sometimes a scaly effect on throat) contrasting with bright yellow lower underparts. Female and immatures duller with grayish or brownish head, throat, and chest (no black); immatures and some females show a broken eye-ring (*in adult males always lacking*).

Similar species: Adult male with its black bib and lack of an eye-ring is readily distinguished, as are those females that lack any eye-ring. Females and immatures with incomplete eye-rings are *not* Connecticuts (which always have complete eye-rings) but can be distinguished from female and immature MacGillivray's only in hand by relatively longer wing. Length of Mourning's wing is 55–67 mm (av. 62); length of tail 43–53 mm (av. 48); wing minus tail equals 10–18 mm (av. 13).

Status and distribution: Fairly common though inconspicuous transient and less common winter resident throughout (late September–mid-May).

Habits: Usually skulks in dense vegetation, but sometimes can be attracted into the open by squeaking. In general it is safe to say that, except in the Chiriquí highlands (where the MacGillivray's is regular, if very uncommon), any *Oporornis* warbler other than a Kentucky is almost certainly this species. Nonetheless, one should remain alert for the others, especially when mist-netting.

Range: Breeds in northeastern and north-central United States; winters from Nicaragua to Venezuela and Ecuador.

MACGILLIVRAY'S WARBLER
(*Oporornis tolmiei*)

Description: 5–5½. Very rare except in Chiriquí highlands. Adult male virtually identical to male Mourning except for *prominent incomplete eye-ring.* Female and immature MacGillivray's indistinguishable in the field from female and immature Mournings. In the hand MacGillivray's wing averages slightly shorter than Mourning's (55–65 mm, av. 61.5) and its tail slightly longer (47–63 mm, av. 52.5) so that wing minus tail equals only 2–10 mm (av. 6.5).

Similar species: All plumages of Connecticut Warbler show complete eye-ring. Wing-to-tail ratio is only way to distinguish between female and immature MacGillivray's and Mournings. On wing-tail ratio criteria, most specimens from Panama reported as MacGillivray's prove to be Mournings.

Status and distribution: Uncommon winter resident in the Chiriquí highlands (early October–early March, but likely also later), though even there much less numerous than Mourning Warbler. Another record is an immature specimen taken at Gatun, Canal Zone, on March 2, 1911 (originally considered to be a Mourning); no recent reports away from Chiriquí.

Range: Breeds in western North America; winters from Mexico to western (casually central) Panama.

COMMON YELLOWTHROAT
(*Geothlypis trichas*)

Description: 4½–5. Male olive above with *black mask extending over forehead and bordered above by whitish or pale grayish band;* throat and breast yellow, *fading to whitish on belly.* Female lacks black mask (sides of head olive), and has *yellow more restricted to throat,* with lower underparts more brownish. Immature resembles female but is often rather brownish above.

Similar species: Both sexes of the Chiriquí and Olive-crowned Yellowthroats have entirely yellow underparts. Male Chiriquí Yellowthroat further differs in having gray (not whitish) border to mask; male Olive-crowned lacks any border at all. See also Kentucky Warbler.

Status and distribution: Rare winter resident (mid-October–late March), probably regular in small numbers in Bocas del Toro and possibly in Chiriquí, but may not be annual in central Panama; not reported from eastern half of Panama, with farthest east being several sightings in the Tocumen/La Jagua area of eastern Panama province (Ridgely *et al.*).

Habits: Typically forages near the ground in shrubbery near water. Its distinctive husky call note, *tchep,* often gives away the bird's presence, but other yellowthroats have similar calls.

Range: Breeds in North America and Mexico; winters from southern United States to Panama and in West Indies, casually to Colombia and Venezuela.

CHIRIQUÍ YELLOWTHROAT
(*Geothlypis chiriquensis*)

Description: 4½–5. Found only in western Chiriquí highlands. Very much like the previous species. Male has *bluish gray mid-*

Left to right (all males), GRAY-CROWNED YELLOWTHROAT, OLIVE-CROWNED YELLOWTHROAT, CHIRIQUI YELLOWTHROAT, COMMON YELLOWTHROAT *crown and border above black mask* (not whitish); both sexes have *entire underparts yellow.* Female has gray forehead and sides of head, but lacks black mask. Immature like female but with olive crown and sides of head.

Similar species: See Common Yellowthroat. Gray-crowned Yellowthroat is somewhat larger with heavier bill, has gray crown but no black mask (even in male). Olive-crowned Yellowthroat has entirely different range.

Status and distribution: Very local but not uncommon where found, usually in loose colonies; in recent years observed only in a few places around Volcán in the lower highlands of western Chiriquí at 3500–4500 feet. Inhabits damp meadows and low marshy growth near streams. Look for it around the Dos Ríos Motel in Volcán.

Habits: Similar to Common Yellowthroat. Its song is a sweet *twicheeteeweeoo tweéchee,* repeated four or five times, then a pause before starting again.

Range: Southwestern Costa Rica and Pacific western Panama.

Note: Often considered a race of the South American *G. aequinoctialis* (Masked Yellowthroat).

OLIVE-CROWNED YELLOWTHROAT
(*Geothlypis semiflava*)

Description: 4½–5. Known only from Bocas del Toro lowlands. Similar in general form to previous two species. Male olive green above with *black mask extending over forecrown onto sides of head* (more extensive than in other Panama yellowthroats), but *without gray or whitish border;* bright yellow below, tinged olive green on sides and flanks. Female olive green above and *bright yellow below* with more olive green on sides and flanks than in male. Immature like female but buffier below (no brownish tone above as in immature Common Yellowthroat).

Similar species: Common Yellowthroat always has whitish belly. Chiriquí Yellowthroat is restricted to Chiriquí.

Status and distribution: Common in tall grass, bamboo thickets, and low bushes especially near water in lowlands of western Bocas del Toro (in Costa Rica ranges up into lower highlands).

Habits: Similar to other yellowthroats. Its song is a loud, sweet warble somewhat suggestive of the Gray-crowned Yellowthroat and the Orchard Oriole (L. Griscom).

Range: Honduras to Caribbean western Panama; western Colombia and western Ecuador.

GRAY-CROWNED YELLOWTHROAT (GROUND-CHAT)
(*Geothlypis poliocephala*)

Description: 5–5½. Known only from western Chiriquí. Somewhat larger than other yellowthroats, with heavier bill and arched culmen, and longer, more graduated tail. Male grayish olive green above with *gray cap* and *black on lores and around eyes* (*no mask*); bright yellow below, fading to buffy whitish on lower belly. Female similar but has gray crown tinged with olive and lacks black on face (lores dusky). In nonbreeding plumage, both sexes have brownish tinge above. Immature resembles adult but has crown olive like back.

Similar species: Female has buffy whitish lower belly and thus can be confused with female Common Yellowthroat except for size, bill shape (pointed with straight culmen in Common Yellowthroat), and brighter yellow underparts. Unless seen clearly, female also easily confused with female Chiriquí Yellowthroat. Immature resembles (except for bill) other immature yellowthroats but the yellow of its underparts extends up over ear-coverts (olive in adults and in other yellowthroats).

Status and distribution: Uncommon and local in grassy pastures and brushy or weedy fields in foothills and highlands of western Chiriquí (2300–7500 feet).

Habits: Skulks in clumps of low vegetation in overgrown and abandoned pastures and cultivated lands. Frequently flicks its tail. Sometimes sings from an exposed tussock of grass, a tree branch, or even a wire.

Range: Northern Mexico (casually southern Texas) to Pacific western Panama.

Note: Sometimes separated in the genus *Chamaethlypis.*

YELLOW-BREASTED CHAT
(*Icteria virens*)

Description: 6½–7¼. Considerably larger than other warblers. *Heavy bill.* Olive green above with *conspicuous white "spectacles";* throat and breast bright yellow, belly white.

Similar species: The yellowthroats are much smaller.

Status and distribution: Uncommon winter resident in lowlands of western Bocas del Toro (early October–late April); only other report is a sighting of one bird on Cerro Campana on September 14, 1961 (R. Ryan and N. Boyajian).

Habits: Generally remains hidden in dense undergrowth of brushy areas and woodland borders. Most readily noted through mist-net captures.
Range: Breeds in United States and Mexico; winters from southern United States to Caribbean western (casually central) Panama.
Note: Some authors doubt its inclusion in the Parulidae.

HOODED WARBLER
(*Wilsonia citrina*)

Description: 5–5½. Male unmistakable with *black hood extending over crown, sides of neck, throat, and chest, and encircling yellow forehead and face;* otherwise olive above and bright yellow below; rather conspicuous white spots on tail. Female lacks the hood, is olive above and bright yellow below and on face and forehead; *white on tail as in male.*
Similar species: Female Wilson's Warbler is smaller and lacks white in the tail.
Status and distribution: Rare winter visitant to lowlands of western and central Panama (late September–early May); reported only from western Bocas del Toro, Coiba Island, and Canal Zone and vicinity.
Habits: Usually forages in lower growth of woodland or borders. Often spreads tail, exposing the white spots.
Range: Breeds in eastern United States; winters from Mexico to central Panama.

WILSON'S WARBLER
(*Wilsonia pusilla*)

Description: 4½–4¾. Male olive green above with *characteristic black cap;* bright yellow below and on face. In female and immatures black cap is reduced or replaced by olive, otherwise like male.
Similar species: Female Hooded Warbler is larger and flashes white in tail. Best distinguished from female yellowthroats with entirely yellow underparts by its yellow forehead and face and different actions. Female Yellow Warbler is also rather similar but lacks yellow forehead and face and has yellow edging on wings and tail.
Status and distribution: Abundant winter resident in highlands of Chiriquí above 3500 feet (mid-September–mid-May), becoming progressively less numerous in highlands and foothills eastward; rare in central Panama, with only three sightings, all males: one on Cerro Campana on September 14, 1961 (R. Ryan), and single individuals on Cerro Azul on December 30, 1967 and December 28, 1973 (Ridgely); so far not definitely reported from lowlands, though a possibility on migration.
Habits: One of the most numerous and conspicuous birds in the Chiriquí highlands during the northern winter months. Very active and noisy, feeding at low and middle levels in bushy clearings and woodland borders.
Range: Breeds in northern and western North America; winters from Mexico to western (rarely central) Panama.

CANADA WARBLER
(*Wilsonia canadensis*)

Description: 5–5½. Male *slaty gray above* with *yellow spectacles* and black on sides of head; bright yellow below, *chest crossed by a necklace of black streaks.* Female similar but duller, with upperparts somewhat more olive; necklace more washed out but still easily visible. Immature resembles female but often shows little or no trace of the necklace.
Similar species: The necklace is the mark; when it is missing, look for combination of gray upperparts and yellow spectacles.
Status and distribution: Uncommon to fairly common transient throughout, including Pearl Islands (early September–late November; late March–early May; most numerous late September–early October and in April); rare winter resident, at least in central Panama (Canal Zone and Cerro Campana).
Habits: Usually forages in lower growth of woodland and borders. At times occurs in small waves, especially on fall migration.
Range: Breeds in eastern North America; winters from Colombia (rarely Panama) and Venezuela to Peru and northern Brazil.

AMERICAN REDSTART
(*Setophaga ruticilla*)

Description: 4¾–5¼. Adult male *mostly black with orange patches on wings and base of tail;* belly white. Female and immatures mostly grayish or olive brown instead of black, with *yellow patches instead of orange.* First-year males are intermediate, usually like female but with orange patches.
Similar species: Readily distinguished by the orange or yellow patches regardless of what plumage it is in.
Status and distribution: Fairly common transient and uncommon winter resident throughout (late August–late April, once May 11) in woodland and borders.

Habits: Extremely active, constantly drooping its wings, fanning its tail, and flitting out after passing insects.

Range: Breeds in North America; winters in Florida and West Indies and from Mexico to Ecuador, northern Brazil, and the Guianas.

SLATE-THROATED REDSTART
(*Myioborus miniatus*) Pl.25

Description: 4¾–5. Highlands. *Slaty gray above and on throat and upper chest,* with chestnut crown patch (sometimes concealed); remaining underparts bright yellow; *outer tail feathers and tail tipping white.*

Similar species: Collared Redstart has all of underparts yellow with chest crossed by black band.

Status and distribution: Very common in forest and woodland, borders, and adjacent clearings in highlands of Chiriquí, Veraguas, and eastern Darién (mostly 3500–7000 feet); recently (July 1973) seen in cloud forest on Cerro Jefe, eastern Panama province (D. Hill).

Habits: Rather similar to American Redstart, very active, making short flycatcher-like sallies, and spreading its tail exposing the white. Has several usually squeaky or sibilant songs, sometimes suggestive of American Redstart, *tseeweech, sweeswee, sweechsweechee,* or *tseeoo-tseeoo, cheewee-cheewee-tsee.*

Range: Northern Mexico to Guyana, northern Brazil, and Bolivia.

COLLARED REDSTART
(*Myioborus torquatus*) Pl.25

Description: 4¾–5. Found only in western highlands. Slaty above with rufous cap (sometimes raised); *face and underparts bright yellow, chest crossed by a narrow black band;* outer tail feathers and tail tipping white.

Similar species: Not likely to be confused. Slate-throated Redstart lacks black chest band and contrasting yellow face and throat.

Status and distribution: Common in forest and woodland borders in highlands of Chiriquí and adjacent Bocas del Toro, mostly above 6000 feet, sometimes down to 4000 feet; found also in Veraguas highlands where regularly comes lower, to 3500–4000 feet.

Habits: Similar to Slate-throated Redstart and often found with it, though outnumbered at lower elevations. Generally stays rather low. Often charmingly tame, sometimes appearing almost curious. The song is a rather soft, slightly musical *tsit-tsit-tsee,* repeated; also has another sweeter and more elaborate song.

Range: Costa Rica and western Panama.

THREE-STRIPED WARBLER
(*Basileuterus tristriatus*) Pl.25

Description: 5. Foothills and highlands locally. Head with *narrow buffy crown stripe enclosed by broad black stripes,* and *buffy superciliary over black ear-coverts;* otherwise olive above; mostly pale yellow below, whitish on upper throat and washed with olive on chest. Birds from eastern Panama (*tacarcunae,* sometimes regarded as a distinct species) have crown stripe more orange, *black ear-coverts reduced to a thin line behind eye,* and yellow throat.

Similar species: Golden-crowned Warbler (found only in western Panama) has yellow or orange crown stripe (not buffy), lacks black ear-coverts, and is entirely yellow below. Also resembles Worm-eating Warbler except for that species' uniform dull buffy underparts.

Status and distribution: Rather rare and local in highlands of Chiriquí and adjacent Bocas del Toro (4000–7500 feet), and also in Veraguas (where ranges lower, 2000–4000 feet); found also (*tacarcunae*) on Cerro Jefe (3000–3300 feet), eastern Panama province (D. Hill, Ridgely) and in highlands of eastern Darién (Cerro Tacarcuna, 3000–5000 feet).

Habits: A bird of forest and woodland (elfin cloud forest on Cerro Jefe), not well known in Panama. Often in small groups, foraging very actively in lower growth.

Range: Costa Rica to northern Venezuela and northern Bolivia.

GOLDEN-CROWNED WARBLER
(*Basileuterus culicivorus*) Pl.25

Description: 5. Known only from western highlands. Head with *yellow or orange crown stripe enclosed by broad black stripes* and olive green superciliary with a dusky spot in front of and behind eye; otherwise olive above (*including cheeks*); yellow below (*including throat*).

Similar species: Three-striped Warbler in western Panama has buffy crown stripe (not yellow or orange), black ear-coverts, and is duller yellow below with whitish throat.

Status and distribution: Fairly common in forest and woodland in highlands of Chiriquí (3500–7000 feet, most numerous below 5000 feet); known also from foothills of Veraguas and Herrera (1600–3500 feet); not reported from Darién, though seems possible.

Habits: Usually forages fairly near the ground in forest or woodland undergrowth. Rather active but often difficult to see clearly. Gives a dry *trrrrrrititit.*

Range: Central Mexico to western Panama; western Colombia to Bolivia, northern Argentina, and Uruguay.

BLACK-CHEEKED WARBLER
(*Basileuterus melanogenys*) Pl.25

Description: 5¼. Found only in western highlands. *Chestnut crown* narrowly margined with black; *long white superciliary above black sides of head;* otherwise grayish olive above; grayish white below, darkest on breast and sides, tinged slightly with pale yellow. Birds from Veraguas (*bensoni,* sometimes treated as a distinct species, Benson's Warbler) have slaty back and no yellowish tinge on underparts.

Similar species: Sooty-capped Bush-Tanager lacks the chestnut crown and has stockier build.

Status and distribution: Common in forest, woodland, and borders in highlands of western Chiriquí, especially above 6000 feet, sometimes down to 5000 feet; found also in highlands of Veraguas (Chitra, 4000–5000 feet).

Habits: Usually seen in pairs or small groups, sometimes with mixed foraging flocks, moving rapidly through the undergrowth. Often quite unsuspicious.

Range: Costa Rica and western Panama.

PIRRE WARBLER
(*Basileuterus ignotus*) Pl.32

Description: 5¼. Known only from eastern Darién highlands. Resembles Black-cheeked Warbler but *superciliary pale greenish yellow* (not white), sides of head greenish yellow mottled with black (not solid black), upperparts greener, and underparts considerably yellower.

Similar species: See Black-cheeked Warbler.

Status and distribution: Recorded only from highlands of eastern Darién (Cerro Pirre, Cerro Tacarcuna).

Range: Eastern Panama.

Note: By some authors regarded as a well-marked race of *B. melanogenys* (Black-cheeked Warbler).

CHESTNUT-CAPPED WARBLER
(*Basileuterus delatrii*) Pl.25

Description: 5. *Crown and ear-coverts chestnut with intervening white superciliary;* otherwise olive green above; bright yellow below.

Similar species: The only *Basileuterus* warbler (apart from the very different Buff-rumped) in most of its Panama range.

Status and distribution: Fairly common in shrubby clearings and woodland borders in lowlands on entire Pacific slope; on Caribbean slope found only in Canal Zone and vicinity; ranges up to lower highlands in Chiriquí (rarely to 5200 feet); found also on Coiba Island.

Habits: Usually found in thickets not far above ground. Often cocks tail in a perky manner. Its song is a fast, dry *chit-cha-chup-cha-chuweep,* sometimes ending with a *chee-weecha,* in pattern reminiscent of a Canada Warbler but in quality rather more like a Chestnut-sided or Yellow.

Range: Guatemala to Colombia and northern Venezuela.

Note: By some authors considered conspecific with *B. rufifrons* (Rufous-capped Warbler) of Mexico and Guatemala, in which case the English name of the entire complex would be Rufous-capped Warbler.

BUFF-RUMPED WARBLER
(*Basileuterus fulvicauda*) Pl.25

Description: 5½. Waterthrush-like in general appearance. Olive brown above with *buff rump and basal two-thirds of tail;* buff below, somewhat mottled with olive on chest.

Similar species: Waterthrushes are streaked below, lack contrasting rump.

Status and distribution: Uncommon to fairly common along rivers and streams, usually rapid and stony, inside forest and second-growth woodland in lowlands and foothills on both slopes; found also in mangroves in Bocas del Toro. Somewhat local, at least in central Panama, and absent from some areas that would appear suitable.

Habits: In many ways reminiscent of a Louisiana Waterthrush, repeatedly flushing ahead when disturbed, finally circling around to its point of origin. Unlike waterthrushes, does not teeter up and down, rather swings its fanned tail from side to side. Also unlike waterthrushes, seems only to hop, rarely if ever actually to walk. The male's song is a rising crescendo of loud

notes, loud enough to be heard over the roar of turbulent streams.
Range: Honduras to Peru and western Brazil.
Note: Sometimes treated as a race of *B. rivularis* (River Warbler) from South America east of the Andes. Some authors place *fulvicauda* and *rivularis* in a separate genus *Phaeothlypis.*

WRENTHRUSHES: Zeledoniidae (1)

The Wrenthrush is a very distinct species of somewhat uncertain affinities, known only from the humid highlands of Costa Rica and western Panama. It was long assumed to be most closely allied to the Turdidae, but recent evidence indicates that it is probably most closely related to the Parulidae (C. G. Sibley, *Postilla* 125: 1–12, 1968). In any case, it is usually placed in a family or subfamily of its own. Short-winged and short-tailed, the Wrenthrush is a small, mostly terrestrial bird that flies little. Remaining in the densest tangles of forest undergrowth, it is a very difficult bird to observe, and only recently have any of its habits become known. It is apparently largely insectivorous. The nest is a domed structure built mostly of moss, concealed within a vertical moss-covered bank (see J. H. Hunt, *Auk* 88: 1–20, 1971).

WRENTHRUSH
(*Zeledonia coronata*) Pl.23

Description: 4½–5. Found only in western highlands. A plump little bird with a rather short tail. *Golden tawny crown* margined with tawny, otherwise dark olive brown above; *face, sides of neck, and entire underparts slaty gray.*
Similar species: Somewhat suggests a small plump nightingale-thrush with a short tail and crown patch, or a heavy-bodied *Basileuterus* warbler. Gray-breasted Wood-Wren lacks crown patch and has white superciliary and black and white-streaked sides of neck and throat. See also Silvery-fronted Tapaculo.
Status and distribution: Rare and local, perhaps overlooked, in dense undergrowth of humid forest in highlands of western Chiriquí (5800–10,300 feet) and Veraguas (Chitra, 3500–4000 feet).
Habits: Lives on or near the ground in thick vegetation, rarely coming out into the open, and likely more numerous than the relatively few Panama records would indicate. Prefers steep ravines and mountainsides in very humid areas. The call is a very high thin *seeeeeeeeep* (G. Tudor), the song a rather squeaky *tseee-del-deet* (J. Hunt); both are easily recognized and are the best way to find the bird. As they hop around they often flick their wings simultaneously (J. Hunt).
Range: Costa Rica and western Panama.

AMERICAN ORIOLES AND BLACKBIRDS: Icteridae (21)

This is a varied family, confined to the New World, with most species in the tropics. They are medium-sized to fairly large birds with rather long pointed bills, in many species with the male larger or more brightly colored. Many species are wholly or predominantly black, some with varying amounts of yellow, orange, chestnut, or red. Many species also have good songs, though others have only harsh strident vocalizations. Great diversity exists in social habits and breeding behavior. Oropendolas and the Yellow-rumped Cacique are gregarious birds whose conspicuous colonies with their long, pendant nests are characteristic in more wooded areas. Other Panamanian caciques are more solitary, usually nesting singly. The Panamanian cowbirds are all brood parasites on other birds, the Giant Cowbird specializing on the colonial oropendolas and caciques, under certain conditions to the host's advantage (N. G. Smith, *Nature* 219: 690–694, 1968). The orioles are the most attractive members of the family in Panama, both resident and migrant species being found in good numbers. Most species have a varied diet of various combinations of fruit and insects, some seeds, with the grackle also taking some small vertebrates (washed up fish, even nestling birds). The arboreal members of the family construct large beautifully woven pouches hanging from branches (sometimes palm fronds, and in some places even radio antennas and wires); the more terrestrial species nest on the ground, while the Great-tailed Grackle constructs a large deep cup nest.

MONTEZUMA OROPENDOLA
(*Gymnostinops montezuma*) Pl.26

Description: ♂20; ♀16. *Basal half of bill black, terminal half bright orange;* bare frontal shield blackish. Iris brown. Head (with narrow crest) and neck black; *patch of bare skin below eye bluish and pink; otherwise mostly rich chestnut,* darker below; tail (except for central two feathers) yellow.

Similar species: Its impressive size alone normally distinguishes it from other oropendolas within its range; in any case, the bicolored bill and largely chestnut body are diagnostic. See Black Oropendola.

Status and distribution: Known only from lowlands on Caribbean slope east to Canal Zone; common locally in Bocas del Toro, less numerous eastward. Since 1969 colonies have been found on Caribbean slope of Canal Zone where it had not been definitely recorded since the nineteenth-century (though occasional individuals were reported in 1964); now can be seen regularly along Escobal and Achiote Roads and should be watched for elsewhere; has occasionally already wandered to Pacific side in Rodman area of southwestern sector (N. G. Smith).

Habits: Similar to those of other oropendolas, sometimes nesting in the same tree with them. The nests are larger and longer than those of the Chestnut-headed Oropendola. Males in display give a series of loud slashing gurgling notes, the bird often leaning forward and sometimes doing a partial forward somersault with wings drooped. The calls resemble those of the Chestnut-headed but are louder and even harsher.

Range: Eastern Mexico to central Panama.

BLACK OROPENDOLA
(*Gymnostinops guatimozinus*) Pl.26

Description: ♂18; ♀16. Found only in eastern Panama. *Bill black with yellow tip;* bare frontal shield black, facial skin bluish and pink. Iris brown. *Mostly black* with only lower back, rump, under tail-coverts, and a little on wing-coverts dull chestnut; tail yellow except for black central pair of feathers.

Similar species: Crested Oropendola is similar but has entirely greenish yellow bill. The larger Montezuma Oropendola has a different range, is mostly chestnut except for black head and neck.

Status and distribution: Fairly common in lowlands of Darién; possibly ranges west into Bayano River valley in eastern Panama province (recent unconfirmed sightings).

Habits: Similar to those of other oropendolas and often with them.

Range: Eastern Panama and northern Colombia.

CHESTNUT-HEADED OROPENDOLA
(*Zarhynchus wagleri*) Pl.26

Description: ♂14; ♀11. Bill whitish ivory to pale greenish yellow (often with dusky tip). Iris pale blue. *Head and neck chestnut;* otherwise mostly black, merging to chestnut on rump and lower belly; tail yellow except for dusky central pair of feathers and outer web of outermost pair. Males have inconspicuous crest consisting of a few hair-like feathers.

Similar species: No other Panama oropendola has a chestnut head and neck (can be hard to see in poor light, however). See Crested Oropendola.

Status and distribution: Common in more humid lowlands on both slopes in forest, second-growth woodland, borders, clearings, and even roadsides with trees; ranges up in reduced numbers in the foothills to about 4500 feet; more local on Pacific slope and absent from drier parts of Azuero Peninsula and southern Coclé; not found on Pacific islands. The most numerous oropendola in the Canal Zone and vicinity, and the most widespread in Panama.

Habits: This species' nesting colonies of up to a hundred (usually 25–50) nests, hung in an isolated or well-exposed tree or grove, are a characteristic sight in much of the lowlands and present a fascinating spectacle throughout the breeding cycle (roughly January to May, occasionally later). At other seasons the birds disperse and wander widely. Both sexes, but especially males in display, emit a variety of loud slashing croaks and gurgling notes, similar to those of other Panama oropendolas. The gurgling notes are rather musical, and suggest dripping water, *plup, plup, plup, plup-loo-upoo.*

Range: Southeastern Mexico to western Ecuador.

CRESTED OROPENDOLA
(*Psarocolius decumanus*) Pl.26

Description: ♂17; ♀15. *Bill ivory yellow to greenish yellow.* Iris pale blue. *Mostly black (including head)* except for dark chestnut lower back, rump, and under tail-coverts; tail yellow except for central pair of feathers. Not really crested; the "crest" consists merely of a few hair-like feathers that protrude from the crown.

Similar species: Smaller and chunkier Chestnut-headed Oropendola has chestnut head and neck. Most resembles Black Oropendola of eastern Panama, but that species has bicolored black-tipped yellow bill and bare facial area.

Status and distribution: Locally fairly common in forest borders, second-growth woodland, and clearings with large trees in lowlands on Pacific slope in western Chiriquí, coastal Veraguas, southwestern Canal Zone, and eastern Panama province (Chepo area) east through Darién; on Caribbean slope known only from Canal Zone and vicinity. Less numerous in western Panama but becomes very common in Darién. Not reported from San Blas but should occur as common in adjacent northern Colombia.

Habits: Similar to the more common Chestnut-headed Oropendola and frequently nests nearby, though apparently not in the same tree; also sometimes nests in association with Yellow-rumped Cacique. Often nests in smallish *Cecropia* trees. Breeding season much like that of Chestnut-headed, but in Canal Zone seems to extend a little later, into late June.

Range: Western Panama to Bolivia, northern Argentina, and southeastern Brazil.

YELLOW-RUMPED CACIQUE
(*Cacicus cela*) Pl.26

Description: ♂11; ♀9½. Bill pale greenish. Iris pale blue. Mostly *glossy black* with *orange-yellow patch on wing-coverts, lower back, rump, basal half of tail, and under tail-coverts.*

Similar species: Oropendolas have yellow only on tail, not on rump, vent, and wings.

Status and distribution: Fairly common in forest, second-growth woodland, borders, and clearings in lowlands on Caribbean slope from Canal Zone area eastward, on Pacific slope from southern Veraguas eastward.

Habits: Similar to the oropendolas and often associating with them, particularly the Chestnut-headed. Frequently nests with oropendolas, but generally in a small group somewhat removed from their main body. Cacique nests are shorter and more oblong than the long, conical ones of oropendolas, and are often clumped together only inches apart or even touching each other. Has a variety of calls ranging from cackles and squawks to squeaks and rather liquid notes.

Range: Western Panama to northern Bolivia and central Brazil.

Note: Birds from Panama and northern Colombia, *C. vitellinus* (Saffron-rumped or Lawrence's Cacique), may be specifically distinct from birds from South America east of the Andes, true *C. cela.* True *Cacicus cela* is known to be a mimic of other birds and even mechanical noises, but this has not been reported from Panama birds.

SCARLET-RUMPED CACIQUE
(*Cacicus uropygialis*) Pl.26

Description: ♂10; ♀9. Rather long bill, greenish white. Iris pale blue. Glossy black with *scarlet rump* (more orange-scarlet in female). Rump patch concealed when perched, but very noticeable in flight.

Similar species: When rump color cannot be seen, can be confused with other all or mostly black forest birds. Yellow-billed Cacique, in particular, is similar in such a situation but is normally found in dense underbrush of clearings and borders.

Status and distribution: Fairly common in forest, second-growth woodland, and borders in lowlands on entire Caribbean slope; less numerous and more local in humid forest and woodland on Pacific slope, becoming fairly common again in eastern Panama province (Bayano River valley) and Darién.

Habits: Usually nests solitarily, though occasionally in small groups, hanging its squarish bag nest from a tree at edge of forest, or even from a bridge or other structure. At other seasons troops about the forest in bold noisy bands, foraging at all levels. Has a variety of loud musical whistles, among them one with a throaty quality *shreeo-shreeo,* and another human-sounding *wheew-whee-whee-whee-wheet.*

Range: Nicaragua to northwestern Venezuela and central Peru.

Note: Birds from Middle America and most of Panama, *microrhynchus* (Small-billed Cacique), may be specifically distinct from birds from most of its South American range. Birds from southern Darién and western Colombia, *pacificus* (Pacific Cacique), may likewise be distinct from nominate form.

YELLOW-BILLED CACIQUE
(*Amblycercus holosericeus*) Pl.26

Description: ♂10; ♀9. *Bill yellowish white or greenish yellow.* Iris pale yellow. *All black.*

Similar species: Perched Scarlet-rumped Cacique, with red rump hidden, looks like this species but has pale blue eye. Male White-lined Tanager is smaller with heavier, shorter, mostly bluish bill, and flashes white under wing-linings in flight.

Status and distribution: Fairly common in thickets and dense undergrowth of clearings and woodland borders in lowlands on both slopes, ranging up in smaller numbers in suitable habitat into the foothills and lower highlands.

Habits: A great skulker, rarely coming into the open, and often difficult to even glimpse. Normally forages close to the ground, but occasionally goes higher to feed in flowering or fruiting trees. Has a variety of liquid whistles and harsh churring notes: a repeated loud clear whistle *pur-weé-pew;* a rather sweet *wreeeeoo* and a harsher *queeyoo;* and an almost duck-like *quack-quack-quack,* varied to *kwok* or a buzzy *kzaak.* Heard more often than seen.

Range: Eastern Mexico to northern Venezuela and Bolivia.

Note: Sometimes placed in the genus *Cacicus.*

GIANT COWBIRD
(*Scaphidura oryzivora*) Pl.26

Description: ♂14; ♀11½. Iris red in western and central Panama, becoming more yellowish orange in eastern Panama. *Thick bill and bare frontal shield black* (occasional juvenals have bill pale flesh or yellowish in whole or in part). Male glossy purplish black with *conspicuous ruff on neck* (often giving it a curiously "small-headed" appearance). Female and immatures duller black with much less prominent ruff. In flight, wings are distinctively long and pointed, and body looks wedge-shaped, the overall effect being apparent at long distances.

Similar species: Male recalls male Great-tailed Grackle but has heavier bill, ruff on neck, and shorter rounded tail; female Giant Cowbird is so much smaller than male grackle that confusion is unlikely. Bronzed and Glossy Cowbirds are considerably smaller than even female Giant Cowbird and have conical bills without frontal shields.

Status and distribution: Uncommon but widespread in more humid lowlands on both slopes where oropendolas or colonial caciques nest; absent from eastern side of Azuero Peninsula, southern Coclé, and most of western Panama province.

Habits: A brood parasite, in Panama its hosts being exclusively the colonial oropendolas and caciques. Most easily seen in the vicinity of these colonies, especially when the hosts are laying. At other seasons, disperses widely and thinly, feeding primarily on the ground in fields or along open banks or sandbars of rivers, also in flowering trees (sometimes with its hosts). The grassy slopes of Gatun Dam are a good place to look for them at this time; there they often forage near, or even with, Great-tailed Grackles.

Range: Southeastern Mexico to Bolivia, northeastern Argentina, and southern Brazil.

BRONZED COWBIRD
(*Molothrus aeneus*) Pl.26

Description: 8–8½. Stout, somewhat conical black bill. *Red iris in both sexes.* Male *all bronzy black* with *prominent ruff on neck.* Female somewhat smaller, duller black and more brownish below, with less conspicuous ruff. Immature more grayish brown, with narrow paler edging below.

Similar species: Though female Giant Cowbird is considerably larger, the two can be confused. Shiny Cowbird is very similar and readily confused, though the two species are not known to occur together. Both sexes of Shiny have dark eye and lack this species' ruff; male in good light shows strong purple reflections (not bronzy); female is grayish brown (not so black as this species), and rather paler below.

Status and distribution: Common in lowlands of Bocas del Toro; uncommon and local in lowlands on Pacific slope from Chiriquí east to eastern Panama province (most numerous in western Chiriquí). Never recorded from Canal Zone, though possible; most central Panama reports are from the Tocumen/La Jagua area of eastern Panama province. Several recent sightings from the María Chiquita/Río Piedras area of eastern Colon province (N. G. Smith *et al.*); also a flock of 8 seen on eastern shore of Madden Lake on February 10, 1973 (Eisenmann). Is perhaps becoming more numerous in central Panama, and spreading eastward.

Habits: Usually seen feeding on the ground, often in flocks, sometimes large, in fields and pastures, sometimes with cattle. A brood parasite on various small birds.

Range: Southwestern United States to central Panama.

Note: Often separated in the genus *Tangavius.*

SHINY COWBIRD
(*Molothrus bonariensis*) Pl.26

Description: 8–8½. Known only from extreme eastern Panama. Short, conical bill. *Iris dark in both sexes.* Male *entirely glossy violet blue-black.* Female dull grayish brown above; *much paler grayish brown below,* with faint dusky streaks on breast. Immature resembles female but is edged with brownish buff above; *yellowish buff below,* streaked with dusky in males.

Similar species: Not always easy to distinguish from Bronzed Cowbird though both sexes lack that species' ruff and red eye; female Shiny is paler and grayer, especially below. Somewhat resembles male White-lined Tanager, but that species has longer bluish bill, lacks glossy violet tones, and has white under wing-linings.

Status and distribution: A rare bird in Panama. Known only from two specimens taken in Tuira River valley of eastern Darién and a sight report of 7–8 birds (3–4 males) east of Puerto Obaldía, in eastern San Blas in June 1965 (D. Sheets). With ever-increasing clearing of forest may become more numerous and even spread westward.

Habits: Similar to Bronzed Cowbird, also feeding mostly on the ground, often among cattle. Likewise a brood parasite on various small birds. Males have a rather pretty whistled song.

Range: Eastern Panama to central Chile and southern Argentina; Lesser Antilles.

GREAT-TAILED GRACKLE
(*Cassidix mexicanus*) Pl.26

Description: ♂17; ♀13. Long, pointed bill. Iris yellow in male, pale brown in female. Male glossy blue-black with *long, creased, keel-shaped tail.* Female much smaller, dull brown above with *buffy superciliary; pale buffy brown below;* tail shorter and less keel-shaped.

Similar species: Male Giant Cowbird can be confused with male but is smaller, with neck ruff, and has normally shaped tail.

Status and distribution: Locally common to abundant in lowlands on Pacific slope from eastern Chiriquí (where scarce) to Darién, especially along coast; on Caribbean slope reported only from just west of Canal Zone eastward in cleared areas through San Blas; common also on Coiba Island, Taboga Island, the Pearl Islands, and other islands off Pacific coast, and on islands off San Blas. Not known from Bocas del Toro or Caribbean slope Veraguas, or from western Chiriquí (where perhaps present in coastal mangroves). Abundant in open residential areas of Canal Zone and Panama city and Colon, especially where there are extensive lawns and along sea shore.

Habits: Feeds mostly on the ground, also as a scavenger along coasts. Roosts in very large, noisy flocks in trees. Male displays, often on ground, with bill up and long neck extended. Has many vocalizations: both sexes have a harsh *chack;* male gives a long strident whistle, *weeek, week,* sometimes drawn out to *weeeeek,* and both sexes also give a rattling *trit-trit-trit.*

Range: Southwestern United States to northwestern Venezuela and southwestern Peru.

Note: Boat-tailed Grackle, *C. major,* of southeastern United States was formerly included in this species with that English name applied to the enlarged complex. Sometimes placed in the genus *Quiscalus.*

ORCHARD ORIOLE
(*Icterus spurius*)

Description: 6–6½. Male *mostly dark chestnut* with black head, neck, back, wings, and tail; wings edged brownish. Freshly molted males have feathers broadly tipped with buff, partially obscuring the chestnut and black. Female olive green above, wings duskier with two whitish bars; *greenish yellow below.* Immature male like female but with *black throat.*

Similar species: Male is only Panama oriole with deep chestnut, not orange or yellow. Female resembles female Baltimore Oriole but is duller and more uniform yellow below (Baltimore is more orange below, especially on chest).

Status and distribution: Common winter resident in lowlands (early August–early April, a few sometimes arriving in late July, most departing by mid-March); occasional transient in highlands to 5500 feet; not recorded from offshore islands. Occurs in light woodland, clearings, residential areas, and semi-open areas with scattered trees.

Habits: Widespread in semi-open areas but especially numerous in residential areas, where it congregates in rather large groups to roost, and to feed in flowering trees, notably *Erythrina.* Adult males seem to predominate numerically.

Range: Breeds from eastern and central

United States to central Mexico; winters from southern Mexico to northern Colombia and northwestern Venezuela.

BLACK-COWLED ORIOLE

(*Icterus prosthemelas*) Pl.26

Description: 7½–8. Found only in western Bocas del Toro lowlands. *Mostly black (including tail)*, with yellow wing-coverts, rump, breast, and belly; a tinge of chestnut between black chest and yellow breast. Immature similar but with yellowish back. In juvenal black is restricted to forehead, sides of head, throat, most of wings, and tail; remaining areas yellowish, brighter below.

Similar species: Juvenal resembles Yellow-tailed Oriole but is smaller, much duller yellow below, and never has yellow in tail. It is also smaller and much duller than Yellow-backed Oriole (not known from Bocas del Toro). Adult is only breeding Panama oriole with wholly black head and neck.

Status and distribution: Fairly common in lowlands of western Bocas del Toro, usually near water.

Habits: Frequents river banks, woodland borders, clearings with trees, and banana plantations. The song is a sweet and rapid, but not very loud, series of whistles.

Range: Southeastern Mexico to Caribbean western Panama.

Note: Sometimes considered conspecific with the West Indian *I. dominicensis,* the Bahama form of which is very similar in appearance to the Middle American form.

ORANGE-CROWNED ORIOLE

(*Icterus aurocapillus*) Pl.26

Description: 8. Known only from eastern Panama. *Crown, nape, and sides of neck orange;* forehead, sides of head, throat, chest, back, wings, and tail black; wing-coverts, rump, and lower underparts orange-yellow. Juvenal has crown and nape yellowish olive, back and tail dull olive, wings dusky with pale yellow edging; pale yellow below, brighter on throat, with some dusky on lower throat.

Similar species: An especially attractive oriole. More orange, especially on head, than Yellow-tailed Oriole and with no yellow on tail. Lacks brownish tinge shown by many Yellow-backed Orioles and with black (not yellow) back.

Status and distribution: Fairly common in woodland borders and shrubby clearings (especially along rivers and streams) in lowlands of eastern Panama province (hills east of Chepo, on Platanares–Jesús María road, eastward) and Darién.

Habits: Most often seen in pairs, regularly feeding high in flowering trees, sometimes with other orioles (Yellow-backed, Northern).

Range: Eastern Panama to northern Venezuela.

YELLOW-TAILED ORIOLE

(*Icterus mesomelas*) Pl.26

Description: 9. *Mostly bright yellow,* with *black back,* wings (except *yellow wing-coverts*), center of tail (with *outer feathers yellow*), and throat and chest.

Similar species: Yellow-backed Oriole has, as name implies, a yellow (not black) back and all black wings and tail, and is more orange-yellow generally. In Bocas del Toro, see juvenal Black-cowled Oriole.

Status and distribution: Fairly common in thickets near water, woodland borders, and clearings with trees in lowlands on entire Caribbean slope; less numerous and more local on Pacific slope from Canal Zone area eastward, becoming more common again in Darién; a pair seen recently (1969–1970) on several occasions near base of Cerro Campana (Ridgely *et al.*) represents farthest west report on Pacific slope.

Habits: Everywhere seems to prefer the vicinity of water. The song is a series of very rich mellow whistled phrases, each phrase usually repeated several times before going on to the next. Usual and distinctive calls are *chup-cheet* or *chup-chup-cheet,* and a *weechaw.*

Range: Southeastern Mexico to northwestern Venezuela and northern Peru.

YELLOW-BACKED ORIOLE

(*Icterus chrysater*) Pl.26

Description: 8½–9. *Mostly rich orange-yellow* with black throat and chest, wings, and tail. In many individuals, the yellow areas adjacent to black bib are more or less tinged with brown.

Similar species: Yellow-tailed Oriole is yellower, has black (not yellow) back, and has yellow in wings and tail (not solid black). In eastern Panama see also Orange-crowned Oriole.

Status and distribution: Fairly common in forest and woodland borders and clearings, and shrubby areas with trees in lowlands on both slopes from Veraguas eastward;

ranges up in smaller numbers into foothills to about 3000 feet. Curiously, no resident oriole has ever been found in Chiriquí; this species would be the most likely. The common resident oriole on Pacific side of Canal Zone and vicinity.

Habits: Often in pairs or small family groups. The song is a series of 4 to 8 loud clear musical whistles moving in a disconnected manner up and down so that it sounds off-key. The usual call is a *teea, cheep-cheep, cheep* (the *cheep*'s nasal); also has a part-chatter, part buzzy whistle *kzwee-kzwee-kzwee-kzwee-kzwee* and a nasal *nyeh-nyeh-nyeh-nyeh*.

Range: Southeastern Mexico to northern Venezuela, though not known from Costa Rica.

Note: There is an old dubious specimen from "Isthmus of Panama" of the Yellow Oriole, *I. nigrogularis,* known from northern Colombia to the Guianas and extreme northern Brazil; if found wild in Panama most likely in Darién or San Blas. Resembles Yellow-backed Oriole but is more lemon yellow overall, with smaller black bib, and has prominent white wing-band and whitish edging to flight feathers and tipping to outer tail feathers.

NORTHERN (BALTIMORE) ORIOLE
(*Icterus galbula*)

Description: 6½–7. Male *orange and black:* entire head, neck, back, wings, and center of tail black; lower back, rump, remaining underparts, and sides of tail bright orange; wings with one white bar and white edging. Female brownish olive above, wings duskier with two white bars; *orange-yellow below, brightest on chest.*

Similar species: Male is only truly orange and black oriole in Panama; Black-cowled Oriole also has entire head and neck black, but it is clear yellow (not orange) on wings, rump, and lower underparts. Female Orchard Oriole resembles female but is uniform greenish yellow below (not orange-yellow).

Status and distribution: Common winter resident throughout (early October–late April, a few sometimes arriving in late September and lingering into early May), mostly in lowlands, but in Chiriquí also in highlands to over 6000 feet; recorded also on Pacific islands. Favors woodland borders and fairly open areas with trees.

Habits: Usually does not feed in such large flocks as Orchard Oriole, but may gather in groups to fly to roost or on migration. Like the Orchard Oriole, feeds a great deal in flowering trees.

Range: Breeds in North America; winters sparingly in eastern and southern United States, mostly from Mexico to Colombia and northern Venezuela.

Note: The form breeding in western North America (*bullocki*), formerly considered a distinct species (Bullock's Oriole) but now considered to be conspecific with *I. galbula,* might occur casually during northern winter (winters mostly in Mexico and Guatemala, casually to Costa Rica). Adult male differs from Baltimore in its orange face and large white patch on wing, female in its olive gray back and whitish belly. Considerable hybridization occurs where the breeding ranges of the two forms overlap, hence sight reports of birds other than adult males must be viewed with some caution. One such female exhibiting the characters of *bullocki* was seen on Barro Colorado Island November 13, 1972 (M. Perrone).

[YELLOW-HEADED BLACKBIRD]
(*Xanthocephalus xanthocephalus*)

Description: 9–11. One recent specimen. Male black with *entire head and chest yellow;* small black area in front of eye; *white patch on wings,* especially conspicuous in flight. Female smaller than male, mostly brown, with *duller yellow sides of head, throat, and chest;* breast streaked with whitish.

Similar species: See only Yellow-hooded Blackbird (below).

Status and distribution: Only record is an immature male taken at Gatun Dam, Canal Zone on November 1, 1972 (J. Strauch, Jr.). It likely was assisted by a ship in its passage to Panama.

Range: Breeds in western North America; winters in southwestern United States and Mexico, rarely in eastern United States; a few records from West Indies, one from Panama.

Note: Yellow-hooded Blackbird (*Agelaius icterocephalus*) of northern and Amazonian South America may occur in marshy areas of eastern Darién and San Blas; it is reported to be common around the Gulf of Urabá in northwestern Colombia, and has been taken within a few miles of the Darién border. Male superficially resembles male Yellow-headed Blackbird, but is smaller (7″), and lacks white on wing; female is more olive above (not so brown) with back streaked black, with superciliary and throat bright yellow, becoming duller yellow on breast and grayish olive on belly.

RED-BREASTED BLACKBIRD
(*Leistes militaris*) Pl.26

Description: 7–7½. Male unmistakable, mostly black with *red throat and breast*. In nonbreeding season (September–March) black feathers edged with brown. Female streaked blackish and buffy above; *buffy below, tinged pink on breast,* with dusky streaks on flanks. Immature like female but more streaked below.

Similar species: Female and nonbreeding male Bobolinks are more yellowish and have a striped crown, never show pinkish breast of female Red-breasted Blackbird. See also Eastern Meadowlark.

Status and distribution: Common on savannas and extensive fields in lowlands on Pacific slope from Chiriquí to eastern Darién (El Real, common in July 1975; Ridgely); recently (since 1972) a small group has been present on France Field on Caribbean slope of Canal Zone (J. Pujals *et al.*). Easily seen along the Pan-American Highway east and west of the Canal Zone.

Habits: Rather like a meadowlark, with which it often associates, and, like it, gathering in fair-sized flocks during nonbreeding season. Even in breeding season seems somewhat gregarious, nesting in loose "colonies" in particularly favorable habitat. The male's song, given from a slightly elevated perch such as a fence post or low bush, consists of two short introductory notes followed by a long rather buzzy trill.

Range: Southwestern Costa Rica (to which it has only recently spread) to Colombia, Venezuela, and the Guianas.

Note: Sometimes placed in the genus *Sturnella.*

EASTERN MEADOWLARK
(*Sturnella magna*)

Description: 8–9. Chunky, with long slender bill and short tail. Brown above streaked with black and buff; head striped blackish and white; *yellow below, chest crossed by broad black "V".* When flushed, *white outer tail feathers* flash out conspicuously. Young birds are duller but still easily recognized as meadowlarks.

Similar species: Female Red-breasted Blackbird can look rather similar, especially when seen from above.

Status and distribution: Common in extensive grasslands and moist savannas and fields in lowlands on Pacific slope from Chiriquí to eastern Panama province; ranges up in diminishing numbers into highlands of western Chiriquí (to about 6000 feet) in suitable habitat; not known from Darién or Caribbean slope.

Habits: Mostly terrestrial, walking on ground. In flight, alternates several flaps with a short sail on stiff wings. Often perches conspicuously on a fence post or low branch of a tree to sing; the song is a pretty, slurred four-noted whistle, *pee-ah, pee-oo,* identical to that of temperate North American birds. Also has a very different warbled song *tleeoo-tleedleeoo;* the usual call is a harsh *zhueet.*

Range: Eastern North America to northern Colombia, Venezuela, the Guianas, and northern Brazil.

BOBOLINK
(*Dolichonyx oryzivorus*)

Description: 6½–7½. Rather short conical bill. Tail somewhat graduated. Female and nonbreeding male brownish buffy above streaked with blackish and with *buffy and dusky stripes on head; yellowish buffy below* with a little brownish streaking on sides. Male in breeding plumage mostly black with *buffy yellow patch on back of neck, white lower back and rump,* and broad white stripe on scapulars. In fresh breeding plumage, feathers broadly tipped with buff, obscuring the pattern; bright plumage is slowly acquired through wearing off of these tips (apparently complete by May).

Similar species: Eastern Meadowlark is chunky, with short tail and long slender bill, and is mostly yellow below; female Red-breasted Blackbird is darker above without head striping, tinged pinkish on breast. Wedge-tailed Grass-Finch lacks stripes on head and has longer more pointed tail.

Status and distribution: Uncommon fall and rare spring transient (mid-September–late October; mid April–early May), mostly along Caribbean coast but also recorded on Pacific slope of central and eastern Panama. Usually noted flying over; when perched, in clearings with grass and in grassy fields.

Habits: Often in small groups but decidedly erratic. In flight often gives a characteristic *pink.*

Range: Breeds in North America; winters in south-central South America; migrates mostly via West Indies, small numbers reaching Middle America.

SWALLOW-TANAGERS: Tersinidae (1)

The one member of this family resembles the tanagers, but differs in its wide flat bill, longer wings and shorter legs, and very different nesting habits. Nonetheless, recent evidence suggests that it may not deserve full family status, and is perhaps best placed in the Thraupidae, most closely related to the genera *Tangara* and *Thraupis* (cf. C. G. Sibley, *Bull.Br.Orn.Club* 93: 2, 1973). It is a South American species extending to eastern Panama; in some parts of its range it is migratory, breeding in forest clearings in foothills and highlands, withdrawing to the lowlands in the nonbreeding season. The bird is gregarious when not nesting, occuring in flocks of only its own species. It eats both insects and fruit, the former caught on the wing (hence the common name). The nest is placed at the end of a burrow dug into a bank or in a hole in a wall or similar structure.

SWALLOW-TANAGER
(*Tersina viridis*) Pl.24

Description: 5½–5¾. Known only from eastern Panama. Broad flat bill. Male *mostly turquoise* with *black mask and throat;* wings and tail black, broadly margined with blue; flanks barred with black, center of belly white. Female *mostly bright grass green* with grayish brown face and throat; wings and tail blackish, broadly margined with green; barring on flanks and center of lower belly yellow.

Similar species: Not likely to be confused. Male might carelessly be mistaken for a male Blue Cotinga, female for a green tanager.

Status and distribution: Apparently rare, with a few records from hill country of eastern Darién (Cana, Tapalisa), and a recent report of 11 in hills north of El Llano, eastern Panama province, on September 3, 1973 (N. G. Smith). Little known in Panama.

Habits: Favors clearings and lighter woodland. Notably gregarious. Regularly captures insects on the wing.

Range: Eastern Panama to northern Bolivia, Paraguay, northeastern Argentina, and southeastern Brazil.

SWALLOW-TANAGER (male)

TANAGERS: Thraupidae (54)

The tanagers are a large group of birds found only in the New World. The great majority of species are found in the tropics, with only four mainly migratory species having spread as far north as the United States to breed. Many tanagers are exceptionally attractive birds, exhibiting a great variety of bright colors and striking contrasts; a few are duller, notably the genera *Chlorospingus* and (in South America) *Hemispingus.* Most tanagers are arboreal birds, and many occur in mixed flocks; several inhabit forest and woodland undergrowth, while one species, the thrush-tanager, is partly terrestrial. In most tanagers song is poorly developed, chief exceptions in Panama being the various *Piranga* sp., the ant-tanagers, and the thrush-tanager. In Panama the two most important subgroups are the euphonias and allied chlorophonia, small chunky birds with short tails and stubby bills, and the genus *Tangara,* containing the typical multi-colored tanagers, most diverse in the Andes but well represented in Panama, especially in foothill areas. Tanagers as a whole eat mostly fruit, with the euphonias specializing in mistletoe (though they eat other fruit as well); most also take some insects, especially to feed their young. The nests of most known species (many are unrecorded) are open cups placed in bushes or trees; euphonias and chlorophonias, however, build covered nests with a side entrance, generally in a niche or hole, while the Palm Tanager constructs its nest in a cranny of some type.

GOLDEN-BROWED CHLOROPHONIA
(*Chlorophonia callophrys*) Pl.27

Description: 5¼. Found only in western highlands. Chunky, like a euphonia, but larger; short bill and tail. Male *mostly bright green above* with light blue crown and nape and *yellow forehead and eyestripe; throat bright green bordered below by a thin black line; remaining underparts bright yellow*. Female and immature male similar in pattern but duller with less blue on head and no black line across chest.

Similar species: See Green Shrike-Vireo of lowlands.

Status and distribution: Uncommon in clearings and forest borders in highlands of Chiriquí and Veraguas, mostly above 5000 feet in Chiriquí, lower (to about 2500 feet) in Veraguas.

Habits: Usually remains well up in trees, often in small groups. The brilliant adult males are greatly outnumbered by females and young males. Has a characteristic nasal call, to some suggestive of the yapping of a small dog, *enk-enk-enk-enk*.

Range: Costa Rica and western Panama.

Note: By some authors considered conspecific with *C. occipitalis* (Blue-crowned Chlorophonia) of southeastern Mexico to Nicaragua. Some feel the genera *Chlorophonia* and *Euphonia* may not belong in the Thraupidae.

BLUE-HOODED EUPHONIA
(*Euphonia elegantissima*) Pl.27

Description: 4½. Found only in western highlands. Male mostly glossy steel blue above with *contrasting bright turquoise crown and hindneck* and chestnut forehead; throat black, remaining underparts orange-tawny. Female similar in general pattern and *with turquoise crown and hindneck;* upperparts bright olive green instead of steel blue; throat buffyish, remaining underparts yellowish olive green.

Similar species: No other Panama euphonia has a light blue crown and nape.

Status and distribution: Uncommon to locally fairly common in clearings with scattered trees and woodland borders in lower highlands of Chiriquí and Veraguas, mostly 3500–5000 feet, less numerous up to about 6500 feet.

Habits: Like other euphonias usually in small groups. Rather quiet, but sometimes gives a single high *chup*, a little reminiscent of a House Sparrow (*Passer domesticus*).

Range: Mexico to western Panama.

Note: By some authors considered conspecific with *E. musica* (Antillean Euphonia) of West Indies and *E. cyanocephala* (Golden-rumped Euphonia) of South America. If so, specific name *E. musica* has precedence.

ORANGE-BELLIED EUPHONIA
(*Euphonia xanthogaster*)

Description: 4¼. Found only in Darién. Male has standard euphonia pattern: yellow crown and steel blue upperparts; throat and upper chest blue-black, *remaining underparts orange-yellow*. Female olive above; *mostly buffy-gray below,* with sides and flanks yellowish.

Similar species: Male very like male Yellow-crowned Euphonia (not known to occur together) but more orange-yellow below, with white on inner webs of tail feathers (sometimes visible in flight—not present in Yellow-crowned); females of the two species are very different. Female resembles female Tawny-capped Euphonia but has *yellowish forecrown* (not a prominent patch of rufous).

Status and distribution: Known only from forest and forest borders in foothills (2000–3000 feet) of eastern Darién (Cerro Sapo, Cana, Cerro Quía).

Range: Eastern Panama to Guyana, Amazonian Brazil, and Bolivia.

TAWNY-CAPPED EUPHONIA
(*Euphonia anneae*) Pl.27

Description: 4¼. Male has *distinctive rich tawny brown cap;* remaining upperparts, throat, and chest steel blue; lower underparts yellow to tawny yellow, under tail-coverts white. Female has *rufous forecrown,* otherwise greenish olive above; *pale gray below* washed with yellowish olive on sides.

Similar species: Female Fulvous-vented,

Spot-crowned, and Olive-backed Euphonias all also have rufous forecrowns, but are yellowish below (not gray) with tawny on lower belly. No other male Panama euphonia has a wholly tawny cap.

Status and distribution: Uncommon to fairly common in second-growth woodland and forest borders in foothills on both slopes, mostly 2000–4000 feet, locally lower and higher. In central Panama most easily seen on Cerro Campana.

Habits: Usually forages within twenty feet of the ground, in pairs or small groups. Has rather harsh conversational notes, but usually silent.

Range: Costa Rica to extreme northwestern Colombia.

WHITE-VENTED EUPHONIA

(*Euphonia minuta*) Pl.27

Description: 3¾. Male has typical euphonia pattern: steel blue upperparts with yellow forecrown; throat and chest steel blue, lower underparts yellow, but with *white lower belly and under tail-coverts.* Female olive above; throat grayish, breast olive yellow, and *belly white.*

Similar species: Male is only male Panama euphonia with white on underparts. Female's white belly sets it apart from other female euphonias except for female Yellow-throated (only in western Chiriquí), but White-vented is yellower below with white restricted to belly (Yellow-throated has most of underparts grayish white, yellowish only on sides).

Status and distribution: Uncommon to locally fairly common in forest and forest borders in lowlands and foothills on entire Caribbean slope; on Pacific slope known from an old specimen taken in lowlands of western Chiriquí (Bugaba), Veraguas foothills (above Santa Fé; Ridgely and G. Stiles), and from eastern Panama province (Cerro Azul/Jefe area) east locally through Darién. Most numerous in foothills; many lowland birds may be post-breeding wanderers, though they are regular in small numbers on Pipeline Road.

Habits: Usually seen high in trees, often accompanying mixed flocks of other frugivorous birds. The calls are much like those of other euphonias, especially that of the Yellow-crowned, *beem.*

Range: Southeastern Mexico to northern Bolivia and Amazonian Brazil.

YELLOW-CROWNED EUPHONIA

(*Euphonia luteicapilla*) Pl.27

Description: 3¾. Male has *entire cap yellow;* upperparts otherwise steel blue; throat and chest steel blue, lower underparts yellow *with no white or tawny.* Female yellowish olive above, *uniform dull yellow below.*

Similar species: Male Spot-crowned Euphonia of Chiriquí has only forehead (not whole cap) yellow, and black (not steel blue) throat and chest. Otherwise male Yellow-crown is only dark-throated male euphonia with all yellow underparts. Female resembles female Thick-billed Euphonia but is more uniform yellow below with typical euphonia bill (not slightly thicker); this hard to see in the field, however. In Darién see also Orange-bellied Euphonia.

Status and distribution: Common in dry scrubby and shrubby areas, savannas, and extensive clearings in lowlands on Pacific slope east at least to western Darién (Santa Fé, Yaviza), ranging up in foothills to about 3000 feet in cleared areas of Chiriquí and Veraguas; on Caribbean slope occurs in small numbers in clearings in lowlands of Bocas del Toro and Canal Zone area.

Habits: Typically forages in small flocks of its own species. Calls almost incessantly, a usually double or triple-noted high-pitched *beem-beem,* from which the species' local name "Bim-bim" is derived. Also has a thin, wiry song. A popular cagebird.

Range: Nicaragua to eastern Panama.

FULVOUS-VENTED EUPHONIA

(*Euphonia fulvicrissa*) Pl.27

Description: 4. Male has yellow forecrown and steel blue upperparts, throat, and chest; lower underparts yellow with *tawny under tail-coverts and usually some tawny on center of lower belly.* Female olive above with rufous forecrown; yellowish olive below with *tawny lower belly.*

Similar species: No other male euphonia with standard pattern has tawny on lower belly. Female probably indistinguishable in the field from female Spot-crowned Euphonia of Chiriquí. Female also resembles both sexes of Olive-backed Euphonia.

Status and distribution: Common in shrubby growth and lower trees in clearings and forest borders in lowlands on both slopes from central Panama eastward, ranging up into foothills on Cerro Campana and in Cerro Azul/Jefe area. Also known from three old specimens taken in western Chiriquí, but no modern records.

Habits: Usually in small groups, often feeding at around eye-level (other Canal Zone euphonias are generally higher up). The usual call is a chattering *treah-treah,* and locally called "Ren-ren" on account of this frequently given note.
Range: Central (western?) Panama to northwestern Ecuador.

OLIVE-BACKED EUPHONIA
(*Euphonia gouldi*) Pl.27

Description: 3¾. Found only in western Caribbean lowlands. Male unlike any other male Panamanian euphonia, and looks "female-plumaged." *Glossy olive green above* (sometimes glossed bluish) with *yellow forehead;* yellowish olive green below with *tawny on center of breast and belly.* Female similar but less glossy, with chestnut forehead and entire underparts yellowish olive, tawny only on under tail-coverts.
Similar species: Male somewhat like female Spot-crowned and Fulvous-vented Euphonias except for *yellow* forehead. Female very like female Fulvous-vented Euphonia (apparently not found together) except that tawny is restricted to under tail-coverts (not on lower belly).
Status and distribution: Common in forest clearings and borders in lowlands on Caribbean slope in Bocas del Toro and western Veraguas.
Habits: Similar to Fulvous-vented Euphonia. The calls are also similar, *treeuh-treah;* it is also known to Panamanians as "Ren-ren."
Range: Southeastern Mexico to Caribbean western Panama.

SPOT-CROWNED EUPHONIA
(*Euphonia imitans*) Pl.27

Description: 4. Found only in Chiriquí. Male has *yellow forecrown* (to just behind eye) *with a few dusky spots;* otherwise steel blue above; *throat and upper chest black,* remaining underparts yellow. Female olive green above with rufous forecrown; mostly yellowish olive below, with *center of breast and belly tawny.*
Similar species: Male's crown spots are visible only at close range, and are not a good field character. It most resembles male Yellow-crowned Euphonia but has yellow only on forecrown (not entire cap) and black throat and chest (not steel blue). Male White-vented Euphonia has white lower belly and vent (not uniform yellow). Female very like female Fulvous-vented Euphonia and probably not safe to distinguish in the field; note Spot-crown's larger patch of rufous on forecrown and more tawny on lower underparts.
Status and distribution: Rare in forest and forest borders in lowlands and foothills of western Chiriquí.
Habits: Little known in Panama. Voice and behavior much like the better known Fulvous-vented and Olive-backed Euphonias (it has been suggested that they are not specifically distinct).
Range: Southwestern Costa Rica and Pacific western Panama.

THICK-BILLED EUPHONIA
(*Euphonia laniirostris*) Pl.27

Description: 4. Has thicker bill than most euphonias, but this is difficult to see in the field. Male has yellow forecrown and steel blue upperparts; *entire underparts, including throat, yellow.* Female olive above; yellow below with *olive wash on breast.* Immature males with black areas but otherwise like females are often seen.
Similar species: In most of Panama, male is the only adult male euphonia with all yellow underparts; in western Chiriquí, see Yellow-throated Euphonia. Female resembles female Yellow-crowned Euphonia, but note latter's uniform yellow underparts (no olive on breast).
Status and distribution: Common and widespread in clearings, gardens, second-growth woodland, and forest borders in more humid lowlands on both slopes, ranging well up into foothills where suitable broken forest habitat occurs, in Chiriquí to about 4000 feet.
Habits: As with other euphonias often in small groups, feeding especially on mistletoe. Generally the most numerous and frequently encountered euphonia in humid lowland areas. Usual calls are a sweet *chweet,* a *wheep,* and a clear *peet* or *peet-peet* much like common note of Yellow-crowned Euphonia. According to E. S. Morton, it imitates the calls of other birds. All euphonias are popular cagebirds, but this is the favorite.
Range: Costa Rica to Bolivia and central Brazil.

YELLOW-THROATED EUPHONIA
(*Euphonia hirundinacea*) Pl.27

Description: 4. Found only in western Chiriquí. Thick bill as in previous species. Male very like male Thick-billed Euphonia but with *smaller yellow patch on forecrown (extending back only to eye)*; like that species, has *entirely yellow underparts.* Female, however, is quite different: olive green above, *grayish white below,* with yellowish restricted to sides.

Similar species: Female Thick-billed Euphonia has mostly dull yellow underparts (no whitish). See also female White-vented Euphonia.

Status and distribution: Rare in partly cleared areas and woodland borders in foothills of western Chiriquí (3000–4000 feet). Very few records and little known in Panama, though it is a common Middle American species. Outnumbered even where it does occur in Panama by the Thick-billed Euphonia.

Range: Eastern Mexico to Pacific western Panama.

Note: Formerly called *Euphonia lauta.*

EMERALD TANAGER
(*Tangara florida*) Pl.27

Description: 5¼. *Mostly golden emerald green,* male with yellow nape; back streaked with black and with black spot in front of eye and black patch on ear-coverts; lower belly yellow.

Similar species: No other Panama tanager is so predominantly *bright* green.

Status and distribution: Uncommon to locally fairly common in humid forest and forest borders in foothills on entire Caribbean slope, mostly 1000–3000 feet; on Pacific slope found in foothills from eastern Panama province (Cerro Azul/Jefe area) east through Darién. In central Panama most easily seen along road near Cerro Jefe.

Habits: Usually seen in small numbers, feeding quite high in the trees, generally accompanying large mixed flocks of other frugivorous birds.

Range: Costa Rica to western Colombia.

SPECKLED TANAGER
(*Tangara guttata*) Pl.27

Description: 5¼. Unmistakable; no other Panamanian tanager is *conspicuously spotted above and below.* Bright yellowish green above spotted with black; yellow superciliary; wings blackish edged with blue; white below, profusely spotted with black, flanks tinged with greenish.

Status and distribution: Fairly common but somewhat local in humid forest and forest borders in foothills on entire Caribbean slope (1000–3000 feet); on Pacific slope known from a few old specimens from the Chiriquí highlands (no recent records) and from eastern Panama province (Cerro Azul/Jefe area) east through Darién. Easily found along road beyond Goofy Lake toward Cerro Jefe.

Habits: Much like the Emerald Tanager and often found with it.

Range: Costa Rica to Venezuela and extreme northern Brazil.

SILVER-THROATED TANAGER
(*Tangara icterocephala*) Pl.27

Description: 5¼. *Bright golden yellow above and below,* streaked with black on back, and wings broadly edged with green; *throat grayish silvery white.* Female similar but duller; immature even dingier, but already showing adult's pattern.

Similar species: The pretty male is easily identified; duller female and immature may possibly be confused with female of smaller Black-and-yellow Tanager, but are streaked above and always show at least a vaguely whitish throat.

Status and distribution: Common in forest and forest borders in foothills and highlands on both slopes from 2000 to 6000 feet; occasionally as high as 7500 feet in Chiriquí; one record from lowlands of western Bocas del Toro, a specimen taken at Almirante, Bocas del Toro, on November 14, 1962 (R. Hinds), doubtless a post-breeding wanderer down the mountains.

Habits: Particularly numerous on Cerro Campana; there it is often one of the most common birds present, sometimes occurring in large flocks of several dozen or more individuals. Elsewhere it is less dominant but still widespread, usually accompanying mixed flocks of other tanagers, honeycreepers, etc. Its call is a characteristically buzzy *bzeet,* rather different from its congeners.

Range: Costa Rica to northwestern Ecuador.

GOLDEN-HOODED (GOLDEN-MASKED) TANAGER
(*Tangara larvata*) Pl.27

Description: 5. *Head mostly golden buff with black facial mask bordered with blue;* back and wings black, latter edged with blue; lower back and rump turquoise; *chest and breast black,* center of belly white, *sides and flanks turquoise.* Immature similar but duller with head light bluish green instead of buff.

Similar species: In Darién see Gray-and-gold Tanager.

Status and distribution: Common in clearings, second-growth woodland, and forest borders in lowlands and foothills on entire Caribbean slope; quite common in Chiriquí (where ranges up to about 5000 feet) and in foothills on entire Pacific slope, also in lowlands from eastern Panama province (Tocumen, Bayano River) east through Darién.

Habits: Usually found in small groups, sometimes among mixed flocks of frugivorous birds. Frequent calls are a single or doubled *tssp* and a repeated *tsit-tsit-tsit-tsit* often given in flight as it moves from tree to tree.

Range: Southeastern Mexico to western Ecuador.

Note: By some authors considered conspecific with *T. nigrocincta* (Masked Tanager) of South America east of the Andes.

GRAY-AND-GOLD TANAGER

(*Tangara palmeri*) Pl.28

Description: 5¾. Found only in eastern Darién. Cap bluish gray, mask black, *back pale golden green;* wings and tail black broadly edged with gray; *throat, sides of head, and upper chest white;* sides of chest black, *band of yellow across breast;* center of belly white, sides and flanks pale gray. Extent and intensity of the green and yellow apparently somewhat variable.

Similar species: See Golden-hooded Tanager.

Status and distribution: Known only from humid forest and forest borders in eastern Darién (Cerro Sapo, Cerro Quía, and Cerro Tacarcuna); apparently rare.

Habits: In western Colombia observed to be a typical *Tangara* tanager, usually associating with flocks of other tanagers, often in pairs (G. Tudor).

Range: Eastern Panama to northwestern Ecuador.

PLAIN-COLORED TANAGER

(*Tangara inornata*) Pl.27

Description: 4¾. Unusual among the colorful and highly patterned *Tangara* tanagers is this dull-plumaged species. *Leaden gray above* with black stripe through eyes; wings and tail black with usually concealed blue lesser wing-coverts; *paler gray below,* fading to white on lower belly.

Similar species: Sulphur-rumped Tanager is also mostly gray with blackish wings and tail but is larger, shows a tuft of white feathers on the sides, and has a yellow rump. The larger Blue-gray and Palm Tanagers can look gray when seen against the light.

Status and distribution: Common in clearings, second-growth woodland, and forest borders in lowlands on entire Caribbean slope; on Pacific slope found from western Panama province (around Cerro Campana) east through Darién; ranges up in reduced numbers into the foothills.

Habits: Seems almost always to occur in groups of four to six individuals, frequently independent of other species. Often feeds in *Cecropia* trees.

Range: Costa Rica to northern Colombia.

BAY-HEADED TANAGER

(*Tangara gyrola*) Pl.27

Description: 5. *Head bright reddish chestnut* with narrow yellow collar on hindneck (sometimes not apparent); most of upperparts bright grass green, rump blue; *most of underparts turquoise,* sides green. Immature duller.

Similar species: See Rufous-winged Tanager.

Status and distribution: Common in forest and forest borders in foothills and lower highlands on both slopes, mostly 2000–5000 feet; ranges in smaller numbers to lowlands in Chiriquí and in Canal Zone and vicinity (where most numerous in Pipeline Road area). Common on Cerro Campana and in Cerro Azul/Jefe area.

Habits: A typical *Tangara* tanager, gregarious, often found among mixed flocks of frugivorous birds. Often one of the most numerous of the Cerro Azul/Jefe area's many tanagers.

Range: Costa Rica to northern Bolivia and Amazonian Brazil.

RUFOUS-WINGED TANAGER

(*Tangara lavinia*) Pl.27

Description: 5. Male has *rich reddish chestnut head* with *broad yellow collar on hindneck;* otherwise bright grass green above, with *primaries prominently edged with rufous; mostly grass green below,* with turquoise stripe down center of breast and belly. Female much duller, lacking (or with just a trace of) reddish head, and with less rufous on wings.

Similar species: The beautiful male is unmistakable, but some females have only a trace of rufous on wings and virtually no chestnut on head, and can be easily passed over. These dull birds most resemble an immature Bay-headed Tanager, but the

Bay-head never shows any rufous on wings (a little is almost always present in Rufous-wing) and usually has some blue on underparts.

Status and distribution: Uncommon and rather local in humid forest and forest borders on Caribbean slope, mostly in foothills (1000–3000 feet); on Pacific slope known from eastern Panama province (Cerro Azul/Jefe area) and foothills of eastern Darién. One specimen taken on Las Cruces Trail in what is now Madden Forest, Canal Zone on August 8, 1931, by R. R. Benson, but no recent reports from Zone. In central Panama, most easily seen on Cerro Santa Rita and in the Cerro Jefe area.

Habits: Very similar to Bay-headed Tanager and often occurs with it, but seems always to be outnumbered by it.

Range: Guatemala to northwestern Ecuador.

SPANGLE-CHEEKED TANAGER
(*Tangara dowii*) Pl.27

Description: 5. Found only in western highlands. *Mostly black above and on throat and chest; spangled on head and especially on ear-coverts with pale green* and with rusty patch on nape, *spangled on chest with buff;* wings edged with blue, rump opalescent green or blue; *lower underparts cinnamon.*

Status and distribution: Rare to locally uncommon in forest and forest borders in highlands of Bocas del Toro, Chiriquí, and Veraguas, mostly 4500–7000 feet.

Habits: Similar to other *Tangara* tanagers, usually in pairs and small groups, often associating with flocks of other highland frugivorous birds.

Range: Costa Rica and western Panama.

GREEN-NAPED TANAGER
(*Tangara fucosa*) Pl.28

Description: 5. Found only in Darién highlands. Closely resembles Spangle-cheeked Tanager but has *pale green* (not rusty) *patch on nape,* and *blue* (not buff) *spangling on chest.*

Similar species: See Spangle-cheeked Tanager of western highlands.

Status and distribution: Known only from highlands of eastern Darién (Cerro Pirre, Cerro Malí). Very little known, with an extremely limited range.

Range: Eastern Panama (probably occurs in adjacent Colombia but not yet recorded).

Note: By some considered a race of *T. dowii* (Spangle-cheeked Tanager).

BLUE-AND-GOLD TANAGER
(*Bangsia arcaei*) Pl.28

Description: 6. *Iris red. Indigo blue above,* brightest on head; wings and tail blackish edged with blue; throat blackish blue; *remaining underparts rich yellow,* mottled dusky on sides.

Similar species: No other Panama tanager (other than the much smaller euphonias) is blue above and yellow below.

Status and distribution: A very local bird of humid forest and forest borders. Recorded from foothills of Veraguas on both slopes, and from the Cerro Jefe area in eastern Panama province. Common near Continental Divide above Santa Fé, Veraguas, on January 4, 1974 (Ridgely and G. Stiles). Status in the Cerro Jefe area unclear, the species being either rare or irregular there (no specimens) (E. S. Morton and P. A. Buckley, N. G. Smith, D. Hill).

Habits: Little known in Panama. Generally seen in pairs or small groups, often with flocks of other tanagers, usually rather high in trees. Rather heavy-bodied and inactive, "suggesting an over-sized red-eyed euphonia" (Slud).

Range: Costa Rica to central Panama.

Note: Sometimes placed in the genus *Buthraupis.*

BLUE-GRAY TANAGER
(*Thraupis episcopus*) Pl.28

Description: 6. *Entirely pale grayish blue,* brightest on wings and tail. In some lights can look peculiarly greenish or grayish.

Similar species: Similar in size, shape, and actions to the Palm Tanager, and often found with it. The olive Palm Tanager can always be known by the black terminal half of its wing. See also Plain-colored Tanager.

Status and distribution: Abundant in gardens, shrubby clearings, second-growth woodland, and borders virtually throughout, up to around 6000 feet in western highlands; common also on Pearl Islands, Coiba Island, and other islands off Pacific and Caribbean coasts.

Habits: One of the most familiar Panama birds. Noisy and active, often becoming very tame around habitations. Its song is an unpatterned series of squeaky notes.

Range: Eastern Mexico to the Guianas, Brazil, and northern Bolivia; southern Florida (recently introduced).

Note: Formerly called *T. virens.*

PALM TANAGER
(*Thraupis palmarum*) Pl.28

Description: 6. *Generally grayish olive,* with glossy violaceous overtones in some lights; forehead and lower underparts more yellowish olive; *terminal half* (flight feathers) *of closed wing black.*

Similar species: Blue-gray Tanager normally looks blue; if not, Palm Tanager can always be known by its black wing. Plain-colored Tanager is smaller, leaden gray (not olive), and entire wing is blackish.

Status and distribution: Common in gardens, shrubby clearings, and woodland and forest borders in more humid lowlands, more numerous on Caribbean slope; absent from drier areas in Pacific lowlands from southern Veraguas to western Panama province; ranges up in foothills to about 4000 feet in Chiriquí.

Habits: Generally associates with the usually more numerous Blue-gray Tanager. Most frequent near habitations, where it often forages under eaves and on screens; also frequently feeds in palms.

Range: Nicaragua to Bolivia, Paraguay, and southeastern Brazil.

CRIMSON-BACKED TANAGER
(*Ramphocelus dimidiatus*) Pl.28

Description: 6¼. In male, *most of lower mandible is silvery.* Male has head, upper back, throat, and chest dark crimson maroon, *becoming blood red on lower back, rump, breast, and belly;* wings and tail black. Female similar but duller, lacking the silvery lower mandible; brownish red where male is crimson maroon, but retains *red rump and belly.*

Similar species: Males of both ant-tanagers are largely brownish red and somewhat resemble female Crimson-back, but lack red rump and belly.

Status and distribution: Common in gardens, scrub, shrubby areas, and clearings in lowlands on both slopes (more common on Pacific) except in Bocas del Toro; ranges up in cleared areas through foothills, rarely to 5400 feet in highlands of Chiriquí; common also on Coiba Island and the Pearl Islands.

Habits: Conspicuous and noisy, often trooping about in groups of three to six individuals, usually with only one fully adult male per group.

Range: Western Panama to Colombia and western Venezuela.

SCARLET-RUMPED TANAGER
(*Ramphocelus passerinii*) Pl.28

Description: 6¼. Found only in west. Male unmistakable, *velvety black* with *brilliant scarlet lower back and rump;* bill pale bluish with black tip. Chiriquí female (*costaricensis*) mostly brownish above, becoming yellowish olive on back and *orange on rump;* throat brownish, *chest orange,* lower underparts yellowish olive. Bocas del Toro female (nominate *passerinii*) duller, with rump dull yellow and chest usually yellowish olive like rest of lower underparts (occasionally with a trace of orange).

Similar species: Female resembles female Yellow-rumped Tanager but is more olive below (Yellow-rumped is entirely lemon yellow below), and has orange on rump.

Status and distribution: Common in gardens and shrubby areas, often near water, in lowlands of Bocas del Toro and western Chiriquí; in Chiriquí ranges up to just over 4000 feet in suitable cleared habitat (readily seen around Volcán).

Habits: Much like Crimson-backed Tanager. Males often perch conspicuously in the open and puff out their vivid scarlet rumps. Males from Chiriquí have a variable but rather pretty song, while Bocas del Toro birds sing less often and less forcefully (A. Skutch).

Range: Southeastern Mexico to western Panama.

YELLOW-RUMPED TANAGER
(*Ramphocelus icteronotus*) Pl.28

Description: 6½. Male unmistakable, *velvety black* with *bright yellow lower back and rump;* bill pale bluish with black tip. Female grayish brown above with *yellow lower back and rump;* throat whitish, *remaining underparts lemon yellow.*

Similar species: Despite their confusingly similar common names, the Sulphur-rumped Tanager is rather different, being mostly gray. See female Scarlet-rumped Tanager.

Status and distribution: Common and conspicuous in shrubby areas, usually near water, in lowlands on Caribbean slope from eastern Bocas del Toro east through San Blas; on Pacific slope at El Valle and from Canal Zone area (where rare, perhaps only seasonal) east through eastern Panama province and Darién. Small area of overlap with Scarlet-rumped Tanager in eastern Bocas del Toro at Cricamola.

Habits: Found in pairs and small groups,

usually near ground. Less often in gardens than Scarlet-rumped Tanager.
Range: Western Panama to western Ecuador.

CRIMSON-COLLARED TANAGER
(*Phlogothraupis sanguinolenta*) Pl.28

Description: 6½. Known only from western Panama. Unmistakable. Sexes similar. Bill pale bluish. Mostly black, with *blood red hindcrown, neck, and chest* (forming the "collar"); small rump patch also red. Immature duller, the black duskier, the red more brownish.
Similar species: The distinctive pattern of the immature, though less clear than in adults, should preclude confusion.
Status and distribution: Local on western Caribbean slope; recorded from western Bocas del Toro lowlands, Veraguas foothills on Pacific slope above Santa Fé (seen and collected, January 4–5, 1974; Ridgely and G. Stiles), and from Caribbean slope north of Cerro Campana (seen along Río Trinidad in March 1966; N. G. Smith).
Habits: Favors shrubby clearings, second-growth woodland, and forest borders, usually foraging within twenty feet of the ground. Generally found singly or in pairs, unlike *Ramphocelus* tanagers.
Range: Southeastern Mexico to central Panama.
Note: Some authors merge this genus into *Ramphocelus,* in which case the specific name would become *R. sanguinolentus.*

HEPATIC TANAGER
(*Piranga flava*) Pl.28

Description: 7¼. *Blackish bill in both sexes.* Male *all brick red,* somewhat brighter below. Female dusky olive above, *bright yellowish olive green below,* sometimes with a tinge of orange on throat and upper chest. Does not show conspicuous dark ear-patch of United States birds.
Similar species: The dark bill distinguishes both sexes from the otherwise rather similar Summer Tanager (with pale bill). Carmiol's Tanager (also with blackish bill) resembles female Hepatic, but is more uniform and darker olive, especially below; the two also differ characteristically in habits.
Status and distribution: Locally fairly common in open woodland and forest borders in foothills on both slopes, mostly 2000–4000 feet. Easily seen in the Cerro Azul/Jefe area and on Cerro Campana.
Habits: Generally found singly or in pairs, usually independent of mixed flocks, feeding rather high in trees, though sometimes comes lower. The distinctive call is a *chup-chitup* or a single *chup,* the song a series of phrases rising and falling in pitch.
Range: Southwestern United States to northern Argentina and Uruguay.

SUMMER TANAGER
(*Piranga rubra*)

Description: 7. *Bill whitish in male, pale yellowish in female.* Adult male *all rose red,* duskier on wings and tail. Female olive above with duskier wings and tail; *deep yellow below.* Immature male resembles female but browner; molting male shows patches of rose red.
Similar species: Hepatic Tanager has dark bill. Female resembles female Scarlet Tanager but is brighter yellow below and lacks Scarlet's blackish wings.
Status and distribution: Very common transient and winter resident (mid-September–late April) throughout, most numerous in lowlands, especially in winter.
Habits: Widespread in gardens, shrubby areas, second-growth woodland, and borders. The distinctive call is often heard, a staccatto *pitichuck* or *pi-tuck.*
Range: Breeds from central United States to northern Mexico; winters from Mexico to northern Bolivia and Amazonian Brazil (accidentally to Chile).

SCARLET TANAGER
(*Piranga olivacea*)

Description: 6¾. Breeding plumage males unmistakable, but seen only on spring migration: *intense scarlet with jet black wings and tail.* Nonbreeding male olive green above with *black wings and tail;* yellowish below. Molting spring male shows scattered splotches of scarlet. Female resembles nonbreeding male but wings not as black. Immature male like female but with black wing-coverts.
Similar species: Female resembles female Summer Tanager but has darker wings and is not as bright yellow below (never orangey).
Status and distribution: Uncommon fall and spring transient throughout (early October–mid-November; April) and rare winter resident in lowlands.
Habits: Favors second-growth woodland and forest borders, not as open terrain as the much more numerous Summer Tanager. The distinctive call, heard regularly, is a throaty *chip-burr.*
Range: Breeds in eastern North America; winters from Panama through western South America to northern Bolivia.

WESTERN TANAGER
(*Piranga ludoviciana*)

Description: 6½. Only one record. *Whitish to yellowish bill.* Male has *red head* merging into yellow of hindneck and throat; *back black,* rump yellow; wings and tail black with whitish wing-bars; most of underparts yellow. In nonbreeding plumage, red on head is reduced, black back is mottled. Female greenish olive above with white or pale yellowish wing-bars; yellowish below.

Similar species: Male closely resembles immature male Flame-colored Tanager but is slightly smaller with more or less black back and no white tips to tail. Female and immature are also similar to female Flame-colored but lack that species' dusky back streaking and white tips to tail. Female White-winged Tanager is smaller, brighter yellow below, with dark bill.

Status and distribution: Only record is a bird taken near Volcán in highlands of western Chiriquí on February 15, 1960. Possibly overlooked due to close similarity to the common Flame-colored Tanager.

Range: Breeds in western North America; winters from Mexico to Costa Rica, casually to western Panama.

FLAME-COLORED (STRIPE-BACKED) TANAGER
(*Piranga bidentata*) Pl.28

Description: 7. Known only from western Chiriquí highlands. Bill whitish. Male *orange-red,* back duller *streaked with dusky;* wings dusky with two white wing-bars; tail dusky, *tipped white.* Female olive above, *back streaked with dusky;* dull yellowish below; wings and tail as in male. Young male resembles female but is brighter; immature male is often rather orange, and usually becomes colored first on head.

Similar species: White-winged Tanager is smaller, rosier red, and lacks back streaking and white tail-tips. See also the very rare Western Tanager.

Status and distribution: Common in forest, forest borders, and clearings in highlands of western Chiriquí, mostly above 4000 feet.

Habits: Usually remains quite high in trees. The song is a rich but somewhat throaty caroling, reminiscent of a Scarlet or Western Tanager; the call is a loud harsh *prreck.*

Range: Northern Mexico to western Panama.

WHITE-WINGED TANAGER
(*Piranga leucoptera*) Pl.28

Description: 5½. Found only in western highlands. Bill dark. Male *bright rose red* with *black through eyes;* wings and tail black, *wings with two broad white wing-bars.* Female yellowish olive above with the same *broad white wing-bars; bright yellow below.* Immature male more orange than adult male.

Similar species: Both sexes can be distinguished from Flame-colored Tanager by their smaller size, unstreaked back, and tail without white tips; males are rosier red. See also Western Tanager.

Status and distribution: Fairly common in forest and forest borders in highlands of Chiriquí and Veraguas, mostly 3000–6000 feet.

Habits: Usually forages well up in trees, generally accompanying mixed foraging flocks of other tanagers, warblers, Furnariids, etc. The call is a distinctive *tsupeét* or *wheet, tsupeét;* it apparently has no real song.

Range: Eastern Mexico to western Panama; Colombia and Venezuela to northern Bolivia.

CARMIOL'S (OLIVE) TANAGER
(*Chlorothraupis carmioli*) Pl.28

Description: 6¾. Bill blackish. *Generally olive green,* somewhat yellower below, especially on throat.

Similar species: Like female Hepatic Tanager but darker olive green overall, especially below. Female Red-crowned Ant-Tanager is olive brown above (not olive green) and has tawny yellow crown patch. Female Red-throated Ant-Tanager is even browner above, with more orange-yellow throat that contrasts with rest of underparts. Ant-tanagers are almost always in pairs or small groups, very rarely alone, so there is usually a male present to confirm their identification.

Status and distribution: Fairly common to locally common in undergrowth of humid forest and forest borders in foothills on entire Caribbean slope; on Pacific slope known from eastern Panama province (Cerro Azul/Jefe area) east into Darién; recorded mostly 1000–4000 feet. Only recently found in Canal Zone, where now known to be a fairly common resident well out on Pipeline Road. One of the most numerous species along the road past Goofy Lake in the Cerro Jefe area and beyond.

Habits: Typically troops about in large bands of up to several dozen individuals. Their incessant calling brings to mind the chattering of Clay-colored Robins.
Range: Nicaragua to northern Bolivia.

LEMON-BROWED TANAGER
(*Chlorothraupis olivacea*) Pl.28

Description: 6½. Found only in eastern Darién. Very like Carmiol's Tanager but darker olive with *conspicuous yellow lores and eye-ring.*
Similar species: See Carmiol's Tanager.
Status and distribution: Known only from forest in lowlands and foothills (to 3600 feet) of eastern Darién (Cerro Sapo, Jaqué, Cerro Quía, Cituro).
Habits: Similar to Carmiol's Tanager.
Range: Eastern Panama to northwestern Ecuador.
Note: By some authors treated as a race of *C. carmioli* (Carmiol's Tanager), and if so the entire complex would be called Olive Tanager.

RED-CROWNED ANT-TANAGER
(*Habia rubica*) Pl.28

Description: 7. Bill blackish. Male *mostly brownish red,* paler below and somewhat brighter on throat; *crown scarlet bordered by distinct narrow black line.* Female olive brown above with *tawny yellow crown* bordered narrowly with black; yellowish olive below, the throat tawny yellowish.
Similar species: Closely resembles Red-throated Ant-Tanager and often confused with it. Male Red-crowns are duller red, more brownish, and usually lack male Red-throat's red throat; Red-throat's red crown is not as conspicuous nor is it bordered with black. Female Red-crowns are more olive above (not so brown), have a distinct tawny yellow crown (lacking in Red-throat), and lack Red-throat's prominent yellow throat. See also Carmiol's and Hepatic Tanagers.
Status and distribution: Uncommon to locally fairly common in undergrowth of second-growth woodland and forest in lowlands and foothills on Pacific slope, ranging up to around 4000 feet in Chiriquí. Decidedly scarce and local in the Canal Zone, where known from the southwestern sector and the Chiva Chiva area; also spills over in small numbers onto Caribbean slope in middle Chagres River valley (Madden Forest, Madden Dam area, and around Summit Gardens). Most numerous in western Panama.
Habits: Tends to forage somewhat higher above ground than Red-throated and not to travel in as large groups. The usual call is a rapid chatter of staccatto notes, *chit chit chit . . . ,* quite unlike Red-throat's harsh, tearing scolds.
Range: Central Mexico to Bolivia, northeastern Argentina, and southeastern Brazil.

RED-THROATED (DUSKY-TAILED) ANT-TANAGER
(*Habia fuscicauda*) Pl.28

Description: 7½. Bill blackish. Male *mostly dull carmine,* with narrow red crown patch; grayer below, tinged with red, but *bright red on throat.* Female more or less brownish above and below with *contrasting ochre-yellow throat.*
Similar species: Easily confused with Red-crowned Ant-Tanager; in Canal Zone, the Red-throat is *much* the commoner of the two. Male Red-throat is somewhat redder above and lacks the narrow black line bordering the red crown; it has more prominent red throat. Female Red-throat is browner above than Red-crown and lacks yellow crown patch; its yellow-ochre throat is its most distinguishing feature. Difference in vocalizations is also helpful. See also Carmiol's and Hepatic Tanagers.
Status and distribution: Very common in undergrowth of second-growth woodland and forest borders in more humid lowlands and lower foothills on both slopes, less numerous westward (particularly on Pacific side).
Habits: Usually in small groups of 4 to 8 individuals, which scold at you in harsh nasal tones, *ahrr* (like paper being torn), from hidden perches in the underbrush; they sometimes appear briefly in the open to soon drop back out of sight. Males have a pretty song, usually of three clear notes, *do, cheh, wheet,* but not too often heard. Neither this species nor the Red-crowned Ant-Tanager seem to be regular followers of army ants in Panama, despite their common names.
Range: Eastern Mexico to northern Colombia.

WHITE-THROATED SHRIKE-TANAGER
(*Lanio leucothorax*) Pl.29

Description: 7–7½. Found only in western Panama. *Bill heavy and hooked at tip.* Male has *black head and neck, upper back yellow;* lower back, wings, and tail black with white patch on wing-coverts; *throat white,* *remaining underparts yellow.* Female has grayish olive head and otherwise *brown upperparts; throat light brown,* remaining underparts yellow with much tawny olive on sides and flanks.

Similar species: The boldly patterned male should be easily recognized; superficially it looks (but does not act) more like an oriole than a tanager. Female bears slight resemblance to Gray-headed Tanager but is brown (not olive green) above and not so bright yellow below.

Status and distribution: Apparently rare in forest and forest borders in lower foothills (1500–2300 feet) of western Bocas del Toro (on trail to Boquete) and in lowlands and foothills of Chiriquí and Veraguas (Santa Fé, Chitra).

Habits: In Costa Rica reported to be noisy and conspicuous, foraging at all levels, mostly inside forest (Slud).

Range: Honduras to western Panama.

Note: By some authors considered conspecific with *L. aurantius* (Black-throated Shrike-Tanager) of northern Middle America; if so, English name would be Great Shrike-Tanager.

WHITE-LINED TANAGER

(*Tachyphonus rufus*) Pl.29

Description: 6¾. Bill bluish. Male *black,* with white under wing-linings (usually visible only in flight). Female *rufous brown above, tawny below.*

Similar species: Male White-shouldered Tanager is also black but shows conspicuous area of white on shoulders when perched. Female rather resembles female Cinnamon Becard but has typical, pointed tanager bill (becard's is stouter and slightly hooked), is larger, and forages at lower levels; also lacks becard's buffy supraloral stripe. See also Shiny Cowbird.

Status and distribution: Fairly common in clearings and shrubby areas in lowlands on entire Caribbean slope; on Pacific slope found in lowlands from western Panama province and Canal Zone area eastward, though scarce and local until Darién. Several recent sight reports from cleared areas around Boquete in lower highlands of western Chiriquí (Ridgely, J. Karr; G. Harrington), apparently spilling over from Caribbean slope.

Habits: As a rule seen in pairs, which facilitates identification. Usually forages rather low.

Range: Costa Rica to Peru and northern Argentina.

WHITE-SHOULDERED TANAGER

(*Tachyphonus luctuosus*) Pl.29

Description: 5. Male *black* with *conspicuous white shoulders* and white under wing-linings. Female olive above with *rather contrasting gray head;* throat grayish white, remaining underparts dull yellow. Birds from western Bocas del Toro (*axillaris*) similar, but male with reduced white on shoulders, female with olive head and yellowish throat. Birds from western Chiriquí (*nitidissimus*) slightly larger with prominent flesh area on lower mandible (especially in males), male with *conspicuous yellow to tawny crown patch* and reduced white on wing, female with olive cap and buffy yellowish throat.

Similar species: Male of larger White-lined Tanager shows no white on closed wing; male Dot-winged Antwren is smaller and slimmer, with white spots on wing (no solid patch) and tail-tips; male Jet Antbird has two broad white wing-bars and white tail-tipping. Females from most of Panama look like miniature Gray-headed Tanager but are duller and have much more arboreal habits; female Blue Dacnis is smaller, with bluish (not gray) head and slender bill. Chiriquí males resemble male Tawny-crested Tanager except for white on shoulders.

Status and distribution: Common in humid second-growth woodland and forest borders in lowlands on both slopes from Caribbean slope Coclé and Pacific slope Canal Zone eastward (nominate *luctuosus*), ranging up to just over 2000 feet on Cerro Azul; uncommon in lowlands of western Bocas del Toro; rare in lowlands of western Chiriquí. Probably occurs in intervening areas but unrecorded to date. Widespread in wooded areas throughout Canal Zone.

Habits: Forages at all levels, but especially at medium heights, and in many areas one of the characteristic members of the mixed foraging flocks of insectivorous birds.

Range: Honduras to northern Bolivia and central Brazil.

Note: More than one species may be involved, both *axillaris* (ranging on Caribbean slope from Honduras to western Panama) and *nitidissimus* (ranging on Pacific slope in southwestern Costa Rica and western Panama) having sometimes been considered distinct.

TAWNY-CRESTED TANAGER
(*Tachyphonus delatrii*) Pl.29

Description: 5½. Male *black* with *orange-tawny crest.* Female *dark olive brown above, brown below.* Immature like female; molting immature male sometimes shows tawny crown before becoming black.

Similar species: In its range not likely to be confused; female is darker brown than any other Panama tanager. Male White-shouldered Tanager from Chiriquí has both tawny crest and white shoulders.

Status and distribution: Locally fairly common in humid forest and forest borders in lowlands on Caribbean slope; on Pacific slope found in Veraguas foothills (Santa Fé—Ridgely and G. Stiles) and Darién. In Canal Zone, easily seen well out on Pipeline Road; also occurs in Achiote Road area.

Habits: Very active and conspicuous, usually foraging at low and middle levels. Seen in good-sized groups of 6 to 12 individuals; generally they are the only species in the flock, but occasionally they are joined by others, particularly the Carmiol's Tanager. Very noisy, with a variety of sharp squeaky notes.

Range: Nicaragua to northwestern Ecuador.

SULPHUR-RUMPED TANAGER
(*Heterospingus rubrifrons*) Pl.29

Description: 6¼. *Mostly gray,* paler below and tinged with yellow on belly; wings and tail blackish; *tuft of white feathers on each side of breast; rump yellow* (most visible in flight).

Similar species: Yellow-rumped Tanager is black (male) or brownish and yellow (female), not mostly gray. Plain-colored Tanager is also largely gray but is smaller and lacks white tuft and yellow rump. In Darién see also Scarlet-browed Tanager.

Status and distribution: Uncommon and local in humid forest and forest borders in lowlands and lower foothills (to about 3000 feet) on entire Caribbean slope; on Pacific slope recorded only in eastern Panama province (Cerro Azul, Bayano River valley) and Darién (Cerro Sapo). In Canal Zone, most easily found well out on Pipeline Road and in clearing on Barro Colorado Island; fairly common also on Cerro Santa Rita.

Habits: Usually forages at high and middle levels, coming lower in clearings. Generally in small groups, often accompanying large mixed flocks of other tanagers, honeycreepers, etc.

Range: Costa Rica to eastern Panama.

Note: Sometimes regarded as a "hen-feathered" race of *H. xanthopygius* (Scarlet-browed Tanager).

SCARLET-BROWED TANAGER
(*Heterospingus xanthopygius*) Pl.29

Description: 6¼. Known only from eastern Darién. Male *black above* with very narrow white line above eye and *prominent scarlet stripe behind eye;* shoulders and *rump yellow;* blackish gray below with tuft of white feathers on sides of breast. Female indistinguishable in field from Sulphur-rumped Tanager (not known to occur together in Panama).

Status and distribution: Recorded from humid forest in lowlands of eastern Darién (specimens from El Real, near Jaqué, Pucro, and Cana; *fide* Wetmore).

Habits: Not well known, but evidently much like Sulphur-rumped Tanager. It is not known whether the two species ever occur together.

Range: Eastern Panama to western Ecuador.

GRAY-HEADED TANAGER
(*Eucometis penicillata*) Pl.29

Description: 6¾. *Head, neck, and throat gray* contrasting with olive green upperparts and *bright yellow underparts.*

Similar species: Female White-shouldered Tanager in central and eastern Panama has same general pattern but is smaller and duller; it is primarily arboreal while the Gray-head is a bird of undergrowth.

Status and distribution: Uncommon in undergrowth of humid second-growth woodland and forest in lowlands and foothills on both slopes, ranging up in diminishing numbers into highlands of Chiriquí to around 5400 feet. Unrecorded on Caribbean slope west of Canal Zone area, though seems likely to occur. In Canal Zone seems most numerous in Fort Sherman/San Lorenzo area, though widespread elsewhere.

Habits: An habitual follower of army ants, though often found independent of them as well. Usually seen singly or in pairs.

Range: Southeastern Mexico to Bolivia and southern Brazil.

DUSKY-FACED TANAGER
(*Mitrospingus cassinii*) Pl.29

Description: 6¾. *Prominent pale iris. Crown olive yellow,* remaining upperparts gray with *blackish mask from sides of head onto forehead and throat;* underparts otherwise olive yellow.

Similar species: Not likely to be confused; one's impression is of an almost comical bird, with its excitable disposition, blackish mask, and staring pale eye.

Status and distribution: Fairly common locally in humid forest and woodland undergrowth in lowlands on entire Caribbean slope; on Pacific slope found in Veraguas foothills (above Santa Fé; Ridgely and G. Stiles), eastern Panama province (upper Bayano River valley; D. Hill) and Darién. Regularly seen well out on Pipeline Road, along Achiote Road, and at Río Piedras.

Habits: Prefers thickets along forested streams or at forested borders; there noisy groups of from 4 to 12 individuals can be found, usually independent of other species. Often difficult to see clearly as they generally remain in dense cover and move very rapidly, but at other times quite bold.

Range: Costa Rica to northwestern Ecuador.

ROSY (ROSE-BREASTED) THRUSH-TANAGER

(*Rhodinocichla rosea*) Pl.29

Description: 7¾. Male slaty black above with rose red superciliary; *underparts mostly rose red,* flanks and lower belly slaty. Female similar but with *tawny replacing male's rose red;* white lower belly.

Status and distribution: Uncommon to fairly common in dense thickets and undergrowth in second-growth woodland and shrubby clearings in lowlands on Pacific slope from Chiriquí to eastern Panama province (east at least to Río Pacora); absent from driest areas in southern Coclé and extreme western Panama province; on Caribbean slope, known only from Canal Zone area and eastern Colon province (Río Piedras); recorded up to 3500 feet in partially cleared areas of western highlands.

Habits: Shy and very hard to see in its dense tangled habitat. Terrestrial, at least in part, hence the common name. Not only is this one of Panama's loveliest birds, it also has an excellent rich song, in quality reminiscent of a Black-bellied Wren's, a loud ringing *cho-oh, chowee* or *wheeo-cheehoh, chweeoo.*

Range: Western Mexico; Costa Rica to northern Colombia and northern Venezuela.

Note: The species' exact taxonomic position is unclear.

YELLOW-BACKED TANAGER

(*Hemithraupis flavicollis*) Pl.29

Description: 5. Found only in eastern Darién. Male *black above* with lower back and rump orange-yellow; *throat and upper chest rich orange-yellow, lower underparts white* with gray sides and yellow under tail-coverts. Female brownish olive above with narrow yellow eye-ring; wings and tail edged yellowish olive; *sides of head and underparts dull yellow.*

Similar species: Male should not be confused; female resembles female Black-and-yellow Tanager but is duller yellow below. See also female White-shouldered Tanager, which in Darién has a gray head.

Status and distribution: Recorded in second-growth woodland and forest borders in lowlands and lower foothills of eastern Darién (Boca de Cupe on Tuira River, Cana).

Habits: Usually seen singly or in pairs, foraging at lower and middle levels. Feeds rather actively, somewhat like a wood warbler.

Range: Eastern Panama to northern Bolivia and southeastern Brazil.

BLACK-AND-YELLOW TANAGER

(*Chrysothlypis chrysomelas*) Pl.29

Description: 5. Male *mostly bright yellow,* with *black eye-ring* (giving it a "big-eyed" look), *back, wings, and tail.* Female olive above, wings duskier and edged with yellowish green; *bright yellow below,* tinged olive on sides.

Similar species: The striking male vaguely recalls a male Prothonotary Warbler. The dull female is more difficult: in most of its range most likely to be confused with female White-shouldered Tanager but lacks gray head and is brighter yellow below. Usually found in small flocks, when presence of males will greatly assist recognition. In Darién, see also Yellow-backed Tanager.

Status and distribution: Locally fairly common in humid forest and forest borders in hill country on both slopes, mostly 2000–3500 feet, more numerous on Pacific slope. In central Panama, known only from Cerro Campana and Cerro Jefe area.

Habits: A very active and spritely arboreal tanager, recalling a wood-warbler. Usually occurs in groups of its own species, which regularly associate with flocks of other tanagers, particularly Silver-throats and Bay-heads.

Range: Costa Rica to eastern Panama.

COMMON BUSH-TANAGER

(*Chlorospingus ophthalmicus*) Pl.29

Description: 5–5¼. Found only in western highlands. Olive green above with *brown* *head and neck* and *conspicuous white spot behind eye;* throat buffy, yellow band across chest (sometimes indistinct), remaining underparts white. Birds from Veraguas and Coclé (*punctulatus,* Dotted Bush-Tanager, often treated as distinct) are similar but have *blackish head and neck* and mostly yellow underparts with throat lightly dotted with dusky.

Similar species: No other similar bird in its range shows such a prominent white spot behind the eye. Sooty-capped Bush-Tanager has long white stripe extending back from behind eye to sides of neck.

Status and distribution: Common to abundant in forest, forest borders, and shrubby clearings in highlands of western Chiriquí and Bocas del Toro (*novicius;* most numerous 5000–6500 feet), and in foothills and highlands on both slopes of Veraguas and Coclé (*punctulatus;* recorded 2800–4700 feet). One of the most common and widespread birds in the western Chiriquí highlands, and the most numerous bird above 3000 feet in cloud forest on Cerro Tute above Santa Fé, Veraguas on January 4–5, 1974 (Ridgely and G. Stiles).

Habits: Rather noisy and active, traveling in flocks, sometimes quite large, often joined by other species. Forages at all levels, but most frequently low. Often very unsuspicious.

Range: Central Mexico to western Panama; Colombia and northern Venezuela to northwestern Argentina.

Note: An exceptionally plastic species through its large range, with many very different appearing races having been described. The following two forms have been treated by some as members of this complex, but are here still tentatively left as distinct species.

TACARCUNA BUSH-TANAGER

(*Chlorospingus tacarcunae*) Pl.29

Description: 5¼. Known only from eastern Panama. *Whitish iris. Mostly olive green,* without white spot behind eye, with *throat and chest yellow.*

Similar species: See other Panama bush-tanagers (none of which has a pale eye): Yellow-throated (not known to occur in eastern Panama) has white and brownish lower underparts (not olive green). Carmiol's Tanager is notably larger and lacks the pale eye, but otherwise is rather similar. Female euphonias are smaller, and none is so uniform olive green on lower underparts.

Status and distribution: Uncommon to fairly common in elfin cloud forest on Cerro Jefe (3000–3300 feet), eastern Panama province (D. Hill, Ridgely); found also in highlands of eastern Darién (Cerro Tacarcuna, 3400–4700 feet).

Habits: Much like other bush-tanagers, usually in small groups, sometimes with other tanagers.

Range: Central Panama to northwestern Colombia.

Note: Often regarded as a race of *C. ophthalmicus* (Common Bush-Tanager) or of *C. flavigularis* (Yellow-throated Bush-Tanager).

PIRRE BUSH-TANAGER

(*Chlorospingus inornatus*) Pl.29

Description: 5¼. Found only in highlands of eastern Darién. Olive green above with *cap and sides of head blackish; mostly yellow below,* with dusky spots on throat, sides and flanks olive green.

Similar species: Rather like Common Bush-Tanager of west-central Panama (*punctulatus*) but without white spot behind eye. See also other bush-tanagers.

Status and distribution: Known only from foothills and highlands of eastern Darién (Cerro Sapo, Cerro Pirre, Cana), recorded 2600–5200 feet.

Range: Eastern Panama.

Note: Perhaps only a race of *C. ophthalmicus* (Common Bush-Tanager).

YELLOW-THROATED BUSH-TANAGER

(*Chlorospingus flavigularis*) Pl.29

Description: 5¼. Found locally in western foothills. Dull olive green above with faint whitish eye-ring; *throat yellow,* chest olive brownish, *lower underparts whitish,* sides and flanks tinged with grayish brown.

Similar species: Other bush-tanagers found in western Panama have either a white spot or a white stripe on head. Tacarcuna Bush-Tanager (of eastern Panama) is similar but has olive green lower underparts.

Status and distribution: Apparently fairly common to common in humid forest and forest borders in foothills of Bocas del Toro and on both slopes of Veraguas, recorded 800–3000 feet. One of the most numerous forest birds above Santa Fé, Veraguas, on January 4–5, 1974 (Ridgely and G. Stiles).

Habits: Similar to other bush-tanagers, usually seen in small groups, often with other tanagers, generally at middle and upper heights.

Range: Western Panama; Colombia to northern Bolivia.

SOOTY-CAPPED BUSH-TANAGER
(*Chlorospingus pileatus*) Pl.29

Description: 5¼. Found only in western highlands. *Head sooty black* with *broad white stripe extending back from over eye to sides of neck;* otherwise olive green above; throat buffy whitish faintly speckled with dusky, remaining underparts yellowish olive fading to whitish.

Similar species: Common Bush-Tanager has merely a white spot behind eye, not a long eyestripe. Black-cheeked Warbler has chestnut crown and long white stripe beginning at bill, but it and this bush-tanager can look deceptively similar and often occur together.

Status and distribution: Fairly common in forest, forest borders, and shrubby clearings in highlands of Chiriquí and Veraguas, usually above 6000 feet in Chiriquí.

Habits: Forages actively at all levels but usually fairly low. Often a numerous member of mixed foraging flocks.

Range: Costa Rica and western Panama.

FINCHES: Fringillidae (42)

The finches form a very large family found virtually everywhere except in Australasia (where some have been introduced), and is well represented in Panama. The taxonomy of the group is disputed, with the traditional A.O.U. treatment, including three subfamilies (Cardinalinae, Emberizinae, and Fringillinae) in the family Fringillidae being followed here. Practically all members of the family (the sole exception in Panama is the Slaty Finch) can be recognized as such by their stout, more or less conical bills; otherwise they exhibit considerable variation in size, shape, and habits. In many species song is well developed, and some species are often kept as cage-birds, frequently for their attractive plumage as much as their song. Most finches eat primarily seeds, but the saltators and grosbeaks especially also take a great deal of fruit, and most species eat some insects and feed them to their young. The nest of most Panamanian species, so far as known (the nests of many are still undescribed), is an open cup, placed on the ground, attached to grass, or placed in a bush or tree. However, the Yellow-faced Grassquit and Black-striped and Orange-billed Sparrows build domed nests with an entrance on the side, while the Saffron Finch nests in holes in trees and crannies in buildings.

BLACK-HEADED SALTATOR
(*Saltator atriceps*) Pl.30

Description: 9¾. Considerably *larger than other Panama saltators. Crown and hindneck black,* superciliary whitish, sides of head dark gray; upperparts otherwise bright yellowish olive; *throat white,* bordered on sides and below with black; remaining underparts mostly gray with brownish sides and bright orange-tawny under tail-coverts.

Similar species: Buff-throated Saltator is smaller and has a buffy throat.

Status and distribution: Locally fairly common in shrubby thickets in clearings and at forest and woodland borders (especially near water) in lowlands on Caribbean slope from Bocas del Toro to eastern Colon province; on Pacific slope locally in hill country of Chiriquí and at El Valle and Cerro Campana; recent sighting of a pair on Bayano River in eastern Panama province a few miles above dam site on August 2, 1972 (Ridgely and J. Pujals). In central Panama most easily seen at Río Piedras and at Achiote Road.

Habits: Noisy and quite conspicuous, often in small groups. The usual call is an arresting harsh smacking note, *tsaak,* much louder than other saltators; it also has a cackling and squawking song.

Range: Central Mexico to central Panama.

BUFF-THROATED SALTATOR
(*Saltator maximus*) Pl.30

Description: 7¾. *Most of head dark gray* with some blackish on crown and with short white superciliary; upperparts otherwise yellowish olive; center of upper throat white, *lower throat buffy,* bordered on sides and below by broad black band; remaining underparts mainly gray with olive brown sides and yellowish buff under tail-coverts. Immature may lack buff throat.

Similar species: Black-headed Saltator is easily distinguished by its notably larger size, more black on head, and white throat

(though throats of some Buff-throats can look very pale). See also Streaked Saltator.
Status and distribution: Common in shrubby clearings and lighter woodland in lowlands on both slopes, ranging up in reduced numbers into foothills and lower highlands (to about 6000 feet in Chiriquí).
Habits: Often found with the Streaked Saltator, but normally outnumbered or even replaced by it in drier areas (which the Buff-throat tends to avoid). Usually found singly or in pairs in lower growth, but also often sings and feeds quite high in trees. The song is a series of repeated sweet musical phrases, *cheéaweet, cheyoo,* or *cheeareet chweyoo,* sometimes suggestive of a *Turdus* robin.
Range: Southeastern Mexico to northern Bolivia and southern Brazil.

STREAKED SALTATOR
(*Saltator albicollis*) Pl.30

Description: 7¼. Olive above with narrow, whitish supraloral stripe and often a vague, whitish eye-ring; whitish below, *broadly streaked with olive* except on throat.
Similar species: Both other Panama saltators have throat patches margined with black and lack streaks below. See Rose-breasted Grosbeak.
Status and distribution: Common in gardens, shrubby clearings, and woodland borders in lowlands on entire Pacific slope, ranging in smaller numbers up into foothills and lower highlands (to about 6000 feet in Chiriquí); on Caribbean slope found only in Canal Zone area; found also on Coiba Island, Taboga Island, and the Pearl Islands.
Habits: Like Buff-throated Saltator, usually found singly or in pairs except at fruiting trees where small groups often gather. Its frequently heard song is a series of three long-drawn sweet whistles, *teéoo, teéoo, teéeeoo,* with distinctive slurred and prolonged final note.
Range: Costa Rica to northern Venezuela and Peru.

BLACK-FACED GROSBEAK
(*Caryothraustes poliogaster*) Pl.30

Description: 6½–7. Known primarily from western Caribbean slope. *Facial area and throat black;* remainder of head yellow, shading into yellowish olive green above with grayish rump; chest yellow *fading to grayish white on belly and gray on flanks.*
Similar species: Should not be confused in western Panama; Yellow-green Grosbeak of Darién is similar but the two are not known to occur together. Streaked Saltator is also mostly olive green but lacks the black and is streaked below. See also Prong-billed Barbet.
Status and distribution: Uncommon to fairly common in forest borders and clearings in humid lowlands and lower foothills of Bocas del Toro and hill country on both slopes of Veraguas; one specimen taken on Río Guabal, Caribbean slope Coclé in February 1962 (Wetmore); 19th century specimens from Canal Zone and hills above Capira, western Panama province, but no confirmed recent records from Canal Zone and vicinity. Recent sightings from Cerro Jefe area require specimen confirmation, as they may refer to the similar Yellow-green Grosbeak or to an intermediate population.
Habits: Usually found in noisy flocks of varying size, sometimes quite large. Often forages at high levels in trees, but also comes lower in clearings.
Range: Southeastern Mexico to western (casually central) Panama.
Note: By some authors considered conspecific with *C. canadensis* (Yellow-green Grosbeak).

YELLOW-GREEN GROSBEAK
(*Caryothraustes canadensis*)

Description: 6. Known only from eastern Darién. Resembles Black-faced Grosbeak, but slightly smaller and with *lower underparts yellow like breast* (not whitish to gray) and an olive green rump (not gray).
Similar species: See Black-faced Grosbeak.
Status and distribution: Known only from foothills of eastern Darién (Cana, 3000 feet).
Range: Eastern Panama; southeastern Colombia, southern Venezuela, the Guianas, and Amazonian and eastern Brazil.

SLATE-COLORED (SLATY) GROSBEAK
(*Pitylus grossus*) Pl.30

Description: 7¼. *Heavy bright red bill. Mostly dark bluish gray,* with center of throat white (often not very noticeable). Male blackish on sides of head; female somewhat paler gray below.
Status and distribution: Fairly common in forest and forest borders in lowlands and foothills on entire Caribbean slope; on Pacific slope found in foothills from Veraguas eastward, in lowlands from Canal Zone (where local) eastward. Widespread

in forested areas on Caribbean side of Canal Zone.

Habits: Usually forages at middle and upper tree levels, dropping lower at forest borders. Seen singly or in pairs, sometimes joining mixed foraging flocks of various birds. Its fine song is a rather variable series of loud deliberate whistles, one version being *witcheeweeoo-cheéoo-cheer,* often questioning at the end. The frequently heard call is a sharp metallic *speek,* quite reminiscent of the call of the Northern Cardinal (*Cardinalis cardinalis*).

Range: Nicaragua to northern Bolivia and Amazonian Brazil.

BLACK-THIGHED GROSBEAK
(*Pheucticus tibialis*) Pl.30

Description: 8½. Found only in western highlands. *Very heavy blackish bill.* Male *mostly golden yellow* with black back, wings, and tail; sides of neck and breast often suffused with blackish; *wings with small white patch on primaries;* tail tipped white. Female less bright yellow. Immature even duller and more olive on head. The thighs are black, but this is hard to see in the field.

Status and distribution: Uncommon and rather local in forest borders and clearings in highlands of Chiriquí, adjacent Bocas del Toro, and Veraguas.

Habits: Usually seen perching in the open in shrubbery or low trees. Has a rich, leisurely song of varied musical phrases interspersed with the phrase *tweek tseéwee.*

Range: Costa Rica and western Panama.

Note: By some authors considered conspecific with *P. chrysopeplus* (Yellow Grosbeak) of western Mexico and Guatemala; others also include the *P. chrysogaster* group (Golden-bellied Grosbeak) of Venezuela to Peru in *chrysopeplus,* then calling the whole complex Yellow Grosbeak.

ROSE-BREASTED GROSBEAK
(*Pheucticus ludovicianus*)

Description: 7–8. Large whitish bill. Breeding plumage male (seen in Panama in late winter and spring) unmistakable: *mostly black above* with white rump and two white wing-bars; throat black, *large inverted triangle of rose red on chest,* remaining underparts white. In nonbreeding plumage, has black mixed with brown, several buffy whitish head stripes (as in female), rose red greatly reduced, and underparts tinged with brownish. Female and immatures are streaked brownish and blackish above, with *buffy whitish crown stripe and superciliary;* whitish below, *streaked with brownish,* without any pink.

Similar species: Nonbreeding male, female, and immature can be known by their chunky grosbeak shape, largely brown coloration, head stripes, and streaking below. Streaked Saltator is mostly olive (not brown), lacks prominent head striping, and is notably slimmer.

Status and distribution: Fairly common transient and uncommon winter resident throughout (late September–late April); also recorded on Pearl Islands.

Habits: Favors forest clearings and second-growth woodland. Often in small groups, especially when migrating. Usually forages rather high in trees. Its call, a distinctive, metallic *pink,* is frequently given.

Range: Breeds in eastern and central North America; winters from Mexico to Venezuela and Ecuador, casually to Peru.

BLUE-BLACK GROSBEAK
(*Cyanocompsa cyanoides*) Pl.31

Description: 6–6½. *Very stout black bill.* Male *entirely blackish blue,* brightest on front of head. Female *rich brown,* a little paler below.

Similar species: Both sexes of the rare Blue Grosbeak have prominent tan or buffy wing-bars. Indigo Bunting is smaller with much less stout bill. Blue-black Grassquit is even smaller, with relatively slender pointed bill. See also Thick-billed Seed-Finch.

Status and distribution: Common in undergrowth of forest, second-growth woodland, and forest borders in more humid lowlands on both slopes, ranging up into foothills to around 4000 feet in Chiriquí and Darién.

Habits: Generally in pairs. A common song is a series of five or six loud clear deliberate whistles, *do-do, deh, dee, deh, do,* sometimes followed by a soft twitter. Also often heard is a distinctive sharp call, *hee-ey.*

Range: Southeastern Mexico to Bolivia and Amazonian Brazil.

BLUE GROSBEAK
(*Guiraca caerulea*)

Description: 6½–7. Rather rare. Stout, dusky bill. Breeding plumage male *deep blue* with *two tan wing-bars* (but looks dull or even blackish in poor light). Fall and winter males have blue feathers edged broadly with brown so that they look essentially brownish. Female brown above, buffier below, with wings and tail dusky, former with *two buffy wing-bars.*

Similar species: Both sexes of the much more numerous and widespread Blue-black Grosbeak lack the tan or buffy wing-bars prominent in this species. Indigo Bunting is smaller and slenderer, with less stout bill, also lacks the wing-bars.

Status and distribution: A rare and local but probably regular winter resident in western and central Panama, recorded mostly at Almirante, Bocas del Toro, and at Playa Coronado, western Panama province; only three reports from Canal Zone: one sighting on Barro Colorado Island (M. Moynihan); one seen at Gatun Locks on March 18, 1973 (D. Engleman and J. Schwartz); and one immature male seen at Frijoles on March 16, 1974 (Eisenmann). Recorded in Panama early October–late March.

Habits: Prefers open scrubby areas and roadsides, usually in low trees and bushes. Frequently twitches its tail to one side (often a good field character). The call is a sharp *chink* (R. T. Peterson).

Range: Southern United States to Costa Rica; winters to Panama.

INDIGO BUNTING
(*Passerina cyanea*)

Description: 5. Small, conical bill. Breeding plumage male *entirely deep rich blue.* In nonbreeding plumage, male mostly brown (like female) but usually with a few patches of blue, becoming bluer as the season progresses. Female and immatures are olive brown above, buffy whitish below with some *indistinct brownish streaks on breast.*

Similar species: Blue and Blue-black Grosbeaks are both larger with much heavier bills; the former also has conspicuous buffy wing-bars (female Indigos sometimes show a trace of them); the latter is a forest bird with which the Indigo does not normally occur. More likely to be confused with the smaller Blue-black Grassquit, which has somewhat slenderer bill and males of which are blacker, females more distinctly streaked below (Indigo's streaks are blurrier). See also Blue Seedeater.

Status and distribution: Uncommon to locally common (in Bocas del Toro and Chiriquí) winter resident (early October–mid-May); much more numerous in western Panama, rather scarce in Canal Zone area, and rare in eastern Panama; ranges well up in Chiriquí highlands to about 6000 feet.

Habits: Frequents open, shrubby country, clearings, roadsides. Often in small flocks.

Range: Breeds in eastern and central North America; winters in Florida, West Indies, and from Mexico to Panama, rarely in Colombia and Venezuela.

PAINTED BUNTING
(*Passerina ciris*)

Description: 5. Small conical bill. Gaudy male unmistakable: *head purplish blue, back bright green,* wings and tail dusky, rump red; *bright red below.* Female and immature male plain dull green above, pale olive yellowish below, becoming yellower on lower belly.

Similar species: Female is simply an all-greenish finch, devoid of any markings. Female Yellow-faced Grassquit is most like it, but is duller (more olive) and has yellowish facial markings.

Status and distribution: Rare to uncommon winter resident (late October–late April) in lowlands of western Panama, recorded primarily in western Bocas del Toro and Chiriquí; only reports from central Panama are two sightings from Playa Coronado, western Panama province: two (an adult male and a female) on November 25, 1962; and one (an adult male) on March 25, 1967 (both Eisenmann).

Habits: Favors undergrowth in shrubby areas and woodland borders; usually shy and often difficult to observe. Frequently in small groups.

Range: Breeds in southeastern United States and northern Mexico; winters in Florida, Greater Antilles, and from Mexico to Panama.

DICKCISSEL
(*Spiza americana*)

Description: 6¼. Breeding plumage male has pale gray head with yellow superciliary; upperparts otherwise brown with black streaking on back and *chestnut patch on shoulders; pale yellow below,* brightest on breast, fading to whitish on belly, with *prominent black "V" on chest* (like a meadowlark's). In nonbreeding plumage duller, with less yellow, and with black chest bib obscure or lacking. Female similar to nonbreeding male with *pale yellowish superciliary, whitish throat,* and a tinge of yellow on breast but no black.

Similar species: Females and winter males

are undistinguished in appearance, but no other Panama bird looks much like them. Often best known by habit of gathering in huge dense flocks.

Status and distribution: Fairly common to locally abundant transient and less common and very erratic winter resident in open country on Pacific slope (late August–May, but mostly September and April); on Caribbean slope, occurs only as an erratic transient in much smaller numbers.

Habits: Often occurs in very large compact flocks, regularly of a thousand birds or more. Calls constantly, a distinctive low raspy *ddrrt* and assorted twitters; a large flock will generate considerable noise.

Range: Breeds in central North America; winters mostly in Panama and northern South America, a few in eastern United States and Central America.

BLUE-BLACK GRASSQUIT

(*Volatinia jacarina*) Pl.31

Description: 4. Bill relatively small. Male *uniform glossy blue-black.* Female dull brownish olive above, wings duskier; brownish buffy below, fading to whitish on belly, *streaked with dusky on chest and sides.*

Similar species: Seedeaters have stouter bills; no female Panama seedeater is streaked below. Female Yellow-faced Grassquit is more greenish olive (not brownish), shows a facial pattern, and lacks streaking below. Indigo Bunting is larger with stouter bill; male is brighter blue than male grassquit and lacks the black overtones, female is browner above and less distinctly streaked below than female grassquit. See also the notably larger Blue Seedeater.

Status and distribution: Abundant in grassy and bushy areas virtually throughout in the lowlands but more numerous on Pacific slope, ranging in smaller numbers into foothills and to around 4000 feet in lower highlands of Chiriquí; common also on Coiba Island and on the Pearl Islands.

Habits: One of the most frequently observed birds in open areas in the lowlands. Males often perch on top of a bush or grass stem and repeatedly come out with an explosive buzzy *dzee-ew,* at the same time jumping a foot or so into the air (sometimes almost seeming to somersault), then dropping back to its original perch. They sometimes call without jumping.

Range: Mexico to northern Chile and central Argentina.

YELLOW-FACED GRASSQUIT

(*Tiaris olivacea*) Pl.31

Description: 4. Male olive above with crown and sides of head blackish; *bright yellow eyestripe, eye-ring, and throat;* chest and breast black, becoming olive on belly. Female similar in pattern but duller, with olive replacing black of head and underparts and with only *a trace of yellowish superciliary, eye-ring, and throat.*

Similar species: Even females have enough facial pattern to be readily recognized. See female Painted Bunting.

Status and distribution: Very common in grassy areas, clearings, and roadsides in foothills and highlands to about 6000 feet; rather scarce and local in lowlands on both slopes, somewhat more numerous on Pacific side, especially in coastal areas; found also on Coiba Island. Very local in Canal Zone, but common on Cerro Campana, Cerro Azul, and at El Valle.

Habits: The male's song is a thin weak trill delivered from a low perch. Usually seen in flocks, often associating with seedeaters and Blue-black Grassquits.

Range: Eastern Mexico to Colombia and Venezuela; Greater Antilles.

SLATE-COLORED SEEDEATER

(*Sporophila schistacea*) Pl.31

Description: 4½. *Conspicuous yellow bill in both sexes.* Male *mostly slaty gray,* with white patches on either side of throat (sometimes lacking in Chiriquí birds) and on wings near base of flight feathers; center of breast and belly white. Female olive brown above, paler below, fading to brownish buffy on lower belly. Immature like female, but with dark bill.

Similar species: All other Panama seedeaters have dark or gray bills. Immature, if alone, cannot be safely identified in the field.

Status and distribution: Rare and local in second-growth woodland and forest borders in more humid lowlands on both slopes, ranging locally into foothills (Cerro Azul and Cerro Santa Rita). Best known from central Panama, though also recorded from western Chiriquí, Veraguas, San Blas, and Darién. Apparently not regular or numerous anywhere in Panama.

Habits: A bird of woodland, much more arboreal than other seedeaters, though the Variable does occasionally feed fairly high in trees and sometimes is found in light woodland. Usually found in pairs or small groups of its own species. The song is a series of fast high sibilant notes, *st-st-st-st-st-st,* sometimes varied to a high thin rattle, very different from songs of other Panama seedeaters and somewhat suggestive of song of Blackpoll Warbler.

Range: Costa Rica to northern Bolivia, very locally in Amazonian Brazil, and the Guianas.

WHITE-COLLARED SEEDEATER
(*Sporophila torqueola*)

Description: 4½. Known only from western Panama. Recalls the more widespread Variable Seedeater. Male mostly glossy black above, with white rump, *two white wing-bars,* and a white spot on primaries; *mostly white below* (often tinged with buff), with black band across chest, white of throat extending onto sides of neck to form a partial collar. Subadult males (which sing and are able to breed) are very buffy below with some brownish above and often have buffy collar. Female brownish olive above with *two whitish wing-bars;* buffy below.

Similar species: The only Panama seedeater with wing-bars.

Status and distribution: First reported from Panama in 1956 (although then already fairly common), now common in grassy areas and clearings in lowlands of western Bocas del Toro, apparently a recent range extension from Costa Rica, probably the result of increasing clearing of forest. In recent years has also spread into Chiriquí in small numbers: the first report was of a singing male and several females near Frontera (about ¼ mile from Costa Rican border) on December 16, 1962 (Eisenmann); it was then recorded near Puerto Armuelles in January 1966 (Wetmore); and four were seen at the David airport on January 18, 1974 (Ridgely).

Habits: Similar to Variable Seedeater, occurring in flocks, often with the Variable. Male's song is quite different, slower, richer, and sweeter, without the twittering effect of the Variable, the last notes resembling those of a canary.

Range: Southern Texas and Mexico to western Panama.

VARIABLE SEEDEATER
(*Sporophila aurita*) Pl.31

Description: 4½. Males vary considerably in plumage. Most birds are basically *glossy black above* with white spot on primaries and often with white rump; *mostly white below,* with black band across chest and blackish on sides and flanks. Birds from Canal Zone and vicinity usually have black instead of white rump and have varying amounts of black below and on center of throat (leaving crescent of white from either side of neck across chest). Birds from western Pacific slope (from Coclé westward) and Darién usually have white throat and rump. Birds from western Caribbean slope (east to western Colon province) are *all black* except for white spot on primaries and trace of white on lower belly; they were formerly regarded

Left to right (all males), GREAT-BILLED SEED-FINCH, WHITE-COLLARED SEEDEATER, VARIABLE (BLACK) SEEDEATER

as a distinct species, *S. corvina* (Black Seedeater). Some males from Caribbean side of Canal Zone approach this plumage. Female dull olive brown, becoming buffy whitish on lower belly.

Similar species: Male is the only black and white seedeater in most of Panama; in western Panama see also the White-collared Seedeater, both sexes of which have prominent white wing-bars. Black males of western Caribbean slope are easily confused with male Thick-billed Seed-Finch except for the latter's almost grotesque heavy bill. Females are probably not safely distinguished in the field from female Yellow-bellied Seedeater, but tend to be less brownish below.

Status and distribution: Abundant in grassy areas in clearings, gardens, and open country virtually throughout but in largest numbers in lowlands; found also on Coiba Island.

Habits: Usually found in small flocks with females and immatures outnumbering males, often associating with Yellow-bellied Seedeaters and Blue-black Grassquits. Male's song is quite varied, a sweet and rapid twittering, usually given from a low perch; a characteristic call is a sweet *seeeu* or *cheeu*.

Range: Southeastern Mexico to northwestern Peru (west of the Andes).

Note: Included is *S. corvina* (Black Seedeater) of southern Mexico to Caribbean western Panama. By some authors considered conspecific with *S. americana* (Wing-barred Seedeater) of northern and central South America east of the Andes, in that case the whole complex being called Variable Seedeater.

YELLOW-BELLIED SEEDEATER

(*Sporophila nigricollis*) Pl.31

Description: 4½. Male has *black head and neck;* otherwise olive above, and *pale yellow to whitish below.* Female olive brown above, buffyish below.

Similar species: Male is unlike any other Panama seedeater in pattern, though whiter individuals may seem poorly named. Female is more difficult and is especially hard to distinguish from female Variable, but tends to be more brownish below and usually (but not always) has slaty (not dusky) bill. The problem is simplified by the flocking habit of both species, when some males are almost invariably present.

Status and distribution: Common in grassy and open shrubby areas on entire Pacific slope, primarily in lowlands but in small numbers up to around 5000 feet; on Caribbean slope recorded only from Canal Zone area; found also on Taboga Island and the Pearl Islands. Often seemingly disappears from many areas during the dry season, when it apparently gathers in flocks in more humid regions (as on Caribbean side of Canal Zone and vicinity).

Habits: Similar to Variable Seedeater, though generally a less familiar bird, and somewhat less partial to residential areas. Male's song is sweet and pretty, shorter than Variable's, often ending with two buzzy phrases, *tzee-tzee-bzeeoo, bzee-bzee.*

Range: Costa Rica to northern Bolivia, northeastern Argentina, and southern Brazil.

RUDDY-BREASTED SEEDEATER

(*Sporophila minuta*) Pl.31

Description: 4. Male ashy gray above, duskier on wings with small white patch at base of primaries; *cheeks and underparts,* and rump, *light cinnamon-rufous.* Subadult male is somewhat browner above, approaching female. Female buffy olive above with pale buff wing-edging; *buffy to pale dull cinnamon below.*

Similar species: Attractive male is easily recognized; female is best known from other female seedeaters by its slightly smaller size and distinctly buffy underparts.

Status and distribution: Common in open grassy savannas in lowlands on entire Pacific slope; on Caribbean slope known only from a few reports from middle Chagres River valley in Canal Zone. Essentially disappears from breeding areas in October and does not reappear in numbers until March and April; where they go during the dry season is uncertain, most probably gathering in large flocks near water.

Habits: The common and (when breeding) conspicuous seedeater of the Pacific slope savannas. Its song is the best of the Panama seedeaters, fairly long, sweet, and deliberate, typically *weet, weet, weet, weet, weet, too-weet-tew,* often given from an exposed perch such as a telephone wire.

Range: Western Mexico to eastern Bolivia and northern Argentina.

BLUE SEEDEATER

(*Amaurospiza concolor*) Pl.31

Description: 5. Male *dull dark blue,* somewhat paler and duller below, with white under wing-linings. Female *rather bright tawny brown,* paler below. Some individuals (probably immature males) are dark rufous brown.

Similar species: Male somewhat resembles male Blue-black Grassquit but is larger, bluer (no black), and has distinctly heavier bill; the grassquit inhabits grassy areas, not woodlands and forest borders. Female is more uniform and brighter brown than other female seedeaters; it resembles Thick-billed Seed-Finch in coloration but that species is a little larger with much heavier bill, and has white under wing-linings. Male Indigo Bunting is brighter blue than male Blue Seedeater; winter male, female, and immature Indigos are a little larger, not as rich or dark a brown as female Blue Seedeater, and generally show indistinct breast streakings.

Status and distribution: Rare and very local. Recorded primarily from foothills and highlands of Chiriquí (2000–9000 feet); known also from Veraguas (2 seen above Santa Fé on April 7, 1975; N. G. Smith), Herrera (Cerro Largo, 1200 feet), and from Pacific slope of Canal Zone (Curundu). Most often noted around Nueva Suiza in western Chiriquí highlands, but scarce even there.

Habits: Little known and local throughout its range. Seems partial to bamboo thickets, at least in the Chiriquí highlands, in which it feeds some ten to thirty feet off the ground.

Range: Southern Mexico; Honduras to western Ecuador.

THICK-BILLED SEED-FINCH

(*Oryzoborus funereus*) Pl.31

Description: 4¾. *Very heavy bill,* the tip forming a right angle. Male *black* with small white spot at base of primaries (often hard to see) and white under wing-linings (visible only in flight). Female *dull brown above, richer brown below,* also with white under wing-linings.

Similar species: Except in western Bocas del Toro (where see also Great-billed Seed-Finch), no other small finch has such an enormously heavy bill. Blue-black Grosbeak is larger with proportionately smaller (though still stout) bill and inhabits forest undergrowth; male is, of course, dark blue, not black.

Status and distribution: Generally fairly common in shrubby areas and woodland borders in lowlands on both slopes, though reports few from Chiriquí and none (so far) from San Blas or Darién; found also on Coiba Island and the larger Pearl Islands.

Habits: Usually found singly or in pairs, not flocking as do the seedeaters. More arboreal than most seedeaters. Male has a fine song, very long and musical, somewhat Indigo Bunting-like; it is usually delivered from a high exposed perch.

Range: Southeastern Mexico to western Ecuador.

Note: By some authors considered conspecific with *O. angolensis* (Chestnut-bellied Seed-Finch) of South America east of the Andes, in which case the entire complex is called Lesser Seed-Finch.

GREAT-BILLED SEED-FINCH

(*Oryzoborus maximiliani*) *page 333*

Description: 6. Known only from western Bocas del Toro. Both sexes resemble the better known Thick-billed Seed-Finch. Male entirely black except for small white spot at base of primaries; *bill enormously thick and yellowish white.* Female essentially a large version of female Thick-billed Seed-Finch but darker brown above and brighter and richer brown below, with much heavier dark bill.

Similar species: Male's pale bill and black (not white) under wing-linings easily distinguish it from male Thick-billed Seed-Finch. Females are more difficult, but are noticeably larger and deeper brown. See also female Blue-black Grosbeak (a forest bird), which has proportionately smaller black (not dusky brown) bill.

Status and distribution: Recently (1960's) discovered in lowlands of western Bocas del Toro.

Habits: Little known. In Nicaragua favors damp open areas and marshes (T. Howell).

Range: Nicaragua to western Panama; northern and central South America east of the Andes.

Note: Wetmore has named the Panamanian population *O. crassirostris loftini;* it is very close to the Nicaraguan *nuttingi,* formerly considered a separate species. I follow de Schauensee's treatment in *Birds of South America* (1970), but simplify the common name as suggested by Eisenmann.

SLATY FINCH

(*Spodiornis rusticus*) Pl.31

Description: 4¾. Known only from western Chiriquí highlands. *Bill rather slender.* Male *dark slaty gray,* somewhat paler below; black wings margined with gray. Female *olive brown above,* wings darker and *edged with rufous; buffy olive below,* faintly streaked with dusky on throat and breast, fading to yellowish on lower belly.

Similar species: Volcano Junco always shows prominent yellow eye and has a more conical bill; it is restricted to very high altitudes.

Status and distribution: Very rare in clearings and forest borders in highlands of western Chiriquí. The few recent records are from the Nueva Suiza/Bambito area; at the former locality, 7 individuals were mist-netted (4 collected) in March–April 1968 (C. Leck *et al.*).

Habits: Little known. In Costa Rica, reported to travel in small flocks, feeding on the ground in lush grass of pastures but near cover of forest (G. Stiles and H. Hespenheide).

Range: Southern Mexico; Costa Rica and western Panama; Colombia and Venezuela south locally to Bolivia.

Note: By some authors placed in the genus *Haplospiza.* The similar Peg-billed Finch (*Acanthidops bairdi*) of Costa Rican mountains may yet be found at high elevations on Volcán Barú. It has a narrower, very pointed, and somewhat upturned bill that almost suggests a flower-piercer's without the hook at the tip; bill bicolored in both sexes, upper mandible black, lower mandible bright yellow (dull yellowish in female). Male Peg-bill is uniform slaty gray (less bluish than Slaty Finch), slightly paler below; female is dull grayish brown, duskier on wings and tail with dull buffy wing-bars and edging. It feeds primarily by gleaning in vegetation and epiphytes in trees (G. Stiles and H. Hespenheide).

SAFFRON FINCH
(*Sicalis flaveola*) Pl.31

Description: 5¼. Apparently restricted to Caribbean coastal Canal Zone and Colon vicinity. Male *mostly bright golden yellow, becoming orange on front of head;* more olive on back and streaked with dusky; wings and tail dusky, edged with olive. Female similar but with orange reduced or lacking. Immature grayish above streaked with dusky, hindneck and back tinged with yellow; wings dusky edged with olive; whitish below with *broad yellow band across chest* and brownish on sides.

Similar species: No similar bird occurs in the restricted area where this bird is found. Grassland Yellow-Finch is known only from Pacific slope grasslands.

Status and distribution: First noted in 1951, apparently introduced; now locally common in residential and park-like areas of Caribbean coast of Canal Zone from Gatun Dam area to Gatun and Coco Solo. Occasional reports of wanderers in the Chagres River valley but not yet established there; unreported from Pacific side of Canal Zone but may eventually spread there.

Habits: Usually seen feeding on lawns, often in small groups. The male's song is an endlessly repeated but rather musical *tzip-tzip-tzee-tzee.*

Range: Colombia south locally to central Argentina; introduced into Canal Zone and Jamaica.

GRASSLAND YELLOW-FINCH (YELLOW GRASS-FINCH)
(*Sicalis luteola*) Pl.31

Description: 5. Known primarily from Coclé grasslands. Male olive above streaked with dusky, wings with two white bars; *facial area and entire underparts bright yellow.* Female similar but duller, browner above, buffier below. Immature resembles female but is paler yellow below with a few faint dusky streaks on throat and chest.

Similar species: No other similar bird in its restricted range is so predominately yellow; female Lesser Goldfinch is smaller with white in wings. Saffron Finch is known only from Caribbean coast of Canal Zone and vicinity.

Status and distribution: Locally fairly common in short grasslands in lowlands of Pacific slope of Coclé; one sighting of 7 birds on February 4, 1967 at La Jagua, eastern Panama province (N. G. Smith). Readily seen from April to November on Pan American Highway west of Río Hato, Coclé; more difficult to find during the dry season.

Habits: Seems to gather in loose colonies during the breeding season and is often absent from other apparently suitable areas. Male has a thin buzzy trill, at times somewhat musical, delivered from an exposed perch, sometimes in flight.

Range: Southern Mexico south locally through Middle America and most of South America to southern Chile and central Argentina; introduced into Lesser Antilles.

LARGE-FOOTED FINCH
(*Pezopetes capitalis*) Pl.30

Description: 8. Found only in higher mountains of west. *Mostly olive green* with *slaty head* and *broad black stripe on each side of crown.* Juvenal similar but has olive on center of crown and is more buffy olive below, streaked with black.

Similar species: A notably large finch that appears very dark in the field. Like a brush-finch in shape and habits. See also Sooty-faced Finch.

Status and distribution: Fairly common in undergrowth of clearings and forest borders in higher mountains of western Chiriquí and adjacent Bocas del Toro, mostly above 7000 feet, locally down to 5000 feet.

Habits: Usually seen on the ground, sometimes in the open (especially on recently ploughed fields) but never far from cover. Scratches with both feet at once, like a towhee; also hops with both feet at once, giving it a peculiar bouncing gait. Generally found singly or in pairs.

Range: Costa Rica and western Panama.

YELLOW-THIGHED FINCH

(*Pselliophorus tibialis*) Pl.30

Description: 7. Found only in western Chiriquí highlands. *Entirely dark slaty,* blacker on head, throat, wings, and tail, sometimes tinged olive on breast; *conspicuous thigh tufts bright yellow.* Immature lacks the yellow thighs.

Similar species: The yellow thighs are readily seen and make this species very easy to recognize. Immatures can be known by their uniform dark slaty plumage; they are usually found with adults.

Status and distribution: Very common in forest undergrowth and borders and clearings in highlands of western Chiriquí, mostly above 5000 feet.

Habits: Very active and noisy, usually in pairs or small family groups, often joining mixed flocks of other birds. Forages mostly at lower levels.

Range: Costa Rica and western Panama.

YELLOW-GREEN FINCH

(*Pselliophorus luteoviridis*) Pl.30

Description: 7. Known only from highlands of eastern Chiriquí and Veraguas. Mostly olive green above with *black cap, wings, and tail,* bend of wing yellow; throat and sides of head grayish, *remaining underparts bright yellowish olive green,* duller on flanks; *conspicuous thigh tufts yellow.*

Similar species: Not found (apparently) with better known Yellow-thighed Finch but could at once be distinguished by its bright yellow-green underparts. See also Sooty-faced Finch.

Status and distribution: Recorded only from highlands of eastern Chiriquí (Cerro Flores) and Veraguas (Chitra, Santa Fé).

Range: Western Panama.

Note: By some authors considered conspecific with *P. tibialis* (Yellow-thighed Finch).

YELLOW-THROATED BRUSH-FINCH

(*Atlapetes gutturalis*) Pl.30

Description: 7. Found only in western highlands. *Head black* with narrow white central stripe on crown; upperparts otherwise blackish olive (browner in Azuero Peninsula birds); *throat bright yellow,* remaining underparts white, shaded with olive on flanks. Immature duller but similar.

Similar species: Prominent yellow throat and basically black and white plumage make identification of this common species easy.

Status and distribution: Very common in shrubby clearings and forest borders in highlands of Chiriquí and Veraguas (including northwestern Azuero Peninsula at Cerro Viejo, 3000 feet); in western Chiriquí mostly above 4000 feet, in eastern Chiriquí and Veraguas down to about 2800 feet.

Habits: Very active and conspicuous birds, usually found in pairs or small family groups. Forages on or near the ground like other brush-finches, but much less of a skulker.

Range: Southern Mexico to western Panama; Colombia.

BLACK-HEADED BRUSH-FINCH

(*Atlapetes atricapillus*) Pl.30

Description: 7½–8. Two forms, formerly often separated specifically, (*A. costaricensis,* Gray-striped Brush-Finch, in Chiriquí; *A. atricapillus tacarcunae* on Cerro Azul/Jefe and in Darién), are here regarded as conspecific. Cerro Azul/Jefe and Darién birds have head black with *very indistinct gray median stripe and stripe behind eye;* upperparts otherwise olive green; *mostly white below,* with sides grayish. Chiriquí birds are quite different, with *more conspicuous gray median stripe and stripe behind eye,* and sides and flanks much more broadly gray (so that, except for throat, *underparts look mostly gray*).

Similar species: Black-striped Sparrow is somewhat similar, especially to Chiriquí birds, but is considerably smaller with merely a narrow black cheek stripe (cheeks not entirely black), and usually shows yellow on bend of wing.

Status and distribution: Uncommon in thickets and forest borders in foothills and lower highlands (mostly 2000–5000 feet) in western Chiriquí; fairly common in dense undergrowth of elfin cloud forest and borders in the Cerro Azul/Jefe area; recorded also from highlands of eastern Darién.

Habits: Rather skulking and difficult to view clearly in its thick tangled habitat, but can sometimes be lured into the open by squeaking.

Range: Southwestern Costa Rica to northern Colombia.

Note: Some authors include this species in *A. torquatus* (Stripe-headed Brush-Finch) of Venezuela and Colombia to northwestern Argentina, and also include a form in Mexico.

CHESTNUT-CAPPED BRUSH-FINCH

(*Atlapetes brunneinucha*) Pl.30

Description: 7–7½. Forecrown and sides of head black, forecrown with three small white vertical stripes (visible only at close range); *crown chestnut,* upperparts otherwise olive green; mostly white below, with *black band across chest,* sides and flanks grayish.

Similar species: A handsome bird, easily recognized by the chestnut crown and black chest band. Sooty-faced Finch also has a chestnut crown, but has breast and belly yellow, black throat.

Status and distribution: Locally fairly common in forest undergrowth in foothills and highlands on both slopes, usually above 3000 feet; known from Bocas del Toro, Chiriquí, Veraguas (both slopes), Cerro Campana, and eastern Darién.

Habits: Though often fairly numerous (as attested to by mist-netting), this shy and inconspicuous species is not seen very frequently. Usually found on the ground, singly or in pairs, inside forest. Flicks leaves aside with its bill, not scratching with its feet.

Range: Central Mexico to southern Peru.

SOOTY-FACED FINCH

(*Lysurus crassirostris*) Pl.30

Description: 7. Found only in highlands. Mostly deep olive green; *cap chestnut, sides of head and throat blackish, conspicuous white moustachial streak;* center of breast and belly yellow. Juvenal dark brown above with paler brown cap; sides of head and throat dusky olive, with indistinct stripe on sides of throat; greenish brown below.

Similar species: Chestnut-capped Brush-Finch has white throat with prominent black band across chest. See also Large-footed Finch.

Status and distribution: Apparently local; known from forest undergrowth and borders of Chiriquí and adjacent Bocas del Toro (mostly 4000–8000 feet), Veraguas (both slopes), Coclé (one old specimen from Río Cascajal, on Caribbean slope), and eastern Darién; recorded mostly on Caribbean slope. Records from Panama are relatively few, but probably not uncommon at least locally; fairly numerous above Santa Fé, Veraguas, on January 4–5, 1974 (Ridgely and G. Stiles).

Habits: Usually found in pairs or small groups on or near the ground in dense tangled undergrowth of ravines and near streams; often not easy to see, though sometimes decoys well to squeaking. The characteristic call is a sharp thin whistled *pu-peee,* generally uttered when hidden in dense undergrowth.

Range: Costa Rica to eastern Panama.

ORANGE-BILLED SPARROW

(*Arremon aurantiirostris*) Pl.30

Description: 6. *Bill bright reddish orange to yellow-orange. Head mostly black* with gray stripe down center of crown and narrow white superciliary; back and sides of neck gray, upperparts otherwise olive green; *mostly white below with broad black chest band,* grayish on sides. Immature much duller with dusky bill and brownish chest band.

Status and distribution: Unusually boldly patterned for a species of the forest interior; the orange bill will make the bird known at once. Both Black-headed Brush-Finch and Black-striped Sparrow have black bills and lack black chest band.

Status and distribution: Fairly common but unobtrusive in undergrowth of forest and second-growth woodland in more humid lowlands and foothills on both slopes, ranging up to around 4000 feet.

Habits: Usually in pairs, on or very near the ground. Male has a rapid, high-pitched song that to some suggests that of the Brown Creeper (*Certhia familiaris*); it is generally given from a low hidden perch.

Range: Southeastern Mexico to northern Peru.

BLACK-STRIPED SPARROW

(*Arremonops conirostris*) Pl.30

Description: 6½. *Head gray* with *black stripe on either side of crown and narrow black* *line through eye onto cheeks;* otherwise bright olive green above, with bend of wing yellow; throat whitish, breast and sides light gray, center of lower underparts also whitish.

Similar species: Though not brightly colored, this neat dapper bird can be easily recognized by its black-striped gray head with contrasting olive green back. Somewhat resembles Black-headed Brush-Finch (especially the Chiriquí race), but is smaller and has much less black on head.

Status and distribution: Common to very common in shrubby clearings, woodland borders, and thickets in lowlands on both slopes, ranging up in smaller numbers into the foothills, to about 5500 feet in the highlands of western Chiriquí; found also on Coiba Island and the Pearl Islands.

Habits: Usually seen singly or in pairs, on or near the ground; generally rather shy, not venturing far into the open. The male's song is easily recognized and often heard, a series of accelerating notes, *cho; cho; cho, cho, cho, cho-cho-cho-ch-chchch,* with rhythm of ball bouncing to a halt. Also has a sharply accented whistle, *ho, wheét,* vaguely suggestive of a bobwhite, and several other less distinctive calls. The species is heard more often than seen.

Range: Honduras to Venezuela, extreme northern Brazil, and western Ecuador.

Note: Does not include *A. chloronotus* (Green-backed Sparrow) of southeastern Mexico to northwestern Honduras.

GRASSHOPPER SPARROW

(*Ammodramus savannarum*)

Description: 4¾. *A flat-headed, short-tailed little sparrow* of grassy savannas. Mostly brown above with a *buffy stripe down center of crown and buffy superciliary;* back streaked with buffy and blackish; buffy below, deepest on chest, paling to whitish on center of lower belly; tail pointed. Immature similar but somewhat streaked on breast and sides.

Similar species: Small size, short pointed tail, and crown striping should clinch identification. No female seedeater has stripes on head. Wedge-tailed Grass-Finch is much larger with long tail, lacks head striping.

Status and distribution: Uncommon and very local in grasslands in lowlands on Pacific slope; known only from western Chiriquí, Coclé, and eastern Panama province (around Pacora). One bird mist-netted and released at Almirante, Bocas del Toro, on November 4, 1967 (V. Kleen) probably was a North American migrant. Most readily found along Pan American Highway between Antón and Penonomé in Coclé.

Habits: Normally very hard to see, crouching in long grass, flushing for short distances with feeble fluttery flight. Most easily noted when males are singing, then perching in the open and emitting an insignificant *pi-tup-tzeeeeeeeeeeeeee,* the first notes inaudible at a distance, very like temperate North American birds.

Range: Central and southern North America south locally through Middle America to western Ecuador; Greater Antilles.

VOLCANO JUNCO

(*Junco vulcani*) Pl.31

Description: 6½. Found chiefly above timberline on *Volcán Barú. Bill pink; conspicuous yellow or orange iris.* Mostly grayish olive, grayest on sides of head, hindneck, and lower underparts; back more olive, *streaked with black;* wings and tail dusky edged with olive; outer tail feathers with pale spot toward tip. Young birds are more streaked.

Similar species: The bright yellow or orange eye is unusual among Panama fringillids; note also the pink bill, overall grayish coloration, streaked back. Unlikely to be confused at the high elevations at which this species occurs.

Status and distribution: Common at and above timberline on Volcán Barú in western Chiriquí (10,000 feet and up; once recorded at about 9,000 feet).

Habits: Rather unsuspicious. Forages mostly on the ground. The most southern and dullest of the junco group.

Range: Costa Rica and western Panama.

RUFOUS-COLLARED SPARROW

(*Zonotrichia capensis*) Pl.31

Description: 5½. Often appears slightly crested. Head mostly gray with a broad black stripe on either side of crown, a narrow black stripe behind eye, and a black "moustache"; *rufous collar on hindneck and sides of chest;* upperparts otherwise brown with blackish streaking; throat white, black patch on either side of upper chest, remaining underparts whitish. Immature much less sharply marked above, with only a trace of rufous collar; buffier below, lightly streaked with dusky on breast.

Similar species: Pert, attractive adults are easily identified by their gray and black-striped heads and prominent rufous collars;

immatures are duller and less distinctive but are the only more or less streaked sparrow-like bird in the areas they inhabit.

Status and distribution: Abundant on shrubby hillsides, agricultural fields, and around habitations in highlands of western Panama, mostly above 4000 feet; in central Panama known only from grassy slopes of Cerro Campana (above 1800 feet) and Cerro Chame in western Panama province; not found in eastern Panama, nor (apparently) on Azuero Peninsula.

Habits: Very tame and familiar. In Panama the song is a pretty whistle, *teéeo, cheéo,* suggesting song of Eastern Meadowlark; it is one of the most pleasant and characteristic sounds of the western highlands. Also has an interminably uttered *tsip . . . tsip . . . tsip. . . .*

Range: Southern Mexico to Tierra del Fuego, but usually not in tropical lowlands; Hispaniola.

LINCOLN'S SPARROW
(*Melospiza lincolnii*)

Description: 5½. Accidental. Grayish brown above streaked with blackish; crown rusty brown with narrow buffy median stripe, *pale whitish eye-ring, sides of head grayish;* whitish below, *strongly washed with buff on chest and finely streaked with dusky on breast and sides* (the streaks sometimes coalescing into a central spot).

Similar species: Though a troublesome bird to identify in its normal North American range, in Panama there are few birds much like it. Immature Rufous-collared Sparrow is the most similar: note especially the gray on the sides of the head of the Lincoln's and the fine (but *distinct,* not blurry) breast streaking; the Lincoln's has a slim, trim look to it and, unlike the Rufous-collar, is a great skulker.

Status and distribution: Only two records: a nineteenth-century specimen taken in the present Canal Zone (McLeannan), and one mist-netted and released at Almirante, Bocas del Toro, on October 31, 1967 (V. Kleen). To be watched for (especially in west) during northern fall and winter months.

Habits: A quiet, unobtrusive bird that would be expected in tangled undergrowth in second-growth woodland and borders.

Range: Breeds in northern and western North America; winters south to Honduras, accidentally to Panama.

WEDGE-TAILED GRASS-FINCH
(*Emberizoides herbicola*) Pl.31

Description: 7. *Bill mostly yellowish; tail long, pointed, and much graduated.* Pale brown above streaked with black, the wings more olive with yellow on bend of wing; *lores and eye-ring whitish;* underparts whitish, tinged with buffy on breast and sides. Immatures more yellowish below.

Similar species: Much larger and with much longer tail than Grasshopper Sparrow; also lacks crown stripes and has pale bill. Rather like female or non-breeding male Bobolink but with longer pointed tail and no dark brown on crown.

Status and distribution: Uncommon and very local in grasslands and on grassy hillsides on Pacific slope; recorded only from foothills of Chiriquí (2000–3600 feet), Cerro Campana, and eastern Panama province (Tocumen/Chepo area). Most easily seen on Cerro Campana.

Habits: Rather inconspicuous, remaining hidden in long grass. Has two songs, a musical *tleedeé, tleedeé, tleedée* with variations, and a very different buzzy *tzit-zeereéa* or *zit-zipzirrree.*

Range: Costa Rica to northeastern Argentina and southeastern Brazil.

YELLOW-BELLIED SISKIN
(*Spinus xanthogaster*) Pl.31

Description: 4½. Found only in western Chiriquí highlands. Male *mostly black* with *lemon yellow breast and belly;* patch of yellow on wings and at base of tail. Female olive green above, wings blackish with *light yellow patch;* light yellowish olive below, somewhat grayer on throat, *fading to white on lower belly.*

Similar species: Resembles Dark-backed Goldfinch, but male has black throat and chest (not all yellow below); female has yellow (not white) patch on wing and white lower belly (not uniform yellow below).

Status and distribution: Fairly common in clearings and forest borders in mountains of western Chiriquí, mostly above 6000 feet, rarely down to 4000 feet.

Habits: Distinctly prefers park-like pastures. Almost always seen in small flocks, usually feeding well up in the trees. The song is a thin but musical warbling twitter, long continued and without distinct form.

Range: Costa Rica and western Panama; Venezuela and Colombia to western Ecuador; northern Bolivia.

DARK-BACKED (LESSER) GOLDFINCH
(*Spinus psaltria*)

Description: 4. Male *glossy black above, bright yellow below,* with *white patches on wing* and near tip of tail. Female olive green above (sometimes streaked with dusky), the *wings black with white patches; uniform lemon yellow below.*

Similar species: Male Yellow-bellied Siskin has black throat and chest; female siskin has yellow (not white) patch in wing and is more olive below with white belly (not uniform yellow). Euphonias lack light patches in wings; a flock of goldfinches (or siskins) in flight can always be distinguished by their undulating flight (direct in euphonias).

Status and distribution: Common locally, but somewhat erratic, in lowlands and foothills on Pacific slope in western and central Panama, most numerous 2000–4000 feet; on Caribbean slope known only from occasional reports from middle Chagres River valley in Canal Zone. Much scarcer in central Panama than in west, with only report from east of Canal Zone area a sighting at Río Tapia, eastern Panama province, in 1934 (R. S. Arbib); most (if not all) individuals in Canal Zone area are probably escaped cage birds. Regularly found in good numbers at El Valle.

DARK-BACKED GOLDFINCH (male)

Habits: Usually found in small flocks in semi-open country. The song is long and musical, rather irregular, with interspersed twittering phrases.

Range: Western United States to Venezuela and northern Peru.

APPENDIX I

Additional Species of Southern Middle America

The following is a list of the resident species (North American migrants excluded) found in the area of Middle America from Costa Rica north through Nicaragua to Honduras which are *not* known to occur in Panama. Included is a brief outline of range and habitat preference. The species of northern Middle America from Mexico to Guatemala and El Salvador are well described and illustrated in the Peterson and Chalif *A Field Guide to Mexican Birds.* For those few species that occur in southern Middle America but not in the regions covered by either the Peterson and Chalif guide or in the main text of this book, a brief description is given. Species recorded only from the far offshore islands (such as the Swan Islands off Caribbean Honduras, and Cocos Island well off Pacific Costa Rica) are not included.

The author has had no field experience in Nicaragua and Honduras. Thus much of the information presented here is second-hand, obtained from various published sources, in addition to the Peterson-Chalif field guide, particularly Eisenmann's *The Species of Middle American Birds,* Monroe's *The Birds of Honduras,* and Slud's *The Birds of Costa Rica,* and to a lesser extent Land's *Birds of Guatemala,* Russell's *The Birds of British Honduras,* Dickey and Van Rossem's *The Birds of El Salvador,* Smithe's *The Birds of Tikal,* and various shorter articles. Supplementary information may be found in Edwards's *A Field Guide to the Birds of Mexico* and Davis's *A Field Guide to the Birds of Mexico and Central America.* Some information is also derived from unpublished data of F. Gary Stiles (for Costa Rica) or E. Eisenmann (for other areas), whose assistance is gratefully acknowledged. For the present, there is no field guide for this southern Central American area that uses the generally adopted English and scientific nomenclature; thus it is felt that this brief synopsis should prove useful.

Most of the abbreviations used should be self-explanatory (spec. = specimen); a list of the more frequent geographic abbreviations follows, proceeding generally southward:

N.Am.—North America
S.Am.—South America
U.S.—United States
Pac.—Pacific
Carib.—Caribbean
Mex.—Mexico
Yuc.—Yucatan Peninsula
Guat.—Guatemala
ElS.—El Salvador
Hond.—Honduras
Nic.—Nicaragua
C.R.—Costa Rica
W.I.—West Indies
Gr.Ant.—Greater Antilles
Col.—Colombia
Venez.—Venezuela

Slaty-breasted Tinamou (*Crypturellus boucardi*)—Carib. slope se. Mex. to C.R.; terrestrial in forest.

Thicket (Rufescent) Tinamou (*C. cinnamomeus*)—Mex. to nw. C.R., also ne. Col. and nw. Venez.; woodland and scrubby areas in semi-arid regions, terrestrial.

Pinnated Bittern (*Botaurus pinnatus*)—locally in fresh marshes se. Mex., Belize, w. Guat., se. Nic., C.R., and S.Am. See main text under American Bittern.

Pearl Kite (*Gampsonyx swainsonii*)—mostly S. Am. with isolated population in w. Nic. A small (8–9″) kestrel-like bird of prey, mostly dark gray above with buff forehead and sides of head, white collar edged chestnut; white below with patch on sides black or rufous; thighs tawny.

White-breasted Hawk (*Accipiter chinogaster*) —highlands s. Mex. to Nic.; pine woodland, cloud forest, borders. Perhaps conspecific with *A. striatus* (Sharp-shinned Hawk).

Plain Chachalaca (*Ortalis vetula*)—s. Texas and e. Mex. to nw. C.R., chiefly Carib. slope (not ElS.); light woodland, shrubby areas, forest borders.

White-bellied Chachalaca (*O. leucogastra*)—Pac. slope lowlands s. Mex. to w. Nic.; woodland borders, shrubby areas.

Black Penelopina (Chachalaca) (*Penelopina nigra*)—highlands s. Mex. to Nic.; cloud forest.

Buffy-crowned Wood-Partridge (*Dendrortyx leucophrys*)—highlands s. Mex. to C.R.; pine and pine-oak woodland, cloud forest.

Black-throated Bobwhite (*Colinus nigrogularis*)—clearings and fields Yuc., Belize, n. Guat., also pine savannas of e. Hond. and e. Nic.

Spot-bellied Bobwhite (*C. leucopogon*)—Guat. to cen. C.R., mostly Pac. slope; open areas, savannas. Perhaps conspecific with *C. cristatus* (Crested Bobwhite).

Singing Quail (*Dactylortyx thoracicus*)—highlands (mostly) cen. Mex. to Hond.; cloud forest, oak-pine woodland.

Ocellated Quail (*Cyrtonyx ocellatus*)—highlands s. Mex. to Nic.; grassy understory in open pine woodland, borders.

Ruddy Crake (*Laterallus ruber*)—e. Mex. to nw. C.R. (sightings); fresh marshes and adjacent areas.

Ocellated Crake (*Micropygia schomburgkii*) —locally in S.Am. east of Andes, one spec. sw. C.R. See main text under Yellow-breasted Crake.

Double-striped Thick-knee (*Burhinus bistriatus*)—s. Mex. to nw. C.R., also Hispaniola and locally in n. S.Am.; open areas, savannas.

Roseate Tern (*Sterna dougallii*)—breeds on islands off Carib. coast of Belize and Hond. (also on coasts locally of e. N.Am., W.I., islands in s. Caribbean, and in Old World). See main text under Common Tern.

Red-billed Pigeon (*Columba flavirostris*)—s. Tex. and Mex. to cen. C.R.; woodland, shrubby areas.

Inca Dove (*Scardafella inca*)—sw. U.S. to sw. C.R.; open and scrubby areas in drier regions. See main text under Mourning Dove.

Common (Scaly) Ground-Dove (*Columbina passerina*)—s. U.S. to cen. C.R., also W.I. and n. and e. S.Am.; semi-open and shrubby areas, gardens, mainly in drier regions.

Caribbean Dove (*Leptotila jamaicensis*)—Yuc. and islands off n. Hond., also Jamaica, Grand Cayman, St. Andrew; scrubby woodland.

White-faced Quail-Dove (*Geotrygon albifacies*)—highlands s. Mex. to Nic.; cloud forest, semi-terrestrial. Perhaps conspecific with the S. Am. *G. linearis* (Lined Quail-Dove), *G. chiriquensis* then also being included.

Green Parakeet (*Aratinga holochlora*)—n. Mex. to Nic., in Cen. Am. mostly in highlands; semi-open areas, scrub, pine woodland.

Pacific Parakeet (*A. strenua*)—Pac. slope lowlands s. Mex. to Nic. Perhaps conspecific with the preceding species.

Orange-fronted Parakeet (*A. canicularis*)—w. Mex. to nw. C.R., mostly Pac. slope; scrubby woodland, open areas.

Yellow-lored Amazon (Parrot) (*Amazona xantholora*)—Yuc. and Belize, Hond. (one spec., Roatán Id.); woodland.

White-fronted Amazon (Parrot) (*A. albifrons*)—w. and s. Mex. to nw. C.R., mostly Pac. slope; scrubby woodland, semi-open areas.

Lesser Ground-Cuckoo (*Morococcyx erythropygius*)—w. Mex. to nw. C.R., mostly Pac. slope; thickets in semi-open areas, scrubby woodland, terrestrial.

Lesser Roadrunner (*Geococcyx velox*)—w. and s. Mex. to n. Nic.; thickets in semi-open areas, scrub, terrestrial.

Spotted (Whiskered) Screech-Owl (*Otus trichopsis*)—foothills and highlands se. Ariz. and Mex. to Hond.; pine and pine-oak woodland.

Pacific Screech-Owl (*O. cooperi*)—Pac. slope s. Mex. to nw. C.R.; scrubby woodland and groves in open arid regions.

Northern Pygmy-Owl (*Glaucidium gnoma*) —w. N.Am. s. in highlands to Hond.; pine and pine-oak woodland.

Fulvous Owl (*Strix fulvescens*)—highlands s. Mex. to ElS. and Hond.; cloud forest, pine-oak woodland. Perhaps conspecific with the Barred Owl (*S. varia*) of North America and northern Mexico.

Stygian Owl (*Asio stygius*)—very locally in highlands Mex., Guat., Belize, Nic., and also Gr.Ant. and S.Am.; forest. See main text under Striped Owl.

Ocellated Poorwill (*Nyctiphrynus ocellatus*) —locally in S.Am., one spec. from ne. Nic. Mostly reddish brown or blackish, white band across lower throat and round white spots on belly, outer tail feathers tipped white (8½–9″).

Buff-collared Nightjar (Ridgway's Whip-poor-will or Cookacheea) (*Caprimulgus ridgwayi*)—se. Ariz. and Mex. to Hond.; open areas with scattered rocks, bushes, trees.

Spot-tailed Nightjar (Pit-sweet) (*C. maculicaudus*)—locally in s. Mex., Hond., e. Nic., and also S.Am.; open grassy areas, pine savannas. See main text under White-tailed Nightjar.

Tawny-collared Nightjar (Chip-willow) (*C. salvini*)—e. Mex. to n. Nic. (not recorded ElS. or Hond.); open areas with scattered bushes, woodland borders.

Black Swift (*Cypseloides niger*)—locally in highlands from w. N.Am. to C.R. and in W.I., perhaps winters in S.Am. (one spec.). See main text under White-chinned Swift.

Spot-fronted Swift (*C. cherriei*)—rare, recorded C.R., n. Col., w. Venez. See main text under White-chinned Swift.

White-throated Swift (*Aeronautes saxatalis*) —highlands w. N.Am. to Hond.

Great Swallow-tailed Swift (*Panyptila sanctihieronymi*)—locally in highlands Mex. to C.R. (sightings).

Wedge-tailed Sabrewing (*Campylopterus curvipennis*)—e. Mex. to n. Guat. and Belize, also e. Hond.; undergrowth in forest, woodland, borders.

Emerald-chinned Hummingbird (*Abeillia abeillei*)—highlands s. Mex. to n. Nic.; cloud forest.

Black-crested Coquette (*Lophornis helenae*) —Carib. slope s. Mex. to cen. C.R.; woodland and forest borders, clearings. See main text under Rufous-crested Coquette.

White-eared Hummingbird (*Hylocharis leucotis*)—highlands extreme sw. U.S. and Mex. to Nic.; pine and pine-oak woodland.

White-bellied Emerald (*Amazilia candida*)—s. Mex. to C.R. (not recorded ElS.); forest, borders, clearings.

Honduran Emerald (*A. luciae*)—endemic to Hond.; "presumably a forest inhabitant" (Monroe). Bill very slightly decurved (1″), lower mandible red basally; metallic green above; throat and chest glittering greenish blue to blue (feathers often with paler edging), sides and flanks green, belly white; tail bronzy green with blackish subterminal band (3½″).

Red-billed Azurecrown (*A. cyanocephala*)—highlands e. Mex. to Nic.; pine and pine-oak woodland, borders, also pine savannas in lowlands of e. Hond. and e. Nic.

Berylline Hummingbird (*A. beryllina*)—highlands s. Mex. to Hond.; pine and pine-oak woodland, borders.

Mangrove Hummingbird (*A. boucardi*)—mangroves and adjacent areas on Pac. coast of C.R. See main text under Snowy-breasted Hummingbird.

Indigo-capped (Blue-fronted) Hummingbird (*A. cyanifrons*)—Col., one spec. C.R. Bill straight (¾″); crown glittering blue, otherwise shining green above, glittering green below; tail blue-black (3½″). ♀ similar but duller.

Blue-tailed Hummingbird (*A. cyanura*)—s. Mex. to Nic., rarely to ne. C.R.; scrubby woodland, borders.

Steely-vented (Blue-vented) Hummingbird (*A. saucerottei*)—w. Nic. and C.R., also Col. and w. Venez.; semi-open country, borders. Bill straight (¾″); mostly dark shining green, lower back and rump more bronzy; tail blue-black (3½″).

Cinnamon Hummingbird (*A. rutila*)—w. and s. Mex. to cen. C.R., mostly Pac. slope; open scrubby areas, woodland borders.

Buff-bellied (Fawn-breasted) Hummingbird (*A. yucatanensis*)—s. Texas and Mex. to n. Guat. and Belize, winters rarely to Hond.; light woodland, shrubby clearings.

Coppery-headed Emerald (*Elvira cupreiceps*) —endemic to Carib. slope C.R. (mostly foothills, lower highlands); humid forest, borders. Bill rather short (½″), decurved; metallic green above, more coppery on crown; shining green below with white under tail-coverts; tail mostly white, tipped with grayish, central pair of feathers bronzy (3″). ♀ metallic green above, whitish below with green spotting on sides, tail as in male.

Amethyst-throated Hummingbird (*Lampornis amethystinus*)—highlands cen. Mex. to ElS. and Hond.; cloud forest, pine-oak woodland.

Green-throated Mountaingem (*L. viridipallens*)—highlands s. Mex. to w. Hond.; pine-oak woodland, cloud forest.

Green-breasted Mountaingem (*L. sybillae*) —highlands Hond. and Nic.; pine-oak woodland, cloud forest. Resembles previous species (with which it is perhaps conspecific), but ♂ with much more green below, ♀ with buff throat.

Garnet-throated Hummingbird (*Lamprolaima rhami*)—highlands s. Mex. to ElS. and Hond.; cloud forest, pine-oak woodland.
Plain-capped Starthroat (*Heliomaster constantii*)—Pac. slope w. Mex. to cen. C.R.; light woodland, clearings, scrub.
Slender Sheartail (*Doricha enicura*)—highlands s. Mex. to w. Hond. (two spec.); woodland, shrubby clearings.
Sparkling-tailed Hummingbird (*Tilmatura dupontii*)—highlands cen. Mex. to Nic.; woodland, shrubby clearings.
Wine-throated Hummingbird (*Atthis ellioti*)—highlands s. Mex. to Hond.; cloud forest, pine and pine-oak woodland, borders.
Cerise-throated Hummingbird (*Selasphorus simoni*)—endemic to highlands of cen. C.R. Very closely resembles C.R. race of Volcano Hummingbird (with reddish purple throat) but ♂ has brighter less purple gorget, and both sexes have central pair of tail feathers mostly bronzy black (not green).
Black-headed Trogon (*Trogon melanocephalus*)—e. Mex. to n. C.R.; second-growth and open woodland. Often considered conspecific with *T. citreolus* (Citreoline Trogon) of Pac. slope Mex.
Mountain Trogon (*T. mexicanus*)—highlands n. Mex. to Hond.; cloud forest, pine-oak woodland.
Elegant (Coppery-tailed) Trogon (*T. elegans*)—extreme sw. U.S. to nw. C.R.; woodland.
Blue-throated Motmot (*Aspatha gularis*)—highlands s. Mex. to Hond.; cloud forest, pine-oak woodland.
Keel-billed Motmot (*Electron carinatum*)—s. Mex. to C.R., mostly Carib. slope; forest. See main text under Broad-billed Motmot.
Turquoise-browed Motmot (*Eumomota superciliosa*)—s. Mex. to nw. C.R.; scrubby and gallery woodland in semi-open areas.
Common Flicker (*Colaptes auratus*)—N.Am. to n. Nic. (from s. Mex. south, one of the "red-shafted" forms, the *mexicanoides* group) in highlands; pine and pine-oak woodland.
Golden-fronted Woodpecker (*Melanerpes aurifrons*)—Texas and Mex. to cen. C.R.; trees in open and semi-open areas. Included is *M. hoffmannii* (Hoffmann's Woodpecker) of s. Hond. to C.R., often regarded as specifically distinct.
Red-vented Woodpecker (*M. pygmaeus*)—Yuc., Belize, Hond. (Guanaja Id.); open scrubby woodland.
Ladder-backed Woodpecker (*Dendrocopus scalaris*)—sw. U.S. to ne. Nic.; trees in open arid areas, scrubby woodland, pine savannas.
Ivory-billed Woodcreeper (*Xiphorhynchus flavigaster*)—Mex. to nw. C.R.; woodland, forest, semi-open areas.
Rufous-breasted Spinetail (*Synallaxis erythrothorax*)—s. Mex. to ElS. and nw. Hond.; thickets in semi-open areas, woodland.
Streak-crowned Antvireo (*Dysithamnus striaticeps*)—Carib. slope se. Hond. to C.R.; forest undergrowth. See main text under Spot-crowned Antvireo.
Gray-headed Manakin (*Piprites griseiceps*)—Guat. (one spec.) to n. C.R., mainly on Carib. slope; humid forest undergrowth.
Long-tailed Manakin (*Chiroxiphia linearis*)—s. Mex. to nw. C.R., mostly on Pac. slope; undergrowth in light woodland.
White-collared Manakin (*Manacus candei*)—se. Mex. to C.R., mostly Carib. slope lowlands; undergrowth in woodland, forest borders.
Lovely Cotinga (*Cotinga amabilis*)—lowlands Carib. slope se. Mex. to C.R.; forest, forest borders. See main text under Blue Cotinga.
Gray-collared Becard (*Pachyramphus major*)—Mex. to e. Nic., largely in highlands; cloud forest, pine-oak woodland.
Rose-throated Becard (*Platypsaris aglaiae*)—extreme sw. U.S. and Mex. to n. C.R.; woodland, borders, clearings with large trees. Some southern males lack the rose throat.
Nutting's (Pale-throated) Flycatcher (*Myiarchus nuttingi*)—w. Mex. to nw. C.R., mostly Pac. slope; woodland, forest borders.
Brown-crested (Wied's Crested) Flycatcher (*M. tyrannulus*)—sw. U.S. to nw. C.R., also S.Am.; scrubby woodland, semi-open country.
Greater Pewee (Coues' Flycatcher) (*Contopus pertinax*)—highlands sw. U.S. and Mex. to n. Nic.; pine and pine-oak woodland.
Buff-breasted Flycatcher (*Empidonax fulvifrons*)—highlands se. Ariz. and Mex. to Hond.; pine-oak and pine woodland.
Tawny-chested Flycatcher (*Aphanotriccus capitalis*)—Carib. slope lowlands Nic. and C.R.; undergrowth of forest borders, woodland. Head slaty gray with incomplete white eye-ring, otherwise olive above with two tawny wing-bars; throat pale gray, chest and sides tawny, lower underparts pale yellow (5″).
Stub-tailed Spadebill (*Platyrinchus cancrominus*)—se. Mex. to nw. C.R.; forest and

woodland undergrowth, mostly in lowlands. Often treated as a race of *P. mystaceus* (White-throated Spadebill), for which see main text.

Northern Beardless Tyrannulet (Beardless Flycatcher) (*Camptostoma imberbe*)—extreme sw. U.S. and Mex. to nw. C.R.; scrubby woodland, semi-open areas.

Yellow-bellied Tyrannulet (*Ornithion semiflavum*)—se. Mex. to sw. C.R.; woodland, forest borders.

Black-capped Swallow (*Notiochelidon pileata*)—highlands s. Mex. to ElS., rarely to w. Hond.; mostly open areas, borders.

Common (Northern) Raven (*Corvus corax*)—N.Am. s. in highlands to Nic., also Eurasia and n. Africa; open areas, cliffs.

Magpie Jay (*Calocitta formosa*)—w. Mex. to nw. C.R., mostly Pac. slope; semi-open areas, light woodland.

Green Jay (*Cyanocorax yncas*)—s. Texas and Mex. to Hond., also S.Am.; woodland, forest.

Bushy-crested Jay (*Cissilopha melanocyanea*)—Guat. to Nic., mostly highlands; open woodland, borders.

Black-throated Jay (*Cyanolyca pumilo*)—highlands s. Mex. to ElS. and Hond.; cloud forest, pine-oak woodland.

Unicolored Jay (*Aphelocoma unicolor*)—highlands s. Mex. to Hond.; cloud forest, pine-oak woodland.

Steller's Jay (*Cyanocitta stelleri*)—highlands w. N.Am. to Nic.; pine and pine-oak woodland, borders.

Brown Creeper (*Certhia familiaris*)—N.Am. s. in highlands to Nic., also Eurasia; pine and pine-oak woodland.

Rufous-naped Wren (*Campylorhynchus rufinucha*)—cen. Mex. to nw. C.R., mostly Pac. slope; thickets in semi-open areas, woodland borders, savannas.

Banded Wren (*Thryothorus pleurostictus*)—Pac. slope sw. Mex. to nw. C.R.; thickets in scrubby woodland, borders.

White-browed Wren (*T. albinucha*)—Yuc., Guat., Nic.; undergrowth in scrubby woodland in drier regions. Perhaps a race of *T. ludovicianus* (Carolina Wren) of e. U.S. to ne. Mex.

Spot-breasted Wren (*T. maculipectus*)—e. Mex. to n. C.R., also Col. to n. Peru; undergrowth in forest borders and woodland.

Rufous-browed Wren (*Troglodytes rufociliatus*)—highlands s. Mex. to ElS. and Hond.; cloud forest, pine-oak woodland.

White-bellied Wren (*Uropsila leucogastra*)—Mex. to n. Guat. and Belize, also n. Hond. (Coyoles); forest, woodland.

Rock Wren (*Salpinctes obsoletus*)—w. U.S. to nw. C.R., mostly foothills and highlands; rocky open areas, cliffs.

Blue-and-white Mockingbird (*Melanotis hypoleucus*)—highlands s. Mex. to ElS. and Hond.; undergrowth in shrubby clearings, woodland.

Black Catbird (*Melanoptila glabrirostris*)—Yuc., Belize, n. Guat., also nw. Hond. (Omoa); undergrowth in woodland, borders.

Brown-backed Solitaire (*Myadestes obscurus*)—highlands n. Mex. to ElS. and Hond.; cloud forest, pine-oak woodland.

Slate-colored Solitaire (*M. unicolor*)—highlands s. Mex. to Nic.; cloud forest.

Rufous-collared Robin (Thrush) (*Turdus rufitorques*)—highlands s. Mex. to ElS. and w. Hond. (one spec.); cloud forest, pine-oak woodland, borders.

Black Robin (Thrush) (*T. infuscatus*)—highlands cen. Mex. to ElS. and Hond.; cloud forest, pine-oak woodland.

Spotted Nightingale-Thrush (*Catharus dryas*)—highlands s. Mex. to Hond., also S.Am.; cloud forest.

Eastern Bluebird (*Sialia sialis*)—e. and cen. N.Am. to Nic., in Mid.Am. mostly in highland pine and pine-oak woodland, also lowland pine savannas of e. Hond. and e. Nic.

White-lored Gnatcatcher (*Polioptila albiloris*)—sw. Mex. to nw. C.R., mostly Pac. slope; scrubby woodland and shrubby areas in semi-arid regions.

Mangrove Vireo (*Vireo pallens*)—mostly along both coasts from w. Mex. and Yuc. to nw. C.R. and ne. Nic.; mangroves and adjacent woodland, also shrubby clearings. Two species may be involved, one on either coast.

Yucatan Vireo (*V. magister*)—Yuc., Belize, Hond. (Bay Ids.), also Grand Cayman; mangroves, woodland.

Warbling Vireo (*V. gilvus*)—breeds N.Am. s. in highlands to Nic., northern birds wintering rarely to C.R.; pine-oak woodland, cloud forest, borders. Mid.Am. breeding forms from s. Mex. s. to Nic. are sometimes included in *V. leucophrys* (Brown-capped Vireo) of C.R. southward, or all are merged in one species (*V. gilvus*).

Cinnamon Flower-piercer (*Diglossa baritula*)—highlands cen. Mex. to ElS. and Hond.; shrubby clearings, woodland and forest borders.

Crescent-chested Warbler (*Vermivora superciliosa*)—highlands n. Mex. to Nic.; cloud forest, pine-oak woodland.

Tawny-headed (Olive) Warbler (*Peucedramus taeniatus*)—highlands sw. U.S. to Nic.; pine (mostly) and pine-oak woodland.

Grace's Warbler (*Dendroica graciae*)—highlands sw. U.S. to n. Nic. in pine and pine-oak woodland, also lowland pine savannas of e. Hond. and e. Nic.

Painted Redstart (*Myioborus pictus*)—highlands sw. U.S. to Nic.; pine and pine-oak woodland.

Fan-tailed Warbler (*Euthlypis lachrymosa*)—Mex. to nw. Nic., mostly highlands; undergrowth in woodland and forest.

Golden-browed Warbler (*Basileuterus belli*)—highlands Mex. to ElS. and Hond.; undergrowth in cloud forest and pine-oak woodland.

Nicaraguan Grackle (*Cassidix nicaraguensis*)—Nic. and n. C.R.; semi-open areas. Much smaller (♂12″; ♀10″) than Great-tailed Grackle, with less creased tail; male glossy blue-black; female brown, paler below.

Melodious Blackbird (*Dives dives*)—e. Mex. to Nic.; semi-open country, borders.

Black-vented Oriole (*Icterus wagleri*)—highlands n. Mex. (casually extreme sw. U.S.) to n. Nic.; scrubby areas, woodland borders.

Spot-breasted Oriole (*I. pectoralis*)—sw. Mex. to nw. C.R., mostly Pac. slope (introduced s. Florida); scrubby areas, light woodland in semi-arid regions.

Black-throated (Altamira or Lichtenstein's) Oriole (*I. gularis*)—s. Texas and Mex. to Nic.; scrubby areas, woodland in semi-open areas.

Streak-backed (Scarlet-headed) Oriole (*I. pustulatus*)—w. Mex. (casually extreme sw. U.S.) to nw. C.R., mostly Pac. slope; scrubby areas in semi-open regions.

Red-winged Blackbird (*Agelaius phoeniceus*)—N.Am. to nw. C.R.; marshes.

Blue-crowned Chlorophonia (*Chlorophonia occipitalis*)—highlands (descending in winter) s. Mex. to n. Nic.; cloud forest borders.

Scrub Euphonia (*Euphonia affinis*)—Mex. to nw. C.R.; woodland, borders, scrubby areas, mostly in semi-arid regions.

Yellow-winged Tanager (*Thraupis abbas*)—e. Mex. to n. Nic.; woodland borders, clearings.

Black-cheeked Ant-Tanager (*Habia atrimaxillaris*)—endemic to sw. C.R. (Golfo Dulce region); undergrowth in forest and woodland. Blackish above and on cheeks with partly concealed red crown patch; dull reddish below, becoming grayish on lower underparts, sexes alike, female duller (7″).

Black-throated Shrike-Tanager (*Lanio aurantius*)—Carib. slope s. Mex. to Hond.; forest and woodland. Perhaps conspecific with *L. leucothorax* (White-throated Shrike-Tanager).

Ashy-throated Bush-Tanager (*Chlorospingus canigularis*)—foothills and lower highlands on Carib. slope of C.R., also S.Am.; humid forest. Drab; olive green above (no white head markings); throat gray, breast and sides yellowish green, lower underparts whitish (5″).

Grayish Saltator (*Saltator coerulescens*)—Mex. to cen. C.R., also S.Am. east of Andes; scrubby areas, woodland borders, around habitations.

Blue Bunting (*Cyanocompsa parellina*)—n. Mex. to Nic.; undergrowth in woodland and forest borders, shrubby clearings.

Peg-billed Finch (*Acanthidops bairdi*)—endemic to montane forests of cen. C.R. See main text under Slaty Finch.

Olive Sparrow (*Arremonops rufivirgata*)—s. Texas and Mex. to n. Guat., also sw. Nic. and nw. C.R.; scrubby areas, undergrowth in light woodland. Southern race (*superciliosa*) much brighter than northern birds.

Green-backed Sparrow (*A. chloronotus*)—s. Mex. to n. Hond.; undergrowth in shrubby clearings and woodland borders. Closely allied to and replaces *A. conirostris* (Black-striped Sparrow).

White-faced (Prevost's) Ground-Sparrow (*Melozone biarcuatum*)—highlands s. Mex. to Hond., also cen. C.R.; shrubby clearings, coffee plantations. The Costa Rican form, *cabanisi*, has been treated as a distinct species (Cabanis' Ground-Sparrow); it differs from the northern populations in having a large black patch on breast, less facial white, more rufous on sides of head, and a black streak on each side of throat.

White-eared Ground-Sparrow (*M. leucotis*)—highlands s. Mex. to C.R. (not Hond.); undergrowth in shrubby clearings, forest borders. C.R. race (nominate *leucotis*) has less prominent eyestripe and more black on underparts than northern birds.

Stripe-headed Sparrow (*Aimophila ruficauda*)—w. Mex. to nw. C.R., mostly Pac. slope; scrub and thickets in semi-arid regions.

Rusty Sparrow (*A. rufescens*)—n. Mex. to nw. C.R.; brushy areas in pine woodland and savanna, grassy fields with scattered trees.

Botteri's Sparrow (*A. botterii*)—extreme sw. U.S. and Mex. to Guat., also lowland pine savannas of e. Hond. and e. Nic., and highlands w. Nic. and nw. C.R.; open grassy areas with scattered bushes or rocks. Birds from lowlands of s. Mex. and Guat. southward have been considered a distinct species, *A. petenica* (Yellow-carpalled or Petén Sparrow).

Chipping Sparrow (*Spizella passerina*)—N.Am. to n. Nic.; in Mid.Am. mostly in pine woodland or savanna.

Black-headed Siskin (*Spinus notatus*)—w. and s. Mex. to Nic., mostly in highlands; pine and pine-oak woodland, also lowland pine savanna of e. Nic.

Red Crossbill (*Loxia curvirostra*)—N.Am. s. in highlands to n. Nic. (not ElS.) in pine woodland, also lowland pine savanna of e. Hond. and e. Nic., also Eurasia.

APPENDIX II

Finding Birds in Panama

Birds are abundant in Panama, and many species can be seen with little or no effort almost "anywhere." But many others can be found only by searching them out in their favored haunts. This section will suggest some accessible areas that have been found especially productive in recent years. Localities in central Panama are emphasized, for I realize that the vast majority of visitors and residents will spend most of their time there; some western Panama localities, particularly several in the fascinating Chiriquí highlands, are also included. Such information is often out of date before it hits the press, especially with regard to the rapidly developing topics, but I hope nonetheless that this compendium will prove useful for a time.

Accommodations are plentiful and good in Panama city, more limited in Colon; English is spoken widely, and food and water are generally perfectly safe. Away from central Panama, adequate lodgings are fewer, though there are good hotels in the Chiriquí highlands. Removed from the influence of the Canal Zone, English is spoken much less, and reasonable caution is advised concerning food and water, especially in the lowlands away from population centers. Though public transportation is available almost everywhere (and is inexpensive), the most convenient way of getting around is a rental car (readily available), though gasoline is costly. 4-wheel drive is useful on some side roads, but not necessary and difficult to procure. Any time of the year is good for birds, though the dry season (January–March) has the most dependably good weather, and the first part of the rainy season (April–June) marks the height of local nesting, with an increase in vocalizing.

Several suggestions may be made regarding effective tropical birding, especially in forest. Perhaps most important is that results will always be best at and soon after dawn. Make every effort to get out as early as possible, then relax during the midday heat, when bird activity often is virtually nil. Birding by ear becomes especially crucial in woodland and forest, where so many species are difficult to see; one should learn as many vocalizations as possible, especially of the common species, in order to pick out the unusual or different sound and track it down to its source. A good tape recorder can be a useful aid under such circumstances; the calls of relatively few neotropical species are available commercially, but it is often possible to record a calling bird on the spot, and then play its own voice back at it, thereby often luring it in for a close view. Wear light-weight and neutrally colored clothing (avoiding bright colors and bold patterns); long pants and sturdy footwear are advised, especially if you plan to "bushwhack" frequently. Finally, while many birds may be seen from the roadside, bear in mind that it is only by actually entering the forest, either on or off a trail, that some of the shyer and more obscure (but also some of the most interesting) species will be recorded, birds such as wood-quail, quail-doves, leaf-tossers, many antbirds, and numerous tyrannids. With a few precautions (the most important simply being sure you are not getting lost), there is nothing especially to fear in so doing. Snakes, for example, are seen only very rarely (unless you are actually looking for them, under logs, etc.), poisonous varieties almost never. Ants are much more numerous, and are more likely to create a problem as most can sting or bite, some viciously, but these can generally be avoided by remaining alert. For a variety of reasons it is best to be careful of where you sit, and never to put your hands anywhere without looking first. It should also be mentioned that annoying flying insects such as mosquitoes are in general remarkably few, though ticks and chiggers may be encountered in some numbers (against them a liberal use of insect repellent seems the best defense).

The foregoing applies especially to forests in the lowlands. In highland forests, snakes, ants, and mosquitoes are much less numerous, and bird activity is greater throughout the day; adjustments can be made accordingly. In more open areas of the lowlands, temperatures rise very rapidly during the morning, and the heat during the middle of the day can be brutal; it is thus all the more important to be in the field early. For waterbirds also, the hours near dawn and dusk are generally the most favorable for observation, not only because of their increased activity at such times but also because of the often severe heat haze that develops during midday. Raptors, too, are especially in evidence during the early morning hours, perching conspicuously on bare branches, later remaining relatively hidden in dense foliage.

The sequence of localities mentioned below starts on the Pacific side of the Canal Zone and vicinity, works north to the Caribbean side of the Canal Zone area, returns to the Pacific slope in eastern Panama province, and finally works west on the Pacific slope to Chiriquí.

Panama city

A number of common and widespread birds can be seen within the city limits. The waterfront along Balboa Avenue, especially toward Paitilla Point, can be good for shorebirds, gulls and terns, etc., particularly at high tide.

Panama Viejo

The ruins of old Panama city, sacked by Henry Morgan in the seventeenth century, dominate this area on the Pacific coast a few miles east of the center of the present city. The vast mudflats offshore are of primary interest to the ornithologist. Low tide is the least satisfactory time for a visit, for the birds are then scattered over the great expanse of mud; at high tide many roost on exposed rocks or inshore (consult local newspaper for tide schedules). The area is thronged with shorebirds at all seasons, but especially during migration periods, with fewer during northern summer months; many other coastal birds will also be seen. One can either walk along the main road and scan or walk out a sandspit (the mud itself is treacherous), sometimes covered at high tide, which starts near the statue of Morelos.[1]

Fort Amador

Fort Amador is a joint Army-Navy post located on the eastern side of the Pacific entrance to the Canal. Access is unrestricted. The grounds of the fort itself are attractively landscaped and good for a variety of the commoner species, but again it is the coastal and shorebirds that are the top attraction here. Soon after driving through the gate, one will notice the large Naval headquarters building on the left; the parking lot behind this building overlooks a lagoon, totally exposed at low tide, which can be excellent for shorebirds, especially at high tide when the birds roost in close. Continuing past Naval headquarters, bear right around a large field on the left and along a row of barracks on the right. Continue straight until passing the Officer's Club, on the left, beyond which a short dirt road to the left leads down to the shore; a walk in either direction is often productive, especially toward the point to the right. Continue out the causeway, watching for birds as you go. The first island is Naos, where the Smithsonian Institution has a marine research facility. The farthest out island and most interesting is Flamenco, but one must have a key to pass its entrance gate. This key is sometimes available at the Smithsonian, or at Building #5 on Fort Amador. The view from the top of the island is superb; watch for boobies and other seabirds, as well as Mangrove Warblers in the scrubby woods; large iguana lizards are common.

Farfan Beach

Farfan lies opposite Fort Amador on the western side of the Pacific entrance to the Canal. Cross the Bridge of the Americas over the Canal, and turn left on a narrow but paved road just on the other side. After almost one half mile, bear right at the only intersection onto an even narrower but still paved road. This whole area is an interesting mosaic of woodland and shrubby clearing habitats, and is often alive with bird

[1] A Guardia Nacional cuartel (local police station) is on the point at Panama Viejo. In August 1975 an American birder was detained for several days here, accused of allegedly "spying" on the Guardia post. Hopefully this unfortunate incident will prove an isoated one, but sensible caution must be urged for the present.

activity in the early morning; watch for Gray-headed Chachalaca, White-necked Puffbird, Barred Antshrike, Masked Tityra, Panama Flycatcher, Rufous-and-white Wren, Golden-fronted Greenlet, Red-legged Honeycreeper, Yellow-backed Oriole, Plain-colored Tanager, Thick-billed Seed-Finch, etc. A little over a half-mile from the fork, the road drops down and skirts a narrow growth of mangroves on the left, with a recently flooded area on the right (hence the many dead trees). Proceed for another half-mile to a small spillway. The flooded area on the right, though unattractive, is good for a variety of fresh water birds and Pale-vented Pigeon and Mangrove Swallow, while the bayshore on the left usually has many coastal birds. Beyond the spillway, the road passes through more extensive woodland. Farfan is best covered on weekday early mornings, as at other times it frequently becomes very crowded.

Balboa and Vicinity

Many birds can be seen in the beautiful landscaped gardens and scattered patches of woodland on the lower slopes of Ancon Hill. The most convenient areas are above the Canal Zone Administration Building, and along Gorgas Road down to Gorgas Hospital. Swifts are usually numerous overhead; watch especially for Short-tailed and Lesser Swallow-tailed. Nearby Albrook Air Force Base offers one of the few extensive open grassy areas in the Canal Zone, and as such holds several savanna species not common in the Zone. A good vantage point is through the fence behind the Canal Zone Library; here one can almost invariably find Yellowish Pipits, among others. The runway area and nearby fields are also good for shorebirds during fall migration.

Fort Clayton

This is a fairly large Army post located north and east of Albrook AFB; access is unrestricted. A good deal of fine second-growth woodland can be found on the fort. The easiest approach is via the "back" or Curundu gate; after entering proceed for about 1¾ miles, following the signs to Fort Clayton (there are many side roads). At this point a road to the left leads back to Albrook AFB, while an unpaved road cuts off to the right (a service station is just beyond, also on the right). Take the right-hand road which, though now unmaintained, is usually traversible. It passes through fine woodland, especially after about a mile, and various smaller roads and trails on either side lead into even more undisturbed areas. About two miles from the start, the road deteriorates rapidly, and must be walked. A fine variety of woodland birds should be found, including White-vented Plumeleteer, Fasciated Antshrike, Dusky Antbird, Lance-tailed Manakin, Southern Bentbill, Black-bellied Wren, and Long-billed Gnatwren, among many others. This virtually untraveled dead-end road is also good for nocturnal birds, especially Pauraque, but also Rufous Nightjar and Common Potoo, and sometimes a few owls.

Southwestern Canal Zone

This is a varied, but mostly wooded, hilly area on the west bank of the Canal, still on the Pacific slope. It is best worked from various side roads branching off the main Pan-American Highway a few miles before Arraijan (one to the left leading to the top of Cerro Galera, at 1205 feet the highest point in the Zone), and from side roads going left off the K-2 Road beyond Cocoli. Birdlife is in general similar to that of Fort Clayton, though there seem to be more species typical of humid forest and woodland, with some here reaching their western limit on the Pacific slope of Panama. Keel-billed Toucans are quite common, as are Rufous and Blue-crowned Motmots; watch also for Slaty-tailed Trogon, Black-headed Tody-Flycatcher, Brown-capped Tyrannulet, and Crested Oropendola.

Chiva Chiva Road

The Chiva Chiva area is reached by driving out the Gaillard Highway along the east bank of the Canal, on past the main gate to Fort Clayton (on the right). About 1¼ miles beyond the gate, lakes appear on both side of the road, and a paved road leads off to the right along one shore of the marshy Miraflores Lake. Scan the lake from vantage points about a half-mile down this road; a variety of freshwater marsh birds should be seen, including sometimes Masked Duck. The road continues on past light woodland and semi-open areas, with a good variety of birds. A large antenna field on the right a little over 1½ miles from the main road has a colony of Red-breasted Blackbirds and an apparently resident pair of Savanna Hawks. Three miles beyond the antenna field, a partially overgrown trail leads off to the left and soon enters a good shady woodland where the local Red-crowned Ant-Tanager and very scarce Sepia-capped Flycatcher can be found.

Summit Gardens and Vicinity

Summit Gardens is a lovely botanical garden maintained by the Canal Zone government; there is also a small zoo, with some of the local fauna exhibited. The Gardens are reached by continuing north on the Gaillard Highway past Pedro Miguel and Paraiso; turn left on the road to Gamboa beyond the Summit Golf Course (going straight leads to Madden Forest, below), and proceed for a little over a mile. A nice variety of birds should be seen in the course of a walk around the Gardens, including a number of hummingbirds if many trees are in flower. Avoid weekends, as the park is then often very crowded.

About a mile beyond Summit Gardens (toward Gamboa), two side roads cut to the right. The second (watch for cement post GMC 12) leads through excellent woodland and forest for about 4¾ miles. Many interesting birds typical of these habitats can be seen; the first part, along a lovely shady stream, is as good as any, with regular Black-throated Trogon, Northern Royal-Flycatcher, Golden-crowned Spadebill, and Buff-rumped Warbler, among others.

Madden Forest Reserve and Madden Lake Area

Madden Forest is a fairly large forest reserve straddling the Continental Divide northeast of Summit Gardens. Continue straight at the Gamboa cut-off (see above); the main road traverses the length of the forest. Traffic on this road is rather heavy, so best birding results will be had by covering various side roads and trails. The most productive is a road to the right not quite 2½ miles past the Gamboa cut-off; it continues for several miles and can be driven with care. The Las Cruces Trail, well marked, about 2¼ miles beyond the above road, also provides access to a portion of the forest. Many birds should be recorded, including Black Hawk-Eagle, trogons, motmots, various antbirds, Purple-throated Fruitcrow, Green Shrike-Vireo (voice), and Scarlet-rumped Cacique.

Another good area can be reached by continuing on to Madden Lake. Proceed through Madden Forest, pass underneath the Trans-Isthmian Highway, and continue for about 5¼ miles. At this point a road to the right leads to the Boy Scout's Camp Chagres, on the shores of Madden Lake. Quite likely, passage will be blocked partway down this side road by a gate, but, just before this, a trail angles off to the right. This trail seems always to have much activity, and is well worth following; there is also a good Chestnut-headed Oropendola colony near the gate. Continuing about a half-mile further on the main road brings one to Madden Dam itself, from which a few waterbirds and kingfishers may be seen.

Pipeline Road

Probably the best area in the Canal Zone for seeing a variety of humid forest birds. To reach it, continue past Summit Gardens to Gamboa; proceed through town, bearing left on a gravel road a few hundred yards beyond (bearing right leads to another Army area). A marshy pond that appears soon on the right is worth a check. Pipeline Road itself begins just beyond; bear right at the only intersection, a few hundred yards past the pond (continuing straight leads to Chagres Air Field). For the first 3 miles, the road leads through second-growth woodland, at times with much activity. About 3½ miles out, a side track to the right leads down to an attractive clear stream, well worth checking. The best areas are further out, however. About a mile beyond, where the road becomes paved, a track angles to the right and into the forest. This leads to the Limbo Hunt Club, situated in a little clearing surrounded by tall forest. Bird activity is usually great around the clearing during the morning, and many interesting and rare forest birds may be seen by walking some of the trails across the little stream. From this point, the now-paved road passes for 6 or 7 miles through superb humid forest; an exciting variety of birds can always be seen. In places the road is steep, but it is readily passable. The road also crosses several beautiful forested streams, which can be waded, sometimes with fine results. The road finally dead-ends on a deserted arm of Gatun Lake, so traffic is virtually nil. A great variety of birds has been recorded here in recent years, far too many for more than a sample to be mentioned here: Great Tinamou (voice), King Vulture, Double-toothed Kite, White and Semiplumbeous Hawks, Ornate and Black Hawk-Eagles, Great Curassow, Short-billed Pigeon, various parrots, Short-tailed Nighthawk (at dusk), Purple-crowned Fairy, trogons, Broad-billed Motmot, Black-breasted Puffbird, araçari and toucans, Cinnamon Woodpecker, Long-tailed and Black-striped Woodcreepers, Spot-crowned Antvireo, many antbirds, Red-capped Manakin, Blue Cotinga, Sirystes, White-ringed Flycatcher, Forest Elaenia, Nightingale Wren (voice), Tawny-faced Gnatwren, Shining Honeycreeper, Scarlet-thighed Dacnis, White-vented and Fulvous-vented Euphonias, and Carmiol's, Tawny-crested, Sulphur-rumped, and Dusky-faced Tanagers, etc. Several mammals may also be seen.

Barro Colorado Island

This famous reserve can be visited only if prior arrangements have been made with the Smithsonian Tropical Research Institute (Box 2072, Balboa, C.Z.), and a fee is charged. The island is located in Gatun Lake and a visit involves taking the Panama Railway from either Panama city or Colon to Frijoles, where a boat takes one out to the island. Entirely covered with forest except around the Laboratory clearing, the island has been a sanctuary since the 1920's. Most visitors are especially impressed with the variety of mammals which can be seen: 4 species of monkeys (Black Howler, Central American Spider, White-faced, and Geoffroy's Marmoset), Two-toed and Three-toed Sloths, *Tamandua* anteater, Coatimundi, Collared Peccary, and even Baird's Tapir, the last coming to the clearing to be fed on many evenings. Birds are also quite numerous, though not as conspicuous as they are at a place such as Pipeline Road; nonetheless, a good assortment should be seen, both around the clearing, and along the well-marked forest trails.

Coco Solo and Vicinity

The naval base of Coco Solo is located on the shore of Manzanillo Bay, opposite Colon, on the Caribbean coast of the Canal Zone. It is reached by turning left at the 4-way stop intersection on the Trans-Isthmian Highway a few miles south of Colon (right if coming from the Pacific side), and is on the left about 2 miles from the intersection. Extensive short grass fields here attract remarkably large and diverse flocks of transient shorebirds during fall migration, and lesser numbers and variety at other seasons (especially when wet). The bayshore itself is also of interest, particularly around the tidal pool near two huge abandoned airplane hangars; here gulls and terns, shorebirds, and frequently a few jaegers congregate. France Field, an abandoned airfield opposite Coco Solo (on the right coming from the 4-way intersection) also has migrant shorebirds in season, and holds a resident flock of Red-breasted Blackbirds, the only such flock on Panama's Caribbean slope. You can drive around the runways.

Gatun Dam and Vicinity

The Gatun Locks of the Panama Canal (which raise ships 85 feet to the level of Gatun Lake) must be crossed in order to reach the interesting forest areas to the west; the route to the locks is well marked. Immediately after crossing the locks, which if a ship is passing through will involve a wait of 10-15 minutes, one comes to a T-intersection. A right-turn puts one on the road to Fort Sherman (below), a left-turn on the road to Gatun Dam and beyond. This latter road proceeds along the edge of the dam itself, with vast open grassy expanses to the left, often literally carpeted with shorebirds during fall migration. After about 1¼ miles, one crosses the Gatun Dam spillway on a rickety bridge; the Chagres River flows 10 miles from here to its mouth at Fort San Lorenzo (below). The immediate area often has many herons and egrets, shorebirds, and other waterbirds, while nearby woodland (conveniently reached via trails behind the Tarpon Club, and near the small boat club, on the opposite side) holds the appropriate species.

Achiote Road and Piña

Achiote Road is one of the best Canal Zone localities in which to see humid forest birds; its only local rival is Pipeline Road (above). Achiote's major drawbacks are its relatively remote location, and the fact that the road itself is often passable only to four-wheel drive vehicles (hence much of it must be walked). To reach it, continue past the Gatun Dam spillway, proceeding straight (the road becomes gravel) for a little over 2 miles to an intersection where the road to Piña (below) cuts back sharply to the right, while the Escobal road continues straight. Take the latter, and proceed through good humid woodland; many birds may be seen, especially in the early morning before traffic becomes too heavy. About a mile past the intersection, a dirt road cuts off to the right; this is often good for forest birds, though Achiote is better. Almost 5¼ miles from the intersection, at a large clearing on the left (the first one comes to), Achiote Road branches to the right; the road to Escobal continues for several miles through partly cut-over country. Achiote Road goes for a little over 3¼ miles in the Canal Zone, then enters Colon province; the contrast between the forested Zone and the open Republic will be obvious. The best procedure is to drive in Achiote as far as one can (or dares), and walk from there; the best part is the last 2 miles in the

Canal Zone, where the road passes through partly swampy forest. Several trails branch off on either side and allow access to the forest interior and a different set of birds; the best (though it is often not easy to find) follows a beautifully forested valley and small stream on the right just before reaching the Republic. A wealth of birds should be seen, including if the weather is decent a good assortment of raptors (Gray-headed and Hook-billed Kites, Tiny, White, Semiplumbeous, Plumbeous, and Crane Hawks, hawk-eagles, all 3 forest-falcons, and Red-throated Caracara have all been recorded) and some of the following specialties: Bronze-tailed Plumeleteer, Pied Puffbird, Spot-crowned Barbet, Tawny-throated Leaftosser, Pygmy and Streaked Antwrens, White-headed Wren, Black-chested Jay, Montezuma Oropendola, Tawny-crested and Dusky-faced Tanagers, and Blackheaded Saltator.

The road to Piña also passes through interesting forested country, but usually is too heavily traveled for good birding. The portions of the road along the Caribbean coast are rather scenic.

Fort Sherman and Fort San Lorenzo

Retracing back to the Gatun Locks intersection (above), take the right turn onto the road to Fort Sherman. A little over one half mile from the Locks, one crosses one of the few extant sections of the French canal effort; a walk along any of its banks may produce Greater Ani, kingfishers, etc. Further on, a number of small roads and trails branch off to the left, each of them leading into good forest and woodland. Nearing Fort Sherman itself, the terrain becomes more swampy, with extensive mangrove areas; watch for Common and a few Great Black-Hawks here and beyond. Fort Sherman is small (though it trained many men bound for the jungles of Vietnam), with an airstrip that holds shorebirds on migration, and surrounding semi-open areas that are often very good for migrant landbirds. The road to Fort San Lorenzo curves for miles through more forest and woodland; Chestnut-mandibled Toucans seem unusually numerous here, and one should record species such as various parrots, White-tailed (and other) Trogons, Long-tailed Tyrant, White-thighed Swallow, and Black-chested Jay. As usual, covering one of the less-used side roads is generally more productive. Fort San Lorenzo itself is beautifully situated on a high promontory overlooking the Caribbean, the mouth of the Chagres River, and miles of unbroken forest. Watch for Brown Boobies and other seabirds. It is a perfect picnic spot.

Río Piedras and Portobelo

To reach this interesting area on the Caribbean coast of eastern Colon province, drive out the Trans-Isthmian Highway to the only Guardia Nacional checkpoint (about 1¼ hours from Panama city, 15–20 minutes from Colon); turn right just before the checkpoint if coming from the Pacific side. Proceed for almost 1¾ miles through thickly inhabited country to the little town of Puerto Pilón; turn right just beyond a church on the right (road marked Portobelo). For the next 6 miles, the road passes through extensively cleared areas, once heavily forested, now grazed by scrawny cattle; birds such as White-tailed Kite, Striped Cuckoo, Golden-hooded and Yellow-rumped Tanagers, and many others may be seen, especially in the early morning. Continue past the little town of María Chiquíta on the left for another ¾ mile, where a dirt road angles off to the right (if you cross a large cement bridge over a river you have gone a little too far). This side road roughly parallels the Río Piedras for several miles and, though increasingly disturbed, is still very good for a variety of birds: all 6 species of kingfishers occur, there is a remarkable diversity of the larger flycatchers (including the only easily found Gray-capped in central Panama), and Olivaceous Piculet and Red-billed Scythebill may be found. The road may be impassable in the rainy season. Wading up some of the river's tributaries may well produce a Sunbittern as well as many other birds. Several tracks can also be followed inland, and they soon lead into relatively solid forest, though selectively logged.

The main road continues for about 12 miles to Portobelo. Though only recently opened, already most of the forest near the road has been felled, and the area is increasingly thickly settled. Common Black-Hawks should still be seen. Portobelo itself is in a lovely setting but is now rather run-down, having reached its heyday in the sixteenth and seventeenth centuries when it was the Caribbean terminus of the Las Cruces Trail, over which poured the riches of Peru. The ruins of the fort are worth a visit.

Cerro Santa Rita

This is a still little-explored foothill area near the Canal Zone in Colon province. Access is difficult, and four-wheel drive mandatory unless the road is fairly dry (not often). Turn off the Trans-Isthmian Highway to the left about ½ mile south (toward Pacific side) of the Guardia Nacional checkpoint. For the first several miles the road is gravel and easily traversed; bear left at the one fork, a little over 1½ miles from the Trans-Isthmian. From about here the road is dirt and can be very slippery and hazardous; it gradually ascends a ridge through clearings at first, but eventually reaches considerable forest before ending about 7 miles from the Trans-Isthmian at about 1500 feet. A sampling of birds seen includes: White-tipped Sicklebill, Great Jacamar, White-fronted Nunbird, Yellow-eared Toucanet, Stripe-cheeked Woodpecker, Rufous-rumped Foliage-gleaner, Russet Antshrike, White-ruffed Manakin, Rufous Mourner, Black-capped Pygmy-Tyrant, and Emerald, Rufous-winged, and Sulphur-rumped Tanagers.

Tocumen Marsh

Returning to the Pacific side, this fine fresh water marsh is readily accessible from the Tocumen traffic circle near the airport. Take the first right off the circle (before coming to La Siesta Hotel), and proceed on this dirt road as it curves for about a mile through open savanna country. This road can be good for nocturnal birds such as Common Potoo, Pauraque, and White-tailed Nightjar. The road ends at a group of buildings overlooking several small ponds and the marsh beyond; request permission to enter (readily given). A number of birds should be seen around the ponds and cattle pens, among them Pied Water-Tyrant. To reach the main marsh, work left around the north side of the larger pond through a small pasture until you come to an obvious red-dirt track continuing in the same direction. Follow this for another several hundred yards, taking the first track to the right you come to. This continues south for over 1½ miles, the outer mile of which is a dike with extensive marsh on either side. Though still excellent for birds, there are signs that the marsh is becoming overgrown with vegetation, which is drastically reducing visibility. A variety of water birds and raptors may be seen, including Bare-throated Tiger-Heron, White-necked Heron (especially summer), Lesser Yellow-headed Vulture, Black-collared Hawk, and regularly Little Cuckoo, Greater Ani, Lesser Kiskadee, and Scrub Flycatcher, among many others. Do this trip early in the morning, for it becomes unmercifully hot before noon.

Cerro Azul/Jefe Area

This is the best area for foothill birds in central Panama. Continue past the Tocumen traffic circle on the road to Chepo for about 3¼ miles; turn left on the paved road to Cerro Azul (so marked). This road soon begins to climb steadily up largely deforested slopes; about 6½ miles from the cut-off, the road enters a partially wooded area where some birds may be found. It then ascends one more slope, then drops down to the incongruous Goofy Lake, at about 2050 feet. Though a few birds may be seen in the Goofy Lake area, the vicinity has in recent years been so highly disturbed that much better results will be had by continuing well beyond. Continue straight past the lake on the (recently) paved road. The paved road continues (as of 1974) for about 2¾ miles, after which it becomes dirt and deteriorates, though usually passable if not too wet. The paved section of the road can be reasonably good for birds, especially in the early morning, but is suffering from increased disturbance and chicken farm development. Beyond the pavement, the road continues for about a mile past clearings and remnant patches of forest, then goes across an extensive clearing before again skirting some more solid forest. This last forest area seems consistently good for a fine variety of tanagers and other birds. Almost 6½ miles from Goofy Lake, a side road to the left leads for about a mile up through a peculiar elfin cloud forest dominated by palms to the summit of Cerro Jefe, at over 3300 feet the highest point in the area. Many interesting birds have recently been found in this isolated forest, including Violet-capped Hummingbird, Slaty-backed Nightingale-Thrush, Three-striped Warbler, Blue-and-gold Tanager, Tacarcuna Bush-Tanager, and Black-headed Brush-Finch. Be forewarned that Jefe is often enveloped in clouds and mist. The "main" (right-hand) road swings around the south slope of Cerro Jefe, soon descending quite steeply, and cuts left at another fork a little over ¾ mile past the Jefe turn-off. This road continues for miles through ever more interesting forested terrain, still with very few inhabitants. A wealth of interesting birds may be found in the Cerro Azul/ Jefe area, especially around Jefe and beyond, including King Vulture, Green Hermit, Spot-crowned Barbet, Yellow-eared Toucanet, Stripe-cheeked Woodpecker, many woodcreepers, Rufous-rumped Foliage-gleaner, Scale-crested Pygmy-Tyrant, Pale-vented Robin, Scarlet-thighed Dacnis, Tawny-capped and White-vented Euphonias, and Emerald, Speckled, Silver-throated, Rufous-winged, Carmiol's, Sulphur-rumped, and Black-and-Yellow Tanagers, and many other rarer species have been found on a few occasions.

Chepo and Points East

The road from the Tocumen traffic circle to Chepo passes through pleasant savanna country, with gallery woodland along the many small streams. Good numbers of raptors and other species typical of these habitats can be seen, especially in the early morning and late afternoon. The area known as La Jagua is now unfortunately difficult of access, but keys might be obtainable from the Panama Audubon Society or Smithsonian; it is located south of the main road, east of the Pacora River. Almost 23½ miles from the circle, the main road cuts to the left, skirting Chepo itself. Continuing straight takes one into town and on to the Río Mamoní, a major tributary of the Bayano. The main road continues east to El Llano through very open country; a side road to the right about 7¾ miles beyond the Chepo turn-off (the Platanares-Jesús María road) leads up into some forested hills which represent the western limit for several species (e.g. Orange-crowned Oriole), and has a number of others of interest, though the road can be difficult without 4-wheel drive and may have to be walked. Another rough road leads up to the Continental Divide north of El Llano; this is projected to continue to San Blas. Beyond El Llano the main road enters increasingly forested country, and will probably soon be open beyond the Bayano River. Ornithological exploration of this whole area has only recently begun, and it promises to be interesting. The present forested aspect of most of this area will likely soon be altered, unfortunately, both because of the effect of the new road, and because of the big dam now under construction on the Bayano at a site several miles above El Llano.

For the present Darién remains inaccessible unless one is willing to mount an expedition. One can fly to El Real, and then proceed up the Tuira River to the remote Cerro Pirre and Cerro Tacarcuna area, still almost entirely forested and little settled, with a superb avifauna including cracids, four species of macaws, even Crested and Harpy Eagles. Eventually the Pan-American Highway may be extended this far east, which will make the area more accessible, but which will also inevitably alter it for the worse.

Cerro Campana

Cerro Campana is an interesting area of cloud forest at about 3000 feet around 30 miles west of Panama city. Take the Pan-American Highway west through the Canal Zone and on to La Chorrera and beyond to the little town of Capira, about 12 miles west of Chorrera. Proceed for a little over 3 miles past Capira to a point where the road curves sharply to the left and drops toward the Pacific; here a gravel road cuts off to the right (sign for Su-Lin Motel). Follow this road as it ascends quite steeply through scrubby woodland and pastures for about 4 miles, then emerging onto dry grassy hillsides with a sweeping panorama out over the Pacific. Continue over these grasslands, watching for White-tailed Hawk, Lesser Elaenia, Blue-and-white Swallow, Wedge-tailed Grass-Finch, etc. In about a mile, it enters woodland, often with some birds, though areas further on are better. The road switchbacks several times, then again comes out into open country, where Rufous-collared Sparrows are numerous. At the fork, take the right-hand road, still following signs for the Su-Lin, a short distance ahead. The motel is a passable place to stay, and its grounds often have many birds. The road goes a short distance further, then peters out into a track that leads through some fairly good forest. Several side trails heading off to the right are usually even better. This area has officially been designated as Panama's sole national park, though to date there is little if any evidence of such special status. Many interesting birds occur, among them several more typical of the western highlands, including Purplish-backed Quail-Dove, Violet-headed Hummingbird, Orange-bellied Trogon, Emerald and Yellow-eared Toucanets, Spotted Barbtail, Slaty Antwren, Black-headed Antthrush, White-ruffed Manakin, Tufted Flycatcher, Scale-crested Pygmy-Tyrant, Olive-striped Flycatcher, White-throated and Pale-vented Robins, Silver-throated, Hepatic, and Black-and-yellow Tanagers, and Chestnut-capped Brush-Finch; other more widespread species will of course be seen.

Western Pacific Slope Lowlands

The drive west from central Panama to Chiriquí on the Pan-American Highway is rather long and hot; to drive non-stop from Panama city to

David takes about 7 hours, if traffic is light. Persons with limited time are advised to fly, but for those with sufficient time, there are a number of places of interest along the way. Accommodations are available at several towns, especially Aguadulce, Santiago, and David. Savanna species will be noted frequently, especially between Antón, Coclé, and Santiago; raptors are quite frequent (be alert for the scarce Aplomado Falcon), and other specialties to watch for include: Crested Bobwhite, Brown-throated Parakeet, Yellow-headed Parrot, Yellowish Pipit, Red-breasted Blackbird, and Grassland Yellow-Finch. South of Aguadulce are some extensive salt flats, always worth a visit, often with large flocks of wading birds (including Wood Stork and Roseate Spoonbill), shorebirds, and gulls and terns. Several good fresh water marshes and ponds are within sight of the road south of Divisa, Herrera, and more can be found with local inquiry; Black-bellied Tree-Ducks and Masked Ducks both occur here, as well as other wading birds, etc. This road south from Divisa continues down the eastern side of the Azuero Peninsula, but is not particularly exciting for birds. The stretch of the Pan-American Highway west of Santiago is especially barren, but soon after crossing the Chiriquí boundary the country becomes lusher and more attractive. The Remedios/Las Lajas area is fairly interesting, especially away from the main highway; a good side road leads down to the coast from Las Lajas (Northern Jacanas replace Wattleds at about this point).

Boquete

This very attractive town at about 3500 feet in western Chiriquí provides a fine base from which to explore the surrounding mountains. Many birds can be seen in the town itself, but most people will want to spend their time in the remaining forest areas searching for quetzals and other specialties. The best such reasonably accessible area is to be found on the Finca Lerida, now owned by the Collins family, who are hospitable to birders if permission is obtained to enter on their land. A 4-wheel drive vehicle is usually needed to negotiate the difficult mountain roads; they can usually be obtained at the hotels in Boquete, with or without the services of a guide/driver. Directions to Finca Lerida are somewhat complicated, and are perhaps best given locally, but essentially the trip involves driving north from the main square of town, bearing left at one fork almost a mile from town, then another left about ¾ mile further. This puts one on a gravel road, which soon begins to ascend quite steeply into the mountains; most of this area has been converted to coffee fincas and vegetable gardens, but some birds can often be seen. About 3¼ miles beyond the second fork, one comes to the driveway in to the Collins house, not visible from the road, on the left; a short distance beyond the road drops down into a forested ravine called El Velo at about 5000 feet. Quetzals have been seen here, and it is a good area for bellbirds and other highland species. Continue up the other side, and turn left on a side track immediately after reaching the top. One can either walk or drive from here, the track ascending gradually first past large fields, then into beautiful forest. Quetzals and bellbirds can be found most anywhere, but the former especially at an area called El Mirador, overlooking a spectacular deep wild ravine. El Mirador is reached by taking the only track to the right after entering the forest; it descends slightly for about ¼ mile to the overlook, used as a picnic area by the Collins family. Many highland species should be seen in the area, and among those possible are: Black Guan, Spotted Wood-Quail, Buff-fronted Quail-Dove, Sulphur-winged Parakeet, Stripe-tailed Hummingbird, White-tailed Emerald, Collared Trogon, many Furnariids, Silvery-fronted Tapaculo, Barred Becard, Dark Pewee, Silvery-throated Jay, Ochraceous Wren, Black-faced Solitaire, Ruddy-capped Nightingale-Thrush, Long-tailed Silky-Flycatcher, Yellow-winged Vireo, Flame throated and Black-cheeked Warblers, Golden-browed Chlorophonia, Flame-colored Tanager, and Yellow-thighed Finch. Even the Bare-necked Umbrellabird has been seen on at least one occasion.

Volcán and the Nueva Suiza Area

The drive up from Concepción to Volcán (c. 4000 feet) involves a trip through largely cleared but still quite attractive country. Numerous birds should be seen, including Crimson-fronted Parakeets and Scarlet-rumped Tanagers, while along the last few miles before Volcán a few patches of woodland begin to appear and a greater variety of species becomes possible (e.g., Smoky-brown Woodpecker, Orange-billed Nightingale-Thrush, Tropical Parula, and Black-headed Brush-Finch). The Dos Rios Hotel just west of Volcán provides good accommodations, and is also a good area for birds, with Chiriquí Yellowthroats in the damp meadows. The road west toward Costa Rica can be good for various lower highland species as well as White-crowned Parrot, Fiery-billed Araçari, and Pale-billed Woodpecker.

A fine variety of highland birds can be seen in the Chiriquí Viejo River valley along the road between Volcán and Cerro Punta, especially around Nueva Suiza (c. 5300 feet). There are now many homes in the valley and much of the forest is now gone, though fortunately patches and scattered tall trees still stand. Birds remain numerous, and it is hard to imagine a more delightful area in which to search for them. Perhaps the best area is upstream from the Florida Audubon Society cabin, on the right (sign marked "Sonrisas Chiricanas") a little over 3 miles from the start of the forested area. The largest patch of forest is owned by a Methodist church group, and lies between the road and the river a few hundred yards above the cabin. Many birds should be recorded here, of which the following are representative: Ruddy Pigeon,

Violet Sabrewing, Green Violetear, Scintillant Hummingbird, Red-headed Barbet, Red-faced Spinetail, Golden-bellied and Yellowish Flycatchers, Torrent Tyrannulet, American Dipper, Slaty Flower-piercer, Golden-crowned Warbler, Slate-throated Redstart, White-winged Tanager, Blue Seedeater, and Yellow-throated Brush-Finch.

Cerro Punta

The Boquete Trail above this agricultural town at about 6200 feet provides convenient access to some high-altitude forest with interesting birds including the quetzal. Continue through town on the only main road for a little over a half mile; at this point the road passes a large horse farm on the right, and descends a steep slope, crossing a stream on a wooden bridge. Boquete Trail starts here, heading up to the right following the stream's valley; the first mile or so can be driven. At this point there is a fork, and you should take the right-hand trail across the stream and on up the valley. From here the trail continues for several miles through alternating forest and cleared areas, with a last very steep forested slope to be climbed before the trail tops off at almost 8000 feet, beyond dropping down eventually toward Boquete. Quetzals will usually be found somewhere along the trail, as will many other species of considerable interest, including perhaps Maroon-chested Ground-Dove, Fiery-throated and Volcano Hummingbirds, Ruddy Treerunner, Buffy Tuftedcheek, Black-capped Flycatcher, Sooty Robin, Black-billed Nightingale-Thrush, Collared Redstart, Sooty-capped Bush-Tanager, Black-thighed Grosbeak, Large-footed Finch, and many others.

Additional information on finding birds in Panama is contained in Edwards' and Loftin's *Finding Birds in Panama,* though some of the data therein are incorrect or out-of-date. Members of the Panama Audubon Society (Box 2026, Balboa, C.Z.) are always ready to help the visiting birder, and may even be willing to take one into the field personally. The group also schedules monthly field trips and meetings, to which the public is always invited. The Smithsonian Tropical Research Institute (Box 2072, Balboa, C.Z.) will be of great assistance to those more professionally inclined, and must in any case be contacted if Barro Colorado Island is to be visited.

APPENDIX III

Addenda and Corrigenda, 1980

I Species Newly Reported From Panama

p. 32. Manx (Common) Shearwater (*Puffinus puffinus*). Hypothetical. One reported seen by an experienced observer in Gulf of Panama (8°44'N, 78°50'W) on 30 Oct 1977 (R. G. Brown). Characters noted would indicate the form *auricularis*. For discussion of identification, see Palmer, *Handbook of North American Birds* I: 188-190, 1962.

p. 42. Reddish Egret (*Dichromanassa rufescens*). Hypothetical. One dark phase adult seen on coastal flats on Coiba Island on 12 Apr 1976 (Ridgely). Photographs taken (with 50mm lens) were not quite recognizable. See North American field guides.

[p. 54. Wood Duck (*Aix sponsa*). Three males seen with wigeon on Volcan Lakes, Chiriquí, on 15 Jan 1976 (J. Pujals et al.) These seem almost certainly to have been local releases, as the species has never been recorded south of Mexico in Middle America.]

p. 58. Pearl Kite (*Gampsonyx swainsonii*). One seen and photographed at Empire Range, Pacific side of Canal Zone, on 12 June 1977 (J. Pujals et al.; *American Birds* 31(6): 1099-1100, 1977). Single individuals have since been noted on several occasions at various localities in central Panama (v. o., fide Eisenmann), and one was also seen near Changuinola, Bocas del Toro, on 24 Apr 1980 (N. G. Smith). Conceivably the species is colonizing Panama. See *Birds of Venezuela*, Plate 5.

p. 115. Yellow-billed Tern (*Sterna superciliaris*). One seen and photographed at Coco Solo, Canal Zone, on 20 Oct 1977 (J. Pujals). See *Birds of Venezuela*, p. 88.

p. 121. Common (Scaly) Ground-Dove (*Columbina passerina*). Recently discovered, with several specimens taken, along Pacific coast in Herrera and Los Santos (V. H. Tejera; F. Delgado). Presumably had been overlooked.

p. 128. Painted Parakeet (*Pyrrhura picta*). A new race of this South American parakeet was discovered in forest at 3300 feet in sw. Los Santos in Feb 1979 (F. Delgado). A series of specimens has since been taken, and are being described. See *Birds of Venezuela*, Plate 9.

p. 132. Dwarf Cuckoo (*Coccyzus pumilus*). Hypothetical. One seen at Tocumen marsh, e. Panama province, on 9 Jan 1979 (V. Emanuel, D. Wolf et al.). See *Birds of Venezuela*, Plate 10.

p. 133. Gray-capped Cuckoo (*Coccyzus lansbergi*). Hypothetical. One seen at Tocumen marsh, e. Panama province, on 10 Feb 1980 (V. Emanuel and M. Braun). Possibly the same bird (though it was reported as a Dark-billed Cuckoo, *C. melacoryphus*) was also seen on 26 Jan (*Toucan* 7(1): 2, 1980). See *Birds of Venezuela*, Plate 10.

p. 145. Ocellated Poorwill (*Nyctiphrynus ocellatus*). Hypothetical. One believed seen along Achiote Road, Canal Zone, on 15 Mar 1978 (R. Ryan). See *Birds of South America*, p. 122.

p. 183. Stripe-billed Aracari (*Pteroglossus sanguineus*). Seen frequently around Río Mono, at base of Cerro Quía, Darién, in July 1975 (Ridgely). A specimen which has been taken here on 18 Feb 1969 (P. Galindo) is an almost pure example of this species (perhaps only a race of *P. torquatus*). Another araçari taken farther down the Tuira River at Matuganti on 20 July 1975 (Ridgely) is an obvious hybrid *P. torguatus* X *sanguineus*. See *Birds of South America*, p. 178.

p. 220. White-collared Manakin (*Manacus candei*). Found to be fairly common at forest edge in lower Teribe and Changuinola River valleys, Bocas del Toro; first recorded in Oct 1978 (J. Pujals), with specimen taken on 17 Feb 1979 (W. Martinez and W. Booth). Additional specimens taken by GML personnel in Jan 1980. No evidence of hybridization with locally sympatric Golden-collared Manakin, but further study needed. See *Field Guide to Mexican Birds*, Plate 26.

p. 226. Rose-throated Becard (*Platypsaris aglaiae*). Hypothetical. One female reported seen at Santa Clara, Chiriquí, on 17 Jan 1977 (A. Greensmith et al.; *Toucan* 4(2): 5, 1977). See *Field Guide to Mexican Birds*, Plate 26.

p. 260. Cave Swallow (*Petrochelidon fulva*). Hypothetical. One seen with other transient swallows at Juan Diaz, e. Panama province, on 10 Mar 1976 (Ridgely). One seen at Tocumen, e. Panama province, on 9 Feb 1980 (V. Emanuel). There is also an old McCleannan "Panama" specimen (Wetmore, MS), the provenance of which has been doubted, though that doubt may not have been altogether warranted. Probably it occurs regularly with other migrant swallows, though identification in the fall would be difficult due to possible confusion with immature Cliff Swallows. See North American field guides.

p. 282. Common Starling (*Sturnus vulgaris*). Hypothetical. One seen at Albrook AFB, Canal Zone, on 10-12 Feb 1979 (J. and R. A. Rowlett et al.). See North American field guides.

p. 292. Nashville Warbler (*Vermivora ruficapilla*). Hypothetical. One reported seen at Santa Clara, Chiriquí, on 2 Jan 1980 (P. Donahue and J. Van Os). See North American field guides.

p. 293. Northern Parula (*Parula americana*). Hypothetical. Two recent sightings from Galeta Island, Canal Zone: one on 21 Jan 1976 (J. Pujals et al.), and one on 4 Mar 1977 (J. Pujals and S. Stokes; *Toucan* 4(4): 7, 1977). See North American field guides.

p. 297. Prairie Warbler (*Dendroica discolor*). Hypothetical. One seen at Volcan, Chiriquí, on 23 Jan 1973 (R. Brownstein and W. George, in litt. to Wetmore). See North American field guides.

p. 334. Lesson's Seedeater (*Sporophila bouvronides*). Hypothetical. Two pairs seen at Yaviza, Darién, on 30 Apr 1979 (J. Pujals; *Toucan* 6(6): 5, 1979). Usually considered a race of the South American *S. lineola* (Lined Seedeater), but recent evidence indicates that *S. bouvronides* is best regarded as a distinct species (P. Schwartz). See *Birds of Venezuela*, Plate 40.

p. 336. Peg-billed Finch (*Acanthidops bairdi*). Large numbers (up to 50–100 were seen per day) invaded forest along Boquete Trail above Cerro Punta, Chiriquí, in Jan-Mar 1979 (V. Emanuel, Ridgely et al.). Recognizable photographs were taken (D. Galinat). All were feeding on seeding bamboo. None were found in 1980.

p. 341. House Sparrow (*Passer domesticus*). Up to 20 were found in downtown David, Chiriquí, on 6-7 Mar 1976 (Ridgely); these would now appear to be established. Since at least Mar 1979, small numbers have also been found in Panama City, with breeding recorded (N. Smith, Ridgely et al.). Finally, 3 were also seen at Changuinola, Bocas del Toro, on 29 Apr 1980 (Ridgely). Whether these represent local introductions, or the birds are spreading unassisted from Costa Rica (where House Sparrows are also slowly increasing), is uncertain. See North American field guides.

II Confirmation of Hypothetical Species

p. 87. Spotted Rail. One adult with a small chick seen at Tocumen marsh, e. Panama province, on 14 Jan 1978; adult recognizably photographed on 21 Jan (V. Emanuel, R. Krebs et al.; *American Birds* 34(2): 214-215, 1980).

p. 295. Townsend's Warbler. One female seen and photographed at Volcan, Chiriquí, on 21-22 Mar 1979 (Ridgely, J. Baird et al.). An adult male was also seen above Cerro Punta, Chiriquí, on 21 Mar.

p. 295. Hermit Warbler. Presumably the same male wintered at the same spot during the winter of 1976: it was seen from at least 16 Jan (J. Pujals et al.) to 6 Mar (P. Miliotis et al.). No subsequent reports.

p. 311. Yellow-headed Blackbird. Up to 8 (no adult males) were seen at Tocumen, e. Panama province, from at least 19 to 26 Jan 1980 (D. Finch, V. Emanuel, P. Donahue et al.). Despite the tremendous gap between Panama and this species' normal wintering range, it now appears likely that they in fact are arriving under their own power (and are not "ship-assisted").

III Notes on Panama Distribution or Status

NB—The area known as "Fortuna" is mentioned repeatedly in the following accounts. It is the site of a projected dam on the Río Chiriquí in central Chiriquí c. 40 km east of Boquete; its elevation is c. 3000 feet. The Gorgas Memorial Laboratory was contracted to produce an ecological impact statement for the project in 1976; the author prepared the study's ornithological component. This previously inaccessible region had not been explored for birds, and it proved to be of exceptional interest, due principally to its avifauna's striking Caribbean slope affinities.

p. 36. Brown Pelican. Nesting colony of c. 150 pairs on Isla Barca Quebrado, an islet off s. coast of Coiba Island, on 10 Apr 1976 (Ridgely). First report of breeding in w. Panama.

p. 38. Neotropic Cormorant and Anhinga. Nesting colony of both species (more cormorants) since 1977 on Bayano Lake, e. Panama province (P. Galindo). First mainland colony for the cormorant.

p. 41. White-necked Heron. One seen on Bohio Peninsula, near Frijoles, Canal Zone, in June 1977 (N. Brokaw and D. Pine). First report from Canal Zone, and farthest west ever. Perhaps only a seasonal visitant to central Panama (including Tocumen), as reports all continue to be from the northern summer months (Apr-Aug).

p. 42. Tricolored Heron. Nesting colony of c. 130 pairs on Taborcilla Island, near Punta Chame, w. Panama province, on 25 Apr 1976 (Ridgely); they were in a mixed heronry with Great and Snowy Egrets, both night-herons, and White Ibis. Had also been seen here in 1975 (N. Gale). First report of breeding in Panama.

p. 45. Fasciated Tiger-Heron. One adult seen along upper Río Pelón on Pipeline Road, Canal Zone, on 31 Jan 1976 (Ridgely and R. Forster). First report from Canal Zone.

p. 47. Wood Stork. Nesting colony in small forest patch adjacent to mangroves on coast S of Las Lajas, Chiriquí, in Feb-Mar 1976 (Ridgely). When first discovered, 40-plus pairs were in attendance, but by 7 Mar only 6–8 pairs remained, evidently due to disturbance by Black Vultures. First report of breeding in Panama.

p. 63. Sharp-shinned Hawk. One adult seen near Cerro Jefe, e. Panama province, on 25 Jan 1976 (Ridgely). First report from central Panama.

p. 63. Tiny Hawk. Appears to have increased in numbers during the past decade at least in central Panama, though some of this increase is perhaps attributable to more complete and sophisticated observer coverage.

p. 71. Great Black-Hawk. Apparent intermediates between *ridgwayi* and nominate *urubitinga* have recently been collected (one at Rodman Naval Base, Canal Zone, on 14 Feb 1974; G. Barrett, Jr.) and seen (pair at Tocumen marsh, e. Panama province, on 23 Feb 1980; V. Emanuel and M. Braun) much farther west than had been realized. Additional investigation is clearly called for, as is care in field identification.

p. 72. Solitary Eagle. One seen near Cerro Quía, Darién, and 15 July 1975 (Ridgely). First report from Darién.

p. 73. Harpy Eagle. Still persists in the Canal Zone, with adult seen on Pipeline Road on 24 Mar 1980 (J. Karr et al.).

p. 74. Ornate Hawk-Eagle. Not uncommon on Coiba Island in Apr 1976 (Ridgely). First report from Coiba.

p. 79. Red-throated Caracara. Fairly common, where forest remains, from e. Panama province (Bayano River valley) eastward. Has apparently now disappeared from all of central Panama, and perhaps western as well, for reasons still unknown. Has also declined rapidly, and inexplicably, farther north in Middle America, but remains numerous in most of its South American range.

p. 85. Black-breasted Wood-Quail. Not uncommon at Fortuna, Chiriquí, in late Feb-early Mar 1976 (Ridgely). Only modern report from Chiriquí, and one of the few definitely from the Pacific slope anywhere in Panama.

p. 88. Rufous-necked Wood-Rail. One seen in mangroves at Fort Sherman, Canal Zone, on 28 Dec 1974 (D. Gardner). First report of this elusive species from central Panama.

p. 89. Yellow-breasted Crake. One seen in small marsh on Coiba Island on 11 Apr 1976 (Ridgely). First report from Coiba.

p. 89. Gray-breasted Crake. One seen and heard in damp meadow near French Canal, Fort Sherman, Canal Zone, on 9 and 14 June 1977 (J. Wall et al.). First report from Canal Zone.

p. 94. Southern Lapwing. Pair seen on several occasions in 1975-1976 along shores of drawn-down Madden Lake (F. Smith et al.; *Toucan* 4(4): 5, 1977). Also one seen at Volcan Lakes, Chiriquí, from at least 24 Jan to 18 Feb 1980 (V. Emanuel, J. Sass et al.; *Toucan* 7(1): 2, 1980). First reports away from eastern Panama.

p. 98. Wandering Tattler. One in non-breeding plumage seen on Isla Barca Quebrado, an islet off s. coast of Coiba Island, on 10 Apr 1976 (Ridgely). Another was seen at the Gatun Dam spillway, Canal Zone, on 18 Mar 1979 (J. Baird, Ridgely et al.). The latter is the first report from the Caribbean coast of this Pacific-littoral species.

p. 102. Dunlin. One in non-breeding plumage seen on the salt flats at Aguadulce, Coclé, on 7 Jan 1977 (A. Greensmith et al.; *Toucan* 4(2): 5, 1977). First report away from central Panama.

p. 105. Long-billed Curlew. One seen and photographed at Coco Solo, Canal Zone, from 23 Nov to 19 Dec 1975 (J. Pujals).

p. 110. Herring Gull. One seen at Fort Amador, Canal Zone, on 7 July 1975 (Ridgely). First report from northern summer. A few now probably occur annually in central Panama.

p. 112. Sabine's Gull. One seen and photographed at Coco Solo, Canal Zone, on 8 Oct 1977 (J. Pujals). First definite record from Caribbean coast.

p. 115. Least Tern. Now occurs annually in small numbers on spring passage along Caribbean coast of Canal Zone area, principally in April (J. Pujals et al.).

p. 116. Caspian Tern. A very few have been found during most northern winters along Caribbean coast of Canal Zone (v. o.).

p. 119. Ruddy Pigeon. Fairly common in upper Bayano River valley, e. Panama province, in late Apr 1976 (Ridgely). First report from so far west of the race *berlepschi.*

p. 121. Maroon-chested Ground-Dove. Became surprisingly numerous, for this typically rare and elusive species (seen daily, up to 6-8/day), along upper part of Boquete Trail above Cerro Punta, Chiriquí, in Jan-Mar 1979 (v. o.). This temporary increase was apparently brought on by the brief seeding of bamboo. None were recorded during the same period in 1980.

p. 126. Scarlet Macaw. Remains, at least as of 1976, common on Coiba Island (Ridgely). Status on the western Azuero Peninsula unknown. No recent records from Chiriquí, where surely now extirpated. A few escapes now roam the Pacific side of the Canal Zone, especially on Ancon Hill (where they probably roost).

p. 127. Chestnut-fronted Macaw. All reports from the Bayano River valley seem uncertain; this macaw is not now definitely known in Panama outside of Darién. A presumed escape was seen at Miraflores Locks, Canal Zone, on 23 Jan 1980 (P. Donahue).

p. 127. Olive-throated Parakeet. An additional, unreported specimen is one taken by R. Hinds at Almirante, Bocas del Toro, on 9 Aug 1961 (in GML collection). Status of this parakeet in Bocas remains uncertain.

p. 128. Barred Parakeet. Occurred in unusually large numbers along Boquete Trail above Cerro Punta, Chiriquí in Jan-Mar 1979 (v. o.). Flocks of up to 50-75 birds were seen. This temporary increase was evidently correlated with the brief seeding of bamboo locally.

p. 128. Spectacled Parrotlet. Two recent reports from Cerro Azul, e. Panama province, apparently indicate a continuing westward spread of this species: a small flock was seen on 1 July 1977 (J. Karr et al.), and 3 were noted on 12 Jan 1978 (J. Rowlett et al.).

p. 129. Red-fronted Parrotlet. One pair was seen at Fortuna, Chiriquí on 27 Feb and 2 Mar 1976 (Ridgely). Only recent report from Panama.

p. 130. Saffon-headed Parrot. There are a number of recent reports from e. Darién, where the species is possibly increasing. The species has been seen near Yaviza in late Jan 1978 (C. Lowe et al.), at Ensenada de Guayabo in the Jaqué region in Feb 1977 (N. Brokaw and W. Glanz), and near Río Mono at bottom of Cerro Quía in July 1975 (Ridgely). Three specimens in GML collection were also taken by P. Galindo on Cerro Nique on 11 Apr 1972.

p. 137. Tropical Screech-Owl. One in GML collection taken by R. Hinds in Apr 1972 on Cerro Nique (2000 feet), Darién. First record from Darién.

p. 138. Least Pygmy-Owl. One seen in forest at IRHE damsite camp on lower Río Changuinola (650 feet), Bocas del Toro, on 26 Apr 1980 (Ridgely). First report from Bocas.

p. 145. Chuck-will's-Widow. Probably more numerous during northern winter than has been thought: GML collection has series of 5, all taken in Panama City during the 1970's.

p. 147. Chestnut-collared Swift. Flocks of up to 75 birds were seen at sea level near Las Lajas, Chiriquí, on 13 and 24 Feb and 7 Mar 1976 (Ridgely). Two were also seen low over the Río Changuinola at the IRHE damsite camp (200 feet) on 28 Apr 1980 (Ridgely). These are the first reports from the lowlands in Panama.

p. 150. Ashy-tailed Swift. One was carefully studied S of Rincón, Herrera, on 26 July 1975 (Ridgely).

p. 156. Brown Violetear. One seen at Boquete, Chiriquí (3500 feet), on 13 Feb 1980 (V. Emanuel and M. Braun). The only recent report from Chiriquí, and the lowest ever.

p. 158. White-crested Coquette. One female seen at *Stachytarpheta* hedge at Santa Clara, Chiriquí, on 6 Mar 1976 (Ridgely). Unusually high elevation for the species, and the only recent Panama report.

p. 158. Green Thorntail. Male seen at Fortuna, Chiriquí, on 3 Mar 1976 (Ridgely). Only modern report from Chiriquí. Female seen at Cerro Jefe, e. Panama province, on 9 Jan 1980 (P. Donahue). First report from e. Panama province.

p. 163. Black-bellied Hummingbird. Uncommon in forest undergrowth and edge at Fortuna, Chiriquí (3000-3500 feet), in late Feb-early Mar 1976 (Ridgely), with one specimen taken, in GML collection. First definite record from Chiriquí; of interest was the absence of Stripe-tailed Hummingbird.

p. 163. Snowcap. Male seen repeatedly near a forest pool on Cerro Campana, w. Panama province, during latter half of 1976 (K. Wells, N. Brokaw). The farthest east report ever.

p. 165. White-bellied Mountaingem. Fairly common in small shrubby clearings and at forest borders at Fortuna, Chiriquí (3000-3500 feet), in late Feb-early Mar 1976 (Ridgely), with two specimens taken (26 Feb and 4 Mar), in GML collection. These are the first Panama specimens with definite locality data.

p. 170. Lattice-tailed Trogon. Male collected of a pair seen at Fortuna, Chiriquí (3400 feet), on 2 Mar 1976 (Ridgely); specimen photographed, but later lost. First modern record from Chiriquí.

p. 174. Amazon Kingfisher. Apparently extirpated from Gatun Lake, where formerly common, evidently due to introduction of "peacock bass." Other kingfishers were also adversely affected (E. O. Willis).

p. 177. Rufous-tailed Jacamar. One male seen on Cerro Azul, e. Panama province, on 24 Feb 1979 (A. Moore). One female seen above Ipetí in upper Bayano River valley on 23 Apr 1976 (Ridgely). These represent the first reports of any *Galbula* jacamar from e. Panama province; they are here listed under this species, though the very similar Black-chinned is not inconceivable (it has not yet been found in e. Panama, however).

p. 183. Fiery-billed Araçari. Persists in encouragingly large numbers in forest patches between Volcan and Santa Clara, Chiriquí; "perhaps more than 40" were seen in late Feb 1978 (C. Lowe et al.; *Toucan* 5(3): 3, 1978).

p. 185. Stripe-cheeked Woodpecker. Male seen at Río Piedras, e. Colon province, on 3 Feb 1976 (Ridgely et al.). Only recent report from central lowlands.

p. 186. Rufous-winged Woodpecker. Male seen in forest at IRHE damsite camp on lower Río Changuinola, Bocas del Toro, on 26 Apr 1980 (Ridgely). Only recent report from Panama, where it appears to be rarer than in Costa Rica.

p. 192. Strong-billed Woodcreeper. Two seen, one of them collected, at Fortuna, Chiriquí, in late Feb 1976 (Ridgely), specimen to GML. Only modern record from Panama.

p. 193. Black-banded Woodcreeper. One seen at Fortuna, Chiriquí (3300 feet), on 29 Feb 1976 (Ridgely). Only modern report from Panama.

p. 196. Slaty Spinetail. One seen at Achiote Road, Canal Zone, on 11 Jan 1979 (J. Pujals; *Toucan* 6(1): 3, 1979).

p. 197. Double-banded Graytail. Pair seen feeding a fledged juvenile in forest above Ipetí in upper Bayano River valley, e. Panama province, on 23 Apr 1976 (Ridgely). First report from as far west as e. Panama province.

p. 199. Rufous-rumped Foliage-Gleaner. Has been seen fairly regularly along outer Pipeline Road, Canal Zone (v. o.). Seen feeding a fledged juvenile on 3 Apr 1976 (Ridgely).

p. 209. Rufous-rumped Antwren. Fairly common in forest at Fortuna, Chiriquí (3000-3500), in late Feb-early Mar 1976 (Ridgely), with one specimen collected but later lost. First modern record from Chiriquí.

p. 211. Immaculate Antbird. Pair seen at Fortuna, Chiriquí (3400 feet), on 2 Mar 1976 (Ridgely), with another collected on 16 Mar (R. Hinds), specimen in GML collection. First modern record from Chiriquí.

p. 214. Rufous-breasted Antthrush. One taken at Fortuna, Chiriquí (3400 feet), on 16 Mar 1976 (R. Hinds), specimen in GML collection. First modern record from Chiriquí.

p. 214. Black-crowned Antpitta. One at an antswarm on Achiote Road, Canal Zone, on 31 Jan and 8 Feb 1979 (J. Arvin, J. Pujals; *Toucan* 6(2): 3-4, 1979). Only recent Canal Zone report away from Pipeline Road.

p. 223. Speckled Mourner. Uncommon in forest above IRHE damsite camp on lower Río Changuinola, Bocas del Toro, in late Apr 1980 (Ridgely), with one specimen taken on 29 Apr (specimen in GML collection). First record from Bocas del Toro.

p. 228. Three-wattled Bellbird. Reported several times from Canal Zone area, especially on Pipeline Road, in late 1976 and early 1977 (v. o.). These are the first reports from central Panama, and possibly reflect a reduction in lowland forest in the west.

p. 229. Black Phoebe. Not uncommon along lower Río Changuinola, Bocas del Toro (150-300 feet), on 22-24 Apr 1980 (N. Smith). Two pairs also seen near Río Diablo, in upper Bayano River valley, e. Panama province, on 24 Apr 1976 (Ridgely). Evidently the Black Phoebe is of very local occurrence in the lowlands, being found only where a large river has cut out steep overhanging banks.

p. 231. Pied Water-Tyrant. Reported nesting at Camp Chagres on Madden Lake, Canal Zone, during summer of 1975, and a pair was seen and photographed at Bayano Lake, e. Panama province, on 28-30 May 1979 (J. Pujals; *Toucan* 6(7): 2, 1979). First reports away from coastal e. Panama province; may be spreading.

p. 231. Vermilion Flycatcher. One male seen at Fort Clayton, Canal Zone, on 22 Jan 1977 (C. Lowe; *Toucan* 4(2): 5, 1977). Several have also been noted in recent years on Caribbean side of Canal Zone (J. Pujals et al.). A specimen is still needed in order to determine the geographic origin of the Panama birds.

p. 251. Rufous-browed Tyrannulet. Quite common in forest at Fortuna, Chiriquí (3000-3500 feet), in late Feb-early Mar 1976 (Ridgely), with one taken on 4 Mar (specimen in GML collection). First record from Chiriquí.

p. 251. Torrent Tyrannulet. One seen along lower Río Changuinola, Bocas del Toro (300 feet), on 23 Apr 1980 (N. Smith). First lowland report from anywhere in Panama.

p. 252. Yellow-bellied Elaenia. Several pairs seen in clearings along lower Río Changuinola, Bocas del Toro, on 25-29 Apr 1980 (Ridgely). First report from Bocas del Toro.

p. 254. Gray Elaenia. Male carefully studied on Pipeline Road, Canal Zone, on 11-12 Jan 1980 (P. Donahue). The only recent Canal Zone report; a specimen is still needed.

p. 254. Mouse-colored Tyrannulet. Two carefully studied at Majé, e. Panama province, on 15 Jan 1976 (F.G. Stiles). First report from eastern Panama. Fairly common in coastal lowlands of Chiriquí (Las Lajas, Estero Rico, etc.) in Feb-Mar 1976 (Ridgely). First report from Chiriquí. Apparently spreading, though possibly overlooked in past years.

p. 258. Bank Swallow. A few now apparently winter locally with the ever-increasing numbers of Barn Swallows at that season: 25 were seen at Tocumen, e. Panama province, on 27 Jan 1976 (R. Forster, Ridgely et al.), and 2 were seen at Aguadulce, Coclé, on 2 Jan 1980 (P. Donahue).

p. 258. Tree Swallow. Very large numbers were recorded during the northern winter of 1975-1976, including many on the Pacific slope: e.g., at least 50 near Rincón, Herrera, on 23 Jan (Ridgely), and many hundreds at both Tocumen and La Jagua, e. Panama province, on 27-29 Jan (Ridgely, R. Forster et al.). Last were two at Gamboa, Canal Zone, on 3 Apr 1976 (Ridgely).

p. 260. Violet-green Swallow. "Invaded" western Panama again in Dec 1976-Jan 1977 A. Greensmith et al. (*Toucan* 4(2): 6-7, 1977) recorded up to 40 on Cerro Campana, w. Panama province, on 27-29 Dec, and up to 80 near Volcan Lakes, Chiriquí, on 13-14 Jan 1977. Evidently all had departed by February.

p. 262. Southern Martin. Two males seen with Brown-chested Martins on Bayano Lake, e. Panama province, on 24 Apr 1976 (Ridgely). Presumed this species (and not Purple Martins) on the basis of date and their associates.

p. 265. Azure-hooded Jay. Fairly common at Fortuna, Chiriquí (3000–3500 feet), in late Feb-early Mar 1976 (Ridgely), with one taken on 4 Mar (specimen to GML collection). First definite record from Chiriquí.

p. 267. Rufous-and-white Wren. Small numbers now occur locally on Caribbean slope of Canal Zone (e.g. at Fort Sherman). Probably a recent immigrant to this region.

p. 269. Rufous-breasted Wren. Small numbers now occur very locally on Caribbean slope of Canal Zone (e.g. at Fort Sherman). Probably a recent immigrant to this region; not previously recorded from anywhere on the Caribbean slope.

p. 292. "Brewster's Warbler." One studied at Volcan Lakes, Chiriquí, on 13 Jan 1977 (A. Greensmith et al.; *Toucan* 4(2): 6, 1977).

p. 294. Cape May Warbler. Female seen at Estero Rico, Chiriquí, on 6 Mar 1976 (Ridgely). One, perhaps two were seen in Colon at least from 24-26 Jan 1980 (P. Donahue et al.).

p. 294. Yellow-rumped Warbler. One of the *auduboni* group was seen at Volcan, Chiriquí, on 5-6 Feb 1976 (Ridgely, R. Forster et al.). First report of "Audubon's Warbler" from Panama.

p. 296. Yellow-throated Warbler. One seen on Cerro Azul, e. Panama province, on 20 Jan 1978 (R. Forster, J. Baird et al.), identified as of the race *albilora*.

p. 309. Shiny Cowbird. Various observers carefully identified up to 200 of this species in the Tocumen area, e. Panama province, in Jan-Feb 1980; Bronzed Cowbirds were not recorded. There are two other recent reports from eastern Panama: a flock of 50 near Yaviza along the lower Río Chucunaque, Darién, in late Jan 1978 (C. Lower et al.; *Toucan* 5(2): 3, 1978), and at least 7 along the upper Bayano River, e. Panama province, on 24 Apr 1976 (Ridgely). Evidently increasing and spreading in Panama (as also in parts of the West Indies).

p. 309. Great-tailed Grackle. Found to be quite common in the town of Changuinola, Bocas del Toro, in late Apr 1980 (Ridgely). Not previously reported from Bocas; it has probably spread south along the coast from Costa Rica.

p. 312. Red-breasted Blackbird. Continues to increase on Caribbean slope of Canal Zone area, now also occurring in adjacent w. and e. Colon province.

p. 319. Blue-and-gold Tanager. Fairly common at Fortuna, Chiriquí (3000-3500 feet) in late Feb-early Mar 1976 (Ridgely), with one taken on 29 Feb (specimen to GML collection). First record from Chiriquí.

p. 322. Western Tanager. Four, two of them adult males, were seen at Santa Clara, Chiriquí, on 22 Mar 1979 (Ridgely, J. Baird et al.). Second Panama record.

p. 325. Tawny-crested Tanager. Also occurs in e. Panama province (El Llano-Carti road, upper Bayano River valley).

p. 334. Ruddy-breasted Seedeater. A few have been noted recently in grassy meadows along Caribbean coast in Canal Zone area, e.g. at least 4 with hundreds of Yellow-bellied Seedeaters near French Canal on Fort Sherman, Canal Zone, on 1 May 1976 (Ridgely and J. Pujals).

p. 335. Slaty Finch. One male was collected at Aguacate (near Capira), w. Panama province, on 16 July 1979; specimen in GML collection. First Panama record away from western Chiriquí. Large numbers were seen in Jan-Mar 1979 feeding with Peg-billed Finches (which see) along Boquete Trail above Cerro Punta, Chiriquí (v. o.).

p. 341. Dark-backed Goldfinch. Has increased in recent years in central Panama, now occurring regularly in small numbers on both slopes, though remaining more numerous on the Pacific. Breeding has also been recorded: a nest under construction was found on Cerro Azul, e. Panama province, on 26 Jan 1976, and a pair were seen feeding three fledged young at Pacora, e. Panama province, on 11 Mar 1979 (both Ridgely).

IV Identification or Description Notes

p. 34. Black Storm-Petrel. Flight style would help to distinguish the still unrecorded Leach's and Sooty Storm-Petrels from this species. Black has a very deep wing stroke and relatively steady flapping (with little gliding); Leach's also has a deep wing stroke, but glides a good deal more (and hence is the most nighthawk-like of the three); Sooty has a much shallower wing stroke, with frequent fairly long gliding periods.

p. 49. Bare-faced Ibis. Actually resembles Glossy Ibis much more than the Green, but is blacker with prominent bare red skin at base of bill.

p. 111. Franklin's Gull. Additional characters separating immature Franklin's from immature Laughing Gulls are its broad but broken white eye-ring (never seen in immature Laughing), and the tapering of the black subterminal tail band such that the outermost retrices are almost always entirely white (in Laughing band extends completely across tail).

p. 116. Elegant Tern. Birds in non-breeding plumage have more extensive black area on rear part of head than does Royal Tern, and it extends anteriorly to include the eye. In the Royal, the dark eye stands out in a white face, with only a narrow streak of black extending back from eye.

p. 123. *Olive-backed Quail-Dove.* In certain lights, nape and back are strongly glossed with purple.

p. 124. Violaceous Quail-Dove. Bill (except for blackish tip), orbital skin, and legs are purplish red (as in Ruddy Quail-Dove).

p. 127. Crimson-fronted Parakeet. Has conspicuous bare white eye-ring. Bend of wing and underwing coverts red, underside of flight feathers yellowish olive.

p. 127. Olive-throated Parakeet. Has conspicuous bare white eye-ring. Flight feathers appear mostly blue from above, are yellowish olive below.

p. 129. Red-fronted and Blue-fronted Parrotlets. Length of each should be 7″ (not 6″).

p. 130. White-crowned Parrot. Has rather conspicuous bare dull pinkish red eye-ring.

p. 135. Pheasant Cuckoo. Feathers of upper tail coverts are long, but reach only to tip of tail (and are not "twice as long as tail itself").

p. 135. Rufous-vented Ground-Cuckoo. Crest is not very prominent, as usually laid flat. Iris is conspicuously yellow.

p. 138. Least Pygmy-Owl. Tempo of call is slower than the actually quite fast series of Ferruginous Pygmy-Owl; Least's series is also notably shorter.

p. 145. Chuck-will's-widow. Adult males have outer three pairs of tail feathers entirely buffy-white (not just terminal half); apparently immature males have tail pattern like female, i.e. entirely tawny barred and dotted with black.

p. 147. Chestnut-collared Swift. Tail usually looks slightly notched (unlike all *Chaetura* swifts).

p. 160. Violet-bellied Hummingbird. Both sexes have lower mandible mostly reddish, a helpful distinguishing point from Crowned Woodnymph (with all-dark bill in both sexes).

p. 163. Black-bellied Hummingbird. Central two pairs of tail feathers are black (not just central pair).

p. 165. Green-crowned Brilliant. Male has conspicuous white post-ocular spot.

p. 196. Pale-breasted Spinetail. Length should be 6″ (not 5½″), the same as Slaty Spinetail.

p. 200. Ruddy Foliage-Gleaner. Most readily confused with Streak-breasted Treehunter, but lacking the streaked effect below.

p. 223. Yellow-billed Cotinga. Ridge of bill in both sexes is black (as in illustration). Male's crown is tinged very pale gray.

p. 225. Cinereous Becard. Female actually is mostly whitish below, washed with buffy only on chest; thus notably *paler* below than the other "brown" becards.

p. 240. Tropical Pewee. When seen closely can be seen to have whitish lores (dark in both migrant pewees), a very useful supplemental field character.

p. 241. Acadian Flycatcher. Length should be 5-5½″ (not 5½-6¾″).

p. 241. Traill's Flycatcher. Both species seem to sing quite regularly while on spring passage, and the Willow also fairly often even during winter. The eye-ring in both species is narrow and inconspicuous, sometimes even lacking. Length should be 5-5½″ (not 5¼-6½″).

p. 242. Least Flycatcher. Apart from its small size, can often be known, even during winter months, by its conspicuous white eye-ring (more prominent than in all other *Empidonax* sp. except a few Yellow-bellies).

p. 255. Southern Beardless Tyrannulet. This small tyrannulet is often most easily known by its bushy-crested look.

p. 293. Northern Parula. In addition to the characters mentioned, can also be distinguished from the Tropical Parula by its broken but prominent white eye-ring (lacking in Tropical), and its more obvious white wing-bars. The two may be conspecific.

p. 327. Pirre Bush-Tanager. Iris is yellow or orange-yellow. Thus both Tacarcuna *and* Pirre Bush-Tanagers have pale eyes.

V Taxonomic and Nomenclatural Notes

p. 42. *Butorides virescens.* Now considered conspecific with *B. striatus.* English name for enlarged complex is Green Heron (33rd Supplement to A.O.U. Check-List, *Auk* 93(4): 876, 1976).

p. 50. White-faced, Fulvous, and Black-bellied Tree-Ducks. All members of the genus *Dendrocygna*, formerly known as tree-ducks, are to be referred to as Whistling-Ducks (33rd Supplement to A.O.U. Check-List, *Auk* 93(4): 876, 1976).

p. 115. *Thalasseus* and *Hydroprogne*. Both genera have now been merged into *Sterna* (33rd Supplement to A.O.U. Check-List, *Auk* 93(4): 877, 1976).

p. 129. Brown-hooded Parrot. Range should be s. Mexico to nw. Colombia, considering Beautiful (or Rose-faced) Parrot, *P. pulchra*, of w. Colombia and w. Ecuador as a distinct species (J. Forshaw).

p. 140. *Speotyto*. Genus has now been merged into *Athene* (33rd Supplement to A.O.U. Check-List, *Auk* 93(4): 877, 1976).

p. 185. *Chrysoptilus*. Genus should perhaps be merged into *Colaptes* (L. Short).

p. 189. *Dendrocopos*. Genus has now been merged into *Picoides* (33rd Supplement to A.O.U. Check-List, *Auk* (93(4): 877, 1976).

p. 212. Bicolored Antbird. *G. bicolor*, ranging from Honduras to w. Ecuador, is probably best considered a distinct species (E.O. Willis).

p. 233. Tropical Kingbird. Range should be s. Arizona and Mexico to central Argentina, considering Couch's Kingbird, *T. couchii*, of s. Texas through e. Mexico to Belize and n. Guatemala as a distinct species (M. Traylor, Jr.).

p. 238. *Nuttallornis*. Genus should probably be merged into *Contopus* (M. Traylor, Jr.).

p. 238. Dark Pewee. On basis of appearance and vocalizations, perhaps the best arrangement for this group would be to consider *lugubris* as conspecific with the South American *fumigatus* group, leaving *C. pertinax* of sw. United States to Nicaragua as a distinct species.

p. 243. Tufted Flycatcher. Range should be n. Mexico to w. Ecuador, considering Olive Flycatcher, *M. olivaceus*, of e. Peru and n. Bolivia as a distinct species (J.D. Webster).

p. 255. Southern Beardless Tyrannulet. Possibly conspecific with Northern Beardless Tyrannulet, *C. imberbe*, of sw. United States to nw. Costa Rica.

p. 269. Rufous-breasted Wren. Taxonomic comment should be "Some consider *T. rutilus* to include *T. maculipectus* (Spot-breasted Wren) of Mexico to nw. Costa Rica and the *T. sclateri* group (Speckle-breasted Wren) of central Colombia to nw. Peru. If so, the enlarged *T. rutilus* would be known as the Speckled Wren."

p. 279. Long-billed Gnatwren. *R. rufiventris* is probably best considered as conspecific with *R. melanurus* from east of the Andes in South America.

p. 288. White-eared Conebill. Sometimes separated in the genus *Ateleodacnis*.

p. 293. Yellow and Mangrove Warbles. Recent evidence indicate that these two groups, along with the "Golden Warbler" complex, are probably best all considered conspecific (S. Olson).

p. 304. Pirre Warbler. This form, *ignotus*, is probably best considered as conspecific with *B. melanogenys* of the w. highlands and Costa Rica.

p. 306. *Gymnostinops* and *Zarhynchus*. Both genera should perhaps be merged into *Psarocolius*.

p. 309. *Cassidix*. Genus has now been merged into *Quiscalus* (33rd Supplement to A.O.U. Check-List, *Auk* 93(4): 878, 1976).

p. 319. Green-naped Tanager. This form, *fucosa*, is probably best considered as conspecific with *T. dowii* of the w. highlands and Costa Rica.

p. 320. Yellow-rumped Tanager. Perhaps conspecific with *R. flammigerus* (Flame-rumped Tanager) of Colombia (C. Sibley).

p. 330. *Cyanocompsa* and *Guiraca*. Both genera should perhaps be merged into *Passerina*.

p. 334. Ruddy-breasted Seedeater. Range should be w. Mexico to nw. Ecuador, Venezuela, and the Guianas, considering Tawny-bellied Seedeater, *S. hypoxantha*, as a distinct species.

p. 337. Yellow-throated Brush-Finch. Perhaps conspecific with White-naped Brush-Finch, *A. albinucha*, of e. Mexico (R. Paynter, Jr.).

p. 341. *Spinus*. Genus has now been merged into *Carduelis* (33rd Supplement to A.O.U. Check-List, *Auk* 93(4): 878, 1976).

BIBLIOGRAPHY

A more comprehensive bibliography concerning the birds of Panama can be found in Eisenmann's *Species of Middle American Birds* (1955); I also understand that Wetmore plans to include a complete bibliography in the last volume of his present work.

Bennett, Charles F. 1968. Human Influences on the Zoogeography of Panama. *Ibero-American 51:* 1–112.

Blake, Emmet R. 1953. *Birds of Mexico: A Guide for Field Identification.* University of Chicago Press, Chicago.

Blake, Emmet R. 1958. Birds of Volcan de Chiriqui, Panama. *Fieldiana:* Zool., Vol. 36, No. 5: 499–577. Field Mus. Nat. Hist., Chicago.

Bond, James. 1971. *Birds of the West Indies.* 2nd ed. Houghton-Mifflin Co., Boston.

Chapman, Frank M. 1929. *My Tropical Air Castle.* D. Appleton & Co., New York.

Chapman, Frank M. 1938. *Life in an Air Castle.* Appleton-Century Co., New York.

Davis, L. Irby. 1972. *A Field Guide to the Birds of Mexico and Central America.* University of Texas Press, Austin, Tex.

Dickey, Donald R., and A. J. van Rossem. 1938. The Birds of El Salvador. *Field Mus. Nat. Hist.*, Zool. Ser. 23, Publ. 406: 1–609.

Edwards, Ernest P. 1972. *A Field Guide to the Birds of Mexico.* E. P. Edwards, Sweetbriar, Va.

Edwards, Ernest P., and Horace Loftin. 1971. *Finding Birds in Panama.* 2nd ed. E. P. Edwards, Sweetbriar, Va.

Eisenmann, Eugene. 1955. The Species of Middle American Birds. *Trans. Linnaean Soc. N. Y., 7:* 1–128.

Eisenmann, Eugene, and Horace Loftin. 1972. *Field Checklist of Birds of Panama Canal Zone Area.* 2nd ed. Russ Mason's Flying Carpet Tours, Inc., Kissimmee, Fla.

Eisenmann, Eugene, and Horace Loftin. 1972. *Field Checklist of Birds of the Western Chiriqui Highlands, Panama.* 2nd ed. Russ Mason's Flying Carpet Tours, Inc., Kissimmee, Fla.

ffrench, Richard. 1974. *A Guide to the Birds of Trinidad and Tobago.* Livingston Publ. Co., Wynnewood, Pa.

Griscom, Ludlow. 1935. The Ornithology of the Republic of Panama. *Bull. Mus. Comp. Zool.,* No. 3: 261–382. Harvard Univ., Cambridge, Mass.

Hellmayr, C. E. *et al.* 1924–1949. Catalogue of Birds of the Americas. *Field Mus. Nat. Hist.,* Zool. Ser. 13, pts 1–11.

Howell, Thomas R. An ecological study of the birds of the lowland pine savanna and adjacent rain forest in northeastern Nicaragua. *The Living Bird,* Tenth Annual (1971): 185–242. Cornell Laboratory of Ornithology, Ithaca, N.Y.

Land, Hugh C. 1970. *Birds of Guatemala.* Livingston Publ. Co., Wynnewood, Pa.

Meyer de Schauensee, Rodolphe. 1964. *The Birds of Colombia.* Livingston Publ. Co., Wynnewood, Pa.

———. 1966. *The Species of Birds of South America with their Distribution.* Acad. Nat. Sci. Phila.

———. 1970. *A Guide to the Birds of South America.* Livingston Publ. Co., Wynnewood, Pa.

Monroe, Burt L., Jr. 1968. *A Distributional Survey of the Birds of Honduras.* American Ornithologists' Union Monograph No. 7.

Murphy, Robert Cushman. 1936. *Oceanic Birds of South America,* Vols. 1–2. Amer. Mus. Nat. Hist., New York.

Peters, J. L. *et al.* 1933–present. *Check-List of Birds of the World,* Vols. 1–15 (several not yet published). Harvard University Press, Cambridge, Mass.

Peterson, Roger Tory. 1947. *A Field Guide to the Birds (East).* Houghton-Mifflin Co., Boston.

———. 1961. *A Field Guide to Western Birds.* Houghton-Mifflin Co., Boston.

Peterson, Roger Tory, and Edward L. Chalif. 1973. *A Field Guide to Mexican Birds and Adjacent Central America.* Houghton-Mifflin Co., Boston.

Rand, Austin L., and Melvin A. Traylor. 1954. *Manual de las Aves de El Salvador.* University of El Salvador.

Ridgway, Robert (and Herbert Friedmann, Parts 9–11). 1901–1950. The Birds of North and Midle America, Parts 1–11. *U.S. Natl. Mus. Bull.* 50.

Robbins, Chandler S., Bertel Bruun, and Herbert S. Zim. 1966. *Birds of North America: A Guide to Field Identification.* Golden Press, New York.

Russell, Stephen M. 1964. *A Distributional Study of the Birds of British Honduras.* American Ornithologists' Union Monograph No. 1.

Skutch, Alexander. 1954–1960–1967. *Life Histories of Central American Birds,* Vols. 1–3. Cooper Ornithological Society. Pacific Coast Avifauna Series, Nos. 31, 34, and 35.

———. 1967. *Life Histories of Central American Highlands Birds.* Publ. Nuttall Ornithological Club, No. 7.

———. 1972. *Studies of Tropical American Birds.* Publ. Nuttall Ornithological Club, No. 10.

Slud, Paul. The Birds of Costa Rica, Distribution and Ecology. *Bull. Amer. Mus. Nat. Hist., 128:* 1–430.

Sturgis, Bertha B. 1928. *Field Book of Birds of the Panama Canal Zone.* G. P. Putnam's Sons, New York.

Wetmore, Alexander. 1960. A classification for the birds of the world. *Smiths. Misc. Coll.* 139: 37 pp.

———. 1965–1968–1973. The Birds of the Republic of Panama, Parts 1–3. *Smiths. Misc. Coll.,* Vol. 150, pts. 1–3.

INDEX

This index lists only the English and Latin bird names mentioned in the main text and the appendices. Alternate names have been included, but subspecies, if they are not referred to in some other context, are not. Persons and places have also not been indexed. Illustration references are given in *boldface*, and follow that species' primary English name only (not its alternate or Latin names), e.g. **Pl.20** for color plate 20, and **230** for a drawing on page 230 of the text.

Library of Congress Cataloging in Publication Data

Ridgely, Robert S 1946-
A guide to the birds of Panama.

"Sponsored by the International Council for Bird Preservation (Pan American and United States Sections), with the support of the Marcia Brady Tucker Foundation."
Bibliography: p.
Includes index.
1. Birds—Panama—Identification. I. Title.
II. Title: Birds of Panama.
QL687.P3R5 598.2'97287 75-30205
ISBN 0-691-08174-3

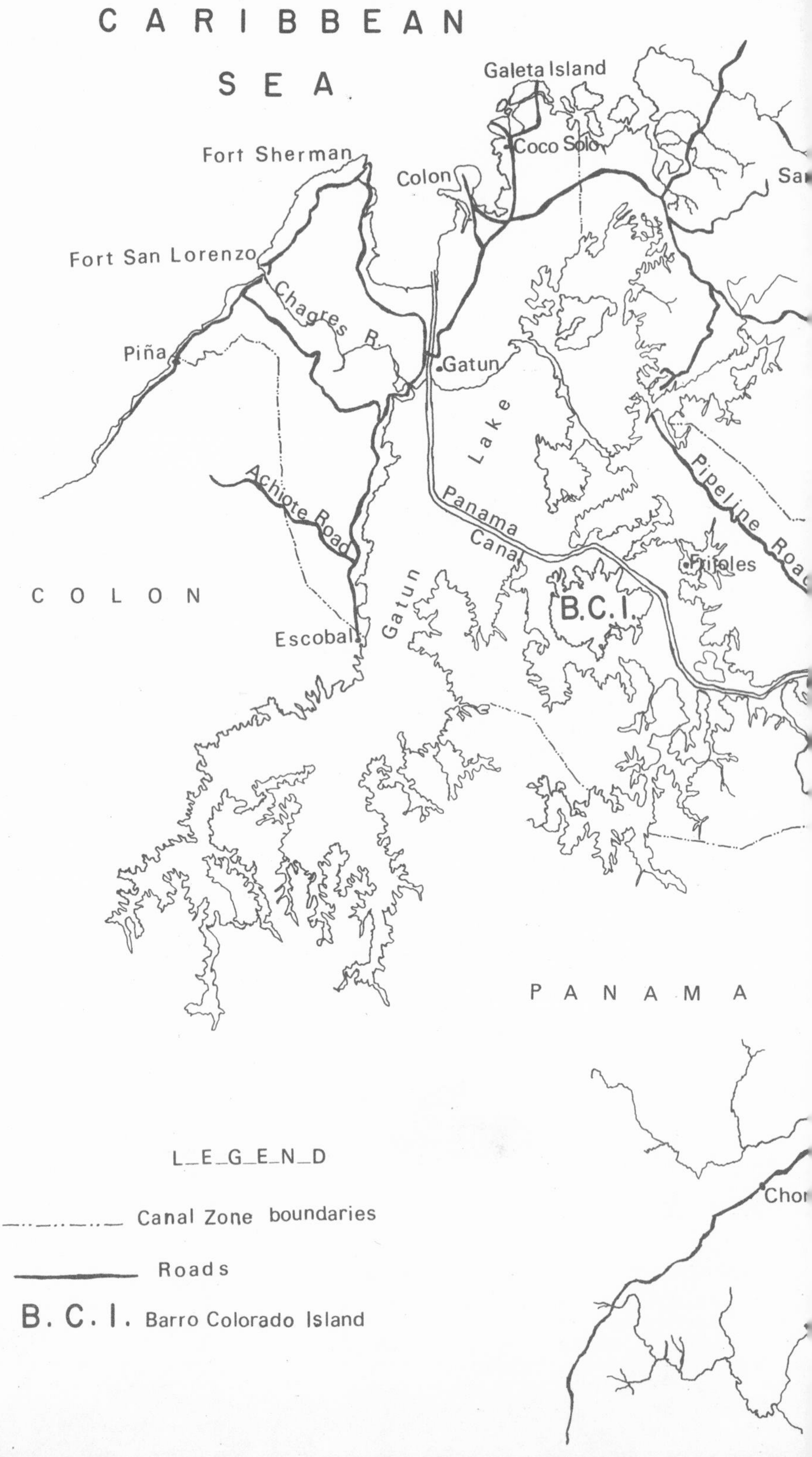
CARIBBEAN
SEA
Galeta Island
Coco Solo
Fort Sherman
Colon
Sa
Fort San Lorenzo
Chagres R.
Piña
Gatun
Lake
Achiote Road
Panama
Canal
Pipeline Road
Frijoles
B.C.I.
COLON
Escobal
Gatun
PANAMA
Chor
LEGEND
Canal Zone boundaries
Roads
B.C.I. Barro Colorado Island